I0816263

THE UNDISCOVERED COUNTRY

ALSO BY PAUL ANDREW HUTTON

The Apache Wars

Phil Sheridan and His Army

Soldiers West

The Custer Reader

Frontier and Region

Roundup!

Western Heritage

THE UNDISCOVERED COUNTRY

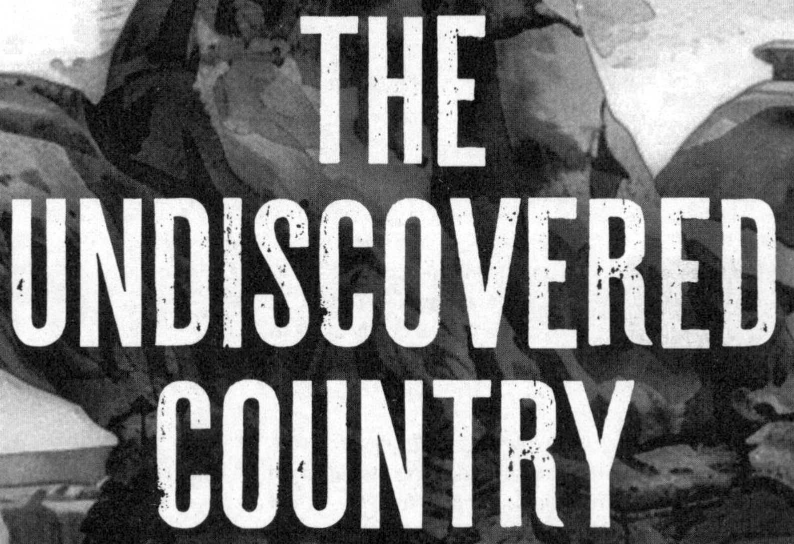

Triumph, Tragedy, and the Shaping of the American West

PAUL ANDREW HUTTON

DUTTON

DUTTON
An imprint of Penguin Random House LLC
1745 Broadway, New York, NY 10019
penguinrandomhouse.com

Maps by Jeffrey L. Ward

Book design by Shannon Nicole Plunkett

LIBRARY OF CONGRESS CATALOGING-IN-PUBLICATION DATA
has been applied for.

ISBN 9781524746131 (hardcover)
ISBN 9781524746155 (ebook)

Printed in the United States of America

2nd Printing

The authorized representative in the EU for product safety and compliance is Penguin Random House Ireland, Morrison Chambers, 32 Nassau Street, Dublin D02 YH68, Ireland, https://eu-contact.penguin.ie.

For my children:
Laura
Caitlin
Lorena
Chelsea
and Paul Andrew
Westerners all

CONTENTS

PART I: THE FOREST

PART II: THE CITY

PART III: THE MOUNTAINS

PART IV: THE PRAIRIE

The undiscovere'd country, from whose bourn
No traveller returns, puzzles the will,
And makes us rather bear those ills we have
Than fly to others that we know not of?
Thus conscience doth make cowards of us all.

—William Shakespeare, *Hamlet*

AUTHOR'S NOTE

There is some confusion, and even controversy, over the proper appellation for Native Americans—"Indian," "American Indian," "Indigenous People," or "Native American." All these names have been used through the years as word preference has changed over time. "Indian" is commonly used, as in the National Museum of the American Indian in Washington, DC; the Institute of American Indian Arts in Santa Fe, New Mexico; or the Plains Indian Museum at the Buffalo Bill Center of the West in Cody, Wyoming. "Indian" is still widely accepted in "Indian Country" in the west, although the name has fallen into disfavor among academics and younger Native Americans, who now prefer "Indigenous." Most Native people prefer to be called by their tribal name. In this book, "Indian" is sometimes used in a quote or within historical context. The more generic "Native" is often used, although wherever possible tribal names are given.

PREFACE

The true point of view in the history of this nation is not the Atlantic coast, it is the Great West," declared Frederick Jackson Turner in 1893. *The Undiscovered Country* tells the epic story of American westward expansion from the era of the American Revolution to 1900. The book's title, a nod to Shakespeare, refers to the dark irony of how the conquest of the West built a new nation, but at the cost of the destruction of another people and the pristine land that had sustained them. For both those coming into this new land and those already there, it became a story of foreshadowing death. The book employs multiple biographies, of both famed American frontiersmen and leading Native Americans, to chronologically tell the story of the triumphs and tragedies that marked the westward movement from Braddock's Defeat in 1755 during the final French and Indian War to the murder of Sitting Bull and the resultant Wounded Knee Massacre in 1890. The seven main protagonists—Daniel Boone, Red Eagle, Davy Crockett, Mangas Coloradas, Kit Carson, Sitting Bull, and William "Buffalo Bill" Cody—are the biographical thread that weaves the narrative together across four generations. These may seem familiar names, yet few know the truth behind their incredible life stories. In some cases their lives interrelate, but in all cases they carry forward the epic tale of this first epoch of American history.

These seven larger-than-life figures were central to the creation of a national myth of progress, redemption, and glorious conquest that became part of the identity of a new nation. At the same time some of them became symbols of heroic resistance. For each of them, save Cody, the "Winning of the West" proved a hollow victory indeed. But the legendary construct that exploited their adventures—both real and imagined—proved irresistible to Americans (no matter where they came from) as well as other peoples around the world. This story was very much an Anglo (or white American) story, yet it appealed to wildly diverse national and international audiences. In form it celebrated men who were masters of both the environment and their own destinies, but in reality the great forces that shaped the West were rarely understood by the main protagonists. By 1900 the story of the West had become an agreed-upon creation myth as Buffalo Bill Cody presented a highly romanticized version to captivated monarchs and common folk alike with his Wild West extravaganza—the story of America.

This narrative also explores "Manifest Destiny," the concept that shaped nineteenth-century American cultural and political thought. Daniel Boone, with the migration up the Cumberland Gap and the Revolutionary War; Red Eagle, the Creek leader who allied with Tecumseh to halt the American pioneers; Davy Crockett, who fought Red Eagle and came to symbolize the rise of the common man and the triumph of the New West as a political movement in Washington; Mangas Coloradas, who united all the Apache bands against the white invaders and led his people in the great battle of Apache Pass, only to then fall victim to American perfidy; Kit Carson, leading America across the Santa Fe Trail, conquering California, fighting the Civil War in the West, and then reluctantly becoming the nation's most famous Indian fighter; Sitting Bull, rallying the final Native resistance, culminating in both the great victory at the Little Big Horn and the catastrophe at Wounded Knee; and Buffalo Bill Cody, who fought the final Indian Wars, before taking it all "on the road" with his celebrated Wild West show, which entertained the world for a quarter century—all contributed to the epic saga of the American West.

It is a tale of both heroic conquest and ghastly violence, of sacrifice and greed, and of man-made wonders and environmental spoliation. That new land—the progenitor of a great nation—finally had no place for any of these legendary figures. They had built something grand, but at a terrible price that quickly morphed into a story that was both wildly romantic and oddly tragic. The American frontier movement has proven eternally fascinating to both American and world audiences. The subject of countless memoirs, histories, poems, paintings, novels, films, and television shows, it has become America's epic—a creation myth as powerful as the tales of Troy or Camelot.

WHY THE WEST MATTERS

During colonial times and in the days of the early republic, frontier folk were disdained by the guardians of American culture (such as it was) as dangerous characters of low breeding, prone to democratic anarchy and fits of violence. Politics were controlled by the elites of New England and Tidewater Virginia. Then, in the 1820s, Americans began to search for a distinctive identity separate from their European ancestors. The powerfully symbolic deaths of both Thomas Jefferson and John Adams on the fiftieth anniversary of the Declaration of Independence (July 4, 1826) was a major impetus, for the new generation felt keenly the passing of the Revolutionary generation (not unlike the present uneasiness at the passing of the World War II generation). Americans turned to the West in search of new figures to lead the country forward—men who were masters of both a hostile environment and their own destiny.

The success of James Fenimore Cooper's "Leatherstocking Tales," and most notably his *Last of the Mohicans* in 1826, along with Timothy Flint's acclaimed biography of Daniel Boone in 1833, helped to create a literary ideal of the American frontiersman as well as encouraged a successful series of "border dramas" on the stage, such as *Nick of the Woods* and *The Lion of the West* (based on Davy Crockett). At the same time the rise of Andrew Jackson, Henry Clay, Sam Houston, Crockett, and other Westerners marked a shift in political power from the East to the New West and ushered in the so-called Age of the Common Man. The martyrdom of Crockett at the Alamo, the celebrated explorations of Kit Carson and John Charles Frémont, the epic migration to Oregon (immortalized by America's first great Western historian, Francis Parkman, in his 1847 *Oregon Trail*), all served to idealize the bold frontiersmen as representative of what an American should and could be. Samuel Woodworth's popular 1822 song "The Hunters of Kentucky," in which, at the 1815 Battle of New Orleans, the Kentucky and Tennessee frontier soldiers were all "half a horse, / And half an alligator," became a campaign ditty for Andrew Jackson. The 1828 election of Jackson marked the culmination of the rise of a new America.

At the same time that Americans celebrated these new frontier heroes, they followed Cooper's lead in lamenting the tragic fate of Indian leaders such as Pontiac, Red Eagle, and Tecumseh. Jefferson's dream of a peaceful merging of the two races was forgotten as greed for land led to a policy of separation, removal, and segregation. Ironically, all of the foremost frontier figures—Boone, Crockett, Carson, Cody—sympathized with and defended the Indians, sometimes even while fighting them. In time they came to see that they often had more in common with their Native foe than with the people of the East who brought on conflict. The story of the West is a tale of contradictions and irony.

Jackson's protégé, the underappreciated James K. Polk, quickly fulfilled Jefferson's "Empire of Liberty" dream by seizing the American Southwest and California from Mexico, acquiring the Oregon Country, and achieving the nation's continental "Manifest Destiny." A ghastly Civil War rent this all asunder until another Westerner redeemed the dream, restored the Union, and again turned the nation westward. Abraham Lincoln, whose grandfather had followed Daniel Boone through the Cumberland Gap and who had been born in the same year just a few miles from the birthplace of Kit Carson, pushed through the Homestead Act and the transcontinental railroad authorization, which would shape the new trans-Mississippi West.

A new epic now arose out of this story that in time united a divided nation and gave a fresh national identity to millions of wildly diverse people from many lands. Printing innovations led to the garish dime novels that horrified parents and literary critics alike. These "penny dreadfuls" celebrated the frontier adventures of a colorful cast of characters, including the hunter, scout, and Indian fighter Buffalo Bill Cody. This story was one of stirring adventure, unbridled optimism, and national progress. When, on May 11, 1887, Cody gave a command performance for Queen Victoria's Golden Jubilee, it seemed as if the United States had finally come of age and that our Western story had indeed conquered the world.

Buffalo Bill, with an able assist from Owen Wister's 1902 classic *The Virginian*, along with the art of Frederic Remington and Charlie Russell, enshrined the cowboy (once a pejorative name) as an American icon and made the story of the West America's story. Theodore Roosevelt, himself the author of the magnificent four-volume *The Winning of the West*, kept the West front and center as our first cowboy president. The onetime rancher and famed Rough Rider now brought a whirlwind of frontier energy to the

White House. His bold efforts at conservation reflected a growing awareness that even at a moment of crowning achievement something important was also being lost. As the Western story triumphed on all fronts, it was increasingly burdened with a melancholy nostalgia. The West was won; now what?

A young historian at the University of Wisconsin, Frederick Jackson Turner, addressed that very question with his 1893 essay "The Significance of the Frontier in American History," which revolutionized the teaching of American history. "American democracy was born of no theorist's dream," Turner declared. "It came out of the American forest, and it gained new strength each time it touched a new frontier." Turner shifted the emphasis of our national story from the East to the West with his bold assertion that the distinctiveness of American cultural and political society, as well as our exceptional national character, emerged from the frontier experience. He refuted the then prevailing theory that American institutions had evolved from so-called European germ cells without regard to environmental factors. It was the frontier—which he characterized as "the meeting point between savagery and civilization"—that explained the unique American character: a rejection of class and aristocracy, of established religion, standing armies, and the other trappings of Europe in favor of adaptation, innovation, invention, individualism, and a rough-hewn democracy. The frontier was not only a process; it was a state of mind.

In some ways it was all an agreed-upon fable, not unlike the tales of Homer, the legends of King Arthur, or the epics of Charlemagne that provided identity and pride to other peoples. Similarly, embracing the story of the American frontier is what helped make people from all across the globe Americans—and defined who they were as a new people. It is a story of conflict—a heroic tale of the building of a nation always shaded by the dark shadow of racism and violence. "The essential American soul is hard, isolate, stoic, and a killer," observed D. H. Lawrence in 1923 in considering the Western hero. "It has never yet melted."

Perhaps the Pulitzer Prize–winning Kiowa novelist N. Scott Momaday put it best when he wrote: "It has something to do with legend, and with the way we must think of ourselves, we cowboys and Indians, we roughriders of the world."

Part I

THE FOREST

THE FOREST
Lake Superior
Lake Michigan
Lake Huron
Lake Ontario
Lake Erie
BRITISH CANADA
WISCONSIN (1848)
MICHIGAN (1837)
NEW YORK (1788)
IOWA (1846)
ILLINOIS (1818)
INDIANA (1816)
OHIO (1803)
PENNSYLVANIA (1787)
MD (1788
MISSOURI (1821)
KENTUCKY (1792)
WEST VIRGINIA (1863)
VIRGINIA (1788)
ARKANSAS (1836)
TENNESSEE (1796)
NORTH CAROLINA (1789)
SOUTH CAROLINA (1788)
MISSISSIPPI (1817)
ALABAMA (1819)
GEORGIA (1788)
LOUISIANA (1812)
FLORIDA (1845)
Mississippi River
Ohio River
Cumberland River
Tennessee River
KICKAPOO
MIAMI
SHAWNEE
CHEROKEE
CHICKASAW
UPPER CREEK
LOWER CREEK
CHOCTAW
SEMINOLE
Detroit
Frenchtown
Fallen Timbers
Fort Dearborn
Fort Wayne
Fort LeBoeuf
Braddock's Defeat
Bushy Run
Fort Pitt
Lancaster
Fort Necessity
Prophetstown
St. Clair's Defeat
New Chillicothe
Point Pleasant
Boone's Lick
Femme Osage
St. Charles
St. Louis
Vincennes
Louisville
Frankfort
Blue Licks
Lexington
Boonesborough
Harrodsburg
WILDERNESS ROAD
Martin's Station
Cumberland Gap
Limestone
Knoxville
Nashville
Dandridge
New Madrid
Rutherford
Nashville
Franklin
Murfreesboro
Lawrenceburg
Chattanooga
Memphis
Kings Mountain
Cowpens
Fort Strother
Tallushatchee
Talladega
Hickory Ground
Tuckabatchee
Holy Ground (Eccanachaca)
Fort Jackson
Coweta
Horseshoe Bend (Tohopeka)
Charleston
Savannah
Fort Mims
Pensacola
Fort St. Marks
St. Augustine
New Orleans
Gulf of Mexico
Apalachee Bay
Atlantic Ocean
0 Miles 300
0 Kilometers 300
Key
OHIO (1803) State name and date of admission to the Union
Towns
Forts
Battle sites
MIAMI Tribes
Trails
© 2025 Jeffrey L. Ward

1

DEATH ON THE MONONGAHELA

Early in the spring of 1774, a solitary figure crossed westward over Kane's Gap into Powell's Valley, far beyond the fragile line of English frontier settlements to the east. Daniel Boone, his hair plaited and clubbed up in Indian fashion, garbed in black-dyed deerskin, had come in search of the rude grave of his eldest son. James Boone and six companions had been killed by a band of renegade Shawnee, Delaware, and Cherokee Indians in October 1773 while hurrying forward with pack animals to rejoin his father's party of Kentucky-bound emigrants. James had called pitifully for his family in his death agony as a Shawnee called Big Jim delighted in torturing him. The slaughter had momentarily ended Boone's dream of a settlement in Kentucky.

The dead had been buried quickly, wrapped only in sheets, and now Boone journeyed alone to this westernmost tip of Virginia to rebury them. His worst fears were soon realized, for the graves had been disturbed by wolves. Under a darkening sky he rewrapped his son's mangled remains in his saddle blanket and reburied him. He wept over the grave as a storm broke above him. "The melancholy of his feelings," his son Nathan later recounted, "mingled with the howling of the storm and the gloominess of the place made him feel worse than ever in his life." Saddling his horse, he mounted and rode in a direction unnatural to his restless spirit—eastward into the evening shadows.[1]

The death of his eldest son proved to be but one of a tragic string of blood payments that Daniel Boone would make to open the American West. In time he will come to be heralded as an American Moses leading the people to their western promised land. His personal travail will be embraced by writers, artists, poets, and filmmakers across the generations to create an epic that becomes the grand creation myth for the founding of a pioneer nation.

Born in what would become Berks County, Pennsylvania, on November 2, 1734 (or October 22 by the Old Style calendar), Daniel was the sixth of Squire and Sarah (Morgan) Boone's eleven children. His Quaker father had come to William Penn's colony in 1713 in search of religious freedom. But Squire Boone, angered when chastised by the Exeter Meeting of Friends for allowing two of his children to marry outside the Church, left the faith and the colony. He took his family to Virginia in 1750 and then to North Carolina, where they settled on the Yadkin River.

By the time the family moved down the Great Valley of Virginia to the Yadkin, young Boone had already made a reputation in Pennsylvania as an accomplished hunter and marksman. The forest, so frightful to others, had early beckoned to the boy. He disdained his father's weaving and blacksmith shop for the freedom he found in the woods. This way of life was in sharp contrast to the rigid sanctity of the Quakers. The natural rhythms of the land appealed to him far more than the contrived rules of the settlements.

Young Daniel's formal schooling was limited, coming to an abrupt end after the teenager knocked down his Irish schoolteacher when the scholar attempted to cane him for some minor transgression. "It's all right, John," Squire Boone declared to his brother after much sober Quaker reflection, "let the girls do the spelling and Dan will do the shooting, and between you and me that is what we most need."[2]

Despite his disdain for formal education, Daniel was not illiterate. He participated in daily readings from the Bible with his family, and like so many on the frontier learned to read in that manner. At first he could but barely scrawl his name, but in time he developed a decent if highly individualistic style of writing. The rules of grammar and syntax could no more contain his restless spirit than the pioneer settlements.

In 1750, with his friend Henry Miller, who was Squire Boone's blacksmith apprentice, Boone pursued his first long hunt. The boys followed the Roanoke Gap through the Blue Ridge and hunted along the Virginia–North Carolina boundary with great success. Deerskins were a valuable frontier commodity—as good as cash—and the terms "buck" and "dollar" quickly became synonymous. Thirty thousand deerskins were exported from North Carolina alone in 1753. The hunters' quarry was primarily the white-tailed deer, and they sought them when the skin was said to be "in the red," usually from April to the first frost. Boone and Miller hunted and trapped for months, eventually selling their hides and furs in Philadelphia. Miller later recalled that he and Boone went on a three-week "general jamboree or frolick" and spent every dollar they had earned. Miller determined to reform but noted that Boone had no such intention, being "very profligate." From 1750 on, Boone was a professional hunter.[3]

Even a young hunter in the distant Yadkin Valley could not escape the pull of international events when, in 1755, the long-festering rivalry between England and France over the rich fur trade with the Natives of the Great Lakes and Ohio River Valley erupted into war. George Washington, a Virginia militia officer but two years older than Boone, had lit the spark the year before.

Virginia lieutenant governor Robert Dinwiddie had been ordered by the king's ministers to repel any French movement onto lands claimed by the Crown. The governor decided to send an emissary to the French with a warning for them to keep out of the Ohio Country. Washington, an inexperienced but eager Virginia militia major, seemed to many an odd choice for such a delicate diplomatic assignment. Dinwiddie, however, recognized the superior characteristics in Washington that others would later come to appreciate. The twenty-one-year-old colonial officer was one of the few Virginians with an affinity for this western country. Washington's surveying work from 1748 to 1750 in the Shenandoah Valley had given him frontier experience as well as a keen eye for the future value of these western lands.

The king's ministers were charmed by the idea of blocking French influence in the western country, and so in 1749 the Crown granted to the Ohio Company 200,000 acres of land somewhere west of the mountains along the "branches of the Mississippi." While the Virginians were obsessed with land, British interests centered squarely on capturing the fur trade with the Ohio Valley tribes. Fur was to the eighteenth-century English what oil would be to their descendants 150 years later. The company, whose sole purpose was the development of lands on the upper Ohio River claimed by Virginia, was founded in 1748 by the first families of the colony, including Dinwiddie and Washington's older half brother Lawrence. Unlike their northern colonial cousins, they did not look to the sea and commerce in order to prosper but rather thought only of more land, more enslaved people, and more expansive plantations. They were joined by English investors with dreams of creating something akin to a new East India Company or Hudson's Bay Company. The only obstacles to these speculative fantasies were the Natives and their French allies.

Major Washington, guided by the experienced frontiersman Christopher Gist, departed Williamsburg on November 1, 1753, with but a handful of companions. He was under orders to deliver Dinwiddie's letter to the French commander of Fort LeBoeuf (some five hundred miles to the northwest, fifteen miles south of Lake Erie). Gist had been one of the principal negotiators the previous year, along with George Croghan of Pennsylvania, of the 1752 Treaty of Logstown, by which the Iroquois had sold their ambiguous claim to the Ohio Valley to the British. He had also scouted out western lands for Lawrence Washington. Gist was held in high regard by the younger Washington as well. "He has had extensive dealings with the Indians, is in great esteem among them, well acquainted with their manners and customs, is indefatigable, and patient, most excellent qualities indeed, where Indians are concerned," he later wrote.

The Ohio Company was anxious to quickly establish a fort and then a settlement at the Forks of the Ohio (present-day Pittsburgh, where the Monongahela and Allegheny Rivers merge to form the Ohio), for which the Crown promised them 300,000 more acres. No one seemed much bothered by Native ownership of this land, although some of the Tidewater aristocrats agreed with Virginia planter and councilman William Byrd II's assessment of the potential new settlers when he fretted in 1736 over the temper and breeding of uncouth frontier folk such as the Boones, who "swarm like the Goths and Vandals of old" down the Shenandoah.

Gist arranged councils between young Washington and prominent tribal leaders Tanaghrisson of the Senecas, also often called the Half King because he represented the authority of the Six Nations, and Shingas of the Delawares in order to request their cooperation in his mission to the French. They were helpful, but these maneuvers also increased the anxiety of some of the Ohio tribes over British intentions and moved them even closer to their French trading partners. Despite their concerns, Tanaghrisson and three other chiefs went north with Washington and Gist as a protective escort.

On a frosty December morning—in terms of both weather and diplomacy—the colonial major delivered Governor Dinwiddie's letter to Captain Jacques Legardeur de Saint-Pierre at Fort LeBoeuf. For the French there was far more at stake than their lucrative fur trade. The British colonies had already swelled to over a million and a half inhabitants, while New France could barely muster 55,000 souls. If British expansion was not halted, they might well sweep aside the French and their Native allies and move on to threaten the Spanish to the southwest. The imperial designs of the great powers now hung in the balance.

Dinwiddie's letter demanding that the trespassing French immediately depart the Ohio Country was met with courteous contempt by the captain, and Washington was soon on his way back to Williamsburg. Despite the intense difficulties of the journey, the young officer paid close attention to the land and river systems. His January report to the governor asserted that the French were undoubtedly plotting a movement south to the Forks of the Ohio, a position Washington felt vital to the overall strategic control of the Ohio Country. He was, of course, absolutely correct.[4]

By the middle of April, Washington, promoted by Dinwiddie to lieutenant colonel, was on his way back to the Forks of the Ohio with a ragtag band of 186 untrained militia troops. Dinwiddie had also employed the services of George Croghan and his partner Andrew Montour to both supply flour to Washington's command and recruit Indian allies. On June 1 the governor appointed Croghan as interpreter for the expedition and urged Washington to rely on him. Washington assured the governor that he would be "particularly careful in consulting Mr. Croghan and Mr. Montour, by whom I shall be advised in all Indian affairs agreeably to your direction." This began an increasingly testy relationship between Washington and Croghan.[5]

Events quickly began to overtake Washington's plans. By May 24, when he reached a boggy valley known as Great Meadows, the young officer had already been greeted by members of a colonial advance party sent to construct the proposed British fort at the Forks. They reported that five hundred French soldiers with eighteen cannons had confronted them at the

Forks and forced their retreat. The French were now busily constructing a formidable bastion that they called Fort Duquesne. Gist arrived on May 27 to report a party of thirty-five Frenchmen advancing on Washington's camp. A Seneca warrior named Silver Heels soon also reached the camp with a message from Tanaghrisson of the French advance. He urged Washington to hurriedly join with him to block the Frenchmen.

Tanaghrisson was playing a dangerous game and cleverly using the young militia officer as his pawn. His position as the Iroquois Confederacy's appointed overlord among the Ohio tribes had been undercut by the French advance, so that many of his followers had drifted away. He needed to strike a blow against the French in order to restore his leadership position within the powerful Iroquois Confederacy.

Washington advanced with forty men through a heavy rain to meet Tanaghrisson and his handful of warriors not far from the French advance camp. By dawn Washington had the little encampment surrounded, and as the Frenchmen crawled out of their blankets someone opened fire; each side, of course, blamed the other. One of the Iroquois warriors later claimed that it was Washington who fired the first shot. The French fled in confusion only to be met by Tanaghrisson's warriors. Within minutes nine Frenchmen were dead and twenty-two were made prisoners.

The wounded ensign who had commanded the French force was brought before Washington. He declared himself but an emissary and attempted to deliver his message that the English must depart this French country. As he was speaking—in French, which Washington did not understand—Tanaghrisson stepped forward and split open the ensign's skull with his tomahawk. As Washington looked on in horror, the Seneca sachem washed his hands in the French ensign's brains while his warriors slaughtered the wounded. And thus, with a single tomahawk blow, did Tanaghrisson incite the Seven Years' War between France and England, as well as the forty-year conflict between the Americans and the Native tribes for possession of the Ohio Country.

Washington retreated back to Great Meadows and hurriedly began construction of the rather pathetic little stockade that he named Fort Necessity. Croghan, with some military stores, joined him there on June 12. Washington dispatched his twenty-one French prisoners to Dinwiddie along with a belabored report of events that sought to cover up the murder of the ensign. He cautioned the governor not to listen to anything the prisoners might say.

Two hundred Virginians soon arrived at Washington's fort with nine small cannons, followed by a company of British regulars from South Carolina with a much-needed herd of forty cattle. Emboldened by these reinforcements, Washington foolishly decided to advance against Fort Duquesne. He left the regulars to defend the fort, since the captain commanding refused to take orders from a colonial militia officer. He expected to be joined by hundreds of Ohio Indians, but at a council arranged by Croghan and Gist he quickly learned that they wanted nothing to do with his plan. Shingas and his Delawares refused to join Washington, and the Shawnees with him quickly departed as well. Croghan could not persuade his Native friends to remain, for they had decided upon neutrality. Tanaghrisson, realizing that his gambit had failed, hurriedly withdrew his people as well. The Half King blamed young Washington for the Indian withdrawal.

Washington, deserted by his Indian allies, wisely decided to retreat back to Fort Necessity. He was pursued by six hundred French regulars and Canadian militia with a hundred Native allies. Commanding this French force was Captain Louis Coulon de Villiers, the brother of the slain emissary. He was determined to extact vengeance. Washington's exhausted command reached Fort Necessity on July 1 and hurriedly attempted to improve the defenses around the frail outpost. The superior French force attacked two days later, and by the end of the day a third of Washington's men were dead or wounded.

As dusk settled over the Great Meadows, Captain de Villiers shouted from the tree line that he was willing to negotiate surrender. Washington hesitated, with the fate of the French ensign still haunting him, but eventually sent one of his militia captains forward to meet with the French captain. The gallant Frenchman offered generous terms if the British would withdraw from the fort, with their arms and colors intact, return the French prisoners previously taken, admit to the assassination of the French emissary, leave two hostage officers, and promise never to return to the Ohio Country for another year. Washington had no choice but to accept.[6]

Washington's bedraggled force departed Fort Necessity on July 4, 1754, a date that would haunt him until it was redeemed as a day of celebration twenty-two years later. Many of the militiamen deserted on the march back to Williamsburg, which only added to the young officer's abject humiliation. Governor Dinwiddie shared in this and even considered resigning. Yet in London the news of Washington's debacle only intensified support for a war to redeem the Ohio Country from French encroachment. Within a week of the arrival of Dinwiddie's official report, King George II had been convinced to send several regiments of British regulars to America. Prince William, Duke of Cumberland, the king's favorite son, handpicked Major General Edward Braddock to command in the colonies and gave him extraordinary powers over the various colonial governors. The Duke of Cumberland, a towering hero in England as a result of his victory over Scottish rebels at Culloden in 1746, had no faith in either the American militia forces or the ability of the disunited and jealous colonies to cooperate in a major war. It was time for the British to take over. The 44th and 48th Regiments were soon on their way from Ireland to America.[7]

Among the items discovered at Fort Necessity by the victorious French was Washington's journal, which eventually reached the hands of the governor general of New France, Ange de Menneville, marquis de Duquesne, in distant Quebec. The marquis forwarded the journal to Paris, where it was "edited" and published in 1756. Duquesne was not impressed by Colonel Washington, whom he characterized as "the most impertinent of all men, but that he has wit only in the degree that he is cunning with credulous savages. . . . There is nothing more unworthy and lower, and even blacker, than the sentiments and the way of thinking of this Washington." Despite the provocation provided by Washington, the French at first attempted to settle the matter through diplomatic channels, but British troop movements quickly ended all talk between London and Versailles, and 3,000 French troops were soon on their way to New France.[8]

The sixty-year-old Braddock had proven to be an experienced and able officer on numerous continental battlefields, although he also had a reputation for being a rather arrogant, haughty commander. His extraordinary powers made him a sort of viceroy over the American colonies while removing colonial defense from the hands of the various governors and placing it squarely under British control. Braddock was charged with raising two more regular regiments in the colonies as well as recruiting provincial troops for one year's service. A British attempt to forge some unity between the disparate and squabbling colonies by calling for a colonial congress to meet at Albany, New York, utterly failed. Benjamin Franklin's "Plan of Union" went nowhere, and British hopes for colonial cooperation between themselves as well as with the regular army and the Iroquois Confederacy were frustrated. Franklin was disgusted, not only irritated by colonial jealousies but also convinced that the British were wary of allowing too much colonial military cooperation lest the Americans come to realize their potential power.

Braddock took control, ordering the colonial governors to raise funds and troops for the campaign against the French. This, the general quickly learned, was easier said than done. His strategic plan called for British troops and their Iroquois allies to capture Fort Niagara near the western edge of Lake Ontario as well as French outposts on Lake Champlain and in Nova Scotia. He would personally lead the most important of these initiatives: the campaign against Fort Duquesne at the Forks of the Ohio.

Braddock had some 1,400 regulars in Sir Peter Halkett's 44th and Colonel Thomas Dunbar's 48th Regiments, as well as another thousand provincials from Virginia, Maryland, and North Carolina. Several hundred civilian teamsters and camp followers also attached themselves to Braddock's command. Benjamin Franklin soon proved instrumental in securing ninety-one wagons and teams and dozens of packhorses from Pennsylvania for Braddock. Franklin, like young Washington, was a firm supporter of western expansion but he had faced considerable difficulty raising funds for frontier defense from the Pennsylvania Quakers.[9]

Franklin visited with Braddock at Frederick, Maryland, soon after the general's arrival in the colonies. His growing international fame preceded him, leading to a most cordial welcome by the general. During Franklin's brief stay, they dined nightly. Franklin was anxious to convince Braddock that he could count on the support of the Pennsylvania Assembly. On April 22, just before Franklin was to depart for home, Braddock received the distressing news that his officers had been able to procure but 25 wagons and teams for the campaign. The expedition could hardly proceed without at least 150 transport wagons, and several officers now suggested that they should seize wagons and stock from the recalcitrant colonials.

The wily Franklin commented that it was a pity that the general had landed in Virginia rather than Pennsylvania, where "almost every Farmer had his Wagon." Braddock quickly wrote out a commission for Franklin to procure 150 wagons as well as hundreds of horses for the expedition and gave him eight hundred British pounds in gold and silver to seal the bargain. Franklin had to advance two hundred pounds more of his own funds as well as post bonds for the return of the wagons, but within two weeks had 150 wagons and over 250 horses on their way to Braddock. He had served the king's military forces well while at the same time protecting his own people from having their property literally seized at sword's point.

Franklin further ingratiated himself with the army by an act of great generosity. While dining with Colonel Thomas Dunbar, Franklin learned that many of the young officers in the 48th Regiment had few financial resources to procure personal supplies for the long journey ahead. Franklin quickly secured funding from the assembly to purchase twenty parcels, each loaded on a packhorse, to send to the officers of both the 48th and the 44th. Each parcel contained several delicacies, including sugar, green tea, coffee, chocolate, biscuits, pepper, butter, mustard, rice, raisins, wine vinegar, cheese, Jamaican spirits, Madeira wines, cured ham, and dried tongues.

Franklin liked Braddock but fretted that the general did not fully appreciate the unique nature of frontier warfare. "This General was I think a brave Man, and might probably have made a Figure as a good Officer in some European War," he later wrote. "But he had too much self-confidence, too high an Opinion of the Validity of Regular Troops, and too mean a One of both Americans and Indians."[10]

One American officer whom Braddock did retain a high opinion of was George Washington. The general invited Washington to join his staff as an unpaid volunteer captain aide-de-camp. British regulations did not allow any provincial field officers to hold superior rank over a regular officer. Thus, no American officer in Braddock's force held a rank above captain, which of course grated on the colonials.[11] The young Virginian, who had resigned his colonel's commission in November 1754 in disgust because "every Captain, bearing the King's commission, every half-pay officer, or other, appearing with such a commission" would outrank him, now welcomed this fresh opportunity and held out hope that it might well lead to a regular commission in the British army.[12]

George Croghan soon came south with fifty packhorses and a small contingent of forty Mingos from Tanaghrisson's old band. Braddock had

had no luck recruiting Native allies, but Croghan's Mingos would prove valuable as scouts. The general could well have made good use of a hundred more but instead infuriated his Native allies by ordering their women out of camp, feeling that they were too much of a temptation to his soldiers. When they departed, their male relatives went with them. Croghan's Native contingent was quickly reduced to eight warriors. Braddock had even less faith in the Indians than he had in his provincial troops. "Savages may indeed be a formidable enemy to your raw American militia," he told Franklin, "but upon the King's regular and disciplined troops, sir, it is impossible they should make any impression."

The Natives thought just as little of Braddock as he did of them. Scarouady, the Mingo leader, held Braddock in total contempt. "He was a bad man," declared the Oneida chief. "He looked upon us as dogs; and would never hear any thing what was said to him."[13]

Braddock ordered the construction of a new fort, which he named for his patron, on the north branch of the Potomac in Maryland. Fort Cumberland was to be the staging area for his expedition. A formidable artillery train was assembled with four light twelve-pounders, six six-pounders, four heavy 8-inch brass howitzers, and fifteen small mortars to reduce Fort Duquesne to rubble. Of course, these cannons, some weighing in at over three-quarters of a ton, would have to be hauled across a forested and mountainous wilderness marked only by the most primitive of trails.

Among the last troops to arrive at Fort Cumberland was Captain Edward Brice Dobbs's North Carolina ranger company. Dobbs's father was the governor of North Carolina and a shareholder in the Ohio Company. These reinforcements, arriving on May 30, completed Braddock's 2,500-man force.[14]

Among the teamsters with Captain Dobbs's company was twenty-year-old Daniel Boone. The accomplished marksman sometimes spent his summers working as a teamster for his father when not out on a long hunt. Daniel Morgan, later to be famed in the American Revolution for Saratoga and Cowpens, was also a teamster on the expedition. Indeed, the expedition had a number of future well-known personalities: Lieutenant Colonel Thomas Gage, who would command British forces at the beginning of the Revolution; Dr. Thomas Walker, the land speculator and explorer who served Braddock as a provincial commissary officer; Horatio Gates, who would later be a controversial general in the Revolutionary army; and of course George Washington. One man who never became famous but who would have a profound impact on the life of Boone, as well as the course of westward expansion, was also with the British column: his name was John Findley.[15]

Braddock's command finally lumbered out of Fort Cumberland at dawn on May 29, 1755, but made only three miles as the artillery and wagon trains crawled up into the Allegheny Mountains. This American forested landscape quickly became an even more formidable foe than the French. It was another 122 torturous miles to Fort Duquesne.

Young Washington soon found himself embroiled in the usual staff jealousies and as the sole American often felt compelled to defend the qualities of the provincial troops to his general and the other officers. The American teamsters, in particular, were a source of constant embarrassment.

These teamsters were a rough, unruly, strong-backed band. Their service to the army was as crucial as were their teams of horses, mules, and oxen. Quick to anger, with short tempers and long memories, they never missed an opportunity for a brawl or a frolic. "These Waggoners are the most irregular set of People I ever had to do with," snorted one British officer. When young Dan Morgan took offense at the tone used by a British officer barking commands, he promptly knocked the man down. He was arrested and sentenced to 499 lashes—enough to kill an ordinary man. Morgan, who carried the scars and a seething hatred for the British for the rest of his life, would one day redeem each lash of that whip with redcoat blood.[16]

Men like Morgan and Boone had to be tough to handle the lumbering Conestoga wagons that formed the bulk of Braddock's massive supply and baggage train. Braddock had purchased, rented, or commandeered every horse, mule, and ox he could get his hands on. These animals were used up at a prodigious rate as they hauled the huge Conestogas, eighteen feet long and four feet wide, across the mountains along the barely passable road that Braddock's men were hacking out of the wilderness. These German-inspired wagons were built to carry loads of up to six tons, with the wagon seams caulked with tar to prevent water damage. A distinctive white canvas or linen cover protected the cargo. The entire boat-shaped wagon was constructed of wood, although the wheels were often iron rimmed. The teamsters did not ride in the wagon but usually walked beside it near the brake handle on the left side or sometimes rode the wheel horse also on the left side. This meant that the Conestogas tended to use the right-hand side of the road—a custom that soon prevailed throughout the American colonies.

The pace of the army was excruciatingly slow. This gave the wagoners plenty of time for idle talk. In this time young Boone made the acquaintance of John Findley, an Irishman with a gift for gab and a seemingly boundless imagination. Findley, who was ten years older than Boone, told the youngster of his journey to the fabled "Kanta-kee" west of the mountains. Findley had only recently returned from a trading expedition to the Shawnee Blue Lick Town, just north of the Kentucky River along a trail called the Warrior's Path. This was an isolated village, for while many tribes hunted in Kanta-kee, few lived there. The Warrior's Path was a well-beaten trail by which parties of Shawnees and Cherokees regularly traversed north and south in raids on each other. The rising tension between France and England had led the Shawnees to abandon Blue Lick Town, leaving Kanta-kee wide open for any hunter bold enough to journey there. This was truly the promised land of milk and honey, rich in game of every kind—a hunter's paradise. Findley fired Boone's imagination with his tall tales, although his description of this new Eldorado was actually not that far off the mark. From that time onward, Kanta-kee was to become the great obsession of Daniel Boone's life.[17]

Braddock, increasingly impatient with the slow pace of his army, determined to split his force. A so-called flying column of 1,200 men, along with eight artillery pieces, teamsters for thirty wagons, and assorted camp followers, would proceed toward the Monongahela while Colonel Thomas Dunbar followed with most of the baggage train and the heavy artillery. Dunbar's men were charged with the arduous work of finishing the road. Within a short time Braddock was sixty miles ahead of Dunbar. Boone went with Braddock's wagon train.

Washington had strongly advised Braddock to make this division of forces, which had been done on June 17. Soon after, the young officer was stricken with the "bloody flux," as dysentery was then called. Braddock, who had grown quite fond of his young American aide, ordered Washington to stay behind at Little Meadows until he was better. Anxious to be with the command when it saw action, Washington was somewhat consoled by the fact that Braddock had marched only twelve miles in four days, "as they were halting to level every mole hill." He had recovered enough by the time they reached the Monongahela to rejoin the column, although he had a pillow over his saddle.

By the afternoon of July 9, 1755, Braddock's advance force had finally reached the Monongahela, just ten miles from the French fort. They had faced little opposition to their advance, having easily brushed aside the few French Indian scouts they met along the way. It was thus with considerable confidence that General Braddock sent his men across the river. The redcoated column, standing out conspicuously against the deep forest green surrounding them, appreciated the cool river water. It was oppressively hot that day. It was at this crossing that the British were most vulnerable, but they met with no resistance. The officers began to think that the French must have abandoned the Forks of the Ohio.[18]

At Fort Duquesne, Captain Claude-Pierre Pécaudy, seigneur de Contrecoeur, had about 1,600 French regulars, Canadian militia, and Indian allies under his command. The fort was so small that it could barely accommodate 200 men, so the rest camped outside. He well knew that they could never withstand an artillery siege, so he ordered Captain Daniel-Hyacinthe-Marie Liénard de Beaujeu forward with 36 officers, 72 regulars, and 146 Canadian militiamen, along with 637 Indians, to ambush the British column.

Lieutenant Colonel Thomas Gage led the advance party of 300 British regulars, along with a company of New York provincials under Captain Horatio Gates, to guard the 250 workers charged with clearing the trail for the army. The thick forest was a green curtain obscuring everything ahead. Croghan, with his handful of Indian scouts, made first contact around one o'clock and gave the alarm. Gage hurried his men forward to unleash several volleys into the enemy force. Captain Beaujeu was among the first to fall. His regulars retreated but the Indians, screened by the forest, quickly dispersed all along the British flanks and poured in a murderous fire. The dense forest was suddenly obscured by the acrid smoke of black powder weapons. The location of the warriors was only apparent from the bright flames spitting from their muskets. Gage's men had no choice but to slowly retreat, while many of the provincial road laborers fled ahead of them in panic. Several of the Americans did rally around Gage's two six-pounders to attempt a stand. In this short time fifteen of Gage's eighteen officers were either killed or wounded.

Braddock, surrounded by his staff and guarded by Captain Robert Stewart's company of Virginia light horsemen, now called up his remaining regular companies from their position guarding the wagon train. As the regulars marched forward, the wagons, stretching back almost a mile, hurriedly attempted to close up for defense. Colonel Peter Halkett received orders to defend the wagons, although he now had but a little over 250 men of his 44th Regiment.

Halkett quickly ordered up a twelve-pounder that was trailing the column, placed it on the right flank of the wagons, and ordered its gun crew into action. Despite Halkett's heroic efforts, the wagons were soon taking a murderous fire from the unseen enemy on both flanks. The gun crew fell one by one and the cannon fell silent. Wounded animals cried out as the wagoners and camp followers huddled together behind the wagons. Christopher Gist saw an Indian leveling his musket at Halkett and shot the warrior, but not in time to prevent him from firing. Halkett's son, a lieutenant in the 44th, rushed to the colonel's side, only to be instantly killed. His body tumbled atop that of his dead father.

The Natives, concealed behind giant old-growth oaks, took careful aim at the British officers, who were on horseback and resplendent with their red coats and gold braid. They made easy targets. Captain Robert Orme of Braddock's staff recalled how the officers "got themselves murder'd by distinguishing themselves in leading their men on." Orme, who had become Washington's closest friend on the staff, soon fell grievously wounded. Captain William Shirley, Braddock's secretary as well as the son of the royal governor of Massachusetts, also fell early in the battle, killed instantly by a shot to the head.

Braddock, with Washington by his side, galloped to the front, where Gates's retreating advance guard collided with their reinforcements. Chaos ruled as the British regulars bunched together to fire volleys at the invisible enemy. Many of the American provincial troops quickly took to the cover of the forest to fight, where they were killed or wounded by the indiscriminate British volleys.

For three tortuous hours the British held the field. Braddock, undeniably brave, was everywhere—encouraging, exhorting, and cursing his soldiers. Washington, at his side, had two horses shot from under him, while four musket balls ripped through his blue coat. He begged Braddock to let him lead the Americans into battle "Indian style" to meet the enemy on his own ground, but the general was certain his regulars would hold. He also needed Washington by his side, for every other member of his staff had been killed or wounded. "I expected every moment to see him fall," declared Virginia regimental surgeon James Craik. "His duty and situation exposed him to every danger. Nothing but the superintending care of Providence could have saved him from the fate of all around him." Many would later agree with the good doctor that Washington's survival was indeed providential.[19]

Then Braddock fell, and all was lost. Four horses had been shot out from under him, and as he mounted a fifth a musket ball slammed into his lungs. Washington and Croghan hurriedly used the general's elaborate sash as a litter to carry him to a cart. Braddock begged for Croghan's pistols so that he might be left on the field to die like an ancient Roman. He was carried back to the wagons, and as the word spread of his fate, the British lines began to disintegrate. A few of the redcoats retreated in order, but as the Indians came rushing out of the trees, screaming war cries and brandishing their war clubs and scalping knives, panic quickly swept the field.

Washington and Croghan placed Braddock in a little two-wheeled cart. Washington's friend Dr. Craik attended to the general as best he could in the midst of the fighting, but the wound was obviously mortal. All was now wild confusion as Washington noted the troops running past them like "sheep before hounds." The rout was unstoppable.

The fleeing soldiers quickly enveloped the wagon train, and the wagoners, under flank attack for hours, now also broke and ran. Boone, sensing that all was lost, cut one of the few surviving horses free of its harness and galloped back toward the Monongahela. "The Wagoners took each a horse out of his Team, and scamper'd; their Example was immediately followed by others, so that all the Wagons, Provisions, Artillery and Stores were left to the Enemy," wrote Franklin of the catastrophe.

Morgan, who was with Dunbar's column over fifty miles southeast of the river, witnessed the pitiful remnants of Braddock's army trickle in.

Washington, having ridden all night, reached Dunbar's camp the morning of July 10 with Braddock's appeal for troops to cover the retreat of the surviving soldiers. "The dead—the dying—the groans—lamentation—and crys along the Road of the wounded for help . . . were enough to pierce a heart of adamant," Washington declared.[20]

The abandoned wagons actually saved the remnants of Braddock's column. The Indians discovered two hundred gallons of rum and a wagon full of trade goods in the wagon corral that Boone had fled and busied themselves with drinking and collecting booty. There were wounded to be dispatched and scalps to be taken. Most of the camp followers were killed, but the Indians took thirteen women as captives. Two of these were badly wounded and so were killed. Few male prisoners were taken, but an unfortunate dozen were marched back to the French fort to be burned at the stake. A handful of the prisoners were rescued by French officers, although this was a delicate business. The French were much more concerned with moving Braddock's captured artillery back to Fort Duquesne than with saving British prisoners.

It was late on the night of July 10 before Braddock reached Dunbar's camp. He was one of the few non-walking wounded brought in, for the rest were left to die where they fell. Dunbar still had a force that outnumbered the French and Indian defenders of the fort, as well as an intact artillery train, but the game was up. He ordered Morgan and the other wagoners to burn the baggage and supplies as well as destroy all the remaining ordnance. The camp went up in flames as the wounded were loaded into the remaining wagons for the retreat back to Fort Cumberland.[21]

Braddock's Road, in time to become an important route to the West, was now but a sorrowful path of defeat. Braddock died on the evening of July 13. Washington and his wounded friend Orme were with the general at the end. "Who'd have thought it?" Braddock gasped out to Orme. "We shall better know how to deal with them another time" were his final words. They buried him under the road that bore his name and the army marched across the grave to hide it from the enemy. Washington kept the general's bloody silk sash as a talisman for the remainder of his life.[22]

Back at Fort Duquesne, Contrecoeur was surprised by Dunbar's retreat but greatly relieved. Most of his Native allies had quickly departed for home loaded down with booty. "If the English had returned," he later wrote, "with the 1000 fresh troops they had in reserve at some distance from them, how far we did not know, we might perhaps have found ourselves distressed." Distressed indeed—but it was not to be. The French and their Native allies had won a stunning victory at a minimal cost, with but 23 dead and 16 wounded. Braddock's command had lost over two-thirds in killed and wounded, including 60 of the 85 officers—a total of 457 killed and 519 wounded.[23]

Washington was mortified by Colonel Dunbar's decision, for he wished yet another advance against the French. The troops, however, were spent in both body and spirit. Once the column reached Fort Cumberland, Dunbar took his regulars north to Philadelphia. He demanded quarters there for his men, which greatly annoyed the populace. Many colonists soon came to agree with Benjamin Franklin's prescient comment on Braddock's Defeat: "This whole Transaction gave us Americans the first Suspicion that our exalted Ideas of the Prowess of British Regulars had not been well founded."[24]

THE FORKS OF THE OHIO

George Washington, promoted to colonel in August 1755, rather reluctantly assumed command of what was left of the Virginia troops. He established his headquarters at the hamlet of Winchester in the Shenandoah. His most pressing problem was how to deal with the flood of frontier refugees fleeing to the east, for the Indians now had a free hand in the backcountry of both Virginia and Pennsylvania. Against Washington's advice, the Virginia House of Burgesses had ordered the construction of a series of small stockades along the frontier line. This used up Washington's few effective troops in the garrison defense of these isolated outposts. The little stockades did not deter Indian raiders but did provide some sanctuary for the frantic refugees. The panic of the frontier folk was well-founded, for by the end of 1756 Indian raiders had killed over a thousand settlers and taken hundreds more—mostly women and children—captive.

Washington still hoped to launch a new offensive against Fort Duquesne but found he could never muster enough men to defend the Virginia outposts, much less take the field. To make matters worse, Governor Dinwiddie held some of the best provincial troops back to guard the Tidewater region against a possible slave revolt. The Africans, Dinwiddie noted, had become "very audacious" since Braddock's Defeat.[1]

Daniel Morgan joined Captain John Ashby's company of Virginia rangers under Washington's command. He was soon at work constructing a blockhouse on Patterson's Creek, just east of the south branch of the Potomac. In April 1756, in one of the scouts just north of Winchester, Morgan and a companion were ambushed. A musket ball ripped through Morgan's neck and came out his cheek, taking several teeth along with it. His companion was killed and Morgan only escaped because the Indians stopped to scalp and loot the dead man. The episode was symptomatic of the fate of the three ranger companies, which Washington disbanded in October. Ashby's company had been a particular problem, for, as Washington noted, the captain could not even control his wife, who engaged in "irregular behavior" with several of the militiamen. Morgan, who was not involved in the scandal, soon returned to his former work as a teamster. Washington regarded the stockades and blockhouses as "more with a view to quiet the fears of the Inhabitants than from any expectation of giving security on so extensive a line to the settlements."[2]

The western land beyond the crest of the Appalachian Mountains was simply called Indian Country in 1755 and for another century and a half to follow as the frontier line continued to advance. By 1700 the Virginia Native population had fallen to less than 10 percent of what it had been at the founding of Jamestown a century before—perhaps less than a thousand people. The once mighty Powhatan Confederacy that had twice nearly wiped out the English colony had now been reduced by disease, war, and migration to a mere shadow of its once formidable power. The romantic fantasy of racial harmony promised by the old story of Pocahontas and John Rolfe had evaporated with the passage of the 1691 anti-miscegenation law that forbade the marriage of whites with "Negroes, Mulattoes and Indians." The punishment was banishment from the colony.[3]

To the south of Virginia and westward to the Mississippi River lay the lands of the Cherokee, Catawba, Chickasaw, Choctaw, and Creek along with their Florida cousins the Seminole. To the northwest, across the Blue Ridge Mountains, were the lands of various tribes still somewhat dominated by the powerful Six Nations of the Iroquois Confederacy of New York (Mohawk, Oneida, Seneca, Onondaga, Cayuga, and Tuscarora). The Shenandoah Valley, increasingly occupied by sturdy German farmers and restless Scotch-Irish frontiersmen, had once been a traditional pathway for Iroquois war parties raiding south against their ancient enemies, the Cherokees and Catawbas. In the summer of 1744, Iroquois leaders had met with a Virginia delegation at Lancaster, Pennsylvania, to resolve competing claims to the Shenandoah. The Iroquois claimed to have conquered every tribal nation in the region, and the Virginians readily agreed to this fiction. For payment in trade goods and cash, the Iroquois ceded their land claim as well as any claims by their alleged client nations. By this Treaty of Lancaster the Iroquois Confederacy ceded not only Virginia land but also the entire Ohio Country. This refocused the attention of Virginia fur traders away from their Cherokee trading partners and toward the Ohio Valley tribes. It also alerted Virginia land speculators to fresh opportunities. The Native inhabitants of these western lands were oblivious to this contrived new order.[4]

All of these Native societies were under increasing stress throughout the eighteenth century. Populations had long been devastated by a series of epidemics, most notably smallpox, which had advanced far ahead of the line of English settlement. French and English fur traders and missionaries inadvertently carried these European diseases to the various tribes. Native migrations also brought disease and war to the Ohio Country. The Shawnees and Delawares were pushed westward from the Susquehanna River over the Allegheny Mountains in response to increasing white settlement, while the Tuscaroras moved north from the Carolinas to join with the Iroquois Confederacy. At the same time splinter bands of the Iroquois Confederacy—mostly Senecas and Cayugas—moved west to the south of Lake Erie. They were branded as Mingos by the neighboring tribes. All of these tribes, increasingly dependent on the fur trade, found their hunting and trapping economy disrupted by the white farmers clearing the forests and planting fields as well as by the incursions of white market hunters like Daniel Boone.

The Miami, Wea, Piankashaw, Kickapoo, Wyandot, Ottawa, Potawatomi, Ojibwa, and other tribes of the Ohio Valley and Great Lakes were all caught up in this political and social chaos, as were the Cherokee, Chickasaw, Choctaw, and Creek to the south. This rapidly changing Native world also led to increased intertribal conflict, which further accelerated population loss. All of these people naturally came to view the Iroquois, French, and British with increasing suspicion.

At the same time, the Natives became increasingly dependent on European trade goods from the French, Spanish, and English. Guns not only assisted the Indians in their intertribal conflicts but were even more critical in their increasing dependence on the fur trade and market hunting. The profits derived from the valuable trade in deerskins alone further tied the Cherokees to English trade goods. By the late 1750s, 200,000 pounds of deerskins were exported from Savannah and another 355,000 pounds from Charleston annually to supply the British tanning industry. The Natives certainly recognized this increasing dependency. In 1750 a Cherokee leader lamented that "the Cloathes we wear, we cannot make ourselves, they are made for us. We use their Ammunition with which we kill Deer. We cannot make our Guns, they are made to us. Every necessary Thing in Life we must have from the white People."[5]

In an attempt to soothe tribal anxiety while also settling their conflicted sense of allegiance, George Croghan had met with various leaders from the Delaware, Shawnee, and Wyandot tribes at Logstown, just to the northwest of the Forks of the Ohio, in June 1752 to sign yet another treaty of friendship. He was aided in this by the Palatine clergyman Conrad Weiser, whose long years of work among the tribes gave him considerable influence. Also critical to Croghan's success in both trading and treaty making was Andrew Montour, the son of the French woman Isabelle Montour and an Oneida chief, who spoke not only English and French but several Native languages as well. Christopher Gist was there with a Virginia delegation to represent Ohio Company interests. Tanaghrisson was also at Logstown to play his usual duplicitous game as the Iroquois representative. The end result was a pledge by the Ohio tribes to support the Crown's interests in the Ohio Country. They also demanded that in exchange for this pledge a fort be promptly constructed at the Forks of the Ohio.[6]

Despite the Treaty of Logstown, Indian affairs were little better in the Pennsylvania backcountry than in Virginia after Braddock's Defeat. Both Virginia and Pennsylvania had been spared much of the Indian warfare that had marked the American fronts in the three previous conflicts between France and England and thus had not developed the same level of military experience as the more northern colonies. North America had been but a sideshow to these dynastic European conflicts, but the Seven Years' War was all about empire and, at least initially, centered in America.

Benjamin Franklin, who had nearly come to financial ruin over the funds he had advanced for Braddock's now lost horses and wagons, was also increasingly frustrated in his attempts to get the Quaker leaders of Pennsylvania to provide funds for frontier defense. Only intervention from England forced the assembly to vote for a defense appropriation. Franklin was among the commissioners appointed by Governor Robert Morris to oversee these military expenditures, including the raising of a militia and supervision of the construction of forts on the northwestern frontier.

Shawnee and Delaware leaders, for so long friendly trading partners with the Pennsylvanians, now ignored the Logstown treaty and unleashed their warriors. The Indians naturally sided with the triumphant French, as it was obvious that the English could not defeat them and that the Quakers would not resist them. Throughout the autumn of 1755, the Pennsylvania line of frontier settlements was thrown back.

"The pannick is inconceivable in every part of the country," provincial secretary Richard Peters wrote Thomas Penn in November. "The number of Indians will most assuredly encrease, & if Croghan or Montour or Scarroyady are worthy of credit, the French have engaged most of the nations of Indians over the Ohio in their interest."[7]

Croghan, who had faced severe criticism for the failure of his Mingo scouts on the Monongahela, was now once again viewed in Pennsylvania as the indispensable man. The Pennsylvania frontier faced even more concentrated Indian raids than did Virginia. Appointed a militia captain, Croghan was ordered to raise troops and build a new string of stockades similar to those in Virginia. Within a few weeks the energetic officer had 180 recruits and was on his way over the mountains to protect the exposed settlers. He prudently armed his men with Pennsylvania long rifles rather than the government-issued smoothbore muskets. While the rifles took three times longer to reload than the sturdy British Brown Bess muskets, they were more accurate at greater range and thus proved far superior in forest warfare. Much of the fighting would be hand to hand anyway, and Croghan's men were well versed in the use of both tomahawk and knife.[8]

Born in Ireland in 1718, Croghan had come to America along with several family members in 1741. Like so many other Irish Protestant immigrants, he worked hard and prospered in this new land of seemingly unbridled opportunity. Within seven years he had established himself as the preeminent Indian trader on the Pennsylvania frontier.

Croghan proved to be a natural Indian trader, for unlike many of his contemporaries he genuinely respected his Native trading partners, readily embraced their elaborate customs, and quickly learned their languages. He also came to understand the vital cultural significance of ritual gift giving and the absolute necessity of honest trading. His obvious personal courage, congenial wit, and sharp intelligence won him the respect of not only the Natives but also his Philadelphia financial backers and even his French rivals.

Within a decade Croghan, headquartered at Carlisle, Pennsylvania, had a cadre of traders working for him, pushing ever westward to establish trading outposts on Aughwick Creek northwest of Carlisle, on the Allegheny; at Pine Creek; at Logstown, eighteen miles south of the Ohio River; and at Oswegle Bottom, on the Youghiogheny River near the Forks of the Ohio. Croghan's men also traveled west to the Wabash River and Lake Erie and south to the Kentucky River. While their French rivals had backing from the military forts they operated out of, they could hardly compete with the superior and cheaper British goods—most notably strouds (cheap cloth blankets) and casks of rum.

Croghan and his men usually traveled in pairs along with a string of twenty or more packhorses, each of which might carry up to 150 pounds of trade goods. These horses were loaded down with strouds, rum, wampum (strings of tubular beads used as currency, as gifts, and to convey messages), linen, ribbons, stockings, awls, needles, buttons, combs, looking glasses, jewelry, pots, kettles, traps, knives, tomahawks, muskets, and powder and lead. These manufactured items were priceless to the Natives. The traders kept their "prices" low in order to undercut both their French and Virginian rivals. The Indians provided payment in the skins of elk, deer, bear, buffalo, fox, mink, otter, and other lesser-prized pelts.[9]

Croghan now personally took command of Fort Shirley, near the junction of Aughwick Creek and the Juniata River, where he had long had a trading post. His second-in-command was the Scottish doctor-turned-soldier Hugh Mercer, later to serve as a general in the Revolutionary army, who was to die heroically at the 1777 Battle of Princeton. The Delaware chief Shingas viewed Croghan as a traitor and kept a dozen warriors lurking about the stockade in hopes of capturing his former friend. Back in Philadelphia many high-placed officials also viewed Croghan with suspicion, believing that he was far too cozy with his old Native trading partners. Croghan's business rivals in the Indian trade fueled these suspicions. When confronted with the accusation that he was working with the Shawnees and other tribes against the colonists, Croghan resigned his commission in disgust and turned command of Fort Shirley over to Mercer.

He traveled north to Albany, New York, where he offered his services to Sir William Johnson, a former Irish trader like Croghan who had risen to prominence as a result of his closeness to and influence with the powerful Iroquois Confederacy. Johnson promptly appointed Croghan as his deputy and they remained closely linked until Sir William's death in 1774. As Johnson's fortunes rose, so did those of his loyal Irish lieutenant. His position allowed Croghan to acquire thousands of acres in western Pennsylvania by both purchase and royal grant. In 1749 he had acquired 200,000 acres to the south and west of the Forks of the Ohio and by 1773 he had another million and a half acres from the Forks stretching north to Venango. These land acquisitions fueled the increasingly bitter rivalry between Croghan and George Washington and the Ohio Company over the Forks of the Ohio.[10]

Events in England now shaped the fate of the war in America. William Pitt, who became secretary of state in the summer of 1757, quickly set in motion a series of military operations on both land and sea that ensured the triumph of British arms around the world. In America he passed over senior commanders to appoint younger, more aggressive officers: James Abercromby, Jeffrey Amherst, James Wolfe, and John Forbes. Newly appointed brigadier general Forbes was charged with taking Fort Duquesne. The overall strategy was to be determined by the visionary, controversial, and undeniably brilliant Pitt.

Forbes was the Scottish colonel of the 17th Regiment, fifty years old, and extremely capable in logistics, diplomacy, and organization. He was unfortunately stricken with a ghastly chronic bowel disease that often left him incapacitated. He thus relied heavily on his able second-in-command, the thirty-nine-year-old Swiss soldier of fortune Henry Bouquet. Forbes planned to abandon Braddock's Road and cut a new road on an old Indian trade route from Carlisle, Pennsylvania, west to the Forks of the Ohio, along which he would construct a string of supply depots.

Washington was horrified, declaring that "all is lost by Heaven!" He repeatedly argued against the new road and strenuously lobbied both military and political figures to advance again up Braddock's Road. Washington knew better than most how military roads might yet shape patterns of migration and commerce into the West. Braddock's Road would help to bolster Virginia's claim, as well as that of the Ohio Company, to the Ohio

Country. Forbes's proposed road would further cement the claims of Franklin, Croghan, and Pennsylvania to the same country.[11]

Forbes became aware of Washington's machinations when "a very unguarded letter of Col. Washington" was given to him. He complained to Bouquet that their Virginia colonel was engaged in "a scheme that I think was a shame for any officer to be concerned in." Forbes's sour mood as his health declined was not helped by Washington's carping, which he characterized as being "no ways like a Soldier."

Colonel Bouquet agreed, writing Forbes that after "an interview with colonel Washington to find out how he imagines these difficulties can be overcome I learned nothing satisfactory. Most of these gentlemen do not know the difference between a party and an army, and find everything easy which agrees with their ideas, jumping over all difficulties."[12]

Forbes proceeded with his road while at the same time engaging in adept diplomacy with the Ohio Country tribes in order to shift their allegiance back to the British. He sent Christian Frederick Post, a Moravian missionary who had lived among the Delaware for ten years, into the Ohio Country to meet with Delaware, Shawnee, and Mingo chiefs. This was a highly dangerous mission. Post was protected by eastern Delaware leaders who were unhappy with the loss of their British trading partners and irritated by the slowness of the arrival of promised French goods, gifts, and military support. By 1757 the French in North America were already in a precarious position because of the successful operations of the British fleet and could barely supply their own armies in the field, much less their Native allies.

Post assured Shingas, Tamaqua, and other important Delaware and Shawnee chiefs that the British desired only to defeat the French, and once that was accomplished, they would protect the Indians from further white settlement in the Ohio Country. The chiefs were skeptical, with one telling Post: "It is plain that you white people are the cause of this war; why do not you and the French fight in the old country and on the sea? Why do you come to fight on our land? This makes everybody believe, you want to take the land from us by force, and settle it."

Tamaqua extracted a pledge from Post that the British would recognize the Native ownership of the western country and would prevent any white settlement there. In return the tribes would not fight alongside the French. Post hurried back to Forbes with this news.

Forbes was elated, for this neutralization of the tribes was a great boon to his ability to advance. "I think nothing can prevent a solid peace being established with most of these Indian tribes as the Indian Claims appear to me both Just and Moderate," he assured Bouquet, "and what no man in their senses or in our situation with regard to the Indians would hesitate half an hour in granting them." He told Pitt much the same and reiterated that it was in the Crown's best interests to protect the Natives in the Ohio Country.

The resulting Treaty of Easton, signed in October 1758, promised the Ohio Country Indian leaders a great deal of autonomy, new trading posts, and a guarantee that the British government would not allow any further settlement beyond the Allegheny Mountains. George Croghan was on hand to represent Sir William Johnson as well as protect the interests of his relatives in the Iroquois Confederacy. (His wife was the head of the Turtle Clan and the daughter of an important Mohawk chief.) The Iroquois, while not particularly pleased with the independent spirit expressed by the Delawares and Shawnees, decided not to block the agreement. This treaty neutralized the various tribes, ended most attacks on the Pennsylvania and Virginia settlements, and opened the way for Forbes to advance against Fort Duquesne.[13]

As Forbes's army finally marched against the French, it suffered two embarrassing reversals. In September, Major James Grant was ordered to move against the French fort with his 77th Highland Regiment as well as men from four provincial regiments and several Indian scouts. Major Andrew Lewis commanded 175 men drawn from Washington's 1st Virginia. Grant arrived undetected with his 800 men but then amazingly ordered his bagpipes and drums to announce their presence before the fort at dawn September 14 when his advance guard became disorganized in the predawn darkness. Grant later explained that the drums were meant "to convince our men they had no reason to be afraid." The French commander, Captain François-Marie Le Marchand de Lignery, was naturally astonished to find kilted redcoats with shrilling bagpipes outside his post. As the Highlanders advanced, supported by the provincial troops, Lignery sent several hundred of his Indian allies forward. It was over quickly. Three hundred of Grant's men were killed or captured, including twenty-two officers, as well as sixty-two Virginians from Washington's regiment. Grant and Major Lewis were among the prisoners. Virginians under Captain Thomas Bullitt saved the day with a rearguard action that allowed the rest of Grant's eight hundred men to safely withdraw. "The Provincials seem to have done very well," Bouquet admitted, "and their good men are more suitable for this warfare than the regular troops."

Bouquet may have had second thoughts concerning the provincials when, a month later, on November 12, the Virginia regiments of Washington and Lieutenant Colonel George Mercer, about a thousand men, were ordered forward to check an Indian raid against Forbes's cattle and horse herd. In the darkness Washington's 1st Virginia and Mercer's 2nd Virginia collided and opened fire on each other. Thirty-eight Virginians were killed or wounded before the frantic Washington could halt the firing.[14]

Despite these setbacks, Forbes was determined to advance. The general was now so ill that he had to be carried forward on a litter, and Bouquet increasingly assumed actual field command. By November 21 the British advance guard was on Turtle Creek, within a dozen miles of Fort Duquesne. From a prisoner Forbes learned that most of the Indians, loaded down with booty and horses from their victories over the British, had gone home to their villages. The French commander had but three hundred Canadian militiamen and a handful of regulars left to defend his fort. Lignery, an experienced and able officer, decided on the better part of valor and determined to abandon Fort Duquesne. He ordered the fort's artillery loaded on boats to be conveyed downstream to the Illinois Country. His soldiers then set fire to the outpost that had caused this great war and hurriedly departed by boat up the Allegheny to Fort Machault.

Despite Washington's rather erratic behavior and unrelenting negativity, Forbes allowed the Virginian to lead an advance column against Fort Duquesne. On the morning of November 24, Washington reached the still-smoldering ruins of the fort that had so impacted his young life. The Forks of the Ohio now belonged to Great Britain.

General Forbes named the location of the remains of the French fort Pittsburgh, after his patron. The desperately ill Forbes now hurried his army back to Carlisle. He was then carried by litter to Philadelphia, where he died on March 11, 1759, at the age of fifty-one. He was given an elaborate funeral at Philadelphia's Christ Church. It was with good reason that Pennsylvania's leading citizens celebrated this most able soldier, for he had not only freed their backcountry from Indian raids; he had also built a road that would ensure a pathway to the West for Pennsylvania Indian traders, land speculators, and pioneer farmers.[15]

Lieutenant Colonel Hugh Mercer, the Scottish doctor turned soldier, with two hundred Pennsylvania provincial troops, was left behind to build a stockade on the banks of the Monongahela to thwart an anticipated French counterattack. Mercer had his crude stockade up by the middle of December. His men also performed the gruesome duty of burying what was left of the remains of Braddock's army. This certainly added to their understandable unease over the return of the French and their Indian allies.

The French counterattack never came. The energetic Captain François-Marie Le Marchand de Lignery put together a formidable force of at least 2,500 men, the vast majority of whom were Great Lakes Indians. Just as the bold captain was about to lead his new army south, he was ordered north to reinforce the besieged French garrison at Fort Niagara. Abandoned by most of his Native allies, Lignery's force of seven hundred French regulars and Canadian militia was intercepted by an overwhelming force of British troops and their steadfast Iroquois allies under Sir William Johnson. The French were slaughtered. Lignery was among the fewer than one hundred prisoners taken. Fort Niagara surrendered soon afterward. This dashed all French hope of ever retaking the Forks of the Ohio.

A new British fort soon arose on the banks of the Monongahela. Fort Pitt was a massive earthen and stone pentagon that, with its extensive ditches and outer works, sprawled across eighteen acres. When completed in the summer of 1761, it was the largest fort on the American frontier. During the months that the post was under construction, French fortunes collapsed all across the colonies. When the French surrendered Montreal to Amherst on September 9, 1760, the war ended in America.[16]

George Washington took no part in these concluding actions of what soon came to be known throughout the colonies as the French and Indian War. After the fall of Fort Duquesne he returned to Virginia, where in July 1758 he was elected to the House of Burgesses and not long afterward resigned his military commission. He then devoted all his time to improving Mount Vernon and to courting the lovely and wealthy widow Martha Custis. They married on January 6, 1759, and from then on, Washington quickly doubled his Tidewater acreage and greatly increased his number of enslaved people to work these new lands. He was now one of the wealthiest men in Virginia.

Washington also remained committed to his dream of the enormous potential of the western frontier. Virginia awarded him 20,000 acres in the Ohio Valley in recognition of his military service, and he purchased 25,000 more acres in land warrants that had been granted to the officers and men who had served under him in the war. In 1767 he hired an old comrade-in-arms, Captain William Crawford, to survey lands on the south bank of the Ohio River. Despite his comfortable life in the East, Washington's gaze was ever toward the West, which he viewed as the future for America.[17]

Daniel Boone was also done with soldiering. And, like Washington, his mind remained fixated on the West. He could not shake off the stories old Findley had told him of the fabled hunter's paradise Kanta-kee. After his narrow escape from Braddock's battlefield, he had headed east to visit relatives near the old family home at Exeter, Pennsylvania. On this solitary journey he came to a bridge straddling a deep gorge cut by the Juniata River through the Pennsylvania mountains. A large besotted Indian man in a foul frame of mind confronted the youngster and blocked his passage over the bridge. "He drew his knife on me," Boone later related, "flourishing it over his head, boasting that he had killed many a Long Knife, and would kill some more on his way home." Boone was unarmed but was in no mood to tolerate this man's drunken threats. He had just witnessed the deaths of countless Long Knives—as the Ohio Indians called whites because of their long hunting knives and sabers—slaughtered by the Natives, and something inside him snapped. Boone concluded that this "blood-thirsty red skin had killed his last victim—that it was high time an end should be put to his bloody career." The enraged Boone lunged at the man, lifting him off his feet and sending him over the bridge and onto the rocks far below. As he looked down on the broken body in the riverbed, he was swept up with horror and remorse—for this was the first man Daniel Boone had ever killed.[18]

3

BUSHY RUN

The French and Indian War essentially ended in North America in September 1760 with the fall of Montreal to British forces. Within a few weeks of Montreal's surrender, Major Robert Rogers with two hundred of his celebrated rangers was westward bound under orders from General Jeffrey Amherst to force the capitulation of the remaining French outposts. Rogers accepted the surrender of Fort Detroit in November 1760 and within a few months all the French forts save those in the distant Illinois Country had also capitulated.

Rogers was warmly welcomed by the local Indians. "All the Rivers would flow with Rum—that Presents from the Great King were to be unlimited—that all sorts of Goods were to be in the Utmost Plenty and so cheap," Rogers assured the assembled Natives.

The ranger commander was deeply impressed by this new western country. "The Country level, the Timber tall, and of the best Sort. Oak, Hickory and Locust," he later wrote. "It is well Watered and for Game, both as to plenty and variety perhaps exceeded by no part of the World." He became, as did so many who ventured into this new land, an apostle for western settlement.[1]

George Croghan and his assistant Andrew Montour soon joined Rogers on this dangerous mission. Croghan sent Native runners ahead to call the various tribal leaders to a council at Detroit, where they would be told of the French defeat in the war. Croghan, like Rogers, was pleasantly surprised by the warm welcome extended by tribal leaders. The Natives were particularly anxious to see a resumption of trade.

Croghan promptly reopened the fur trade. All traders were to be regulated by the government and only allowed to trade at fair prices to be set by Croghan. The Irishman declared the going currency to be a buck's worth, or one fall male deerskin. The equivalent of a buck was to be two spring bucks, two does, six raccoons, four foxes, two otters, and so on with lesser furs. A blanket was to be traded for four bucks, a pint of powder was worth one buck, as were one hundred wampum beads. The Indians now nicknamed Croghan the "Buck."

This admirable system quickly broke down as numerous Pennsylvania traders infested the Great Lakes and Ohio Country. At the same time General Amherst made such deep cuts in Croghan's budget that it became impossible to employ agents to enforce the new price rules or regulate the trade. These men brought inferior goods and charged exorbitant prices. "The most worthless men in the Provinces," one British official labeled them, "being proficient in all sorts of vice and debauchery." A fee to a colonial governor was all that was needed to enter the trade. As Native dissatisfaction grew, Sir William Johnson traveled to Detroit in the fall of 1761 to meet with and calm northwestern tribal leaders, but it was too little, too late.

By the 1763 Treaty of Paris ending the war, France ceded all of its American possessions save New Orleans to England. The French gave to their ally Spain the vast and unexplored Louisiana Territory west of the Mississippi River as a reward for joining them against the British. The French were thus driven out of North America. This all looked grand on paper but of course neglected to consider that these western lands were rightfully owned and still controlled by a host of Native nations.[2]

The British victory over the French had only increased suspicions among the various tribes that their lands would soon be overrun. A prophet now arose among them with a message of cultural revitalization. Neolin warned against their dependence on English trade goods and most especially rum and other spirits that enabled the white man to insidiously break down Native society. Neolin's call for cultural rebirth also included the expulsion of the English. "Those who come to trouble your lands—drive them out, make war upon them . . . send them back to the lands which I have created for them and let them stay there." His messianic message traveled wide and found many willing audiences. In time it would help to unite the tribes of the Great Lakes with those of the Ohio Valley.[3]

The Indians came to understand that the loss of their French trading partners left them at the mercy of the voracious British traders. Without competition and with scant imperial regulation, many traders raised the prices of their goods while lowering the market value of furs and hides. Nor were the Natives oblivious to scores of surveyors marking out their lands for the great companies controlled by Washington, Franklin, Croghan, and other leading colonists. To make matters worse, the new military commander in America, Sir Jeffrey Amherst, followed a policy of strict economy in dealing with the tribes, whom he held in unconcealed contempt. With the war over, they had ceased to be of military use. Despite the warnings of Sir William Johnson and Croghan, he refused to finance the annual ceremonial gift giving among the tribes. He also ordered Croghan to secure the release of white captives taken in the late war, many of whom had no wish to return to the frontier settlements and their former lives.

A Chippewa leader now perfectly stated the Native view: "Although you have conquered the French you have not conquered us! We're not your slaves. These lakes, these woods, these mountains were left to us by our ancestors. They are our inheritance; and we will part with them to none."[4]

Croghan soon learned that wampum war belts were being circulated in Indian villages from the Great Lakes south to the Ohio River and as far west as the Mississippi. Leading this call to war was a charismatic Ottawa leader named Pontiac. Building on Neolin's spiritual message, he now called for pan-tribal unity to confront the British claim to all the Native lands upon which they lived. The French had no right to transfer tribal lands to the British, Pontiac declared at a great council held on April 27, 1763, not far from Fort Detroit. At fifty years of age, Pontiac was past his prime as a warrior, but his previous deeds in war were spoken of with awe around Ottawa campfires and throughout the western country. He was taller than most and imposing in bearing, with "a proud, vindictive, warlike countenance." His hair was combed in a narrow pompadour which diminished from the front to the back. His body was marked with typical Ottawa tattoos. A shrewd politician and master orator, Pontiac mesmerized the assembled Hurons, Potawatomis, Ottawas, and Chippewas with his bold call to unite and "drive off your lands those dogs clothed in red who will do you nothing but harm."[5]

Croghan's repeated warnings to Amherst and Colonel Henry Bouquet fell on deaf ears. He was certain by late 1762 that war was imminent. The Indians were jealous of British power, resented the many forts built in their country, were insulted by the refusal of Amherst to engage in the annual ritual of gift giving, and were outraged at the demand to repatriate their white captives, whom they now regarded as family. Croghan was certain that his French fur trade rivals were encouraging the Natives to strike with promises of the return of French soldiers. Amherst responded by cutting Croghan's budget for a supply of gifts to the tribes—which he regarded as bribes—and dismissing all talk of French intervention. "I look upon the intelligence you received of the French stirring up the western Indians of little consequence, as it is not in their power to hurt us," he responded to Croghan. To Colonel Bouquet the general wrote that "the post of Fort Pitt or any others commanded by officers, can certainly never be in danger from such a wretched enemy." Sir Jeffrey could not have been more wrong.[6]

On May 9, 1763, Pontiac led eight hundred warriors from half a dozen tribes against the wooden walls of Detroit and, although initially repulsed, laid siege to the fort. Within a few weeks, eight small British forts—Sandusky, St. Joseph, Ouiatenon, Michilimackinac, Venango, LeBoeuf, Presque Isle, and Miami—were taken by a broad coalition of Great Lakes and Ohio Valley tribes. The garrisons were mostly slaughtered, some after surrendering.

Fort Pitt, with its garrison of 250 soldiers, was attacked on June 22. The steady commandant, Swiss-born Captain Simon Ecuyer, had heeded the rumors of war. He hurriedly gathered nearby civilians into his fort and burned their ramshackle cabins clustered around the post. Ecuyer soon found his garrison cut off from any communication with the outside world, although a handful of haggard survivors from Presque Isle and LeBoeuf arrived to report the fall of those outposts. Several settlers who had not come to the fort were slaughtered as well. Ecuyer sent a courier off to Bouquet with a desperate message. "I think the uprising is general. I tremble for our posts," he wrote. "I think according to reports that I am surrounded by Indians. I am neglecting nothing to give them a good reception."

Within days, Fort Pitt was ringed by over four hundred Shawnee, Mingo, and Delaware warriors, and the Swiss captain had no way of knowing if his couriers had reached Carlisle some two hundred miles to the east. While most of the warriors besieged the fort, small raiding parties moved east against the isolated farms and small settlements. Many of these farmers were recent immigrants who had little knowledge of firearms and no money to purchase them. Others were recently freed indentured servants whose poverty dictated they scratch out a living on this distant frontier. They fled eastward in panic as the Indian raiders burned their cabins and slaughtered their livestock. Many did not escape in time, with some 2,000 killed or carried off into captivity.[7]

Bouquet had hurried from Philadelphia to Carlisle after sending dispatches to Amherst in New York. The general at first dismissed what he considered unfounded frontier rumors, but enough fresh intelligence had reached him by June 12 that he wrote Bouquet: "I find the Affair of the Indians, appears to be more General than I had Apprehended." Amherst ordered two companies of light infantry from the 42nd (the famed Black Watch) and 77th Highlander Regiments to reinforce Bouquet.

As Bouquet mobilized his troops at Carlisle, he bitterly complained of the refusal of the Pennsylvania Assembly to offer support or of the frontier militia to join with him. At the same time that he struggled to consolidate his supply chain, he found himself inundated with a flood of refugees that he felt compelled to feed. "I find myself utterly abandoned by the very people I am ordered to protect," Bouquet reported.

The indifference of the provincials to the east, and especially of the elites, puzzled the Swiss soldier, but he had to put them out of his mind and deal with the very real crisis at hand. "The despair of those who have lost their parents, relatives, and friends, with the cries of distracted women and children who fill the streets, form a scene painful to humanity and impossible to describe," he wrote Amherst. Bouquet reported that "a general Panick has Siezed this extensive country."[8]

One of the refugees, Phoebe Byerly, was well known to Colonel Bouquet. She, too, was from Switzerland, and they had often met at Bushy Run Station to reminisce about the old country. Bushy Run was a relay station where army couriers and troops moving between Carlisle and Pitt could rest and water their horses. After the Indians struck the farms to the east of Fort Pitt, Phoebe's husband, who operated Bushy Run Station, went to bury a family slaughtered at a nearby farm. Mrs. Byerly, who had given birth to her fourth child but three days before, remained behind with the children. An Indian friend suddenly appeared at the cabin and warned Phoebe to depart at once. She scrawled a note and left it on the cabin door for her husband, strapped the newborn to her breast and her two-year-old to her back, mounted a horse, and headed east to Fort Ligonier. Her two older boys, ages twelve and three, followed along, driving their milk cows. After an all-night journey they reached the doubtful sanctuary of the Ligonier stockade. She would live to laugh with Bouquet about the Alps yet again.[9]

Such was the mettle of the pioneer stock so easily dismissed by the Quaker elites and Tidewater gentry to the east. These brave souls had left the past far behind to become the vanguard of a glorious future. They had traveled far to what they saw as an undiscovered country at the edge of the world. Many would die, but more would come.

Bouquet, forced to linger for over two weeks at Carlisle to deal with the refugee crisis, finally departed with his kilted Highlanders on July 18 along with a herd of one hundred cattle and two hundred sheep. It was August 2 before Bouquet reached Ligonier over the Forbes Road he had helped construct.

The little stockade at Ligonier, which he had himself directed the construction of, was in such a sad state of disrepair that it could offer scant refuge if the column was ambushed on the two-day march to Fort Pitt. The Swiss colonel heard nothing from Pitt, for indeed all of Ecuyer's recent Indian couriers had been killed or forced back. Bouquet decided to leave his wagons, artillery, and invalid troops behind while he advanced in a reconnaissance in force to Pitt. The only certainty that Bouquet had was that he would undoubtedly be attacked somewhere in the dense forest ahead.

On July 26 an impressive delegation of Native leaders—including the Delaware chiefs Grey Eyes and Shingas and the Shawnee chief Big Wolf—approached Fort Pitt to demand its surrender. They called on Ecuyer to withdraw to his own country, for they now realized that British forts were not there to protect the Indian nations but to oppress them. The fact that the British had refused to trade any muskets, powder, and lead was a clear sign to them that they had really come to dispossess them of their lands. A Delaware chief held forth a wampum belt from the Ottawas far to the west and proclaimed that all the Indian nations were now united against the English.

Ecuyer was unmoved. "I will not abandon this post," he angrily retorted, "and we shall not abandon it as long as a white Man Lives in America."[10]

The next day hundreds of warriors assaulted the fort. Fire arrows struck several houses, but the women of the post set up bucket brigades while the men manned the ramparts. Although a handful were wounded, including Captain Ecuyer, Fort Pitt held. Then suddenly the warriors abandoned the attack. On the afternoon of August 1 the puzzled garrison watched as hundreds of Delaware, Huron, Shawnee, Mingo, and Ottawa warriors crossed over the Ohio River toward the east.

Bouquet, with less than five hundred men, departed Ligonier on August 4 for the final push to the Forks of the Ohio. Andrew Byerly and his oldest son joined the column in hopes of reopening the Bushy Run relay station. Lieutenant James Dow of the 60th Royal American Regiment led the way into the dark forest of old-growth oaks and chestnuts. The shade of the towering trees meant that there was little undergrowth amidst the emerald shade cast across the ground. Bouquet, the wisest of all the British officers in America, relied upon his light infantry and American rangers to confront the Natives with their own style of forest warfare. Round of face and soft of flesh, Bouquet did not much resemble the ideal of a soldier, but he had proved himself on countless battlefields. His men trusted him. He hoped to make Bushy Run Station before nightfall on August 5.

The column, although stretched out for nearly a mile, made good progress and by one o'clock was but a mile from Bushy Run. It was hot that day, and both the men and pack animals desperately needed the water at the relay station. It was then, between two rolling hills, that the ambush was sprung. Dow's advance column held their ground and returned fire. The lieutenant was among the first to fall. Bouquet sprang instantly into action. As soon as he heard the desultory musket fire of the warriors, he ordered two companies of the Black Watch forward to reinforce Dow. He then hurriedly organized his main column for action.

Although the Natives melted back before the cold steel of the Highlanders' bayonet charge, they quickly shifted their position to the flanks of the main column. This forest encirclement was just the type of tactic that had shattered Braddock's force on the Monongahela.

Bouquet was no Braddock. He ordered his Highlanders to dislodge the Indians from the high ground before him. The Indians again fell back only to suddenly appear to his rear, where the vulnerable packtrain and livestock herd waited. Bouquet had no choice but to call back his men and retreat to the packtrain. It was an orderly withdrawal, but the packtrain was a chaotic scene, with scores of animals killed and the civilian packers in a panic.

Bouquet spotted a likely defensive position nearby; he called it Edge Hill. He would make his stand on this spacious hill of ten or so acres. It had a precipitous drop-off on one side, thus the name. He ordered his men to herd the remaining animals to the hill and to pile flour bags and packsaddles up to form a defensive perimeter. The Highlanders and Royal Americans unflinchingly stood their ground to ward off the warriors while this makeshift redoubt was thrown together.

As darkness fell, the firing slackened, although the warriors could still be heard moving about in the woods. Bouquet took stock of his rather desperate situation. He had sixty men killed or wounded. Many of his packhorses had been slain or driven off. His men had no water, not even for their wounded comrades. He established his pickets and sat down to write a dispatch to Amherst. Sir Jeffrey had been dismissive of this war, but at least now he would learn that it was indeed serious business. The colonel may well have thought this to be the last letter he would ever write: "Whatever our Fate may be I thought it necessary to give your Excellency this early Information, that you may, at all Events, take such measures as you will think proper with the Provinces for their own Safety, and the Effectual relief of Fort Pitt, as in case of another Engagement, I fear insurmountable difficulties." He closed with warm praise of his troops, whose "cool and steady behavior" had driven "the Enemy from their Posts with fixed Bayonets." After dispatching a courier eastward, the intrepid Swiss officer settled into the darkness to devise a plan for the morning's bloody work.[11]

At dawn the warriors resumed their assault on the redoubt. The Highlanders answered these attacks with bayonet charges. The warriors withdrew each time only to resume the assault from a different direction. Each counterattack left more redcoats dead or wounded, which encouraged their foe to even greater fury. A British officer later remembered these assaults as "very smart, and bloody, many being killed and wounded on both Sides, the Indians still continuing to behave with uncommon Bravery."

The British held firm amidst the Indian war cries and dense, acrid black powder smoke that helped conceal their enemy. When they did emerge from the smoke, they presented a frightful sight, with bodies painted crimson and black and long scalp locks floating in the wind. A warrior now shouted out in perfect English to Bouquet that "they would have his scalp before night." The colonel thought differently.[12]

At ten that morning Bouquet called his exhausted officers together to lay out his plan. Two companies on the western flank were to withdraw into the hilltop circle. Men from the north and south would adjust their position to help fill in their gap in the line. Bouquet felt certain that his Native foes would instantly recognize this weakness and, sensing a retreat, come rushing forward en masse. Meanwhile, Major Allan Campbell, an old veteran with the 42nd Regiment, was to quietly lead the two "retreating" companies over the eastern edge of the hill into the forest to circle back to flank the attacking warriors. It all worked perfectly. The Indians came rushing forward to confront Bouquet's weakened west line, expecting to roll the redcoats up. Campbell's men suddenly appeared on their right flank to deliver a devastating volley. No strangers to bloodcurdling war cries of their own, the Highlanders now crashed into the shocked Indians with claymore and bayonet.

"We met them with our fire first," recalled one of the Scots, "and then made terrible havock amongst them with our own fixt bayonets, and continuing to push them everywhere, they set to their heels and were never able to rally again." The ferocious Highlanders pursued the Indians for over a mile before they halted. The game was up.

The retreating Indians left over twenty slain on the field, which was highly unusual, as they always carried off their dead. Bouquet had won a great victory, but at a considerable cost. The butcher's bill numbered fifty dead and another sixty wounded, including Lieutenant Dow and three other officers. "The Highlanders are the bravest Men I ever saw," noted the Swiss colonel, "and their behavior in that obstinate affair does them the highest honor."[13]

Bouquet pushed on the short distance to Bushy Run and the desperately needed water for his wounded men. With so many packhorses killed or scattered, he had no choice but to burn most of the flour bags meant for Fort Pitt. On the evening of August 10 the bloodied but unbowed command finally staggered into Fort Pitt. The Indians had departed and the siege was lifted. The Forks of the Ohio were once again under British control.

Bouquet tarried at Fort Pitt for two more months as he attempted to enlist the support of the Pennsylvania militia in order to take the war to the Delaware, Mingo, and Shawnee villages west of the Muskingum River. Bouquet's plans were further complicated by a directive from London to cut the number of troops stationed in the colonies to save money. Amherst promptly complied, ordering a drastic reduction in the Black Watch, the disbandment of the 77th Highland Regiment, and the transfer of three companies of the Royal American Regiment to South Carolina.

This was the final straw for Croghan. He was already disgusted by the general's determination to resort to war over negotiation. "Indeed," Sir Jeffrey had lectured Croghan, "their total extirpation is scarce sufficient atonement for the bloody and inhuman deeds they have committed." Croghan was now particularly outraged by Amherst's refusal to enlist both Indian and provincial volunteers to continue the war. "The General seems determined to neither accept of Indian serving nor provincials," he wrote Bouquet on October 11, 1763. "I have resigned out of the service . . . as no regard was had to any intelligence I sent, no more than to my opinions."[14]

Although the Native leaders had abandoned the siege of Pitt following their defeat at Bushy Run, they continued to send a steady stream of raiding parties against the frontiers of Pennsylvania and Virginia. In one particularly ghastly incident, Delaware warriors descended on a log schoolhouse in Pennsylvania's Conococheague Valley on July 26. The schoolmaster held forth his Bible and pleaded with the Indians to spare the children. A Delaware promptly shot him dead and scalped him. The warriors then methodically butchered the children and scalped them. When the horrified parents rushed into the school, they found nine dead children sprawled across the room. A little girl, although scalped, escaped and was discovered at a nearby stream, washing the blood from her body. Little wonder that these pioneer folk called for the extermination of this enemy. The number of settlers slaughtered or captured was appalling, especially considering the relatively small population on the exposed frontier.[15]

Amherst came up with a novel solution to his Indian problem. "Could it not be contrived to Send the Small Pox among those Disaffected Tribes of Indians?" he inquired of Bouquet. The Swiss colonel responded that he could try, but that smallpox was deadly to the British as well as to the Indians. "You will Do well to try to Innoculate the Indians, by means of Blankets, as well as to Try Every other Method, that can Serve to Extirpate this Execrable Race," Amherst ordered.

Neither officer knew that Captain Ecuyer at Fort Pitt was one step ahead of them. On June 24 he had presented gifts to two Delaware chiefs who had come to beg him to surrender. The gifts included liquor and rations, as well as two blankets and a handkerchief from the smallpox section of the post hospital. This early attempt at biological warfare failed, for neither the two chiefs nor their people were infected. There were indeed smallpox outbreaks among the western and Great Lakes tribes during this period, but that was not unusual, since the disease had long been among them. Over the preceding decades thousands had perished from this pestilence, while many others had survived to carry the marks of the disease on their faces. Amherst's devious plan had minimal if any impact.[16]

The reaction of the settlers of western Pennsylvania to the Indian uprising did not involve biological warfare but was equally cruel. These frontier folk were outraged by the inability of either British or provincial troops to protect their families, as well as by the persistent indifference of the Philadelphia Quaker elites to their plight. They began their protest with murder.

On December 14, 1763, a mob of fifty armed men from Paxton Township descended upon a small settlement of Christian Indians at Conestoga Manor and brutally slaughtered six, scalping and mutilating the bodies. Refugees from Conestoga fled to nearby Lancaster, where they found sanctuary in the community workhouse. On December 27 a large band of Paxton men attacked the workhouse. Fourteen Indian men, women, and children were cut down and their bodies horribly mutilated. The local authorities offered no resistance and the killers rode away unmolested.

Several other Christian Indian settlements were hurriedly abandoned as the people fled to the east. Pennsylvania governor John Penn offered the Natives sanctuary on an island in the Delaware River. Penn also posted a large reward for the capture of the ringleaders of the so-called Paxton Boys. The law had no trouble locating these culprits, for they soon led 250 heavily armed men in a march on Philadelphia.

The Philadelphia elites now got a taste of the panic sweeping over the backcountry. The Quaker-dominated assembly, suddenly awakened to a keen interest in military defense, authorized Benjamin Franklin to raise nine militia companies to defend the city. The Paxton Boys halted at Germantown and settled in to await a delegation from Philadelphia headed by Franklin.

This Scotch-Irish and German rabble in arms seemed quite formidable to the Quaker residents of Germantown. A local citizen described them as "a set of fellows, dressed in blanket coats and moccasins, like our Indian traders, or back-country waggoneers: they were armed with rifles and tomahawks, and some of them had a brace of pistols besides."[17]

Franklin, ever the consummate diplomat, soothed the rebels with a promise to present their "Declaration of Remonstrance" to the governor and assembly. The declaration demanded the removal of all Indians from the colony, the immediate repatriation of white captives, a stronger frontier defense force, and a dramatic increase in backcountry representation in the assembly. They then returned peaceably to their homes. Their charge that the Quakers cared more for the Indians than for the white citizens resonated with the electorate, and in the next election the Quaker faction in the assembly was soundly defeated. This was perhaps the first time that frontiersmen came east to challenge government authority, but it would hardly be the last.[18]

At Detroit, Pontiac faced mounting difficulty in holding his tribal coalition together. A prolonged siege did not fit well into the standard norms of tribal warfare. The British helped Pontiac's cause a bit in July with an ill-advised sortie out of the fort against their villages. Amherst had sent his trusted aide-de-camp, the aristocratic Captain James Dalyell, with a relief column to Fort Detroit. The captain arrived with twenty boats at Detroit on July 28. Anxious for action and contemptuous of his Native foe, Dalyell immediately requested permission of Major Henry Gladwin to attack the Indian villages. Major Robert Rogers, despite misgivings about the raid, accompanied the young captain along with 247 men. They marched in the fog-shrouded darkness of the early morning hours of July 31 toward Pontiac's village and right into a well-laid ambush. Within the hour twenty-three men were dead and another thirty-five wounded. The remainder were saved only by a desperate rearguard action commanded by Major Rogers. Dalyell was among those slain, supposedly killed by Pontiac's brother-in-law. His head was impaled on a stake in Pontiac's camp for all to see.

Amherst, furious when he learned of the death of his young aide, placed a two-hundred-pound bounty on the head of Pontiac. "His Death would be some small satisfaction for the loss of poor Dalyell," wrote the grieving general.[19]

Amherst's days in America were numbered. The repeated military setbacks and added expense of the Indian war were too much for London. On October 7, 1763, he was recalled. This news was greeted with elation in the colonies and among many British soldiers. "What universal cries of joy and what bumpers of Madeira are drunk to his prompt departure," Captain Ecuyer confided to Colonel Bouquet.[20]

General Thomas Gage was appointed to take Amherst's place. The old soldier had seen considerable action on the continent as well as at the Battle of Culloden that crushed the Jacobite rebellion in 1746. Although his appointment to replace Amherst was meant to be temporary, Gage would serve as the North American commander in chief from September 1763 until June 1775.

A fellow officer cautioned Gage on his new command: "I am sorry to see you charged with the cares of such a harassing war; the honor that you may acquire cannot be compared to the unpleasantness to which you will be exposed, and what is even worse, no one in Europe will realize the difficulties you must surmount."[21]

The war now proceeded on three fronts. Sir William Johnson negotiated with the Six Nations to abandon their neutrality and again join with the British in order to regain their dominance over the Delawares, Shawnees, and Mingos in the Ohio Country. Johnson's successful diplomatic gambit also isolated the hostile Senecas and brought them back under the power of the Iroquois Confederacy. Johnson ordered Andrew Montour out with a force of two hundred Iroquois warriors to attack Delaware and Shawnee towns along the Susquehanna River. These successful raids forced the surviving Delawares and Shawnees to flee to the Scioto and Muskingum Rivers deep in the Ohio Country.

Even though Johnson's diplomacy had undercut Pontiac's fragile Native alliance, Gage still proceeded with Amherst's plan for a two-pronged military campaign. In the north, Colonel John Bradstreet was to lead a formidable force across Lake Erie from Fort Niagara to Detroit. At the same time, Bouquet was to march to the west of Fort Pitt to destroy the Delaware, Mingo, and Shawnee Ohio villages.

As these military expeditions very slowly organized as a result of the colonial governments' recalcitrance in providing militia forces, Sir William Johnson sent messengers deep into Indian Country to invite all the tribes to come to a great council in July at Fort Niagara. Although Pontiac did not attend, 2.000 others did. Johnson generously distributed gifts to the assembled chiefs and warriors and reached an agreement whereby they would "bury the hatchet," return all prisoners, and resume trade with the British. The trade in both gunpowder and shot as well as alcohol was to be resumed.

Bradstreet proceeded to Detroit with 1,400 men and there met with several important Indian leaders and attempted to negotiate a new peace. Pontiac did not attend but sent a wampum peace belt. Bradstreet shocked the assembled Indians by hacking the belt to pieces. He then demanded the immediate surrender of the leaders of the rebellion. The Indians left in disgust. Bradstreet's campaign collapsed in on itself from a lack of supplies, mutinous troops, and disaffected Native allies. Bradstreet hurriedly retired back to Fort Niagara with his half-starved command.[22]

By September 1764, Colonel Bouquet had managed to assemble nearly 1,200 troops at Fort Pitt. He anchored his force around the 42nd Regiment and the Royal Americans, along with around 600 Pennsylvania militia troops and a detachment of 200 Virginia volunteers. The colonel was determined to fight the Indians in their own way and so organized several of the Pennsylvania men into rifle companies. Bouquet, unlike other British officers, respected the talents of his men and prized marksmanship over the standard musket volleys.

On October 3, Bouquet led his little army across the Allegheny River into Indian Country. His men hacked out a pathway straight for the Indian villages on the Muskingum. About a mile above the forks of that river, Bouquet had a small stockade built around his military camp. This show of force so deep in their homeland led the Shawnee, Delaware, Seneca, and Mingo leaders to meet with the Swiss colonel on October 17, 1764, and ask for peace. Bouquet brushed aside the chiefs' attempts to blame the war on Pontiac and the western bands and accused them of a string of crimes, including the siege of Fort Pitt and the murder of the schoolmaster and his young students. "Your conduct has always been equally perfidious," the colonel declared. "You promised at every former Treaty, as you do now, that you would deliver up all your Prisoners . . . but you have never complied." Bouquet now demanded that they cease all hostilities, surrender their white captives to him within twelve days, and then travel east to meet with

Sir William Johnson to formally conclude a peace treaty. The assembled chiefs sullenly agreed to these terms.[23]

The Delawares and Mingos soon brought to Bouquet more than two hundred white prisoners, while the Shawnee brought in thirty-six and promised to come into Fort Pitt in the spring with all of the rest of their prisoners. The return of the prisoners proved to be highly emotional, for many of them had no desire to be repatriated. A good number of the white children had only known their Native parents. Several of the women had accepted their new lives with loving Indian husbands, had had children by them, and did not wish to return to a judgmental white society. Others, however, were overjoyed to find their white husbands among the troops and were delighted at their liberation. As the troops marched back to Fort Pitt, several of the Indian men accompanied them to linger as long as possible near their white wives and children. Bouquet and his officers were all touched by these poignant scenes.

"We have taken as much care of these prisoners, as if they were our own flesh and blood," declared a Shawnee chief. "They are become unacquainted with your customs and manners; and therefore, we request you will use them tenderly and kindly."[24]

Bouquet was treated as a conquering hero upon his return to Fort Pitt. Both the Pennsylvania and Virginia Assemblies passed resolutions of thanks to the colonel. General Gage and Sir William Johnson were equally lavish in their praise of this judicious officer who had ended the Indian war without firing a shot.

Of course, the war was not quite over, for Pontiac and his Illinois Country followers were still determined to resist the British. Gage and Johnson realized that a military campaign in that distant country was impossible but that one man might yet bring about peace. That man was, of course, George Croghan.

"This fellow [Pontiac] shou'd be gained to our Interest, or knocked in the head," Gage bluntly stated. Croghan knew what he had to do.[25]

Croghan, as wily as he was bold, fully realized that while negotiating a peace with these far western nations he might also scout out potential lands as well as assert his right to corner this distant fur trade. He met with several tribal leaders, including the prophet Neolin, at Fort Pitt in the early spring. The assembled Natives brought in two dozen more white captives as a sign of their goodwill and again agreed to go meet with Sir William Johnson. They also provided the Irishman with an escort of ten warriors to accompany him to the Illinois Country.

On May 15, Croghan and his Indian escort departed Fort Pitt in two boats laden with gifts for Pontiac and his followers. As they made camp on the Ohio not far from the mouth of the Wabash River, they were attacked by a large Kickapoo war party. Croghan fell with a severe tomahawk blow to the head, while five of his companions—two whites and three Shawnees—were killed. The Kickapoos took Croghan and his remaining men as prisoners to their village on the Wabash River.

"I got the stroke of a Hatchet on the Head, but my Scull being pretty thick, the hatchet would not enter," Croghan would later joke with a friend, "so you may See a thick Scull is of Service on some Occasions."[26]

The Kickapoo leaders were horrified to learn that their young warriors had killed the three Shawnees, for it might well mean a blood feud between the tribes. Croghan managed to purchase sixty-four gallons of rum from French fur traders at Vincennes as a gift for his Kickapoo captors. After a brief debate they promptly set Croghan and his men at liberty. The envoy then reached an agreement with the Kickapoos as well as the nearby Miamis to open peace negotiations with the British.

On July 18, Pontiac arrived to meet with Croghan. The British emissary had met the Ottawa chief before but was even more impressed by him now. He determined Pontiac to be "a shrewd Sensible Indian of few words." He allowed himself to be convinced that Pontiac "commands more respect amongst those Nations, than any Indian I ever saw could do amongst his own tribe." Although Croghan was correct in his estimation of Pontiac's sway over the western tribes, the chief's influence with the Great Lakes and Ohio nations was already waning.

Pontiac agreed to travel with Croghan to Fort Detroit for a council with the leading men of all the Great Lakes tribes. More than five hundred warriors and headmen from various tribes—Ottawa, Chippewa, Potawatomi, Huron, Miami, Kickapoo, and others—responded to messages from Pontiac and Croghan and came to Detroit in late August for this grand council. Pontiac, who spoke only for the Ottawas, promised a lasting peace with the British if only they would reopen trade, most notably in guns and rum, and properly compensate the Indian nations for the forts and trading posts they wished to construct in their lands. He agreed to meet with Sir William Johnson in July of 1766 at Oswego on Lake Ontario.

The elevation of Pontiac by Croghan and Johnson only served to weaken the chief's position with the jealous leaders of other tribal groups. Croghan realized this possibility and welcomed it, writing to his assistant Alexander McKee that "I am mistaken if I don't ruin his influence with his own people before I part with him." This erosion of the once mighty chief's position was further exacerbated by Johnson's private negotiations with him at Oswego.[27]

The final peace negotiated by Johnson with Pontiac at Oswego did indeed bring temporary peace to the western country, but all involved recognized it as tenuous at best unless the British could stem the advance of the American land speculators and settlers. In London, British officials were already hard at work on a plan to prevent further occupation of the western country even before Pontiac's rebellion.

Pontiac returned to the Illinois Country to find his position significantly eroded by local tribal jealousies. The great chief whose words had once directed the actions of eighteen tribes from the Great Lakes to the Mississippi River was by 1768 an outcast from his own people. His new warm relationship with the English—and especially Sir William Johnson and George Croghan—had cost him everything. He now hunted alone with but a handful of relatives and steadfast friends. A fur trader at Detroit had warned Sir William Johnson in August 1766 that "Pontiac would be killed in less than a year, if the English took so much notice of him." On April 20, 1769, Pontiac was indeed murdered in the village of Cahokia on the Mississippi River by a young Peoria warrior.[28]

Pontiac was dead, but the spark he had ignited would soon grow into a great conflagration that, in time, would help to change the history of the world.

4

CUMBERLAND GAP

Dr. Thomas Walker was a man of many talents: physician, merchant, farmer, land speculator, and surveyor. In the year 1750 he was also to become an explorer. The year before, the Loyal Company of Virginia, or Loyal Land Company, had been formed by Dr. Walker, John Lewis, Joshua Fry, Peter Jefferson (father of Thomas), and several other prominent Virginians. The House of Burgesses, of which several of the company founders were members, promptly granted to the Loyal Land Company 800,000 acres of land to the west of the Blue Ridge Mountains along the Ohio River watershed. This grant did not stipulate that the company need establish settlements in the new land, as did the Ohio Company royal grant, but only that it survey the land within four years.

The thirty-five-year-old doctor was selected to explore this new domain and with five companions traveled to the west in March of 1750. The little party had two packhorses and a fine pack of hunting dogs. From Charlottesville, Virginia, Walker's band traveled up the valleys of the Holston, Clinch, and Powell Rivers to the ancient "Athiamiowee," which the Americans came to call the Warrior's Path.

This ancient warpath connected the Shawnees of the Kentucky Blue Licks and their Iroquois overlords with their Cherokee and Catawba enemies east of the Blue Ridge to the south. This route was passable because of a great gap in the Appalachians near the juncture of the future American states of Virginia, North Carolina, Kentucky, and Tennessee.

Buffalo and elk had once used this V-shaped notch in the rock wall of the mountain in their migrations over the centuries. Native peoples sought out these animals for sustenance, both physical and spiritual. From north of the Ohio River came Shawnees, Delawares, and Miamis and from the south came Cherokees and Creeks. They followed the buffalo traces to the many salt licks and rich hunting grounds south of the Ohio and north of the gap. They battled each other for these hunting grounds, and raiding parties soon journeyed both north and south through the gap along the Athiamiowee—"the path of the armed ones."[1]

Walker noted massive swarms of honeybees—or "English flies," as the Cherokees called them—already established in this wilderness as he moved west. The bees were a clear sign of the pioneer farmers to follow. He noted both elk and buffalo along his route but lamented that they were already becoming scarce, as Native hunters had slaughtered so many for their hides to serve the English market. As they journeyed farther to the west, Walker found the land well-timbered with ancient stands of trees. One great elm measured some twenty-five feet around. Along the Holston they also found several abandoned Indian towns. The weather proved dismal and the men struggled through tangles of holly, laurel, and ivy.

On April 9 the little party reached the Clinch River, where they had to build a raft to carry their supplies across. They then followed a small stream that Walker named Beargrass but which later hunters named after Ambrose Powell, who had carefully carved his name into beech-trees all along their route.

On April 13, 1750, Dr. Walker noted in his journal his discovery of a pass through the mountains, and that others had been there before him: "We went four miles to a large creek. Which we called Cedar Creek, being a Branch of the Bear-Grass, and from thence Six miles to Cave Gap, the land being Levil. On the north side of the Gap is a large Spring, which falls very fast. . . . On the South side is a plain Indian Road. On the top of the Ridge are Laurel Trees marked with crosses, others Blazed and several Figures on them. . . . A Beech stands on the left hand, on which I cut my name. . . . This Gap may be seen at a considerable distance, and there is no other."[2]

Walker named this pass the Cumberland Gap, after the hero of Culloden. Although the Warrior's Path beckoned to the north, Walker turned to the west to follow a river he also named Cumberland. As if to foreshadow the travails to follow, Powell was soon mauled by a bear and his leg was badly lacerated. On April 22 they crossed the river and Walker ordered the construction of a cabin to mark their claim to this new land. Walker, along with the wounded Powell and another man, followed the river to the west but found no inviting agricultural lands, just tangled woods rich with game. The land was rocky and so thick with hemlocks, cedars, and laurel that even the horses could not graze. They retraced their tracks back to the cabin.

By mid-July, after considerable suffering, the discouraged party finally reached Dr. Walker's home in Louisa County, Virginia. In frustration the good doctor wrote a rather negative report for the Loyal Land Company. Since he had found no promising agricultural land—because he had failed to push north into the rich bluegrass country—he could only report on the abundant wildlife. In the gleefully wastrel hunting practices that would mark the American advance across the continent, Walker reported that his party had killed 13 buffalo, 8 elks, 53 bears, 20 deer, 4 geese, and 150 turkeys. Walker felt that he had failed in his mission, but his was actually a magnificent triumph. He had located the great gateway to the West, placed it on a map, and given it a name. Others would follow.[3]

The ambitions of the Loyal Land Company, as well as those of the rival Ohio Company, would eventually be frustrated by Pontiac's rebellion. Even though Pontiac had been killed and his Native coalition defeated, the rebellion prompted a sharp turn in royal policy concerning colonial western lands. Even before Pontiac's war the British government had contemplated prohibiting frontier settlement as a way to protect the Indian trade as well as control the independent American frontiersmen who were moving beyond imperial control. The promise made by the Treaty of Easton to limit the advance of white settlement as reiterated to the Indians by both Colonel Bouquet and Sir William Johnson, as well as the actions of Pontiac, now pushed the government toward a fateful decision.

The Proclamation of October 7, 1763, attempted to provide order and control over the lands won from France and so recently contested by the confederated tribes. The royal proclamation established four new colonies in the territory wrested from France and Spain: Quebec, East and West Florida, and Grenada in the West Indies. In response to powerful fur trade interests in London, as well as some small regard for promises previously made, the Natives were now to be protected in their lands west of the Appalachian Mountains. No white settlements were to be allowed west of the mountain chain, and those settlers already there were ordered to depart. Nor were private purchases of Indian land to be allowed, for all the land from the Appalachian highlands to the Mississippi River belonged to the Crown. The Indian trade was to be strictly regulated, with all traders to be licensed by the British government. This system broke down immediately, as the colonial governors insisted on their right to issue trading licenses—and collect both fees and bribes connected to them. The trade increasingly came to be dominated by veteran French traders in the Illinois Country who sent their goods south down the Mississippi to Spanish New Orleans. Thus, the British were frustrated in their attempt to control the trade and enhance Crown revenues.[4]

The cost of the war as well as the need to garrison the west with 10,000 troops had the British treasury stretched thin. Royal officials now began to ponder just how to tax the colonies in order to pay for all this. The Stamp Act of 1765 was their answer. This, of course, only further enraged the American colonists.

"The British colonies are to be regarded in no other light," noted one British memorialist, "but as subservient to the commerce of their mother country; the colonists are merely factors for the purpose of trade, and in all considerations concerning the colonies, this must be always the leading idea." Indeed it was.[5]

Sir William Johnson met in council with over 2,000 representatives from some twenty-four tribes at Niagara in the summer of 1764 to inform them of the royal proclamation. The Indian nations were well pleased by this. To the south, John Stuart, Johnson's newly appointed southern counterpart, met with nearly a thousand Cherokees, Chickasaws, Creeks, Choctaws, and Catawbas at Augusta, Georgia, in November to inform them of the new order of things.[6]

While the Indian nations were pleased with the proclamation, the American colonists were horrified, and none more so than the land speculators. George Washington had just joined with several other prominent Virginians in June 1763 to form the Mississippi Land Company and to petition the British government for 2.5 million acres of land around the junction of the Mississippi and Ohio Rivers. Much of this speculation by Washington and his Tidewater friends was in the purchase—at steeply discounted value—of land bounties granted to veterans of the late war. Western lands were granted to veterans based on rank, from 5,000 acres for officers to 50 acres for private soldiers. Washington naturally assumed that he was to be granted a considerable share of the 200,000 acres of western lands claimed by Virginia that Governor Dinwiddie had set aside for provincial veterans.

While Washington worked diligently in the House of Burgesses to protect the land bounty claims of men who had served under him in the war, he was also quick to purchase rights to these same bounties from willing veterans. "Could I purchase 12,000 or 15,000 acres upon the same terms," he wrote, "I would do it, considering of it as a lottery only." He fully understood the delicate nature of these transactions, writing his brother Charles that if he could purchase "any of the Rights of those who continued in the Service... at the Rate of about five, Six, or Seven pounds a thousand acres I shall be obliged." He enjoined his brother to be cautious "in the whole of your transactions.... [D]o not let it be known that I have any concern therein."[7]

The former colonel was already one of the largest landowners in Virginia, with 9,831 acres by the summer of 1763. Despite these holdings, he was in debt and hard-pressed for funds. Like most of the Tidewater planters, Washington's main crop was tobacco—which also served as a form of currency—but the Virginia soil was being depleted and the "leaf," as it was called, was of increasingly lower quality. New land, and fresh western soil, were critical to his future fortunes.

Washington did not take the proclamation line seriously. "I can never look upon that proclamation in any other light (but this I say between ourselves) than as a temporary expedient to quiet the minds of the Indians," he wrote his old friend William Crawford in September 1767. "It must fall, of course, in a few years, especially when those Indians consent to our occupying the lands. Any person, therefore, who neglects the present opportunity of hunting out good lands, and in some measure marking and distinguishing them for his own, in order to keep others from settling them, will never regain it."[8]

Washington proposed a partnership with Crawford to secure claim to lands beyond the Appalachians. Crawford, with Washington's financial backing, was to explore and survey prime western lands not yet open to settlement so that they might secure a preemptive claim once the proclamation line was adjusted westward or abandoned altogether. This was dangerous work, for the Indians viewed the surveyors—with their chains, compasses, and logbooks—with hostility. They well knew that these men were the outriders of the white advance into their country.

Crawford was to locate prime lands in western Pennsylvania that might be opened by the ongoing survey then being conducted by Charles Mason and Jeremiah Dixon to ascertain the correct boundary between the colonies of Pennsylvania and Maryland. Washington promised his friend "a reasonable proportion of the whole" in compensation for him to undertake this risky venture. The Indians were not the only worry. "I recommend that you keep this whole matter a secret," he warned Crawford, "because I might be censured for the opinion I have given in respect to the King's proclamation." He urged Crawford to pursue his explorations "under the guise of hunting game." Crawford readily agreed.[9]

Washington's new partner had been born on September 2, 1722, in Westmoreland County, Virginia, not far from where Washington was born a decade later. Crawford's father died when the boy was only three. His mother soon remarried and the family moved west to Frederick County in the Shenandoah Valley. When Crawford turned eighteen he was apprenticed to a local surveyor. In 1750 he met young Washington, who was surveying for his benefactor, Lord Thomas Fairfax. They often worked together on surveys and Washington became a frequent guest in the Crawford home at Cattail Run on the Shenandoah River. The two men were remarkably similar—both tall for their time, with sandy hair and piercing blue-gray eyes. They formed a lifelong friendship while surveying in the Shenandoah. Unlike Washington, however, Crawford was not a wellborn aristocrat with powerful connections.

Crawford later served with Washington during the Fort Necessity campaign and again as a member of Captain Adam Stephen's company on the Monongahela, acting as rangers for Braddock's column. Crawford was part of the rearguard defense that saved the retreating British regulars. In the reorganization of the Virginia militia that followed Braddock's Defeat, Washington secured Crawford an officer's commission. The new officer served under Washington in the Forbes campaign, emerging with the rank of captain after the capture of Fort Duquesne.[10]

In early October 1770 Washington set out with his friend Dr. James Craik and two servants to meet with Crawford at his home on the Youghiogheny River in western Pennsylvania. Crawford's simple log home, which he called Spring Garden, was at Stewart's crossing on Braddock's old road. As Washington rode there he passed through Great Meadows, where he had both built Fort Necessity and buried General Braddock. In a rare burst of nostalgic sentimentality he asked Crawford to secure the Great Meadows for him. This was soon done.

On October 15, Crawford took Washington to the land along the Youghiogheny that had been purchased and surveyed for him. Washington was greatly pleased, noting in his diary that this was "as fine a land as ever I saw." The next day Washington, Crawford, Dr. Craik, and several companions departed for Fort Pitt.[11]

At the fort Washington met with George Croghan. Over dinner Washington learned that Croghan was equally busy acquiring western lands and that he was also a partner in the ambitious attempt to found a new colony called Vandalia south of the Ohio River. This grand enterprise, which was supported in London by Thomas Walpole and other important politicos, called for the establishment of a new colony of some 20 million acres extending from the Forks of the Ohio south to the Greenbrier River and west to the Scioto River. Walpole's enterprise steadily advanced and was accepted by King George III and his Privy Council on August 14, 1772.

Croghan offered to sell his proprietary share in the Walpole Company, as the Vandalia scheme was called, to Washington. The Virginian was at first quite interested, but Crawford was dubious. Washington came to agree with his friend that "the unsettled state of this country renders any purchase dangerous." This proved a wise decision. The whole Vandalia enterprise eventually collapsed, not as a result of unsettled conditions in the West, but because of increasingly shrill agitation in the colonies over British regulation and taxation.

Washington, Crawford, and company departed Fort Pitt on October 20 in canoes with an interpreter and two Native guides provided by Croghan. They proceeded down the Ohio with Washington making careful notes on the land and Crawford marking likely claims for his friend. After eight days they came to a small Native village. To Washington's surprise it was the hunting camp of old Guyasuta. The Seneca chief had accompanied Washington to the French fort LeBoeuf in 1753. Washington was greeted warmly despite the fact that his host had fought alongside both the French and Pontiac. He was detained a day by, as he put it, "the kindness and Idle ceremony of the Indians." Guyasuta, noted Dr. Craik, spoke of the invulnerability of his old friend to Indian bullets on the Monongahela and prophesied a grand future for him.[12]

The party continued by canoe on the Ohio to the juncture with the Great Kanawha River, where ancient Indian mounds dotted the landscape. Washington took no note of them in his journal, for he only jotted down entries when the land offered potential for agriculture. He worried about others who were marking out choice land parcels. "A few Settlements in the midst of some of the large Bottoms," he noted, "would render it impractacable to get any large qty. of Land Together."[13]

On November 5 the party turned around and paddled back up the Ohio River for a dozen days to the Mingo town. Once there they procured horses and after a day's ride reached the relative comfort of Fort Pitt. Bidding Crawford farewell, Washington headed back to Mount Vernon. Crawford was now to survey the lands Washington had selected between the Great Kanawha and Little Kanawha Rivers and report to Washington at Mount Vernon when the surveys were completed. Washington reached home on December 1, 1770, after a western journey of almost nine weeks.

His journey had reaffirmed the colonel's conviction that the future of America lay in the West. While he remained determined to secure the lands promised to his veterans, he also became even more committed to the purchase of bounty claims from men anxious to have cash in hand rather than a dubious promise of future landholdings. In this enterprise Washington met with considerable success, but he was always cognizant that such purchases were a gamble. He was determined to pay as little as possible for these bounty land promissory notes, declaring to a friend that the veterans must "take a trifle for it, and more than a trifle circumstanced as things are, I will not give." In such a way did Washington obtain the potential rights to thousands of acres of bounty lands from his former soldiers.[14]

One thing that bothered the colonel was the potential for frontier squatters to move onto these lands in total disregard of prior claims (white claims, that is; not Indian claims). The frontiersmen posed a threat to the plans of Washington and his land company compatriots, for "people in numbers that have no property and of bad reputation generally are bursting daily thro' the bounds of the settled Colonies, and fixing on the Waters of the Ohio, both lawless and useless to their Country."[15]

These "lawless and useless" folk who so fretted the good colonel and his Tidewater friends were backcountry frontiersmen from Pennsylvania, Virginia, and North Carolina. They had been held in check for a while by the hostility of the Natives and their French allies as well as by the sheer majesty of the seemingly impenetrable Appalachian Mountains. The British now added the legal barrier of the proclamation line, but this they simply ignored. Poor but proud, independent yet clannish, uneducated save in the ways of the land and the forest, they were rightly disdainful of all authority. They now formed a relentless tide of humanity that crashed up against the mountains and then swept over them. In this grand enterprise they sought a better life for themselves, for their children, and for their children's children. They represented the future of a new nation yet unborn.

The man who, in time, came to symbolize their travail was Daniel Boone. After his narrow escape from the slaughter of Braddock's army, Boone had returned to North Carolina's Yadkin Valley in the summer of 1755. He again took up the hunter's life but, in his pursuit of wild game, found instead an enduring love.

The story, retold countless times so that folks came to accept it as fact, recounted how Daniel and several friends were out at night with torches, "firehunting." Deer would be transfixed by the light and stand frozen to make an easy target. Rebecca Bryan, a tall, dark-eyed beauty of seventeen years, was in the forest in search of a stray cow when the hunter's torch caught her eye. Boone leveled his rifle at the reflection of the eyes but held his fire. She called out and he realized that he had almost shot this beautiful girl. It was, as they say, love at first sight.

It may well have been love at first sight, but the first meeting more likely occurred at the wedding of Boone's sister Mary and one of the sons of Morgan Bryan who lived ten miles north of the Forks of the Yadkin. Daniel and Rebecca married on August 14, 1756, with Daniel's father, Squire Boone, officiating as justice of the peace. He was twenty-one and she seventeen. This union would last fifty-six years and Rebecca would bear him ten children—six sons and four daughters. Daniel built a snug cabin for his bride, whom he always called "my little girl," on a little stream called Sugartree not far from Morgan Bryan's settlement. They took in the two orphaned sons of his brother Israel, who had died of consumption that year, and their first son, James, was born nine months after their wedding in May 1757.[16]

It was on Sugartree Creek that they would live for ten years. While they put in crops and boiled maple sap for syrup, it was Boone's hunting and trapping that provided most of the household income. Unlike some of their relatives and neighbors, they did not own slaves to help work their little farm.

Although devoted to Rebecca and their growing family, Boone was more often than not away on long hunts sometimes extending for more than a year. He was a man of contradictions: a family man who was rarely with his family; a man who loved the wilderness but who was instrumental in bringing about its destruction; a man who fled the constraints of civilization and yet who became a pathfinder for that very civilization.

Boone, now in his prime, impressed all who met him. "His large head, full chest, square shoulders, and stout form are still impressed upon my mind," recalled a neighbor. "He was (I think) about five feet ten inches in height, and his weight say 175. He was solid in mind as well as in body, never frivolous, thoughtless, or agitated; but was always quiet, meditative, and impressive, unpretentious, kind, and friendly in his manner. He came very much up to the idea we have of the old Grecian philosophers."[17]

His long hunts took him across the Blue Ridge into the Cherokee lands of eastern Tennessee and south into the Florida swamps and the country of the Seminoles. Boone borrowed much from these Natives, especially their keen sense of nature's rhythms. Like the Indians, he and the other long hunters sought the white-tailed deer. Their skins were best when "in the red." In this business they became direct competitors of the Native hunters.

Boone and his companions were armed with the Kentucky or Pennsylvania long rifle, the product of immigrant German gunsmiths. In the old country only aristocrats could afford guns, and hunting was strictly limited. In America, especially on the frontier, a good rifle was essential. For the long hunters, hunting was not for sport but rather to supply the rich European leather market. These long rifles weighed around nine pounds and were about five feet long. They were, thanks to their rifled barrels, incredibly accurate. Phrases associated with these rifles soon entered the American vernacular: terms such as "lock, stock, and barrel," "flash in the pan," and "going off half-cocked."

The hunter needed to carefully clean this treasured weapon and always carried on him a number of items for that work. This included a good supply of fine cloth patches for loading, bullet molds, extra locks, lead, powder, and small tools for repair work. These were carried in a leather pouch or knapsack, or loaded on pack animals. A powder horn, often personally decorated, kept the hunter's powder dry. These were made from the horns of cattle or buffalo, with the cores boiled out. They might carry one or two pounds of powder. The powder would be poured into a small antler measure before being placed down the barrel. A good knife, and sometimes a tomahawk, was essential equipment.

The technology required to rifle a gun barrel was German in origin and dated back to the mid-1500s. These early, stocky guns were expensive and meant only for wealthy sport hunters. In France, flintlock ownership was forbidden to commoners. German immigrants had brought the skill set necessary to make a rifle to Pennsylvania in the 1750s. These weapons were handcrafted by master gunsmiths. The American weapons were sleeker than their European cousins, with longer barrels and a reduced bore size, usually around .50 caliber. Although the rifles took longer to load than a smoothbore musket, an experienced hunter could still get off two and sometimes even three shots a minute. The hand-cast ball was covered in a cloth patch greased with tallow and thumbed into the barrel before being rammed home with a hickory ramrod. Priming powder then was set in the frizzen and the gun set at half cock.

Boone and others typically wore caped hunting shirts that reached to mid-thigh. Sometimes these were made from buckskin but more often than not were of cloth, with bone or antler buttons. The hunters wore leggings and sometimes Indian-style cloth breechclouts. They also often adopted Indian leather moccasins. Headgear was sometimes a coon- or fox-skin fur cap and often a tricorn, although many preferred, as Boone did, a wide-brimmed, low-crowned beaver hat. The goal was to keep the hunter dry in an unforgiving wilderness.[18]

So famous did Boone become for these extended hunts that a bit of frontier humor grew up around him. The truth of this tale—called "Boone's Surprise"—will never be known. When Daniel returned home in the autumn of 1762, after a nearly two-year hunt, he found Rebecca suckling a newborn baby girl at her breast. Rebecca began to weep and proclaimed she thought him dead and so had sought comfort in the arms of another man. Daniel inquired just who the father might be. She replied that it was his own brother Ned, who, after all, "looked so much like Daniel, she couldn't help it." Boone picked up the baby, looked her over, and with a broad grin proclaimed, "So much the better, it's all in the family." He cherished that baby, whom he named Jemima, as his own and in time she became his great favorite.[19]

In the spring of 1768, an unexpected guest arrived at Boone's cabin door in search of shelter. It was old John Findley, who thirteen years before had regaled young Daniel with tales of the fabled Kanta-kee during Braddock's ill-fated march. Findley, who had become an itinerant peddler, stumbled upon the Boone cabin quite by accident but received a warm welcome from his young friend. He settled into the Boone cabin, where he regaled his host with more tales of the hunter's paradise called Kanta-kee. John Stewart, who was married to Boone's sister, took part in these discussions. He had crossed the Appalachians the year before with a large party of hunters into what is now Tennessee and was anxious to return. Findley urged the two men to seek out the Warrior's Path as the best route across the mountains. Once over the mountains, he felt certain that he could lead them north to the great meadows that had led the Iroquois to name the land Kanta-kee.[20]

Boone was anxious to explore this new land. He hoped to move farther west, for the North Carolina backcountry was rapidly filling up. As these newcomers cleared the land, they drove off the game. Most of the new settlers were Germans and Scotch-Irish.

The Germans were the descendants of the Palatines who had fled the Rhinish Palatinate to England in 1708 after the devastation of the Thirty Years' War and a particularly brutal winter. The English had pledged transport at no cost to any foreign Protestant who wished to emigrate to the New World. Three thousand Palatine Germans were conveyed to New York in 1709, while others went to the Carolinas. Some of these Germans settled along the Hudson River but most moved west to the Mohawk Valley, where they came into conflict with both fur traders and land jobbers who controlled the area. Pushed south into Pennsylvania, where they were welcomed by the ever-tolerant Quakers, the Palatines wrote glowing reports home of this new American Eden. Within twenty years over 100,000 more Germans, widely referred to as Dutch by the other settlers, had made their way to Pennsylvania and began to pour south into the Great Valley of Virginia. In 1713 they had laid out the town of Winchester, and within a decade their settlements had pushed south to the James River. A group of German Moravians purchased 100,000 acres in 1751 in the Yadkin Valley, so that a line of German farmers bordered the colonies from the Mohawk Valley to the Carolinas. George Washington was not particularly impressed by these folk, describing them in 1748 as "Ignorant a Set of People as the Indians. They would never speak English but when spoken to they all speak Dutch."[21]

Washington and the other Tidewater planters were even less impressed by the Scotch-Irish who came south hard on the heels of the Germans. These people were mostly lowland Scots, with a smattering of Highlanders and Englishmen, who had been forced to settle in Ireland early in the seventeenth century in a vain attempt to quell the overly independent Irish. Restless under English trade regulations and the suppression of their Presbyterian faith, they began to migrate to America in the early eighteenth century so that by 1750 over 300,000 lived in the colonies. Like the Germans before them, they flocked to Pennsylvania, but with most of the best farmland already occupied they drifted into the hill country and then southwest to the James River in Virginia and farther south to the Carolinas. Along the banks of the Watauga, Holston, and Nolichucky they built crude cabins where no one else dared to settle. Isolated and constantly threatened by enemies both real and imagined, they were a self-reliant, independent people unimpressed by those who lived in comfort or occupied any sort of high station in life. They were not a people to be trifled with, or cheated, or wronged in any way.

The prosperous colonists in the Tidewater region were horrified. "The clothes of the people," wrote a traveler from the East, "consist of deer skins, their food of Johnnycakes, deer and bear meat. A kind of white people are found here who live like savages. Hunting is their chief occupation." Suspicious of all authority, these clannish pioneers bragged of how they would devoutly keep the Sabbath and anything else they could lay their hands on. They disliked the Tidewater people to the east and the Native people to the west with an equal fierceness. Armed with axes and long rifles, they were as untamed as the land they illegally squatted on. They girdled the trees to let in sunlight, planted their corn, built their rude cabins, and raised great crops of children.[22]

Politics also played a role in Boone's renewed wanderlust. The backcountry settlers of North Carolina, like the settlers of western Pennsylvania, were unhappy with their lack of representation in the colonial assembly, excessive legal fees, and the ever-increasing taxes levied on them. The Eastern elites dominated political life and paid scant attention to the frontier folk. In 1768 the armed "Regulators," as they called themselves, had taken over the courthouse in Hillsboro, driven out the sheriff and other officials, and asserted their rights. They would keep the backcountry in a state of agitation until May 1771, when the colonial governor led troops against them in a brief but bloody skirmish on the Alamance River. Although defeated, with six of their leaders hanged, the frontiersmen remained sullen and ripe for further rebellion. Boone took no part in any of this, but several members of Rebecca's family were actively involved. The events of the Regulator Movement left a bad taste in everyone's mouth.[23]

On May 1, 1769, Boone, Findley, Stewart, Joseph Holden, James Mooney, and William Cooley departed the Yadkin in search of the fabled Kanta-kee. They traveled across the Blue Ridge to the Clinch River and the Powell River valley. In the valley, much to their surprise, they discovered Joseph Martin and several men erecting a trading post. Martin's Station was the only white settlement west of the Blue Ridge. From there the party moved south along the Powell River to the formidable cliffs of the Cumberland Mountains. It was there that the Warrior's Path cut across the V-shaped notch through the mountains that came to be called Cumberland Gap. This was the great gateway to the West.

They moved slowly, packhorses loaded down with extra rifles, ball, and powder, as well as traps, kettles, and salt. On June 7, 1769, Boone stood atop Pilot Knob and for the first time viewed "Kanta-kee." It was all he had ever dreamed of and more.

"From the top of an eminence, saw with pleasure the beautiful level of Kentucke," he later recalled. "We found everywhere abundance of wild beasts of all sorts, through this vast forest. The buffalo were more frequent than I have seen cattle in the settlements, browsing on the leaves of the cane, or cropping the herbage on those extensive plains, fearless, because ignorant of the violence of man."

Boone declared to Findley, "We are as rich as Boaz of old, having the cattle of a thousand hills."[24]

They hunted with great success for the next six months. The three camp keepers could barely keep up with the deerskins and buffalo robes the hunters brought in. This idyllic existence suddenly changed in late December when Boone and Stewart, hunting along the Kentucky River, were surrounded by Shawnees from north of the Ohio. They demanded to be taken to the hunters' main camp. The Shawnees viewed these men as poachers in their land and were determined to confiscate their furs and robes. When they reached the main camp it was deserted. The delighted Shawnees loaded all of the peltry and supplies onto Boone's packhorses. Before they departed, they gave the hunters two pairs of moccasins, some powder, lead, doeskin patches, and an old French trade gun.

"Now brothers," declared the Shawnee leader, "go home and stay there. Don't come here anymore, for this is the Indians' hunting ground, and all the animals, skins and furs are ours. And if you are so foolish as to venture here again, you may be sure the wasps and yellow-jackets will sting you severely."[25]

Boone did not take this warning to heart, for he and Stewart were soon on the trail of the Shawnees. They caught up with the Indians after nightfall and recovered their horses while the Shawnees slept. Galloping south, they finally rested just after dawn only to find themselves again surrounded. The Shawnees found this whole situation hilarious and with considerable whooping and laughing tied the two men together and marched them north toward the Ohio River. The men managed to escape, but this time the Shawnees did not pursue.

After several days the fugitives caught up with Findley and the rest of the party. To Boone's delight, his brother Squire, along with a young companion, Alexander Neeley, had arrived from the Yadkin with supplies and fresh horses.

"I have come in search of the Western world," declared Squire, and "my brother Daniel Boone!"

Despite this reinforcement, Findley, along with the camp keepers Holden, Cooley, and Mooney, had had enough. They headed back to the Yadkin. Boone never saw Findley again. The old man returned to Pennsylvania, outfitted himself for another trading venture, and headed west again in 1772, where he vanished.[26]

The Boone brothers, along with Stewart and Neeley, moved their main camp north near the long-deserted Shawnee Blue Lick Town. They again trapped beaver and otter and hunted the numerous buffalo that invariably gathered at the salt licks. The beaver and otter pelts might bring three to five dollars in North Carolina, while deerskins were worth a dollar or less. The pelts also weighed less than deerskins and were more easily packed out.

This was a wondrous time for Boone. He hunted by day and at night read Jonathan Swift's *Gulliver's Travels*, his favorite book next to the Bible, to his companions by the campfire. He even christened a nearby creek after a city in Swift's fantasy. In a moment worthy of Swift, Boone came upon the Big Bone Lick, where the fossilized bones of ancient mammoths and giant sloths protruded from the ground. Some of the tusks were over five feet long, while large teeth weighed over four pounds. "Nature was here a series of wonders, and a fund of delight," Boone later declared.[27]

In late December, Boone and his brother-in-law were laying their traps along the Kentucky River when Stewart failed to return to their camp. Boone searched for several days but could find no sign of his companion save the initials "J.S." carved into a tree. Boone then returned to the base camp and reported Stewart's disappearance to his companions. Neeley became unnerved and suggested an immediate return to the Yadkin. The brothers decided to stay but wished Neeley well on his journey home. The hunter made it back to the Yadkin safely. In later years, like Findley, he would return west only to be killed by Indians.

The Boone brothers continued to hunt and trap throughout the winter. That May, Squire returned to the Yadkin with their furs to trade for fresh horses, ammunition, and supplies. Daniel remained in Kentucky alone for three months. In this time he carefully explored the country. Although he was at first "disposed to melancholy," his travels soon renewed his spirit, for the wilderness was a tonic to Boone.

"The diversity and beauties of nature I met with in this charming season, expelled every gloomy and vexatious thought," he long remembered.

He often saw signs that the Indians were about and so regularly changed his campsites, sometimes sleeping in caves or in the thick cane.

"In this situation I was constantly exposed to danger and death," he recalled. "How unhappy such a situation for a man tormented with fear, which is vain if no danger comes, and if it does, only augments the pain. It was my happiness to be destitute of this afflicting passion with which I had the greatest reason to be affected."[28]

Squire Boone returned in late July to their base camp as promised. Since the Indians had obviously visited their rude cabin, the brothers decided to abandon the site. They used several caves as new base camps but generally kept on the move. Their trapping and hunting were once again highly successful, and in the fall Squire again returned to the Yadkin with the furs to purchase more supplies.

Daniel again remained alone to explore the country. He was too short on powder and lead to engage in any market hunting and so simply hunted to sustain himself. He had no encounters with the Indians save two. He came across an old Indian man who, too feeble to travel, had been left by his companions to die. Boone had recently killed a deer and gave the meat to the starving man. The Indian warmly thanked his white benefactor as Boone moved on. On the other occasion, Boone discovered Indian signs all around his campsite. He attempted to quietly slip away but was blocked in his effort to cross a nearby stream by an Indian fishing from the bank.

"While I was looking at him," Boone later told his son Nathan, "he tumbled into the river and I saw no more of him." Nathan and the other Boone children who heard the story assumed that their father had shot the Indian fisherman. The incident seems out of character for Boone, but the frontier was often a place of contradiction.[29]

Upon Squire's return, the brothers again took up the hunt for deer as well as trapping beaver. Increasing signs of Indian hunters led the brothers to finally pack up their hides and pelts and head back to the Yadkin in March 1771. South of Cumberland Gap, in Powell's Valley, they encountered a party of "Northern Indians" who entered their camp at night. At first feigning friendship, the Natives suddenly turned their rifles on the brothers and stole everything they had. Like the Shawnees in Kentucky, the warriors allowed the brothers to depart.

The Boone brothers—bearded, bedraggled, and unkempt—reached the Yadkin settlements in May. A frolic was taking place and they pushed into the crowd, where Daniel saw Rebecca. He approached her to extend his hand and request a dance. She indignantly refused, which made Daniel laugh. "You have danced many a time with me," he declared. Recognizing her husband, she threw her arms around him. The crowd closed in around the couple, all anxious to hear of Boone's adventures across the mountains in Kentucky.[30]

Rebecca soon learned that her husband had made a fateful decision. "I returned home to my family," he later told John Filson, "with a determination to bring them as soon as possible to live in Kentucke, which I esteemed a second paradise, at the risk of my life and fortune."[31]

5

THE WILDERNESS ROAD

On September 25, 1773, Daniel Boone set out with a party of fifty souls to establish the first American settlement in his Kentucky paradise. He had with him Rebecca and their eight children, including four-month-old Jesse, as well as Squire Boone with his wife and their three young sons. Several other families joined the emigrant party as well, along with a number of adventurous young men from the Yadkin settlements. Several of Rebecca's relatives pledged to join up with them in Powell's Valley.

Boone's mother, along with her daughter Mary, traveled with them for the first half day. She was now in her seventies and well knew that she might never see Daniel and her grandchildren again. "They threw their arms around each other's necks and tears flowed freely," recalled an eyewitness to this last farewell. "[H]is dear old Mother held him around his neck weeping bitterly." Boone, not a man to display emotion, wept. He would never see his mother again.[1]

Boone had farmed, hunted, and fretted for two years over a return to Kentucky. He had good reason to worry, for the land speculation mania sweeping the Ohio Country had shifted to Kentucky. The Proclamation of 1763 was now universally ignored as surveyors and speculators descended on the rich Kentucky lands just south of the Ohio River.

On the very day that Boone's party departed the Yadkin, George Washington wrote from Mount Vernon to his friend William Crawford to hurry his survey work "lest some new revolution should happen in our political system." The colonel had heard that Thomas Bullitt, a prominent Virginia surveyor, was at work in Kentucky and now urged Crawford to consider traveling to the Falls of the Ohio (the future Louisville, Kentucky), cooperate with Bullitt, and secure "ten thousand acres for me, of the most valuable land you can." Washington was particularly interested in acquiring rights to the bottomlands south of the Ohio as well as a salt lick on the Kentucky River, which, he assured Crawford, "I would immediately turn to an extensive public benefit, as well as private advantage."

The long-gestating issue of military bounty lands had finally been settled by Virginia's governor and council, with Washington well rewarded for his hard work. In November 1773 he received 18,500 acres for himself and had also purchased bounty claims for another 5,600 acres. This land was to be located where Crawford had surveyed along the Kanawha as well as the left bank of the Ohio. Washington, however, was far from satisfied. Along with many others, he now turned his gaze toward Kentucky.[2]

Boone had partnered with a prominent Virginian who shared his passion for Kentucky. Captain William Russell of Castle's Woods, in southwest Virginia, while not as renowned as Washington, was also a member of the House of Burgesses, was married to Patrick Henry's sister, and was regarded by Virginia's governor, John Murray, Lord Dunmore, as a "gentleman of some distinction." Lord Dunmore, who would serve as Virginia's last royal governor, was puzzled by these strange Americans who "acquire no attachment to Place: But wandering about Seems engrafted in their Nature; and it is a weakness incident to it, that they Should forever imagine the Lands further off, are Still better than those upon which they are already settled."[3]

Boone's party reached Russell's Clinch River settlement in mid-August. Russell provided several more men, including a number of enslaved people, to accompany the party. He planned to join Boone at a later date with even more men.

All of their worldly goods were loaded onto pack animals for the perilous journey, for there was as yet no wagon road through the wilderness. The youngest children, along with piglets and chickens, were placed in hickory baskets tied across packsaddles. A few of the women rode but most walked. The men and boys drove the cattle and hogs. This proved slow going and it took two weeks to cover the hundred miles to Powell's Valley, where Rebecca's relatives from the Yadkin waited for them as promised. Realizing that they would need more supplies, Boone sent his sixteen-year-old son, James, along with John and Richard Mendinall, back to Castle's

Woods. Captain Russell promptly organized a little caravan of additional packhorses loaded with flour and other supplies as well as a few additional head of cattle. He sent his son Henry, together with trusted guide Isaac Crabtree, his hired man Drake, and two slaves named Adam and Charles, back with young Boone and the Mendinall brothers. Russell promised to follow shortly with even more supplies and men.

On the evening of October 9, the little party camped beside Wallen's Creek at the eastern edge of Powell's Valley. As the boys huddled around their campfire, wolves could be heard howling a short distance away. Crabtree joked with the nervous boys that they would hear far worse sounds once they reached the wilds of Kentucky and told them to turn in. Little did they know that wolves were the least of their worries. There were two-legged predators watching them from the surrounding woods.

The Indians—fifteen Delawares, two Shawnees, and three Cherokees—attacked the sleeping men at dawn. The Mendinall boys died still wrapped in their blankets. The shots stirred the camp into wild confusion and all the men fled toward the woods. Crabtree and Drake, both wounded, managed to escape into the covering forest. The slave Adam also got away and concealed himself in the woods. He now watched in horror as events unfolded.

Boone and Russell were both shot through their legs and could not run. The Indians were quickly upon them, slashing at them mercilessly with their knives. James recognized a large and distinctive Shawnee named Big Jim who had often visited with his father and called out to him for mercy. Big Jim laughed. He proceeded to tear out the boy's fingernails. As James cried for his mother, another Indian took pity upon him and crushed his skull with his tomahawk. The Russell boy suffered a similar fate. The bodies were then further mutilated—a gruesome calling card.

The killers gathered up their booty and hurriedly departed. They took the Black man Charles with them. The Cherokees, in particular, had long understood the value of these enslaved people. An argument soon ensued over the ownership of Charles. The matter was settled when a warrior cleaved in his skull and left him to die.

Crabtree managed to escape detection and eventually reached Castle's Woods, as did Adam, who had borne witness to the slaughter. The hired man, Drake, mortally wounded, died alone in the forest not far from the massacre site.

Boone's main party was encamped but three miles away. A young deserter from the camp, who had stolen a horse and was on his way back to the settlements, came upon the horrific scene that morning. He galloped back to warn the camp. Boone, not knowing how many warriors they might be facing, quickly organized the camp for defense. He sent Squire and several men to investigate the murder site and bury the boys. Rebecca supplied two of her finest linen sheets for Squire to wrap the bodies in.

When Squire reached the scene, he found Captain Russell and his party already there. They carefully wrapped the brothers in one sheet and James and Henry in the other. The boys were buried in a common grave over which the men piled rocks and logs in hopes of preventing wolves from getting to them. Then they all hurried to reinforce Boone's camp.

A council was convened, and although Boone wanted to push on, all the others were far too discouraged to join him. They gathered their remaining stock and retreated to Russell's little settlement on the Clinch River. There the grief-stricken Boone family was to remain for nearly two years.[4]

The news of the killings spread quickly across the frontier and back to Virginia. "The Murder of Russells, Boones and Drakes Sons," noted a militia officer, "was in every ones mouth." Lord Dunmore demanded that the Cherokees surrender the culprits. In response, the Cherokees executed two men, which pacified the Virginia governor. Dunmore then turned his attention to the Shawnees.[5]

The Shawnee chief Colesquo, whom the British called Cornstalk, was a tall, impressive man respected by all. He attempted to placate Dunmore, but to no avail. Random killings were by now becoming common all along the Ohio River. This culminated with the ghastly slaughter of the family of Tachnechdorus, the Mingo leader whom the Americans called John Logan, at a trading post on Yellow Creek near the Ohio River. The killers, led by Daniel Greathouse, murdered Logan's wife and sister along with eleven other women and children. Logan's sister, who was pregnant, was stripped and strung up by her wrists. The men then cut open her womb and impaled the unborn child on a stake. They also carried off her infant daughter. Crawford, who rescued the child, wrote to Washington that "a war is every moment expected."[6]

Crawford was correct. He was soon commissioned a major in the Virginia militia by Lord Dunmore. The governor called out the western militia on June 10, 1774. Lord Dunmore's War, as it came to be called, proved highly controversial. Pennsylvanians viewed it as a land grab by the Virginians and pointed out that the governor himself had speculated heavily in Ohio Country land. Dunmore was also interested in securing Kentucky for Virginia, but the Shawnees refused to recognize the Iroquois land cession made in the 1768 Treaty of Fort Stanwix. Others suggested that Dunmore had started the war as a way to distract Virginians from the political crisis in the East.

Even before he set his troops in motion, Dunmore sent Daniel Boone and fellow frontiersman Michael Stoner into Kentucky to warn surveyors of the impending conflict. The two men journeyed over eight hundred miles in sixty days. When Boone returned to Castle's Woods, he was placed in command of a company of rangers and soon afterward commissioned as a captain of militia.[7]

John Logan, seeking revenge for his family, led Mingo raiders against the Clinch River settlements. The warriors slaughtered horses and cattle, killed a handful of settlers, and captured two slaves—whom they called "bearskins"—before retiring back to the Ohio Country. Boone, with a party of two dozen men, pursued the Mingos but failed to overtake them. Logan had left a message at the scene of one of his attacks attached to a Mingo war club. It made reference to the killings by the Paxton Boys in Pennsylvania as well as the recent Ohio murders.

"Captain Cresap, What did you kill my people on Yellow Creek for? The white people killed my kin, at Conestoga, a great while ago; and I thought nothing of that. But you killed my kin again, on Yellow Creek, and took my cousin prisoner. Then I thought I must kill too; and I have been three times to war since; but the Indians are not angry; only myself. Captain John Logan."[8]

Dunmore ordered two columns out against the Shawnee and Mingo villages in Ohio. He led eleven hundred Virginians west from Pittsburgh while Colonel Andrew Lewis, with a thousand militiamen, advanced down the Great Kanawha River to where it joined the Ohio River at a place called Point Pleasant. Here Dunmore planned to rendezvous with Lewis and then advance against the Shawnee and Mingo towns along Ohio's Scioto River.

Cornstalk moved south against Lewis's army at Point Pleasant, hoping to attack and defeat the divided colonial forces. He was greatly outnumbered, having been able to gather but seven hundred men, for the Iroquois Confederacy and the Delawares continued to adhere to the British. Only the Mingos sided with the Shawnees.

Cornstalk's warriors silently crossed the Ohio on rafts and struck the militia camp at dawn on Monday, October 10, 1774. The Virginians faltered at first but then rallied and pushed the Indians back to the river. This was pure frontier warfare, with every man on each side "finding his tree" and pressing forward. It was also in many places hand to hand. This was entirely an American battle, for no British officers or troops were involved.

Cornstalk could be heard above the din of battle exhorting his warriors. "I could hear him the whole day speaking very loud to his men," recalled Captain John Stuart, "and one of my company, who had been a prisoner, told me what he was saying; encouraging the Indians, telling them 'be strong, be strong!' "

At dusk, Cornstalk, with powder and shot running low, withdrew his warriors back across the Ohio. Lewis claimed victory, since he held the field, but it had been costly: seventy-five men, including the colonel's brother and several other officers, had been killed and twice that number wounded. Shawnee losses were somewhat less but included many prominent chiefs and warriors. The Americans could sustain such losses but the Shawnees and Mingos could not.[9]

Back on the Scioto, Cornstalk called a council and again argued that peace talks with the Long Knives, while bitter to contemplate, were nevertheless essential. Although many of the young men wanted to continue fighting, cooler heads prevailed. Cornstalk sent a messenger to Lord Dunmore requesting a peace council.

Dunmore had established Camp Charlotte—named for his wife—on Scippo Creek, not far from several Shawnee villages along the Scioto River. Cornstalk and the other chiefs and leading warriors arrived there on October 19. The militia officers were all impressed by the commanding presence of the Shawnee chief. "His looks while addressing Dunmore, were truly grand and majestic; yet graceful and attractive," noted one militia colonel. "I have heard the first orators in Virginia, Patrick Henry and Richard Henry Lee, but never have I heard one whose powers of delivery surpassed those of Cornstalk on that occasion."

The Scottish governor dictated hard terms to Cornstalk and the assembled Natives: they were to return all captives (both white and Black), all captured stock and other plunder, cease attacking boats on the Ohio River, and recognize the Fort Stanwix cession of Kentucky. The Indians were to cease hunting south of the Ohio, and Dunmore promised to also stop white hunters from crossing north of the river. As an act of good faith, the Shawnees were to give up four hostages, one of whom was to be Cornstalk's son, for Dunmore to take back to Williamsburg.[10]

Cornstalk and the Shawnees begrudgingly agreed to these terms, but the Mingos remained sullen and uneasy. Dunmore was particularly concerned that Logan had not come to the council and so sent the Indian trader John Gibson, whose wife, Logan's sister, had been murdered by Daniel Greathouse's men, to bring him in. Logan refused to join the treaty negotiations but instead dictated a speech to Gibson and sent it back to Dunmore. Struck by Logan's words, the governor read the speech to his assembled officers:

> *I appeal to any white man to say if ever he entered Logan's cabin hungry and he gave him not meat; if ever he came cold and naked and he clothed him not? During the course of the last long and bloody war, Logan remained idle in his camp, an advocate for peace. Such was my love for the whites that my countrymen pointed as I passed and said, "Logan is the friend of the white man." I had even thought to have lived with you, but for the injuries of one man. Colonel Cresap, the last spring, in cold blood and unprovoked, murdered all the relations of Logan, not even sparing my women and children. There runs not a drop of my blood in the veins of any living creature. This called on me for revenge. I have sought it. I have killed many. I have fully glutted my vengeance. For my country I rejoice at the beams of peace; but do not harbor a thought that mine is the joy of fear. Logan never felt fear. He will not turn on his heel to save his life. Who is there to mourn for Logan? Not one.*

It was quite a gathering of frontier notables that listened as the words of the brooding Logan were read. Among the assemblage were Crawford, Captains Daniel Morgan, William Campbell, and Isaac Shelby, famed scouts Simon Girty and Simon Kenton, young George Rogers Clark, and Captain

Michael Cresap himself. Everyone knew that Daniel Greathouse, not Cresap, had led the slaughter of Logan's family at Yellow Creek. Clark joked with Cresap that he was so famed as an Indian fighter that every killing was laid at his feet. Cresap was not amused and threatened to hunt down Greathouse and kill him.

The letter was widely circulated, soon appearing in several Pennsylvania and Virginia newspapers. Thomas Jefferson, who was busy establishing the Virginia Committee of Correspondence to protest British actions against Massachusetts after the Boston Tea Party, would later learn of Logan's speech from John Gibson, soon to be a general in the Revolutionary army. Jefferson was struck by the power of "Logan's Lament," as the speech came to be called, comparing it to the classical eloquence of Cicero. He would later quote it in his *Notes on the State of Virginia*, published in 1785. Jefferson saw the speech as a perfect statement of the nobility of a vanishing race. His book immortalized the speech, which became a famed example of rhetoric memorized by generations of schoolchildren from McGuffey Readers.[11]

Logan's eloquence did not deter Dunmore from his determination to strike a blow on the nearby Mingo villages to force them to surrender all prisoners. Since his column of the army had seen no action, he ordered Major Crawford, along with Captains Daniel Morgan and George Rogers Clark, out with 240 men against the Salt Lick Town at the forks of the Scioto River. Crawford hurried his men some forty miles up the Scioto, reaching the Mingo town after nightfall on the second day. Crawford planned a dawn attack, but his force was discovered and most of the village inhabitants escaped in the darkness. The Virginians killed six, captured fourteen, rescued two white captives, and burned the village. The plunder from the village and the captured horses were sold and the proceeds divided among Crawford's men. Such was the custom on the frontier.

"I think we may with propriety say we have had great success; as we have made them sensible of their villainy and weakness, and, I hope, made peace with them on such a footing as will be lasting," Crawford wrote Washington soon after returning from his expedition. Peace, of course, might well result in more land cessions. Crawford gleefully concluded his letter with optimistic comments on the surveys and improvements he had made on Washington's Kanawha landholdings.[12]

Events in London once again conspired to frustrate the plans of Washington and the other land speculators. In June 1774, Parliament passed the Quebec Act, which attempted to provide a more tolerant government to the French Canadians while also extending the boundaries of the province south and west to the Ohio and Mississippi Rivers. This enraged both the Virginians and the Pennsylvanians by wresting the Ohio Country lands from them and placing them under the control of unelected British officials in distant Montreal. They now denounced the new law as one of the hated "Intolerable Acts" promulgated by the British to abridge American liberties.

Dunmore's frontier militia also made their loyalties clear. Andrew Lewis, who had served with Washington during Forbes's campaign and had since been promoted to colonel, encouraged officers to set down resolutions on the Eastern political crisis. An address was drafted at Fort Gower on November 5, 1774, and soon after printed in Virginia newspapers. The soldiers thanked Lord Dunmore for his bold leadership during the campaign. The men also swore their loyalty to King George so long as "he delights to reign over a brave and free people" but asserted that their love of liberty outweighed all other considerations. They made it abundantly clear that their fellow Americans need have no fear that such a large body of armed men would ever allow themselves to be used against their own countrymen. They had been on the frontier for three months and were unaware of the recent British outrages in Boston or of the actions of the Continental Congress then meeting in Philadelphia. They assured their fellow citizens that they were battle-tested and ready to fight if called upon by their countrymen.

"We as an army victorious formed ourselves into a society pledging our word of honor to each other to assist our brethren of Boston in case hostilities should commence," declared Captain Daniel Morgan.[13]

These Westerners indeed stood ready to defend American liberty. In time many of them would come to see the Battle of Point Pleasant as the opening shot of the American Revolution. Before long, Colonel Lewis found himself leading militia forces into battle against Lord Dunmore's Loyalists. Dunmore had infuriated the Virginia Patriots by encouraging the Indians he had just defeated to now attack the exposed frontier settlements. He also offered freedom to any enslaved people who would join his Loyalist forces. He was not particularly successful with either gambit, although he did raise a small force of what he called "Loyal Ethiopians." In July 1776 the governor was forced to abandon the colony and seek sanctuary on a British warship. Dunmore soon sailed for Great Britain.[14]

One man who was undaunted by the political crisis—or who at least hoped to take advantage of it—was Judge Richard Henderson of North Carolina. "Even in the superior courts where oratory and eloquence are as brilliant and powerful as in Westminster-hall," noted one of the judge's English friends, "he soon became distinguished and eminent, and his superior genius shone forth with great splendour, and universal applause." Another observant traveler referred to the colonial judge as "one of the most singular and extraordinary persons and eccentric geniuses in America."

Henderson, who had been one of the most hated of the jurists during the Regulator Movement, now decided to become the champion of the western settlers. The judge proposed an outrageous scheme to purchase Kentucky from the Cherokees and create a fourteenth colony with himself as the main proprietor. In the winter of 1774–1775 he organized what eventually became the Transylvania Land Company with several prominent investors. Lands in this new colony were to be allocated by Henderson and the other proprietors to settlers for twenty shillings for one hundred acres and an annual quitrent of two shillings. It is quite remarkable that Henderson and his gentry cronies somehow convinced themselves that they could collect rents from the stridently independent frontier folk who had so recently rebelled against them. But such is human nature.

Henderson, the former superior court judge for North Carolina, knew full well that this purchase was illegal under both Crown and colonial law. He also knew that any Cherokee claim to Kentucky was nebulous at best. Kentucky was a common, if often contested, hunting ground that was not "owned" by any tribe. He contacted Attakullakulla, known as Little Carpenter, a highly influential chief who, although nearing eighty, held great sway over the Cherokees. The chief, who had once crossed the great water and visited the "King of all the English," assured Henderson that the Cherokee claim to the so-called Bloody Grounds, as the tribes called Kentucky, was indeed valid. The Iroquois Confederacy had given up their claim long ago at Fort Stanwix, and Dunmore's War had ended the Shawnee claim. So now Little Carpenter met with Henderson to set a price.

Henderson and Little Carpenter decided to call for a grand council of Cherokee chiefs and leading warriors at the Sycamore Shoals on the south side of the Watauga River. This location, some fifteen miles southeast of the Long Island of the Holston, was a favorite Cherokee meeting ground. Henderson hired Daniel Boone, who had recently been commissioned a captain in the Virginia militia, to help arrange the treaty negotiations. By the second week of March 1775 over a thousand Cherokees were gathered at Sycamore Shoals. Several other prominent frontiersmen, including James Robertson, John Sevier, and Isaac Shelby, also journeyed to Sycamore Shoals.[15]

Little Carpenter, whose name derived from his diplomatic talent with both Indian and white people, opened the council with a speech defending the Cherokee claim to the "Bloody Grounds." Future congressman Felix Walker, at this time but a very young man, was deeply impressed by the oratorical skill of the small-framed and seemingly frail old chief: "Like as a white carpenter could make every joint and notch fit in wood, so he could bring all his views to fill and fit their places in the political machinery of his nation." He was also in awe of his appearance. "He was marked with two large scores or scars on each cheek," noted the youngster, "his ears cut and banded with silver, hanging nearly down on each shoulder, the ancient Indian mode of distinction in some tribes and fashion in others."[16]

For 10,000 pounds sterling's worth of trade goods, Little Carpenter and the other Cherokee chiefs agreed to sign away 20 million acres of land stretching from the Ohio and Kentucky Rivers down to the Cumberland River watershed. They also agreed to sell a corridor between the Watauga River and the Cumberland Mountains so that settlers from North Carolina heading for the Cumberland Gap would not trespass on Cherokee land.

Little Carpenter of course knew full well that his people had no real claim to the "Bloody Grounds." "Brother," he said to Boone, "we have given you a fine land, but I believe you will have much trouble in settling it."[17]

When Lord Dunmore heard of the Treaty of Sycamore Shoals, he promptly declared it illegal and labeled Henderson as an "evil disposed and disorderly person." John Stuart, the southern Indian superintendent, agreed and berated the Cherokees for selling land they had but slight claim to. Even George Washington, who by now shared few sentiments with Dunmore, expressed concern. "There is something in that affair which I neither understand, nor like, and I wish I may not have cause to dislike it worse as the mystery unfolds," he wrote a Virginia friend. North Carolina governor Josiah Martin branded Henderson a "land pirate" and denounced the treaty council as "null and void." He warned that Henderson was attempting to create "an Asylum to the most abandoned fugitives from the several colonies." The British officials might well vent their outrage, but distracted as they were by the colonial political crisis they did nothing to stop Henderson.[18]

Dragging Canoe, the son of Little Carpenter, was also furious over what he witnessed at Sycamore Shoals. Tall and imposing, he towered over his frail and bent father and the other older chiefs. His face, stern and hard, was marked with smallpox scars. Like his father, he possessed a gift for oratory, and his voice seethed with righteous indignation as he spoke. He opposed the sale and warned his people that the American appetite for land was insatiable and that they would soon come for the Cherokee homelands. He prophesized that his people would one day "be compelled to seek a retreat in some distant wilderness." When the sale proceeded, he warned Henderson that while the Cherokees might not molest the white settlers, the other tribes could not be restrained. "There was a dark cloud over that country," he declared.[19]

Even before the negotiations were finalized, Henderson sent Boone north in command of thirty men with orders to mark out a road along the ancient Warrior's Path to the Kentucky River, some 112 miles distant. There Boone was to construct a fort to protect the rent-paying settlers who Henderson hoped would soon flock through the Cumberland Gap and up this new Wilderness Road.

Boone had with him his brother Squire; his new son-in-law William Hays (who had just married his oldest daughter, fifteen-year-old Susannah); the always reliable German Michael Stoner; Captain William Twitty with his enslaved man, Sam; and eight more riflemen, including young Felix Walker, who would later write an account of their adventure; the wellborn Colonel Richard Callaway; and, as Boone put it, "a number of enterprising men, well armed." Susannah and an enslaved woman belonging to Callaway were to serve as camp keepers.

Boone's company gathered near the Long Island of the Holston and on March 17, 1775, began the difficult job of cutting a way through the canebrakes, tangled vines, fallen timber, and undergrowth that obstructed the ancient Warrior's Path. Boone was ever in the lead, marking the trail and continuously hunting to feed the men.[20]

Not far from the Cumberland Gap they came upon Captain Joseph Martin, busily engaged in constructing a trading post. His first effort at establishing an outpost had been frustrated by the hostility of the Cherokees back in 1769. Martin's Station was soon to be a vital way station on the Wilderness Road. Boone purchased some supplies from Martin and then pushed on the remaining twenty-five miles to the Cumberland Gap.

By the time they reached the gap it was apparent that Henderson's dream of a wagon road would have to wait for another day. The path Boone's men now cut through the wilderness remained suitable only for pack animals for another twenty years.

Beyond the gap the old trail followed a broad buffalo trace to the Cumberland River and beyond it to Big Flat Lick. Here Boone turned northwest, leaving the Warrior's Path to follow his 1769 hunting trail. This was hard going across hill country thick with laurel, rhododendron, and brush. While hacking out their primitive road, one of the axmen made a grim discovery. In the hollow of a sycamore tree a skeleton was discovered with a powder horn marked with the initials "J.S." Boone instantly recognized the horn as belonging to his missing brother-in-law, John Stewart.

Young Walker was deeply impressed by his leader. Walker later wrote, "Colonel Boone conducted the company under his care through the wilderness, with great propriety, intrepidity, and courage; and was I to enter an exception to any part of his conduct, it would be on the ground that he appeared void of fear and of consequence—too little caution for the enterprise."

They cut their way north to cross the Rockcastle River, where they finally left the hills and soon after emerged into lush open country. The grassland was covered with blooming clover, and wild animals were everywhere. A huge flock of turkeys strutted about and buffalo calmly grazed, seemingly unconcerned with these intruders into their domain.

"As the cane ceased, we began to discover the pleasing and rapturous appearance of the plains of Kentucky," noted Walker. "A new sky and strange earth seemed to be presented to our view." He thought he had found Eden but would quickly learn otherwise.[21]

They encamped for the night beside Taylor's Fork of Silver Creek, some fifteen miles from their final destination on the Kentucky River. Just before dawn on March 25, 1775, all were suddenly awakened by gunfire. It was too dark to see anything but the spits of flame from the Indian muskets. Captain Twitty, shot through both knees, went down in a heap. As his slave, Sam, rushed to his side, he, too, was shot and tumbled into the smoldering campfire. The warriors rushed forward to scalp Twitty but the captain's bulldog leapt up and seized one of them by the throat. Another warrior tomahawked the faithful dog and they hurriedly retreated in the face of the return fire from Boone's men.

The Indians, satisfied with a few of Boone's horses, hurriedly departed. As Boone and his brother slowly advanced back into camp, they discovered young Walker also dangerously wounded. It was felt that his wounds, as well as Twitty's, were mortal. Several of his demoralized men promptly headed for home, but Boone would not leave the two wounded men and ordered the construction of two crude wooden cabins, which he named Fort Twitty.

Twitty lingered for three days before succumbing to his wounds. The melancholy mood only increased when Boone, out hunting, discovered the scalped remains of two more of his party. The gloom was somewhat tempered by the rather miraculous recovery of Walker. Boone tenderly nursed the boy.

Walker warmly recalled the care he received from Boone: "He was my father, my physician, and friend; he attended me as his child, cured my wounds by the use of medicines from the woods, nursed me with paternal affection until I recovered, without the expectation of reward."

It now began to appear that even nature was conspiring against them. As they hunkered down in Twitty's Fort, they boiled their meat in large camp kettles and the smell attracted packs of wolves. One night a rabid wolf came in amongst the sleeping men and bit one of them. Although the wolf was shot, the poor man fretted over his wound and indeed later went into a fit and died.

On April 1, Boone wrote Henderson requesting reinforcements. "My advice to you, Sir, is, to come or send as soon as possible," he scrawled out as best he could. "Your company is desired greatly, for the people are very uneasy, but are willing to stay and venture their lives with you; and now is the time to flusterate their [the Indians'] intentions, and keep the country whilst we are in it. If we give way to them now, it will ever be the case."[22]

With Walker slung on a litter between two horses, Boone's men made the final push to the Kentucky River on April 6. Boone had already scouted the site for a fort sixty yards south of the river and near a salt lick. Walker, rising from his litter, was greeted with a remarkable view: "On entering the plain we were permitted to view a very interesting and romantic sight. A number of buffaloes of all sizes, supposed to be between two and three hundred, made off from the lick in every direction: some running, some walking, others loping slowly and carelessly, with young calves playing, skipping, and bounding through the plain. Such a sight some of us never saw before, nor perhaps ever may again."

Walker was prescient, for the days of the buffalo in Kentucky were indeed numbered. Boone's men could not be restrained from shooting the beasts, as often as not just for sport, and later settlers were even more indiscriminate in this wholesale slaughter. The buffalo were indeed a major threat to newly planted crops, but the killing often had little to do with protecting a future harvest.

"We found it very difficult at first and indeed yet, to stop the great waste in killing meat," Henderson later jotted in his journal for May 9, 1775. "Others of wicked and wanton dispositions, would kill three, four, five or half a dozen buffaloes, and not take half a horse load from them all."

Boone proposed that a law be enacted to "halt the wanton destruction of game" and especially the "wild cattle," as he called the buffalo. "Boone's Law" was passed during the first convention of the Colony of Transylvania on May 17, 1775, but proved impossible to enforce. Within a little more than a decade the once vast herds were down to a pathetic remnant. Even those pitiful last few were soon gone, to be replaced by the settlers' hogs and cattle.[23]

Boone's fort was to be constructed on a broad, open floodplain just to the south of the Kentucky River. A large salt lick, the magnet that attracted both man and beast, was nearby near the mouth of Otter Creek. Sycamores and elms lined the banks of both the broad river and the smaller creek. This gave to the valley a sense of natural protection. Several nearby springs were situated to provide fresh water for future settlers. This land was everything the men had dreamed of and more.

"We felt ourselves as passengers through a wilderness just arrived at the fields of Elysium, or at the garden where was no forbidden fruit," Walker gushed.[24]

It was difficult for Boone to keep his men focused on the task at hand, for they were all anxious to scout out land claims, to hunt, and to put in a corn crop. A number of crude cabins went up, but they were not connected by a stockade wall. The killing of yet another of Boone's companions by Indians helped to sharpen the men's focus on the need to work on the fort.

Henderson was but a few miles south of the Cumberland Gap—delayed by a spring snow—when Boone's letter reached him on April 7. The letter caused considerable consternation among the judge's party. Several men immediately turned back and retreated to the relative safety of Martin's Station. Henderson had started out with thirty well-mounted men, several wagons, and a long horse packtrain but had left the wagons back at Martin's Station. There he had been joined by Benjamin Logan, a Virginian who had served under Bouquet, and several others, so that his party numbered almost fifty by the time he reached the gap.

The judge hurriedly composed a letter to his fellow investors back in North Carolina. "You observe from Mr. Boone's letter the absolute necessity of our not losing one moment," he wrote. "We are all in high spirits, and on thorns to fly to Boone's assistance, and join him in defense of so fine and valuable a country."

Not long after crossing the gap, Henderson's party was met by several of Boone's men in headlong flight south. This further unnerved some of Henderson's men. "The general panic that had seized the men we were continually meeting, was contagious; it ran like wild fire," the judge noted. Most of the men they met were not from Boone's party but rather were independent hunters or potential settlers searching out good land. Nevertheless, their panic was quite demoralizing to Henderson's group.

Henderson now sent a message forward to alert Boone that help was on the way. It took the nervous rider four days to reach the Kentucky River. A greatly relieved Boone sent Michael Stoner back to guide Henderson's party on in.[25]

At Hazel Patch, just north of the Laurel River, Benjamin Logan left Henderson. At this point Boone's road turned north, away from the Warrior's Path. Logan, with a companion and several enslaved people, turned instead to the west on the old trace and followed it to a broad and well-watered valley on the southern edge of the Bluegrass Region. Here Logan and his companions erected a crude fort that in time became the little settlement of St. Asaph.

Logan's route eventually became a major branch of the Wilderness Road. It led westward from Logan's fort, some twenty-two miles to Harrodsburg. This settlement had been established by Pennsylvanian James Harrod in June 1774 but was quickly abandoned at the outbreak of Lord Dunmore's War. Harrod, traveling down the Monongahela and Ohio Rivers, returned with a party of men and reestablished his settlement in March 1775. Along with Logan's Station and Boonesborough, it formed the westernmost part of the triangle of American settlements founded along the Wilderness Road in 1775.[26]

Henderson's party reached Boone's encampment at noon on April 20. They were warmly greeted by a ceremonial volley of rifle fire from Boone's men. Little did Boone and his men know as they gathered in martial array to fire that welcoming volley that they were actually at war. The day before, the opening shots of the American Revolution had been fired at Lexington and Concord.

Henderson acknowledged that the survival of his Kentucky dream "was owing to Boone's confidence in us, and the people's confidence in him, that a stand was even attempted." Henderson now took command of the settlement, which he named Boonesborough, and set the men to constructing a proper fort on higher ground fronting the Kentucky River. The former judge drew up a detailed plan that called for blockhouses on all four corners of the large stockade. The stockade walls would connect several cabins and a powder magazine. This fort was to cover almost an acre of ground. Boone was placed in charge of the construction, but it remained difficult to get any of the eighty men to devote much time to such hard labor.

The aristocratic Henderson came to regard his men as "a set of scoundrels who scarcely believe in God or fear a devil if we were to judge from most of their looks, words, and actions." Boone's character had been forged in the same frontier environment as his men and he identified with their desire to find and mark off good plots of land on which to plant their corn. He felt that they had made decent progress on the fort throughout April and May. Still, it would be nearly two years before construction on the fort was completed.[27]

Boone's pretty young daughter Susannah—the only white woman in the camp—became the object of great interest and considerable gossip among the men. One of Henderson's gentrified business partners huffed that Susannah was "a notorious prostitute." That was certainly debatable, but there was no question that she was a high-spirited young woman: she was said to have flirted with the men by saying that "every Kentuckian ought to try her gait, since she was the first white woman in Kentucky."

When Will Hays had first approached Boone to ask permission to marry Susannah, he received a stern warning from his prospective father-in-law that she was quite a lively girl who often tended to frolic with the boys. Boone urged Hays to beware, for Susannah would undoubtedly prove unfaithful. Hays dismissed such talk and he and Susannah were married in March 1775, just before they all departed for Kentucky.

Alas, Boone well knew the temper of his daughter, and his warning to Hays proved prophetic. The young man soon came to him to complain of his wife's behavior.

"Didn't I tell you," Boone replied with a smile, "trot father, trot mother, how could you expect a pacing colt?"[28]

Henderson called for a general convention to meet at Boonesborough on May 23, 1775, to officially establish a government for his new colony of Transylvania. The Boone brothers, Colonel Callaway, and three others were elected to represent Boonesborough, while four delegates each were sent from Harrodsburg, a second Harrod settlement at Boiling Springs, and Logan's Station. James Harrod and Benjamin Logan refused to recognize that the Transylvania Land Company had any authority over their people, who actually outnumbered the eighty inhabitants of Boonesborough.

The eighteen delegates met under the shaded canopy provided by a giant elm. Henderson opened with an impassioned if long-winded speech on how all power was of course derived from the people but then proceeded to lay out a charter of government that vested almost all power in the hands of the proprietors. The delegates were naturally skeptical of Henderson's grandiose plan and so appointed Boone and Harrod to engage the judge in further discussions in order to clarify the details of land sales and proposed rents. They were also anxious to make certain that the company did not make large land sales to outside investors not involved in the actual settlement of Kentucky. The delegates set up a court system as well as a local militia. Boone's proposals for a law to preserve wildlife and another to encourage the proper breeding of horses both became law. The former was generally ignored, of course, while the latter was enthusiastically embraced.[29]

News of Lexington and Concord reached Boonesborough on May 29, the day after the convention adjourned. The company now scrambled to deal with this new political reality by appealing to the Continental Congress to recognize Transylvania as a fourteenth state. This was met with either studied indifference or outright hostility. Quitrents, noted Thomas Jefferson, were a "mark of vassalage." Congress kicked the question over to Virginia and North Carolina, where the Treaty of Sycamore Shoals was declared illegal and Transylvania once again invalidated.

In Kentucky, twenty-four-year-old George Rogers Clark, only recently arrived at Harrodsburg, promptly began to act as an agent for his political friends back in Virginia. The tall, red-haired agitator roused the Harrodsburg settlers into a frenzy against the Transylvania Land Company. Henderson and his fellow proprietors assisted young Clark by suddenly raising land prices as well as by selling off several large tracts of land to favored speculators in North Carolina. Meanwhile Clark's powerful friends in Virginia, who included Jefferson and Governor Patrick Henry, helped to establish Kentucky County in December 1776, with its seat in Harrodsburg. The revolutionary Virginia Assembly also authorized funds to purchase much-needed powder and lead for the Kentucky County militia.

Henderson's grand scheme was shattered. Even if the hostile Revolutionary assemblies in Virginia and North Carolina had not acted, the company effort to sell land and collect rent collapsed in the face of hundreds of new settlers who arrived in the summer of 1775 and totally ignored the proprietors.

Henderson's visionary efforts did not go unrewarded. The Virginia Assembly granted him 200,000 acres along the Ohio north of the Green River, while his friends in North Carolina secured him a similar grant in Powell's and Clinch Valleys. Henderson's Transylvania Land Company passed into oblivion with the creation of Kentucky County, and with it went all grants of land made by the company, including the 2,000 acres promised Daniel Boone in payment for his service in marking the Wilderness Road and laying out Boonesborough.[30]

On June 13, Boone left the new settlement in company with Richard Callaway. They each intended to recruit new settlers in Virginia and lead them back to Boonesborough. Boone had even more pressing personal business to attend to at the Clinch River settlement. Rebecca, who was now thirty-six, was in the ninth month of a difficult pregnancy. William, her ninth child, was born in late July but did not live for long. Boone, although anxious to return to Kentucky, would not leave without his family, and Rebecca was in no condition to travel. Boone urged the men he had recruited to go on without him, but they did not care to dare the Wilderness Road without him.

Henderson, back at Boonesborough, was helpless without Boone. The men would not follow his orders, construction on the fort was barely underway, and land claims were a tangled mess. He took to his cabin to seek solace in his private supply of good whiskey.

"We are informed that Mrs. Boone was not delivered the other day, and therefore do not know when to look for him," he wrote in his journal entry for July 18, "and until he comes, the devil himself can't drive the others this way."

Henderson's frustration boiled over in early August when he left Boonesborough for the more congenial climes of North Carolina. There he pleaded his case before the assembly in the old colonial capital at New Bern, but without success.

By the middle of August, Rebecca felt well enough to travel and the party set off for the Cumberland Gap. Along with his wife and children, Boone had seventeen well-armed young men and a long horse packtrain. Squire Boone and his family followed shortly afterward, as did several of Rebecca's Bryan relatives. Also but a few weeks behind were Richard Callaway with his family and an additional forty new settlers from Virginia. This was just the beginning of a great human migration.

In Powell's Valley, Boone was joined by Hugh McGary with his family and two other families from the Upper Yadkin in North Carolina. Boone guided this large band of pioneers through the Cumberland Gap and up the Wilderness Road. For Boone this was a journey both physical and spiritual, for he saw a grand future beyond the mountain barrier—for himself, his family, his people, and his nation. He was determined to seize that future.

They reached Boonesborough on September 8, 1775. Boone took considerable pride in the fact that Rebecca and his daughters were "the first white women that ever stood on the banks of the Kentucke river." He set to work building a substantial cabin with wooden floors and glass windows for Rebecca near the fort.[31]

Others followed—only a trickle at first, but it soon became a human flood. By the time of Kentucky statehood in 1792, well over 200,000 had traced Daniel Boone's footsteps through the Cumberland Gap and up the Wilderness Road. Already the remarkable partnership between the aristocratic land speculator and the pioneer long hunter was paying rich dividends as the little Kentucky settlements became the westernmost outposts of liberty in the coming American Revolution.

6

THE DARK AND BLOODY GROUND

Jemima Boone did not listen to her father. Instead, the spirited thirteen-year-old recruited Colonel Callaway's daughters—Betsy, sixteen, and Fanny, fourteen—to join her for a river float in a dugout canoe. Daniel had repeatedly warned his daughter, as well as all the young people of Boonesborough, about venturing out from the settlement and especially about the dangers that might well be lurking on the far bank of the river.

It was hot and humid that July 14, 1776, Sabbath day. Jemima dangled a sore foot in the cool water while the other girls took turns paddling. The cumbersome dugout began to drift in the current toward the north bank of the river, and Jemima warned her companions to paddle in the other direction. The girls laughed, one suggesting that Jemima was "more afraid of the yellow boys [Indians] than she was of disobeying her father."

As the canoe closed on the north bank, an Indian suddenly appeared, grabbed the mooring tug, and pulled it in to shore. The girls screamed while Fanny bashed the man across the head with her paddle. She broke the paddle over his head, but just as it looked as if they might yet escape, several other warriors jumped into the shallow water and grabbed the girls. One of them threatened to cut Betsy's throat if they did not cease their yelling and resisting.

This was a mixed party of three Shawnees and two Cherokees. They were watching the settlement, hoping for a target of opportunity, when the three girls drifted into view. They now hurriedly cut off the bottoms of the girls' dresses to make the cloth into leggings. They also gave them moccasins.

Jemima recognized the oldest Indian in the band as a Cherokee called

Hanging Maw, whom she had seen with her father back in the Watauga settlement. She told him who she was and he asked in broken English if the other two girls were her sisters. Thinking this might work to their advantage, she replied that they were.

"We have done pretty well for old Boone this time." Hanging Maw laughed.

The little war party hurried their prisoners north, being careful to conceal their trail. That night they camped about six miles north of Boonesborough. The girls had made every effort to drop pieces of cloth and break twigs or trample the earth to leave a trail, but the Indians were no fools and repeatedly threatened them if they did not stop. They securely tied all the girls together for the night.

Boone was enjoying a late-afternoon nap when he heard the young brother of the Callaway girls shouting the alarm. Grabbing his rifle and powder horn, he rushed to the riverbank. He now saw the empty dugout canoe floating aimlessly downstream. He was soon joined by Samuel Henderson, the judge's son and the fiancé of Betsy Callaway, who had been shaving when he heard the alarm and still had half his face covered in lather. John Gass, a bold teenager, plunged into the river and swam out to retrieve the dugout. Boone and Henderson needed the canoe to cross the deep river while keeping their powder dry.

Colonel Callaway, distraught and flustered, arrived on horseback with a party of armed men. They galloped on to a ford a mile or so below Boonesborough while Boone, Henderson, Gass, John Floyd, and two others crossed in the dugout to the far side of the river. Boone's party immediately picked up the trail. Callaway and his mounted companions soon caught up with them. Boone convinced Callaway to proceed on horseback to the Lower Blue Licks, where the Warrior's Path crossed the Licking River. He was to wait there in ambush. Boone and his party would follow the kidnappers' trail on foot. Boone knew full well that the noise made by Callaway's horsemen would alert the Indians and place the captives in grave danger of being tomahawked on the spot. Callaway was also obsessed that the Indians might rape the girls, which further clouded his judgment, though Boone knew that this was not culturally condoned by most of the tribes and was thus highly unlikely.

Boone's party made about five miles before darkness halted them.

Young Gass now volunteered to backtrack to Boonesborough to retrieve breechclouts, moccasins, powder and shot, and some food. Boone was barefoot and wearing his tight Sunday-best pantaloons. The heroic lad returned before dawn as promised. The little party, reinforced by three hunters, headed north at daybreak.

The Indian trail was well hidden by thick cane, and Boone quickly realized that they were falling behind. He felt certain that the warriors would head for the traditional river ford at the Blue Licks and now decided to cease tracking and head rapidly for the crossing. This decision fretted his nervous companions, but they wisely deferred to his experience. Within a few hours they again encountered the trail, well marked by the clever girls, and hastened their pace until again halted by darkness.

The Indians were rather indulgent and surprisingly gentle with their captives. They came across a stray horse, captured it, and had the girls take turns riding. But Jemima, who was an experienced rider, pretended to be unable to handle the horse. The other girls played along, pinching and kicking the animal to annoy it. The warriors thought this hilarious at first but soon caught on that the girls were playing a charade of delay. They released the old nag and hurried the captives along on foot.

Hanging Maw proved particularly solicitous of Jemima. At the evening camp he asked the "pretty squaw" if he might take the combs from her hair. Her long black locks fell well below her waist, much to the delight of the old Cherokee. He asked her to comb his hair and inspect his scalp for lice. Jemima complied but later admitted that she was so tired and distraught that she "could not have found a louse, had it been as large as her thumb."

The Indians were so certain that they had outdistanced and eluded any pursuit that they paused a few miles below the Upper Blue Licks to shoot a buffalo. They cut off part of the hump and soon after settled down to cook their first meal since the capture of the girls. They relaxed a bit, certain that they would soon unite with other war parties and be safe from the whites.

Boone was elated when his party came upon the buffalo carcass. It was still dripping blood. He assured his companions that the Indians would stop to cook the buffalo hump at the next good water.

The Indians made camp in a small glen, built a fire, and put the buffalo hump on a spit. One warrior stood watch while another tended to the spit.

Hanging Maw went down to the nearby creek to get water; another warrior set off to collect firewood. The girls settled down against a fallen log just a few feet from the fire. Jemima and Fanny laid their heads in Betsy's lap. As Betsy unconsciously searched through their hair for lice, the girls all wept. Jemima, as she had done countless times since being kidnapped, swore to herself that if only they were rescued, she would never again disobey her father.

Through her tears, Jemima suddenly saw her father "creeping upon his breast like a snake" upslope above the glen but a few yards away. Their eyes met and he motioned her to be silent. The sentinel who had returned to the fire to light his pipe suddenly pitched forward into the flames; his companion was shot in the chest at the same time. Fanny, who had been watching the Indian cook, "saw the blood burst out of his breast before she heard the gun."

"That's Daddy!" screamed Jemima.

Boone and his men came storming down into the camp, yelling and whooping. Betsy, rushing toward them, felt a tomahawk breeze by her head as she stumbled up to Boone. In the haze of the black powder, one of the men mistook her for an Indian and raised his rifle to club her.

"For God's sake don't kill her when we've travelled so far to save her," Boone exclaimed as he grabbed the man's arm.

The startled Indians vanished into the canebrake, leaving behind most of their weapons and scant supplies. Boone and Floyd had each hit their mark, as proven by two trails of blood. So overcome with emotion were all that no pursuit of the Indians was contemplated.

"Thank Almighty Providence, boys," Boone declared, "for we have the girls safe. Let's all sit down by them now and have a hearty cry."[1]

BOONE, HIS COMPANIONS, AND THE GIRLS ARRIVED BACK in Boonesborough on July 17 for a joyful reunion with family and friends. They did not know that the Continental Congress had declared for independence just thirteen days before. Boone and the majority of the Kentucky settlers identified as Whigs (as the rebels were commonly known), although there was a small Tory (or British loyalist) element among them. Several of Rebecca's Bryan relatives remained loyalists, which was awkward for

Boone and even caused some to question his own loyalties. Many on the frontier remained neutral, for they had little in common with Boston rabble-rousers or the Williamsburg gentry. Boone and his fellow settlers, Whig, Tory, or neutral, were of course far more interested in basic survival on this distant frontier than in Eastern political turmoil. The Indians certainly made no distinction between the Whigs and Tories among the Kentuckians. Every white settler was viewed as just one more hated invader.

With perhaps 150,000 Indians living to the east of the Mississippi River—plus some 12,000 warriors north of the Ohio River and another 14,000 to the south—it was imperative for both sides to gain their support or at the very least ensure their neutrality. The British had already taken steps to enlist the Natives, both north of the Ohio and south of the Cumberland Gap, to their cause. The always scheming Lord Dunmore, as soon as he had heard of Lexington and Concord, immediately sent messages to Cornstalk and other Shawnee and Mingo leaders to enlist them in the service of the Crown. He also ordered the withdrawal of Virginia militia forces from the frontier posts at Pittsburgh, Wheeling, and Point Pleasant. This would leave the settlements defenseless. Many of the militiamen did indeed return to the East, where they promptly drove Dunmore from Virginia. The wise counsel of Cornstalk held the Ohio tribes to uneasy neutrality. The young warriors now sullenly waited to see what the Americans would offer.[2]

American commissioners had traveled to Pittsburgh in the autumn of 1775 in an effort to placate the Ohio tribes and ensure their neutrality. Virginia was represented by Thomas Walker, Andrew Lewis, James Wood, and two others, while James Wilson and Lewis Morris (both eventual signers of the Declaration of Independence) came as representatives of the Continental Congress. The Virginians were to take the lead in the negotiations. Simon Girty and Andrew Montour's son John agreed to serve as interpreters.

Among the Indian leaders present were the Shawnee leader Cornstalk, Guyasuta representing the interests of the Iroquois Confederacy, White Mingo of the Mingos, the Delaware sachems White Eyes and Captain Pipe, and Pontiac's son Shaganaba leading the Ottawa delegation. Some six hundred Indians from the various tribes gathered at Fort Pitt to hear what the Americans had to say.[3]

Several men for so long prominent in Indian Country were now absent.

Sir William Johnson had been felled by a stroke on July 11, 1774. Andrew Montour had been murdered in January 1772. George Croghan had resigned his position as deputy Indian agent back in November 1771 in order to pursue his extensive land speculations as well as his ambitious Vandalia scheme. That grandiose effort to create a new colony soon imploded in the face of the colonial political crisis. Croghan now found his loyalty questioned by both sides. He was placed under house arrest by the British before they evacuated Philadelphia because he had briefly chaired Pittsburgh's Committee of Correspondence. Later he offered his services to the rebel government to assist in negotiations with the Indians, but he found himself under arrest in the summer of 1778 on a charge of treason against both Pennsylvania and the government of the United States. His old rival Washington did not trust him and the general's opinion had prejudiced many others against him. Although Croghan was eventually acquitted of the charge, he was nevertheless ruined. Impoverished and in ill health, he was to die a forgotten man four years later.[4]

The great council at Fort Pitt began on September 26, 1775, with the arrival of the Shawnee delegation. Many ceremonial speeches followed, most accompanied by insincere pledges of eternal fraternity by both sides. Although the stated goal of the Americans was to ensure the neutrality of the tribes north of the Ohio, considerable time was given to the return of all captives, both white and Black. The Virginians, led by Walker, were obsessive on the issue of the return of captive enslaved people.

"Brothers we Expect you have brought with you and are ready to Deliver up all our Flesh and Blood, our Negroes and all that belongs to us," Walker demanded.

Cornstalk replied for the Shawnees, reminding the Americans that all captives, both white and Black, had been repatriated at the recent conclusion of Lord Dunmore's War. The only whites now with the Indians were redeemed captives who had run away from their white families and returned to the villages north of the Ohio. The tribes were happy to allow white family members to come and attempt to convince these people to return home, but they would not cast these people out as they had been forced to do by Bouquet. The Shawnees and Mingos held only a handful of Blacks, and they would try to return them if they did not flee into the forest.

Cornstalk adamantly refused to give to the Americans the children born of Black women fathered by Indian men. They would not allow these children of their blood to become slaves to the Americans.

Walker became quite belligerent on this issue, but all knew that the Virginians were in no position to do much beyond issuing empty threats. Considering the importance of the central issue of neutrality that was the purpose of the council, it was surprising that the Virginians remained so adamant on the question of a handful of runaway slaves and their mixed-race children, but such was indeed the case. With the negotiations stalled, both sides pulled back and agreed to allow a select group of Indian leaders to travel to the various towns to inquire about captives, both Black and white. The Americans then proceeded quickly to yet again guarantee the Ohio River as the eternal boundary between white settlement and Indian Country. In return, the Natives pledged to remain neutral in the war between the Americans and the British.

Guyasuta promised to use his influence with the Iroquois to ensure the neutrality of that powerful confederacy. "We must be fools indeed to imagine that they [the British] regard us or our interests who want to bring us into an unnecessary war," he declared. At the same time he warned that his people "will not suffer either the English or the Americans to march an army through our country."

The Americans also received an interesting insight into divisions within the tribal alliance when the Delaware sachem White Eyes angrily disputed the right of Guyasuta to speak for his people. The Delawares, he declared, were no longer to be subordinate to the Iroquois Confederacy. It became clear to the American commissioners that the solid front the Natives presented was more fragile than it first appeared to be.[5]

While Guyasuta may well have been sincere, most of the other tribal leaders were simply biding their time. The American invasion of Canada had cut the St. Lawrence trade route between Montreal and the Ohio Country. Until that vital supply line could be reopened, the Indians had no real choice but to remain neutral. It would be early 1777 before the British, having finally repulsed the American invaders, could reopen the old trade route to the south.

Cornstalk did his best to hold his young men in check, but it became increasingly hopeless. Other chiefs, most notably Blackfish (Cottawamago) of the Chillicothe Shawnees, now challenged Cornstalk for leadership. The new British commandant at Detroit, Henry Hamilton, had sent a war belt to the Shawnee. Rumors persisted that he had offered the Mingos a bounty for every American scalp they brought to him. While Hamilton had actually urged restraint on the tribal leaders who had visited Detroit, he confessed to his superiors that the warriors could not long be held back from "falling on the scattered settlers on the Ohio." It was, he lamented, bound to be "a deplorable sort of war, but which the arrogance, disloyalty, and impudence of the Virginians has justly drawn down upon them."[6]

In October 1777, a frustrated Cornstalk, along with two Shawnee companions, traveled to Fort Randolph, which was built on the Kanawha River not far from the site of the Battle of Point Pleasant. There he related to the post commander, Captain Matthew Arbuckle, his inability to exercise control over his young men anymore.

"When I speak to them they will attend for a Moment and sit still whilst they are within my Sight," he confessed. "At night they steal their Blankets and run off to where the evil Spirit leads them."

Captain Arbuckle decided to hold the chief and his two companions as hostages to discourage the Shawnee from joining forces with the British. When Cornstalk's son arrived soon after to inquire about his father, he was also placed under arrest. The Shawnees were all housed in one of the cabins inside the fort walls. They were treated well and the post officers often talked with them. Captain John Stuart, an experienced officer who, like Arbuckle, had battled Cornstalk at Point Pleasant, enjoyed visiting with his former foe. Stuart greatly admired the old chief, whom he found to be quite friendly but stoic and somewhat fatalistic.

"When I was a young man and went to war, I thought it might be the last time, and I would return no more," he told Stuart. "Now I am here amongst you; you may kill me if you please; I can die but once; and it is all to me, now or another time."[7]

On November 10, 1777, a young militia officer, hunting just across the river from the fort, was set upon by a Mingo warrior, killed, and scalped. His outraged companions decided to kill the Shawnee hostages in revenge. Stuart and Arbuckle attempted to stop the mob but were pushed aside at gunpoint. As the men burst into the room, Cornstalk calmly rose to meet them only to be shot down in a hail of gunfire. His son died by his side. The men killed the two other Shawnees and hurriedly left the bloody scene, well satisfied with their handiwork.

"Thus died the great Cornstalk warrior," lamented Captain Stuart, "who from personal appearance and many brave acts was undoubtedly a Hero."[8]

The murders compromised the work of the peace commission and outraged the American civil and military leaders. Governor Patrick Henry was determined to bring the killers to justice in order to prove the good faith of the Virginians to the Shawnee Nation, but every order he issued for their arrest was ignored by frontier officers. Even sympathetic officers such as Stuart and Arbuckle refused to cooperate. Sentiment among the frontier militia forces would not countenance any arrests.

Governor Henry sent several contrite messages of apology to the Shawnees while loudly condemning the murders to anyone who would listen, but it was all to no avail. "If we had anything to expect from that Nation it is now vanished," a frontier commander reported to the governor.[9]

More bad news soon followed when, in March 1778, Alexander McKee, the British Indian agent who had replaced Croghan, escaped from house arrest at Fort Pitt in the dead of night with the assistance of Matthew Elliott and Simon Girty. They quickly made their way to join Colonel Hamilton at Detroit. These three would form the core of the British Indian Department north of the Ohio. To the Americans, Girty and Elliott now became notorious renegades.

The Shawnees, with their Mingo and Delaware allies, could muster over 3,000 warriors to hurl at the isolated and vulnerable Kentucky settlements. They needed no encouragement from the British to attack the Americans, although the muskets, powder, and ball that began to flow south once the St. Lawrence trade route was reopened were most welcome. It was obvious to all the Natives, even to those who distrusted the British, that the American settlers were a direct threat to their survival. Even Guyasuta now allied himself with the Crown.

A Seneca chief spoke for many members of the various northern tribes when he warned that "the Rebels, who notwithstanding their fair speeches, wish for nothing more than to extirpate us from the Earth, that they may possess our Lands, the Desire of attaining which we are convinced is the

Cause of our present War between the King and his disobedient Children." It was difficult to argue with his logic.[10]

IT HAD BEEN RELATIVELY QUIET ACROSS THE KENTUCKY frontier following the abduction and rescue of Jemima Boone and the Callaway girls. An uneasy calm now settled in on both sides of the Ohio River throughout late 1776. George Rogers Clark, anticipating a renewal of hostilities, had returned to Kentucky following his successful argument before the Williamsburg assembly to admit Kentucky as the westernmost Virginia county. While the debate over county status dragged on for weeks until finally passed on December 7, 1776, young Clark had busied himself securing five hundred pounds of powder for the settlements. This was sent to Pittsburgh to await delivery to Kentucky. With a handful of volunteers, Clark eventually moved the powder by boat from Pittsburgh to the mouth of Limestone Creek, where it was buried rather than risk transporting it overland with so few men. Clark then arrived just in time to help defend McClelland's Station and Harrodsburg from Mingo attacks. Although the Natives were repulsed, the settlers decided to abandon McClelland's Station. James Harrod, with thirty riflemen, managed to retrieve Clark's cached gunpowder in January 1777, and now his fort, Logan's Station, and Boonesborough remained as the only Kentucky settlements.

The Virginia authorities had appointed Clark as militia major for the new county. He now promptly selected James Harrod, John Todd, Benjamin Logan, and Daniel Boone as his captains. Clark and his officers had only 121 men available for militia service at the three outposts. Many settlers, with both powder and morale low, and with renewed Indian attacks inevitable, had already abandoned Kentucky. Boone had but twenty-two men to defend the fifty other souls gathered inside the stockade walls of Boonesborough.[11]

Although the Shawnees remained bitterly divided over a course of action between the war faction and the smaller but more influential peace faction, they stepped up their campaign against the Virginians in the spring of 1777. Perhaps a thousand members of the tribe, with little faith in the British and none in the American colonists, moved to the northwest, nearer to the lands of their allies the Miami along the Little Miami, Great

Miami, and Mad Rivers. Some moved even farther to the west. Their effort at neutrality would not last long, for this was in fact the beginning of a twenty-year war for the Ohio Country.[12]

Blackfish now led some two hundred warriors south across the Ohio against the Kentuckians. His advance parties scouted around both Boonesborough and Harrodsburg. Two men were killed near Boonesborough on March 7, while at Harrodsburg the Shawnees killed Hugh McGary's son not far from the fort. McGary was so horrified upon finding the boy's mutilated body that he began to spiral into madness. The very next day he and his men overtook the Shawnees and killed several of them. When McGary found that one of the dead warriors was wearing his son's shirt, he hacked the man into pieces and fed the body parts to his hounds.

Blackfish's warriors took a heavy toll on the three Kentucky outposts—butchering cattle, destroying crops, and holding the settlers as virtual captives inside their stockades. On April 24, 1777, the Shawnees ambushed several men outside Boonesborough, and Boone, rushing to their rescue, went down with a shattered ankle. He was saved by Simon Kenton, a young Virginia giant with a mysterious past, who hoisted the wounded man over his shoulder and made for the fort gate amidst a hail of arrows and musket balls. Boone, confined to his cabin for several weeks, would ever after limp from the wound. The post barely held on until finally relieved by reinforcements from Virginia.

By the time Blackfish lifted his siege late that summer, the settlers were near starvation. Daniel Trabue, newly arrived from Virginia, was shocked by what he found. "The people in the fort was remarkable kind and hospetable to us with what they had," he noted, "but I thought it was hard times—no bred, no salt, no vegetables, no fruit of any kind, no Ardent sperrets [spirits], indeed nothing but meet."[13]

With their crops destroyed, the settlers were now desperate for salt to preserve the game meat that provided their only food. In January 1778, Boone decided to take thirty men to the Lower Blue Licks to boil salt for the settlements. This was hard work, for it took six to eight hundred gallons of brine water to produce a fifty-pound bushel of salt. While the men toiled at the salt licks, Boone hunted game to feed them. The weather was brutal, with a half foot of snow on the ground and game scarce, but Boone managed to down a large buffalo. As he butchered the beast and loaded the meat on his horse, he was surprised by a party of Shawnee hunters. They took their prize captive back to Blackfish's encampment, which was but a few miles from the Lower Blue Licks. Blackfish, with 120 warriors, was headed south on a raid to avenge the recent murder of Cornstalk.

As Boone was brought into the Indian camp, he was recognized by Captain Will, the Shawnee who had captured him and Stewart eight years before, taken all their furs and skins, and then released them with a warning never to return.

"Howdydo," he exclaimed as he firmly grasped Boone's hand in greeting. Captain Will laughingly chastised Boone for not heeding his warning about yellow jacket stings. He then introduced the celebrated chief of the Long Knives all around to his curious companions.

Boone was then taken before Blackfish. Pompey, an enslaved Black man captured by the Shawnee as a child and raised among them, acted as interpreter. Boone, too wise in his forty-fourth year for forlorn hopes, managed to convince Blackfish to allow him to take the Shawnees back to the American camp, where he would convince his men to surrender. Blackfish listened patiently to Boone's proposal and then turned to confer with his leading men. He argued that this would be an easy, bloodless victory and that the white captives would bring a good price from the British at Detroit. It was agreed.

The warriors reached the camp of the salt boilers the following day around noon and Boone was sent forward. The Shawnees silently encircled the camp as Boone talked to the men. The salt boilers were naturally wary and several murmured that Boone had betrayed them, but they finally agreed to the surrender. As the men reluctantly put their weapons aside, the Shawnees quickly moved in from every direction. It now became apparent that they would all have been slaughtered had they resisted.

Blackfish was now confronted by several prominent warriors who demanded that the whites be killed to avenge the death of Cornstalk. Blackfish, even though a great chief, led by consensus and so now called a council to discuss this life-and-death question. Boone was allowed to sit within the council circle with Pompey at his side to interpret. The debate became heated, and when it finally ended, Blackfish called on Boone for a closing statement.

"You have got all the young men," Boone told the warriors as Pompey translated. "To kill them, as has been suggested, would displease the Great Spirit, and you could not expect future success in hunting nor war. If you spare them, they will make fine warriors, and excellent hunters to kill game for your squaws and children. I consented to their capitulation on the express condition that they should be made prisoners of war and treated well. I now appeal both to your honor and your humanity: spare them, and the Great Spirit will smile upon you."

As Boone sat back down the warriors debated the point and then voted. It was a close-run thing. Fifty-nine voted for death and sixty-one for life.

To satisfy the losing faction, Blackfish ordered Pompey to tell Boone that he must run the gauntlet. The warriors, armed with clubs, now formed two long lines that Boone would have to run between. If he fell, he might well be beaten to death.

"I set out full speed," Boone later told his grandson, "first running so near one line that they could not do me much damage, and when they give back, crossed over to the other side, and by that means was likely to pass through without much hurt." Despite a blow to the head that clouded his vision with blood, he retained the strength to ram into the final warrior who blocked his path. Boone sent the man sprawling.

A great shout of acclaim went up from the Shawnees. They pressed in around their captive to clasp his hand and praise his daring. Boone had first won them over with his words and now once again by his actions. The next morning they began the one-hundred-mile journey to Blackfish's village at Chillicothe on the Little Miami River. Once there, some of the prisoners were dispersed to other villages. Most of them eventually managed to escape. Ten of the men, including Boone, were taken farther north to Detroit to be sold to the British.[14]

At Detroit, Boone was warmly received by Lieutenant Governor Henry Hamilton, who had many questions for the famous frontiersman. Boone ingratiated himself to Hamilton by declaring his Loyalist sympathies. He assured Hamilton that many at Boonesborough shared his views and if given the chance he could convince them to surrender just as he had done with the salt boilers. He also provided his host with the first news of the British defeat at Saratoga the previous October and of the surrender of General John Burgoyne's army. Hamilton relished his time with Boone and offered Blackfish a rich ransom of one hundred pounds sterling for him, but the Shawnee leader refused to part with his prize captive.[15]

At this time Boone learned that one of the warriors killed in the rescue of Jemima the previous year was the son of Blackfish. The chief now decided to adopt Boone as a replacement for his lost son. In an elaborate ceremony, Boone was scrubbed by several Indian women as if to wash away his whiteness, and his hair was all plucked out save for a traditional Shawnee topknot. He was painted and befeathered with much fanfare before this initiation was complete. Blackfish gave him the name Sheltowee, or Big Turtle.

"I was adopted," Boone later related, "according to their custom, into a family, where I became a son, and had a great deal of affection for my new parents, brothers, sisters, and friends."[16]

Early in June of 1778, Boone traveled with his adoptive father to the Shawnee and Mingo villages along the Scioto River, where he uncovered a plan for a large number of warriors to attack Boonesborough. Upon their return to Chillicothe, Boone promptly made his escape at dawn on June 16. Despite his bad ankle, he managed to outdistance the Shawnees sent in pursuit in a mad dash to the Kentucky River. Boone covered over 160 miles in four days to reach Boonesborough on June 20. There he discovered that many of the disheartened settlers, including Rebecca and all his children save Jemima, had departed. Boone's son-in-law Flanders Callaway had been away from the salt boilers' camp hunting on the day of the surrender, and he had brought the news of the captured men back to the fort. It was assumed that the men would all be killed. Several of those who remained at the fort now viewed Boone with suspicion, for reports had reached Boonesborough that he, like the renegade Simon Girty, had gone over to the Indians.

Boone found the fort in a terrible state of disrepair and so immediately organized both work and hunting parties to prepare for a siege. Boone penned a letter to Virginia authorities asking for reinforcements. "Both French and Indians coming against us to the number of near 400," he wrote. He also sent runners to the two other settlements. A few men came over from Harrodsburg and Logan's Station to join in the defense, but it would be three months before a small contingent of Virginia militia arrived.[17]

Arms and ammunition were passed out to the enslaved men as well as all the boys old enough to shoulder a rifle. Boone commanded some sixty men. Inside the stockade were another dozen women and twenty young children. Boone set the women to work in the preparation of bandages, the molding of rifle bullets, and the gathering of all wild greens and other foodstuffs from the nearby woods.

On July 17 one of the salt boilers stumbled up to the stockade. William Hancock had escaped from Captain Will, who had told him that the planned attack on Boonesborough had been delayed while Blackfish awaited the arrival of arms and ammunition from Hamilton in Detroit. Captain Will had told Hancock that the Natives intended to offer the whites a chance to surrender but that if they refused, all the men were to be killed and the women and children taken captive.

Blackfish, with over four hundred men—not only Shawnees but also Mingo, Wyandot, Miami, and Delaware warriors—as well as a small company of Canadian militia sent by Hamilton from Detroit, arrived before Boonesborough on September 7, 1778. Blackfish immediately asked for a parley, where he presented Boone with a wampum belt and a letter from Hamilton with a promise of safe conduct to Detroit for the settlers if they surrendered. Otherwise, no quarter would be given. Pompey again translated. The talks went on for two more days some sixty yards from the gate of the fort near the sulfur lick. Nothing was settled, as both sides were wary and mistrustful. Boone had placed sharpshooters on the palisade to cover the parley area, and Blackfish had done the same with select warriors in the nearby forest line.

Finally Blackfish made a surprisingly generous offer. The whites might remain at Fort Boonesborough if they promised to swear allegiance to King George and to never again cross the Ohio River onto Shawnee land. Boone, anxious to stall for time, agreed to this. Blackfish gave a speech to his assembled warriors and then turned back to Boone and the eight other white negotiators. It was customary for each man to embrace two warriors to seal the bargain. This was a new custom to Boone, but before he could object, Blackfish and one of his warriors had him by both arms. As other Shawnees seized hold of the other white men, a great wrestling match ensued. Boone slammed his Indian father to the ground and broke free just as gunfire erupted from both the fort and the tree line. Squire Boone went down with a shot in the shoulder but quickly rose and sprinted for the fort. Boone received a nasty gash to the back of his head from a tomahawk blow but also managed to escape. The sharpshooters on the walls dropped several Indians as all of their comrades staggered back into the fort. Blackfish sent his warriors storming after the men but they were repulsed, with heavy losses.

For nine days and nights the battle raged. The Indians boldly assaulted the fort at night with burning torches and flaming arrows, but the defenders held on. It was as desperate a defense as any ever waged on the frontier. Finally on September 18 the warriors, after suffering nearly forty dead and many more wounded, withdrew. Among the Shawnee dead was Pompey. Inside the fort, two lay dead, with four more wounded, including Daniel and Squire Boone. A small contingent of Virginia militia reinforcements arrived a few days after the departure of the Indians. This tiny outpost of the Revolution had held, and in time it helped to secure the new republic's claim to the West.[18]

No sooner had the last Shawnee stragglers departed than a court-martial was convened at Logan's Station. Richard Callaway and Benjamin Logan brought charges of treason against Boone for his surrender of the salt boilers, his negotiations with Hamilton at Detroit, and his aborted peace parley with Blackfish at Boonesborough. Callaway, long jealous of Boone, now saw his chance to discredit his rival. His bitterness toward Boone was intensified because his nephew, one of the salt boilers, remained a prisoner. Callaway now insisted that Boone "was in favour of the britesh government, that all his conduct proved it . . . and he ought to be broak of his commission."

Boone mounted a spirited defense. He had surrendered at the Blue Licks both to save the lives of his men as well as to prevent an attack on the unprepared settlement. He had indeed ingratiated himself to Hamilton and lied to him that he was prepared to surrender Boonesborough. He had told Blackfish the same story and had in that way delayed a Shawnee assault on Boonesborough. Once he learned of the planned British and Indian attack, he had escaped from the Chillicothe village to warn Boonesborough, repair the palisades, gather provisions, and lead the defense of the fort.

The court-martial officers not only acquitted him of all charges; they also secured his immediate promotion to major in the militia as a reward for both his heroism and his wisdom. Despite this result, Boone felt deeply embittered by the whole affair as well as by the continuing scorn and distrust of several of his former compatriots. He and Colonel Callaway would never speak again despite the family connection through Flanders and Jemima. Their feud finally ended in March 1780 when Callaway was killed by an Indian raiding party.[19]

Callaway had not been entirely wrong concerning Boone's divided loyalties. His stated affection for his Indian family was well-known among the settlers, many of whom could not begin to fathom this seeming contradiction. Boone's sympathy for the Indians, and his personal identification with them, remained constant throughout his life.

Soon after this ordeal, Boone departed for North Carolina to reunite with his family. Accompanied by Jemima and Flanders Callaway as well as Will Hays, Boone's little party reached the Yadkin early in November 1778. It would take all of his considerable powers of persuasion to convince Rebecca to return to Kentucky. They then spent a year on the Yadkin living with Rebecca's Bryan relatives. During this time Boone hunted both wild game and fresh recruits for his planned return to Kentucky. Tensions were on the rise in the North Carolina backcountry between Tory and Patriot families. Many loyalists, including several of Rebecca's Bryan relatives, decided that the very real threat of Carolina backcountry strife made the dangers of Kentucky pale in comparison. A compelling feature of Kentucky was a new commission set up by Virginia governor Thomas Jefferson to both regulate new land claims and validate old ones. Boone was entitled to four hundred acres at $2.25 per hundred acres, with a preemption right to yet another thousand acres at $40 per hundred. He needed to return to Kentucky during the winter of 1779–1780 to meet with these commissioners.

Boone's large party departed the Yadkin in September 1779. With Boone came all of his remaining brothers and sisters with their families, along with many of the Bryans. Numbered among the one hundred men, women, and children were Captain Abraham Lincoln and his wife, Bathsheba, of Rockingham County, grandparents of the future president. Boone led them all over the Cumberland Gap and up the trace toward the Bluegrass. They reached Boonesborough in late October.

Boone, uncomfortable in the community he had founded, met with the land commissioners in December and then quickly departed with his family for land some six miles northwest of Boonesborough. The new settlement was to be called Boone's Station. With Boone were his daughters Jemima and Susannah and their husbands, six young orphaned Bryan cousins, as well as the five Boone children: twenty-year-old Israel, the teenage girls Rebecca and Levina, and the younger boys Daniel Morgan and Jesse Bryan. Boone's brothers Edward, Samuel, and Jonathan and their families all settled nearby. Rebecca's Bryan relatives moved to the north on Elkhorn Creek (near present-day Lexington), where they founded Bryan's Station.[20]

Between fifteen and twenty families settled near the little stockade that was Boone's Station. Many others now came through the Cumberland Gap, so that by the time of Kentucky statehood in 1792, nearly 300,000 pioneers had followed in Boone's footsteps up his Wilderness Road. This increasing American population so infuriated the Indians that they stepped up their raids. Among the most dramatic and consequential of these attacks was the capture by Miami warriors of thirteen-year-old William Wells in 1784. Taken north to the Wea villages along the Eel River in present-day Indiana, the redheaded, freckled-faced boy was adopted and given the name Apekonit (Wild Carrot). He adapted to Indian life quickly and accompanied the Miamis on raids into Kentucky. In time he married the daughter of Little Turtle, the war leader of the Miami Confederacy, and rapidly rose to prominence as a warrior. He fought alongside his adopted people in the crushing defeat of General Arthur St. Clair's 1,400-man American army on the Wabash in November 1791. Over six hundred Americans were slaughtered and the army routed.[21]

White raiding parties now retaliated, crossing the Ohio River to attack the Shawnees. The men knew each other, and they now sought retribution in a brutal, unrelenting war on both the white settlements in Kentucky and the Shawnee villages to the north. One such raid was against Moluntha's Shawnee town, where Girty was reported to be visiting. Girty escaped, but Boone soon spied a more personal target running away from the village. "Mind that fellow!" he called out to Simon Kenton. "I know him. Big Jim, who killed my son in Powell's Valley!" Big Jim, hearing his name called, turned and shot one of the Kentuckians near Boone. As the Cherokee reloaded, Kenton dashed forward and plunged his knife into the renegade's chest.[22]

The Indians also extracted a heavy price in blood. In October 1780, warriors ambushed Daniel and his brother Ned while they were hunting. Boone escaped but Ned was killed. As Boone hid in a nearby canebrake he heard one of the Shawnees shouting, "We've killed Daniel Boone!" The Shawnees beheaded Ned so that they could prove their kill and collect the British bounty on the celebrated Patriot. Indeed, as Rebecca had declared years before, Ned looked very much like Daniel.[23]

Boone, elected to represent the frontier peoples, traveled to Richmond, Virginia, for the opening of the legislative session in 1781. At the same time he was promoted to colonel in the militia by Governor Thomas Jefferson. The troops of Lord Cornwallis were then sweeping through Virginia in their retreat—which their commander labeled an invasion—after the American triumphs at Kings Mountain and Cowpens. Colonel Banastre Tarleton's British dragoons captured Boone on June 4 but soon released him, so that he was back in the legislature later that month. Assigned to a committee charged with dealing with frontier issues, he proved so indifferent to the work and was absent so much on hunting trips that the sergeant-at-arms was ordered to find him and return him to his duties. While in the assembly, Boone learned of the surrender of Cornwallis at Yorktown on October 19, 1781, and carried that news back to Kentucky in February 1782. It must have seemed to Daniel Boone that his Kentucky dream had finally come true. It was not to be.[24]

7

KINGS MOUNTAIN

They called it the "Bloody Year of the Three Sevens." In that cruel year the Revolutionary struggle to the east swept across the mountains, fully engulfing the trans-Appalachian country. The Chickamauga warriors of Dragging Canoe struck repeatedly at the exposed settlements of the *unakas*—the whites—of eastern Tennessee. Dragging Canoe was relentless in his wrath. He had become an outlier to many of his own Cherokee people, breaking with his father, Little Carpenter, and the other older leaders at Sycamore Shoals in 1775, refusing to sign away yet more land, and ominously warning Richard Henderson that the settlement of his new purchase would be a bloody enterprise. Dragging Canoe proved true to his word.

The new year, however, had brought prospects of peace to the scattered settlements along the Holston River. The summer of 1776 had been marked by a three-pronged Cherokee invasion of the eastern Tennessee country. The settlers blamed the British—and indeed British arms and supplies moved north from Mobile, Pensacola, and St. Augustine—but Cherokee grievances predated the outbreak of the Revolution. British Indian agent John Stuart had studiously disobeyed General Thomas Gage's orders to set the Indians against the western settlers, only to have an intemperate and ill-timed letter from the Virginia Revolutionary government threatening the Cherokees with extinction should they make war undercut all his efforts to restrain the passing of the war belt. Friends among the Cherokees, most notably Nancy Ward, the niece of Little Carpenter, warned the settlements to the east near the Long Island of the Holston, in Carter's Valley, and to the south in the Watauga and Nolichucky region, so that the whites were able to retreat into their forts. The Cherokee offensive was repulsed, to be promptly followed by an already planned invasion of the Overhill Cherokee country by 1,800 Virginia, North Carolina, and Watauga troops. This force, under the able command of Colonel William Christian, who would himself perish battling Indians on the Beargrass in Kentucky in 1786, destroyed several abandoned Cherokee towns, and so overawed the principal chiefs that a truce was promptly announced. The Cherokees agreed to come to the Long Island of the Holston in the summer of 1777 to negotiate a new land cession treaty. Ominously, Dragging Canoe refused to be party to this appeasement, leading his followers westward to establish a new town on Chickamauga Creek.[1]

Among the pioneers of Carter's Valley, north of the Holston River, was the family of David Crockett. He was Scotch-Irish and, like so many of that hardy Presbyterian breed, had migrated to the New World in the middle of the eighteenth century. David Crockett had the wanderlust and, like many others, moved from Pennsylvania down into the lower Shenandoah Valley of Virginia. By 1771, David had moved his family to North Carolina, where he purchased 250 acres south of the Catawba River in Tryon County, but they did not remain long. The year of the Declaration of Independence found the Crocketts and their five sons in Carter's Valley on the Holston.[2]

Inspired by the news of Lexington, Concord, and greater battles to the east, and worried about Indians close around them and Tories in their midst, members of the Watauga Association, including David and his son William Crockett, petitioned North Carolina for protection and annexation on July 5, 1776. In this petition, signed but a day after the announcement of the Declaration of Independence in Philadelphia, these frontiersmen boldly pledged themselves "to the glorious cause in which we are now struggling," promising to "contribute to the welfare of our own or ages yet to come." These men had a crystal-clear self-image. "We are the Advanced Guard of Civilization; Our way is across the Continent," bluntly declared James Robertson, one of their leaders.[3]

The Crocketts had come to this troubled but promising land on the eve of revolution, settling in Carter's Valley not far from the confluence of the Holston and Watauga Rivers. They hacked out a clearing and built their earthen-floored log cabin not too distant from the "great Trading Path," the ancient Indian warpath that became the entry for white traders seeking out the Cherokees. Eventually it became a rough-hewn highway for pioneer emigrants like the Crocketts. The Wilderness Road took form nearby and traced west and north through the Cumberland Gap to the Kentucky settlements of Boonesborough and Harrodsburg.

John Carter was one of those early Indian traders, establishing an outpost on the north bank of the Holston in 1769, the same year that Daniel Boone first went north through the Cumberland Gap. The settlers trickled in after him, making the lush valley that bore Carter's name their home. Many of them, like the Crocketts, came from North Carolina, where the bloody May 1771 defeat of the backcountry "Regulators" had sent refugees in search of new homes and greater freedom to the west.

They raised corn in their stump-strewn fields, ran hogs and cattle that fattened on the rich native grasses, and carefully guarded their wiry horses—some of them traded from the Chickasaws far to the west. Horses and cattle quickly became valuable trade commodities. Wild game was the source of much food, but corn sustained them. Johnnycake, hominy, pone, mush, and eventually, once mills were built, corn liquor all came from this true staff of life.

These hardy folk could be clannish, suspicious, and wary but also warm, generous, and hospitable. They lived by the ancient code of an eye for an eye, and toward their rivals for this land—the Indians—they developed an implacable hatred. They had purchased or leased title to wilderness tracts—or in many cases simply squatted on the land—had then cleared the forest and planted their crops, and cared little for any previous claimants. They were not to be frightened away and were prepared to meet any enemy on his own terms. They did not view mercy as a virtue.[4]

Among the Cherokees there were many who returned this hatred in kind. On Chickamauga Creek, various bands of disaffected Indians—Cherokees, Creeks, Shawnees—rallied to Dragging Canoe. It had been but a generation since the Cherokees had driven the Creeks and Shawnees from eastern Tennessee, but now they united to confront a common enemy. Even as the older chiefs prepared to negotiate a new treaty with the whites, Dragging Canoe's followers took the black drink to purge and purify themselves for war. They were well armed and supplied by their British friends for the cruel war to come. Still limping from wounds sustained the previous July in a battle at the Long Island of the Holston, Dragging Canoe led his warriors northeastward toward Carter's Valley.

Spring was just beginning to take hold of the valley in early April 1777 when Dragging Canoe's warriors swept in as silently as a killing frost. Many of the settlers had pulled out after earlier raids, but not the family of David Crockett. Three of his sons had cabins of their own by this time, and so the homestead of the elder Crockett could offer little resistance to Dragging Canoe's onslaught. It must have been over quickly. David and his wife died together, but their son Joseph, with an arm broken by a musket ball, managed to escape into the forest. Young James, who could neither speak nor hear, was carried off into captivity by the murderers of his parents. He remained among them for seventeen years.[5]

John Crockett served as a member of one of the frontier ranging companies and was on duty when his parents were killed. He was still away in August 1778 when his brothers William and Robert administered their father's estate. He may well have ridden westward with old Colonel Evan Shelby and six hundred volunteers against the Chickamauga towns in April 1779. Eleven villages were burned and great stores of arms, ammunition, and food captured, but there was no real fighting, for Dragging Canoe and most of his warriors were away with their British allies in Georgia. Dragging Canoe's unrelenting hostility toward the frontiersmen would continue unabated until his death in 1792. Deprived of his leadership and harried by American troops, his people finally rejoined the Cherokees in 1794 and at last made peace with their enemies.[6]

By this time John Crockett had his own family to look after, for soon after his father had migrated to Carter's Valley he had married Rebecca Hawkins. She was a Marylander, probably born at Old Joppa, between York, Pennsylvania, and Baltimore, to Joseph and Anneke Jane Edwards Hawkins. Joseph Hawkins's forebears were English, and had come to Virginia in 1658. His wife was a Quaker. They had nine children, and another of their daughters, Sarah, married flamboyant John Sevier, the hero of Kings Mountain, who would serve as Tennessee's first governor. John Crockett would follow him to Kings Mountain and there extract a full measure of vengeance for his parents.[7]

The fifth year of the war for America was also the darkest year for the Patriot cause. It was the year of Benedict Arnold's treason. It was a starvation year for General Washington's ragged little army encamped at Morristown, New Jersey, where rumors of mutiny were rampant. And it was a year of unrelenting defeat for Patriot forces as British North American commander Sir Henry Clinton shifted the war to the south in expectation of strong Loyalist support. In July of 1779, the royal government had been reinstated in Georgia—the only one of the thirteen colonies restored to Crown rule—and in early October an assault on Savannah by a combined French and Patriot force had been repulsed with heavy losses. On May 12, 1780, Charleston (called Charles Town at that time), America's fourth-largest city, with its 5,500-man garrison, fell to the British in the worst American defeat of the war. British regiments now swept through South Carolina, establishing a chain of posts from Georgetown on the coast to Augusta on the Savannah River and north to the Star Fort ("Old Ninety Six") on the Saluda River near the western border of the colony.[8]

In the forefront of this British advance was twenty-five-year-old Lieutenant Colonel Banastre Tarleton, the energetic commander of the British Legion, a mixed force of green-coated dragoons and light infantry renowned for their ruthlessness. Tarleton had no sympathy for those who opposed his king and volunteered to join the force under Lieutenant General Lord Charles Cornwallis that was to embark for America in February 1776. He quickly distinguished himself by the serendipitous capture of General Charles Lee at Widow White's Tavern in Basking Ridge, New Jersey. This won him a promotion to captain. Despite being caught quite literally between the sheets with the mistress of his regimental major, Tarleton's heroics at the Battle of Monmouth on June 28, 1778, brought him to the attention of General Clinton and secured his promotion to lieutenant colonel of the British Legion in August.

Tarleton cut quite the romantic figure, although some officers, both British and American, dismissed him as an arrogant, aristocratic dandy. The young officer was not without military talent but mostly relied on sheer audacity and aggressiveness for his success. He represented everything about the British that the Americans hated.[9]

A great favorite with the British high command, Tarleton was often commended in dispatches for his dash and daring and as a result quickly became the darling of the British press. The Patriots nicknamed him "Butcher Tarleton" and heartily agreed with the assessment of the man by their French ally the Comte de Rochambeau that "Colonel Tarleton has no merit as an officer—only that bravery that every Grenadier has—but is a butcher and a barbarian."[10]

At the Waxhaws, near the North Carolina border, Tarleton surprised 350 Virginians under the command of Colonel Abraham Buford, who had marched south to reinforce Charleston. Upon hearing of its fall, Buford had retreated to the north only to be surprised by Tarleton's Legion. The Americans attempted to surrender but were ruthlessly cut down by the British dragoons. One hundred and thirteen Americans were killed, while another 150 were badly wounded and left for dead on the field. Tarleton's loss was but 5 killed and 12 wounded.

Clinton, in Charleston, was delighted with Tarleton's victory. He now prepared to return to New York, turning command of the southern theater over to Lord Cornwallis. Clinton was confident that Loyalists throughout the Carolinas would rally to the Crown. Just before departing, he wrote to Lord George Germain, "With greatest pleasure I further report to your lordship that the inhabitants from every quarter repair to declare their allegiance to the King. I may venture to assert that there are few men in South Carolina who are not either our prisoners, or in arms with us."[11]

He was wrong. From the Carolina swamps and forests, from eastern valleys and western hills, small bands of resolute men rallied to the call of partisan leaders Francis "Swamp Fox" Marion, Thomas "Gamecock" Sumter, and Andrew "Wizard Owl" Pickens. They would strike, vanish, and strike again. A bloody civil war between Tories and Patriots soon ravaged the Carolinas.

In London, the British government had become convinced that the American South was a hotbed of Tory sentiment. Deeply in debt and confronting serious domestic political problems, the king's ministers could squander no more men or treasure on the American war. They were anxious to have loyal Americans fill the ranks of the king's army and suppress the rebellion once and for all. Cornwallis, who had long feuded with Clinton, did not trust any of the Americans and opposed this policy. Sir Henry circumvented Cornwallis and gave an independent command to a remarkable thirty-five-year-old major of the 71st Highland Regiment—Patrick Ferguson—whose new title became inspector of militia in the southern provinces. Ferguson was given orders to raise a force of 4,000 Loyalist militia and to put a thousand of them into the field, ready for action.

Clinton trusted Ferguson to employ a much more benevolent policy toward the colonists than Cornwallis or Tarleton: "You will pay particular attention to restrain the militia from offering violence to innocent and inoffensive people, and by all means in your power protect the aged, the infirm, the women and children of every denomination from insult and outrage."[12]

Patrick Ferguson was admirably suited by both temperament and training for the task. Few officers in the British service were as widely admired as the Scottish major, known throughout the army as the "Bull Dog." In July 1759 a commission was purchased for Ferguson in the Royal North British Dragoons—the Scots Greys—and the youth won distinction on the battlefields of Germany. Promoted to captain in 1768, Ferguson was soon battling Native rebels on the West Indies island of Tobago before a fever felled him, placing him on inactive service for some time. While convalescing in England, he turned to the study of firearms. A noted hunter and marksman—widely regarded as the best shot in the British army—he developed a reliable breech-loading rifle for the army. He displayed the new weapon to King George III at Windsor. The king was amazed at this remarkable rifle that could fire six accurate shots in one minute.

Ferguson, who had been issued patents on his rifle in December 1776, was soon on his way to America in command of a hundred handpicked soldiers. Armed with the new weapon, his green-uniformed troops arrived in New York in May 1777. Ferguson distinguished himself at the Battle of Brandywine on September 11, 1777, but was horribly wounded, his right elbow shattered by a musket ball. Some nine months after being wounded, Ferguson finally returned to active duty, although he could no longer bend his arm and carried it in a sling. Promoted to major in the 71st Regiment, he went on to again distinguish himself at the battles of Monmouth and Charleston.

Ferguson's new appointment as inspector of militia in the southern provinces delighted him, for he relished an independent command. He was confident of raising a large Loyalist army and hoped to win the Americans over by his justice and fairness. Disgusted with Tarleton's no-quarter campaigns, Ferguson hoped to bring the Americans back to their king, not terrorize and further alienate them. This behavior toward the colonists did not endear him to Cornwallis or Tarleton.[13]

While Ferguson recruited his Loyalist militia, Lord Cornwallis advanced northward with his main army, establishing a chain of fortified posts throughout South Carolina, with the northernmost one at Camden. Congress, without consulting General Washington, assigned command of all southern forces to General Horatio Gates, the hero of Saratoga. The ambitious Gates, who hoped to replace Washington as army commander, assumed command of 1,100 Continentals in North Carolina on July 25, 1780, and immediately advanced toward the British outpost at Camden. Although reinforced by North Carolina and Virginia militia, he had but a little over 3,000 hungry, ragged, and mostly ill-trained men. At Camden on August 16, 1780, Cornwallis confronted him with 2,200 battle-tested veterans.

The battle was over within an hour as the British quickly routed the American militia and then cut down the stalwart Continentals. Tarleton's Legion did bloody work in a bold flank attack on the Continentals that ended the battle. He then pursued the fleeing Americans for twenty miles. General Gates was among those who first fled the field of battle—his northern laurels, as one wag later put it, turning to southern willows. At least 650 Americans were killed, wounded, or taken prisoner. The victory was complete and the road to North Carolina wide-open.[14]

General Nathanael Greene, the new American commander in the South, had but a handful of troops to face Lord Cornwallis's victorious army. He required time to build his forces, and he desperately needed some kind of victory to inspire his militiamen to rejoin the fight. Guerrilla warfare raged everywhere—with looting, burnings, and murders the order of the day. Greene was horrified by this level of brutality, commenting that "the whole country is in danger of being laid waste by the Whigs and Tories who pursue each other with as much relentless fury as beasts of prey."[15]

Cornwallis, although frustrated by the raids of Marion and the other rebel partisans, was nevertheless determined to extend the war into North Carolina. He called Major Ferguson to Camden for a war council where he announced a three-pronged thrust northward. The British right wing, on the coast, was to move against Wilmington to secure the flow of supplies, while Cornwallis was to advance with the main army toward Charlotte, North Carolina. Ferguson, with his provincial volunteers and Loyalist militia, was to sweep to the left, guarding against the worrisome frontiersmen west of the mountains. Ferguson eagerly looked forward to proving the value of his Loyalist militia. He was looking for a fight and did not have far to look.[16]

On August 19, at Musgrove's Mill on the Enoree River, Patriot militia under Colonels Isaac Shelby, Elijah Clarke, and James Williams surprised Ferguson's provincials and Tory militia and inflicted punishing casualties: sixty-three dead and ninety wounded Loyalists, with only four killed and eight wounded among the Patriots. Enraged by this attack, Ferguson composed a message and sent it over the mountain to Colonel Shelby: "If they do not desist from their opposition to the British arms, I will march my army over the mountains, hang their leaders, and lay waste their country with fire and sword."[17]

Isaac Shelby was not a man to be trifled with. Of commanding physical presence, he was well-known throughout the western settlements as a surveyor, community leader, and, when the need arose, Indian fighter. He had served with distinction at Point Pleasant and afterward surveyed Kentucky lands for Judge Henderson.

Upon receiving Ferguson's warning, Shelby promptly saddled his horse and rode some forty miles to consult with the leader of the Nolichucky and Watauga River settlements, John Sevier. No man in the western country was better known than Sevier—adventurer, land speculator, warrior, politician, and born leader. "Chucky Jack," as he was called, after his cabin on the Nolichucky River, lived up to his frontier reputation. As one fellow frontiersman put it, "He can outride and outshoot—and, it is said, outswear—the best and worst of the men who followed him." Sevier and Shelby decided that the best defense was a strong offense. They sent out a call to arms to all the over-mountain settlements.[18]

The Holston and Watauga men responded to Ferguson's ultimatum by rallying at the Sycamore Shoals of the Watauga on September 25, 1780. It was much like a gathering of the clans in the old country. They brought their horses, their long rifles, and their seething anger to the rendezvous—a deadly trinity. Each wore a fringed and tasseled hunting shirt girded with a beaded belt in which his knife and tomahawk were thrust. Many carried a Dickert rifle, while a shot pouch, powder horn, knapsack, and blanket completed the outfit. Some of the men wore fur caps, some with long tails hanging in back, while others sported the favored broad-brimmed felt hat with a buck tail or evergreen sprig attached. There was not a uniform, a bayonet, or a tent to be found among them. Rawboned, hard-edged, and undisciplined in the extreme, they were as dangerous and wild a body of men as ever congregated to give battle. They were indeed the new Americans.

One of those frontier warriors later described the martial mindset of the pioneers. While anathema to professional soldiers, his sentiments clearly encapsulated the spirit of the western citizen-soldier from the Revolution to the Alamo:

> *Every man considered himself a soldier. He had his horse and his rifle, which he knew well how to use, and he was always ready at short notice to join his fellows in any emergency. All had a common interest, and that most vital: their homes, their families, and everything dear to man. Thus there was formed among them a pride of tacit league and covenant, which all regarded as most binding. When fighting came on, everyone fought for himself, officers as well as men. The best officers were those who fought best; as among the Indians, the officers were leaders rather than commanders. . . . It would surprise men of this generation to see the power these leaders exercised over their followers. It was power conferred by God and nature, much more effective than that on parchment.*[19]

John Sevier, along with Isaac Shelby, William Campbell, and Charles McDowell, shared command—at least so much as any man commanded this magnificent rabble. Over nine hundred strong, they prepared to march eastward on the morning of September 26. Before departing, they stood grimly, caps in hand, as the black-coated Presbyterian preacher Samuel Doak railed at them as John Knox himself must have done generations before in the old country. With a zealot's fire he called on them to smite the British and Tories with "the sword of the Lord and Gideon." With his words ringing in their ears, they rode off along the Doe River and up over the snow-covered pass between Roan Mountain and Big Yellow Mountain to

Gillespie Gap and passage over the Blue Ridge to the Carolina settlements beyond.

Tory spies hurried to Ferguson with word of the march of the over-mountain men. He sent out a call to arms among the Carolina Tories, warning of an "inundation of barbarians" who would mutilate the men and rape their women. "The Backwater men have crossed the mountains.... If you choose to be pissed upon forever and ever by a set of mongrels," he closed, "say so at once, and let your women turn their backs upon you and look out for real men to protect them."[20]

Colonel Shelby addressed his frontier soldiers at about the same time. He offered any man who wished to depart the chance to step out of ranks. Not a man moved. "I am heartily glad," Shelby proclaimed, "to see you to a man resolved to meet and fight your country's foes. When we encounter the enemy, don't wait for the word of command. Let each one of you be his own officer, taking every care you can of yourselves, and availing yourselves of every advantage that chance may throw in your way. If in the woods, shelter yourselves and give them Indian play! Advance from tree to tree, pressing the enemy and killing and disabling all you can."[21]

They finally rested east of the mountains on the Catawba River. At Quaker Meadows they were reinforced by 350 North Carolina militia under Colonels Benjamin Cleveland and James Williams.

Shelby, Campbell, and Sevier selected the best riflemen with the strongest horses for the final pursuit of Ferguson. John Crockett was numbered among these riflemen. On October 6 they pushed on, not halting but once in thirty-six hours. At the Cowpens they were again reinforced by 400 men of the South Carolina militia. Another choice selection was made by the officers of the best riflemen and horses, and that night 910 mounted men rode forth, followed by 85 determined men on foot. They pressed on through a driving rain toward flat-topped Kings Mountain. They knew that they had to bag Ferguson before he could be reinforced.

Ferguson and his army were encamped atop Kings Mountain, a rough hill, forested and rocky, rising some sixty feet above the plain less than two miles south of the border between the two Carolinas. He expected reinforcements at any time but was certain he could handle this backcountry rabble with his well-trained provincials and Tory militia. He could have retreated but refused, and his contempt for his foe sealed his fate. Cornwallis and Tarleton, both ill at the time, ignored his request for aid.

The rain continued throughout the morning of October 7, but as the over-mountain men tied their horses in the forest at the base of Kings Mountain, the sky began to clear. The frontiersmen primed their rifles and silently moved into the forest to surround the hill. Sevier's men were on the west, Shelby's on the north, Campbell's on the southwest, while the North Carolinians moved off to the northeast. It was well past midday when they scrambled up the rocky terrain toward the waiting enemy.

Ferguson had nearly a thousand men, mostly Carolina Tories but also over one hundred red-coated New Jersey and New York volunteer provincials: King's Rangers and Queen's Rangers. All were well armed, some with Brown Bess muskets and bayonets, others with rifles, knives, and swords. They calmly held their fire as the over-mountain men moved toward them. Finally, at near three o'clock, they fired a volley at Shelby's men, but their position atop the crest sent their shots high.

Onward came the resolute Americans, holding their fire until the last possible moment. Finally, Shelby let out with an Indian yell, the signal to fire. "Here they are boys! Shoot like hell and fight like devils!" he shouted.[22]

Down charged the Tories with bayonets fixed. The mountaineers melted before them, falling back out of reach to reload and come again. Again and again Ferguson's men fired volleys that went high and then charged with the bayonet. The American fire was desultory but remarkably accurate, and always the frontiersmen retreated before the bayonets, only to reload and return. The Tory ranks thinned, their bayonet charges weakened, and their hope vanished. The Americans tightened the ring. Ferguson, conspicuous on a white horse, galloped along his lines roaring encouragement and twice cutting down white flags raised by his own men. The air was foul with the smell of black powder, smoke obscured all vision, and the desperate defenders soon found their lines pressed back-to-back.

FERGUSON AND TWO OF HIS OFFICERS SUDDENLY GALloped into view of Sevier's men. "There's Ferguson—shoot him!" went up the cry. Hit repeatedly, Ferguson reeled in the saddle and fell. His foot caught in a stirrup and the panicky horse dragged the limp body through the American lines. The white flag again went up, but the frontiersmen paid no heed. "Give them 'Tarleton's Quarter'!" the men shouted as they advanced. Rifle, tomahawk, and knife took a terrible toll among the helpless Tories until bloodlust was satiated and the exhausted frontiersmen reckoned they had killed enough. It had all taken but an hour.

Sevier and Shelby regained as much control as they could and tallied losses. They had lost fewer than 50 while killing over 150, wounding nearly as many, and taking over 800 prisoners. Among the American dead was Colonel Williams. Ferguson's body and those of his slain comrades were thrown into a shallow trench and slightly covered with earth and a few stones. Wolves soon found the spot, dug up the bodies, and feasted heartily. They made it a haunt, hoping for another banquet, so that for some time afterward wolf hunters found Kings Mountain a prime spot.

The over-mountain men, undisciplined to begin with, now became totally unmanageable with the battle won. Nine Tory prisoners were hanged before Sevier could halt the killing. Turning their prisoners over to the lowland militia, Sevier and Shelby, still worried about Dragging Canoe's warriors, hurried their men back to their cabins along the Holston, Watauga, and Nolichucky. They had won a stunning and decisive victory.[23]

Colonel Arthur Campbell, with four hundred of his Virginia militia, soon reinforced Sevier, who had intercepted a large Cherokee war party near the French Broad River, and the combined command marched westward against the Cherokee towns in central Tennessee, where they destroyed several villages as well as great quantities of foodstuffs. Campbell then called on the Cherokees to come to a treaty council on the Long Island of the Holston in July. "Never did a people so happily situated, act more foolishly," noted Campbell in his report of the campaign, "in loosing their livings, and their Country, at a time an advantageous neutrality was held out to them, but such is the consequences of British seduction."[24]

AS SOON AS NATHANAEL GREENE ASSUMED COMMAND of the Southern Department from Horatio Gates that December, he wisely turned over a third of his 1,600-man army to Brigadier General Daniel Morgan. Greene now ordered Morgan to march southwest into South Carolina with a "flying army to consist of Infantry and horse." It was hoped that

Kings Mountain would reinvigorate the local militia and encourage them to take the field. From Charlotte, Morgan planned to move south across the border to unite with militia units under Thomas Sumter and Andrew Pickens and threaten the British left flank.[25]

Cornwallis, shaken by the loss of Ferguson and his men at Kings Mountain, had retreated back into South Carolina. There his army waited to be reinforced by 2,200 troops sent south by Clinton. This would swell the British ranks to about 4,000 men. Clinton, in New York, upon finally hearing of Kings Mountain, was surprised at the cavalier manner in which Cornwallis had refused to respond to Ferguson's call for reinforcements. The British commander was hardly sanguine about the future of the southern campaign. He felt that Ferguson's defeat had "so encouraged that spirit of rebellion in both Carolinas that it never could be afterward humbled. For no sooner had the news of it spread through the country than multitudes of disaffected flew to arms from all parts, and menaced every British post on both frontiers."[26]

When Lord Cornwallis learned of Greene's division of forces, he promptly ordered Tarleton to advance west toward the Broad River to protect the vital post Old Ninety Six and hopefully engage Morgan. Cornwallis promised to closely follow and support his favorite with the main army. Morgan was not near Ninety Six but rather some distance to the northeast, encamped along the Pacolet not far from the west bank of the Broad River. He soon learned from Greene of the British movement. "Col. Tarleton is said to be on his way to pay you a visit," wrote the Quaker general. "I doubt not but he will have a decent reception and a proper dismission."[27]

Tarleton, much like an unleashed hound on a scent, was confident of success if only he could force Morgan to stand and fight. He had 450 men of his own legion (infantry and dragoons), 334 of the 71st Regiment of Foot, 100 redcoats of the 17th Light Dragoons, and an amalgam of 250 additional light infantry regulars (7th Fusiliers, 16th Foot, and the Prince of Wales Regiment) sent by Cornwallis, as well as two light artillery pieces with gun crews. Heavy rains slowed Tarleton's column but hardly dampened his spirits. "The more difficulty, the more glory," he declared.[28] Morgan now turned from prey to predator. Unable to cross eastward over the swollen Broad River, the wily "old wagoner" retreated north to a backcountry grazing commons to the west of Kings Mountain called the Cowpens.

Here, reinforced by Andrew Pickens with several hundred South Carolina militiamen on the evening of January 16, 1781, Morgan decided to stand and fight.

"Captain," he declared to one of the South Carolina militia officers, "here is Morgan's grave or victory."[29]

With Pickens's militia reinforcement, Morgan now commanded nearly 2,000 men. That night he moved about the camp from campfire to campfire, laying out his plan to the officers and men. He recognized that his raw militia would not be able to stand for long against the bayonets of Tarleton's regulars and so he had devised a plan by which Pickens's men were to hold their fire as long as possible and then unleash two volleys into the advancing British. He urged both the forward skirmishers and the militia line to take careful aim and to pick off the British officers and then fall back behind Lieutenant Colonel John Eager Howard's Continentals, who stood some 150 yards away on the crest of the gently sloping ridge. The Continentals, supported by seasoned Virginia militia, would then surprise the British advance. Morgan planned for Tarleton to take the militia retreat as bait and then when charging forward to be enveloped by the Continentals, the re-formed militia, and Lieutenant Colonel William Washington's dragoons. Like the man, Morgan's plan was boldly unorthodox.

As he talked to the men, he pulled up his hunting shirt so the firelight could dance off the deep scars from the British lashing he had received during Braddock's campaign over twenty years before. Now, the "old wagoner" declared, he would crack his whip over Tarleton in the morning. "Just hold your heads, boys, three fires," he told then, "and you are free, and then when you return to your homes, how the old folks will bless you, and the girls kiss you, for your gallant conduct."[30]

Tarleton had kept up a relentless pursuit. The troops had to navigate dense thickets, flooded streams, and the broken terrain that passed for a road in name only. Just at dawn the advance guard encountered Morgan's 120 skirmishers blocking the Green River Road at the edge of the Cowpens pasture. The grassy meadow was some five hundred yards long and just about as wide, bordered by marshland.

The battle opened according to Morgan's plan. His militiamen in the advance line got off two well-aimed rifle shots. Several British officers were promptly brought down. The riflemen then rapidly withdrew 150 yards to re-form on the flanks of Pickens's militia line. As Morgan had hoped, Tarleton plunged headlong toward the thin American line, sending fifty of his dragoons to ride down the skirmishers. Fifteen of these were shot out of their saddles and the rest turned back.

Tarleton now hurriedly formed his infantry into line: the red-coated 16th Foot and Fraser's Highlanders, some 110 men, formed on the right, while to their left he placed 250 green-coated provincial regulars of his legion. The 7th Regiment of Royal Fusiliers formed on the far left. Both flanks were held by 50 men of the 17th Light Dragoons. He kept a battalion of Fraser's Highlanders, 250 strong, to the rear as a reserve, along with 200 of his Green Dragoons. Even as the men were extending their line, their impatient commander ordered his little three-pounders—called grasshoppers—to open fire on the militia line.

"About sunrise, the British line advanced at a sort of trot, with a loud halloo. It was the most beautiful line I ever saw," remembered Thomas Young of the South Carolina militia. "When they shouted, I heard General Morgan say 'They give us the British halloo, boys, give them the Indian halloo, by God,' and he galloped down the lines, cheering the men, and telling them not to fire until we could see the whites of their eyes."[31]

Pickens's men coolly held their fire until the British were within fifty yards. Two ragged volleys followed. The withdrawal was not as orderly as Morgan might have hoped for, but Pickens's men had played their part well.

Tarleton sensed that the retreat marked the battle's climactic moment and so sent his troops surging forward. They would finish the job with the bayonet. As he turned downslope to bring up the 71st, Tarleton ordered the cavalry on the right to charge and outflank the rebel left. The Highlanders now advanced to the shrill wail of their bagpipes, which added to the wild cacophony of sound on the field.

"They are coming on like a mob," exclaimed William Washington as he reined his horse in beside Morgan. "Give them one fire and I'll charge them!" Howard's Continentals, who had seemed for a moment to be retreating, suddenly turned about to let loose a sheet of flame and then advance with bayonets fixed. The stunned British line paused and then broke just as Washington's dragoons struck their flanks.

"An unaccountable panic extended itself along the whole line," Tarleton grimly noted. His frantic efforts to rally the men were to no avail, so he turned back to bring up his Green Dragoons. He made a prominent target as he dashed along the lines, and Morgan's sharpshooters blazed away at him. As his horse went down under him, he could hear the repeated shouts of "Tarleton's Quarter" from the advancing Americans. An officer offered him his mount, and as Tarleton leapt into the saddle, several of his dragoons rallied around him. With forty men and a handful of officers he cut his way out—engaging in a brief saber duel with Lieutenant Colonel Washington—and galloped down a back trail toward the Pacolet.[32]

"I was desirous to have a stroke at Tarleton," Morgan gleefully wrote a friend, "and I have given him a devil of a whipping, a more compleat victory never was obtained." Quite a whipping indeed, with nearly 90 percent of Tarleton's force destroyed: 110 dead, over 700 prisoners, including 200 wounded men, as well as 70 people enslaved by British officers. The two grasshoppers were among the captured plunder, along with eight hundred muskets, two regimental standards, one hundred horses, and thirty-five wagons. Morgan reported but a dozen of his men killed and sixty wounded.[33]

The crestfallen Tarleton reached Cornwallis's camp on Turkey Creek, some thirty-five miles southeast of the Cowpens, the next day. He had with him but two hundred men of his once proud command. Many of the older British officers agreed with Major Archibald McArthur, the Highlander commander, who bitterly noted that he had been "an officer before Tarleton was born, that the best troops in the service were put under 'that boy' to be sacrificed."

"That he possesses personal bravery inferior to no man is beyond doubt," grumbled Cornwallis's chief commissary officer of Tarleton. But, he asserted, "during the whole period of the war no other action reflected so much dishonor upon the British arms. . . . The defeat of his majesty's troops at the Cowpens formed a very principal link in the chain of circumstances which led to the independence of America."[34]

Cornwallis made his report to Clinton on January 18, 1781. He was more than kind in his assessment of his pet Tarleton, praising his gallantry and blaming the debacle on the troops. He did grimly note that "it is impossible to foresee all the consequences that this unexpected and extraordinary event may produce."[35]

Cornwallis, more determined than ever to bring Greene to bay, refitted at Hillsborough to await the arrival of North Carolina Loyalists. The Tory militia forces failed to materialize, for after Kings Mountain and Cowpens the fight had gone out of them. Finally, on March 15, 1781, Cornwallis managed to eke out a costly victory over Greene at Guilford Courthouse. While the British held the field, it cost Cornwallis nearly a third of his army in killed and wounded. Greene, with most of his force intact, retreated back into South Carolina, while the British retired to the relative safety of the coast at Wilmington.[36]

"One more such victory would prove the ruin of the British army," the leader of the opposition party in Parliament quipped. Unable to corner Greene, the frustrated earl abandoned the Carolinas and in exasperation turned northward toward his fate and the complete surrender of what was left of his army at Yorktown, Virginia, on October 19, 1781.[37]

Sir Henry Clinton later wrote that the road to Yorktown had begun at Kings Mountain and Cowpens: "The instant I heard of Major Ferguson's defeat, I foresaw most of the consequences likely to result from it. The check so encouraged the spirit of rebellion in the Carolinas that it could never afterward be humbled. It was the first link in a chain of evils that followed each other in a regular succession until they at last ended in the total loss of America."

The rough frontiersmen of Kings Mountain and Cowpens had won stunning victories that had altered the course of the war. "That memorable victory," wrote Thomas Jefferson, "was the joyful annunciation of that turn in the tide of success which terminated the Revolutionary War with the seal of independence."[38]

THE WAR MAY HAVE ENDED TO THE EAST, BUT NOT SO on the frontier. In June 1782, Colonel William Crawford, General Washington's land agent, was captured by the Delawares during a disastrous engagement on Ohio's Sandusky River. On June 11 he was slowly burned at the stake in a four-hour ordeal that horrified even the most seasoned frontiersmen when they heard of it. Simon Girty was there and watched impassively his old friend's death agonies. At one point Crawford begged Girty to shoot him. The renegade responded with a laugh.[39]

In August 1782, Girty led a large Indian force that attacked Bryan's Station to the north of Boonesborough. Daniel Boone and his twenty-one-year-old son, Israel, rode with Colonel John Todd's militia force in pursuit of the Indians. Boone fretted that the trail was too easy to follow and at the Licking River, near the Blue Licks, argued against an attack, fearing a trap. Major Hugh McGary accused Boone of cowardice. Boone was now overruled by Todd, who was among the first of over seventy Kentuckians to fall when Girty sprang his ambush.

Boone ordered a retreat but stood his ground to cover his men. Israel, who refused to leave his father's side, was shot down. Although Boone tried to protect his son's body, his position was quickly overrun by warriors and he was forced to flee. The price of Kentucky, and of his own obsession to open this new land, had finally proven too high. He never again would speak Israel's name without weeping.

"Two darling sons and a brother have I lost by savage hands," he lamented. "Many dark and sleepless nights have I been a companion of owls . . . an instrument ordained to settle the wilderness."[40]

The Battle of the Blue Licks proved to be the last great Indian raid into Kentucky as well as the final battle of the Revolutionary War. The Shawnees, abandoned by the British, soon moved westward beyond the Mississippi River. The Indian confederacy was finally crushed by General Anthony Wayne at the Battle of Fallen Timbers in August 1794.

Wayne's victory was helped immensely by a remarkable detachment of scouts—made up almost exclusively of former Indian captives—led by Captain William Wells. After St. Clair's defeat, young Wells had joined the Americans in exchange for the release of his Miami wife, who had been captured. His scouts—or spies, as they were called—engaged in a series of daring adventures that made their captain something of a frontier legend. Wayne appointed Wells as the chief Indian agent for the Miamis, Delawares, Potawatomis, and smaller bands. His loyalty to the Miamis soon led Wells into conflict with both the young Indiana territorial governor William Henry Harrison, who pressured the Indians to sell more land, and the bold Shawnee warrior Tecumseh, who dreamed of a new Indian confederacy. This would soon lead to a new crisis north of the Ohio.[41]

It was not long before Boone, finding himself a stranger among the new settlers flooding into Kentucky, and beset by lawsuits over land claims and surveying lines, followed the Indians westward. In 1799, at age sixty-four, he traveled toward the setting sun, settling in Spanish territory in the

Femme Osage Valley, some forty miles west of St. Louis. When asked why he had left Kentucky, he replied, "Too many people! Too crowded. . . . I want more elbow room."

The Spanish granted him over 8,000 acres of land and in 1800 appointed him as syndic, or magistrate, at Femme Osage Valley. A popular little book published in 1784 by schoolteacher John Filson had made Boone an international hero, and the Spanish proved anxious to honor him. Not so his own people, however, for when the Louisiana Purchase was made in 1803, Boone's land grant was nullified. Finally, in 1814, a parsimonious Congress granted him 850 acres in recognition of his service to the republic. He sold it all off to repay his Kentucky creditors, declaring in 1817: "I have paid all my debts and no one will say when I am gone 'Boone was a dishonest man.' I am perfectly content to die."[42]

Boone died in his eighty-fifth year at dawn on September 26, 1820, at the Femme Osage Valley home of his son Nathan. They buried him next to Rebecca, who had died in 1813, in a nearby cemetery, but in 1845 they were exhumed and reburied amidst much ceremony in Frankfort, Kentucky. The state he had forged with blood finally recognized him. As his fame grew, the national government also tardily honored him. The politicians who had disdained to vote him the land he had so dearly purchased for the republic now placed him in marble on the east steps of the U.S. Capitol, where Horatio Greenough's epic statue stood until 1958, and also immortalized him in a fantasy scene of combat in the Capitol's Rotunda dome.

Filson's book, and countless others that followed, celebrated Boone's deeds and transformed him into the embodiment of Jefferson's ideals on the frontier. A new nation found their first Western hero in Boone, the Jeffersonian pioneer, and at the same time discovered a new identity for themselves. Boone became the Revolutionary founding father of the American West and all it had yet to offer to an expansive people. He was the true founder of an American West that Thomas Jefferson rightly proclaimed "an empire for liberty."

Fame was but moonglow to Boone. "Many heroic actions and chivalrous adventures are related of me and only exist in regions of fancy," he declared near the end of his life. "With me the world has taken great liberties, and yet I have been but a common man."[43]

8

THE COUNCIL FIRE

Far to the south, in the Upper Creek village of Coosauda, a son was born in 1781 to the Scottish trader Charles Weatherford and his Native wife, Sehoy. They named the boy William, although among the Creeks he was called Lamochatee and later, by the Americans, Red Eagle. In time these names came to reflect his often tortured position caught between frontier societies in conflict.

Sehoy was something akin to Creek aristocracy through her membership in the important Wind Clan. Her grandfather had been a French officer and her Indian father a chief of the Tukabatchee band of the Creek Confederacy. Her mixed-race mother, also called Sehoy, took as her second husband the wealthy Scottish trader Lachlan McGillivray, by whom she had a son and three daughters. The son, Alexander McGillivray, rose to prominence as an influential and powerful Creek leader and would play an important role in the upbringing of his young nephew Lamochatee.

Charles Weatherford, a slippery man of elastic ethics, had built an impressive trading post on the bluffs above the west bank of the Alabama River, some three miles below where the Coosa and Tallapoosa Rivers joined. Not far from his house were five earthen mounds, the remnants of a long-vanished civilization that some thought to be the ancient ancestors of the Creeks.[1]

Sehoy was the absolute ruler of the household. Benjamin Hawkins, the American Indian agent to the Creeks and other southern tribes from 1796 until 1816, visited with the Weatherfords on several occasions. He was impressed by Sehoy, whom he referred to as "Mrs. Weatherford," noting that she "lives well in some taste, but expensively. Her negroes do but little, and consume everything in common with their mistress, who is a stranger to economy." In the matrilineal Creek society, children belonged to their mother's clan and had a much closer relationship with her and her relatives than with their biological father. Hawkins was not opposed to mixed marriages but was shocked that "the women have invariably the habit of governing absolutely in all cases when connected with a white man." Still, such marriages, and there were many, furthered the government's goal of assimilating the Creeks into the larger American society. Hawkins appreciated the attraction Sehoy and other Creek women had for white men, musing that "if the concurrent testimony of the white husbands can be relied upon, the women have much the temper of the mule, except when they are amorous, and then they exhibit all the amiable and generous qualities of the cat."[2]

Women held a rather exalted position in Creek society. "You may depend upon my assertion that there is no people anywhere who love their women more than these Indians do," the noted naturalist William Bartram declared, "or men of better understanding in distinguishing the merits of the opposite sex, or more faithful in rendering suitable compensation. They are courteous and polite to the women. . . . I never saw or heard of an instance of an Indian beating his wife or other female, or reproving them in anger or in harsh language. And the women make a suitable and grateful return; for they are discreet, modest, loving, faithful, and affectionate to their husbands."[3]

Despite their high standing, Creek women still labored long hours. They tended their fields in the morning, almost always with the assistance of children both male and female, while later in the day they would often gather in the town plaza with the other women to sew, cook, construct pots and baskets, rub and scrape skins, and gossip. As the day wore on, the plaza filled with people, and there were often dances as well as games, gambling, and drinking.[4]

There was little prejudice in Creek society against people of mixed heritage. This, of course, was just the opposite of white society. Lamochatee, despite his light complexion and reddish hair, was thus reared as the privileged child of an important family with a level of comfort and security far above that of most white frontier families. He essentially grew up in two worlds—one the small frontier planter class of his father and the other the complex Indian culture of his mother. Charles Weatherford's holdings at the Hickory Ground were substantial, with his racehorses, fenced fields, cattle, and hogs all worked by some thirty slaves. Since each enslaved person had his or her own cabin, it gave the plantation the appearance of a small village. Sehoy was mistress of this estate, although the trading business that financed it was run by her Scottish husband. As a Creek woman of the Wind Clan, Sehoy was anxious to instill in her son the customs and lifeways of her people.[5]

Lamochatee, like all Creek children, was mainly reared by his mother. When young, he helped her in the planting of the corn, sweet potatoes, beans, and pumpkins that were mainstays of the tribal diet. He also spent considerable time in the stoop labor of weeding the planted fields. The clearing of the thick canebrakes—some of them towering above the heads of tall men—was no easy task. It was hard work to keep the resilient cane from sprouting again, though the introduction of European livestock helped to finally eradicate much of the cane. Native women rotated their fields, so that fallow "old" fields, as they were called, were a common sight in Creek Country.

The gathering of the plentiful berries, fruits, and nuts found throughout the forest also fell to Creek women and children. The chestnut, oak, black walnut, and hickory trees—all growing to astonishing heights—provided a rich bounty. The nuts were stored in the hull for year-round use. Hickory nuts were also made into oil by boiling the cracked nuts. This was used in cooking as well as for a broth. In the summer there were also wild strawberries and grapes, as well as blackberries and huckleberries, and in the fall persimmons were plentiful. The collected seeds of the cockspur grass and the chenopodium were ground in stone bowls into a meal and stored for later use. A variant of chenopodium, often called Jesuit's tea or wormseed, was used for deworming the children, since it was mildly toxic.[6]

The center of Creek life was the *tvlofv*, or town, and there were over seventy of them at the time of Lamochatee's birth. The Upper Creeks lived in forty-eight towns with populations of from twenty to over two hundred families along the Tallapoosa, Coosa, and Alabama Rivers in what is now Alabama, while the Lower Creeks resided in twenty-five towns along the Chattahoochee and Flint Rivers in Georgia. There were perhaps as many as 20,000 people living in these communities, with the Upper Creeks greatly outnumbering the Lower Creeks. Because the Natives lived beside the great rivers and numerous creeks, the English colonists came in time to refer to them all as Creek Indians. The Creeks called themselves Muskogees after the common language that eventually gave them a fragile sense of unity, although quite distinct dialects were spoken among the scattered towns.

Coosauda, like the other major Creek towns, was arranged around a square where four low buildings with open fronts faced inward. On one side of the square was a tall, cone-shaped *chakofa*, or communal house, where the ceremonial council fire was kept. A large field for games was adjacent. It was in this square that the most important ceremony of the year was held. The Green Corn Ceremony, or Busk (from *poskita*, "to fast") was an eight-day period in August, with many traditional rituals and much oratory, as well as dancing and celebration. In the Busk both body and soul were purged of impurities, and past transgressions were forgiven. The purging was more than simply symbolic, for the men all took the sacred black drink (a tea made from caffeine-rich yaupon), which acted as both a stimulant and a diuretic and was accompanied by purposeful vomiting.

The old council fire was extinguished and a new fire started. The same was then done in every household. The square was surrounded by communal compounds that consisted of several wooden houses. Gardens were interspersed among the compounds, and the families inhabiting a compound were all of the same clan. Since marriage within the same clan was prohibited and a male child belonged to his mother's clan, he looked to his uncles, not his father, for his training as a hunter and warrior.[7]

Creek boys were naturally anxious to leave the hard work in the fields behind them and get on with learning the ways of the warrior. These boys were often wild and undisciplined, and it was the duty of their uncles to punish any transgressions. Thorns or the sharp tooth of a gar were used to scratch open the skin to let out the evil spirits. This also taught the boy to endure pain and the loss of blood, important attributes for his future life as a warrior. The Creek people were indulgent with their children and so such punishment was not that common. This led many Creek elders to agree with the old warrior who lodged a universal complaint to a visiting Englishman: "Young people are not so orderly and obedient to the old people now as they used to be.... [W]hen we tell them to do anything they seem to stop and think about it. Formerly they always went at once and did as they were told."[8]

Young boys used miniature bows and arrows to kill small game. As they grew older they sought bigger game. The hunting of the white-tailed deer was the center of every town's wealth in Lamochatee's time as well as a major source of food. Boys would often help the hunters with the setting of fires in the forest underbrush. This made better feeding grounds for the deer. A boy's uncles taught him to hunt while at the same time preparing him for his future life as a warrior. Both the killing of game and the taking of scalps were vital steps on the journey to manhood. Creek society venerated the warrior and rewarded the best fighters with esteem and social position. Before killing an enemy, a teenage boy was relegated to menial tasks, including lighting the pipes for warriors and helping to make the black drink. A young man was not permitted to marry until he had brought back a scalp, or, as the Creeks termed it, "bring in hair." The return of the successful neophyte warrior was a cause for public celebration. His trophy was suspended atop the end of a red painted stick. He marched with the scalp into the town square, where amidst war songs it was inspected by the elders as they listened to the tale of his heroics. The boy was then given a war name and a seat in the square for the black drink ceremony.[9]

Much attention was also given to ball play, and this was another way for young men to distinguish themselves. Nearly all Creek towns had a ball field measuring twenty by two hundred feet with two poles six feet apart at each end. Using two ball sticks, the object of the game was to get a small leather ball through the goalposts. These were rough-and-tumble affairs as the players ran or passed the ball forward. Injuries were common. The contests were between towns and there was heavy gambling on the outcome. After the game, the bloodied opposing players celebrated long into the night. The Creeks called ball play "the little brother of war," and in this game Lamochatee excelled.[10]

Lamochatee was quite fortunate in that one of his uncles was the Creek leader Alexander McGillivray. Alexander had been born in 1759 to the Scottish immigrant Lachlan McGillivray and the highborn Creek woman Sehoy Marchand, daughter of the French commander of old Fort Toulouse on the Coosa River, and the belle of the village of Otciapofa. Lachlan prospered greatly in the Indian trade—which by this time was mostly in deerskins—and wielded an influence over the southern tribes that was similar (albeit to a lesser degree) to that enjoyed by Sir William Johnson with the northern tribes. His trading post at Little Tallassie (Hickory Ground) took on the trappings of a Southern plantation with an apple grove and extensive fields worked by dozens of enslaved African Americans. He also had extensive landholdings in Georgia. Alexander, like his nephew Lamochatee, was partially raised as a Creek and mastered the language and culture of his mother's people, although a slender build and frail constitution prevented him from excelling at the hunt or ball play. Despite his delicate health, he presented an imposing figure at over six feet, with a high forehead and dark, piercing eyes. His delicate hands—long and tapering—were reflective of his mastery of a graceful writing style.

At fourteen, Alexander was sent by his father to Charleston to be educated in Greek, Latin, and English history and literature. When the Revolution broke out, he hurriedly returned to Little Tallassie, while his father, an ardent Loyalist, was forced to flee back to Scotland. The Patriot forces eventually confiscated much of his property. Alexander, named Hoboi-Hili-Miko, or the Good Child King, by the Creeks, was accorded status as a *miko*, or chief, when he returned to the Coosa River country. He was also commissioned as a colonel by the British, who designated him as their agent to secure the loyalty of the Creeks. He battled both the Americans and the Spanish, participating in the battle for Pensacola. He was never considered a great war leader by the Creeks. His French brother-in-law, Louis Milfort, noted that "when one has so much administrative capacity and so many qualities of heart as Alexander McGillivray, he does not need the military virtues to be a great man."[11]

After the war he quickly proved himself to be a master of diplomacy with both the Americans and the Spanish as well as with the neighboring Indian nations. He adroitly manipulated his connections with the Europeans and Americans to establish himself as the sole distributor of their gifts and trade goods to the Creek people. This helped cement his position as "Great Beloved Man" with many of the Creeks. Through astute diplomacy as well as occasional brute force, he came to control the trade with the Spanish and English. So persuasive was he with the Spanish that he amazingly got them to allow his English friend William Panton, of Panton, Leslie and Company, to have a monopoly over their trade with the Creeks. This added to his personal wealth as well as his political power. The British, of course, had far superior trade goods, in terms of both quality and quantity, compared to the Spanish.

Despite the fact that McGillivray sometimes frustrated their designs, the Europeans as well as the Americans liked having an intelligent, forceful single leader to deal with rather than numerous chieftains. He moved seamlessly between the world of the colonizers and that of the Creeks, aided by his strong personality, graceful manners, and personal charisma. McGillivray had "the good sense of an American, the shrewdness of a Scotchman, and the cunning of an Indian," an aide explained to President Washington. He charmed Abigail Adams, wife of the vice president, when he visited New York in 1790. "He dresses in our own fashion, speaks English like a Native," she noted, "& I should never suspect him to be of that Nation, as he is not very dark."[12]

McGillivray's loyalty to the British Crown during the war began to wane after the Treaty of Paris. He felt that the British had betrayed the Creeks, and in fact all the Indian Nations east of the Mississippi, by blithely ceding their lands to the Americans in the peace treaty. The Creeks had not only lost the major source of their economic well-being in the loss of their British trading partners; they had also lost the protection that the Crown had provided against the expansive American frontiersmen. The Treaty of Paris, which ended the war, made no provision for any of the Crown's Indian allies. McGillivray bitterly protested that the British had "no right to transfer us with their former possessions to any power whatever contrary to our inclination and Interest."[13]

Britain had ceded Florida to Spain, and McGillivray now looked to the south for a new trading partner. The new masters of Florida hoped to use the Creeks as a buffer against the Americans, and McGillivray was quick to oblige them if they would agree to the trade concession for his friend Panton. By the Treaty of Pensacola on June 1, 1784, the Spanish agreed to McGillivray's requested trade concession and also pledged to defend Creek lands west of the Flint River and south of the Tennessee River—land that Spain also claimed.

He was quick to establish a decent, if not exactly cordial, working relationship with the new American government. He was anxious to have the federal government rein in the aggressive Georgians who constantly threatened the lands of the Lower Creeks. Despite his public posture, McGillivray viewed the denizens of the new republic with studied contempt. "The whole Continent is in confusion," he wrote Arturo O'Neill, governor of Spanish West Florida, in response to backcountry resistance to taxation. "Before long I expect to hear that the three Kings must Settle the matter by dividing America between them." In 1785 he remarked to O'Neill on the fighting that had broken out between the new nation and the Barbary pirates: "The Americans and the Algerines are both alike and one is not better than the other. I think they are well matched."[14]

He had a special hatred for the Georgians. This was personal, of course, since the state had confiscated his father's property during the war. It was made doubly so when he learned that the Georgia agent to the Creeks had attempted to hire assassins to kill him. McGillivray was determined to expel these "crackers" (so called because of the way they cracked their long whips) and "gougers" (in reference to their practice of growing their fingernails long so as to gouge out an opponent's eye in their constant brawling) from Creek land.

An illegal treaty between Georgia and a handful of pro-American Creek leaders at Augusta in 1783 gave over eight hundred square miles of land along the Oconee River to the Georgians. In 1786 the Georgians secured even more land concessions through bribery and intimidation, and as settlers rushed in to occupy these new lands, clashes with the Creeks became inevitable. A series of unprovoked murders of Creeks by Georgians soon made the situation untenable.

The federal government, anxious to avoid an Indian war, sent Benjamin Hawkins, Andrew Pickens, and two other prominent commissioners to broker a peace between the Creek Nation and Georgia and establish a just boundary line. McGillivray held them at arm's length. In a letter to Pickens he defended his alliance with Spain and made clear the position of his nation. "We know our limits, and the extent of our hunting-grounds," he lectured the commissioners. "As a free nation, we have applied, as we had a right to do, for protection, and obtained it. We shall pay no attention to any limits that may prejudice our claims that were drawn by an American, and confirmed by a British negotiator." He then succinctly stated the position of the Creek Nation: "We want nothing from you but justice. We want our hunting grounds preserved from encroachments. They have been ours from the beginning of time, and I trust that, with the assistance of our friends, we shall be able to maintain them against every attempt that may be made to take them from us."[15]

McGillivray declined to meet with Pickens and Hawkins and they sullenly returned home. Georgia, furious with this interference by the federal government in what they saw as a local issue, responded by negotiating yet another bogus treaty with two pro-American *miko*s that gave to the state even more valuable Creek land.

In July 1787, McGillivray wrote Arturo O'Neill at Pensacola requesting arms and ammunition to enable him to send six hundred warriors east against the Georgians as well as north to attack James Robertson's Cumberland River settlements. "All the different Towns are now getting Ready to Celebrate their yearly New Fires," he informed O'Neill; "directly after that we mean to give the Georgians a hearty Chastisement." He assured O'Neill that his warriors would also "ravage the Settlement of Cumberland & destroy their houses & plantations." And indeed they did just that.[16]

The Creek assault on Robertson's Cumberland settlements—which now numbered nearly 4,000 people in some forty scattered stations—proved devastating. They were aided in these wide-ranging strikes by Dragging Canoe's Chickamauga warriors. The settlers held on, but just barely. All cultivation was halted and many farms abandoned. Casualties were so high that Robertson wrote McGillivray hoping to arrange a peace conference. By August 1786, McGillivray could truthfully and rather exultantly write O'Neill that "the Cumberland people are begging hard for peace." In order to consolidate his forces against the far more numerous and dangerous Georgians, McGillivray concluded a truce with Robertson.

The Georgia settlers in the newly opened Oconee lands now paid the price for the perfidy of their state authorities. Within a brief period Creek warriors drove the Georgia frontier line back: over seventy were killed, another thirty wounded, while over one hundred settlers and their slaves were taken captive. Eighty-nine settler cabins were burned and there were extensive livestock losses. The Georgia authorities attempted to bribe McGillivray with an offer to return his father's confiscated estates in exchange for peace, but he turned them down. They then attempted to assassinate him but also without success. Georgia then appealed to the federal government for troops but was flatly turned down. The government, then in transition under the new constitution, had no funds with which to wage war against the Creeks—the largest and best-organized Indian nation east of the Mississippi River, with well over 4,000 warriors—even if it had been willing to. And it was not. In one area the Georgians had some success. Their loud complaints to the Spanish over the provisioning of the Creeks with guns and powder led Governor O'Neill, nervous about further angering the aggressive Americans, to curtail the supply of armaments.[17]

Now, with victory in his grasp, McGillivray found himself in a desperate situation. A reliable supply of armaments was critical to his goal of Creek unity as well as military success against his enemies. This led McGillivray to lead a delegation of Upper Creek *miko*s to a council with the Lower Creeks at the village of Coweta. Just at that moment, succor appeared from a rather surprising source in the form of a remarkable young man.

William Augustus Bowles was a flamboyant twenty-five-year-old adventurer of profound ambition. In his short lifetime he performed remarkable feats of acting on both the stage of the theater and the living stage of the American frontier. Strikingly handsome, quick-witted, boldly daring—with charm to spare—he was also seemingly devoid of any scruples whatsoever. He was, at times, a soldier, actor, artist, diplomat, pirate, and self-styled "Director General of the Creek Nation."

Born in Maryland in 1764 to a prominent family, he had enlisted in a Tory regiment at age fourteen. He was quickly promoted to ensign and ordered to Pensacola, Florida, where a dispute with another officer led him to desert. He headed northeast into Creek Country, where he went native, embraced the culture, mastered the Creek language, and married the daughter of a prominent village leader. This union produced a son. He later married a Chickamauga woman who also bore him a son.

In 1780, Bowles had gone with hundreds of Lower Creek warriors to the aid of Pensacola, then besieged by Spanish forces. Over a thousand Indians, including Choctaws and Chickasaws, as well as Upper Creeks under young McGillivray, rallied to Britain's banner. In the fighting that followed around both Mobile and Pensacola, Bowles distinguished himself with feats of reckless daring. This won him reinstatement as ensign in his former Maryland Loyalist regiment just in time to become a prisoner of war when the British commander surrendered to the Spanish on May 10, 1781.

Bowles and his fellow prisoners were taken to Havana, where they were quickly paroled in a prisoner exchange and transported to New York City.

With the 1783 Treaty of Paris, many Loyalist soldiers migrated to Canada. Most of the remaining Marylanders went north to New Brunswick, but Bowles headed south to Nassau with a theatrical company he had joined in New York City. This placed him much closer to his Creek family and friends. He also made a powerful new friend in Nassau: former Virginia governor John Murray, fourth Earl of Dunmore, now appointed governor of the Bahamas. Lord Dunmore, as a silent partner with the powerful merchant prince John Miller, hoped to break the monopoly over the Creek trade held by Panton, Leslie & Company. McGillivray was, of course, a not-very-silent partner with his friend William Panton. London had made Nassau a free port and as colonial governor Dunmore had every expectation of lining his pockets with a cut of the lucrative Indian trade. Bowles was to be his agent in this enterprise.[18]

Bowles and a handful of associates were carried by a British warship to Florida and then made their way to the Lower Creek villages. Reunited with his Creek family on the Chattahoochee, Bowles recruited several Creek and Seminole warriors to accompany his party to Coweta. McGillivray was relieved to receive the munitions Bowles brought and flattered by the twenty-five-pound-sterling silver sword he was gifted. He had known Bowles during the Pensacola campaign and, while happy to see him again, remained wary. This all seemed a bit too good to be true. Still, McGillivray and the assembled *miko*s were delighted with the weapons Bowles had brought and eagerly agreed to open up trade with him for more. While Bowles returned to Nassau for more goods, McGillivray adroitly wrote his Spanish friends that a new source of presents and trade had opened for his people and that they would no longer need Spanish weapons. Charles Weatherford, who had come to feel slighted by McGillivray, now provided the Spanish with an unflattering account of the Bowles-McGillivray relationship. The nervous Spanish promptly backtracked and agreed to resupply the Creeks with munitions, but Weatherford's report compromised their trust in McGillivray.

Bowles returned to Florida with more arms and powder in January 1789, accompanied by thirty armed men recruited from the dregs of the Nassau docks. He quickly discovered that Spanish spies had uncovered his scheme, that he was in danger of arrest, and that McGillivray had soured on him. McGillivray came south to again meet with Bowles but this time to warn him to "seek adventures in other climes." McGillivray did not wish to harm an old comrade-in-arms, but he nevertheless left Louis Milfort behind to keep an eye on the American, who now wore the uniform of a British colonel and sported the turban of a Creek *miko*.

"Bowles has too many irons in the fire and has conducted himself of late very foolishly," McGillivray assured his friend Panton.[19]

Bowles did indeed depart but not before meeting at Coweta in a grand council with the Lower Creeks and the Seminoles. Dragging Canoe and Hanging Maw led a Chickamauga delegation to the council. Bowles promised them all British arms and ammunition with which to fight both the Americans and the Spanish. He now set himself up as a rival to McGillivray, declaring himself "Director General of the Creek Nation," or Eastajoca ("Writings Person") in the Muscogee language, and proposed to take a delegation to London to meet with King George III. Eight Creek and Cherokee leaders accompanied him on one of Miller's ships to Nassau and from there to Quebec, where he met with General Guy Carleton, now Baron Dorchester, who agreed to secure passage for Bowles and the Indians in a British merchantman bound for Plymouth. By October 1790, Bowles was in London, meeting with Home Secretary William Grenville, and soon after the Prince of Wales. The Indian delegation caused a sensation in London high society, and no one more so than the dashing Bowles, decked out in full Creek regalia. Within a few months a biography appeared: *The Authentic Memoirs of William Augustus Bowles, Esquire, Ambassador from the United Nations of Creeks and Cherokees, to the Court of London*.[20]

While Bowles hobnobbed with London high-society swells, his rival McGillivray embarked on a diplomatic mission of his own. In the summer of 1790, McGillivray led a delegation of twenty-six Creek leaders to New York to meet with President Washington and Secretary of War Henry Knox. (Indian affairs in the new government were under the War Department.) An alarmed Spanish agent in the city reported that McGillivray and his people "were received hardly less highly than royal persons."

McGillivray hoped to secure federal recognition of Creek national independence, protection of Native territory from the encroachment of the Georgians, and a trade agreement under his management. He achieved these goals and more, although he had to recognize the sovereignty of the U.S. government over the Creek Nation and concede lands obtained by Georgia through spurious treaties with minor *miko*s. Because of white settlement, the ceded land had already lost any value as hunting land for the Creeks. The Treaty of New York guaranteed the Creek Nation to be under the protection of the federal government, forbade the sale of Creek land to any individual state, and gave the Indians the right to expel white squatters or hunters from their lands. Two secret articles in the treaty commissioned McGillivray as a brigadier general in the U.S. Army with pay of $1,200 a year and gave to him authority to import trade goods duty-free through any American port and control their distribution.[21]

McGillivray was accompanied to New York by his ten-year-old nephew. This may well have been Lamochatee. They stayed at the home of Secretary of War Knox, and that portly gentleman took a liking to the boy. Since Lamochatee already spoke English fluently, as well as a smattering of French and Spanish, the minister requested that the boy stay on for a while to receive some additional schooling. McGillivray agreed to this, thinking it best for his nephew, although the boy's feelings on that matter were hardly considered. Whatever the case, unlike his uncle, Lamochatee never mastered written English.[22]

The Treaty of New York was a triumph for both McGillivray and Washington but infuriated the Georgians, the Spanish, and several of the Lower Creek *miko*s. Georgia congressman James Jackson was apoplectic, thundering on the floor of Congress that Washington and Knox had ceded "three million acres of land guaranteed to Georgia by the Constitution" and betrayed his state. The new federal government had "given away her land, invited a savage of the Creek nation to the seat of Government, caressed him in a most extraordinary manner, and sent him home loaded with favors." James Seagrove, the federal Indian agent in Georgia, warned President Washington that the frontier people "now consider the troops and servants of the United States nearly as great enemies as they do the Indians." He added that the country "is unfortunate in having the worst of people on her frontiers."[23]

The long-contested Oconee River boundary line between Georgia and Creek territory remained a festering wound. "We see that we have been imposed on, perhaps by our beloved man," noted several prominent chiefs, "that land which McGillivray defrauded us out of, we know not if he had money for it; we never received a farthing for it."

Many agreed with the Hallowing King of the Cowetas, a Lower Creek tribe, that the people could ill afford to cede any more land to the Georgians: "These last strides tell us they never mean to let their foot rest; our lands are our life and breath; if we part with them, we part with our blood. We must fight for them." The Frenchman Milfort began to worry that the discontent might lead the Lower Creeks to assassinate his brother-in-law. The new Georgia boundary line, along with demands for the repatriation of white and Black captives as well as the return of fugitive African Americans added to McGillivray's difficulty in bringing the Lower Creeks around to accept the treaty. He now warned Knox: "You will recollect, sir, that I had great objection to making the south fork of the Oconee the limit, and when you insisted so much, I candidly told you that it might be made an article, but I could not pledge myself to get it confirmed, or that of the restoration of the negro property which has so often changed hands."[24]

The Spanish were determined to use the Creeks as a buffer against the encroaching frontiersmen, and McGillivray's sudden rapprochement with the Americans fretted them. Carlos Howard, a Spanish agent sent from Florida to New York to spy on the treaty negotiations, chastised McGillivray over leaving his young nephew with Knox, for he feared that "to give one's nephew in that manner to the Americans was to manifest a decided predilection for that nation." Howard also worried about Caleb Swan, a prominent army officer sent home with McGillivray by Knox to serve as Indian superintendent to the Creeks. Aware of Spanish suspicions, McGillivray wrote the captain general in New Orleans a reasonably full accounting of the treaty (with some important omissions of secret articles) in order to "not incur the most distant suspicion of duplicity." The Creek leader truthfully assured the Spanish authorities that his utmost goal was "in defending ourselves & defeating the inordinate ambitions of the American emigrants Westwardly, encroaching on the Territory of the King as well as on ours."

In the midst of this swirling controversy, Bowles suddenly reappeared to stir the pot and further exacerbate McGillivray's troubles. Beset, McGillivray wrote his friend Panton, "that fellow Bowles . . . is making a great noise in the Chetaws, & has perfectly Confused & distracted the foolish & inconsiderate part of the Indians thereabout."[25]

Bowles was indeed making a great noise, for he had grand plans for the Creek Nation. He was determined to replace the ailing McGillivray as leader, unite the Upper and Lower Creeks along with the Seminoles and Chickamaugas, block the running of the new Georgia boundary line, and—if need be—lead his followers against both the Americans and the Spanish. He hoped to accomplish all this by uniting the southern tribes in a great confederacy with the tribes north of the Ohio. The northern tribes, with British aid, were already enjoying success against American armies. In this bold enterprise, the Creeks were to be supplied by Dunmore and Miller, although Bowles now claimed to have the complete backing of Whitehall as well.

Bowles's rhetoric fired the fighting spirit of the young men of the Lower Creek towns and Seminole villages. McGillivray responded by sending three trusted warriors to kill Bowles, and when that failed, he placed a $100 bounty on his rival's head. He assured his Spanish backers that Bowles "must be taken or killed or run away before long." Word of the crisis soon reached New York, where Secretary of War Knox, highly perturbed, fretted to one of his generals that "it seems probable, that either McGillivray or Bowles must fall."[26]

McGillivray correctly discerned that Bowles had overplayed his hand. The promised supplies from the Bahamas were tardy in arriving and then failed to materialize in the quantities promised, so Bowles, his influence dissipating, decided on a reckless move. With a hundred Indians and a handful of white brigands, he descended on Panton's warehouse near the small Spanish fort of St. Marks on Apalachee Bay. Bowles easily seized the undefended warehouse on January 16, 1792. While the impotent Spanish garrison watched, the rich stores were loaded on packhorses for distribution among Bowles's adherents to the east.

Francisco Luis Hector, baron de Carondelet, who had recently replaced Esteban Miró in New Orleans as Louisiana governor, promptly sent reinforcements to St. Marks. The cunning baron also sent a message to Bowles that he was willing to open negotiations with him to recognize his authority over the Creeks and form an alliance against the Americans.

Bowles took the bait. With a promise of safe conduct from Carondelet, he boarded a Spanish ship for New Orleans. At first Carondelet treated Bowles as a guest but, souring on the negotiations, he soon had him arrested and shipped to Havana. After a brief imprisonment in Morro Castle, Bowles found himself on a ship bound for Spain. His traveling companions included former governor Miró and his lovely wife, Celeste. Bowles charmed them both. When the ship reached Spain, they intervened on Bowles's behalf but could not save him from a cell in the royal prison at Cádiz.[27]

With Bowles finally out of the picture, McGillivray sent Milfort south with a large contingent of warriors to liberate Panton's warehouse and overawe the discontented among the Lower Creeks and Seminoles. He also cleverly used the Bowles affair as an excuse to block the Americans from running the new Georgia boundary line. Although his health was rapidly deteriorating, he nevertheless made the arduous journey to New Orleans to negotiate a new treaty with Carondelet in July 1792 that guaranteed a steady supply of Spanish arms and ammunition to the Creek Nation.

McGillivray's triumph was short-lived. His health, fragile for so long, now collapsed altogether. He hurried to his friend Panton's home in Pensacola in the vain hope of securing better medical care and died there on February 17, 1793. He was but thirty-four years old.[28]

McGillivray's main objective among the Creek people had been to shape their loose political alliance—bound only slightly by language, customs, and geography—into a strong, centralized confederacy in order to blunt the advance of the land-hungry Americans. His efforts to strengthen the Creek National Council, despite the daunting challenges posed by entrenched local leaders and bitter clan rivalries, had met with considerable success. His powerful oratory held sway at National Council meetings at the Hickory Ground, Tuckabatchee, and Coweta. While his influence over the Upper Creeks was nearly absolute, it also extended to many of the Lower Creeks and even, to a lesser extent, the Florida Seminoles. This movement toward Creek unification in the face of American expansion was dealt a fatal blow by McGillivray's untimely death. Some hoped that McGillivray's son might pick up the mantle of leadership, but he was still a child and was sent to Scotland by Panton to be educated. It would be up to young Lamochatee—now called William Weatherford—to take up his uncle's dream.

9

THE HEARTH

The forest defined his world. Beyond the cabin loft he shared with his brothers, beyond the warmth of the hearth his mother tended, beyond the great stone at the doorway, beyond the tiny clearing that opened their homestead to the light, the mighty trees loomed, dark and ominous. They crowded the little valley in which he had been born and carpeted the mountains to the south in a luxurious green that turned as colorful as Joseph's coat with the first hint of frost.

Adults viewed this forest as the enemy, and the child could not help but sense their anxiety. In that forest, beyond the safety of the hearth, lived the beasts that preyed upon the family's livestock—fox, wildcat, panther, wolf, and bear. Worse yet, the trees provided the means of surprise as well as escape for Indian raiders like those who had killed his grandparents. It concealed them, sustained them, and nurtured them. Its destruction would mean their end as well. All pioneer families feverishly labored to fell the trees, to clear the land, to open the vista, to destroy that which they could not, or would not, understand.

Ancient stands of timber, some struggling toward the sun since before Columbus set sail, were felled in a twinkling. It was a marvel of destructive power that men of so few numbers and so crudely armed could so rapidly wreak such havoc. A French traveler in the western country commented that these pioneers seemed "to have declared war on the whole species of [trees]." Only when the land was cleared might they express satisfaction. "When his patch of ground is completely naked," noted a British visitor, "he tells you that it looks *handsome*."[1]

They might well appreciate the forest bounty provided by the logs for their cabin, barn, and outbuildings, the split rails for the meandering worm fences, the kindling and fuel for the hearth that gave warmth and cooked their food, the wild fruits and nuts that helped vary their diet, and the birds, varmints, and deer so essential to their larder. Still, they anticipated the day when they would clear away the trees altogether to make room for their fields and to open up grazing for their flocks. Nature's bounty was but transitory, to be replaced by their livestock, vegetables, corn, and wheat.

Already, by the time the young child became aware of this world, the land had changed. The buffalo and elk that had made trails through the woods in his grandparents' time were gone, soon to be followed by the predatory wolf, bear, and panther. The deer were becoming scarcer in the river valleys, for the hunters and the roaming dogs took a fearful toll. The forest still echoed with the sounds of the insects, birds, and squirrels but now also with the low grunts of the pioneers' half-wild hogs, the chiming of cow and horse bells, and the singing of axes.

After Kings Mountain, John Crockett had moved to Brown's Purchase in Washington County, North Carolina. With the war over, a new county, named after General Nathanael Greene, was created from a portion of Washington County. It grew rapidly, so that by 1795 the county boasted a population of 7,172 free whites and 466 enslaved Blacks. Prosperity seemed likely for Crockett as he made a name for himself in the new county. He served as constable three times, in 1783, in 1785, and again in 1789. His brother Robert also served as constable in the new county. As a leading citizen of Greene County, John Crockett was often called on for jury service and eventually served as a road commissioner and as a magistrate. A young backwoods lawyer by the name of Andrew Jackson received his first law license from the court where John acted as magistrate.[2]

Crockett followed his former commander John Sevier in supporting the movement to secede from North Carolina and establish the state of Franklin. That eventually futile effort was supported by several important land speculators, and John Crockett played that risky game as well. In 1783 he invested in a two-hundred-acre homestead, which he sold in 1787 for a tidy profit. He also purchased, or was granted, a three-hundred-acre tract on Mossy Creek in Jefferson County, but this land was sold at a sheriff's auction in 1795, as debt had finally overwhelmed its owner.[3]

Even as John Crockett's fortunes waned, his family grew. By 1786 he had leased land from Colonel George Gillispie at the confluence of Big Limestone Creek and the Nolichucky River in Greene County. Up on a bank of high ground above the river line he built a crude cabin and fur house for Rebecca and their five children. It was in this log cabin that their fifth son was born on August 17, 1786. In honor of John's father, they named him David.[4]

John Crockett, with the aid of his brothers and neighbors, had felled what trees he could and girdled others so that they would soon die, opening up the ground below to the sun. If need be he could plant in this eerie landscape of dead and dying trees until he had time to burn them and pull up the stumps.

Most of his rented acreage was devoted to corn. In the spring he broke the ground and planted, needing but a hoe to make a hole into which seeds were dropped and quickly covered with his heel. The boys helped in this work. He and other pioneer farmers first planted Indian-style, turning their cornfields into a garden. Pole beans were planted around cornstalks, climbing up them, while gourds and pumpkins littered the ground throughout the field. Only later would fields be devoted to single crops.

Corn provided an early bounty. Rebecca Crockett watched the green ears closely, pinching them often to discover if they were yet plump and milk-filled enough to serve as "rosen yers" (immature field corn for roasting). When they were ripe she might boil, roast, or fry them, seasoning them with milk and butter for the family table. They served both as vegetable and as a substitute for bread.[5]

By the middle of August, and sometimes earlier, it was time to harvest ears for gritted bread. Rebecca and the girls did the hard work—rough on knuckles and fingers—of rubbing the corn against the gritter (often a piece of tin punched through to create small, sharp jags that stuck out on one side). More often than not, the meal was tinged red from their cut hands before it was baked with buttermilk and eggs, creating a nutty and somewhat sweet-tasting bread. A corn pounder, or hominy block (a wooden mortar and pestle), might also be used to create a finer meal for bread, with coarser meal used for hominy. Such labor was Rebecca's lot until a horse mill was built in the neighborhood. Eventually, of course, a water mill marked the countryside as becoming settled and exceedingly civilized. But during Davy's years on Limestone Creek it was still a wilderness. After the

French botanist François André Michaux spent the night at John Collier's home on the creek in March 1796, he traveled for twenty-three miles the next day without seeing a house.[6]

In his first years, the cabin hearth was the center of Davy's world, as it was much of the time for his mother. The warmth of the fire in the big stone fireplace, never allowed to go out, and the aroma of his mother's cooking were among the first and finest experiences for Davy. He was lord of the cabin and the pride of his mother, and her world was his world. The warmth of the hearth, the sweet smells and new tastes, were all an extension of his mother's protective embrace.[7]

Eyes wide, he watched in wonder as she made simple bread from meal, salt, and water—hoecake, he later learned to call it. She baked it on a slanted board sloped toward the fire, and it was a marvel to watch her turn it without dropping a bit into the ashes. She also made corn bread, a pioneer staple, in a Dutch oven covered over with hot coals. Made from stone-ground undried corn mixed with eggs and fresh buttermilk, with a pinch of lye obtained from corncob ashes, it was served at every meal. In the fall, pumpkin and persimmon bread added to her table's variety.

Another staple of Rebecca's and every southern pioneer's table was hominy. There was pride to be derived from the difficult and delicate chore of creating fine hominy from good white corn. Of course, pioneer corn was rarely white, and much searching went into the task of selecting proper ears without red or blue kernels. Once Rebecca selected the ears, she placed them in an iron kettle, mixing in just enough fireplace ashes to yellow the corn hulls. These clean ashes came from the hearth, and Rebecca constantly had to guard against the menfolk spitting into her fireplace. She cooked it for just the proper length of time, then rinsed it thoroughly with spring water, leaving only plump white grains. After cooking and rinsing it again, she had tender raw hominy for the table. Davy might sometimes accompany Rebecca and the younger children into the woods to pick a mess of salat greens (any green leafy cooked vegetable). Pioneer women in search of wild greens had to beware of poison plants and so sometimes followed the cows to pick whatever they ate. Tips of wild grape shoots, blue root, and wild lettuce were all prized, but it was the balance of salat greens that countered the natural bitterness—and this fine distinction came from the common sense of the pioneer mother.

From the garden patch came beans and peas, turnips and cabbage, and potatoes—especially sweet potatoes. The latter Rebecca could roast in the ashes of the hearth, fry, or mix with milk, eggs, and spices as pie filling. Fresh milk was abundant, and the chore of milking rarely fell to Davy, for it was universally considered girls' work.

Davy, like most frontier boys, learned early on to expect meat three times a day. That meat was almost always pork. Hog-killing time came with the first sharp cold snap, and then the Crockett table overflowed with fresh pork, cracklin' bread, and spicy sausage. Much of the hog was salted down and smoked for later use.[8]

CHILDREN OF COURSE FIND JOY IN THE HUMBLEST OF surroundings, and while the Crocketts were not wealthy in material goods or high position, they nevertheless enjoyed a decent life. Hunger did not dog them, for the land was rich and gave easily of its bounty. The large family, both nuclear and extended, provided support, protection, and nurturing love. There was no note of unhappiness in Davy's earliest years.

Of course, this hardly means that pioneer life was idyllic. The frontier could be hard, brutal, and dangerous even by the harsh standards of the time. Travelers to the western country were horrified by pioneer living conditions. "They take so much Care in raising a Litter of Piggs," noted South Carolina governor James Glen in a 1753 remark often repeated by visitors to the frontier, "their Children are equally naked and full as Nasty." Fifty years later, François André Michaux, visiting eastern Tennessee, noted but slight improvement in living conditions: "Their ragged clothes, and the miserable appearance of their children, who were bare footed and in their shirts, was a plain indication of their poverty." Michaux's extensive travels in the western country, however, had taught him that the riches of the inhabitants were not in specie, for "not one in ten of them are in possession of a single dollar; still each enjoys himself at home with the produce of his estate."[9]

"A miserable cow and a few pigs . . . distinguish the more prosperous dwellings," according to English novelist Frances Milton Trollope, "and on the whole I should say that I never witnessed human nature reduced so low."[10]

Exposure, disease, an unbalanced diet heavy in corn and meat, and a total lack of concern for the most rudimentary hygiene left pioneer folk with jaundiced and pasty complexions. Illness was viewed as a natural part of life, as inescapable as the changing seasons. Measles, mumps, chicken pox, and other childhood diseases were considered a part of growing up. If they struck a frontier settlement during a temperate season, healthy children might be deliberately exposed to get the disease over with while taking advantage of the strength derived from the seasonable weather. Loss of teeth and rheumatism were likewise considered a natural part of advancing years. Malarial fevers were so commonplace that coming down with the "ager" or "ague" or "shakes" was not thought of as being sick at all. The ague, however, could be deadly: cold chills alternating with raging fevers, with spells lasting days or weeks. Davy's life was dogged by this pestilence.[11]

The family toilet was the nearby stream or, in particularly cold weather, just a few feet beyond the cabin door. No hole was dug, although a pole strung between two forked stakes was provided to sit on, and privacy in such matters was not a consideration. Good hounds were invaluable in keeping the yard clean of the excrement. "That's the biggest thing the dogs had to eat," noted one old-timer in the east Tennessee hills. "They didn't have enough food for the children, let alone the dogs."[12]

Such pitiful sanitation made typhoid epidemics common on the frontier. The pioneers called it bilious fever, brain fever, or autumnal fever and supposed its cause to be rotting vegetation or the chill night air, never dreaming that their own living conditions brought on the scourge.[13]

Considering the level of sanitation, it was a great boon to the settlers of Davy's youth that the housefly had yet to cross the mountain barrier. Yet the pioneers still dealt with a profusion of insect pests that made life miserable. Horseflies and mosquitos bled humans and their stock alike, while fleas and lice found snug homes among these intruders into their country. Rebecca waged a constant war against lice, with a rough scrubbing with boiled sarsaparilla root proving a powerful weapon against both lice and nits (louse eggs). A temporary victory over the lice did not ensure comfort, for the drafty cabin was a welcome home to "chinches," or bedbugs. No sooner were candles extinguished at night than the bedbug legions marched forth to feast. While these critters gnawed on the outside, many a pioneer child also played host to roundworms and pinworms on the inside. "Oh, they'd killed lots of children," lamented an old Tennessean. "I've been to children's buryings where they wasn't nothing in the world wrong with them but worms. Oh, God that was trouble! Poor little ole boney children."[14]

Doctors were unknown in the backcountry of Davy's childhood, although, considering the medical practices of the day, that was in many cases just as well. Every settlement had some man or woman versed in the folk arts of healing; "yarb and root doctors" they were called. Many of their cures were learned from the Indians, making good use of local herbs and roots as emetics, purgatives, and poultices.[15]

Every frontier mother—she was in charge of home doctoring—kept a bottle of bitters on hand as a cure for just about every type of ailment as well as a general tonic for all to purify the blood with in the spring. Various combinations were used in the concoctions, although whiskey or brandy was a standard and major ingredient. The stronger the brew, the more it was esteemed.

Whiskey was regarded not only as a healthful beverage and essential dietary supplement but also as a cure-all. Anne Royall, the professional traveler and insightful chronicler of Crockett's generation, put it succinctly: "When I was in Virginia, it was too much whiskey—in Ohio, too much whiskey—in Tennessee, it was too, too much whiskey!"[16]

Whiskey, as commodity, beverage, and medicine, was universally celebrated in the West. It was highly regarded as an antidote to snakebite and, in a land teeming with copperheads and rattlesnakes, was quite often needed. Many a child shrewdly developed regular stomach complaints in order to get an extra toddy. With whiskey so regularly administered as a healthful tonic, it is small wonder that Davy and others of his generation developed a taste for it early and remained addicted throughout life.

Indian medicines, folk cures, and charms in a most wonderful and weird profusion were current on the frontier. Some worked, some did no harm and little good, while others might wreak serious damage on weakened constitutions. They were part and parcel of frontier life, reflective of a self-reliant people proud of their folk wisdom, quick to embrace the sensible customs of their Indian neighbors, and suspicious of professional men such as doctors. In time, as their society became more complex, that would change, but the forest world of Davy's childhood was a place steeped in empirical folk wisdom and deep-seated superstitions.

Like most children, Davy's first conscious memory was of a dramatic, near-tragic event. It was an incident reflective of the casual and commonplace dangers that awaited children who ventured beyond the security of their mother's hearth, past the great stone at the cabin door, and into the forest.

He was playing beside the creek with his four older brothers and a much older neighbor boy by the name of Campbell. The older boys, much to Davy's chagrin, left him on the stream bank and paddled off in John Crockett's canoe. Caught in the swift current, they were rapidly carried out of control toward dangerous rapids. A neighbor plunged into the swift current and, after much exertion, gained the canoe and pulled the terrified boys to shore. Comforted by the ashen countenance of his shaken brothers, Davy took it all as suitable punishment for their having dared leave him behind.[17]

Soon afterward another incident again demonstrated the dangers of the forest, deeply impressing Davy. One fall, Rebecca's brother, Joseph Hawkins, visited and went off into the forest to hunt for deer. Some movement in a grape thicket led Hawkins to fire, shooting through the body of a neighbor picking grapes. The wounded man, Absalom Stonecipher, was carried to the Crockett home, where John Crockett patched him up as best he could. Davy watched, awestruck, as his father passed a silk handkerchief through the wound and entirely through Stonecipher's body. To everyone's amazement, he eventually recovered.[18]

It was about this time that John Crockett's brother James, captured by the Indians at the time of the killing of his parents, was redeemed from the Cherokees after seventeen years of captivity. The purchase of "Dumb Jimmie," as the vernacular of the time referred to him, since he could neither speak nor hear, was arranged by Indian traders among the Cherokees.[19]

When Davy was eight, the family moved to the mouth of Cove Creek, where John Crockett entered into a partnership with Thomas Gilbreath to build a mill on the creek near the road to Greenville. Gilbreath was a prominent Greene County settler and, like John Crockett, a Revolutionary War veteran. This partnership boded well for John Crockett's fortunes, but nature intervened, delivering a crippling blow from which he never recovered. In the late spring of 1794, a great flood washed away the nearly completed mill, inundating the Crockett home as well. John Crockett was ruined. Thrown on the mercy of others, the family lived for a time in a cabin provided by the kindly Gilbreath while John Crockett labored to retrieve his shattered fortunes. It was hopeless, and the family plunged ever deeper into debt. As a result, Crockett's three-hundred-acre tract on Mossy Creek in Jefferson County was sold at a sheriff's auction on November 4, 1795.

The loss of that land, his reward for Revolutionary War service and his only legacy for a growing family, broke John Crockett. He sought comfort more and more in the bottle and never again held a prominent position in his community. Still, he did not give up entirely and continually cast about for opportunities. His friend Gilbreath pointed him westward. Nicholas Hays, Gilbreath's father-in-law, operated a ferry across the French Broad River some five miles east of Dandridge in Jefferson County. The settlements in Jefferson County were growing, and there was money to be made off the county's most traveled roads leading to Knoxville. Gilbreath would eventually settle his family at Banner's Mill, a mile east of Dandridge.

So John Crockett moved his family westward to Jefferson County in search of the opportunity that so far had eluded him. He rented a little land on the Knoxville-to-Virginia road from a prosperous Quaker farmer named John Canaday. This was over Bays Mountain to the northeast of Dandridge, near Panther Creek, near present Morristown, Tennessee. There he opened a modest tavern.

The road tavern was among the most popular types of business in the early republic, and next to deep ruts they were the most common product of America's primitive but growing roadway system. A prodigious number of taverns of widely diverse quality sprang up along every major thoroughfare. The Philadelphia-to-Lancaster turnpike numbered sixty-two taverns along its sixty-two miles. The Great Western Turnpike from Albany, New York, westward numbered fifty taverns on its fifty-two-mile length. Along the 271 miles of the National Road from Baltimore to Wheeling, there were four hundred taverns. Only the finest of these—and that is a relative term—serviced stagecoach traffic. Far more numerous were the "wagoner" or wagon stands, serving the teamster trade. Finally, there were "drover stands," which catered to the many herdsmen from the backcountry moving their cattle and hogs to Eastern markets. These drovers naturally preferred less traveled roads where their cattle and hogs could move more freely. It was this latter group that John Crockett's establishment served.[20]

Tradition and common sense would have Davy constantly employed in the forest, bringing in fresh game for the table while developing the unerring skill with a long rifle that was to make him famous from Nashville to New Orleans and from New York to London. But if such was the case, he never made mention of it. Rather he worked, and worked hard, serving tables, cutting wood, shoveling muck, and performing whatever other menial tasks his father could think of. This was a far cry from the idyllic days on Limestone Creek, warmed by his mother's hearth, excited by the vastness and beauty of a green and fragrant world just beyond the great cabin stone. It was a hard burden for a lad not yet twelve, and for the first time in his young life he was indeed unhappy. Yet, even in his newfound misery, he could not imagine the hard times yet to come.

John Crockett was beset by debt, for this tavern was hardly a profitable concern. Perhaps it could have been if better managed, or if managed by a man not inclined to drink up all the profits. He could not even keep up with his rent payments to Canaday, much less provide for his family.

A frequent customer of Crockett's tavern was Jacob Siler, a Dutchman, as every human of German descent was called in the backwoods, who lived some four hundred miles to the east in Rockbridge County, Virginia. Siler regularly herded cattle from Tennessee to Virginia and he proposed to John Crockett that he might purchase the labor of one of his young sons to act as drover on this long journey. The prospect of one less mouth to feed, coupled with hard money in his pocket, was far too tempting for Crockett to resist.

And so it was that in the cold winter of his twelfth year, Davy Crockett learned that he was to leave his mother, his family, and his home to go on a long journey and work for a complete stranger—as was the custom of the day he had been sold as a bond servant.[21]

Siler was a kind master and, being happy with the boy's labor, attempted to keep him on once they reached Virginia. The homesick lad worked for Siler for another month before running away in a driving snowstorm, meeting up with some kind wagoners, and making his way home. In this journey the boy not only used his wit and determination to gain his freedom but also came to deeply appreciate the kindness of strangers. This would no doubt help to develop his later determination to use government to assist those in need.

Davy's return home was not as happy as he had anticipated. To his chagrin, his father decided to send him to a newly established school run by a stern schoolmaster by the name of Benjamin Kitchen. The boy did not warm to the schoolmaster and so spent his days cavorting in the woods. His truancy was quickly discovered, and John Crockett decided to beat some education into the boy.

"My father had been taking a few *horns* and was in a good condition to make the fur fly," Crockett remembered. "He gathered about a two-year-old hickory, and broke after me."[22]

The boy won the ensuing footrace and did not look back for three long years. He hired on as a drover and made his way to Baltimore, where he almost took work as a cabin boy on a ship bound for London. Hard circumstances prevented him from setting sail and in time he worked his way back to his father's tavern.

"I often thought of home, and, indeed wished bad enough to be there," he related, "but when I thought of the school-house, and Kitchen, my master, and the race with my father, and the big hickory he carried . . . I was afraid to venture back; for I knew my father's nature so well, that I was certain his anger would hang on to him like a turkle [turtle] does to a fisherman's toe."

He need not have worried, for his homecoming was warm. At first, upon reaching the tavern late in the evening, the now well-grown fifteen-year-old held back and mingled with the drovers. He was not at first recognized. Suddenly his sister hugged him and exclaimed, "Here is my lost brother!"[23]

Crockett set to work to pay off his father's debts to the Quaker Canaday. He also now determined to at least learn to read and write and so enrolled himself in the local school, which was run by the Quaker's son. He worked for Canaday to pay his tuition and concluded that after six months, having "learned to read a little in my primer, to write my own name, and to cypher some," he had education enough.[24]

Now with education under his belt, the eighteen-year-old turned his attention to obtaining a wife. He was frustrated in several romances and with his "heart bruised" and "spirits broken down" concluded that "I was born for hardship, misery, and disappointment." At a frolic he was introduced to Mary "Polly" Finley, the seventeen-year-old belle of the backwoods. This lovely Irish girl won his heart at first glance.

"I must confess, I was plaguy well pleased with her from the word go," he confessed. "She had a good countenance, and was very pretty, and I was full bent on making up an acquaintance with her."[25]

The young couple were married on August 12, 1806, and settled nearby in the rolling hill country near Finley Gap. His in-laws gave the couple two cows and calves, and Quaker Canaday presented them with fifteen dollars in credit at the local general store (a substantial sum in those days in the backwoods).

"I thought I was completely made up, and needed nothing more in the whole world," Crockett recalled. "But I soon found this was all a mistake—for now having a wife, I wanted everything else; and, worse than all, I had nothing to give for it."

Times were hard for the young people, who lived on rented ground and barely scraped by. "In this time we had two sons," Crockett related, "and I found I was better at increasing my family than my fortune."[26]

With the help of Polly's father, they packed up in 1811 and moved across the mountains to Lincoln County on the head of the Mulberry Fork of the Elk River. The Crocketts lived there for two years before again pressing westward to Bean's Creek in Franklin County. It was here that Crockett began to make a reputation for himself as a hunter.

Crockett proved far more adept at hunting than farming, for deer and bear were plentiful in this new country. Not only did these animals provide essential food for families such as the Crocketts, but their skins were also a marketable cash crop. The extra venison and bear meat Crockett gave to his neighbors.[27]

"Whenever I had anything, and saw a fellow being suffering, I was more anxious to relieve him than to benefit myself," he later wrote. "And this is one of the true secrets of my being a poor man to this day."[28]

Crockett eventually won widespread fame as a hunter, killing 105 bears in one season alone (although one wag suggested that Davy could not count that high). This is an impressive record in our wastrel environmental history, although in Crockett's time bears were not only a threat to livestock and even humans on occasion but were also a source of a great deal of meat, as well as hides for clothing, blankets, and rugs, and lard for cooking, grease, and soapmaking.

The black bears of the Tennessee hills were large in those days, and

Crockett was credited with many a five- or six-hundred-pound behemoth. In his hunting days he was known to run wild risks but mostly remained levelheaded. Bears were, after all, dangerous beasts.

Crockett often told a tale on himself that contradicted the popular image of him wrestling a bear into table meat. He had followed his dogs for a considerable distance, thinking them on the trail of a large bear, but each time he reached them they were barking up an empty tree. Then off they would go again with the increasingly frustrated hunter following along. Finally he found that the dogs had treed "about the biggest bear that ever was seen in America."

Crockett put a shot in his breast and he came tumbling out of the tree. The dogs were instantly on him, so Crockett could not get off a clear shot for fear of hitting them. He set his rifle aside and took hold of his tomahawk and big butcher knife and went after the critter. He got within a few paces when the bear rose up, scattering the dogs and staring straight at Crockett.

"I got back in all sorts of hurry," Crockett declared, "for I know'd if he got hold of me, he would hug me altogether too close for comfort."

Crockett ran back for his rifle, took careful aim, and "killed him good."[29]

Some hunts did not end as well. On one occasion the country was so rough from tornado or flood—a "harricane," Crockett called it—that Crockett had a hard time keeping up. The bear led the hounds across the Obion River, Crockett's favorite, old Carlow, in the lead, and before the hunter could catch up there was a terrific tussle between bear and hounds. Crockett finally reached the scene of the struggle.

"My dogs were all lying down under him, and I don't know which was the most tired, they or the bear," Crockett recalled. "I knew I had him. . . . I got up and old Betsy thundered at him. I shot him right through the heart, and he fell without a struggle."

It was only then that Crockett could see that his three hounds were all bleeding, and that old Carlow could not get up. Crockett rushed to his side to find a large puddle of blood under him.

"He was cut into the hollow, and I saw he was dying—nothing could save him," Crockett related. "While I was feeling 'bout him, he licked my hand—my eyes filled with tears—I turned my head away, and to ease his sufferings, plunged my knife through his heart."

The cost of this hunt had been too high. "This is all I hate in bear hunting," Crockett noted. "I didn't git over the death of my dog in some time; and I have a right to love him to this day, for no man ever had a better friend."[30]

Crockett's skill with his rifle became legendary in the backwoods. His favorite rifle he named "Betsy." A visitor to his cabin, James S. French, left a description of this frontier Excalibur: "Betsy, as he termed her, I had the pleasure of shooting. She is a large, coarse, common rifle, with a flint lock, and from appearance has been much used. In her breech there is a wire hole or two with feathers in them, and several parts of her may be found wrapped with a wax thread, for the purpose of healing up wounds which she has received in her passage through life."

It was natural in those days to compare men like Boone and Crockett to the literary hero of James Fenimore Cooper's creation. "One who is little accustomed to shooting, can form no idea of the skill of the backwoods marksman," wrote French. "Even the fiction of Cooper, in the skill of his far-famed Hawkeye, I have seen surpassed. And were the deeds of La Longue Carabine and old Betsy brought into comparison, an impartial judge would have to decide in favor of the latter."[31]

In September 1813, Crockett learned of the slaughter of American settlers at Fort Mims by the Creek Indians. Old Betsy would soon engage in a new kind of hunt—after that most dangerous of game: men.[32]

10

FORT MIMS

All through the sweltering night of August 30, 1813, under a dim crescent moon, Red Eagle—William Weatherford—had quietly mobilized nearly a thousand warriors—heavily armed, stripped to loincloths and painted red and black—in the tall grass around Fort Mims. "Fort" was certainly an exaggerated description of the flimsy stockade that surrounded the blockhouse, cabins, and barns of wealthy planter Samuel Mims. Located on the western edge of the homeland of the Lower Creeks, Fort Mims had become the only place of refuge for American settlers, their enslaved people, and their mixed-blood Creek friends after war had erupted in July 1813 between the Upper Creeks and the United States. The American militia, defeated at Burnt Corn Creek by the Creeks on July 27, 1813, had retreated in disarray, leaving the Alabama frontier defenseless.

Major Daniel Beasley had but 106 men of the Mississippi Territorial Volunteers and 41 of Captain Dixon Bailey's Creek militiamen under his command to protect the 300 refugees crammed into the one-acre stockade. The major was remarkably casual concerning the peril they all faced. When warned by an enslaved young man about a nearby Creek war party on August 29, Beasley not only dismissed the report but had the poor youngster tied to a post in the middle of the fort and whipped. When Red Eagle sent his warriors storming forward at noon that steamy Monday, Beasley was among the first to fall as he attempted to close the gate he had so carelessly allowed to be left open. The Cassandra-like slave, still tied to the post where Beasley had placed him, died there.

Red Eagle, at the head of his gaudily painted warriors, spied Bailey. "Dixon Bailey, today one or both of us must die," he shouted above the din of battle. The settlers retreated into the larger cabins and set up a stiff defense, but Red Eagle unleashed a torrent of flaming arrows on them; those who fled outside were quickly clubbed to death, while the rest were burned alive. Bailey and his men put up a heroic resistance before attempting to break out. They were all killed. Although Red Eagle tried to halt the slaughter, he found it difficult to restrain his warriors. He managed to protect only a few survivors—mostly women, children, and slaves—while the Creeks burned the fort and tortured the captured soldiers to death. It was all over by late afternoon.[1]

This day of horror marked the greatest victory won by the Creeks in their war with the Americans. It also made their leader, Red Eagle, who was also known by his Creek name, Lamochatee, and his American name, William Weatherford, into one of the most famous of all Indian chiefs. It also changed what had been a civil war among the Creeks into a war between Upper Creeks—called Red Sticks because of their crimson-painted war clubs—and the United States. Many Lower Creeks, under their mixed-blood leader William McIntosh (who was Red Eagle's cousin), allied with the Americans. McIntosh, who would fight alongside General Andrew Jackson at Horseshoe Bend, would later be executed by the Creeks for his loyalty to the Americans.[2]

Red Eagle had risen rapidly in Creek society, not only as a result of his distinguished lineage but also through the patronage of Benjamin Hawkins. In 1796 the former senator from North Carolina had reluctantly accepted the appointment as general superintendent of Indian affairs for all the Indian tribes south of the Ohio River. President Washington, impressed with Hawkins's contribution to the 1790 Treaty of New York and the important work he had done in running the new boundary line between Georgia and the Creek Nation, convinced his friend "to sacrifice a few years of your life in making the experiment which you have suggested, and try the effects of civilization among them." Hawkins thought of the appointment as temporary, but it became his life's work. He settled on the Flint River with his common-law wife, Lavina Downs (who may have been part Creek), where his careful study of Creek language and customs made him popular among the Natives. He was adopted into the tribe and quickly assumed the leadership vacuum left by the death of Alexander McGillivray. Like McGillivray, Hawkins assiduously worked to strengthen the Creek National Council, which he soon controlled, but unlike McGillivray his goal was to undermine tribalism through his civilization plan rather than enhance Creek nationalism. In this work Hawkins, who genuinely cared for the Creek people and was absolutely honest, proved quite successful, although his actions increased tensions between the Lower Creek towns and the more traditional Upper Creek towns.[3]

Hawkins's first challenge came with the unexpected return of the flamboyant William Augustus Bowles in the autumn of 1799. Bowles had escaped his Spanish captors and after a series of remarkable adventures from Cádiz to Peru and the Philippines to Sierra Leone, made it back to London. He was soon lobbying friends in the government to sponsor him in an effort to take Florida and Louisiana from the Spanish before the French revolutionaries did. He was frustrated in his efforts to get full backing from Whitehall, but some funds as well as passage to the Bahamas on a British warship were provided. Instructions were sent to officials in the West Indies to assist the unofficial British agent in his triumphant return to Florida. Unfortunately, the British warship carrying Bowles, along with a sizable cargo of powder, lead, and trade items for the Creeks and Seminoles, was caught in a storm in Apalachee Bay, ran aground, and broke up off the Florida coast at St. George Island. Bowles and the survivors of the shipwreck managed to salvage about half of the powder and lead as well as some trade goods. After seven years he had returned to regain leadership of the Creeks as their "Director General." He was soon reunited with his Creek wife and young son. He sent runners north to call for a great council at Wekiva. The representatives of the Lower Creeks and Seminoles, unhappy with the recent Pinckney's Treaty between Spain and the United States, which had established the 31st parallel as the new northern boundary of Florida (which further divided their land), were delighted to see Eastajoca. They promptly "with one voice" elected him "Director of our nation."[4]

Bowles cleverly played off Native dissatisfaction with the new treaty, with the high prices of Panton, Leslie & Company, and with how the Spanish had betrayed and imprisoned him. Most importantly, he promised them that the British were about to return to seize Florida and Louisiana. This was not entirely far-fetched, for the British had contingency plans in the works for just such an action. Bowles, as energetic as ever, soon had construction of warehouses underway at the forks of the Apalachicola River and sent word to his merchant friends in the Bahamas that the Creeks were eager to trade deerskins for British goods.

The return of Bowles naturally alarmed the Spanish, who promptly placed a huge bounty of $4,500 on him, dead or alive. Spanish patrols were soon on the hunt for the adventurer, but Bowles turned the tables on the Spanish. In April, with a small force of Seminoles and Creeks, Bowles captured Panton's warehouse. He then turned his attention to the nearby Spanish fort at St. Marks. With a large force of Seminoles, Lower Creeks, and even a few Upper Creeks, Bowles laid siege to the fort, captured two reinforcement provision ships, and forced the capitulation of the post on May 19 after a six-week siege. The Spanish garrison, numbering just under one hundred, were allowed to depart with their arms, but Bowles had the fort and its dozen artillery pieces. Large numbers of young Creeks now rallied to his banner.

The already anxious Americans, along with the Spanish and to some extent the British, were quite shocked. "This news has been received here and below with extravagant joy," Hawkins wrote William Panton. "All contemplate British times and British presents, and many have flocked down for that purpose." Bowles had turned the American Indian agent and the British merchant into allies. Hawkins, like McGillivray before him, realized that Bowles had to be removed. Bowles and the Wekiva Council now ordered all Americans off Creek lands, chief among them Benjamin Hawkins.

"Mr. Hawkins is the man, who if he is not gone, must go immediately," Bowles declared in a proclamation from Wekiva, "as he is a dangerous man and will cause some mischief."[5]

Hawkins was not a man to be trifled with. He entered into correspondence with the Spanish as well as with Panton and made it clear to his superiors in Washington that Bowles must be eliminated one way or another. The Spanish wanted him assassinated and reminded Hawkins of the bounty on the adventurer's head. Hawkins, who realized Bowles had broken no American laws, preferred for the Creeks to take care of him.

International affairs had undercut Bowles's position. The 1802 Treaty of Amiens between England and France had ended any hope of British military intervention in Florida. Even worse, a change of administration in the

Bahamas had cut Bowles off from the trade goods he so desperately needed for his Seminole and Creek allies. With his influence waning, he decided on a desperate gamble: he would attend the great council at the Hickory Grounds, a hundred miles north of the 31st parallel, and win the assembled Creeks, Seminoles, Cherokees, Choctaws, and Chickasaws over with his celebrated oratory. This was just what Hawkins had hoped for.

The tribes began to gather in May. Hawkins was there, of course, but was joined by a Panton representative as well as the son of the Spanish governor at Pensacola. The Seminoles arrived last, with Bowles at their head. He boldly spoke of the many grievances the people had against both the land-hungry Americans and the devious Spanish. Only a united front could save the tribes, and he was willing to assume leadership of this coalition. He reminded the assembled Natives that he was the representative of their great friend King George III of England. If only they would make him their leader once more, he could stop the American advance, restore their pride as warriors, and open up fair and lucrative trade with the British. It would be a return to the old ways. Bowles was a master orator, which the Creeks highly prized, and there were murmurs of approval as he finished his speech.

With the approval of several older chiefs, most notably Hopoie Micco, the "Speaker of the Creek Nation," Hawkins had selected a small group of enforcers that included William Weatherford, his friend Sam Moniac, and three others to seize Bowles. That evening Weatherford and Moniac boldly advanced into the Cherokee village where Bowles and the Seminoles were camped. As warriors reached for their weapons, the two youths seized Bowles and clapped him in irons made for them by Hawkins's blacksmith.

Many of the *miko*s were unhappy and embarrassed by this act of betrayal at a council; Bowles's captors hurried him away down the Alabama River before anyone could intervene. Their pirogue made good speed in the journey to Mobile, and on the fourth night out they camped on an island near present-day Salem. The wily prisoner managed to free himself in the night, steal the pirogue, and escape to the opposite shore. They discovered his absence at dawn, and Weatherford was quickly on his trail. The still-shackled prisoner was recaptured by noon. They were warmly greeted by the Spanish governor in Mobile and paid the bounty price for the prized prisoner. Bowles was soon on a ship to Havana and imprisoned in Morro

Castle. He died there under mysterious circumstances two years later, a sad end to a spectacular if quixotic career.[6]

The capture of Bowles greatly enhanced Weatherford's position among the Creeks. Hawkins kept in the background to make certain his young protégé received all the credit for the elimination of the "Director General."

"I had seen Billy Weatherford before the war, but only knew him from character," noted the Georgian Thomas Woodward, who later became a confidant of Weatherford. "The circumstance of him and Moniac aiding Col. Hawkins in the arrest of Bowles, made them generally known to the people of Georgia."[7]

Now widely recognized as a bold leader for the new generation of Creeks, Weatherford established a plantation on the Alabama River some forty miles south of Coosada. In 1801 he married his friend Sam Moniac's sister Mary, called Polly. Moniac wed William's sister Elizabeth Weatherford. The union was happy but brief, for Polly took a fever and died in 1804. Weatherford did not remarry until 1813. He then married his dead wife's niece, Supalamy Moniac, who was a noted adherent of the Red Stick cause. His plantation, worked by dozens of enslaved Africans, prospered and became famous for the open-handed hospitality of its owner to both Creeks and Americans. Like his father before him, he had a keen eye for horseflesh and kept a stable of fine animals. He usually could be found in the clothing of any white plantation owner of the time.

He cut a striking figure at over six feet, with auburn hair, a light complexion, and dark eyes. "The squaws would quit hoeing corn," remembered a Creek woman, "and smile and gaze upon him as he rode by the corn patch."[8]

With the capture of Bowles, a decade of relative peace followed as Hawkins promoted his civilization plan among the Creeks. He had more success among the Lower Creeks, where he kept his headquarters, than with the more nativistic Upper Creeks. One of his gambits to turn the Creeks into "white farmers" and thus free up excess land for purchase by the American government was to encourage African slavery among them. Creeks were also employed to capture escaped slaves at $12.50 a head. This proved to be a lucrative business, especially as the bounty increased with the passing years. Many escaped African Americans found sanctuary with the more welcoming Florida Seminoles.[9]

The growing economic and political power of the Southern cotton planter class as well as the 1803 Louisiana Purchase put increased pressure on Creek landholdings. Hawkins negotiated several land cessions that angered Creek traditionalists. The efforts of the Americans to put roads through Creek territory to connect coastal states with the newly acquired Louisiana Territory further agitated the Natives, most notably the Upper Creeks, through whose country the roads passed.

Then, in 1811, the great comet appeared. For 260 days after it first appeared in March, it lit up the heavens and caused a worldwide sensation. It was at this time when all were captivated by this celestial visitor that the Shawnee leader Tecumseh came to the country of the Creeks. It was lost on no one that his name in Shawnee translated as Shooting Star, for he had been born under an earlier comet in 1768. The Shawnee chief, whose mother was Creek and may well have been a relative of Weatherford, came south in search of allies to join in a great Native confederacy to unite all the tribes from the Great Lakes to the Gulf of Mexico to act as one to resist the American advance. This was the old dream of Pontiac, whom Tecumseh's older brother had fought alongside, and like that previous nativistic movement Tecumseh wrapped his effort in spiritualism. His younger brother, the one-eyed Tenskwatawa—called the Prophet or the Open Door—called for a revival of ancient customs and a rejection of white influences. The way to salvation lay only through him—the Open Door. This powerful combination of mysticism and political unity appealed to many in the north, so that by 1808 the brothers had gathered nearly 6,000 followers at Prophetstown, their pan-Indian village on Indiana's Tippecanoe River (near present-day Lafayette, Indiana). Now Tecumseh hoped to bring his mother's people into the fold.[10]

He had already visited with the Chickasaws and Choctaws, traditional enemies of the northern tribes, but had met with scant success among them. Now the visionary Shawnee visited several Creek villages in the fall of 1811, including the Hickory Ground, before joining a great council at Tuckabatchee on the Tallapoosa River. Many young Upper Creek warriors now joined Tecumseh's retinue. Hawkins rushed north upon hearing that thousands of Creeks and Cherokees were gathering at Tuckabatchee to hear Tecumseh speak. Sam Dale, one of the most noted of Georgia frontiersmen, joined Hawkins and left an account of the council: "The day after the council met, Tecumseh, with a suite of twenty-four warriors, marched into the center of the square, and stood still and erect as so many statues.... Their faces were painted red and black. Each warrior carried a rifle, tomahawk, and war-club.... Tecumseh was about six feet high, well put together, not so stout as some of his followers, but of an austere countenance and imperial mien. He was in the prime of life."[11]

Big Warrior, the leading *miko* at the council, showed Tecumseh and his followers to their lodgings. They were expected to speak the next day but declined to do so, although they put on a "wild dance of the northern lakes" every evening under the dim light of the comet. Finally, Hawkins, weary of waiting, departed, but he left Dale behind. With the Indian agent gone, Tecumseh came forth the next day at noon. The ceremony went on all day until finally, as darkness fell, Tecumseh began to speak. Dale hung back in the shadows to watch. "I have heard many great orators," Dale later declared, "but I never saw one with the vocal powers of Tecumseh." Dale related an obviously embellished version of Tecumseh's speech:

> *Accursed be the race that has seized on our country and made women of our warriors. Our fathers, from their tombs, reproach us as slaves and cowards. I hear them now in the wailing winds. The Muscogee were once a mighty people. The Georgians trembled at your war-whoop, and the maidens of my tribe, on the distant lakes, sung the prowess of your warriors and sighed for their embraces.*
>
> *Now your very blood is white; your tomahawks have no edge; your bows and arrows were buried with your fathers. Oh! Muscogees, brethren of my mother, brush from your eyelids the sleep of slavery; once more strike for vengeance—once more for your country.... Let the white race perish.... Burn their dwellings! Destroy their stock! Slay their wives and children! The Red Man owns the country, and the Pale-faces must never enjoy it.*
>
> *War now! War forever! War upon the living! War upon the dead! Dig their very corpses from the grave. Our country must give no rest to a white man's bones.*
>
> *This is the will of the Great Spirit, revealed to my brother, his familiar, the Prophet of the Lakes. He sends me to you.*

All the tribes of the north are dancing the war-dance. Two mighty warriors across the seas will send us arms.

Tecumseh will soon return to his country. My prophets shall tarry with you. They will stand between you and the bullets of your enemies. When the white men approach you the yawning earth shall swallow them up.

Soon shall you see my arm of fire stretched athwart the sky. I will stamp my foot at Tippecanoe, and the very earth shall shake.[12]

His rhetoric had a profound effect on the assembled *miko*s and warriors. Dale worried that even the old chief Big Warrior might be swayed. As Tecumseh resumed his seat, the pipe was passed while several of his followers again did the dance of the northern lakes, sometimes writhing and going into a trancelike state.

Red Eagle then rose. This was all madness, he declared; to follow Tecumseh would mean the ruin of the Muskogee nation. When the Americans were much weaker they had defeated the British, who then proved faithless to the Creeks who had fought alongside them. The British cared no more for the Indian people than did the Americans. Were they not both white? The wise choice was to remain neutral, but if there was to be war, then the Muskogee should fight alongside the Americans. Staring directly at Tecumseh, Red Eagle demanded that the Shawnee depart from the land of the Muskogee.

Tecumseh was furious that this Creek leader Red Eagle, dressed like a white man and called by the white name Weatherford, would dare to speak to him in such a way. The tide had turned, as Sam Moniac and several other Lower Creek leaders now also spoke to denounce Tecumseh. With his support slipping away, Tecumseh returned to his lodging at midnight.

Big Warrior, his backbone restored, now proposed that they kill Tecumseh. Red Eagle would have nothing to do with such a rank betrayal of a distinguished visitor who had come in peace. The proposal was dropped. Tecumseh soon departed, accompanied by some thirty Creek warriors, including the important Hickory Ground *miko* Little Warrior. He left behind Seekaboo, a Creek prophet who was a firm disciple of Tenskwatawa, to proselytize among his people. This proved to be a fateful decision.

On December 16, 1811, near New Madrid, Missouri, there occurred a devastating earthquake of such magnitude that it forced the Mississippi River to momentarily flow retrograde. The quake was even felt on the East Coast. In Tuckabatchee, most of the village buildings were leveled. The prophecy had come true, for Tecumseh had stamped his foot and it was a sign of war. The proselytizing work of Seekaboo suddenly won over many converts.

Hawkins had dismissed Tecumseh's visit, assuring Washington that the new Creek prophets had no influence and that he could control the situation. He was wrong.

"He believed that it would be a mere civil war for power among the chiefs and tribal factions, and that he would be able to restrain them," Sam Dale sadly noted. "He continued to cherish this opinion until menaced with danger that compelled him to remove his family into Georgia and withdraw from his post."[13]

War had already broken out in Indiana, where Governor William Henry Harrison had defeated the Prophet's forces at Tippecanoe and burned his village. Tecumseh, furious over his brother's preemptive attack on Harrison, carefully rebuilt his Native coalition and, once war was declared in June 1812 between the United States and Great Britain, formally allied himself with the British.

"Among the Indians whom I found at Amherstburg were some extraordinary characters," Major General Isaac Brock reported to his superiors. "He who attracted most my attention was the Shawanese chief, Tecumseh, brother to the prophet, who for the last two years had carried on, contrary to our remonstrances, an active warfare against the United States. A more sagacious or more gallant warrior does not exist."[14]

In a stunning victory, Brock and Tecumseh forced the surrender of Detroit on August 16, 1812. The day before, Fort Dearborn (present-day Chicago) had fallen to the Potawatomis. Captain William Wells, Anthony Wayne's famed scout, died in a heroic effort to save the doomed garrison. The vital post Fort Mackinac, at the northern tip of Lake Huron, also fell to the British. When a detachment of Major General William Henry Harrison's army under General James Winchester of Tennessee moved north against the British and Indians, they were defeated at Frenchtown (now Monroe, Michigan) on the River Raisin on January 21, 1813, with heavy losses. Winchester surrendered what was left of his eight-hundred-man force and they were marched north into Canada. A number of the American wounded—perhaps as many as one hundred—were left in Frenchtown, where, once the British troops left, they were slaughtered by the Indians.

Little Warrior and his band of Creeks had participated in what has become known as the River Raisin Massacre, and they now headed home bearing many American scalps. Tenskwatawa told Little Warrior that now was the time to attack the Americans in the South, and Tecumseh promised that as soon as he defeated Harrison, he and the British would come to help the Creeks. On the Ohio River south of Illinois, Little Warrior's people slaughtered two white families. One of the Creeks stripped a pregnant white woman and sliced open her belly with his knife. As she lay dying, he impaled her fetus on a post. This atrocity was not without purpose, for Little Warrior well knew the temper of his enemies. The Americans would blame all the Creeks and war would be most certainly assured.[15]

Hawkins quickly learned of the murders, for Little Warrior proudly displayed his scalps upon his return to his village, and he finally realized that events were moving beyond his control. The Creeks were already in an ugly mood, for the war-strapped American government had failed to make its 1812 annuity payments.

Hawkins wrote Big Warrior that "the guilty must suffer for their crimes or your nation will be involved in their guilt." Hawkins wanted the Upper Creeks to kill Little Warrior and his accomplices, but just to make sure they did not backslide he sent William McIntosh and several of his Lower Creek warriors to assist them. The council at Tuckabatchee ordered the murderers put to death, and McIntosh and his men, along with several Upper Creek warriors, tracked them to their village on the Coosa River and surrounded them in a cabin. The killers were defiant, one shouting out how he had cut open the white woman on the Ohio. They offered stiff resistance. Finally, McIntosh ordered the cabin set afire and the men were burned alive or shot down as they fled the flames. Little Warrior, who fled to a nearby swamp, died in a hail of bullets. He became an instant martyr to the Red Sticks.[16]

More Creek prophets now rose to prominence. Peter McQueen, a nephew of Alexander McGillivray, was one of the new prophets; others included Josiah Francis and Paddy Walsh. They spoke as one, telling the people to discard the ways of the whites—except for guns—and to slaughter the cattle and hogs introduced by the whites. This they did, so that soon the people began to starve. They also ordered the slaughter of the pro-American chiefs. Big Warrior and his followers soon fled east to Georgia. Many other older *miko*s and their families were killed in a reign of terror.

In July 1813, McQueen led three hundred Red Sticks and a train of packhorses to Pensacola to acquire muskets and powder from the Spanish as promised by Tecumseh. The commander at Pensacola had little enough powder and lead to sustain his own command, much less any to spare for the Creeks. McQueen and his followers, including a particularly fanatical prophet called Jim Boy, now threatened the Spanish commandant, who had no choice but to relent. He provided the Red Sticks with 1,000 pounds of powder, over 2,000 pounds of musket balls, 2,000 flints, and a wide assortment of foodstuffs. In thanks, McQueen's prophets regaled the Spanish with the bizarre dance of the lakes. Watching all this from a hideaway was David Tate, Weatherford's half brother, acting as an American spy.

Tate's report alerted the Americans at Fort Stoddert, to the northwest above Mobile, to what had transpired at Pensacola. Militia colonel James Caller volunteered to intercept the Creeks and capture their munitions. Brigadier General Ferdinand Leigh Claiborne, a veteran of the Battle of Fallen Timbers, agreed to Caller's plan, although he had no regular troops to spare save one army captain to act as an advisor. Sam Dale, who by chance was at the fort, agreed to go along as well. Caller's 125-man militia force was joined on the trail by Dixon Bailey and thirty Creek volunteers.

On July 27, 1813, Caller's scouts brought back word that the Red Sticks were encamped just ahead on Burnt Corn Creek. Despite words of caution from Dale, Caller decided to attack at once without further scouting. His troops, more like a mob, galloped in among the Red Sticks, who were cooking breakfast. A volley killed only a woman and a Black slave as the warriors retreated into the nearby canebrake. Most of the men stopped to loot the Indian packhorses while only Dale and Bailey pressed on with a few men after the Indians. The Red Sticks had divided into several groups on the return from Pensacola, and this band of eighty, led by Jim Boy, was poorly armed. They now put up a spirited resistance. Dale was wounded and two others were killed, which unnerved Caller, who ordered his men to regroup. Seeing this, the Red Sticks poured out of their hiding places as the militiamen fled in panic. Caller, unhorsed, fled into the canebrake, where he wandered for two weeks until finally rescued by a search party. The "battle" of Burnt Corn Creek, according to Weatherford's relative George Stiggins, "gave them an exalted opinion of their own valor and prowess and a most contemptible opinion of the Americans."[17]

At about this time, Weatherford and Sam Moniac were returning from a cattle-trading trip to the Chickasaw in Mississippi Territory when, upon reaching Coosada, they discovered their homes looted and their families taken hostage. They hurried to nearby Hoithlewalee, where the Red Sticks were taking the black drink and preparing for war. Weatherford, despite threats made against him by the prophets, had avoided taking sides, believing that the religious fervor would blow over. This neutrality had led to suspicions of his motives on both sides.

Weatherford and Moniac found their families held in the square, surrounded by Red Stick warriors. Among them were several members of Moniac's family, including his sister, who had embraced the prophets' religion, as well as Peter McQueen and Jim Boy. The prophet Josiah Francis demanded that they join the Red Sticks on penalty of instant death. Moniac bolted from the square and mounted his horse. Francis, who was his brother-in-law, grabbed the bridle, but Moniac snatched his red war club from his hand and struck him with it. He galloped away in a hail of bullets.

Weatherford, now to become the embodiment of a great war leader as Red Eagle, declared that while he did not agree with their new religion or their goals, he was yet still a Creek and he would fight with them against the Americans. His speech swayed them, although several of the religious fanatics remained skeptical. To allay their fears, he soon married the Red Stick sister of his friend Moniac. The Red Sticks now began to plan the attack on Fort Mims.[18]

11

THE WAR OF THE RED STICKS

Young Davy Crockett was among the first to volunteer for war when news reached the Tennessee settlements that the Creeks had wiped out the garrison of Fort Mims. Crockett left his wife, Polly, with their two little boys back at his small farm ten miles south of Winchester and enlisted as a volunteer in Captain Francis Jones's company of the Tennessee Volunteer Mounted Riflemen at Winchester on September 24, 1813. Polly begged him not to go, but he was determined.

"My countrymen had been murdered, and I knew that the next thing would be, that the Indians would be scalping the women and children all about there, if we didn't put a stop to it," he declared. "The truth is, my dander was up, and nothing but war would bring it right again."[1]

Major General Andrew Jackson, particularly outraged by the Creeks even before Fort Mims, had written Tennessee governor William Blount that the Creeks "must be punished—and our frontier protected—and as I have no doubt but they are urged on by British agents and tools, the sooner they can be attacked, the less will be their resistance." He requested 2,500 volunteers and permission to advance "and lay their Towns in ashes." Blount did not at first allow Jackson to proceed, but once war was declared on Great Britain in June 1812, the governor relented, so that militia major general Jackson became Major General of U.S. Volunteers Jackson and began to recruit his army. The news from Fort Mims was a great boost to recruitment.[2]

Tall, rawboned, rail-thin Andrew Jackson was a passionate hater. He particularly hated the British. His parents had come from northern Ireland to America in 1765, settled in the hill country of South Carolina, and had just begun to prosper when the senior Andrew Jackson, aged twenty-nine, died in 1767 just before the birth of his namesake son. His widowed mother, Elizabeth, supported by a large extended family, raised young Andrew and his two brothers as best she could. The boys received as good an education as the backwoods Waxhaws country provided. Andrew was eight when the Revolution began, and he was but thirteen when his older brother Hugh died in the war. That same year Banastre Tarleton's Tories ravaged the Waxhaws and slaughtered the Patriot militia. The teenage Andrew carried messages for the militia and was captured; when he refused to polish the boots of a British officer, he was savagely assaulted, his left hand cut to the bone and his forehead deeply gashed. The external scars would heal but not the burning internal ones.

Andrew and his older brother Robert were placed in a British prison camp in Camden, where they both contracted smallpox. Elizabeth secured their release, but Robert died on the way home. Andrew slowly recovered, but his mother, stricken while nursing ill soldiers, died in November 1781.

"I felt utterly alone," the orphan boy declared, "and tried to recall her last words to me."[3]

The boy went to Salisbury, North Carolina, where he read for the law. This led him to follow a friend who had just been appointed judge for North Carolina's western district—Tennessee—where he was appointed public prosecutor. Thus began a grand career that saw the hot-tempered lawyer become a planter, land speculator, judge, politician, and soldier. At age thirty-five the hotspur, despite a total lack of military experience, was elected a general of the Tennessee militia.

Captain Jones's company marched to a rendezvous point just south of Huntsville, Alabama, where they joined with several other mounted militia companies that were organized into part of Colonel John Coffee's cavalry division, over a thousand strong. General Jackson was not yet with them, for he had been terribly wounded in a Nashville brawl with the Benton brothers (Jesse and Tom) on September 4, 1813. Jackson lay near death for several days, his left arm useless from Jesse Benton's pistol shot (he would carry the ball in his shoulder for twenty years and finally have it removed by surgeons in Washington when he was president), and he remained bedridden for weeks. It would be the end of the month before he could head south to join Coffee's advance guard.

After the fight, the Benton brothers were upbraided by a guest at the City Hotel where the fight took place, who railed at their careless behavior. A bullet had passed through the wall above the bed where his young son was sleeping. The baby was John Charles Frémont. The chagrined Bentons profusely apologized.[4]

Coffee decided to send scouts across the Tennessee River while he waited for Jackson and asked Captain Jones for the best woodsman in his company. Jones selected Crockett and sent him over to join Major John Gibson's scouting party. Crockett brought young George Russell with him and they were soon off into Creek Country. The major divided the group, with Crockett and five others scouting south to the Coosa River, where they discovered that large numbers of Creek warriors were moving north. Crockett and his men rode all night to inform Coffee. To Crockett's chagrin, his report made little impact on the colonel.

"When I made my report, it wasn't believed, because I was no officer; I was no great man, but just a poor soldier," he later wrote. "But when the same thing was reported by Major Gibson!! Why, then, it was all as true as preaching, and the colonel believed it every word. [This] convinced me, clearly, of one of the hateful ways of the world."[5]

Coffee sent an express to Jackson at Fayetteville to hurry south with his infantry, and the general reached Coffee on October 24, at Camp Deposit on the Tennessee River. Jackson soon learned of a Creek force at the nearby village of Tallushatchee and promptly ordered Coffee out with nine hundred men to attack it. Before dawn on November 3, 1813, Coffee's men surrounded the Creek village and attacked. Quite a number of women and children came forward to surrender, but as they were being helped by the soldiers to the rear of the line, several warriors suddenly opened fire. The volunteers returned a devastating fire on the Indians. "We now shot them like dogs," recalled Crockett with dismay. The battle quickly turned into a massacre.

Fifty warriors took shelter in a wooden house and the volunteers set it ablaze, burning the Creeks alive inside. Crockett watched in horror as the warriors sang their death songs and were consumed. The next day, as the soldiers searched the Creek town, they discovered a potato cellar beneath the burned house. The men were starving and Crockett and others crawled down into the cellar. "We found a fine chance of potatoes in it, and hunger compelled us to eat them, though I had a little rather not," Crockett later wrote, "for the oil of the Indians we had burned up on the day before had run down on them, and they looked like they had been stewed with fat meat."[6]

This grim moment soured him on war and would have a profound impact on his life. He realized that in both a real and a metaphorical sense the pioneers were drawing sustenance from the Indian dead—cannibalizing them to build a new nation. The episode forever haunted him.

All of the men—Coffee reported 186—had been killed, while 84 women and children were taken captive. "We found as many as eight or ten dead bodies in a single cabin," noted an army lieutenant in his journal. "Sometimes the dead mother clasped the dead child to her breast, and to add another appalling horror to the bloody catalogue—some of the cabins had taken fire, and half consumed human bodies were seen amidst the smoking ruins. In other instances dogs had torn and feasted on the mangled bodies of their masters. Heart sick I turned from the revolting scene."[7]

A crying toddler was found wandering across the field of carnage. An interpreter with Coffee's column took the child up behind him and rode to Jackson's headquarters at Fort Strother to present the boy to the general. Jackson's angry heart melted, for he knew an orphan's pain. He used his one good hand to dissolve brown sugar in water for the little boy. He sent the child to Huntsville to be cared for until he could arrange to send him north to his childless wife, Rachel, at the Hermitage. The ladies in Huntsville gave the baby boy the name Lyncoya, which was their imaginary idea of an Indian name.

"I therefore want him well taken care of," Jackson instructed Rachel upon sending Lyncoya to her, "he may have been given to me for some valuable purpose—in fact when I reflect that he as to his relations is so much like myself I feel an unusual sympathy for him."[8]

The Jacksons raised the boy as a son and the general hoped to secure him an appointment to West Point. Unfortunately, the youngster contracted tuberculosis and wasted away, dying in the summer of 1828 when but sixteen years old.[9]

A week after Tallushatchee, word reached Jackson that friendly Creeks were besieged by Red Stick warriors at Talladega. Crockett was soon riding south with the rest of Coffee's command to rescue their Indian allies. At least a thousand of Red Eagle's warriors encircled the Talladega stockade, and they were in turn surrounded by Jackson's 1,200 infantry and 800 mounted riflemen on November 9, 1813. In the bloody battle that followed, over 300 Creek warriors fell before the rest made a break through the lines of a militia regiment and escaped. Jackson, with but seventeen dead, might have pursued and crushed the Red Sticks if he had not run out of supplies. With his troops facing starvation and with talk of mutiny among both the militia and the volunteers, Old Hickory had no choice but to retrace his steps to Camp Deposit. Jackson ordered Coffee's mounted volunteers back to Tennessee to refit and get fresh horses while he remained to face down his increasingly mutinous militia. Crockett happily returned to Polly and the boys and, along with all the other volunteers, refused to return when recalled by Coffee, since they had less than two weeks left to serve. He was paid $65.59 and discharged on December 24, 1813.[10]

While Jackson haltingly advanced from the north, Brigadier General Ferdinand L. Claiborne, with his Mississippi Territorial Volunteers, moved up from the south. The Red Stick prophets had established their stronghold Eccanachaca on the south bank of the Alabama River, just to the east of present-day Selma, in a heavily forested area not easily accessible. Josiah Francis and Seekaboo were both there, and they assured their followers that their invisible "wizard circle" would keep all the whites out. Red Eagle was not so easily convinced, and he only reluctantly brought his warriors there when his scouts reported the advance of Claiborne's army. The old veteran of Fallen Timbers had 550 regulars of the 3rd Regiment, as well as 80 more Mississippi Volunteers and smaller detachments of militia and Choctaw warriors, for a total of 950 men. Captain Sam Dale was with the militia. Sam Moniac was the chief scout.

On the freezing morning of December 23, 1813, Claiborne's column reached the Holy Ground (as the whites called Eccanachaca) and were divided into three columns in hopes of encircling the Red Sticks. Scouts under Red Eagle discovered the soldier columns and hurried back to warn the village. While the 200 Red Stick warriors calmly awaited the attack, certain that the divine intervention promised by the prophets would protect them, Red Eagle and a few clear-eyed warriors gathered up the women, children, and elderly to try to get them to safety. Red Eagle also urged the thirty Blacks in the village to arm themselves and fight for their freedom. Red Eagle gathered his Black recruits and about eighty warriors together to face an equal number of Mississippi Volunteers advancing against the northeastern edge of the village. They unleashed a cloud of arrows against the white soldiers.

"A prophet was seen in the midst," one of the volunteers related, "frantically running to and fro, waving a cow tail dyed red in each hand and giving vent to the most unearthly yells."

A Mississippi volunteer took careful aim and silenced the prophet. The shocked Creeks, already mystified that the white soldiers could pass the "wizard circle," now began to flee. Red Eagle, with a few warriors and the desperate Black men, held their ground for as long as possible. The fight lasted about a half hour before Red Eagle and his friend Malcolm McPherson turned from their log barricade, mounted their horses, and galloped away with the soldiers in hot pursuit.

Red Eagle reached the bluffs above the turgid river and pulled up his horse, Abbanonair. It was a twenty-foot drop to the water below. He wheeled his horse about—he well knew the mettle of the steed—and galloped back a few yards toward the soldiers. As the soldiers fired at him, he turned again, put spurs to Abbanonair, and flew over the cliff into the icy river. His friend followed. As Dale and the other soldiers watched in amazement, the men and horses swam the river to the far bank. Red Eagle calmly inspected his horse to make sure he was all right and then mounted and rode away. This tale, which lost nothing in the retelling, quickly became something of a frontier legend.[11]

Jackson lived up to his nickname of Old Hickory in those trying days of December and January as he continuously dealt with mutinous troops and a total failure of logistical support, as well as none of the promised reinforcements from Blount. He overcame every obstacle through dogged determination and was finally rewarded on January 14, 1814, when 850 recruits reached him at Fort Strother. Without hesitation the determined general immediately marched these raw recruits into Creek Country, where two indecisive battles, at Emuckfau and Enotachopco, bled the enemy while seasoning his new soldiers. The Americans, with nearly a hundred casualties, retreated to Fort Strother. At this dark moment in Jackson's fortunes a sudden turnaround occurred. The U.S. 39th Regiment under Colonel John Williams reached the fort on February 6. Among the ranks of this force of regulars was young ensign Sam Houston. They were soon joined by more

Tennessee volunteers sent south by Governor Blount as well as five hundred Cherokees under their chief, known as Major Ridge (or The Ridge), and one hundred Creeks commanded by McIntosh. With his ranks now swelled to over 5,000 men, Jackson felt confident enough to advance against the main Red Stick village of Tohopeka, at Horseshoe Bend on the Tallapoosa River.[12]

Menawa, or Great Warrior, commanded the Creeks at Tohopeka, along with Red Eagle and several other chiefs and prophets of the Upper Creeks. Over three hundred cabins occupied the land on this natural peninsula formed by a great bend in the Tallapoosa River. A massive log barricade guarded the 350 yards of the narrow land entrance, while water protected the flanks. Here the Creeks had gathered over a thousand poorly armed warriors and nearly four hundred women and children. They felt confident that their land fortifications and the river barrier would protect them from their enemy. Of course, the prophets among them were busy with their fervent incantations.

Jackson approached Horseshoe Bend on the morning of March 27, 1814, and promptly opened fire with his artillery battery (a six-pounder and a three-pounder), but the small cannons had little impact on the stout wooden barricade. He had sent Coffee with his seven hundred horsemen, along with McIntosh's one hundred Creeks and the five hundred Cherokees, to cross the Tallapoosa below the bend and surround the peninsula to prevent any escape. Hearing the artillery fire, several of the allied Indians swam across the river and seized the Creek canoes. With these they began to ferry men across to attack the village from the rear while Coffee's men provided covering fire. Within minutes three hundred Indians had crossed and were engaged in sharp fighting with the defenders. They set the Creek cabins on fire and under this smoke screen more of Coffee's men crossed to join the fray.

Jackson, hearing the gunfire and seeing the plumes of smoke, ordered the long roll sounded and sent his 2,000 infantrymen forward at 12:30. The regulars took the lead, supported by the militia. They were met by brisk fire from the barricade. Major Lemuel Montgomery of the 39th was the first to mount the barricade, only to be shot dead atop the fortification. He was followed by Ensign Sam Houston, who, despite a barbed arrow wound to his thigh, dropped into the fort and cut down several Creeks with his saber.

As more soldiers joined him, the young ensign reluctantly retired from the fray to seek a surgeon. As Houston's wound was being treated, Jackson rode up and asked how he was and ordered him not to return to the battle. This was the beginning of a warm friendship that would forever alter the destiny of the American West.

The Creeks, outnumbered and outgunned, fought tenaciously and disdained surrender. Twice Jackson offered quarter only to be met by musket fire. Houston, limping back into battle, led a charge on a Creek redoubt and was wounded twice more. "Not a warrior offered to surrender, even while the sword was at his breast," Houston later recalled. The slaughter now became general as the warriors were cut down. Menawa, wounded several times, hid under a pile of the dead until he could slip into the river and escape. He was among the few to get away, for at least eight hundred Creek warriors died at Tohopeka before darkness halted the killing. Jackson deeply regretted the deaths of a handful of women and children, but almost all of the Indian families were taken prisoner. Of the 350 prisoners taken, only 3 were warriors. Jackson's losses totaled 26 killed and 107 wounded among his regulars and militia, with 18 killed and 36 wounded among the Cherokee allies, and 5 killed and 11 wounded among McIntosh's Creeks.

The decisive victory at Horseshoe Bend ended the Creek War, at the same time denying the British the Native allies they needed to assist in a planned invasion, but Jackson was not satisfied. He wanted Red Eagle, and his scouts combed the forest for him after the battle. The captured Creeks were offered bounties to betray their leader to the Americans, and Jackson made it clear that there could be no peace until Red Eagle was killed or captured. Jackson did not know that his prey had left Tohopeka for Hoithlewalee two days before the battle to gather more warriors.[13]

On April 18, 1814, a solitary Indian rode into the American camp near the fork of the Coosa and Tallapoosa Rivers. He was not molested as he guided his gray stallion toward Jackson's tent, for despite his Creek garb he had long red hair and sunburned skin and was thought to be a scout. He had the eye of an eagle "and moved with the regal air of a king," noted one who knew him. As Red Eagle reined in his horse before Jackson's large tent, he was recognized by Creeks allied with the Americans. As Jackson came out of his tent Red Eagle gave an eloquent speech offering up his life if only Jackson would spare the starving Red Stick families. Moved by this speech,

Jackson shouted down the mob that had gathered with ropes to hang the prisoner: "Any man who would kill as brave a man as this would rob the dead!" the general declared.[14]

Jackson, who recognized a kindred spirit, invited his prisoner into his tent. He possessed, the general later wrote, "in a most preeminent degree the elements of true greatness, and for reckless personal courage was the Marshal Ney of the Southern Indians." Thomas Woodward, who witnessed the surrender, later wrote: "General Jackson, as if by intuition, seemed to know that Weatherford was no savage and much more than an ordinary man by nature, and treated him very kindly indeed." Red Eagle agreed to bring in as many of his warriors and their families as possible and also to secure the release of white and Black American prisoners. When Jackson finally returned to his Tennessee estate, he took Red Eagle with him in order to protect him from retribution.[15]

The return of the heroes from Horseshoe Bend encouraged Davy Crockett to rejoin the volunteers. Word was that, with the Creeks defeated, the Tennesseans would now travel to the Gulf Coast to take on the British. "I wanted a small taste of British fighting," declared Crockett. He enlisted on September 28, 1814, in Major William Russell's Tennessee Mounted Gunmen and was promptly promoted to sergeant. Russell's command of 130 men hurried south from Fayetteville to join General Jackson's force advancing on Pensacola. Jackson, now a major general in the regular army and commander of the 7th Military District, was charged with halting any British attack on the Gulf Coast. By the time Russell's men arrived on November 8, 1814, Jackson had taken Pensacola and Crockett and the newly arrived troops had only the solace of witnessing the departure of the British ships from the harbor. Crockett's company was then sent into the Florida swamps in search of recalcitrant Creeks and their Seminole allies. They saw some fighting but for the most part had to deal with swamp fevers and meager rations. Crockett's skill as a hunter was now much in demand. He returned home to Polly and the boys in February and hired a young friend to serve out the remaining month of his enlistment. "This closed my career as a warrior," he later wrote, "and I am glad of it, for I like life now a heap better than I did then, and I am glad all over that I lived to see these times, which I should not have done if I had kept fooling along in war, and got used up at it."[16]

For the Creek people there would be only hard times to come.

The Madison administration assigned Benjamin Hawkins and Thomas Pinckney to offer generous peace terms demanding but modest land cessions to help pay for the cost of the war. Reparation payments were to be made to the Creeks who had stood with the United States to compensate them for property losses during the war.

Jackson, along with most western men, was horrified by these treaty terms. In particular, he did not trust Hawkins, whom he perceived as far too sympathetic toward the Indians. Although he felt the Creek uprising to be crushed, he was fully aware that Josiah Francis and Peter McQueen had fled into the West Florida swamps with over a thousand Red Stick warriors and their families. He correctly surmised that the British would supply and arm these Creeks and their Seminole allies, and indeed a detachment of marines had landed at Pensacola to train the warriors. Josiah Francis was soon on his way to London to request additional assistance. The British, as usual, promised much and delivered little. Francis returned to Florida, where he was eventually captured by Jackson's troops and hanged.

Jackson wanted an American buffer between Spanish Florida and Creek territory. At Fort Jackson on August 5, 1814, Jackson presented his peace terms to the assembled *miko*s and warriors, almost all of whom were from friendly or allied villages. The general actually had little respect for those Creeks who had fought with him, believing them to be dishonorable traitors to their own people not unlike the American Tories who had destroyed his family. He now demanded a vast land cession of nearly 22 million acres—over half of all Creek land—to pay the cost of the war. To protect the southern border with Florida, much of this land would come from the allied Lower Creeks. It was, as Jackson described it, "the cream of the Creek country." This rich land would in time form the heart of the cotton kingdom of Georgia and Alabama and help ensure the rise of the slavocracy that would bring on the Civil War. On August 9, a stunned group of thirty-six chiefs led by Big Warrior signed the Treaty of Fort Jackson. This was just the beginning of the removal of the Creeks from their homeland to west of the Mississippi River.[17]

The War of 1812 soon ended in a blaze of glory with Jackson's stunning victory at New Orleans on January 8, 1815. Although unknown to the battle's participants, a peace treaty with Britain had already been signed. That treaty guaranteed that Indian land boundaries would be returned to what they had been in 1811. The Americans ignored this provision and the British, even if they cared to, had no power to enforce it. The Battle of New Orleans convinced most Americans that they had won the War of 1812 and set Old Hickory on the road to the White House.

Red Eagle, now again known as William Weatherford, returned to Alabama to rebuild his shattered fortunes. In 1817 he was married for the third and final time, to Mary Stiggins, and she would bear him five children. He resettled in Monroe County, Alabama, where he prospered as an American planter with hundreds of acres under cultivation worked by two hundred slaves. His children married into the families of local gentry and a nephew, David Moniac, graduated from West Point.

He was forgiven by his new white friends, if not by many of the Creeks. Sam Dale, now a colonel in the Alabama militia, asked him why he had moved away from Creek land: "He said that his old comrades, the hostiles, ate his cattle from starvation; the peace party ate them from revenge; and the squatters because he was a damned Red skin. 'So,' said he, 'I have come to live among gentlemen.' "

In the first week of March 1824, Weatherford went out on a deer hunt with several friends. When one of his companions came upon an albino deer and killed it, the old warrior was horrified. He immediately left the party to return to his plantation. He told his hunting companions that the killing of the albino deer was a grave mistake and that one of them would be called to the spirit world to atone for it. The day after his return home, he fell ill. In his delirium he saw a vision of his second wife, who had died in childbirth giving him his namesake son, William, motioning to him to come join her in the spirit world. He died March 4, 1824.

"Nature had endowed him with a noble person, a brilliant intellect, and a commanding eloquence," declared Dale,

He was buried just to the west of Little River, under a large stone marker erected by his admiring white neighbors. He did not live to see the forced removal of his people from their homeland.[18]

Part II

THE CITY

12

THE LION OF THE WEST

In December of 1833, Colonel David Crockett of Tennessee, recently elected to his third term in the House of Representatives, went to the theater in Washington City. The colonel did not necessarily approve of theaters and stage acting. "I have heard some things in them that was a little too tough for good women and modest men," he declared, "although it is said that high people don't mind such things." While the colonel certainly did not classify himself among the "high people," he was nevertheless most anxious to view actor James Hackett's performance as Colonel Nimrod Wildfire in *The Lion of the West*.[1]

Hackett, a noted comedic actor celebrated for his portrayal of Falstaff, had offered a prize in 1830 for a new play featuring a distinctly American character. Frontier America was fast becoming all the rage in literary circles, the first three of James Fenimore Cooper's "Leatherstocking Tales"—*The Pioneers* (1823), *The Last of the Mohicans* (1826), and *The Prairie* (1827)—having already captivated the reading public. Samuel Woodworth's song "The Hunters of Kentucky," celebrating the prowess of Kentucky and Tennessee militiamen at the Battle of New Orleans, had swept the nation since its introduction in 1822. The frontiersman, once disdained by the guardians of American culture as a symbol of low breeding and anarchy, was fast becoming idealized as the very essence of the evolving American character. James K. Paulding, future secretary of the navy in the Van Buren administration, capitalized on this interest to win Hackett's prize with his play *The Lion of the West; or, A Trip to Washington*.

Paulding, while writing the play, asked a friend for help "by furnishing me with a few sketches, short stories, and incidents of Kentucky or

Tennessee manners, and especially some of their peculiar phrases and comparisons. If you can add, or invent, a few ludicrous scenes of Col. Crockett at Washington, you will be sure of my everlasting gratitude." The end result was the blustering yet commonsensical Colonel Nimrod Wildfire. Paulding, who was no admirer of Crockett, had meant to parody the Tennessee congressman, but the hilarious persona created by Hackett brought the character to life as the quintessential American. The play was a grand success in both its November 1831 New York premiere and in London (where it was reworked and retitled *The Kentuckian; or, A Trip to New York*) before Hackett brought it to the capital city.[2]

It was a grand evening. Crockett was escorted by the theater manager through the overflowing audience to the front seat reserved for him by Hackett. The crowd roared their cheers as he made his way down, for all knew that Hackett's Nimrod Wildfire was but a caricature of Colonel Crockett. "Go Ahead!" they roared as Crockett waved. When the cheering subsided, the curtain rose and out strode Hackett, resplendent in hunting shirt and fur cap. Hackett noted the applause of the crowd and then turned toward Crockett and bowed. The colonel, equally resplendent in his best city suit, rose and bowed right back. The crowd went wild with applause as legend met reality right before their eyes. Then the play went on.[3]

Crockett had come a long way from his bear-hunting days in the Tennessee canebrakes. A widely circulated Eastern newspaper story of the time put it succinctly: "He attracted the general gaze by his grotesque appearance, his rough manners, and jovial habits, at the same time that he exhibited uncommon indications of a strong though undisciplined mind. He became, indeed, the object of universal notoriety—and to return from the capital without having seen Col. Crockett, betrayed a total destitution of curiosity, and a perfect insensibility to the 'Lions' of the West."[4]

CROCKETT'S RETURN FROM THE CREEK WAR HAD BEEN met by what he forever considered "the hardest trial which ever falls to the lot of man" when his beloved Polly died in the summer of 1815. While devastated, he was ever the practical and resourceful man. With three small children to care for, he promptly began to scout the countryside for a new wife. He followed a hot trail to the "snug little farm" of a young widow,

Elizabeth Patton, whose husband had been killed in the Creek War. Not only was her farm considerably more impressive than his own, she was well-connected to a prominent North Carolina family so that, as he put it, he "began to pay my respect to her in real good earnest; but I was as sly about it as a fox when he is going to rob a hen-roost." They were married on May 22, 1816.[5]

Soon after the wedding, Crockett moved his family, which now included Elizabeth's two children as well as his three (to which they together added three more), to Shoal Creek in Lawrence County in west-central Tennessee. It was there that Crockett began his political career, first as magistrate, then as justice of the peace, as elected lieutenant colonel of the 57th Militia Regiment in 1818, and finally as representative to the state legislature in 1821. It was the militia election that gave him the title of Colonel Crockett for the remainder of his life.[6]

Crockett was a natural for the rough-and-tumble world of backwoods electioneering. His equal measures of common sense and honesty, combined with a good dose of self-effacing good humor, endeared him to the voters. His campaign style was simple and direct, perfectly fitted to an era where political meetings opened with a barbecue and ended with a dance—with the candidate expected to buy drinks all around. Elizabeth worked the farm, raised the children, and provided the cash to support her husband's political career.

"I was able to buy a little of 'the *creature*,' to put my friends in a good humour, as well as the other gentlemen," Crockett noted, "for they all treat in that country; not to get elected, of course—for that would be against the law." Elizabeth also sewed her husband a large buckskin hunting shirt with two great pockets. "In one I would carry a great big twist of tobacco, and in the other my bottle of liquor," Crockett declared, "for I knowed when I met a man and offered him a dram, he would throw out his quid of tobacco to take one, and after he had taken his horn, I would out with my twist and give him another chaw. And in this way he would not be worse off than when I found him; and I would be sure to leave him in a first-rate good humour." This simple but exceedingly practical political style worked wonders.[7]

Crockett, elected to represent Hickman and Lawrence Counties in the state assembly convening in Murfreesboro on September 17, 1821, journeyed north via Pulaski, where he encountered James K. Polk, newly selected as clerk of the Tennessee Senate. No one was to have more influence over Crockett's political fortunes than this stern, taciturn, humorless man. Polk served in the state legislature alongside Crockett from 1823 to 1825, where their relationship was quite cordial. In 1825 Polk, a firm disciple of Andrew Jackson, won the first of seven successive terms in the U.S. House of Representatives, being elected speaker twice. Although nine years younger than Crockett, Polk was from a wealthy family and had graduated three years before from the University of North Carolina.[8]

"I was in Pulaski, where I met with Colonel Polk," Crockett later recalled, "and in a large company he said to me, 'Well, Colonel, I suppose we shall have a radical change of the judiciary at the next session of the Legislature.' 'Very likely, sir,' says I, and I put out quicker, for I was afraid some one would ask me what the judiciary was; and if I knowed I wish I may be shot. I don't indeed believe I had ever before heard that there was any such thing in all nature; but still I was not willing that the people there should know how ignorant I was about it."[9]

Retreat was not in Crockett's nature, and when the legislature joined in session he was again challenged by a more direct assault on his qualifications for office. During the opening days of the session Crockett, ill at ease and awkward, rose to speak. In response to his speech a fellow representative alluded to him as "the gentleman from the cane," which brought laughter from the other legislators. Humiliated, Crockett sought out his tormentor to thrash an apology out of him. His colleague properly noted that such direct action was not acceptable under the rules of the legislature, which forced Crockett to resort to a remedy that never failed him: humor. The following day he appeared with a cambric ruffle, so common among the so-called gentlemen of the day, attached to Elizabeth's roughhewn hunting shirt. When Crockett rose to speak, his ruffle so disdainfully displayed, the entire House was convulsed with laughter and his rival's pretensions totally discredited. Thereafter the "gentleman from the cane" appellation became a badge of honor and Crockett became recognized as one of the most acclaimed members of the legislature.[10]

Nature interrupted Crockett's legislative sojourn when a flood on Shoal Creek swept away his gristmill and distillery. He hurried home to find his finances in ruin. Elizabeth stood firm, urging him to make the best of a bad situation and pay off their debts at whatever cost. This inspired

Crockett. "This was just such talk as I wanted to hear," he declared, "for a man's wife can hold him devlish uneasy, if she begins to scold, and fret, and perplex him, at a time when he has a full load for a rail-road car on his mind already. . . . I determined not to break full handed, but thought it better to keep a good conscience with an empty purse, than to get a bad opinion of myself, with a full one. I therefore gave up all I had, and took a bran-fire new start."[11]

In September 1822, Crockett moved his family west to new lands he had explored in the Obion River country of northwestern Tennessee. These were rich hunting grounds reshaped by the great earthquake of 1811 and still called "the shakes." There, in a simple log cabin, the Crocketts made their new home.

It did not take Crockett long to return to the political arena, successfully running for the state legislature as the representative of four West Tennessee counties in 1823. His opponent was Dr. William Butler, a leading citizen of the area and a kinsman by marriage to Andrew Jackson. Crockett's political tactic was to portray Butler as an aristocrat out of touch with the pioneer settlers of the western country. He often told voters of his visit to Butler's fine home and of the lush carpet on the floor that so contrasted with the bearskins used for rugs in his dirt-floored cabin. "Fellow citizens, my aristocratic competitor has a fine carpet," he declared, "and every day he *walks* on truck finer than any gowns your wife or your daughters, in all their lives, ever *wore!*"[12]

In the legislature he won high marks for his strong defense of squatter's rights in the western country. His effort to ensure that the impoverished settlers might have the right to purchase at a reasonable price the land they had cleared and settled became the central cause of his political career.

A wealthy friend, Memphis mayor Marcus Winchester, the son of General Winchester of the Battle of the River Raisin, encouraged Crockett to run for Congress in 1827. Despite Winchester's financial backing, Crockett was still out-financed in his campaign but made up for this lack of cash with a plentiful supply of wit. His opponent was a man famed for his smile. From the stump, Crockett regaled the crowd with a tale of how he no longer wasted powder and ball on raccoons but rather simply grinned them out of a tree. He declared his concern over his competitor's countenance to the crowd, worrying aloud that "he may get some votes by *grinning*, for he can *out-grin* me. . . . Now, fellow citizens . . . you must be convinced that, in the *grinning line*, I myself am not slow—yet, when I look upon my opponent's countenance, I must admit that he is my superior. . . . Therefore, be wide awake—look sharp—and do not let him grin you out of your votes."[13]

Crockett could be reasonably serious when he needed to be. After he was insulted in a letter to the editor of the *Jackson (TN) Gazette*, he wrote to the paper to remind the voters of the district just who he was. "I am the Dave Crockett who volunteered and shouldered his knapsack and gun, and served twelve months under the immortal Old Hickory, in endeavoring to put down the enemies of our country who spared neither age nor sex. . . . I am the self same Dave Crockett who has had and now has the daring impudence to oppose the immaculate Adam R. Alexander, or any body else, for a seat in the next Congress of the United States," he wrote in December 1826. The attack on him had been signed "Cotton Planter" and Crockett could not resist taking a class-conscious swipe at his opponent. "Cotton Planters may find time to scribble, and ridicule the common farmers and bear hunters, as they call me, when they attempt to come before the people. I am a poor man. . . . I never had the opportunity of college learning, like cotton planters' boys;—No, I have been raised in the humble walks of life—but I have been taught the glorious privileges of American freedom and independence." He signed "David Crockett" but used "Dave"—his spelling of "Davy"—in the letter to remind folks he was one of them.[14]

The *Nashville Republican Banner* was soon reporting that Crockett was on his way to Washington City and that the folks there had best watch out, for the new congressman had "looked a wild cat to death, swam the Mississippi towing a steamboat, and did a great many other feats."[15]

Henry Clay of Kentucky, Jackson's political rival in the West, was quite interested in this new congressman. It had been Clay who, when Jackson won the popular vote in 1824 but failed to get the necessary votes in the Electoral College, had maneuvered in the House of Representatives to elect John Quincy Adams as president. Clay was then appointed secretary of state (then the stepping stone to the White House) by Adams. James Erwin, Clay's son-in-law, had met Crockett in Nashville and sent a full report. "Colonel Crockett is perhaps the most illiterate Man, that you have ever met in Congress Hall," Erwin wrote the secretary of state. "He is not only illiterate but he is rough & uncouth, talks much & loudly, and is by far, more in his proper place, when hunting a Bear, in a Cane Break, then he will be in the Capital." Yet, noted Erwin, Crockett was "independent and fearless & has a popularity at home that is unaccountable. He is the only man that I now know in Tennessee that could openly oppose Genl. Jackson in his District & be elected to Congress."[16]

THE NEW CONGRESSMAN FROM THE NINTH CONGRESSIONAL District, the second largest in the republic, took rooms at Mrs. Ball's boardinghouse, where he met Congressman Thomas Chilton of Kentucky. They quickly became fast friends even though Chilton was a Clay man. Crockett, naturally nervous upon reaching Washington, slowly began to get his bearings. "I think I am getting along very well with the great men of the nation much better than I expected," he wrote his friend James Blackburn in February. He also felt confident of the passage of his land bill: "Mr. Polk and myself are getting along very well with our vacant land bill; and I have no doubt but we shall effect a relinquishment early this session." His alliance with Polk would be short-lived.[17]

Crockett created a sensation in Washington, becoming a picturesque figure and providing wonderful copy for the press. Anti-Jackson newspapers portrayed him as a hopeless country bumpkin devoid of manners, refinement, or education and warned that the government would be overrun with such creatures should Jackson be elected president in 1828. Such criticism only endeared Crockett all the more to the voters back home.

Crockett now began to emerge as a symbol of the dawning "Age of the Common Man." His generation, the first to face the future without the guidance of the republic's Founding Fathers, looked to the frontier for the regenerative values once associated with the Revolutionary generation. Westerners like Crockett were the flag bearers of a national destiny reaffirming that the members of this new generation were masters of both the environment and their own future. The rise of the West—along with men like Jackson, Clay, Harrison, Houston, and Crockett—represented the triumph of American democracy and a final rejection of decadent European values of class and aristocracy. These were self-made men—indeed, Clay is credited with coining the phrase, while Crockett never missed an opportunity to emphasize his humble origins—in a nation that had long embraced the concept as almost a secular religion, thanks to the writings of Benjamin Franklin. Crockett built on Franklin's legacy, at the same time visibly defining an emerging national character. He soon came to symbolize a rough egalitarianism, a wild freedom of economic and social opportunity, and a solid reaffirmation of the cherished principles of equality in the Declaration of Independence.

Of course, not everyone was impressed. "Two years ago the inhabitants of the district of which Memphis is the capital," grumbled Alexis de Tocqueville in 1831, "sent to the House of Representatives in Congress an individual named David Crockett, who has no education, can read with difficulty, has no property, no fixed residence, but passes his life hunting, selling his game to live, and dwelling continuously in the woods. His competitor, a man of wealth and talent, failed."[18]

The first biography of Crockett—*Sketches and Eccentricities*, published in 1833—had the colonel introduce himself to folks in a tavern on his way to Washington when first elected thusly: "I'm that same David Crockett, fresh from the backwoods, half-horse, half-alligator, a little touched with the snapping turtle; can wade the Mississippi, leap the Ohio, ride upon a streak of lightning, and slip without a scratch down a honey locust; can whip my weight in wild cats—and if a gentleman pleases, for a ten dollar bill, he may throw in a panther—hug a bear too close for comfort, and eat any man opposed to Jackson."[19]

Although identified with Jackson (who would win the presidential election in 1828), Crockett grew increasingly restive under the rigid party control James K. Polk exerted over the House. He found the business of being a congressman hard work. "There's too much talk," he grumbled. "Many men seem to be proud they can say so much about nothing. Their tongues keep working, whether they've got any grist to grind or not."[20]

"There are some men whom you cannot report," declared *Niles' Weekly Register* in May 1834. "The Colonel is one. His leer you cannot put upon paper—his curious drawl—the odd cant of his body and his self-congratulation. He is an original in every thing."[21]

He soon drifted from the Jackson camp over the question of squatter's rights in the western country, rightly convinced that Jackson and Polk were far more concerned with looking after the interests of the slave-owning planters and land-speculating interests. His Tennessee Vacant Land Bill proposed that the federal government relinquish all vacant public land in Tennessee for educational funds. His plan was that the land would then be sold at low prices by the state to the poor squatters who had pioneered it: Crockett's constituents in western Tennessee. Essentially what Crockett wanted was free land for the western pioneers—a dream that Abraham Lincoln would bring into reality with the 1862 Homestead Act. Crockett wanted an affordable preemption price of 12½ cents an acre to the people who had pioneered the land and even proposed an outright donation of 160 acres to pioneers who had improved on the land they squatted. Polk betrayed Crockett on the land bill, insisting on high land prices only the planters could afford. When Crockett denounced this, pointing out that the Tennessee state legislature that would oversee any land sales was in the hands of the planters and speculators, Polk was outraged.

"I forbear to comment in detail, on the disgraceful and disrespectful terms, in which Crockett was in the habit of speaking of his own State and her Legislature, further than to say that the whole delegation feel humiliated," Polk wrote back to friends in Tennessee. "We can't trust him an inch."[22]

Despite this, Crockett easily won reelection in 1829 over Polk's handpicked opponent, garnering 64 percent of the vote.

He finally broke completely with Jackson and Polk in 1830 over the hotly debated question of Indian removal. As the representative of the westernmost congressional district in Tennessee and an undisputed symbol of the frontier, Crockett's opposition to Indian removal proved highly embarrassing to the Jackson administration. Crockett's position on this issue reflected his high sense of honor and principle. He had long been disgusted by the pork-barrel projects and partisan political machinations of the Jacksonians, but until this time had still resided uncomfortably in their camp. He was unable, however, to go against his heart on Indian removal even though he knew it to be favored by almost all of his western colleagues and constituents. The memory of the massacre at Tallushatchee haunted him, for he disdained the advice of others, as well as good common political sense, and engaged in a forlorn quest for justice for the Indians.

The great Westerner, the famed Indian fighter—the man from Jackson's own state—spoke boldly against removal on May 19, 1830. His speech was reported on in a pamphlet in defense of the Indians widely distributed throughout the East:

> *He knew the Indians were unwilling to go; and therefore he could not consent to place them in a situation where they would be obliged to go. He could not stand that. He knew that he stood alone, having, perhaps, none of his colleagues from his state agreeing in sentiment. He could not help that. If he should be the only member of the House who voted against the bill, and the only man in the United States who disapproved it, he would still vote against it; and it would be a matter of rejoicing to him till the day he died, that he had given the vote.*[23]

The vote cost Crockett his job, for the Jackson and Polk forces worked diligently and successfully to defeat his reelection bid. For the two years after this defeat he bided his time, hunting bears, mending his political fences back home, and watching the astonishing growth of his legend in the East.[24]

By the time Crockett won reelection to Congress in 1833, he was more famous than ever and more clearly allied with Jackson's enemies. Eastern audiences had been applauding Paulding's play, *The Lion of the West*, since its April 1831 New York premiere. The anonymously authored biography *Sketches and Eccentricities of Col. David Crockett of West Tennessee* was published in Cincinnati in 1833, and within a year it was republished in both New York and London. Amazed at the book's success, Crockett decided to write his own account. Assisted by his friend Kentucky congressman Thomas Chilton, Crockett began writing in 1833. Clearly influenced by Benjamin Franklin's classic autobiography, the book became an instant bestseller when published by the Philadelphia house of Carey & Hart early in 1834. Like Franklin's book, it was very much the success story of a self-made man, but it was also a skillful and often hard-edged account of frontier life. With fabulous hunting tales, delightful frontier humor, and acerbic political blustering in equal amounts, Crockett's book did much to cement his status as an authentic American hero. It also gave to the world his motto: "Be always sure you're right—Then Go Ahead!"

Crockett promoted the book on a grand Eastern tour arranged by the emerging Whig political party. The Whigs, despite the fact that they shared few common interests with Crockett, now worked studiously to build his image, hoping to use him as their authentic log cabin Westerner to beat Jackson at his own symbolic game. Crockett's head was turned by their flattery, so that he actually came to believe their loose talk of running him for president. In 1835 he allowed his name to be attached to two Whig ghostwritten books: an account of his Eastern tour that at least used his actual speeches, and a bitterly partisan biography of Martin Van Buren that he had no hand in. Also, in 1835 came the first of nearly fifty Crockett almanacs. Once again the debt to Ben Franklin was obvious, for *Davy Crockett's Almanack, of Wild Sports of the West, and Life in the Backwoods: 1835* was a direct descendant of *Poor Richard's Almanack*. Originating in Boston, Philadelphia, and New York, the booklets mixed predictions on wind and weather with Crockett hunting stories and Western tales. Expanding on Crockett's own writings, the almanacs created a tall-tale trickster and comic superman celebrating both the virtues of the common man and the expansionist impulse. These little publications proved enormously popular, ensuring Crockett a rare immortality while further defining the emerging national character.[25]

Crockett responded to all this by becoming increasingly self-conscious, more often than not playing to the crowd. One writer noted how Crockett terrified a zookeeper by attempting to crawl into an animal cage to "grin down the British lion," while another remembered him confronting an opposition newspaper editor and declaring that "he had a great mind to grease and swallow him." While the artist John Gadsby Chapman attempted to paint a portrait of Crockett, they were interrupted by visitors who had come a great distance just to meet the famed frontiersman. Chapman noted how Crockett put on his hat, threw a leg over his chair, and greeted the strangers warmly, regaling them with a tall tale. When they departed, the colonel dropped his dramatic pose and murmured, "Well!—they came to see a bar, and they've seen one—hope they like the performance—it did not cost them anything any how—Let's take a horn."[26]

Crockett, not happy with Chapman's original portrait, urged his young friend to try again, suggesting that by portraying him "on a bear-hunt in a 'harricane,' with hunting tools and gear, and team of dogs, you might make a picture better worth looking at." Chapman did just that, and so the "Go Ahead" man—and the unbridled spirit of a young nation—was captured.[27]

Despite his increasing fame, Crockett made no progress in Congress with his land bill. His contention that the government ought to "at least occasionally, legislate for the poor," met with studied indifference from both his Democrat and Whig colleagues. He was blocked at every turn by the ever-efficient Polk. "I have no other feelings towards Col. Crockett than those of pity for his folly," declared the future president. The current president was even blunter, demanding that Tennessee rise "from her degraded attitude of abandoning principle to sustain men who have apostatised from the republican fold." Jackson made it clear to all that he wanted "Davy Crockett & Co., hurled as they ought, from the confidence of the people." What Andrew Jackson wanted in Tennessee he usually got.[28]

Crockett's reelection campaign in 1835 was a bitter one, for Jackson's forces devoted all their resources to defeating him. That year also marked the return of Halley's comet, and a widely circulated newspaper report declared that Crockett and Jackson had agreed to a temporary political truce in the face of this celestial invader. Old Hickory had given Crockett a special commission to scale the Alleghenies and wring the tail off the comet before it could scorch the planet. When asked about Jackson's commission, Crockett retorted: "I'll be damned if I had a commission, if I didn't wring *his* tail off!"[29]

Despite such bluster, Crockett soon had an opportunity to help save Old Hickory's life. They both attended the funeral of a South Carolina congressman on January 30, 1835, in the House chamber. As Jackson, accompanied by most of his cabinet, filed past the casket and out into the Capitol rotunda, a heavily bearded but well-dressed gentleman approached him. Crockett followed closely behind the president. The bearded man not six feet from Jackson suddenly pulled a pistol and fired. The shot echoed through the chamber as he pulled a second pistol and fired again. Both pistols misfired. Crockett pounced on the assailant, aided by naval lieutenant Thomas R. Gedney (later famous in the *Amistad* affair). An infuriated Jackson began to beat his assailant with his walking cane. It took several men to restrain the sixty-eight-year-old president. As they rushed him off to his carriage Crockett and Gedney handed the would-be assassin over to the law. He was an Englishman named Richard Lawrence, who claimed to be the rightful heir to the British throne. He was soon after lodged in an asylum. This was the first known attempt on the life of a president.[30]

Crockett's electoral opponent in 1835 was Adam Huntsman, a West Tennessee lawyer of talent and considerable wit. Nicknamed "Blackhawk," he had lost a leg fighting in the Creek War, was a steadfast Jacksonian, and was a backwoods character cut from the same cloth as Crockett, although not quite as homespun or coarse. He felt confident that he could defeat Crockett, writing Polk on January 1, 1835: "I begin to believe I can beat Davy. . . . I have been in all the counties but one in this District and Crockett is evidently losing ground or otherwise he never was as strong as I supposed him to be. . . . If he carries his land Bill it will give him strength. Otherwise the conflict will not be a difficult one."[31]

Crockett's land bill indeed failed again to pass. He gave his last speech in Congress on February 18, 1835, in a desperate attempt to bring the bill to the floor but was defeated 82 to 90. Thanks to Polk, Crockett had failed even to rally the entire Tennessee delegation to his cause.

Throughout the summer, Crockett and Huntsman traveled together throughout the district, giving stump speech after stump speech, exchanging barbs with considerable wit and good humor. One evening they boarded together at the house of an influential farmer who was known to be partial to Blackhawk Huntsman.

As they retired for the night, Crockett came up with a clever if devious plan to embarrass his opponent. Now, the farmer had a beautiful young daughter, whom Huntsman, a notorious ladies' man, had paid particular attention to at dinner. The two men were bunking together in a room on one end of a long wooden front porch. The young lady's room was at the other end of the porch. Once Huntsman was sound asleep, Crockett crept out of the room with a straight-back wooden chair and proceeded across the porch. He jiggled the knob on the daughter's door and pushed on it as if to gain entry. She awoke and let out an unearthly scream. Crockett raced back to his room, tapping the wooden chair loudly on the planks of the porch, and hopped back into bed. The angry farmer soon burst into the room to confront the startled Huntsman. He had heard Huntsman's damn wooden leg knock-knocking on the porch and also well knew his reputation. Crockett intervened on Huntsman's behalf and promised to keep an eye on him for the rest of the night. The farmer could well see the type of men he was dealing with and not only pledged his vote to Crockett but promised to bring as many of his friends over to the colonel as possible.[32]

Alas, such wit still could not win the day, for in August, Crockett was defeated by 233 votes. Upon such slim numbers the fate of men—and legends—resides. Crockett, convinced that he had been "completely Raskeled out of my Election," was uncharacteristically bitter.

"Since you have chose to elect a man with a timber toe to succeed me," he declared, "you may all go to Hell and I will go to Texas."[33]

13

THE TEXAS

I am on the eve of Starting to the Texes—on tomorrow morning my self Abner Burgin and Lindsy K Tinkle & our Nephew William Patton from the lowar country," Crockett wrote his brother-in-law George Patton on October 31, 1835, "this will make our Company we will go through Arkinsaw and I want to explore the Texes well before I return."[1]

He was soon in Memphis, where a large crowd of friends attached themselves to him. He was naturally a great curiosity to all. "Crockett, who cannot blow his nose without a query remark or observation, was regarded as a passing comet, not to be seen again," noted an admirer as the colonel passed by, "and every hand extended either in courtesy or regard. This occasion proved him to be more of a Lion than I had supposed." Halley's comet at that time lit up the night sky—surely an omen.

A grand farewell tour of the Bluff City's finest taverns was proposed, and so, in company with old friends Marcus Winchester, Gus Young, C. D. McLean, and others, the colonel made his way from the Union Hotel on Front Street to Hart's Saloon on Market Street. The crowd grew larger and rowdier as they progressed. Crockett had to intercede to prevent a fight between Hart's bartender and Gus Young over the eternal question of cash or credit. It was decided to decamp to the more congenial climes of McCool's Saloon next door. The exuberant crowd promptly hoisted Crockett atop Neil McCool's bar counter and demanded a speech.

"My friends," the colonel declared, "I suppose you all are aware that I was recently a candidate for Congress. I told the voters that if they would elect me I would serve them to the best of my ability; but if they did not, they might go to hell, and I would go to Texas. I am on my way now!"

The crowd shouted in delight—that is, all save the fastidious barkeeper, Neil McCool. The sight of Crockett in muddy boots atop his freshly oil-clothed counter was too much. In a rage, he lashed out with a club. Crockett had jumped down by then, and McCool managed only to fall over the counter into the arms of a dozen half-drunken revelers. Amid many oaths he ordered everyone out.

Crockett now advocated retiring for the night, for, while he admittedly "was in hunt of a fight," he said he "did not want it on this side of the Mississippi river." The crowd would have none of that, and they whisked their hero off to Cooper's, on Main Street. Now, Cooper only sold his liquor by the barrel or cask, but that proved a scant problem for Crockett's company. "It is needless to say we all got tight—I might say, yes, very tight," noted one participant. It was the greatest saloon crawl in the celebrated history of Memphis inebriation.

Early the next morning Crockett and his three companions, in good spirits and not too terribly hungover, walked their horses down to the ferry landing at the mouth of the Wolf River. His Memphis friends were still with him, and the group attracted the curious. Young James Davis watched the warm farewells, somewhat in awe of the noted hunter turned politician. "He wore that same veritable coon-skin cap and hunting shirt, bearing upon his shoulder his ever faithful rifle," Davis recounted. "No other equipments, save his shot-pouch and powder-horn, do I remember seeing."[2]

Crockett stepped onto the ferry-flat, and the elderly Black ferryman, Limus, cast off and pushed away from the shore. Limus worked his snatch oars as the little flatboat floated lazily down the Wolf, into the Mississippi and toward the distant shore. In retrospect, it was something of a scene out of ancient mythology, with old Limus standing in for Charon on the River Styx.

"Be always sure you're right—Then Go Ahead!" was Crockett's motto, and he reflected that self-assurance as he traveled westward. He had added three more to his party by the time he reached Little Rock on November 12. The city fathers heard of his arrival and sought him out, finding him busily skinning a deer he had just shot. He was invited to a dinner in his honor at Jeffries Hotel, where he regaled those gathered with a talk described by a local newspaper as "simply rough, natural, and pleasant." The war news from Texas was now ominous, and while Crockett could not help but direct a few barbs at President Jackson, he aimed his real enmity at the president of Mexico, quipping that he intended to "have Santa Anna's head, and wear it for a watch seal!"[3]

The next morning Crockett's company departed Little Rock, joined by several young men anxious for adventure in Texas. Texas was on every American tongue by 1835 as a land of grand opportunity. American settlers there were growing increasingly restless under Mexican rule that was at best incompetent and at worst despotic. Once the Mexican shackles were discarded, there would be plenty of free land for those bold enough to take it. They crossed the Red River at Lost Prairie and entered Texas, where Crockett, strapped for funds, traded a gold watch to Isaac Jones for his watch and $30.[4]

He led his men on to the tiny hamlet of Clarksville, some twenty-five miles south of the Red River, where his old friend Captain William Becknell lived. Becknell, the famed father of the Santa Fe Trail, lived on Sulphur Fork Prairie, and Crockett stayed there for several days while a large buffalo-hunting party was organized. Ignoring warnings of Indian war parties, Crockett and his companions pushed farther westward, exploring the country and searching for buffalo. Crockett loved this wide-open prairie country, so different from Tennessee. "Good land and plenty of timber and the best springs and wild mill streams, good range, clear water and every appearance of good health and game aplenty," he wrote his daughter.[5]

Near the headwaters of the Trinity River, Crockett's party was met by James Clark, the founder of Clarksville, who turned the hunting party back with tales of raiding Comanches. Crockett called the area Honey Grove because of its swarming bees, a name it came to be forever known by.

Many old friends from Tennessee were in the Red River country, and Crockett agreed to meet several of them for a grand hunt at the falls of the Brazos River in December. He then pushed southeast along Trammel's Trace to Nacogdoches. News of his coming had preceded him, and yet another dinner in his honor was planned. He delighted the Texans with another version of his hell-and-Texas speech.

In Nacogdoches, Crockett swore an oath of allegiance "to the Provisional Government of Texas or any future *republican* Government that may be hereafter declared." He had Judge John Forbes insert the word "republican" before he would sign the oath. The political situation in Texas was confused, with the provisional government divided into factions favoring the governor, Henry Smith, with the governing council on the other side. The military situation was equally confusing, for although armed conflict had erupted between the settlers and Mexican forces on October 1, and General Martín Perfecto de Cos had surrendered San Antonio de Béxar to the rebels on December 11 and retreated with his army south of the Rio

Grande, there was no real Texas army, no goal of independence declared to fight for, and no unity of command. General Sam Houston, the new army commander, was unable to exert authority over his scattered and wildly undisciplined forces, while rumors abounded that Santa Anna was leading a large army northward.[6]

ANTONIO LÓPEZ DE SANTA ANNA PÉREZ DE LEBRÓN HAD been born in the city of Jalapa, in the province of Veracruz, on February 21, 1794. His family was of modest wealth and, most importantly, of Spanish blood (called *criollos* in Mexico). Even before his commission as a "gentleman cadet," a title of some honor, into the Permanent Infantry Regiment of Veracruz in 1810, he had become enamored with the career of Napoleon Bonaparte. He modeled his career on his idol, and in years to come would refer to himself as the "Napoleon of the West." This Mexican Bonaparte was soon in the thick of Indian fighting in Tamaulipas, where he received an arrow wound, and then against American freebooters in Texas in 1813, where he received a citation for gallantry. He secured another award for bravery in the desultory campaigns running to ground the last remnants of Father Miguel Hidalgo's revolt.

By 1821, Santa Anna was a captain in the Veracruz lancers and soon won promotion to lieutenant colonel for his exploits against the insurgents. He proved to be the most effective of the royalist combat commanders. Augustín de Iturbide soon rose against the new liberal Spanish constitution that threatened the status of the Catholic Church and the colonial elites. Iturbide had once been Santa Anna's commander, and the promising young officer now switched sides—taking six hundred soldiers with him—and joined the revolutionaries. They soon claimed victory over their Spanish colonial overlords. Iturbide rewarded him with a promotion to general and command of the vital port of Veracruz, with its lucrative customshouse.

In May 1822, Iturbide proclaimed himself emperor of Mexico, a victory for the conservatives over the longtime revolutionaries, and began to fret over his ambitious young commander in Veracruz. He soon ordered Santa Anna to report to Mexico City, but the young officer joined rebel forces instead.

On December 6, 1822, Santa Anna proclaimed for a Republic of Mexico from his Veracruz headquarters. Joining with liberal insurgents, he endorsed the Plan of Casa Mata, which called for the overthrow of Iturbide and the establishment of a congress and a federal republic. Years later, Santa Anna would confess that in 1822 he did not actually know what a republic was. Iturbide soon abdicated the throne, was banished, but returned in 1824 when he received word of a Spanish plan to reconquer Mexico. He was promptly arrested and executed by firing squad on July 18, 1824.

IN OCTOBER 1824, GUADALUPE VICTORIA BECAME THE first president of the Mexican Republic under the Constitution of 1824 (modeled on that of the United States). Santa Anna provided crucial support, so that Guadalupe Victoria became the only Mexican president before 1860 to serve a full four-year term. That ended Santa Anna's support for the republic, for in 1829 he helped overturn the election and installed the losing candidate, the popular old revolutionary Vicente Guerrero, as president. He received promotion to the rank of general of division (the highest rank in the army) as his reward and promptly proved his worth at Tampico in September 1829 when he defeated a Spanish invasion force from Cuba.

While Santa Anna faced down this foreign threat, intrigue ruled in Mexico City. President Guerrero was deposed by his vice president and executed. The government collapsed in chaos. It was a moment made for Santa Anna. He marched on Mexico City, overthrew the illegitimate government, and restored order. Now the undisputed hero of the hour, Santa Anna easily won election as president in 1833 as a liberal committed to the federal constitution of 1824. He declined to take an active role in politics, leaving the details of government to his vice president while he retired to his estate in Veracruz.

In his absence Vice President Valentín Gómez Farías unwisely attacked the special position of the army and the Catholic Church. The generals, who supported the Church and a centralized government, rebelled and called on Santa Anna to assume the role of dictator. Once again Santa Anna marched on Mexico City to restore order. He now deposed his vice president, dissolved the congress, overthrew the Constitution of 1824, and declared himself dictator.

Federalist militias in five states rose against the dictator, but the army and the Church rallied to him. Santa Anna quickly defeated his enemies. By 1835 the only remaining federalist stronghold was in the northern part of Coahuila—the province known as Texas.

Texas had long been troublesome to both Spain and Mexico. In 1821 there were fewer than 3,000 settlers in Texas. Constantly harassed by the Comanches, the settlers lived precarious lives distant from any markets for their produce or cattle. In 1825 the Mexican government offered large land grants and favorable tariff and tax incentives to get foreign colonists to settle in Texas. They hoped that these colonists might blunt the Comanche raids that devastated the other northern Mexican states as well as breathe some economic life into the beleaguered province. Stephen F. Austin was the most prominent of a number of so-called *empresarios* who brought colonists into Texas. These new settlers were required to swear allegiance to Mexico and convert to Catholicism but were otherwise left alone by the government in Mexico City. By 1830 these colonists, almost all of them Americans, outnumbered the Hispanics in Texas ten to one and were increasingly restless under Mexican rule. All their trade, mostly in cotton, went east to the United States. They flagrantly ignored the Mexican law against slavery and were openly contemptuous of the Catholic faith.

The government in Mexico City responded with a new law in 1830 that outlawed all immigration from adjacent countries (only the United States was adjacent to Texas), banned future colonization, ended tariff exemptions, and reinforced the ban of slavery. The outraged Texans, both Americans and wealthy Hispanics, began to organize to protest this new law. Many of these Texans supported Santa Anna in his 1833 election as president.

Santa Anna proved no friend to Texas, and in August 1835 he sent General Martín Perfecto de Cos, his brother-in-law, to Texas with five hundred troops. Cos soon dissolved the Coahuila legislature and announced his intention to drive all Americans who had been in Texas fewer than five years out of the province. When Cos sent troops to Gonzales in October to confiscate a little cannon, the Texans hoisted a flag with the words "Come and Take It" emblazoned on it, shots were fired, and the Texas Revolution was underway. Stephen Austin soon led a disorganized but effective militia force against Cos in San Antonio de Béxar, the largest town in Texas, and on December 10, 1835, the Mexicans surrendered. Cos and his men were paroled and, under promise not to return, were allowed to march south in peace.[7]

This humiliation stained not only Mexican military honor but Santa Anna's family name as well. To make matters worse, his longtime political ally, Lorenzo de Zavala, had resigned his position as minister to France to return to his estate in eastern Texas to join the rebels against Santa Anna. At a dinner with the French ambassador, Santa Anna boasted that "if the Americans do not behave themselves, I will march across their country and plant the Mexican flag in Washington."[8]

CROCKETT'S WARM RECEPTION IN TEXAS LIFTED HIS spirits. On January 9, 1836, he wrote his daughter Margaret from San Augustine. He had joined the army, he told her, and planned to depart soon to join the Texan forces to the south on the Rio Grande. He still had politics on his mind.

"But all volunteers is entitled to vote for a member of the convention or to be voted for, and I have but little doubt of being elected a member to form a constitution for this province," he told her. Now he was to be a founding father of a new nation. "I am rejoiced at my fate. I had rather be in my present situation than to be elected to a seat in Congress for life," he reassured her. "I am in hopes of making a fortune yet for myself and family, bad as my prospects have been. Do not be uneasy about me, I am among friends."[9]

Micajah Autry, a Tennessee lawyer and sometime poet, wrote his wife on January 13 from Nacogdoches that "Colonel Crockett has joined our company." Although Lindsey K. Tinkle and Abner Burgin had returned home, Crockett and his nephew, along with many of those who had attached themselves to him, now joined with a dozen other volunteers into a company dubbed the "Tennessee Mounted Volunteers" in honor of the colonel. On January 16 they headed toward San Antonio. "We go with arms in our hands," wrote young Daniel Cloud of Kentucky, "determined to conquer or die."[10]

Crockett's company reached Washington-on-the-Brazos in late January. There Crockett hoped to meet with Sam Houston, his old friend from

Tennessee politics. He had last seen Houston in Nashville in April 1829, on the very day that the young governor had resigned his office as a result of a marital scandal of epic proportions. "He told me that he was going to leave the Country and go up the arkensaw and live with the Indians as he Calls them his adopted Brothers," Crockett wrote a friend at the time.

Houston, drinking heavily and on the verge of a complete breakdown, had then boarded the steam packet *Red Rover*. That night he had roamed the deck of the steamboat "reflecting on the bitter disappointment I had caused General Jackson and all my friends, and especially the blight and ruin of a pure and innocent woman who had entrusted her whole happiness to me." As the sun began to set, he gazed at the swirling waters and decided to throw himself overboard "and end my worthless life." Suddenly an eagle swooped down just above his head and soared aloft with the wildest of screams. "I knew then," he declared later, "that a great destiny waited for me in the West."[11]

Houston had missed Crockett because he was at Goliad, attempting, without much success, to establish some order in the chaotic Texan army. On January 17 he had ordered Colonel James Bowie to San Antonio with thirty men to destroy the fortifications at the old mission Alamo and withdraw the garrison and artillery eastward.

Bowie, a swashbuckling adventurer who had given his name to a deadly knife, was a legend all across the Old Southwest. A towering figure, the sandy-haired giant's physical stature was matched by an equally imposing personality. Men recounted his countless deeds of daring: roping wild mustangs, riding alligators, smuggling slaves with the pirate Jean Lafitte, outrageous land speculations, battling Indians, and searching for the fabled San Saba silver mine. Men spoke in awed whispers of his knife—a monstrous double-edged blade—and of the men he had slain with it. As his fame spread, especially after the Vidalia Sandbar fight (the O.K. Corral of its time), he became notorious as a mankiller.

Bowie and his brother Rezin had first come to Texas in 1819; there they fell in with Lafitte, who, after helping Jackson win the great victory at New Orleans, had set up a lucrative slave-smuggling operation on Galveston Island. The Bowie brothers worked with Lafitte for some time and used their ill-gotten gains to engage in land speculations in Louisiana and Mississippi. Despite his checkered reputation, Bowie eventually was welcomed in

Texas in 1828 and began moving in the elite circles of San Antonio society. In 1831 he married the beautiful Ursula Veramendi, the seventeen-year-old daughter of the vice-governor of the joint state of Coahuila y Tejas. Through his new family connections, Bowie soon acquired dubious title to thousands of acres of prime Texas real estate. His idyllic life came crashing down in 1833 when a cholera epidemic claimed the lives of his wife and in-laws. Devastated, Bowie took more and more to the bottle to ease his pain.

While Austin distrusted Bowie as a reckless adventurer, Houston became his warm friend. The former Tennessee congressman and governor first met Bowie in 1833. Houston, in Texas as a representative of American land companies but actually an agent for his mentor Andrew Jackson, took an immediate liking to Bowie. Himself broken by marital scandal and an addiction to the bottle, Houston understood a man like Bowie.

"There is no man on whose forecast, prudence, and valor I place a higher estimate," Houston declared of Bowie.[12]

Crockett tarried in Washington-on-the-Brazos for a few days, perhaps hoping for Houston's return or delaying in order to find some role for himself in the convention of independence that was to meet there on March 1. Finally, on January 24, he pushed on toward San Antonio de Béxar. Crockett's company entered the town from the west, through an old Catholic graveyard amidst a rainstorm. They were met there by Colonel Bowie and his aide Antonio Menchaca. Upon arriving at the Alamo, Bowie had disregarded Houston's orders, writing to Governor Smith that "The salvation of Texas depends in great measure in keeping Bexar out of the hands of the enemy. . . . [W]e will rather die in these ditches than give it up to the enemy." He was naturally delighted to see Crockett.[13]

Bowie escorted Crockett to Béxar's main plaza, where a large crowd had by now gathered. A speech was naturally in order. Crockett's hell-and-Texas story was greeted with enthusiasm, and he finished it with a democratic flourish. "I have come to aid you all that I can in your noble cause," he told them. "I shall identify myself with your interests, and all the honor that I desire is that of defending as a high private, in common with my fellow-citizens, the liberties of our common country."[14]

Crockett found quarters near the Plaza de Armas and surveyed the town, so different and exotic from what he knew, with its adobe huts, ancient missions, and large Mexican population. The ditches that his new friend Bowie was so determined to defend were hardly imposing. The Alamo was a sprawling mission compound founded in 1718 by Franciscans as the Mission San Antonio de Valero, which had been converted in 1801 into a fort for Spanish troops. After the Mexican revolution of 1821, the mission was abandoned, many of its buildings occupied by local citizens. Like most of the Spanish missions in the Southwest, there was a large rectangular plaza of about three acres lined by nine-to-twelve-foot stone walls. A series of rude buildings formed the west wall, facing toward the town, while the east wall was marked by a two-story building called the long barracks. South of these barracks was the ruined church, with twenty-two-foot-high walls. The roof had collapsed sixty years before. The main gate was west of the church, through a single-story building called the low barracks. Between the church and the low barracks was a fifty-yard gap fortified with earth and logs. This would be the area Crockett would eventually be assigned to defend.

Although the old mission was crumbling and in disrepair, the Texans had twenty-one pieces of artillery of various sizes captured from General Cos. They also had a good supply of British Brown Bess muskets and 16,000 rounds of ammunition left by the Mexicans. If they could hold the Alamo, it might yet prove a rallying point for all of Texas. That was certainly Bowie's hope.

On February 10 a grand fandango was held in Crockett's honor. Around midnight word arrived from ranchers on the Rio Grande that Santa Anna had reached the river with a large army. Bowie took the warning seriously, but his rival for command of the 150-man garrison, William Barret Travis, dismissed the report. Arguing that he was about to dance with the loveliest lady in all Béxar, Travis declared, "Let us dance to-night and to-morrow we will make provisions for our defense."[15]

The Mexican army was but ten days away, and as the men sobered up the next morning they found Travis and Bowie in contention for command. Travis was a twenty-seven-year-old South Carolina lawyer of Byronic temperament and soaring ambition. More than perhaps any other man in Texas, he had helped foment the rebellion, and now he was determined to command this frontier outpost of dubious honor. By February 14, they reluctantly agreed to share command—Bowie the volunteers and Travis the regulars.

While the Texans bickered, the Mexicans rapidly advanced. In Saltillo, Santa Anna had organized several thousand men into a poorly equipped army that then endured a heartbreaking march to the Rio Grande, dogged by disease, poor rations, and brutal weather. Cos and his troops were ordered to violate their parole and rejoin this invasion force. Santa Anna proclaimed that all rebel leaders were to be executed and all foreigners captured under arms were to be considered pirates. All land grants were to be nullified, all Americans expelled, their property confiscated, and all enslaved people freed.

February 21, 1836, which was Santa Anna's forty-second birthday, found his army some twenty miles from San Antonio. In hopes of surprising the Texans in the town, the general ordered Joaquín Ramírez y Sesma to take an advance guard of 160 lancers of the Dolores Regiment and make a surprise attack. A rainstorm delayed the lancers, so that the Texans were warned in time to retreat into the Alamo.

Béxar was a community in motion on the morning of February 23, with a steady stream of wagons and carts moving the citizenry out of town. A sentinel in the bell tower of the San Fernando Cathedral soon spied the reason for the exodus: Mexican troops. Two scouts, John W. Smith and Dr. John Sutherland, rode out to investigate. They soon came galloping back, Sutherland's horse taking a tumble along the way. Mexican cavalry were not far behind them. The Texan garrison hurriedly retreated to the doubtful sanctuary of the Alamo. "Poor fellows," a Mexican woman called out to them, "you will all be killed."[16]

Travis, busy in his headquarters room in the Alamo, looked up to find Crockett and Sutherland before him. Sutherland had injured his leg when his horse fell, and Crockett was supporting him. "Colonel, here am I," declared Crockett. "Assign me to a position, and I and my twelve boys will try to defend it." Travis promptly assigned him a post of honor: the wooden palisade between the church and the low barracks. It was the most dangerous and vulnerable spot in the Alamo.[17]

Eight-year-old Enrique Esparza, the young son of Alamo defender Gregorio Esparza, remembered well the grand entry of Santa Anna into San Antonio. "Riding in front was Santa Anna, *el Presidente!*" he recalled years later. "This man was every inch a leader. I was very impressed." The boy then fled with his family into the Alamo.[18]

Within hours Santa Anna had occupied Béxar with a strong force. Much of his 5,000-man army was still strung out back to the Rio Grande, but he would soon have several thousand men concentrated before the Alamo. He had a bloodred flag—signifying no quarter—raised over the San Fernando Cathedral and sent emissaries to the Alamo to demand unconditional surrender. Travis answered with a cannon shot.

All the next morning Travis sequestered himself in his west-wall quarters and hurriedly wrote letters requesting aide. He well knew that Colonel James Fannin was but ninety miles away at Goliad with four hundred men, and that Houston was somewhere in the north recruiting. One letter, addressed "To the People of Texas & All Americans in the World," would ring down through the ages:

I am besieged, by a thousand or more of the Mexicans under Santa Anna—I have sustained a continual Bombardment & cannonade for 24 hours & have not lost a man—The enemy has demanded a surrender at discretion, otherwise, the garrison are to be put to the sword, if the fort is taken—I have answered the demand with a cannon shot, & our flag still waves proudly from the walls—I shall never surrender or retreat. Then, I call on you in the name of Liberty, of patriotism & everything dear to the American character, to come to our aid with all dispatch—The enemy is receiving reinforcements daily & will no doubt increase to three or four thousand in four or five days. If this call is neglected, I am determined to sustain myself as long as possible & die like a soldier who never forgets what is due to his own honor & that of his country—Victory or Death

William Barret Travis
Lt. Col. comdt

P.S. The Lord is on our side—When the enemy appeared in sight we had not three bushels of corn—We have since found in deserted houses 80 or 90 bushels & got into the walls 20 or 30 head of Beeves—Travis

Albert Martin rode out of the gates of the Alamo and delivered the letter to Gonzales. He then joined thirty-two volunteers under George Kimbell and John W. Smith and led them back to the Alamo. James Butler

Bonham had less success with Fannin at Goliad, who, after an abortive attempt to reach Travis, hunkered down in his post. Bonham returned to the Alamo to report to his friend Travis.

On February 25, Santa Anna probed the Alamo's defenses, only to have his forces thrown back. Travis, now in complete command, since Bowie had taken ill with a fever, sent a sortie of his own out against the Mexicans, burning some nearby huts that had given them cover. In a dispatch he sent to Houston that night with Captain Juan Seguín, Travis noted of the day's battle, "The Hon. David Crockett was seen at all points, animating the men to do their duty."[19]

Enrique Esparza described the fighting many years later. "Crockett seemed to be the leading spirit," he remembered. "He was everywhere. He went to every exposed point and personally directed the fighting. Travis was the chief in command, but he depended more upon the judgement of Crockett and that brave man's intrepidity than upon his own."[20]

The enemy also seems to have taken note of Crockett. "A tall man, with flowing hair, was seen firing from the same place on the parapet during the entire siege," wrote Captain Rafael Soldana. "He wore a buckskin suit and a cap all of a pattern entirely different from those worn by his comrades. This man would kneel or lie down behind the low parapet, rest his long gun and fire, and we all learned to keep at a good distance when he was seen to make ready to shoot. He rarely missed his mark . . . This man I later learned was known as 'Kwockey.' "[21]

Reinforcement swelled Santa Anna's army to more than 2,500 men as he tightened the ring around the Alamo, keeping up a continual bombardment. Travis's many appeals for aid went unanswered, save for thirty-two bold men from Gonzales who came in early on the morning of March 1. The reinforcement cheered the garrison, as did Crockett, who often played his fiddle, told tall tales, and exhibited his homespun humor. But finally even Davy despaired. "I think we had better march out and die in the open air," he lamented on March 4 to Susanna Dickinson, wife of an artillery captain. "I don't like to be hemmed up."[22]

Travis also called a meeting of his entire garrison late on March 5. He spoke to his men as militia commanders often had done to their democratic forces since Kings Mountain onward: of their free will, of their duty, and of their possible fate. He now offered anyone who chose to depart the right to do so. He drew a line in the dust with his saber. Susanna Dickinson watched as her husband and every man crossed over and joined Travis save one. That night the Frenchman Moses Rose vanished into the darkness beyond the walls of the Alamo. Travis now had but 185 men.

On March 4, 1836, Santa Anna called his officers together for a war council. In the contentious meeting General Manuel Fernández Castrillón, a Cuban soldier of fortune with a great shock of white hair, argued that any assault should be postponed until heavier artillery arrived and then joined with Colonel Juan Almonte to protest the red flag declaration that no quarter would be given the rebels. The general dismissed these protests and ordered his officers to prepare for a predawn assault.

The assault came on the freezing morning of March 6, 1836. Santa Anna sent 1,500 of his best troops storming against the Alamo. Colonel Juan Morales led a column of one hundred men against the stockade defended by Crockett and his boys. More than seven hundred men under General Cos and Colonel Francisco Duque assaulted the northeastern and northwestern walls while Colonel José Maria Romero's three hundred men attacked from the east.

The darkness was lit by the fire from the Texan artillery, blowing great gaps in the Mexican ranks. Duque fell wounded and the columns faltered as the men bunched under the Alamo's walls, seeking protection from the defenders' guns. Santa Anna now ordered General Castrillón to take over Duque's column while he sent in four hundred reserves to bolster the attack. He ordered the Mexican bands to play the "Degüello," the ancient Spanish cutthroat tune signifying no quarter.

Castrillón rallied the faltering troops and, with the added pressure of the reserves, they swept over the north wall. Here Travis was killed; he was one of the first Texans to fall. His men retreated from the wall and into the long barracks.

Morales's column, hit hard by Crockett's men at the stockade, had veered to the left and now swept over the southwest corner. Crockett's company, flanked and caught in the open, fell back to the long barracks and the church. Several defenders bolted over the wall, attempting to cut their way out, only to be slaughtered by Mexican lancers.

The Mexicans turned the Texan cannons around, firing point-blank into the barracks doors. The dazed and wounded defenders inside were then bayoneted. In one of these rooms Bowie was slain in his sickbed. The enraged Mexicans tossed his body atop their bayonets like hay. Finally, the heavy doors of the church were battered down, and after brief but fierce hand-to-hand combat the last defenders were killed. In a nightmarish aftermath, the Mexicans murdered the wounded and mutilated the dead.[23]

General Castrillón, however, stopped his advancing soldiers before a handful of bloodied, exhausted defenders. Offering clemency, he convinced them to surrender. Among this pitiful remnant was Crockett.

The sun had just come up as Castrillón marched his prisoners, seven in number, into the Alamo courtyard. Santa Anna and his staff had finally dared to enter the fort, and the Mexican leader busied himself haranguing the troops on their glorious victory. Having lost almost a third of their number in killed and wounded while taking the Alamo, the soldiers were not in a particularly vainglorious mood.

Lieutenant Colonel José Enrique de la Peña saw Castrillón's approach, noting in particular one man with him: "Among them was one of great stature, well proportioned, with regular features, in whose face there was the imprint of adversity, but in whom one also noticed a degree of resignation and nobility that did him honor. He was the naturalist David Crockett, well known in North America for his unusual adventures."

Santa Anna flew into a rage as Castrillón presented the prisoners. Turning to the troops nearest him, the sappers, he ordered the execution of the Texans. No officer or soldier moved. They had had enough of killing. Humiliated, Santa Anna ordered his staff officers and personal guard to carry out the murders. As Castrillón and de la Peña watched in horror, the officers used their sabers on the defenseless prisoners.

Castrillón stormed off to his tent and did not speak to Santa Anna. Not long after the captives were slain, Mrs. Dickinson was brought out of her hiding place in the church. "I recognized Col. Crockett lying dead and mutilated between the church and the two-story barrack building," she recalled years later, "and even remembered seeing his peculiar cap lying by his side."[24]

Crockett's body was then thrown into a funeral pyre with his fellow

Alamo defenders. From these ashes rose—phoenixlike—a legend and a battle cry.

Santa Anna later met with the handful of noncombatant survivors of the battle: Susanna Dickinson and her daughter and Ana Esparza and her four children, as well as Travis's slave Joe and a half dozen Hispanic women. Santa Anna gave Mrs. Esparza two silver dollars and a blanket. Young Enrique stared at the man responsible for his father's death: "He had a hard cruel look and his countenance was a very sinister one. It has haunted me ever since I last saw it and I will never forget the face or figure of Santa Anna."[25]

Despite the tally of six hundred dead or wounded, including twenty-six officers killed, Santa Anna was well pleased. "Much blood has been shed but the battle is over," he commented to staff officer Fernando Urriza. "It was but a small affair." Captain José Juan Sánchez-Navarro, adjutant to Cos, lamented that "with another victory like this one we may all end up in hell."[26]

Santa Anna tarried for a month in San Antonio, seeking the affections of a local beauty. In the meantime General José de Urrea's column overtook Colonel James Fannin's retreating force from Goliad and forced their surrender. When Urrea protested Santa Anna's order to execute the prisoners, he was sternly rebuked by his commander. On March 27, 1836, Fannin and 342 rebels were murdered by their Mexican captors. A handful escaped in the confusion of the mass slaughter to carry the tale of Santa Anna's perfidy to the world.

Santa Anna, finally in pursuit of the retreating rebel army with 700 men, soon outdistanced supporting columns under Vicente Filisola, Urrea, and General Antonio Gaona, burning Texas towns as he advanced. On April 20 he thought he had trapped Houston's eight-hundred-man force on the San Jacinto River near the coast. Reinforced on the morning of April 21 by Cos with 540 men, complacent and contemptuous of his foe, Santa Anna settled in for an afternoon siesta. He was surprised by Houston's ragtag force at 4:30 that afternoon. The initial battle was over in less than twenty minutes, although the pursuit of the routed Mexican army lasted several hours. While Santa Anna fled the field, over 600 of his men were killed and 500 more taken prisoner. Among the dead was the gallant Castrillón. The next day the general was captured and brought before the wounded Houston. In exchange for his life he agreed to order all Mexican troops out of Texas and to urge his government to recognize Texas independence. Houston then sent his prisoner east to Washington, where the defeated general met with President Andrew Jackson. In one of his final acts as president, Jackson recognized the new Republic of Texas. Sam Houston was elected as the republic's first president.

As Houston led his men forward on April 21, he had shouted, "Remember the Alamo!" and all down the advancing line they repeated the ringing battle cry. Soon it would be heard all across the nation.

Part III

THE MOUNTAINS

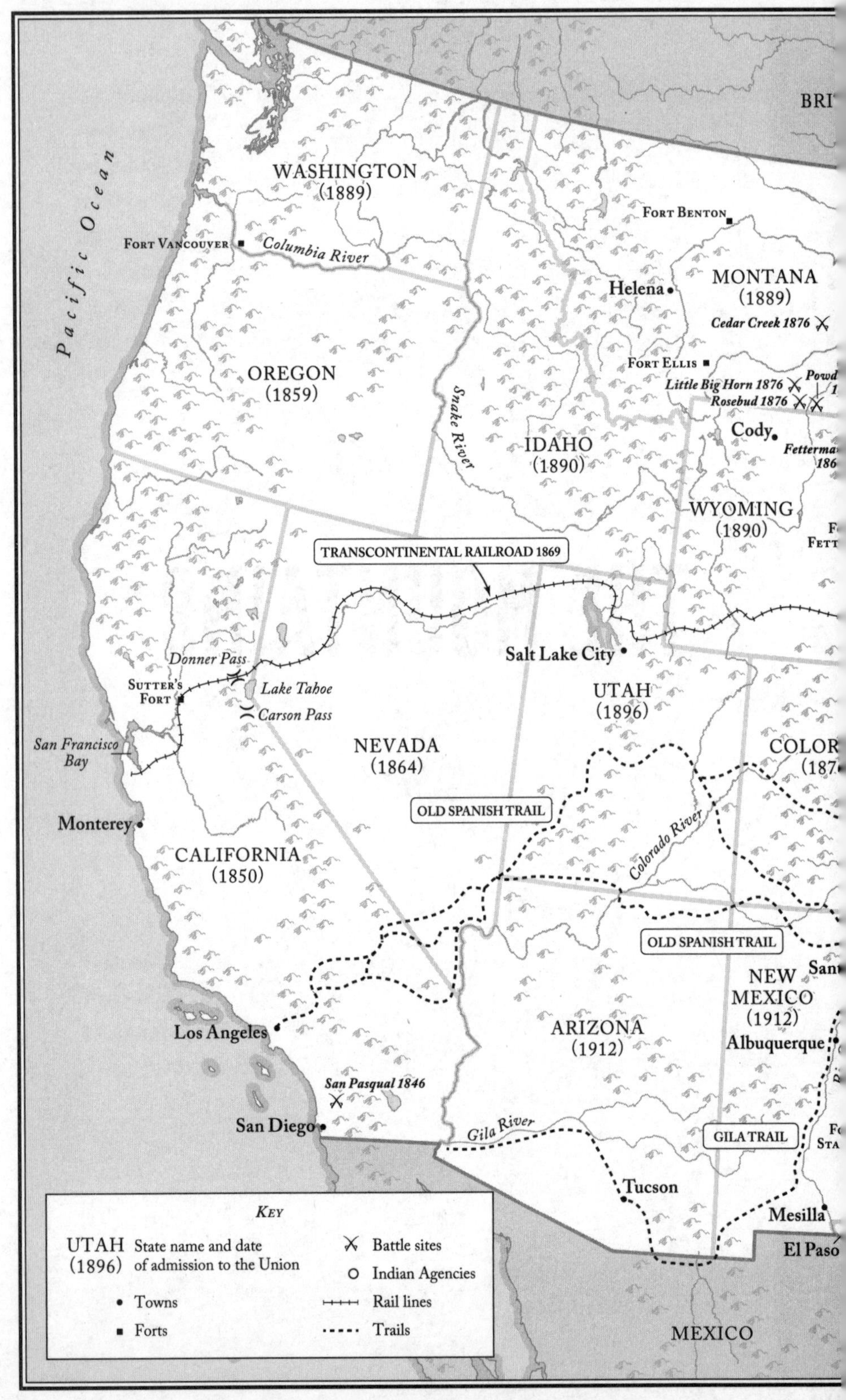

Pacific Ocean
WASHINGTON (1889)
FORT VANCOUVER
Columbia River
OREGON (1859)
Snake River
IDAHO (1890)
FORT BENTON
Helena
MONTANA (1889)
Cedar Creek 1876
FORT ELLIS
Little Big Horn 1876
Rosebud 1876
Cody
WYOMING (1890)
TRANSCONTINENTAL RAILROAD 1869
Donner Pass
SUTTER'S FORT
Lake Tahoe
Carson Pass
San Francisco Bay
Salt Lake City
UTAH (1896)
NEVADA (1864)
OLD SPANISH TRAIL
Colorado River
Monterey
CALIFORNIA (1850)
OLD SPANISH TRAIL
NEW MEXICO (1912)
Los Angeles
ARIZONA (1912)
Albuquerque
San Pasqual 1846
San Diego
Gila River
GILA TRAIL
Tucson
Mesilla
El Paso
MEXICO
KEY
UTAH (1896) State name and date of admission to the Union
Towns
Forts
Battle sites
Indian Agencies
Rail lines
Trails

GREAT PLAINS AND THE MOUNTAIN WEST
NORTH DAKOTA (1889)
SOUTH DAKOTA (1889)
NEBRASKA (1867)
KANSAS (1861)
OKLAHOMA (1907)
TEXAS (1845)
MINNESOTA (1858)
IOWA (1846)
MISSOURI (1821)
ARKANSAS (1836)
LOUISIANA (1812)
WISCONSIN (1848)
ILLINOIS (1818)
MICH. (1837)
INDIANA (1816)
KENTUCKY (1792)
TENNESSEE (1796)
MISSISSIPPI (1817)
ALA. (1819)
Lake Superior
Lake Michigan
Mississippi River
Missouri River
Platte River
Arkansas River
Red River
Sabine River
Fort Buford
Fort A. Lincoln
Fort Rice
Fort Yates
STANDING ROCK AGENCY
CHEYENNE RIVER AGENCY
Slim Buttes 1876
Fort Sully
Deadwood
War Bonnet Creek 1876
Wounded Knee 1890
PINE RIDGE AGENCY
ROSEBUD AGENCY
Fort Robinson
SPOTTED TAIL AGENCY
RED CLOUD AGENCY
North Platte
Fort McPherson
Fort Kearny
Summit Springs 1869
Beecher Island 1868
KANSAS PACIFIC RAILROAD
Fort Leavenworth
Fort Hays
Fort Riley
Hays City
Fort Harker
Kansas City
St. Louis
Fort Lyon
Fort Dodge
Bent's Fort
Fort Larned
Adobe Walls 1864
Washita 1868
Soldier Spring 1868
Fort Sill
0 Miles 500
0 Kilometers 500
© 2025 Jeffrey L. Ward

14

THE MOUNTAIN MEN

It was a large rodent that determined the destiny of the mountain men and much of the American West. The North American beaver, the second largest rodent in the world, was prized for its luxurious fur. Beaver pelts were particularly useful in the manufacture of malleable felts for hats of all types. The pelts were prized throughout Europe, with the industry centralized in Russia from the fifteenth century onward. The fine quality of these hats, and their expense, led to their identification with wealth. During the English Civil War the broad-brimmed beaver hat became symbolic of the royalist Cavalier faction, while in the Catholic Church it became the headgear of cardinals. By the late sixteenth century, however, European beavers had been trapped to near extinction.

The colonization of the New World opened up a fresh and cheaper supply of beaver pelts. This new market was controlled by the French and the British, who in time fought a series of wars in order to monopolize the fur trade. The triumphant British attempted to keep their American colonies hemmed in to the east of the Appalachian Mountains in order to better control this valuable trade, and this contributed to the outbreak of revolution in 1775.

An increased supply of high-quality beaver pelts from America, as well as the introduction of demi-castors (or half beaver mixed with wool or hare pelts) led to a drop in price. This cut in price led to market expansion throughout Europe and the colonies. The hats were now affordable to most consumers, and almost everyone needed a hat. Not only was the familiar top hat made, but also a wide variety of clerical and military headgear, including the naval cocked hat, the tricorne, and the army shako. Since this was an era of almost constant warfare, there was a huge market for military headgear. The English dominated this trade after 1750, and it was indeed big business.

The new American government looked to the western fur trade as a critical source for economic growth. When Thomas Jefferson sent Lewis and Clark westward in 1803, they were charged with ascertaining the potential of the fur trade beyond the Missouri River. John Colter, one of the members of that expedition, would soon become famous for his exploits as a new type of frontiersman: the mountain man.[1]

Christopher "Kit" Carson, who would emerge as the most famed of all the mountain men, was born on Christmas Eve 1809 in Madison County, Kentucky. Lindsey Carson, with his second wife, Rebecca Robinson Carson, moved his large family westward in 1811, following the trail of old Daniel Boone to Boone's Lick, in Howard County, Missouri. Lindsey was killed in an accident while clearing out trees in 1818, leaving a pregnant wife and thirteen children. Three years later Rebecca apprenticed young Kit to David Workman, in nearby Old Franklin. The boy was to learn the saddler's trade. Workman was a kind master, but the boy was unhappy with the labor and, as he later put it, "being anxious to travel for the purpose of seeing different countries, I concluded to join the first party for the Rocky Mts."[2]

Old Franklin was an outfitting center for wagon trains heading west over the Santa Fe Trail. In August 1826, young Carson joined the Santa Fe–bound caravan of William Wolfskill and Andrew Broadus. Workman placed a one-cent reward for the runaway in the October 6, 1826, *Missouri Intelligencer*: "Notice is hereby given to all persons, that Christopher Carson, a boy about 16 years old, small of his age, but thick-set; light hair, ran away from the subscriber, living in Franklin, Howard County, Missouri, to whom he had been bound to learn the saddler's trade. . . . All persons are notified not to harbor, support, or assist said boy under penalty of the law. One cent reward will be given to any person who will bring back the said boy." This would be Kit Carson's first appearance in a newspaper.[3]

THE NEGLECTED SPANISH PROVINCE OF NEW MEXICO, rich in silver, horses, and furs while starved for manufactured goods, became a magnet for enterprising Americans in the early 1800s. Watchful

Spanish troops turned back all interlopers who dared to cross the plains. Fur trappers brought back exaggerated tales of the wealth and beautiful senoritas to be found in the glittering capital city of Santa Fe, nestled in the foothills of the snowcapped Sangre de Cristo Mountains. While the senoritas were indeed lovely, the sunbaked, mud-brick town tended to disappoint most visitors.

In 1821, William Becknell of Franklin, Missouri, led a party of twenty frontiersmen to the Arkansas River in search of wild mustangs. At Raton Pass they encountered a party of New Mexico soldiers who informed them that Mexico had thrown off the Spanish yoke and now welcomed commerce with the Americanos. Becknell followed the soldiers to Santa Fe, where he traded his meager goods for substantial profits. In late January 1822, Becknell returned to Franklin loaded down with silver and anxious to return to Santa Fe. On May 22 he led twenty-one men and three wagons westward from Franklin. They did not follow the Arkansas to drop down through Raton Pass—soon to be known as the "Mountain Branch"—but cut south of the Arkansas on the "Cimarron Cutoff." When they reached Santa Fe after nearly a month's journey, it seemed as if all 3,000 inhabitants turned out to greet them. Enormous profits were again made—despite the corruption of the local politicos and customs officials—and even more importantly Becknell had proven that wagons could traverse the buffalo prairies to the New Mexico mountains. Even larger trade caravans were to follow. Becknell—"father of the Santa Fe Trail"—and those who followed him had pioneered a new road west into that unknown country that would soon become a pathway for conquest.[4]

Carson reached Santa Fe in November 1826 and immediately headed north to Taos, then the seat of the southwestern fur trade. The trappers preferred Taos to Santa Fe because it was more distant from the prying eyes of Mexican officials. He wintered there with Matthew Kinkead, a trapper who was also from Boone's Lick, and in the spring joined on as a teamster with an El Paso–bound wagon train. Upon his return to Taos, Kit met Ewing Young, who had come to Santa Fe with Becknell's expeditions and by 1828 was famed for his daring trapping forays throughout the Southwest. Young employed the boy as a cook but soon promoted him to trapper. It was from Young that Carson learned not only how to be a trapper but also the cruel reality of life on the far-flung edges of the frontier. In the spring of 1829 he accompanied Young and forty other trappers on a dangerous journey to trap beaver along the headwaters of the Gila River. This was Apache country, and the trappers had to dodge Mexican army patrols—fur trapping by Americans was illegal—as well as Indian scouts. The American trappers were notorious for selling powder and guns to the Apaches for safe passage, although Young declined to do so. Along the Salt River the trappers were attacked by a large band of Apaches but repulsed their foe. In this fight the nineteen-year-old boy killed his first man. As was the trappers' custom, Carson scalped the Apache.

Young's party pushed westward to trap along the Verde River, but they were continually harassed by various bands of Indians. In frustration Young sent a party of men back to Taos with the beaver pelts they had secured, while he headed to California with Carson and sixteen others in search of safer trapping country.

A difficult journey followed in which their passage was blocked by the Grand Canyon. They fortunately encountered a band of Mojaves who traded corn and beans with the trappers and guided them south to a crossing of the Colorado River. This was the same crossing of the river where the Mojaves had slaughtered most of Jedediah Smith's band of trappers two summers before. Young's party reached the Mission San Gabriel Arcángel (near present-day Los Angeles) and then turned north to trap the Central Valley of California before returning to Taos with 2,000 pounds of beaver pelts in April 1831. This was the first party of Americans to have crossed from the Rio Grande settlements to California and then back again, and in this epic journey young Kit Carson became a full-fledged member of that daring and eccentric breed that came to be called mountain men.[5]

In the autumn of 1831, Carson signed on with Thomas Fitzpatrick, head of the new Rocky Mountain Fur Company. Called "Broken Hand" by the Indians because of a gunshot wound to his left wrist, Fitzpatrick had immigrated to America from County Cavan, Ireland, in 1816 at age seventeen. He had gone up the Missouri in 1823 with William Henry Ashley's company—a band that included Jed Smith, Jim Bridger, Hugh Glass, William Sublette, and James Clyman. Some of these men were already on the Yellowstone with Ashley's partner, Major Andrew Henry. Fitzpatrick took part in a great battle with the Arikara that June on the Missouri, in which a dozen trappers were killed and as many more wounded.[6]

Many trappers pulled out of the trade after Ashley's fight, but Fitzpatrick—along with Jed Smith, William Sublette, James Clyman, Edward Rose, and six other bold adventurers—decided to bypass the river route and strike westward to find a pass across the mountains and open up a land route between St. Louis and the rich beaver country on the far side of the Continental Divide. They crossed the Black Hills and made for Absaroka, the land of the Crows. Rose, who was intimate with the Crows, went ahead to meet with his friends. While he was gone, Smith was horribly mauled by a grizzly bear along the Cheyenne River. His detached scalp and dangling right ear were stitched back on by Clyman. Fitzpatrick now went ahead with most of the men while two stayed behind to nurse Smith, and they trapped along the branches of the Powder River. The party, eventually rejoined by Smith, then wintered with the Crows just north of Wyoming's Wind River Valley.

The Crows told their guests that the beaver were so plentiful in the Green River to the south that they would not need traps but could club them. The trappers headed south in February to find this beaver Eden and, after an arduous journey, rediscovered South Pass. Others had been there before—most notably the eastbound Astorians led by Robert Stuart in 1812—but it was the Smith-Fitzpatrick party that put South Pass on the map. In time it became the key point on the great road of western empire. They trapped with great success, and while Smith and some of the men remained in the mountains, Fitzpatrick carried their beaver pelts back to Fort Atkinson on the Missouri in what is now Nebraska and reported the discovery of South Pass to Ashley.

Fitzpatrick now led Ashley and a large party of trappers back into the mountains. Ashley divided the trappers into smaller parties and marked a spot along the present Utah-Wyoming border (at the mouth of Henry's Fork of the Green River) where they would all meet at the end of their hunts. The result was the first great mountain man rendezvous, held on the Green River in July 1825. Some 120 men attended this first of sixteen such mountain fairs. Most were Ashley-Henry trappers like Fitzpatrick, Clyman, and Smith, but twenty Hudson's Bay Company deserters joined in, as did a band of trappers up from Taos under Étienne Provost. Ashley hauled in 9,000 pounds of beaver pelts, worth $50,000 in St. Louis (over a million dollars in today's money). Beaver skins traded for around $5.00 each, but trade coffee or sugar was $2.00 a pint, gunpowder was $2.00 a pint and lead $1.00 a bar, tobacco was $2.00 per pound, a good knife was $2.50, while a common blanket was $20.00. Whiskey was not plentiful at this first rendezvous, but that would change.

After the 1826 rendezvous, held in Cache Valley, in present-day Utah, Ashley sold out to Smith, Sublette, and David Jackson. Smith then led expeditions southwest from Utah into California, where he trapped north up the San Joaquin to the American River and then east across the Sierras to reach the 1827 rendezvous at Bear Lake, in Utah. His remarkable expeditions made the teetotaling, Bible-reading Smith a legend in the mountains. In 1830, Smith sold out to Fitzpatrick, Bridger, and three others, who now formed the Rocky Mountain Fur Company. It was with this outfit that young Kit Carson signed on in 1831.

After purchasing the fur company, Fitzpatrick traveled to Missouri for the first time since 1823. Much had changed, including the construction of Fort Leavenworth in 1827 and the rapid growth of Independence, Missouri, which had become the jumping-off point for expeditions to the West. Fitzpatrick met with his old friends Smith, Jackson, and Sublette, who agreed to sell him the trade goods he needed for his men in the mountains. He joined their twenty-three-wagon caravan to Santa Fe. Despite their long experience in the mountains, the leaders of the wagon train were unfamiliar with the dangers on the Santa Fe Trail. Smith, who had decided to quit the mountains after so many narrow escapes, was killed by Comanches on the Cimarron that May while scouting ahead of the wagon train in search of water. The wagons reached Santa Fe on July 4.[7]

Late in July 1831, Fitzpatrick and some forty men, including young Carson, headed north up the front range to the North Platte and then westward toward the Green River Rendezvous. Fitzpatrick soon returned to St. Louis, but Carson and the others trapped the Green and then wintered in Idaho near the headwaters of the Salmon River. With the thaw, Carson and a handful of companions moved east to trap the central Colorado streams, where they had several sharp engagements with the Native people, endured considerable privation and hardship, but still returned to Taos in October 1833 laden down with fur.

Trapping was, needless to say, hard and dangerous work. Carson's friend Joe Meek left a clear account of the techniques employed by the trappers: "[The trapper] has an ordinary steel trap weighing five pounds, attached to a chain five feet long, with a swivel and ring at the end, which plays round what is called the *float*, a dry stick of wood, about six feet long. The trapper wades out into the stream, which is shallow, and cuts with his knife a bed for the trap, five or six inches under water. He then takes the float out the whole length of the chain in the direction of the centre of the stream, and drives it into the mud, so fast that the beaver cannot draw it out; at the same time tying the other end by a thong to the bank. A small stick or twig, dipped in musk or castor, serves for bait, and is placed so as to hang directly above the trap, which is now set. The trapper then throws water plentifully over the adjacent bank to conceal any foot prints or scent by which the beaver would be alarmed, and going to some distance wades out of the stream."[8]

The animal was generally skinned immediately after removal from the trap. (If the trap worked properly, it had drowned). The meat was discarded and only the pelt and castor glands (for future bait) were harvested. The tail was often kept, for beaver tail was considered a delicacy in the mountains. The discarded carcasses were quickly consumed by wolves, bears, bobcats, and eagles, all natural predators of the industrious but ill-fated rodents.

The mountains were becoming crowded. In the far northwest the British Hudson's Bay Company ruled, and their trappers pushed south into the central Rockies with the goal of trapping out the beaver and keeping the Americans from coming north. Empire was at stake as well as money. The Americans had no such monopoly, for rival free trappers competed with the men of Fitzpatrick's Rocky Mountain Fur Company and John Jacob Astor's older American Fur Company for furs in the mountains and from the river Indians. In this reckless enterprise the beaver population was soon destroyed, as was the self-sufficiency of the Native peoples. The diseases inadvertently introduced by the trappers also decimated the Indian population, especially among the river tribes. Astor, who operated several important fur-trading posts on the western rivers in competition with the St. Louis trappers, came to dominate the trade. He made a fortune but wisely left the business in 1834 just before its rapid decline.

To Kit Carson, these youthful years as a mountain man were remembered as the happiest days of his life. In March 1834 he rejoined Fitzpatrick and Bridger in northwestern Colorado and, although a free trapper, agreed to work with the Rocky Mountain Fur Company. While out hunting alone late one afternoon, Carson shot an elk but was almost immediately confronted by two grizzly bears that seemed to desire a two-course dinner of both hunter and elk. Carson, with no time to reload, ran for his life and climbed a nearby tree. The bears could not climb the tree but one remained awhile to study Carson. "He finally concluded to leave," Carson recalled, "of which I was heartily pleased, never having been so scared in my life."[9]

Bears might well have been Carson's most terrifying foe that trapping season, but the Blackfeet also made life miserable for the trappers. In February 1835, Carson was shot through the shoulder in a fight with the Blackfeet along Idaho's Snake River. He recovered well enough to join Bridger in the spring hunt before heading to the Green River Rendezvous. This spring hunt (the trappers also did a fall hunt) was quite successful, although it was damaging to the future of the mountain men because it depleted the beaver population by killing the mothers before they could nurture their kits (baby beavers who remained in the lodge for the first month of life).

The August 1835 Green River Rendezvous was to be one of the last of the great mountain man gatherings. It proved, however, to also be one of the most notable. Lucien Fontenelle had departed from Bellevue, in present-day Nebraska, in late June with six wagons, over fifty men, and nearly two hundred horses, meeting up with Fitzpatrick at Fort William on the Laramie River (the future Fort Laramie) on July 26. He had with him two missionaries—Dr. Marcus Whitman and Reverend Samuel Parker—bound for the Oregon Country. The trade goods were transferred to pack mules for the journey to the rendezvous and, under the command of Fitzpatrick, the party set out on August 1, reaching the Green River eleven days later.

Over two hundred mountain men came in, along with several large bands of Arapahos, Shoshones, Nez Perces, Flatheads, and Utes. All attention was quickly riveted on Dr. Whitman, who with great surgical skill removed a three-inch iron arrow point from Jim Bridger's back. The Blackfoot barb had been lodged in Bridger for three years. Whitman, the hero of the hour, was now much sought after by many an ailing trapper in the camp.

Reverend Parker was delighted to find so many potential Indian converts at the rendezvous, but he had no hope for the white heathens he found there: "They appear to have sought for a place where, as they would say, human nature is not oppressed by the tyranny of religion, and pleasure is not awed by the frown of virtue." He recognized their skill at trapping, sin, and blasphemy. The latter impressed him with its inventiveness: "They disdain common-place phrases which prevail among the impious vulgar in civilized countries and have many set phrases, which they appear to have manufactured among themselves, which they have committed to memory, and which, in their imprecations, they bring into almost every sentence and on all occasions. By varying the tones of their voices, they make them expressive of joy, hope, grief, and anger."[10]

The good reverend was soon treated to a dramatic display of mountain man anger. A great crowd gathered to wager on and watch a duel between two of the mountain men. "A hunter, who goes technically by the name of the great bully of the mountains, mounted his horse with a loaded rifle, and challenged any Frenchman, American, Spaniard, or Dutchman, to fight him in single combat," he later wrote. "Kit Carson, an American, told him if he wished to die, he would accept the challenge. Shunar [*sic*] defied him—C. mounted his horse, and with a loaded pistol rushed into close contact, and both almost at the same instant fired." Carson, who was slightly wounded above the ear, put a ball through his opponent's wrist that went up his arm before exiting. Joseph Chouinard, the wounded French trapper, who worked for Astor's company, then begged Carson for his life. Parker did not know that Carson and Chouinard had previously quarreled in the Arapaho camp over the affections of an Arapaho girl, Waa-nibe, or Singing Grass, and that she was the cause of the duel. In good time Carson asked her father for the girl's hand, paid a substantial bride price, and took her away into the mountains.[11]

With the rendezvous winding down and most of the Indian bands departing, Fitzpatrick headed back to Fort William with 120 beaver packs and 80 bundles of buffalo robes. He was accompanied by over eighty men—the beaver were playing out and many trappers were quitting the business—as well as Dr. Whitman, who was returning east to recruit more missionaries. Reverend Parker continued on to Oregon in company with Bridger, who soon headed to Jackson Hole with his men to trap while Flathead and Nez Perce Indians conducted the missionary westward. Parker explored the Oregon Country and met with several Indian bands before returning to the East Coast by sailing ship via Hawaii and Cape Horn. His memoir of his adventures—*Journal of an Exploring Tour Beyond the Rocky Mountains*—published in New York in 1838, contained his account of Carson's duel with Chouinard. It would be Carson's first appearance in a book but hardly the last.

By mid-September 1835, Carson was trapping with Bridger along the Yellowstone and Big Horn Rivers on the fall hunt. For a while he even worked briefly for the Hudson's Bay Company. The Blackfeet were out in force and the trappers found themselves constantly harassed until a smallpox epidemic in the spring of 1837 reduced the once mighty tribe by two-thirds. The Mandans were almost completely wiped out. Astor's men had inadvertently carried the pestilence up the Missouri River.

Waa-nibe soon bore Carson a daughter, whom they named Adaline, and they decided to quit Blackfoot country and go south to Fort Davy Crockett in Brown's Hole of what is now northwestern Colorado. Many of the mountain man marriages with Indian women were unions of economic convenience, but Carson and Waa-nibe were a real love match. Many years later Carson would attempt to explain their devotion to each other to his navy friend Edward Beale in simple mountain man terms. "She was a good woman," he explained. "I never came in from hunting but she had warm water for my feet."[12]

She bore Carson another child in 1840 but became ill with fever and soon died from the complications of childbirth. A devastated Carson, with two small children to care for, decided to leave the mountains. "Beaver was getting scarce, and, finding it was necessary to try our hand at something else, [I and other trappers] concluded to start for Bent's Fort on the Arkansas," he later declared.[13]

Bent's Fort, which stood near the confluence of the Arkansas and Purgatoire Rivers, had been completed in 1833 by the Bent brothers, Charles and William, and their urbane partner Ceran St. Vrain. The fort was substantial, with thick adobe walls fifteen feet high that enclosed a courtyard 100 by 180 feet. Circular bastions some 30 feet tall guarded the array of trading rooms, warehouses, and quarters. There was even an icehouse to service the bar and billiard room on the second story. It came to rank in importance with the northern fur trade posts—Forts Union, Laramie, and Hall—and in a short time dominated the expanding buffalo robe trade on the southern plains as well as proving to be an important way station on the Mountain Branch of the Santa Fe Trail.[14]

Carson was warmly greeted at the trading post in 1841 and was offered employment as a contract hunter by St. Vrain and the Bent brothers at a dollar a day. The buffalo robe trade was quickly supplanting the beaver trade as the moneymaker. In Europe the silk hat had come into favor, while the beaver hat fell out of fashion. The beaver had been all but wiped out by the trappers by 1840 anyway.

"Come, we are done with this life in the mountains—done with wading in beaver dams, and freezing or starving alternately—done with Indian trading and Indian fighting," said old mountain man Robert Newell to Joe Meek. "The fur trade is dead in the Rocky Mountains, and it is no place for us now, if ever it was."[15]

And so, one by one, the trappers quit the mountains. The great era of the mountain man had come to an end. Later writers would turn Carson into the king of the mountain men, but that was false, for he was never a leader among them. He came to the mountains late, and men like Young, Smith, Fitzpatrick, Sublette, and Bridger were the true leaders of that rare breed. Backing them, of course, were the men with the money: Astor, Ashley, Pierre Chouteau, and the Hudson's Bay Company. All of them contributed to a bold enterprise that had blazed a trail across the wilderness that would in time give rise to a continental nation.

At Bent's Fort, Carson looked about for a new wife to tend to his two infant daughters. He found his bride among the Cheyennes camped near the trading post. His time with Making Out Road proved to be brief, for she soon divorced him Cheyenne-style by tossing all his property outside their tepee. Not long afterward Carson's youngest daughter was killed in a horrible accident when the toddler was scalded to death by falling into a pot of boiling water. Determined to make a better life for his surviving child, he took young Adaline to St. Louis in April 1842 to be educated in a Catholic school. After visiting relatives, he decided to board a steamer heading up the Missouri, where by chance he encountered a young army lieutenant of the army topographical corps by the name of John Charles Frémont.[16]

15

THE OREGON TRAIL

Lieutenant John Charles Frémont was looking for a guide for an expedition to travel the Oregon Trail to map and examine South Pass and the Rocky Mountains to the Wind River. His goal was to encourage emigration to the Oregon Country—jointly occupied by the United States and Great Britain—by American settlers. The mountain men had discovered South Pass and laid out a rudimentary trail, but Frémont's plan was to create a much-needed guide to the wagon route.

"On the boat I met Kit Carson," Frémont later wrote. "I was pleased with him and his manner of address at this first meeting. He was a man of medium height, broad-shouldered and deep-chested, with a clear steady blue eye and frank speech and address; quiet and unassuming."[1]

"I informed him that I had been some time in the mountains and thought I could guide him to any point he would wish to go," Carson declared. "His object was to survey the south Pass and take the height of the highest peaks of the Rocky Mountains."[2]

Thus began a grand collaboration between these two men that would change forever their own lives as well as dramatically alter the destiny of the American West. Frémont, handsome, impetuous, and charming, cut a striking figure. He possessed a somewhat volatile temper, which he usually kept in check, and a soaring ambition that far outstripped his grasp. He was most fortunate in his marriage to the beautiful and talented Jessie Benton Frémont, daughter of the powerful Missouri senator Thomas Hart Benton (who in his youth had violently feuded with Andrew Jackson). She proved to be a skilled writer, astute politician, and tireless promoter of her husband. She was in many ways his strongest asset.

Frémont, born under a cloud of scandal on January 21, 1813, in Savannah, Georgia, managed to live down his illegitimate birth and acquire a decent education through the kindness of men who recognized his early potential. His most important patron proved to be Joel Poinsett, the South Carolina congressman who served as the first United States minister to the new Republic of Mexico. In March of 1837, Poinsett was named secretary of war and in 1839 he secured young Frémont an appointment as second lieutenant in the army Bureau of Topographical Engineers. One of his earliest assignments as a civilian employee before his commissioning was to assist with a survey of Cherokee lands in anticipation of the removal of that tribe to the Indian Territory. Frémont then served an invaluable apprenticeship under the renowned French scientist Joseph Nicollet in his exploration of the lands between the Upper Mississippi and Missouri Rivers. In two expeditions with Nicollet, Frémont learned to draw careful sketch maps, observe botany and the condition of the soil, and make accurate astronomical observations. Nicollet also opened doors into St. Louis and Washington society for his assistant. Frémont was now moving in rarified social circles.[3]

Among those Frémont met in Washington was the senior senator from Missouri, Thomas Hart Benton. They shared a fascination with the western frontier and Frémont quickly became a disciple of Benton's vision of the nation's continental destiny. The young officer soon found himself a frequent dinner guest in the elegant Benton home. Upon first meeting the senator's vivacious fifteen-year-old daughter, the lieutenant was smitten. The feeling was mutual, much to the discomfort of the senator and his wife. As the couple drew closer, the alarm of the parents, despite their admiration for Frémont, grew stronger. The senator cautioned the young lovers; they ignored him and soon eloped. They were married on October 19, 1841, by a Catholic priest (which led to reports that the groom was a secret Catholic during his 1856 presidential campaign). "All Washington was horror struck," the seventeen-year-old bride noted with glee.[4]

Benton fumed for a few months but could not long be estranged from his favorite child. At a family dinner on January 1, 1842, he announced to the young couple that he had secured for John Charles the position as head of an expedition to explore the Rocky Mountains and map the Oregon Trail. As head of the Senate Committee on Military Affairs, the senator had enormous influence. Texas may well have been wrested from Mexico by

Sam Houston, but the great prize of Oregon was still in question. The way to this great prize must be mapped.

By the first week of June 1842, Frémont had all the preparations ready for the departure of his expedition to South Pass, the storied gateway to the far West. He had brought with him to St. Louis a cranky but able German cartographer named Charles Preuss as well as Jessie's younger brother, Randolph, and his cousin Henry Brant. With the good advice of Pierre Chouteau and other fur trade contacts, he had put together an impressive twenty-six-man crew that included Lucien Maxwell as hunter; Basil Lajeunesse and Auguste Janisse, the only Black member of the crew, as voyageurs; Jean Baptiste Dumes as cook; and Kit Carson as guide.

Frémont's party departed Chouteau's Landing at the mouth of the Kansas River and traveled north following the already well-rutted emigrant trail along the Platte River, making a strong twenty to twenty-five miles a day. The travel was relatively easy, and Carson kept the camp well supplied with venison, although the German Preuss constantly complained about the food prepared by the French cook Dumes. They had been warned of hostile Pawnees and one morning young Brant galloped up to the head of the column in a panic, shouting "Indians!" Carson hurried off in the direction Brant was pointing, only to discover a small herd of elk. There would be fresh meat for supper as well as a bevy of jokes at the expense of the nineteen-year-old boy.

By June 27 they reached Grand Island (in present-day Nebraska), which split the Platte into two channels. They followed the north fork into buffalo country, where they had their first hunt and downed several of the shaggy beasts. Not long afterward they were met by a small party of trappers led by Carson's old friend Jim Bridger. Around the campfire that night, over a feast of buffalo hump roast, the two boys sat in rapt attention as Bridger and Carson swapped tall tales and talked of the good old days in the mountains before the beaver played out. Bridger had gone up the Missouri River with Ashley and Henry in 1822 when not much older than Randolph Benton. He had lived a life of wild adventure that showed plainly in his craggy face. He now frowned and warned Carson that the Sioux beyond Fort Laramie were in a foul mood and spoiling for a fight; he had already tangled with them and was lucky to have kept his scalp. The men were nervous but pressed on to the safety of Fort Laramie, which Frémont reached on July 15.

The formidable fort, owned by the American Fur Company, had been built in 1834. Various bands of Indians camped outside its whitewashed wooden walls. Frémont, who, along with Maxwell, had been away from the main column for ten days in order to explore the South Platte and visit St. Vrain's small trading post on the river to see if it might be useful as a future military post, now found many of his men uneasy about continuing on. Rumors of Sioux hostility at the fort had confirmed the story told by "Old Gabe" Bridger. On July 19, Frémont gathered the party and offered to release any man who did not wish to go forward. To his great relief, only one man took his offer. To be safe, he decided to leave the boys Henry Brant and Randolph Benton at Fort Laramie.

On July 21, the expedition departed Fort Laramie for South Pass. Frémont had met with several Sioux chiefs at the fort who warned him of possible trouble ahead and provided him with a young warrior as guide. They also traded him a large tepee, which proved much stouter and more mosquito resistant than the thin army tents. Told that a drought had left the trail to South Pass barren of grass and thus buffalo, they warned Frémont that his party might well starve.

"We'll eat the mules," declared Frémont's favorite among the voyageurs, Basil Lajeunesse.[5]

Carson now led them up the Sweetwater to South Pass without incident. The broad pass sprawled across a relatively flat plain bounded by low hills on both sides. "The ascent had been so gradual that, with all the intimate knowledge possessed by Carson, who had made this country his home for seventeen years, we were obliged to watch very closely to find the place at which we had reached the culminating point," Frémont would shrewdly write in his report. He wanted to make it clear to future readers just how accessible South Pass would prove for emigrant wagon trains.[6]

From South Pass, which they had reached on August 8, Frémont pushed on up the Green River Valley to the towering Wind River Range. His orders from Colonel John Abert had called for him to map the Oregon Trail to South Pass and return. Frémont now established a pattern by which he treated orders as mere suggestions. From a campsite at Boulder Lake in western Wyoming, Frémont, with Preuss and a small party, set out in search of the highest peak in the nearby mountain range. Through rough, jagged terrain, and suffering from altitude sickness, the young officer ascended a

13,500-foot mountain that he presumed to be the highest in the Rocky Mountain chain (he was wrong) and planted a special flag of thirteen stripes and twenty-six stars with an image of an eagle clutching both arrows and a peace pipe. It was August 15, 1843.

He naturally named the mountain Frémont Peak and from it he could survey the vast western empire: the snowcapped Grand Tetons to the northwest, and to the northeast the spectacular Wind River Range. It was to the west that Frémont fixed his gaze. A restless romantic, he saw his future—and that of the nation—in that "undiscovered country."

They returned to Fort Laramie on the last day of August after a difficult journey that had seen the loss of much of their scientific equipment and notes in the Platte River. Carson soon left the party and headed south to Taos, where he had been courting the fifteen-year-old beauty Josefa Jaramillo. The hundred dollars a month pay he had received from Frémont might well place him in a better position to overcome the objections to his suit from her parents.

Frémont's party retraced their steps across the prairie to the confluence of the Platte and Missouri, where they acquired a Mackinaw boat for the journey down the Missouri to Chouteau's Landing. They passed it on October 10, four months and 2,000 miles since departing, and followed the Mississippi back to St. Louis, which they reached seven days later.

Frémont hurried on to Washington, arriving on October 29, just in time for the birth of his and Jessie's first child, a girl they named Elizabeth after her mother but always called Lily. John gallantly brought his bedridden wife the expedition flag.

"Spreading over me a wind-whipt flag," Jessie remembered, "he said, 'This flag was raised on the summit peak of the highest point of the Rocky Mountains. I brought it to you.'"

Frémont set to work on his report, but the bold explorer soon retreated before the looming blank page, only to receive a welcome reinforcement from Jessie. He dictated and she wrote and often rewrote his narrative statements. It was a perfect collaboration. The end result was a compelling work of literature as well as an excellent travel guide for the Oregon Trail through South Pass. One nimble touch that may or may not have really happened was the appearance of a solitary bumblebee that came "winging his flight from the eastern valley and lit on the knee of one of the men" just after Frémont had returned from raising his flag over the lofty peak looming above them.

"It was a strange place, the icy rock and the highest peak of the Rocky Mountains, for a lover of warm sunshine and flowers," either Frémont or Jessie wrote in the report, "and we pleased ourselves with the idea that he was the first of his species to cross the mountain barrier—a solitary pioneer to foretell the advance of civilization."

As metaphor builds on metaphor, Frémont then relates how "we carried out the law of this country, where all animated nature seems at war," and killed the poor creature—this "herald of civilization"—and pressed him in a book. Thus did exploration and destruction work hand in hand.[7]

The report, presented to Colonel Abert on March 1, 1843, was a triumph. It was promptly printed as Senate Document number 243 by the 27th Congress, 3rd Session, but such was the demand that a thousand additional copies were distributed. Frémont's part consisted of but 76 pages, with the rest of the 215 pages consisting of Preuss's careful charts and a catalog of geologic animal and plant specimens, weather records, and other scientific data. The attached map was of great interest to those heading west. The report, with its romantic view of the West, helped to intensify a growing spirit in the land for expansion.

"The Oregon fever is raging in almost every part of the Union," editorialized the May 6, 1843, issue of *Niles' National Register*. "It would be reasonable to suppose that there will be at least five thousand Americans west of the Rocky Mountains by next autumn."

The "Oregon Fever," as they called it, proved highly contagious all across the Mississippi River Valley in the early 1840s. Why would thousands of people leave snug little farms in fertile midwestern lands to endure a 2,000-mile, six-month journey to distant Oregon? There were expelling as well as compelling factors, of course: a dream of greater and better land, a healthier climate, financial or romantic problems at home, disgust with politics and especially the rising slavery question, legal problems, or a simple desire to reinvent oneself in a new land. And certainly there was the romance of the frontier—of "Westering"—that had dominated American society since Jamestown and Plymouth Rock.

Those who traveled the Oregon Trail were different from the overland emigrants who flocked to California after the discovery of gold. They were for the most part sturdy pioneer families holding fast to the dream of a better life in the Far West. They came with a vision of long-term settlement for themselves and their children, not a quick buck in the goldfields. Some, of course, came for adventure, for they had been raised on the romanticized tales of Daniel Boone and Davy Crockett and Cooper's fictional Leatherstocking Tales. They even coined a phrase for it—"seeing the Elephant"—although its origins remain obscure.

Small parties pioneered the trail at first, and the reports they sent home along with the reports of missionaries like Dr. Marcus Whitman encouraged others. In the spring of 1843, the first truly great migration began—encouraged no doubt by Frémont's report—when nearly a thousand people converged on Independence, Missouri, to join Peter Burnett's Oregon-bound wagon train. The march divided into two columns of sixty wagons each, with over 5,000 head of oxen, horses, and cattle. (The Oregon emigrants used oxen to pull their wagons, while those headed to California after 1848 wanted faster horses.) Many thought the migration sheer lunacy, but its ultimate success convinced the naysayers, and in 1845 there was a migration of over 5,000 in a series of caravans. This doubled the American population in Oregon, with most of the settlers going to the lush Willamette Valley to the south of the Columbia River.

It was not inexpensive to make the journey, for it cost around $1,500 for a wagon for a typical pioneer family. In time the trail was littered with the debris of the migration—furniture, plows, trunks, stoves—along with the bones of dead oxen and horses and the graves of fallen emigrants. Merchants in Independence even organized scavenger parties to go out on the trail and collect salvageable goods for resale. While Indians were a threat to stock, they really were more of an annoyance than a real threat to large parties. The Native peoples watched in dismay as thousands passed across the open prairie, killing off the buffalo and eating up all the grass. Prairie fires, sudden storms, insects that tormented the stock, accidents, and especially the dreaded cholera took a frightful toll.

The wagon trains followed the south bank of the Platte River through what is now Nebraska and southeastern Wyoming to Fort Laramie (purchased by the government from the American Fur Company in 1849 for $4,000) to South Pass and over the Continental Divide to the Snake River and along it to Fort Boise and from there overland to the Columbia and

Oregon. In 1847, Brigham Young established the north bank of the Platte River as the "Mormon Trail" for his people as they fled westward to the Salt Lake Valley in hopes of avoiding further persecution. Nearly 13,000 Saints (the Mormon Church is the Church of Jesus Christ of Latter-day Saints) followed the forty-three-year-old Young's pioneer band, and they were in time followed by many thousands more Scandinavian, German, and British converts. Many of these European immigrants pulled their meager possessions along in handcarts. This was an orderly and highly disciplined migration as the Mormons moved out in small caravans to conserve grass and water on the trail. Improvements were made on the trail, especially at the difficult mountain crossing into the Salt Lake Valley, and a church fund was established to assist the new converts in their migration. The Mormon Trail would be in use for twenty years until the railroad reached Utah Territory.

Over 300,000 pioneers would travel across the prairies and mountains on the Oregon Trail and its branches, the California and Mormon Trails, before the coming of the transcontinental railroad in 1869. This was a massive human migration for a nation of but 25 million people. The pioneers who dared to make that difficult journey to the Pacific Northwest assured the peaceful transfer of that valuable region to the United States.[8]

Benton already had a far more ambitious second expedition in the works for his son-in-law. This time Frémont was to go in search of another route westward south of Wyoming as well as explore south of the Columbia River all the country between California and the Rocky Mountains. Abert's March 10, 1843, orders instructed Lieutenant Frémont to make "a Circuit" that should "embrace within its limits the heads of the Colorado, the Columbia, some of the heads of the Missouri proper, the Yellowstone and the Platte." This was to tie neatly with naval officer Charles Wilkes's 1841 reconnaissance from the Oregon coast to the fur-trading post Fort Walla Walla.

Frémont immediately began his preparations. In St. Louis he recruited several men—including Basil Lajeunesse and Lucien Maxwell—from his first expedition. From the East he had brought back mapmaker Charles Preuss as well as eighteen-year-old Jacob Dodson, a free African American who was a servant in the Benton household and who was to be his personal assistant. Dodson was paid the same as the white men, a novelty at the time. Another eighteen-year-old Frémont hired was Theodore Talbot, the son of a former senator from Kentucky, anxious for adventure and military training. He also hired mountain man Tom Fitzpatrick as a guide at a salary of $1,750.

Frémont requested four pistols, thirty-three carbines, and five kegs of gunpowder, as well as a mountain howitzer and five hundred pounds of artillery ammunition from Jefferson Barracks. Colonel Stephen Watts Kearny approved the order but the ordnance officer, Captain James Bell, was suspicious of Frémont's motives. He promptly wrote army headquarters in Washington to inquire just what a peaceful exploring expedition might need with artillery. Abert, equally puzzled, considered recalling Frémont, but Jessie intercepted his letter and promptly sent a messenger to her husband to depart immediately before he could be recalled.

On May 30, 1843, Frémont hurriedly led his party westward, mingling with several emigrant parties heading for Oregon. Young Talbot was enthralled with what he referred to as Colonel Crockett's "Go Ahead" spirit inspiring "those hardy pioneers of the march of civilization, whose every delight would seem to be in the hardships and privations which encompass the early settler of the western wilds."[9]

The expedition left the main Oregon Trail, which Frémont had surveyed on his previous expedition, and pushed west across present Kansas to St. Vrain's Fort on the South Platte. Frémont reached the little outpost on July 4 and bought supplies and hoped to purchase fresh horses and mules from St. Vrain. He was disappointed in this, for stock was low. Marcellin St. Vrain, the post bourgeois (head trader), told Frémont that a large herd of fresh mules had recently arrived in Taos, so Maxwell was sent south to obtain a dozen of these animals. Frémont then pushed to the southwest with fifteen men to search for a southern version of South Pass. In this he would be frustrated, for no such pass existed. Turning back eastward, they reached the new settlement of Pueblo, Colorado, on July 14. The famous Black mountain man Jim Beckwourth had founded the village the year before. At Pueblo, Frémont was greeted by Kit Carson, who had learned from Maxwell about the expedition. Frémont immediately offered Carson a position as guide and hunter at a hundred dollars a month. He then promptly sent him off to Bent's Fort for supplies and mules.

Frémont returned to St. Vrain's Fort to rejoin Fitzpatrick and the main party. Carson soon joined them with ten mules and some additional supplies. Maxwell never returned, for he was forced to remain in New Mexico to look after his family as a result of a crisis caused by an invasion of Texas freebooters; Frémont replaced him with Alexis Godey, a remarkable young French Canadian. In time Godey would impress Frémont as almost an equal to Carson.

Frémont again divided his party, sending Fitzpatrick with most of the men north to follow the Oregon Trail to Fort Laramie and South Pass. He would proceed west with Carson and a dozen men, including Preuss, Lajeunesse, and Dodson, to continue the search for another pass through the mountains. They were to reunite at the Hudson's Bay Company fur trade post of Fort Hall on the Snake River, in present-day Idaho.

Carson led them over the Continental Divide to the Bear River. Frémont sent Carson on to Fort Hall to purchase supplies while he and the rest of the party moved south to follow the Bear River to the Great Salt Lake. Not far from the Promontory Mountains, where in 1869 the famed meeting of the rails completing the transcontinental railroad would take place, they were rejoined by Carson with supplies from Fort Hall. A few days later they reached the Great Salt Lake. "We wander around Salt Lake like children around hot porridge," grumbled Preuss. "Uncertain whether we shall reach it at all."[10]

Frémont's brief exploration of the lake and the surrounding landscape as related in his published report would have a profound effect on future settlement. Brigham Young's decision to bring his Latter-day Saint (Mormon) people to the valley of the Great Salt Lake was heavily influenced by Frémont's positive report on the availability of perpetual water from the Bear River as well as mountain streams and "good soil and good grass, adapted to civilized settlements." Mormon legend recounts that upon first viewing the Great Salt Lake Valley from the Wasatch Mountains in July 1847, Young declared, "This is the place." Many of his companions were dismayed by the inhospitable desert landscape they saw before them—"the paradise of the lizard, the cricket and the rattlesnake"—and recalled Jim Bridger's offer of a thousand dollars for the first bushel of corn grown in that arid land. That first migration saw 1,800 Mormons settled along the shores of the Great Salt Lake, and within a dozen years that population would swell to over 40,000. Through cooperative irrigation farming and construction efforts overseen by Brigham Young and his theocratic government, the Mormons indeed made the desert blossom in a remarkably short time. Old Bridger lost his bet, for in 1850 alone over 100,000 bushels of wheat were harvested by the Mormon settlers.[11]

After his exploration of the northern end of the Great Salt Lake, Frémont turned north for Fort Hall, which his party reached on September 18. Eleven of the men were now discharged to return to the states, and they carried letters back home for Frémont, Preuss, and Talbot. Frémont purchased a few horses and oxen from the British factor at Fort Hall and promptly pushed westward on September 22, to follow the Snake River to Fort Walla Walla on the Columbia.

Their journey proved uneventful, although the perpetually unhappy German complained that he was forced to sleep in the open air outside the command tent because of Dodson's infernal snoring. Preuss, whose appetite was prodigious, was comforted by the salmon they purchased from the river tribes.

"These miserable Indians are a happy, harmless people," he jotted in his diary at Salmon Falls on October 2. "Here, too, only wealth makes them insolent and arrogant, as it does the Sioux with their long buffalo skins, their nice lodges, etc. . . . Below the falls the fish rise in such multitudes that the Indians can pierce them with their spears without looking."[12]

On October 25 the party reached the Whitman Mission. Preuss was not impressed, finding the little settlement "not much better than all the miserable country which we have crossed." Dr. Marcus Whitman was not present to greet the visitors. Here, four years later, on November 29, 1847, Dr. Whitman, his wife, Narcissa, and eleven others would be murdered by Cayuse Indians. The so-called Whitman Massacre would give great impetus to the granting of territorial status to Oregon several months later.

Frémont pushed on along the Columbia, mapping Mount St. Helens and Mount Hood before going ahead of the main group to reach Fort Vancouver by Indian canoe on November 5. "We were a motley group, but all happy: three unknown Indians; Jacob, a colored man; Mr. Preuss, a German; Bernier, a creole French; and myself," noted Frémont.[13]

He was graciously greeted by John McLoughlin, the tall, white-haired Hudson's Bay Company factor, who was already a legend in the Pacific Northwest. McLoughlin must have sensed that the tenuous British hold on this land was fast slipping away. Frémont's arrival, howitzer in tow, was yet more confirmation of American intentions. McLoughlin offered the hospitality of the fort to the young officer, who was delighted at the prospect of an actual bed and a roof over his head. Necessary supplies and fresh stock for the return journey were also provided, at a cost of $2,000. Old McLoughlin was as famous for his business acumen as for his hospitable nature. Frémont bid Fort Vancouver and McLoughlin farewell on November 10 and headed back upriver to rejoin Carson, Fitzpatrick, and the main party. He had reached the point of exploration concluded by naval Captain Wilkes in 1841 and had completed his expedition.[14]

The men expected to return home along the Oregon Trail, but Frémont had a much grander plan. He was not a man to backtrack. They would travel south from the Columbia to Klamath Lake, which he incorrectly thought might be the source of the Sacramento River, explore the western portion of the Great Basin (which he had named), and search for the mythical Buenaventura River, which supposedly crossed the mountains into California. He then planned to reach the headwaters of the Arkansas River and follow the river back to Bent's Fort. For Frémont, this was truly undiscovered country, a land "absolutely new to geographical, botanical, and geological science . . . which inflamed with desire to know what this *terra incognita* really contained."

They pushed south to Klamath Lake and by January 10 had reached Pyramid Lake (which Frémont named) in present Nevada, where they feasted on large trout. Frémont now made the fateful decision to turn to the west and cross the formidable Sierra Nevada to Sutter's Fort at the confluence of the American and Sacramento Rivers. Perhaps this incursion into Mexican California had always been on his mind, developed around Senator Benton's dinner table.

Carson had made this journey before and must have known its dangers, but he nevertheless supported Frémont, as did Fitzpatrick. "We were nearly out of provisions and cross the mountains we must," Carson remembered, "let the consequences be what they may." They attempted to hire Indian guides, but none would go, for they all said it was impossible to cross the mountains in winter.[15]

The midwinter crossing was harrowing, with the men subsisting on mule flesh. Many of the horses and mules floundered in the deep snow and had to be shot. The remainder were so hungry, they ate each other's tails and even chewed on the saddlebags. Half of the stock eventually died. They reached what is now known as Lake Tahoe and agonizingly crossed over what Frémont named Carson Pass. Most of the baggage, as well as the cumbersome howitzer, was left behind as they finally reached the 9,000-foot-high mountain summit and saw the lush Sacramento Valley far in the distance. It was February 20, 1844, before they all staggered up to the summit and March 6 before they reached Sutter's Fort.

"When we arrived at the fort, we were naked and in as poor a condition as men possibly could be," noted Carson. "We were well received by Mr. Sutter and furnished in a princely manner, everything we required by him."[16]

John Sutter, although born in Baden, Germany, was of Swiss descent. He had come to America in 1834, settled in St. Louis, and was soon engaged in the Santa Fe trade. Four years later he arrived at San Francisco Bay, where he became a Mexican citizen. Blessed with considerable charm and some financial resources and business savvy, he quickly ingratiated himself with the Mexican authorities. The governor granted him nearly 50,000 acres in the Sacramento Valley, where he had constructed a substantial mud-and-brick fort as the headquarters of what he christened "New Helvetia." He also purchased Fort Ross from the Russian-American Fur Company and moved its goods, livestock, and cannons to the Sacramento Valley. Sutter employed hundreds of Indian, Mexican, and American workers.[17]

Frémont paused for over two weeks at Sutter's Fort, engaging in long, friendly talks with his host about the conditions in California. Sutter was pleased with the hundreds of Americans who had migrated to the rich lands surrounding his outpost. Frémont sensed that Sutter was not averse to further American settlement. The California Mexican population of around 10,000 lived well on sprawling ranches that provided the cattle hides and tallow for the rich trade with Boston shipowners. High tariffs and negligent Mexican rule left these people as dissatisfied with the government in Mexico City as were the new American settlers, who numbered about a thousand. The life led by these people, despite their political discontent, seemed perfectly idyllic.

On March 22, Frémont led his refreshed party south. Five men were allowed to stay behind. Sutter, who rode along with Frémont for a few miles, had provided the Americans with 130 horses and mules and a nice herd of 30 cattle. The Americans kept away from the coast to avoid any encounters with the Mexican authorities. They followed the San Joaquin Valley south to strike the Old Spanish Trail, which had long connected Los Angeles with Santa Fe. It was a wonderful place, rich with game and well-timbered, with green pastures often covered with a luxurious growth of flowers. The Sierras were toward the east, while the San Joaquin River flowed to the west. Frémont knew that this would be a paradise to industrious American pioneers.

Carson led them across a series of sandy hills that marked the juncture of the Sierras and the Coast Ranges and into the Mojave Desert. This journey convinced Frémont that there was no Buenaventura River linking the Great Basin to California. On April 24, the camp was surprised by a Mexican man and boy. The distraught man—Andreas Fuentes—declared that his small party of five (his wife, the boy's mother and father, and another man), driving a herd of thirty horses from Los Angeles to Santa Fe ahead of a larger caravan, had been attacked by Indians some eighty miles distant. He and the boy—Pablo Hernandez—had been mounted on horse guard and managed to escape. He begged Frémont for assistance and the lieutenant asked for volunteers.

"Godey and myself volunteered with the expectation that some men of our party would join us," Carson later related. "They did not. We two and the Mexican took the trail."[18]

Fuentes's horse soon gave out and he returned to Frémont's camp, while Carson and Godey pushed ahead. They followed the Indian trail until dark and resumed the pursuit at dawn. Within two miles they discovered the Indian camp and slowly crept up to it. The Indians, some thirty in number, were feasting on some of the captured horses when the two frontiersmen suddenly charged their camp. Carson and Godey fired, killing two warriors and stampeding the rest. The Indians must have assumed that they were being attacked by a much larger party. Godey scalped the two dead.

With a war whoop, Carson and Godey rode back into camp, driving the recaptured horses before them. Godey carried the two scalps attached to his rifle. Preuss was horrified.

"To me, such butchery is disgusting, but Frémont is in high spirits," he wrote in his diary. "I believe he would exchange all observations for a scalp taken by his own hand."

Frémont was indeed in awe. "This expedition of Carson and Godey may be considered among the boldest and most disinterested which the annals of Western adventure, so full of daring deeds, can present," he later wrote. "Two men, in a savage desert, pursue day and night an unknown body of Indians into the defiles of an unknown mountain—attack them on sight, without counting numbers—and defeat them in an instant—and for what? To punish the robbers of the desert, and to avenge the wrongs of Mexicans whom they did not know."[19]

As Frémont's party marched to the north they came upon the camp of Fuentes, where they found the mutilated bodies of two Mexican men, including the boy's father. There was no sign of the two women. Only the boy's little lapdog had survived. The dog leapt into the arms of the weeping boy.

Fuentes and the boy, along with his dog, joined Frémont's party. Later they would learn that a caravan had discovered the bodies of Fuentes's wife and Pablo's mother, both murdered by the Indians. Fuentes would later serve with Frémont on his third expedition, while eleven-year-old orphan Pablo would be taken into the Benton household to be educated in the East. Juan Almonte, the Mexican minister in Washington, offered to take the boy back to Mexico, but Pablo preferred to stay with the Bentons. He was well cared for and educated in the best schools.

The Indians, who were assumed to be Paiutes, soon got their revenge when they killed Baptiste Tabeau, who had been waylaid while hunting alone for a lost mule. The men were anxious to avenge Tabeau, but the worn-out condition of their horses made pursuit impossible.

Preuss now had a change of heart concerning the Indians. "May God have mercy on the Paiutes who fall into our hands now," he wrote. "They lurk like wolves between rocks along the road. . . . We must guard against the Paiutes until we have crossed the Colorado; beyond it the land is free of the wolves of the desert."[20]

They moved north to Mountain Meadows, a lush camping spot on the Old Spanish Trail well-known to Mexican traders and not yet infamous as the site of the ghastly 1857 Mormon massacre of the Fancher wagon train, where they met up with mountain man Joe Walker and several companions. Walker and his men had also had trouble with the Indians and he was anxious to join Frémont's larger party. He agreed to guide them north to explore the freshwater Utah Lake, just south of the Great Salt Lake, and the nearby Wasatch and Uinta Mountains. They then crossed over to Brown's Hole and then across the Continental Divide to move down the mountain chain south to Pueblo. They soon reached the Arkansas River and followed it to Bent's Fort, which they reached on July 1. George Bent gave them a warm welcome. "On the 4th, Mr. Bent gave Fremont and party a splendid dinner," Carson later recalled. "The day was celebrated as well, if not better, than in many of the towns of the States."[21]

Carson and Walker remained at Bent's Fort, while Frémont and the rest of his party followed the Arkansas to the east and home. On August 6 they reached St. Louis, where the expedition party was disbanded. In fourteen months, through soaring adventure and incredible hardship, the expedition had circuited almost the entire American West. The expedition would prove to be not only a triumph of exploration and science but also a pivotal point in national expansion. Frémont proved to be much more than a conventional army explorer, for he was an avid booster and promoter who saw in that great unsettled land he had traversed the future of the American republic.

MANIFEST DESTINY

In the December 27, 1845, issue of his *New York Morning News*, journalist John L. O'Sullivan perfectly captured the national mood when he editorialized on the American need to annex both Texas and Oregon "by right of our manifest destiny to overspread and to possess the whole of the continent which Providence has given us for the development of the great experiment of liberty and federated self-government entrusted to us." Manifest Destiny quickly became the catchphrase of the day. It was hardly a new doctrine, dating back to the Puritan fathers and their "city upon a hill" and up through Thomas Jefferson's dream of a continental "empire for liberty." Similar sentiment had certainly helped to bring on the War of 1812. This combination of expansionism and nationalism, with the added benediction of divine providence, now reached its aggressive climax in the 1840s. The doctrine's casual disregard for the rights of those already living in the coveted lands (Indian and Hispanic) was somewhat alleviated by the guarantee of the eventual extension of full political rights. The young republic was almost exclusively Anglo-Saxon Protestant (with the notable exception of enslaved African Americans) and the people—no matter their station in life—possessed a keen sense of racial superiority. Some Americans at the time viewed it as brutal and unsavory—unworthy of a righteous and moral republic—but they were a distinct minority. By far the vast majority of the people endorsed Manifest Destiny wholeheartedly. The exuberant young nation, bursting with cockiness and pride, swelling in population, was quick to embrace western expansion as both a mystical calling and a practical duty.[1]

James K. Polk was a firm disciple of Manifest Destiny. In this, as in most things, he followed in the footsteps of his mentor Old Hickory—so much so that he had been nicknamed "Young Hickory." Davy Crockett's old political nemesis had served as the thirteenth Speaker of the House of Representatives from December 1835 to March 1839 but had left Congress in 1839 to run for governor of Tennessee. Polk hoped that the governorship might better position him for national office. While he won election, he faced a bitterly divided Tennessee as Whig political strength grew. Defeated for reelection in August 1841, he tried to regain the governorship in 1843 only to again be beaten at the polls. It appeared that his political career was over. Jackson attempted to revive his protégé's fortunes by securing him the vice presidential nomination in 1844 alongside Martin Van Buren to oppose the Whig candidate Henry Clay. Van Buren then stunned Jackson and most southern Democrats by coming out in opposition to Texas annexation. Clay had made the same political misstep in an effort to pander to northern antislavery voters. Van Buren's Texas declaration led to gridlock at the Baltimore convention until Polk emerged as the first "dark horse" candidate in history to win the Democratic nomination on the ninth ballot. In the campaign that followed, Texas and Oregon, along with the tariff, were the key issues, with slavery emerging as an increasingly prominent and uncomfortable topic (although both Polk and Clay were slave owners). Polk won by a mere 38,000 votes out of 2.5 million cast, carrying fifteen states to Clay's eleven. Expansionist sentiment had provided the margin for victory.[2]

President John Tyler and his secretary of state John C. Calhoun now moved forward with annexation. "Nothing but Texas has engrossed all minds," a congressional ally reported to Polk upon the passage of an annexation resolution by the House on January 25, 1845. Tyler hoped to sidestep the slavery question, which had been instrumental in the Senate defeat of an annexation treaty the previous June, by securing Texas with a joint resolution of both houses of Congress that needed but a simple majority. The president-elect hurried to Washington to lobby for the annexation resolution. Senator Willie Mangum of North Carolina praised Polk for riding to the rescue of the resolution, declaring that Polk "is for Texas, Texas, Texas, and talks of but little else." On February 27 the Senate passed a slightly amended resolution by two votes, 27 to 25, and the next day the House agreed with a vote of 132 to 76. President Tyler signed the resolution on March 1, three days before Polk's inauguration.

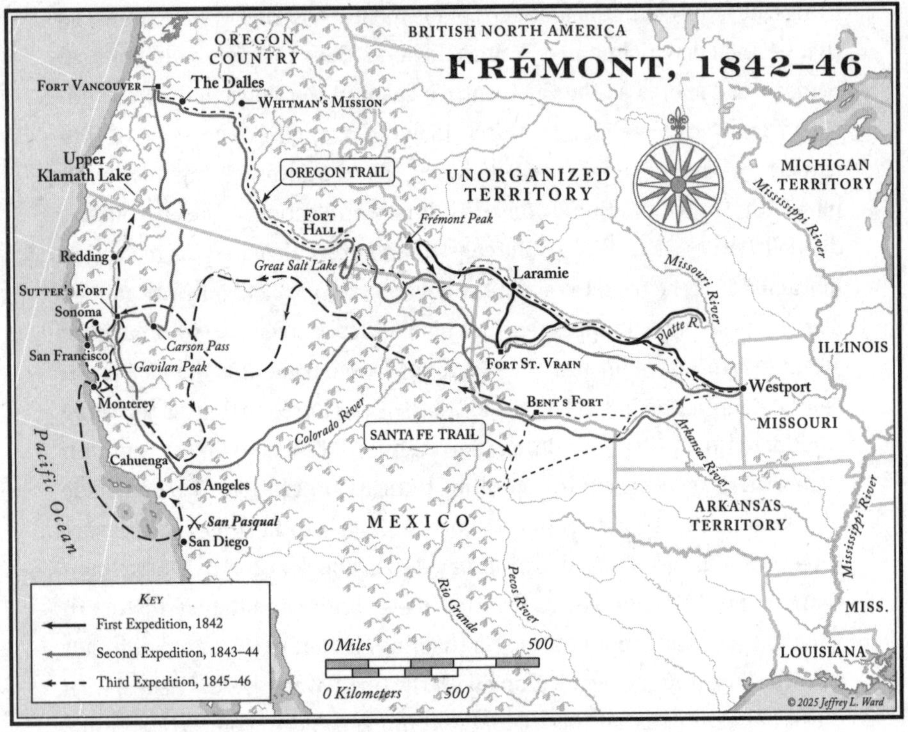

During its decade of independence, Texas had steadily grown in population. Generous land bounties to newcomers had increased the population to over 140,000 by 1845 (with some 12,000 enslaved African Americans). Hoping to block American expansion, the British pressured Mexico to finally recognize Texas independence in exchange for a pledge never to accept annexation. Texas president Sam Houston had disingenuously courted the British, knowing full well it would fret the expansionists back in Washington to no end. It worked. Houston assured his ailing mentor, Andrew Jackson, who had only months to live, that Texas was being offered to the United States "as a bride adorned for her espousal," but that quick action was essential. Polk took care of that. When Congress convened in December 1845, the new president reported that Texas had accepted annexation and had submitted a state constitution. Congress reported a joint resolution on December 10, 1845, declaring Texas a state by a vote of 141 to 56 in the House and 31 to 14 in the Senate. Polk signed the resolution on December 29, 1845, and Texas officially entered the Union.

In the hamlet of Austin, Texas, on February 19, 1846, the new and last president of the republic, Anson Jones, took to the speaker's platform to declare: "The final act in this great drama is now performed. The Republic of Texas is no more." As he lowered the Lone Star flag, the pole broke and the banner fluttered down into the waiting arms of Sam Houston. "The Magnificent Barbarian," as Houston had come to be known, was soon on his way to Washington as the first senator from the new state.[3]

Within a matter of weeks Mexico broke off diplomatic relations with the United States. Juan Almonte, who had been Santa Anna's aide-de-camp at the Alamo, was the Mexican minister. He denounced annexation as "an act of aggression, the most unjust which can be found recorded in the annals of modern history" as he left Washington. He hurriedly returned to Mexico, where he began to plot the restoration of his old commander to power.[4]

Mexico was anxious for war, although it was woefully unprepared. The republic's government was dysfunctional, its economy marginal, and its treasury empty. Its population of 7 million, which had stagnated since independence from Spain because of warfare, disease, and starvation, was but a third of that of the robust United States. Mexico indeed had a large albeit ill-equipped army that had been seasoned in the unrelenting internecine conflicts that had marked the young nation's twenty-year history since independence. Santa Anna, now in exile in Cuba, had dominated much of this turbulent period since 1821. The butcher of the Alamo and Goliad was older though hardly wiser. He remained as chronically devious and dangerously charismatic as ever. From Havana he carefully monitored political affairs in Mexico much as a fox might study a henhouse.

In Mexico City, President José Joaquín de Herrera realized that his bankrupt nation was in no position to fight a war with its northern neighbor. Despite the jingoistic rantings of the Mexican press, he agreed to entertain the American diplomatic mission of John Slidell to settle the Texas boundary dispute and to purchase California and New Mexico, which at the time included present-day New Mexico, Arizona, Utah, Nevada, and part of Colorado. The former congressman was authorized to pay Mexico as much as $40 million for the coveted lands, although Polk hoped to pay half that if possible. Polk completely misjudged the Mexicans. He blithely thought they would readily sell a sparsely populated land that they actually ruled in name only.[5]

JOHN FRÉMONT, HAVING RETURNED TO ST. LOUIS FROM his second expedition early in August 1844, was naturally delighted to hear of the growing excitement about the West. He and Jessie had hurried on to Washington, where Frémont reported to General Winfield Scott and began a brief period of relaxation. They stayed in Benton's spacious house but also rented a small cottage nearby where they could work without interruption on his report of the expedition. Once again Frémont dictated and Jessie wrote. Her graceful prose turned what could have been a dry report into something of a minor literary masterpiece. This was no simple journal of the expedition but rather a promotional tract on the glories of Oregon and California, the relative ease of traveling there, and the enormous potential to be found there. The report not only contradicted but dismantled the army explorer Stephen Long's contention that the West was but a "Great American Desert." Part guidebook, part promotional tract, and part tale of high adventure, Frémont's book would cause a national sensation when published.

Frémont presented his report to the War Department on March 1, 1845, and two days later a Senate resolution maneuvered by Senator Benton arranged for the printing of 5,000 copies. Pennsylvania senator James Buchanan, soon to receive appointment as Polk's secretary of state, praised Frémont as "a young gentleman of extraordinary merit, great energy, and ability to serve the country" and moved to double the print run. Newspapers across the country published long extracts from the report, while commercial houses hurried their own editions into print. The press now co-opted the title of James Fenimore Cooper's 1840 bestseller and applied it to the explorer. The "Pathfinder" soon emerged as a national hero, as did his intrepid scout Kit Carson.

Benton took Frémont, who had just been promoted to brevet captain, to meet the new president. Polk was amazed at just how young the famed explorer was. Frémont spun a marvelous tale for the president about the wonderful potential of both Oregon and California for settlement but came away from the meeting a bit chagrined with Polk's doubting attitude over his geographic pronouncements. Polk "found me 'young,' and said something of the 'impulsiveness of young men' and was not at all satisfied in his own mind," Frémont later wrote. That first impression would have important later consequences.[6]

Washington was now swirling with excitement and intrigue as the fate of Texas, California, and Oregon was on everyone's mind. The Benton home was the meeting place for many of the expansionists. Secretary of State Buchanan, who could not read Spanish, often brought letters and documents over so that Jessie could translate them for him. He worried about security in his own office. Secretary of the Navy George Bancroft, a far more ardent expansionist than the often vacillating Buchanan, was more than willing to fight a war with Mexico to fulfill America's continental destiny. Senator Benton respected Bancroft, who at the time was the nation's most famous historian, and saw him as an important political ally, although the senator hoped to avoid war. He was not as committed to Texas annexation because of slavery but was exceedingly enthusiastic over Oregon, which he saw as the gateway to the China trade. Bancroft had played an instrumental role in securing Polk the Democratic nomination and had emerged as the new president's closest advisor. At glittering dinner parties or over drinks in Benton's library, the questions of expansion and war were discussed at great length. Frémont listened attentively. As the thirty-two-year-old captain began to plan his third expedition, he recognized that this would be a different kind of "exploration."

Frémont's February 1845 orders from Colonel John Abert of the topographical corps made no mention of California. He was directed to explore and map the Arkansas and Red Rivers, with particular attention to the headwaters of the Arkansas. In fact, Abert's instructions seemed designed to limit Frémont's field of operations: "Long journeys to determine isolated geographical points are scarcely worth the time and the expense which they occasion; the efforts of Captain Frémont will therefore be more particularly directed to the geography of localities within reasonable distance of Bents Fort, and of the streams which run east from the Rocky Mountains, and he will so time his operations, that his party will come in during the present year." For the most part Frémont ignored these official orders, and it remains unclear if they were perhaps simply issued for diplomatic cover. He seems to have left Washington determined to act upon his conversations with Bancroft and Benton, whom he rightly perceived to have the ear of the president.

"In arranging this expedition," Frémont later declared, "the eventualities of war were taken into consideration." He added that "my private instructions were, if needed, to foil England by carrying the war now imminent with Mexico into the territory of California." He assumed much, or he simply assumed what he wished to believe.[7]

The captain was back in St. Louis by May 30 to complete the recruitment of his party already begun by Theodore Talbot. Within a week they had recruited fifty-five men and headed south to Westport Landing by steamboat. The volunteers, many of them quite green, were issued a Hawken rifle, two pistols, a knife, saddle, bridle, pistol holsters, and two blankets. Each man was also given a horse or mule to ride and two pack animals to care for. Auguste Archcambeau, a noted hunter who had joined Frémont late in the second expedition, gave the recruits a quick tutorial on mule packing, although it took them some time to master that fine art.

"For a month or two after our start much amusement was caused by the awkward attempts at packing of some of the company," recalled the green Tennessean recruit Thomas Martin. "In time however, they all became more or less expert."[8]

On June 26 they headed west, driving two hundred horses and mules as well as a small herd of cattle. By the time the expedition reached Bent's Fort on August 2, it was a seasoned band. Several of the men had served with Frémont before: Talbot and Archcambeau of course, along with Frémont's favorite Frenchman, Basil Lajeunesse, Lucien Maxwell, Tom Fitzpatrick, Joseph Walker, Bill Williams, and the always reliable Alexis Godey. Frémont's young valet Jacob Dodson again accompanied his employer. Edward Kern, an accomplished artist, took the place of Preuss, who had reluctantly remained behind in Washington. A dozen Delaware Indians, led by the chiefs Segundai and Swanuck, formed Frémont's personal bodyguard. It was a formidable crew.

One indispensable man was missing and so Frémont sent a galloper south to Kit Carson's new ranch on the Little Cimarron. Carson had promised Frémont that he would join him if there was a third expedition, and so he and his partner, Dick Owens, sold their improvements at a considerable loss and, leaving Josefa with her sister's family in Taos, headed north.

Frémont was elated: "This was like Carson, prompt, self-sacrificing, and true. I received them both with great satisfaction. That Owens was a good man it is enough to say that he and Carson were friends. Cool, brave, and of good judgment; a good hunter and good shot; experienced in mountain life; he was an acquisition, and proved valuable throughout the campaign."[9]

In compliance with his orders, Frémont dispatched Lieutenant James Abert, the colonel's son, along with Fitzpatrick and a thirty-four-man detachment to survey south through Raton Pass to the headwaters of the Canadian River and then east to its junction with the Arkansas. Frémont, with sixty men, then departed Bent's Fort on August 16 to proceed westward up the Arkansas toward the towering Rocky Mountains.

BACK IN WASHINGTON, HOPES FOR A DIPLOMATIC SOLUtion to the Texas question were fading. The new president had campaigned on an expansionist platform calling for the annexation of Texas and the Oregon Country. He was determined to purchase New Mexico and California—or to fight a war for them if need be. Polk and Bancroft fretted over the intentions of England concerning California: Mexico had threatened to declare war if Texas was annexed, and Polk and Bancroft worried that the British would seize the prized harbor at San Francisco Bay if war broke out. On March 21, 1845, Bancroft sent orders to Commodore John D. Sloat, commander of the Pacific Squadron, to proceed to the west coast of Mexico and soon after instructed him to promptly seize San Francisco Bay if he heard of a declaration of war. The settlement of the Oregon question now seemed more important than ever. The British, in an effort to reduce tensions, decided to accept the long-standing American offer of the 49th parallel boundary. With Americans flooding in over the Oregon Trail and the fur trade in such sharp decline that the Hudson's Bay Company had removed its headquarters from Fort Vancouver on the Columbia River north to Vancouver's Island, the disputed territory was no longer considered particularly valuable. In the spring of 1846, the British foreign office agreed to the 49th parallel and to the channel separating the coast from Vancouver's Island as the new boundary line between the United States and Canada. "Fifty-four Forty or Fight" was promptly abandoned by the United States and a boundary treaty was accepted on June 15, 1846.[10]

Herrera's stance to open negotiations had incensed Mexican nationalists, and General Mariano Paredes promptly seized power, pledging to retake Texas. The new Mexican government naturally refused to treat with Slidell. The envoy reported this to Washington and urged stronger measures. When word of the failure of Slidell's mission reached Washington on January 12, 1846, the president ordered Major General Zachary Taylor, with 3,500 troops, to Corpus Christi, Texas. When Mexican troops moved north to the Rio Grande, Taylor was ordered to advance his army into the disputed Nueces Strip. He did so in early March. Taylor had been instructed to avoid conflict unless attacked. The general received a strongly worded note from the Mexicans ordering him to withdraw to the Nueces or prepare to fight. On April 23, 1846, Paredes declared that a "defensive war" existed between Mexico and the United States. Mexico considered the Nueces River, not the Rio Grande, to be the border of Texas. General Mariano Arista, an old military rival of Santa Anna's, was sent to take charge of the 5,000 Mexican troops at Matamoros on the Rio Grande. He now sent a polite note to Taylor to announce that "hostilities have commenced."

The two armies warily watched each other. Finally, on April 24, 1846, General Arista sent a 1,600-man force across the Rio Grande to cut off the American supply line to Port Isabel on the coast. Taylor dispatched an eighty-man dragoon detachment to investigate, and they rode into an ambush. Eleven men were killed, six more wounded, and the rest captured.

President Polk had been working on a war message to Congress as a result of Mexico's refusal to pay its debts to the United States or to consider his generous offer to purchase New Mexico and California when news of the Rio Grande skirmish reached him on May 9, 1846. He hurriedly revised his message: "Now, after reiterated menaces, Mexico has passed the boundary of the United States, has invaded our territory and shed American blood upon the American soil." Two days later Congress declared that "by the Act of the Republic of Mexico a state of war exists" and authorized President Polk to raise an army of 50,000 men. Eventually nearly 116,000 men, mostly volunteers from the South and West, would serve.[11]

Despite the declaration of war, Polk still hoped to negotiate a quick settlement. In a last-ditch effort to end hostilities, he opened secret negotiations with Santa Anna. Naval officer Alexander Slidell Mackenzie traveled to Havana in July to meet with the exiled Mexican dictator. Through back channels Santa Anna had made it clear to Polk that he would be open to a negotiated peace on terms favorable to the Americans if he were back in power. He now informed Mackenzie that he would consent to the purchase of New Mexico and California and be willing to settle the disputed Texas boundary at the Rio Grande. He also requested $500,000 for expenses. Santa Anna pledged his commitment to liberal republican principles and assured Mackenzie that only he could promptly end the political anarchy in Mexico. The naval officer came away deeply impressed. "General Santa Anna appeared in excellent health and condition, strong and active, notwithstanding his mutilation, and capable of enduring great fatigue. He had the air of a man of forty well preserved," Mackenzie reported to Washington on July 11. "I believe in the entire sincerity of his views and his intentions as imparted in his note to the President," the officer gushed.

Polk, long renowned for his political cunning, might well have been expected to view Mackenzie's report with a jaundiced eye, but surprisingly he embraced it. Bancroft sent secret instructions to the commander of the blockading squadron to allow Santa Anna to pass freely to Veracruz on a small British steamer.

Santa Anna had been in close communication with the Mexican liberal faction led by his former vice president Valentín Gómez Farías. Almonte had also been working to ensure his old commander's return to power. This was a bitter pill for many Mexican liberals. "I detest no man more than I do pegleg Santa Anna," declared a prominent liberal leader, "but in spite of that I would gladly throw myself in his arms if he wanted to come back and fight the dangerous faction that dominates us."[12]

Santa Anna entered Mexico City in triumph on September 15, 1846, proclaimed his newfound admiration for the federalist constitution of 1824, and with his usual energy and administrative skill began to raise a new army. He was appointed commander of the Mexican army and soon after elected president by the Congress, with Gómez Farías as his vice president.

"The war is a necessity of immediate importance," he declared, "every day's delay is an age of infamy."[13]

There can be little doubt that Santa Anna was a Mexican patriot of the highest order, especially when such patriotism coincided with his own soaring ambition. On September 28, 1846, he departed Mexico City at the head of 3,000 men to confront General Taylor at Buena Vista. Polk's folly in trusting Santa Anna quickly became apparent.

FRÉMONT KNEW NOTHING OF ANY OF THIS WHEN IN OCtober he announced the extension of his exploration westward beyond the Great Basin and over the Sierras into California. The perceptive Theodore Talbot had surmised that California was their ultimate destination early in June back in St. Louis, and it may well have been an open secret among the men. Before this they had crossed the Continental Divide just east of Homestake Peak at over 10,000 feet, explored the headwaters of the Colorado River, and surveyed the Great Salt Lake. Frémont then sent Carson, with Maxwell, Archcambeau, and Lajeunesse, to blaze a trail across the white-sand desert to the west. Bill Williams declined this dangerous crossing and left the party. Frémont was convinced that his was the first body of white men to make this crossing, not knowing that Jed Smith with two companions had done so back in 1827. Frémont divided his force in late November, sending Talbot and most of the men, with Joe Walker as guide, south along the eastern Sierra foothills to cross the mountains at a pass Walker had discovered a decade before and enter the San Joaquin Valley. He and Carson, with fifteen men, would follow the Truckee River over the mountains at a place soon to be known as Donner Pass and then down to the south fork of the American River. Frémont's party reached Sutter's Fort on December 10, 1845.

Frémont felt certain that Sutter, who had extended his hospitality to him eighteen months before during the explorer's second expedition, would again warmly greet him. They had discussed the future of California back in 1844, so Frémont knew that Sutter welcomed American emigrants and shared the captain's dream of an American California. Still, Sutter was in a delicate position and needed to carefully balance his relationship with the army captain and his Mexican benefactors.

With rumors of war over Texas rife, the eight hundred Americans in California were viewed with suspicion. The Californios outnumbered them ten to one (and the Indians, although but a pitiful remnant of the vast population that had existed when the Spanish first arrived in 1542, greatly outnumbered both groups by several thousand), but they were bitterly divided north and south. General José Castro in Monterey ruled over the north, while Governor Pío Pico, headquartered in Los Angeles, was the power in the south. The two men disliked each other intensely but at least agreed on their mutual disdain for the government in Mexico. They both acted independently of the central government.

Sutter was absent when Frémont first arrived but returned in a few days to welcome the newly arrived Americans. Frémont needed mules and cattle, which Sutter provided. Frémont then explored the countryside, met with local settlers, skirmished with some local Indians, and fretted over Talbot's party. It soon became abundantly clear to the young captain that California was not only exceedingly ripe fruit; it was quite low hanging as well.

In January, Frémont crossed the San Joaquin Valley to Yerba Buena and gazed in amazement at the wide opening in the Coast Range where the San Francisco Bay met the Pacific Ocean. He named it the Golden Gate. He then rode south to Monterey to meet with the American consul, Thomas Larkin. The transplanted New England merchant took Frémont to meet General Castro, who was quite cordial but advised Frémont to stay away from the coastal towns and remain in the interior. The American officer assured Castro that his peaceful party was solely devoted to mapmaking. He found a moment to write a brief letter to Jessie extolling the beauty of the country but confessing that "many months of hardships, close trials, and anxieties have tried me severely, and my hair is turning gray before its time.[14]

Frémont and his men then traveled some sixty miles north to San José, where they heard that the Talbot and Walker party were on the San Joaquin. Carson and Owens were sent to guide them back to San José. They found Talbot's men camped beside the Calaveras River, where they had been joined by an old mountain man friend of Walker's named William Fallon, called Le Gros because of his size, who had told them where Frémont was. The reunited party then moved back south to Monterey. Sixty heavily armed Americans approaching General Castro's provincial capital naturally worried him: he sent an order to them to promptly depart California. Then the general issued a call to arms to the Californios on March 8, in order "to lance the ulcer which (should it not be done) would destroy our liberties and independence." On that very same day, in Texas, General Taylor had moved his army across the Nueces River into the disputed land north of the Rio Grande.[15]

Frémont moved his force northeast of Monterey to Gavilan Peak in the Coast Range, where the men commenced to build a rude log fort. Frémont hoisted the American flag and prepared to fight. Larkin sent a message to Frémont urging restraint and warning of the mobilization of a large Mexican force. Frémont responded with a note of romantic bravado reminiscent of Travis at the Alamo: "We have in no wise done wrong to the people or authorities of the country, and if we are hemmed in and assaulted, we will die every man of us, under the Flag of our country."[16]

Rhetoric aside, Frémont now began to think that discretion might well be the better part of valor—and that, as a junior officer, he probably should not initiate a war between the United States and the Republic of Mexico. When a breeze blew over the impoverished flagpole on March 9, Frémont took it as an omen and ordered his men to prepare to move out under cover of darkness. Joe Walker, unhappy with this turn of events, demanded and received his discharge. As Frémont's party headed north, Walker headed south. The Mexicans did not pursue.

Frémont's party leisurely moved north past Mount Shasta to reach Oregon's Klamath Lake on May 6. They were met there by Klamath Indians, who traded dried fish and salmon with the newcomers. The Indians were friendly but wary. Frémont led his men farther north between the lake and the mountains and on the night of May 8 camped in a forest on a little creek not far from the lake. Standing alone by the campfire, Frémont was startled to hear the muffled sound of approaching horses' hoofs. Two exhausted men emerged from the shadows into the firelight with a remarkable tale to tell. Frémont instantly recognized Samuel Neal, who had been with him on his second expedition before settling in California. Reinforced with hot coffee, Neal told Frémont that he had been sent forward by Lieutenant Archibald Gillespie of the United States Marines, who was in search of Frémont, with important dispatches from Washington for the explorer. The men had been trailed by Indians and were worried for the safety of Gillespie and his three other companions who were camped south of Upper Klamath Lake. Frémont decided to leave at dawn with ten handpicked men to make up a rescue party: Carson, Owens, Godey, Maxwell, Joe Stepperfeldt ("Stepp"), Basil Lajeunesse, Segundai, Denny (an Iowa mixed-blood), and two other Delawares.

The next day they found Gillespie camped some forty miles away at the lower end of the lake. The young marine officer had traveled from Washington across Mexico and then by ship to Monterey. He had been sent on this dangerous secret mission by President Polk with messages for Larkin and Frémont. Fearing that he might be intercepted in Mexico, he had memorized Polk's written instructions and then burned the originals, but he did carry letters to Frémont from Jessie and Senator Benton. The message and the marine officer's own observations in Mexico made it clear that war was imminent. (They did not know it, but the war had already begun on the Rio Grande.) Polk and Benton were worried about British intentions over California and wanted Frémont to be ready to claim the province for the United States the instant he heard of a war declaration.

The two officers talked well into the evening, making plans, and were interrupted only by the arrival of several Klamaths bearing salmon. The Klamath chief handed a fine fish to Gillespie and then led his men out of the camp. As the men settled into their blankets, Frémont stayed up pondering his next move. He felt himself but a pawn in a grand chess game, but as a pawn he must make the first move. "I saw the way opening clear before me," he later wrote. "This decision was the first step in the conquest of California."[17]

Carson heard them first. "What the matter over there!" he called out to Lajeunesse. Then he heard the sickening sound of an axe striking flesh and shouted the alarm: "Indians!" Crane, one of the Delawares, jumped to his feet but his rifle misfired, and he was instantly struck by four arrows. Carson, Stepp, and Maxwell all fired, and the Klamath chief went down.

Godey stepped into the light of the campfire to check his gun. This astonished Carson, who yelled out, "Look at the fool. Look at him, will you?" Godey gave Carson a dirty look and continued to tinker with his gun as arrows whizzed by. "He was the most thoroughly insensible to danger of all the brave men I have known," remarked Frémont.

With the death of their leader, the Indians withdrew. Carson and his companions lay under cover all night. At dawn the gray light revealed that Lajeunesse (whose head had been bashed in with an axe), Crane, and Denny were dead and another of the Delawares wounded. The Klamath chief who the day before had given Gillespie salmon lay dead by the smoldering campfire.

"He was the bravest Indian I ever saw," Carson remarked. "If his men had been as brave as himself, we surely would all have been killed." The chief had a British axe tied to his wrist. Carson took the axe and knocked the chief's head to pieces after Segundai scalped him. In Indian fashion he intended to leave the mutilated body as a message to the Klamaths. "The Indians had commenced the war with us without cause," Carson declared. "I thought they should be chastised in a summary manner."[18]

Frémont, who suspected that the British had incited the Klamaths, was now determined to exact revenge. The Delawares in particular demanded vengeance. Once the command was reunited, Carson went ahead with ten men and promptly found and attacked a Klamath village of fifty lodges near where the Williamson River emptied into Upper Klamath Lake, scattered the people, and set everything on fire. Carson led his small band into the river in pursuit of the fleeing Natives but misjudged the depth of the water so that the men were soon floundering about.

"All of us had got our powder wet and we would have been in a fine fix, if the rest of our party had not arrived at this moment," grumbled Tom Martin.[19]

Frémont hurriedly brought the rest of his men up to reinforce Carson, but the Klamaths had all fled from the burning village. About a mile from the village he made camp and had the men build a strong corral. Word soon reached the camp that the Klamaths were returning, and the men hurriedly mounted. Frémont and Carson led them out into the thick forest, where Frémont's horse, a gift from Sutter named Sacramento, made a daring leap over a fallen oak. "Captain, that horse will break your neck someday," Carson shouted.

Minutes later a Klamath scout emerged from behind the trees and drew a bead on Carson with his bow. Carson fired at him but his rifle snapped. Frémont spurred Sacramento and they rode the Indian down so that his arrow shot went wild. Segundai then leapt upon the Klamath and smashed in his skull with his war club. It was all over in a moment, but it was a close call for Carson, who now developed a keen appreciation for Sacramento. "I owe my life to them two," declared Carson. "The Colonel and Sacramento saved me."

"By Heaven, this is rough work," Gillespie exclaimed. This was the first combat he had witnessed since joining the marines. He would soon see much more.[20]

Frémont's party reached Peter Lassen's ranch on Deer Creek in the Sacramento Valley on May 24 after skirmishing with Indians during much of the journey south. Frémont found the American settlers in an uproar following a decree from Castro threatening all non-Mexican citizens with expulsion and by recent raids by Indians from the nearby hills. Some of these raiders were descendants of mission Indians who had retreated to the mountains rather than work as serfs for Sutter or the Mexican ranchers. Others were Maidu, Wintu, and Yana people who had lived in the Sacramento Valley long before the Spanish first arrived. They numbered several thousand and sometimes raided the American and Mexican ranches for livestock.

Frémont was at first reluctant to lead a campaign against them but relented to the settlers' pleas when he received a message from Sutter warning that Castro had sent messengers to incite the Indians against the American settlers. "I resolved to anticipate the Indians and strike them a blow which would make them recognize that Castro was far and that I was near." He convinced himself that it would be unwise to leave a potentially hostile force to his rear. Frémont's combined force of settlers and his own men, numbering over sixty, struck several Wintu rancherias along the Sacramento River, killing dozens of Natives and driving the rest into the hills. While the Indians were numerous, they were poorly armed and it was over quickly. Martin put the number killed at 175. Many of the victims were women and children who drowned or were shot attempting to cross the river. The Americans suffered no casualties.

This one-sided affair disturbed even Carson. "The number killed I cannot say," he declared. "It was a perfect butchery."[21]

With the Indians neutralized, Frémont turned his attention to the Californios. He encouraged Ezekiel Merritt, William Fallon, and William Ide, with thirty American settlers, to capture the Mexican garrison and cannons at Sonoma, the northernmost settlement. The Americans found no Mexican soldiers, and the town's nine brass cannons were hardly serviceable, but they did capture the former commanding general of California, Mariano Vallejo, and seventeen Sonoma residents. Vallejo, who was sympathetic to the American annexation of California, offered his captors some brandy and his sword. They let him keep his sword but readily drank all the brandy. Vallejo and his compatriots were taken to Sutter's Fort and imprisoned. When Sutter objected to this, Frémont seized the fort and put Edward Kern in command.

Merritt quickly emerged as a leader of the American rebels. The forty-year-old former mountain man, who had a pronounced stutter, was notoriously quarrelsome, loudmouthed, and often inebriated. Frémont described him as "a rugged man, fearless and simple, taking delight in incurring risks, but tractable, and not given to asking questions when there was something he was required to do. Merritt was my field-lieutenant among the settlers." To the young captain, this unprincipled rounder seemed the perfect specimen to be the founding father of a new state.

Merritt, along with Daniel Boone relative Granville Swift and a dozen more men, intercepted a Mexican patrol herding a large remuda of horses from Vallejo's Sonoma ranch south to Castro in Santa Clara. They seized the horses but allowed the Californios to go free with a message to Castro that if he wanted his horses back, he should come and take them.

Back in Sonoma, the rebels issued a proclamation declaring the overthrow of the Mexican regime and announcing the Bear Flag Republic. One of the volunteers was William Todd, a cousin of Abraham Lincoln's wife, Mary Todd Lincoln, and a descendant of Levi Todd, one of the pioneer founders of Kentucky. He had written his father a few months before: "There will be a revolution before long and probably this country will be annexed to the United States. If here, I will take a hand." He designed a crude flag with a star, a grizzly bear, and the inscription "California Republic." Todd was not much of an artist, and one wag noted that the bear looked more like a pig. Art critics aside, they raised the flag over Sonoma on June 14.

James Marshall, one of the Bear Flaggers later famous as the discoverer of gold at Sutter's Mill, described his rebel compatriots as a particularly diverse crowd: "There were Americans, French, English, Swiss, Poles, Russians, Chileans, Germans, Greeks, Austrians, Pawnees, native Indians, etc." It was a veritable melting pot of armed humanity, ready for a fight.[22]

Ide sent two of his men, Tom Cowie and George Fowler, to the Russian River to find Moses Carson, Kit's half brother, in hopes of acquiring arms and gunpowder from him. When the two men failed to return, a search party was sent out. The Americans skirmished with a Mexican patrol and captured a soldier who confessed that the men had been captured, tortured, and then killed. Godey was among those who, along with Moses Carson, discovered their bodies. They had been disemboweled, with their throats cut and their genitals cut off. Cowie was a great favorite of Frémont's men, and they were enraged by his fate.

A detachment of Bear Flaggers—or "Los Osos" ("the Bears"), as the Californios called them—led by Henry L. Ford and Granville Swift, soon after skirmished with a detachment of Castro's lancers at Camilo Ynitia's Rancho Olompali on the Petaluma River and rescued William Todd and another rebel from them. Todd and his companion had been on a similar mission to Cowie and Fowler's when captured but had been spared their fate. The Mexicans suffered one dead and several wounded in what turned out to be the only real battle fought by the Bear Flaggers.

On June 25, Frémont, Carson, and Gillespie, with Segundai and the Delawares, led the way as the little army rode into Sonoma. From there, Frémont decided to journey south to the Golden Gate to see what Castro's forces were up to. He soon moved south to the mission at San Rafael, sending out scouting parties to probe toward Sausalito. Carson, with Sam Neal, Tom Martin, and Granville Swift, intercepted three Californios on the estuary near San Quentin. The men, one of whom was the elderly father of the alcalde of Sonoma, were bearing dispatches from Castro.

Carson rode back to report the prisoners to Frémont. "I want no prisoners, Mr. Carson," the captain replied. Carson returned to his men and had the three Californios summarily shot. "Their bodies laid there for three or four days, as we passed and repassed them," Martin recalled. Cowie and Fowler had been avenged.[23]

The Bear Flaggers held a grand July 4 fandango in Sonoma, where they organized the 250-man California Battalion and appointed Frémont as its commander. Archibald Gillespie was to be his adjutant. The little army was split into four companies, with Dick Owens commanding a company comprising Frémont's men and the three other companies made up of settlers under Captains Henry L. Ford, John Grigsby, and Granville Swift. Affairs were moving rapidly now and Frémont had given up any pretense of neutrality. He was now leading a rebellion. Of course, he was still ignorant of any declaration of war and so wrote a letter of resignation from the army just in case it was needed for diplomatic cover.

Two days later, navy captain William Mervine hoisted the American flag over the Monterey customshouse while offshore three American warships under Commodore John D. Sloat fired a twenty-one-gun salute. As 225 sailors and marines occupied the town, Sloat issued a proclamation annexing Alta California to the United States and assuring the local inhabitants of just and fair treatment. Soon after, the Bear Flaggers lowered their flag and raised the Stars and Stripes. Castro wisely withdrew his small force south to Los Angeles.[24]

On July 19, 1846, Frémont led his grizzled band into Monterey. They rode in two by two, Frémont, Carson, and the Delawares in the vanguard, all of the men armed to the teeth, their long rifles cradled in their arms. Offshore, the British eighty-gun *Collingwood* ominously lay at anchor. The British, who would take no action, were as awestruck over Frémont's tough band as were the American sailors and marines. Lieutenant Frederick Walpole, RN, left an account:

> *During our stay in Monterey, Captain Frémont and his party arrived. They naturally excited curiosity. Here were true trappers, the class that produced the heroes of Fenimore Cooper's best works. . . . Frémont rode ahead, a spare active-looking man. . . . He was dressed in a blouse and leggings, and wore a felt hat. After him came five Delaware Indians, who were his bodyguard. . . . The rest, many of them blacker than the Indians, rode two and two, the rifle held by one hand across the pommel of the saddle. . . . He has one or two with him who enjoy a high reputation in the prairies. Kit Carson is as well known there as the duke is in Europe.*[25]

FRÉMONT AND GILLESPIE PROMPTLY BOARDED SLOAT'S flagship to meet with the commodore. Sloat was shocked to learn that Frémont had acted on his own authority without any news of a declaration of war. Sloat had received word of the battles at Palo Alto and Resaca de la Palma before departing the Mexican coast, but he had no official word that war had been declared. Old and ill, Sloat now vacillated about cooperating with Frémont's land operations. Fortunately, Commodore Robert F. Stockton had just arrived with full authority to supersede Sloat, which he did. As bold as Sloat was timid, he was also politically ambitious, self-assured, well-connected in Washington, and determined not to allow this opportunity for glory to pass. He and Frémont immediately formed a mutual admiration society.

Stockton mustered the Bear Flaggers into the service of the United States as the California Battalion with Frémont in command as major, Gillespie as captain and second-in-command, Ezekiel Merritt as quartermaster, Dick Owens as captain, and Alexis Godey as lieutenant. Stockton and Frémont now turned their full attention to the south, where Castro and Governor Pico were raising an army.

Frémont, with 120 men, was to sail to San Diego on Captain Mervine's *Cyane* while Stockton, on the *Congress*, would land his force at San Pedro, just south of Los Angeles. The voyage on the *Cyane* was not particularly rough, but most of the men still became terribly seasick. Carson was particularly downtrodden and swore never to leave land again. The three-day voyage ended with an uncontested landing in San Diego. In fact, the local officials welcomed Frémont warmly and aided him in acquiring horses and cattle for his march north to Los Angeles. As the Americans moved north, General Castro and Governor Pico moved on.

On August 13, 1846, Stockton occupied Los Angeles without a struggle. The leading citizens, Andrés Pico (the governor's brother) and José María Flores, surrendered and promised never to bear arms against the United States. Stockton issued a proclamation announcing that California was now part of the United States, that the people were now U.S. citizens, and that a civil government with free elections would soon follow. California was conquered, or so it seemed.[26]

17

CALIFORNIA

With California conquered, Commodore Robert Stockton developed even grander visions of glory. The self-proclaimed "commander-in-chief and Governor of the Territory of California" now proposed to sail south to Acapulco, establish a supply base there, and then march to the east to join with American troops near Mexico City. The commodore divided California into three districts and placed Gillespie as commander of the southern district with headquarters in Los Angeles. He would be left with fifty men to garrison the town. Frémont was sent north to the Sacramento Valley to take command there as well as recruit men for Stockton's Mexican invasion force. Stockton, who stationed himself at Monterey, promised Frémont that upon his departure for Mexico the young officer would assume the governorship of California.[1]

Frémont selected Carson to carry dispatches with the news of the conquest of California back to Washington. "It was a service of high trust and honor, but of great danger also," Frémont later wrote. "Going off at the head of his own party with *carte blanche* for expenses and the prospect of novel pleasure and honor at the end was a culminating point in Carson's life." Carson was to report directly to Senator Benton, who would then take him to meet Secretary of the Navy Bancroft and President Polk. Carson's party consisted of his trusted friend Lucien Maxwell and fourteen men, including several of Segundai's Delawares, as well as a train of pack mules. He felt he could reach Washington in sixty days.[2]

The journey along the Gila River was rough, with many of the mules giving out. There was no time for hunting and so they subsisted on mule meat and pinole (parched cornmeal and a flour paste made from mesquite beans). Near the Santa Rita del Cobre mines in southwestern New Mexico they encountered Mangas Coloradas and a large encampment of Apaches preparing a revenge raid into Mexico. Mangas, who knew Carson from the fur trade, was pleased to hear from him that the Americans were now also fighting the hated Mexicans. Mangas informed Carson that a white man he called the "Horse Chief of the Long Knives" had taken New Mexico from the Mexicans.[3]

Mounted on fresh mules provided by Mangas, Carson pushed on toward the Rio Grande. On October 6, 1846, he encountered Brigadier General Stephen Watts Kearny with three hundred dragoons a few miles from the little village of Socorro. The "Horse Chief" had marched across the Santa Fe Trail with his 1st Dragoons, the 1st Regiment of Missouri Mounted Volunteers under Colonel Alexander Doniphan, and the Mormon Battalion of five hundred men whose services had been essentially rented from Brigham Young at Council Bluffs, Iowa—a strange conglomeration grandiosely dubbed the Army of the West—and bloodlessly conquered New Mexico. Now he was on his way to conquer California.

Kearny was undoubtedly the greatest frontier soldier of his day. A veteran of the War of 1812, he had spent almost his entire career on the western frontier, had established Jefferson Barracks near St. Louis, and served as the second commanding officer of the 1st Dragoons. That regiment, essentially mounted infantry, was the forerunner of the United States Cavalry. It had been formed in 1833 by President Jackson to meet the needs of westward expansion across the Great Plains. Kearny had been selected by Polk and Benton to protect the Santa Fe Trail, conquer New Mexico, and then proceed to California.

Kearny was well liked in both military and civilian circles, and people as diverse as Francis Parkman, the future historian, and Susan Shelby Magoffin, the wife of a famed Santa Fe trader, testified to his affable personality and gentlemanly demeanor. Yet he could also be something of a martinet—a stickler for regulations with a temper as short as his stature.

Carson informed the general that Frémont and Stockton had already taken California. As a result, Kearny sent two hundred of his dragoons back to Santa Fe under the command of Major Edwin Vose Sumner and ordered Carson to lead him back to California. Carson protested but to no avail. His dispatches were carried east by his old friend Tom Fitzpatrick, who was Kearny's guide. Carson was so angry, he considered slipping away in the night, but Maxwell talked him out of it.[4]

Kearny had kept but two companies of dragoons—about one hundred men—commanded by Captain Benjamin Moore, as well as two mountain howitzers under the watchful care of Lieutenant John Wynn Davidson. The dragoons were mostly mounted on mules. Kearny also retained Lieutenant William H. Emory and his fourteen-man topographical unit to map the new territory to be covered. Carson had convinced the general of the impossibility of taking wagons across the Gila route and so the command paused to wait for Sumner to send packsaddles. Kearny expected Captain Philip St. George Cooke, with the Mormon Battalion, to follow them to California with wagons by a longer, more southern route.

Carson's disappointment was not shared by Kearny's men. "Taking leave of the fellows left behind, we put out, with merry hearts and light packs on our long march—Carson as guide, every man feeling renewed confidence in consequence of having such a guide," Dr. John S. Griffin, a Virginian who served as regimental assistant surgeon, noted in his diary.

While Carson certainly felt honor bound to carry the dispatches to Washington, much of his frustration over this change of plans had to do with the fact that he was but days away from being reunited with Josefa in Taos. This was not lost on Kearny's officers, themselves so far from family and friends. Carson "consented and turned his face to the west again . . . after his arduous trip and when he had set his hopes on seeing his family," dragoon Captain Abraham Johnston confided in his journal. "It requires a brave man to give up his private feelings thus for the public good; but Carson is one such. Honor him for it."[5]

On October 18, Carson led Kearny's party to the abandoned copper mines at Santa Rita del Cobre. While the soldiers set up camp, Carson sent up smoke signals to invite Mangas to come meet with the "Horse Chief of the Long Knives." Mangas arrived later that evening with but a single companion. Kearny presented Mangas with several presents and the Chiricahua chief pledged "good faith and friendship to all Americans." Carson, who was standing next to Lieutenant Emory, winked at the lieutenant and whispered, "I would not trust one of them."

Two days later Mangas again met with the soldiers, this time at Santa Lucia Springs. He brought thirty of his people as well as a fine herd of mules freshly stolen from Sonora. Kearny's officers were fascinated by the Apaches, whom they found quite different from eastern Indians. "They were armed—some with guns, bows and arrows and all with lances, they are said to be very formidable with these weapons, they are finely mounted, expressed the greatest friendship, and lasting hostility against the Mexicans," noted Dr. Griffin.

Lieutenant Emory felt that the Apache warriors reminded him "of pictures of antique Grecian warriors," although he frowned at a warrior who wore "a jacket made of a Henry Clay flag, which aroused unpleasant sensations, for the acquisition, no doubt, cost one of our countrymen his life." Both Emory and Griffin were impressed by how shrewd the Apaches were at trade. It proved to be a productive and congenial meeting; it ended with Kearny presenting Mangas with a paper setting forth their mutual pledge of eternal friendship.

In return, the general received some sage Apache advice: "You have taken New Mexico, and will soon take California; go then and take Chihuahua, Durango, and Sonora. We will help you. The Mexicans are rascals; we hate and will kill them all."[6]

Mangas Coloradas was the undisputed leader of the Chiricahua Apaches as well as one of the few Apache leaders who could unite the wildly independent tribal bands. He had been born in 1790 into the Bedonkohe band of the Chiricahuas, who lived near the headwaters of the Gila River. His father was a renowned warrior and his mother a Spanish captive. As he grew to towering manhood—he was over six feet tall—he was given the name El Fuerte ("Strong One") in honor of his impressive physique. He eventually married into the Chihenne band, and since Chiricahua custom led a man to live with his wife's people, he came to be identified with that band even more than his own Bedonkohe people. These were a mountain people who lived in southwestern New Mexico, eastern Arizona, and northern Chihuahua and were identified by their favorite village (rancheria) locations: Mimbres, Warm Springs, Copper Mines, and Gilas.

The Apaches, who called themselves Dine or Indeh—"the people"—embraced the cult of the warrior and lived by raiding their neighbors—Navajos, Pueblos, Pimas, Papagos, and most especially the Spanish invaders. The Apaches were divided into many independent tribal groups: the Mescalero of southeastern New Mexico; the Jicarilla, who lived in the mountains of northern New Mexico but ranged eastward onto the Great Plains; the Lipans, who lived along the Pecos River in Texas; the Chiricahuas, who occupied the Gila and Dragoon Mountains of western New Mexico and southeastern Arizona as well as the Sierra Madre in northern Mexico; and the Western Apaches of the central and eastern mountain ranges of Arizona. Although united by language, custom, and religion as Apaches, these groups lived in proud isolation, with loyalty given first to family and clan rather than to the tribe. At the time of the rise of Mangas Coloradas, the Apache people numbered between 8,000 and 10,000.

El Fuerte came to prominence as a warrior early in life, but it was the brutal 1837 massacre of an Animas Mountain Apache village by American scalp hunters in the employ of the governor of Sonora that elevated him to a leadership role. El Fuerte escaped the carnage, swore vengeance, and led reprisal raids deep into Mexico. In this bloody work, the warrior Fuerte earned a new name: Mangas Coloradas, or "Red Sleeves," because of the blood that stained his shirt as he slaughtered his Mexican enemies.

The Spanish had been unable to defeat the Apaches and so had long paid tribute in order to secure a fragile peace. The successful Mexican Revolution of 1821 ended the tribute payments and that doomed the peace. The new central government in Mexico City quickly descended into chaos and civil war, so that in the northern Mexican states warlords rose to power. Unable to stop Apache raiding parties, they hired mercenary scalp hunters, many of them Americans, to kill Apaches. The bounties for Apache scalps ranged from $100 for an adult male to $50 for a female and $25 for a child. There was always Mexican silver to be had for Apache slaves as well. This only enhanced the bitter enmity between the Apaches and the Mexicans.

Unprotected by the army, the Mexican settlers in northern Sonora and Chihuahua were helpless against the Apaches. They had few weapons and so resisted as best they could with clubs and improvised lances. Hundreds were killed and scores more carried off into captivity, so that their fields became barren and skeletons lined the roads and the abandoned haciendas. All of this would greatly assist the Americans in their war with Mexico.[7]

When Kearny and Carson met with Mangas at Santa Lucia Springs, the Apache leader was preparing for a great revenge raid against the Mexican town of Galeana. In July 1846 the Irish-American scalp hunter James Kirker, in the employ of the governor of Chihuahua for 100,000 pesos, had lured a large group of Chiricahuas into Galeana with promises of a peace treaty and presents. The Apaches negotiated with the Mexicans of Galeana while Kirker and his men lay in wait. When the Apaches went to sleep that night, Kirker's land pirates butchered 130 of them. Mangas, along with his son-in-law Cochise of the Chokonen and Chihenne leaders Cuchillo Negro (Black Knife) and Delgadito, led their warriors in a war that all but obliterated Galeana and forced the Mexicans to abandon their presidios at Fronteras and Tubac. The vengeance of Mangas Coloradas was indeed terrible.

Captain Henry Smith Turner, the general's adjutant, was remarkably prescient in his observations of the Apaches who inhabited the country that was to become Arizona: "Should this country ever get in the possession of the U.S. there will be much difficulty in keeping these Indians in order—their only subsistence is the stolen cattle, etc. from Sonora, and if they are cut off from this resource I cannot perceive how they are to live—the U.S. may buy them up with annuities, and cause them to be subsisted, and in this way purchase permanent peace with them—they live in such a rough country their hiding places are in such fastnesses that a war with them would be almost as endless as was the Florida war with the Seminoles."[8]

CARSON GUIDED KEARNY'S DEPLETED ARMY WESTWARD from the Rio Grande, through the mountains and along the Gila River, to its juncture with the Colorado without incident. It was rough going, with so many of the mules giving out that most of the men had to walk. "We marched 500 miles down that river, having most of the way a bridle path, but over very rough and barren country," Kearny later wrote to his wife. "It surprised me to see so much land that can never be of any use to man or beast."

Dr. Griffin echoed the sentiments of his commander: "Every bush in the country is full of thorns—and every piece of grass so soon as it is broken becomes a thorn at both ends—every rock you turn over has a tarantula or centipede under it, and Carson says in the summer the most beautiful specimens of rattle snakes are scattered around in the greatest profusion."

Captain Turner was equally disgusted with the landscape but was a bit more sanguine about the potential of Arizona: "The United States will place a high value on this country, as affording a highway from the United States via New Mexico to California." He also noted that "the country is healthy to a degree far surpassing in this respect all parts of the United States and perhaps all other parts of the world—there was never a purer atmosphere than I am breathing at this moment, but having said this there is nothing more to be said in favor of the country. Invalids may live here when they might die in any other part of the world, but really the country is so unattractive and forbidding, that one would scarcely be willing to secure a long life at the cost of living in it." History would prove him correct on both the road and the invalids.[9]

By November 23 they had neared the junction of the Gila and the Colorado. In the evening as they approached the river they came across the tracks of a large number of horses. The assumption among Kearny and his officers was that this must be a Mexican force up from Sonora sent to intercept them. Kearny called for Carson.

"Find them Carson and we will fight them tonight," the general declared.

Griffin thought this a wildly optimistic plan. "Our men are nearly naked and barefooted," noted the good doctor. "Their feet are sore and leg weary—they have been marching many of them for the last four or five hundred miles. Our mules are all so that they can scarcely get along with a pack or a man on their backs. Only the sick have been allowed to ride lately. This is rather a bad picture for men who have a hard campaign before them."[10]

It was nearly dark when Carson returned to report that he had discovered scattered horse tracks along with the footprints of both men and women. This was no military formation. Lieutenant Emory led a patrol out and soon returned with four Mexicans. They were part of a larger party herding some five hundred horses south to Sonora. They told an alarming story of how the Californios had risen against the Americans, driven Gillespie from Los Angeles, and now fielded a force of several hundred men. This was confirmed the next day when Emory captured a Mexican soldier with dispatches for General Castro.

Kearny paid the Mexican herders for twenty-five horses and a few mules and released them. The army then moved on two miles to ford the Colorado River. Carson warned that beyond the river lay nearly a hundred

Colonel George Washington

Author's collection

Braddock's Retreat by Alonzo Chappel from John Schroeder, *The Life and Times of Washington* (1857)

Author's collection

Henry Bouquet and the battlefield at Bushy Run from a 1903 postcard

Author's collection

Daniel Boone. Engraving based on Chester Harding's 1820 portrait.

Author's collection

Boonesborough. Postcard circa 1920s.

Author's collection

Gateway to the West—Daniel Boone Leading the Settlers Through the Cumberland Gap, 1775 (2002)

Courtesy of David Wright

Engraving based on Karl Bodmer's *Deliverance of the Daughters of Daniel Boone and Callaway* (1852)

Author's collection

"Torture of Colonel Crawford" by J. Steeple Davis from *The Indian Wars of the United States* by Edward S. Ellis (1902)

Author's collection

Daniel Morgan

Author's collection

"Battle of Cowpens—Conflict Between Cols. Washington & Tarleton" by Alonzo Chappel from *Battles of America on Sea and Land* (1859)

Author's collection

"Death of Major Ferguson at Kings Mountain" by Alonzo Chappel from *Battles of America on Sea and Land* (1859)

Author's collection

"Massacre at Fort Mims" by Alonzo Chappel (1859)

Author's collection

Menawa by Charles Bird King

Author's collection

William McIntosh by Charles Bird King

Author's collection

Crossroads to Destiny by David Wright (1999) depicts General Andrew Jackson, Ensign Sam Houston, David Crockett, and Dr. Charles McKinney at Camp Blount in October 1813 at the beginning of the Creek campaign.

Courtesy of David Wright

Surrender of Weatherford (Red Eagle) to Jackson by John Chapin (1814), engraved by W. Ridgway for *Battles of America on Sea and Land* (1859)

Author's collection

Young Davy Crockett by John Nava (1994)

Courtesy of David Zucker

"Sporting Anecdotes—'Clear Out My Buck'—David Crockett's Elk Hunt" by H. Alken (1839)

Courtesy of David Zucker

David Crockett by Anthony Lewis De Rose, engraved by Asher Durand (1834)

Courtesy of David Zucker

David Crockett by Charles Osgood (1834)

Courtesy of David Zucker

The U.S. Capitol as it looked during Crockett's time in Congress.

Author's collection

James Hackett as Colonel Nimrod Wildfire in *The Lion of the West* (1831)

Courtesy of David Zucker

Davy Crockett's 1837 almanac copied its cover from a portrait of actor James Hackett. It is our first image of Crockett in a fur cap.

Author's collection

Crockett speaking in Congress from Davy Crockett's 1844 almanac.

Author's collection

The cover of Crockett's 1842 almanac was based on the 1834 portrait by John Chapman.

Author's collection

"Ruins of the Alamo, 1845," by U.S. Army engineer Jacob E. Blake

Author's collection

Susanna Dickinson

Author's collection

Santa Anna

Author's collection

Sam Houston

Author's collection

"Remember the Alamo" by F. C. Yohn. Continental Fire Insurance calendar art, 1913.

Author's collection

Kit Carson circa 1850

Author's collection

John C. Frémont

Author's collection

James K. Polk

Author's collection

In 1888 John and Jessie Frémont and daughter, Lily, visited the tree in California where he had camped in 1846.

Author's collection

Thomas Hart Benton

Author's collection

George Bancroft

Author's collection

Commodore Robert Stockton

True West Archives

Stephen Watts Kearny, from *The History of the Military Occupation of the Territory of New Mexico from 1846 to 1851* by Ralph Emerson Twitchell (1909)

Author's collection

"Navajos" by Heinrich Balduin Möllhausen (1861) from Lt. Joseph Ives's "Colorado River Expedition 1858" report

Author's collection

Navajo chief Manuelito

Author's collection

Mangas, son of Mangas Coloradas. No picture of his father exists.

Author's collection

Mescalero Apaches from *Harper's Weekly*, May 29, 1886

Author's collection

Kit Carson, 1868

Author's collection

Buffalo Bill Cody,
cabinet card circa 1872

Author's collection

Cody holds Lucretia Borgia as he poses with Lord Adare, later the fourth Earl of Dunraven, and 5th Cavalry officers Francis Michler and Walter Schuyler at Fort McPherson in 1871.

Buffalo Bill Center of the West, Cody, Wyoming

Colonel Eugene Carr

Author's collection

The Summit Springs Rescue by Charles Schreyvogel (1908)

Buffalo Bill Center of the West, Cody, Wyoming

The grand duke Alexis kills his first buffalo as depicted in *Frank Leslie's Illustrated Newspaper*, 1872.

Author's collection

The Scouts of the Prairie cast: Ned Buntline, Buffalo Bill, Giuseppina Morlacchi, and Texas Jack, 1872

Buffalo Bill Center of the West, Cody, Wyoming

Bill and Louisa Cody with daughter Arta in Rochester, New York

Buffalo Bill Center of the West, Cody, Wyoming

Annie Oakley

Buffalo Bill Center of the West, Cody, Wyoming

First Scalp for Custer by Robert Lindneux (1928)

Buffalo Bill Center of the West, Cody, Wyoming

Back row: White Eagle, William F. Cody, Adirondack the naturalist. Front row: William Halsey (interpreter), Sitting Bull, and Johnny Baker.

Author's collection

Sitting Bull and Cody, 1885

Author's collection

Sitting Bull argues in defense of Lakota land at Standing Rock in 1888, *Frank Leslie's Illustrated Newspaper.*

Author's collection

"The Triumph of the West" cartoon by Charles Dana Gibson in *Life*, December 15, 1887

Author's collection

Buffalo Bill's Wild West program, 1899

Author's collection

Frederick Jackson Turner

Courtesy of Huntington Library

miles of brutal desert with neither water nor forage. Kearny did not hesitate to order an advance.[11]

Kearny had decided to march to San Diego rather than Los Angeles. Carson led them across the unforgiving desert, tough on men and mules, to Warner's Ranch (a commercial center somewhat similar to but not as elaborate as Sutter's Fort in the north) in the first week of December. From there Kearny sent a message off to San Diego with the news of his arrival.

The Californios were indeed in full revolt against their new American overlords. José María Flores and Andrés Pico had broken their parole, declared California free of all foreign control, and driven Gillespie out of Los Angeles and forced him and his small force to seek sanctuary on an American merchant ship at San Pedro. Merritt, with nineteen men in San Diego, took sanctuary on an American whaler. Talbot, with but nine men in Santa Barbara, cut his way out to the north. News of the rebellion quickly reached Stockton and Frémont in the north. Stockton promptly sailed in the *Congress* down the coast to San Diego while Frémont, with his California Battalion, was to march south from Monterey to Los Angeles. Flores had only a few hundred untrained men with which to resist the Americans. Andrés Pico, with nearly two hundred well-mounted Californios, was to guard San Diego.

Stockton sent Captain Gillespie and navy lieutenant Edward Fitzgerald Beale with thirty-five men and a little four-pounder cannon to reinforce Kearny. This well-traveled cannon was Russian and had been purchased by Sutter from Fort Ross. He had taken it to Los Angeles in 1845 and left it there. Gillespie had retrieved it. The two parties met on a gloomy Saturday, December 5, and Gillespie informed Kearny that Pico with a hundred lancers was camped just nine miles away at an Indian village called San Pasqual. Despite the jaded nature of both his men and his horses, as well as a steady rain, Kearny decided to attack.[12]

Kearny sent a dragoon patrol forward under Lieutenant Tom Hammond to scout the enemy position, but they were spotted. With the element of surprise lost, he now foolishly prepared to attack the Californios at dawn. The officers were all anxious for action, although some agreed with Captain Benjamin Moore, who fretted that the paper cartridges for the men's Hall breech-loading carbines were wet. Kearny had but 160 men.

Captain Abraham Johnston, with Kit Carson and a dozen dragoons, led the advance into a dense fog. Kearny, who was behind Johnston with Beale and the other officers, gave the order "Trot!" Johnston instead shouted, "Charge!"

"O heavens!" exclaimed the exasperated general. "I did not mean that!"

Johnston's little band were mounted on the command's best horses and they quickly distanced themselves from their commander and his dragoons on their broken-down animals. Pico's men waited in a gully just in front of the Indian village so that the Americans did not see them until almost upon them. The Californios, mostly lancers, sent a volley into the advancing dragoons and then wheeled and fled. Johnston was shot out of the saddle; Carson's horse stumbled, throwing him. He regained his bearings after nearly being trampled by the charging dragoons, found the weapon of a fallen dragoon, and tried to join the fight, but he was soon left behind. The Americans on their exhausted animals were so strung out that their charge proved ineffective.

Captain Moore, with fifty men, pursued the retreating Californios for nearly a mile when they suddenly turned and encircled the dragoons. Moore charged into them, confronting Pico himself. As the two men dueled with sabers, two of Pico's men lanced Moore from behind. As he fell, a third man shot him dead. Lieutenant Hammond, Moore's brother-in-law, tried to cut his way through to his assistance but went down with several lance wounds. "For God's sake, men, come up!" he gasped as he fell mortally wounded near Moore. The captain's men attempted to retrieve his body but their carbines only snapped harmlessly because of the wet powder. They used their carbines as clubs, but they were no match for the long lances of their opponents. Other Californios used their reatas to lasso the dragoons and jerk them from their saddles.

Kearny could only watch in horror. "They are admirably mounted & the very best riders in the world—hardly one that is not fit for the Circus," he later declared.

Gillespie now hurried forward with thirty men of the California Battalion, the little Sutter four-pounder in tow. Davidson followed with his two mule-drawn six-pounder howitzers. They reached the field as the dragoons were falling back.

"Rally men, for God's sake rally!" Gillespie shouted. "Show a front, don't turn your backs! Face them, face them, follow me!"

No one listened. The mule with one of the howitzers bolted and carried it into the Californio ranks. They killed one of the crew and lassoed the field-piece and dragged it away. The crew of the second gun went down before the Californio lances. Gillespie, smeared in blood from several wounds, including one that punctured a lung, staggered toward the howitzer and fired it into the advancing lancers before fainting. Some of the California Battalion men fired the little Sutter four-pounder at the same time. The lancers pulled up and then hurriedly abandoned the field. They left eighteen Americans dead and fifteen more, including Kearny, wounded. Amazingly, Kearny would later claim San Pasqual as a victory since he held the field.

Lieutenant Emory, who had saved his general's life during the fight, was more realistic: "Our provisions were exhausted, our horses dead, our mules on their last legs, and our men, now reduced to one third of their number, were ragged, worn down by fatigue, and emaciated. . . . Our position was defensible, but the ground, covered with rocks and cacti, made it difficult to get a smooth place to rest, even for the wounded."[13]

Kearny, with a severe lance wound to his buttocks and another to his arm, briefly turned command over to Captain Turner. They then spent a cold and damp night on the battlefield. No one slept. Dr. Griffin, who had feverishly labored over the wounded all day, somehow managed to lose only one of them. To the nearby melancholy howl of wolves attracted by the smell of death, they buried their comrades in a common grave by a little willow to the east of the camp.

By morning Kearny had recovered enough to resume command. "Kearny concluded to march on," Carson noted, "let the consequences be what they would." Godey was dispatched with two men to ride the thirty miles to San Diego to report the situation to Stockton. Turner took command of what was left of Kearny's dragoons, who were now consolidated into a single company. The wounded were placed in the center on improvised travois stretchers, but the forward movement over the rocky trail proved excruciating for them. It was equally uncomfortable for their general, mounted on a mule with his most delicate and embarrassing wound. Carson led the advance guard.[14]

The Californios hovered on the nearby hills but did not dispute the column's passage. Within a few miles they reached the rancheria of San Bernardo. The place was deserted save for a handful of Indians. Kearny ordered a halt and the men managed to locate some chickens to make into a broth for the wounded. They also collected a few cattle. As the column resumed the march, several lancers dashed forward to seize a rocky hill that commanded passage to San Diego. Emory, with but six men, charged the lancers and drove them off. As the column came up, Kearny decided to camp on the hill for the night to rest the wounded before attempting to cut their way through to San Diego. In the rush up the hill the cattle had scattered, so that the Americans had the high ground but little else. While some of the men piled rocks up as a crude battlement, others slaughtered several of the loyal mules for food. They named their sad encampment Mule Hill.

The next morning a flag of truce appeared before the huddled Americans. Kearny sent Lieutenant Emory forward. He met with Andrés Pico, whom he found to be "a gentlemanly looking and rather handsome man," and was informed that the Californios had Godey and three other prisoners that they were prepared to exchange. The Americans had but one Mexican officer to trade and Pico was willing to part with only one of his prisoners. Thomas Burgess returned with Emory to Mule Hill, where all anxiously awaited his report. He said that they had reached San Diego but that Stockton had no troops to spare. They had been returning to rejoin the column when they were captured that morning.[15]

Kearny called a conference with Carson and his few remaining officers. Their situation was hopeless, he declared, and they must cut their way out. Dr. Griffin protested that the wounded could not possibly survive such a movement. Navy lieutenant Beale assured them all that Burgess must be mistaken, for Commodore Stockton would never abandon them.

Kearny agreed to wait a bit longer. Carson stepped forward and volunteered to slip through the ring of Californio pickets and again seek help from Stockton. Young Beale and his Indian striker Chemuctah offered to join Carson. Kearny reluctantly agreed, although he doubted that the men could get past the surrounding Californios.

Under cover of darkness, the three men slipped down the hill. They removed their boots and discarded their canteens to muffle the sounds as they passed so close to the Californio lines that they could smell the smoke of their *cigarritos*. They lay quietly, and as pickets passed by, Carson could hear Beale's heart pounding. Pico had learned from Godey that Carson was with the soldiers and had warned his guards to be wary.

"Carson is there," he declared. "*Se escapara el lobo*" ("The wolf will escape").

The messengers managed to get through the lines and into the open valley below. Carson never doubted their escape. "I have been in worse places before," he told Beale, "and Providence has always saved me."

They separated in hopes one would get through. They had lost their boots in the hills and now had to cross thirty-five miles of hills, cactus, and rock in their bare feet. As they neared San Diego, Carson had them travel in different directions. Chemuctah reached San Diego first, Beale following, and Carson arriving last. Stockton had already sent two hundred of his sailors and marines to rescue Kearny.

Carson's feet were so cut and bruised that it would be a week before he could walk again. Beale was carried to the infirmary on the *Congress* in a deranged state. He would remain there for a month. Carson visited him and worried that he would not survive. Chemuctah, it was reported, did not live for long after.[16]

What was left of the Army of the West limped into San Diego in a drenching rain on December 12. Kearny placed his men under Stockton's command, although friction between the two officers quickly developed. It was December 29 before the combined American force was on the march north toward Los Angeles. Stockton's naval band from the *Congress* led the way, followed by Stockton and Kearny with forty-two officers, five hundred sailors and marines, fifty-seven dragoons under Captain Turner, a mounted detachment of volunteers under Captain Gillespie (now recovered from his wounds), and six pieces of ordnance.

At San Luis Rey Mission, they were met by three emissaries for José Flores proposing a suspension of hostilities. Stockton responded that Flores was a rebel who had broken his parole and now faced execution. The commodore was in no mood to parley, but he was nervous about the size of the force he might confront. And where was Frémont? Rumors had him at Santa Barbara, and so Stockton sent a message north by sea to hurry the California Battalion south.

Frémont, recently promoted to lieutenant colonel, had finally led his 430-man California Battalion south from Monterey on November 30. They were a colorful but rough-looking lot, reminiscent of the volunteers of old Kentucky, New Orleans, and the Alamo. Many of them wore blue sailor shirts courtesy of the United States Navy, with buckskin trousers sometimes trimmed with red flannel. A broad Mexican sombrero was the favored headgear. Mountain men, settlers both American and Mexican, recent emigrants from the states, and contingents of Paiute, Walla Walla, and California Indians—along with Delaware scouts—made up this wildly diverse army.

It had taken time to recruit this force and gather horses for them, and now their march south was slowed by torrential rains as well as three pieces of ordnance, wagons, and a large horse remuda and cattle herd. On the night of December 14 they reached San Luis Obispo in a driving rain, surrounded the old mission, and captured thirty Californios. Numbered among the prisoners was José de Jesús Pico, a cousin of Andrés Pico, who despite being on parole had skirmished with Frémont's forces at the La Natividad rancho the previous month, when four Americans had been killed. Frémont ordered an immediate court-martial, which unsurprisingly sentenced Pico to be executed the next morning.

As the hour of execution approached, Owens brought before Frémont the wife and children of Pico. This elegant woman now fell to her knees weeping and pleading with Frémont to spare her husband. Deeply moved, the young officer raised her up and told her to go to her home. He told Owens to bring the condemned man before him.

Pico appeared ashen but did not otherwise show any sign of nervousness. Frémont was impressed by such calm bravery in the face of certain death. "He was a handsome man, within a few years of forty," the colonel recalled, "with black eyes and black hair."

"You were about to die," Frémont told Pico, "but your wife has saved you. Go thank her."

Don Jesús made the sign of the cross, thanked Frémont, and promised to serve him faithfully.

"When the march was resumed he accompanied me and remained with me until I left California," Frémont noted, "always an agreeable companion and often rendering me valuable service—perhaps sometimes quite unknown to myself."[17]

Frémont, anxious to curry favor with the Californios, also released the other prisoners. He then led his column south, and while the weather briefly cleared, the going was still slow. Fearing ambush, they skirted Gaviota Pass leading to Santa Barbara and took a treacherous trail, little better than a goat path, through the Santa Ynez Mountains above the town. They lost over a hundred horses in the journey and spent a frigid, rainy Christmas Day surmounting the ridgeline. They entered Santa Barbara on December 27 after three nightmarish days in the mountains only to find that the Californio forces had abandoned the town. They raised the Stars and Stripes and settled in to rest and refit. Frémont gave strict orders that the local population was not to be disturbed in any way. This good behavior was soon rewarded when many Californios came into the American camp to surrender.

On January 3, 1847, Frémont ordered his troops south again. This time they traveled along the shoreline, accompanied by the naval schooner *Julia*, which kept abreast and in cannon range of the column. They were shadowed to the east by fifty or more Californios but no hostile action was initiated by either side. On January 9, George W. Hamley, the captain of the whaler *Stonington* out of New London, Connecticut, reached Frémont's camp with a message from Stockton dated January 3 with news that his force would soon "march for the City of the angels." Stockton informed Frémont of Kearny's defeat, which the colonel had already learned of from Don Jesús Pico, and warned him not to underestimate the Californios.

"My advice to you is, to allow them to do all the charging and running, and let your rifles do the rest," Stockton warned. "In the art of horsemanship, of dodging, and running, it is in vain to attempt to compete with them."[18]

Stockton's army, moving north, was confronted by Flores and Pico at a ford of the San Gabriel River, twelve miles to the northeast of Los Angeles. The Californios numbered near five hundred, but they were poorly armed and the gun crews manning their four cannons were untrained. Stockton took personal charge of the American artillery and quickly silenced Flores's guns. Kearny then led the Americans in a wild charge that took the Californio positions on a bluff above the river crossing.

The men, shouting "New Orleans!" as they scrambled up the bluff, sent the enemy into a disorderly retreat. It was January 8, the anniversary of Jackson's great victory at New Orleans. The victorious Americans camped on the battlefield. They had lost but two killed and eight wounded.

The next morning at nine the Americans advanced across a mesa between the San Gabriel and Los Angeles Rivers. They soon discovered the

Californio position. Flores had drawn his men up in a horseshoe formation. After an ineffective artillery barrage, Flores sent his lancers galloping forward. Kearny had his dragoons and Stockton's sailors in a hollow square bristling with steel worthy of Wellington.

"Ready, aim, pick your men, boys, fire!" exclaimed the old dragoon.

The lancers reeled and fell back in disorder, but Flores rallied them. Again they came on, swirling around the American square, only to be met by several volleys from the sailors, volunteers, and dragoons as well as well-placed grape from Stockton's cannons. Bravery and horsemanship were not enough for the Californios that day.

"We all considered this the beginning of the fight," Emory noted, "but it was the end of it."

That evening Stockton and Kearny crossed the Los Angeles River and camped some three miles from the pueblo. Their force had suffered but nine wounded—one of whom was poor Gillespie—and none killed. The next morning three citizens from the town approached the American camp to promise no resistance if only the citizens might be protected in their persons and property. Stockton promptly agreed, although he still distrusted Flores and Pico, and at noon on January 10 the little American army entered the City of Angels. Gillespie was given the honor of raising the Stars and Stripes.[19]

Frémont had missed all the action, but he arrived with his California Battalion just in time to accept the surrender of Andrés Pico. He encountered Pico's Californio army just to the north of Los Angeles. Flores, it was soon learned, had fled south to Sonora. Don Jesús Pico now proved to be an invaluable emissary. Frémont offered generous terms that forgave previous transgressions and allowed all Californio officers and men to return to their homes after surrendering their arms. All were to be guaranteed their full rights as American citizens. Frémont, looking to the future, hoped now to win the peace. Talbot drew up the Treaty of Cahuenga (so named because Frémont and Pico met near Cahuenga Pass just to the north of Los Angeles) in both English and Spanish and it was signed on January 13, 1847. The war for California was now truly over.

"We took the wind out of Frémont's sails by capturing the Puebla—and whipping the enemy on the 8th & 9th, but he has shown himself the better politician by negotiating first with the enemy," grumbled Dr. Griffin.[20]

Kearny, already humiliated by his "victory" at San Pasqual, and nursing wounds both physical and mental, was outraged by Frémont's action in accepting the surrender without first consulting with his superior officers. He was then further enraged when Frémont, officially appointed governor by Stockton, declared that he would take orders only from the commodore. Kearny seethed and bided his time. Ambiguous orders to both Stockton and Kearny from Washington had set up this army-and-navy conflict over command, but they were soon clarified by new dispatches appointing Kearny governor of California. Stockton soon sailed away and Frémont was left to face Kearny's wrath.

On February 25, Frémont sent Carson, along with Beale, Theodore Talbot, Joe Stepperfeldt, and seven others, east along the Gila with dispatches to Benton and Polk, giving his side of the command controversy. Kearny had already dispatched Emory by sea with his version of the imbroglio. Stockton also sent his account of the affair to Bancroft, urging the recall of Kearny to "prevent the evil consequences that may grow out of such a temper and such a head!"[21]

It proved to be a difficult journey, made even worse when they reached Santa Fe the first week of April only to learn of the January 19 uprising in Taos by Mexicans and Taos Pueblo Indians. Carson's brother-in-law, Governor Charles Bent, had been murdered in his own house and his scalp carried through the streets of Taos. Twenty others, both American and Mexican friends of Carson, had also been killed, while Josefa and her now widowed sister had barely escaped. Ceran St. Vrain, with 60 New Mexico Volunteers, had joined with Colonel Sterling Price of the 2nd Missouri Mounted Volunteers—some 353 men all told—to march from Santa Fe to defeat over a thousand insurgents at La Cañada and at Embudo Pass before reaching Taos on February 2. Price, reinforced by Captain John H. K. Burgwin's company of the 1st Dragoons, attacked the ancient Taos Pueblo the next day. Several hundred defenders barricaded themselves in the large adobe church. Price's four little mountain howitzers proved ineffective against the stout walls of the church, so the place had to be assaulted. Captain Burgwin and 6 others were killed and over forty wounded in taking the church, while over 150 insurgents perished. The revolt was crushed and 28 of the rebels, including the main ringleaders, were tried and promptly hanged.[22]

Carson comforted Josefa as best he could but after a ten-day delay had to hurry on with his dispatches. If he had been home, he probably would have suffered the same fate as Bent, but that was but slight comfort to assuage the guilt he felt for being away when his wife, relatives, and friends were in such danger.

Carson's party reached St. Louis toward the end of May. Beale and Talbot proceeded on while Carson remained briefly in St. Louis to confer with Benton. The senator was in a fury over the dispatches carried by Emory that had reached Washington in April with Kearny's one-sided account of his "heroic victory" at San Pasqual and his argument with Stockton and Frémont over command. The dispatches had been leaked to the press and widely reported. Benton read Frémont's measured account of the controversy with great interest and hurried Carson on to Washington by train to report to President Polk.

When Carson descended from the train onto the platform in Washington, he was startled to be approached by a beautiful young woman whom he had never met but who recognized him instantly. It was Jessie Benton Frémont. She took charge of the scout and escorted him to Senator Benton's spacious Washington home. He preferred to sleep outside on the veranda rather than in the house but otherwise enjoyed the Bentons' warm hospitality. Jessie introduced him to all her society lady friends. They all wanted to meet the famous scout. This embarrassed Carson and also made him uncomfortable because he felt these high-toned ladies would not wish to associate with him if they knew he had been married to an Indian woman. He confessed his uneasiness to Beale.

"She was a good wife to me," he told his friend. "I never came in from hunting that she did not have the warm water ready for my feet."[23]

On June 7, Jessie took him to meet with President Polk and to give Frémont's side of the California controversy. Polk, delighted to meet the famous scout, listened attentively but remained noncommittal. Jessie could sense that the president would not support her husband. He just wanted the whole dispute to go away, but both Kearny and Benton were determined to have it all aired in a formal court-martial.

"Mrs. Frémont seemed anxious to elicit from me some expression of approbation of her husband's conduct, but I evaded making any," Polk confided in his diary that evening. "In truth I consider that Col. Frémont was greatly in the wrong when he refused to obey the orders issued to him by General Kearny. . . . I saw Kit Carson again after night, and had a full conversation with him concerning the state of affairs in California, and especially in relation to the collision between our land & naval commanders in that distant region."[24]

Carson spent three weeks in Washington—a true fish out of water—and came to have a dim view of many of the government officials he met. After a visit with Buchanan at the State Department, he was particularly gloomy.

"He is such a fair-looking gentleman—who would think he is not to be trusted!" he complained to Jessie. "With their big houses and easy living they think they are princes, but on the plains we are the princes—they could not live there without us."[25]

Back in California, Colonel Richard B. Mason, an old dragoon comrade of Kearny's, arrived in San Francisco on February 13, 1847, with orders from General Winfield Scott investing all government authority in Kearny. Scott also instructed Kearny to muster the California Battalion into the army and to send Frémont home: "It is desired that you do not detain him, against his wishes, a moment longer than the necessities of the service may require." After Kearny had established a civil government and ensured tranquility in California, he was to turn over command to Colonel Mason and return to St. Louis. Kearny, who had moved his headquarters to Monterey in February, was now in the catbird seat. He placed Lieutenant Colonel Philip St. George Cooke, who had finally arrived with his Mormon Battalion, in command in Los Angeles and ordered Frémont to report to Monterey. Kearny and Mason proceeded to do everything in their collective power to humiliate the chastened lieutenant colonel. The tension between the two officers was compounded when Kearny offered the men of the California Battalion the opportunity to be mustered into the army and none would accept because of the manner in which their commander was being treated. When Frémont requested permission to return to St. Louis with the remaining members of his exploring party, it was denied, as was his request to be allowed to join his regiment, the Mounted Rifles, in Mexico. Both denials were in direct violation of Scott's orders to Kearny.

Mason, who was a notorious martinet, took particular pleasure in insulting and abusing Frémont, whom he did not consider a real soldier, threatening at one point to clap him in irons. Frémont responded with a formal challenge to a duel. Kearny ordered both men to stand down. When the time finally came on May 31 for his army to depart California, Kearny further humiliated Frémont by ordering him and his topographical corpsmen to follow in the rear of the column and camp separately. His men stood loyally by their commander. "We would not trust him with Kearny," declared Alexis Godey. "We were not under Kearny's orders—the prairies were free and we came along to watch over the Colonel." When they reached Fort Leavenworth on August 22, 1847, Kearny had Frémont arrested on charges of mutiny and disobedience of orders.[26]

At a cabinet meeting on June 8, 1847, Polk had reached consensus with his cabinet that Kearny had indeed been in the right in California. It was decided to separate Kearny and Frémont by sending Carson back to California with dispatches making clear the command structure but allowing the new lieutenant colonel of the Mounted Rifles to join his regiment in Mexico. In this way Polk had hoped to bring the whole affair to a quick resolution.

When Jessie and Carson again called on the president on June 14, Polk assured her that her husband could either remain in California or go to Mexico and that Carson would carry this news along with other important dispatches west to Santa Fe and Monterey. Polk also appointed Carson a lieutenant in Frémont's regiment, the Mounted Rifles. The morning of his departure, Jessie entrusted to Carson a hand-painted miniature of herself to carry west, along with a short note:

> *Kit Carson is waiting to take a letter to you. Nothing I can say will express in the littlest degree the love and yearning in my heart—the grief that I cannot be with you. It hurts too much even to write. Besides, I would not make you unhappy by my repining. Kit will tell you everything. I am sending you myself—in miniature. I lay with it over my heart last night. I pray you wear it over yours until le bon temps viendra. Your devoted wife, Jessie.*[27]

In October, Carson, after a brief visit with Josefa, arrived in Los Angeles, where he learned that Kearny and Frémont had departed for Fort Leavenworth months before. He proceeded north to Monterey to deliver his dispatches to Colonel Mason. This was considered to be the first overland mail to reach California.

Carson delivered his mail to Mason's adjutant, a young redheaded lieutenant who was thrilled but a bit disappointed upon meeting the frontiersman. "His fame was then at its height, from the publication of Frémont's books, and I was very anxious to see a man who had achieved such feats of daring among the wild animals of the Rocky Mountains, and still wilder Indians of the Plains," recalled William Tecumseh Sherman. "I cannot express my surprise at beholding a small, stoop-shouldered man, with reddish hair, freckled face, soft blue eyes, and nothing to indicate extraordinary courage or daring. He spoke but little, and answered questions in monosyllables. . . . He spent some days in Monterey, during which time we extracted with difficulty some items of his personal history."[28]

At the very time that Carson was meeting with Sherman and Mason in Monterey, the court-martial of Frémont was getting underway at the Washington Arsenal. Polk's hope of avoiding a trial had been dashed, as had his long friendship with Senator Benton, and he now "resolved that Col. Frémont shall be tried as all other officers are tried. . . . I will grant him no favours or privileges which I would not grant to any other officer, even though I should incur his displeasure & that of his friends."[29]

Polk would incur considerable "displeasure," and not just from the agitated Benton, but from the public at large. Frémont, a dashing national hero, received wide support from the people and the press. Kearny was often portrayed as a jealous and vindictive old soldier well past his prime. The embarrassing trial became a national cause célèbre and often overshadowed the war news from Mexico in the newspapers. The proceedings were to drag on from November 2, 1847, until the last day of January 1848, but the verdict was a foregone conclusion. The military officers, most of whom had been in the army since before Frémont had been a schoolboy, backed Kearny. Frémont was convicted on all charges and ordered to be dismissed from the service. A majority of the court recommended leniency and on February 16, 1848, Polk, dismissing the charge of mutiny but approving the charges of "disobedience of lawful commands" and of "conduct to the prejudice of good order and military discipline," remitted the penalty of dismissal from the service "in consideration of the peculiar circumstances of the case, of the previous meritorious and valuable services of

Lieutenant Colonel Frémont." Frémont was ordered to rejoin his regiment.[30]

Feeling that to accept clemency would be tantamount to an admission of guilt, the proud officer promptly resigned his commission on February 19, 1848. It was a sad end to a glorious and consequential military career.

"My path of life led out from among the grand and lovely features of nature, and its pure and wholesome air," an embittered Frémont later wrote of his fall from glory, "into the poisoned atmosphere and jarring circumstances of conflict among men, made subtle and malignant by clashing interests."[31]

Not long after Frémont's resignation, Jessie collapsed. She had been suffering through a troubled pregnancy, made all the more difficult by the stress of the court-martial. A dangerous fever ensued and the doctors ordered her to remain in bed for the remainder of her pregnancy. On July 24, 1848, she gave birth to a fragile baby boy whom they named Benton. He lived but three months.

Jessie would not let go of her baby's lifeless form. Frémont finally had to pry the infant from her arms.

"Grief was new to me then and I could not bear to give him up," she later wrote the baby's godfather, Kit Carson.[32]

Jessie felt certain that the court-martial was to blame for her difficult pregnancy and the infant's death. She blamed Kearny. While she lay bedridden and prostrate with grief, her physician brought her a remarkable note from another of his St. Louis patients. Following the court-martial, General Kearny had been ordered to Veracruz, Mexico, where he had contracted yellow fever and dysentery. He had returned to St. Louis, where he now lay dying at the nearby home of his brother-in-law, Meriwether Lewis Clark, the son of another famous explorer. He begged Jessie to come and visit him so he might make his final peace with her.

She declined: "There was a little grave between us I could not cross."[33]

ON MARCH 4, 1848, TWO MEN CAME TO COLONEL RICHARD Mason's Monterey headquarters with a message from John Sutter. They presented the colonel with about a half ounce of placer gold.

"What is that?" Mason asked young Sherman.

"Is it gold?" a puzzled Sherman replied as he bit into a piece. He then took a hatchet to beat the largest piece flat. It was pure gold.

Sutter had hired Bear Flagger James Marshall, along with a crew of former Mormon Battalion men, to build a sawmill some forty miles up from his fort on the south fork of the American River. Sutter was certain that a fortune was to be made in milled lumber with all the new emigrants that would flock to California, now that it was in American hands. On January 24, 1848, Marshall had discovered gold in the millrace at the sawmill site.

Sutter wanted Mason to grant him the right to lease the land and its mineral rights from local Indians where the mill was being constructed. Since California was still a conquered Mexican province, the colonel refused to give Sutter title to the land, as American land laws were not yet in effect. Mason wrote Sutter that he had nothing to worry about because his sawmill was so far from any settlements and there would certainly be no trespassers. This decision proved to be the ruination of John Sutter, for his sawmill would never be built, his lands would be overrun, and his dream of New Helvetia would be lost along with his fortune.[34]

By that spring the rush was on to the new diggings. Crews deserted their ships and the hulks were soon hauled ashore to form the first storefronts of the new city of San Francisco. Soldiers deserted the army in droves. In July, Colonel Mason and his aide Sherman ventured into the goldfields on an inspection tour along the American River.

"There the gold was in every conceivable shape and size," Sherman reported, "some of the specimens weighing several ounces. . . . We spent nearly a week in that region, and were quite bewildered by the fabulous tales of recent discoveries."

The soldiers who had provided their escort to the diggings got "gold fever" and all deserted. The problem of desertion was so great that Mason began granting liberal furloughs so long as the men promised to eventually return. Hardly anyone returned.

They returned to Monterey, where Sherman prepared a report on the goldfields for Mason to send to President Polk. An empty oyster can was procured and 230 ounces of gold were packed inside it. Army lieutenant Lucien Loeser was sent with this treasure and Mason's report aboard a schooner going south in August. He crossed the Isthmus of Panama, caught a sailing ship to New Orleans, and from there a stagecoach to Washington, always carefully watching over his oyster can. He arrived in late November, where the contents of the oyster can caused an immediate sensation.[35]

Kit Carson had also been sent overland with dispatches. He departed Los Angeles on May 4, 1848, with a twenty-five-man escort. They followed the Old Spanish Trail. With Carson rode Lieutenant George Brewerton, who would later write of their journey together. Brewerton, like Sherman, had been surprised upon meeting Carson to find him so unlike the romantic conception he had previously formed.

"The Kit Carson of my *imagination* was over six feet high—a sort of modern Hercules in his build—with an enormous beard, and a voice like a roused lion," Brewerton later wrote. "The *real* Kit Carson I found to be a plain, simple, unostentatious man; rather below the medium height, with brown, curling hair, little or no beard, and a voice as soft and gentle as a woman's. In fact, the hero of a hundred desperate encounters, whose life had been mostly spent amid wildernesses, where the white man is almost unknown, was one of Dame Nature's gentlemen."[36]

Upon reaching New Mexico, Carson learned that his appointment to the Mounted Rifles had not been approved by the Senate. His friends urged him to remain with his family and send the dispatches on with another courier.

"I determined to fulfill the duty," Carson declared. "That mattered not to me if, in the discharge of a duty of service beneficial to the public, whether I was of the rank of Lieutenant or holding the credit of an experienced mountaineer."[37]

Carson's party avoided the usual Arkansas River route because of Comanche raiding parties and followed instead the Republican River eastward, reaching St. Louis safely on July 31, 1848. He hurried on to Washington to deliver his dispatches and to enjoy a melancholy reunion with the Frémonts. In his saddlebags he carried military dispatches and private letters with the first news of the discovery of gold at Sutter's Mill—news that would forever alter the destiny of California, the American West, and the United States.

18

LINES ON PAPER

In April 1851, John C. Cremony, chief Spanish interpreter for the U.S. Boundary Commission, rode ahead of the main column of the expedition to explore an impressive canyon and locate a nearby spring. Cremony, an experienced soldier, should have known better than to be out alone ahead of the others in the midst of Apache country. As he neared Cooke's Canyon, some forty miles east of the Mimbres River, he was suddenly confronted by Apaches.

Cuchillo Negro appeared with twenty-five warriors to block Cremony's passage. Well armed with two belt and two holster Colts, a Sharps carbine, and a large Bowie knife, Cremony was not about to be stampeded. He pulled a pistol and spurred his horse forward to meet the Chihenne chief.

"We do not permit people to enter our country without knowing their purpose," declared Cuchilla Negro.

Cremony, with his pistol leveled on the Apache, assured the chief that "we come in peace, and will always act peaceably, unless you compel us to adopt other measures; if you do, the consequences will do you great harm."

Cuchillo Negro scoffed at Cremony's bold talk, but the sudden appearance of Captain Louis Craig's infantry column in the distance ended the conference and undoubtedly spared Cremony's life. With an expression of friendship, Cuchillo Negro galloped off, followed by his warriors.

Several days later, some twenty miles east of Santa Rita del Cobre, Cremony again had an Apache encounter of some consequence. He was hunting antelope near a hot spring and drew a bead on a fine buck. Just as he was about to fire, the antelope stood erect and called out in Spanish to him. It was a young Apache hunter wearing an antelope skin with head and

APACHERIA
Cieneguilla
Canyon de Chelly
Fort Defiance
Little Colorado River
Rio Grande
ARIZONA
(1912)
Fort Wingate
NEW MEXICO
(1912)
Camp Reno
Sierra Ancha
Fort Tularosa
San Mateo Mountains
Fort Apache
Salt River
Cuchillo Negro
San Francisco R.
Camp Ojo Caliente
Fort Craig
Fort Stanto
Superstition Mountains
Cañada Alamosa
Black Range
Fort McRae
Gila Mtns.
Black Range
Gila River
Gila River
Jornado del Muerto
Hembrillo Canyon
Camp Grant Massacre
Fort Breckenridge/ Camp Grant
Pinos Altos
Fort Webster
Dog Canyon
Fort Thomas
Fort Bayard
Santa Rita del Cobre
Pinaleño Mtns.
Fort Grant
Burro Mtns.
Fort McLane
Fort Thorn
Penasco Canyo
Santa Catalina Mtns.
Dos Cabezas Mtns.
Fort Cummings
Cooke's Canyon
Fort Selden
San Andres Mtns.
Doubtful Canyon/ Steins Peak
Fort Lowell
Willcox
Mesilla
Tucson
Fort Bowie
BUTTERFIELD OVERLAND MAIL ROUTE
Dragoon Springs
Apache Pass
Santa Rita Mtns.
Bonita Canyon
Florida Mtns.
Cochise Stronghold
East Stronghold
Western Dragoons
Tombstone
Texas Canyon
Fort Bliss
Chiricahua Mtns.
Mule Mtns.
Tubac
Paso del Norte
TEXA
(1845
Rio Grande
Fort Buchanan
Fort Huachuca
San Bernardino
Candelaria Mtns.
Santa Cruz
Canyon de los Embudos
Fronteras
MEXICO
Sierra Madre
KEY
ARIZONA (1912) State name and date of admission to the Union
Towns
Forts
Battle sites
Trail
Geographic sites
0 Miles 50 100
0 Kilometers 10
© 2025 Jeffrey L. Ward

horns. Cremony was amazed. "The Apaches frequently adopt this method of hunting," he learned from the lad, "and imitate the actions of the antelopes so exactly as to completely mislead those animals with the belief that their deadliest enemy is one of their number." It was not lost on the astute Cremony that the ruse of the hunt could also be applied by the Apaches in war. The boy turned out to be the son of Ponce, an important leader of the Chihenne band, and by holding his fire Cremony had made an important new friend.[1]

The Americans returned to Santa Rita del Cobre on May 2, 1851. John Russell Bartlett, who had been appointed the United States boundary commissioner to settle the new international line with Mexico, led them. A Rhode Islander with no qualifications for this vital position beyond solid political connections, Bartlett was a studious man with a literary bent and a romantic temperament. He had lived in New York City since 1836, operating a small publishing company and running a bookstore located in the Astor Hotel. His shop became a focal point for the city's men of letters, including Albert Gallatin, Henry Schoolcraft, and Edgar Allan Poe. Bartlett and Gallatin founded the American Ethnological Society.[2]

By September 1850, Bartlett was in San Antonio, Texas, where he assembled over one hundred members for his party, along with eighty-five men of the 3rd Infantry under Captain Craig as escort. He decided on the abandoned mines at Santa Rita del Cobre as his headquarters. Among his most fortunate recruits for the expedition were two able interpreters. Cremony, an exceptionally bright and thoughtful former newspaper correspondent for the *Boston Herald*, as well as a veteran of the Mexican War, would prove invaluable. He would later write an important memoir of his time with the Apaches. The other interpreter was Santiago Brito, a Mexican soldier from Janos who developed a good rapport with the Apaches and eventually settled at Pinos Altos. His son Frank would serve with Teddy Roosevelt's Rough Riders in 1898.[3]

Mangas Coloradas was in Sonora when Bartlett's main party set up their base camp at the abandoned copper mines on May 2. Captain Craig's troops had already established their encampment around the ruins of the old triangular presidio. On June 23, Mangas met Bartlett. Here at last was the sort of Indian leader who fulfilled the expectations of Bartlett's literary fantasies: he was a great admirer of James Fenimore Cooper's frontier romances and fully subscribed to the ideal of the "noble red man." Mangas not only appeared physically imposing to the American commissioner but also seemed to be a leader "of strong common sense and discriminating judgment." Bartlett treated Mangas with respect and bestowed a fine blue military frock coat on the chief. He also informed Mangas that under the provisions of the treaty ending the war with Mexico, the United States government was now obliged to protect Mexico from Indian raids originating within its boundaries. Mangas, perplexed by this, reluctantly agreed not to attack the Mexican boundary party operating on the border under García Conde. He agreed to no more but nevertheless departed in a fine mood with his new coat. This foreshadowed great troubles to come.[4]

As word spread, more Indians arrived in the vicinity of the commissioner's encampment. Delgadito and nearly three hundred Chihennes united with Mangas's band, which was of equal strength. Delgadito's people camped along the Mimbres River some twenty miles away. Even more surprising was the arrival of nearly four hundred Navajos who made camp along the Gila River some thirty miles from Santa Rita. Although Bartlett was delighted at the arrival of so many Indians, more experienced frontier hands became a bit nervous.

Cremony was also puzzled as to why the Navajos, so often the bitter enemies of the Apaches, would dare venture so far to the south. His Apache friends explained that it was Mangas's diplomacy that had secured peace with the Navajo. On a raid in Sonora, Mangas had "carried off a handsome and intelligent Mexican girl, whom he made his wife, to the exclusion of his Apache squaws," the Apaches told Cremony. This forced Mangas to fight duels with two of the outraged relatives of his Apache wives, but this domestic turmoil eventually yielded rich diplomatic dividends. "By his Mexican wife Mangas had three really beautiful daughters," the Apaches explained, and through his diplomatic ability, he married one of them to a chief of the Navajos. The other two married important Apache chiefs and in this way, as Cremony put it, Mangas became "undoubtedly the most prominent and influential Apache who has existed for a century . . . and carried his influence from the Colorado River to the Guadalupe Mountains."[5]

Although the Navajos visited the American encampment, they never spoke with any of the Apaches. This perplexed Cremony, and so under cover of darkness he ventured to spy on Mangas's camp. There he could see the leading men of the Navajos in animated conversation with Mangas and his leading warriors, all illuminated by the Apache campfires. He later learned that the Navajo son-in-law of Mangas had sent his warriors south to assist the Apaches in overpowering the Americans if conflict should erupt. The first signs of that conflict soon came as a direct result of Cremony's actions.

Late in the evening of June 27, 1850, Cremony and several others noticed the flickering of a campfire a few hundred yards from their encampment. Apaches were forbidden to camp so close, and Cremony armed himself and sallied forth with a companion to see who dared break this prohibition. As they cautiously approached the campfire, Cremony saw a strikingly beautiful young Mexican girl laboring over a cooking pot, preparing a meal for a party of Hispanics. She was, Cremony observed, "clothed in a tattered chemise, with a buckskin skirt, and another skin thrown over her shoulders." He walked forward and asked who she was. She put her fingers to her lips, for she dared not speak. Cremony pressed the point, and she whispered that her Apache captors had just sold her to these New Mexican traders. Cremony quickly retreated from the suspicious party, but he soon returned with several of Captain Craig's soldiers. The New Mexicans were detained and the fifteen-year-old Mexican girl, Inez Gonzales, was housed in Bartlett's spacious quarters.

Inez, along with two other girls and a boy, had been taken the previous September in an Apache ambush that had left her uncle and a ten-man Mexican military escort dead. A band of New Mexicans had purchased her three companions, but she had been retained by the Apaches as a slave. It was later rumored that she had been in the village of the Western Apache chief Eskiminzin. An old Apache woman saved Inez from sale or abuse until she was finally sold to another band of New Mexicans, who were taking her to Santa Fe when Cremony intervened.

Bartlett closely questioned the leader of the trading party, Peter Blacklaws of Santa Fe. He and his Hispanic companions all had different explanations for how they had obtained Inez from the Apaches. Bartlett saw through their lies and, with considerable sanctimony for the official representative of a government that still allowed chattel slavery to exist, noted that "the purchaser belonged to a people with whom the system of peonage prevails, and among whom, as a general thing, females are not estimated as with us, especially in a moral point of view." The Apaches had not raped the girl, but Bartlett was probably correct in his assumption of her fate if left in the hands of the New Mexicans. This was Bartlett's first exposure to the traffic in humans that was a mainstay of the economy of both the New Mexico settlements and the Apaches. Bartlett and Cremony eventually had the pleasure of restoring Inez to the welcoming arms of her distraught mother in Santa Cruz.[6]

The next intervention on behalf of Mexican captives would not have so happy an ending. The day following the rescue of Inez, two frantic Mexican boys appeared at Cremony's tent in search of sanctuary. Word of his rescue of the girl had quickly gotten around. The boys were both around twelve years old, and one, José Trinfan, had been with the Apaches for six years, while the other, Savero Aredia, had been captured only five months before. As Cremony conversed in Spanish with the boys, he saw a large party of Apaches approaching his tent.

"For God's sake, do not deliver us again among them," cried out one of the boys. Cremony reached over for two Colt revolvers and thrust them into his belt. His Mexican servant José, not much older than the captive boys, slung a carbine over his shoulder and cocked Cremony's double-barreled shotgun. With a pistol in each hand, Cremony led the captive boys out of his tent and toward Bartlett's headquarters. José brought up the rear with his shotgun at the ready. They passed through a menacing gauntlet of about thirty angry Apaches, who brandished their weapons and demanded the release of the boys. Cremony ordered José to unload both barrels into the first Apache that bent his bow. It was a long two hundred yards to Bartlett's tent. Several of Cremony's companions rushed to the scene with pistols drawn, and the grumbling Apaches dispersed. Under cover of darkness Bartlett sent the boys, with a strong guard, to the nearby encampment of General Conde, the Mexican boundary commissioner. The general eventually restored the boys to their families.[7]

Five days later, on July 4, 1851, Mangas, along with Delgadito, Ponce, and the Apache owner of the boys, appeared with a large force of warriors at Santa Rita. Bartlett was delighted, for this was his chance to impress upon the Apaches the new order of things. Both sides were heavily armed as they sat down to smoke tobacco in a grand semicircle. Inez had not caused a problem with the Apaches because she was no longer their property when rescued, but the two boys were another matter altogether. Finally, Mangas rose to speak, as did Cremony, to translate.

"Why did you take our captives from us?" Mangas demanded.

"Your captives came to us and demanded our protection," Bartlett replied.

"You came to our country. You were well received by us. Your lives, your property, your animals were safe," said Mangas. "We were friends! We were brothers! . . . We believed your assurances of friendship and we trusted them. Why did you take our captives from us?"

Bartlett's carefully worded response—that the Americans had promised protection to the Mexicans once the war had ended—was lost on the assembled Apaches. Ponce, one of the more moderate chiefs, was particularly outraged.

"Yes, but you took our captives from us without beforehand cautioning us," Ponce exclaimed, all the while pointing menacingly at Bartlett. "They were made prisoners in lawful warfare. They belong to us. They are our property. Our people have also been made captives by Mexicans."

Bartlett lost his temper. He called Ponce a "squaw" and repeated that the United States would honor its promises to Mexico and return all redeemed captives. Infuriated, Ponce demanded that Bartlett be quiet, for he wanted only Cremony to speak. With tension rising, Cremony ordered Ponce to be seated and called on Delgadito to speak.

Delgadito was calm. He knew the temper of the Americans. With them, everything had a price. At first he proclaimed poverty: "The owner of these captives is a poor man; he cannot lose his prisoners, who were obtained at the risk of his life, and purchased by the blood of his relatives. He justly demands his captives. We are his friends, and wish to see this demand complied with. It is just, and as justice we demand it."

Bartlett replied that while the Americans could not purchase a captive, the Mexicans might pay a reasonable ransom for the boys.

"The brave who owns these captives does not wish to sell," Delgadito replied. "He has had one of those boys six years. He grew up under him. His heart-strings are bound around him. He is as a son to his old age."

Warming to his subject, Delgadito ended with a flourish: "Money cannot buy affection. His heart cannot be sold. He taught him to string and shoot the bow and to wield the lance. He loves the boy, and cannot sell him."

Bartlett was unmoved. The boys were already in the hands of the Mexican authorities. "Our brother has fixed his affection on the child of his enemy," Bartlett said as Cremony translated. "It is very noble. But our duty is stern. We cannot avoid it." To Bartlett it was simple—the law demanded their return to Mexico and that was the end of the matter.

"Let our Apache brother reflect and name his price," Bartlett concluded with perfect Yankee logic.[8]

The Apaches departed in a foul mood. Three days later a few returned to accept a payment of $200 in trade goods for the boys. Bartlett thought he had taught the Indians a valuable lesson, but Cremony realized that they had accepted payment only because they recognized the sad reality of their situation. He was convinced that they would soon claim a greater recompense for their loss.

Two days later, the bad temper of the Apaches was intensified when a Hispanic teamster shot and desperately wounded an Apache in an argument over a whip he had taken from the Indian. The gunfire roused the camp. The Apaches, with the duplicity of Johnson and Kirker still fresh in their minds, fled to a nearby hill and began to fortify the area. A clash seemed imminent when Captain Craig and Cremony boldly walked up the hill to confer with the Apaches. Mangas and several others followed him back to the American camp, where they found the teamster, Jesús López, in chains. Mangas was momentarily satisfied, but he warned Bartlett and Cremony that if the Apache died, they would expect swift justice. The wounded Apache was carefully tended by Dr. Thomas H. Webb, the commission physician, but died thirteen days later.

Mangas conferred with Bartlett on July 21, demanding that the murderer be turned over to the Apaches for justice. Bartlett refused but promised to send López in chains to Santa Fe for trial. Mangas thought this a pretty good joke, made all the more tiresome by the fact that to the Apaches the murderer was a hated Mexican. This was the final straw for Mangas. He decamped with his people the next day for the springs at Santa Lucia.[9]

The following day, Ponce and Delgadito brought the mother of the murder victim to meet with Bartlett. It was Ponce who rose to demand Apache justice. "The Apaches will not be satisfied to hear that the murderer has been punished in Santa Fé. They want him punished here, at the Copper Mines, where the band of the dead brave may see him put to death—

where all the Apaches may see him put to death," demanded Ponce, making a sign with his fist of a hanging man. "Then the Apaches will see and know that their American brothers do justice to them."

Bartlett again promised that López would be punished in Santa Fe and also offered compensation to the dead warrior's mother. He had made the same offer back in Texas when one of his teamsters killed a Hispanic from San Antonio. This inflamed Ponce all the more. "Would money pay you, Señor Commissioner, for the loss of your child?" he asked. "No; money will not bury your grief. It will not bury ours. The mother of the dead brave demands the life of his murderer. Nothing else will satisfy her. She wants no money."

Bartlett once more offered payment in gold or goods to the woman. Again Ponce expressed outrage: "If an Apache should take the life of an American, would you not make war on us and take many Apache lives?"

Ponce stated the obvious, but Bartlett denied it, proclaiming the righteousness of American justice. Still, the frustrated commissioner ended the conference with a grim and prophetic warning of what would happen if the Apaches did not bend to American will: "War will then follow; thousands of soldiers will take possession of your lands, your grazing valleys, and your watering places. They will destroy every Apache warrior they find, and take your women and children captives."

Ponce and Delgadito quickly departed from Santa Rita. Within days, horses and mules began to vanish from the American camp. The Navajos soon returned to their own country, trailing a large herd of Bartlett's animals with them. Cremony estimated the number of lost horses and mules at nearly three hundred. Bartlett decided to abandon Santa Rita in late August and move westward. His stay among the Apaches had ended in rancor and lingering bitterness that foreshadowed events to come.[10]

Captain Craig, recognizing the strategic potential of Santa Rita del Cobre, recommended to his military superiors that a permanent post be built at the copper mines. In response, Captain Israel Richardson with a company of the 3rd Infantry occupied Santa Rita in late January 1852, renaming the old presidio Fort Webster. When Ponce and several Chihenne warriors approached the new post under a white flag, Captain Richardson opened fire, wounding several Apaches. Three days later Ponce returned, reinforced by warriors under Delgadito. Young men stampeded the American horse and oxen herd, which led Captain Richardson to foolishly sortie out of his fort in pursuit. Ponce and Delgadito waited in ambush. Richardson was fortunate to save his small command, but he left two soldiers dead on the field and another captured: Nicholas Wade, a redheaded sergeant of the 3rd Infantry, who was turned over to the relatives of the dead Apaches. What was left of him was recovered a few days later. "No funeral is a pleasant one," noted one of Wade's companions. "But a funeral at a lonely frontier military fort after a skirmish in which the comrades who are buried have been killed and one tortured by savages is a sorrowful affair."[11]

The bands of Ponce, Delgadito, and Cuchillo Negro were now at war with the Americans. All along the Rio Grande, travelers were attacked, and when American dragoons from Laguna responded, the Apaches ambushed them. Five were killed and three more wounded. A supply train of eight wagons returning from Fort Webster had all its stock stolen. The teamsters abandoned their wagons and fled toward the Rio Grande. Unable to supply the post at Santa Rita, the army relocated Fort Webster east, to the west bank of the Mimbres River. A log-and-adobe fortification was hurriedly constructed, although most of the infantrymen lived in tents. The Apaches saw this as a victory of sorts and now approached the Americans with an olive branch, but Cuchillo Negro informed the American commander at the new Fort Webster that he could agree to nothing until Mangas Coloradas returned from Sonora. "Some of the young chiefs are therefore sent after Mangas," a soldier jotted in his diary, "and told to instruct him to come in and attend a peace council."[12]

In a surprising show of military efficiency, the new commander in Sonora, Miguel Blanco de Estrada, simultaneously sent forth columns from Santa Cruz, Tucson, Bavispe, and the reoccupied Fronteras. Over five hundred Mexican soldiers were in the field by March 1852. They kept up operations against the Chiricahuas throughout the spring and into the early summer months.

Mangas realized that he could not sustain a two-front war with the Americans and the Sonorans. On July 11, 1852, he met with Lieutenant Colonel Edwin Vose Sumner of the 1st Dragoons and New Mexico Indian agent John Greiner far to the north at the pueblo of Acoma. Greiner was feuding with the imperious dragoon colonel, but they managed to present a united front upon meeting the Apaches. Mangas deeply impressed Greiner, who thought him a "magnificent looking Indian" and "undoubtedly the master spirit of his tribe."[13]

Sumner was as tough a soldier as the American army ever produced. A musket ball had glanced off his skull at Cerro Gordo during the Mexican War, earning him the nickname "Bull" from his troops. He was a complete martinet, for which his soldiers both loathed and admired him. He was generally despised by all the civil authorities in New Mexico, who referred to him contemptuously as the "Big Bug at Albuquerque."[14]

The Chiricahua leader could match Sumner in both arrogance and boldness. Wearing the uniform coat of a Mexican artillery officer whom he had recently slain, Mangas greeted the colonel and got right to business: "You are chief of the white men. I am chief of the red men. Now let us have a talk and treat."

The treaty that they jointly signed, the first by the Chiricahuas with the United States, recognized the jurisdiction of the Americans and allowed the government to establish military posts and Indian agencies in the lands of the Apaches. The tribe would liberate all Mexican captives and cease raids into Mexico. In exchange, the Americans promised to give goods to the Chiricahuas at a future, unspecified time.

Mangas, although willing to sign the treaty on behalf of his people (at least the Bedonkohes and Chihennes), expressed his objection to the clause on raiding Mexico. He was prepared to pledge peace and friendship with the Americans but not the hated Mexicans.

"Are we to stand by with our arms folded while our women and children are being murdered?" he asked Sumner. The colonel had only recently written a letter to Secretary of War Charles Magill Conrad in which he called the Hispanics of New Mexico "idle and worthless." He saw no hope for any improvement and had seriously recommended the withdrawal of all American troops from the territory in hopes the Hispanics and the Indians would kill each other off. If possible, the colonel had even more contempt for the citizens of Sonora and cared little if the Chiricahuas slaughtered them. Mangas and Sumner were kindred warrior spirits, and the chief later claimed that the colonel gave a wink and nodded in approval of his demand to continue the war against Mexico despite the treaty forbidding it.[15]

The festering problem of Apache raids into Mexico was soon partially rectified by diplomatic and political developments in the East. Bartlett's boundary line became controversial even before his survey with General Conde was completed. By accepting Conde's interpretation of where the boundary line would depart the Rio Grande and go due west, Bartlett conceded New Mexico's valuable Mesilla Valley to Mexico. The boundary was soon caught up in presidential politics as Democrats accused Bartlett, a Whig, of giving up the valley in order to prevent construction of a southern transcontinental railroad. Bartlett and Conde were actually quite correct in their interpretation of the southern boundary of New Mexico as stated by the Treaty of Guadalupe Hidalgo. It was not Bartlett but the U.S. Senate, in accepting the boundaries stipulated in that treaty, who had blundered. William H. Emory of the U.S. Army Corps of Topographical Engineers and other military officers joined in the chorus of criticism of Bartlett, which played into the hands of the expansionists in Congress. Democrats soon cut funding for the boundary commission, which had indeed been quite inefficient, and Cremony and others were forced to depart from it. President Franklin Pierce finally dismissed Bartlett in March 1853. The much-maligned commissioner returned East to compile his notes and journals, which were published to great acclaim in 1854. The lingering controversy over Bartlett's U.S. and Mexican Boundary Commission contributed to a diplomatic initiative that would have an enormous impact on Mangas, the Apaches, and the future shape of the American Southwest: the Gadsden Purchase.[16]

WITH THE 1848 DISCOVERY OF GOLD IN CALIFORNIA, THE subsequent population explosion, and the admission of California to statehood in 1850, it became increasingly urgent to establish overland mail and protected transportation routes to the West Coast. Sectional rivalry over which route a future transcontinental railroad would take led to bitter debates in Washington. Secretary of War Jefferson Davis, the most powerful and influential member of President Pierce's administration, was determined that the railroad route be a southern one, and he indeed had logic, climate, and geography on his side in the debate. The problem for Davis and his allies was that the controversial boundary established by the 1848 Treaty of Guadalupe Hidalgo ending the Mexican War had failed to secure for New Mexico the Mesilla Valley or the land south of Arizona's Gila River—land that army explorers had reported as the most suitable route for a wagon road or a future railroad.

In 1853, Davis secured the appointment of South Carolinian James Gadsden as the American minister to Mexico. Pierce and Davis instructed Gadsden to secure the lands south of the Gila for the railroad and even more Mexican territory if the opportunity presented itself. He was also to obtain nullification of Article XI of the 1848 treaty, which obligated the United States to protect Mexican citizens from cross-border raids by American Indians and to pay an indemnity when failing to do so. It had become quite apparent that it was not even remotely possible to halt Apache and Comanche raiders from crossing the border.

Gadsden arrived in Mexico City early in August 1853 and promptly met with President Antonio López de Santa Anna. The general was once again momentarily back in power and desperately in need of funds to pay his army and bolster his shaky position. Santa Anna's lack of both scruples and money led Gadsden to be quite optimistic. "This is a government of plunder and necessity," he reported back to Washington. While Gadsden's cynical characterization of Santa Anna's corrupt regime was not totally misplaced, the Mexican dictator faced serious problems, with a soaring national debt and a weak army that simply could not defend the northern sections of the states of Sonora and Chihuahua. The Apaches had made the situation so untenable for Mexico that to the government it made far more sense to sell this land rather than continue to defend the indefensible.[17]

The most ambitious of Gadsden's offers to Santa Anna was a payment of $50 million for Baja California as well as substantial parcels of the northern Mexican states of Sonora, Chihuahua, and Coahuila. This would have secured a vital outlet to the sea for Arizona as well as enough territory for a potential new slave state. Santa Anna was tempted by this offer, but the expressions of outrage by both Mexican nationalists and American opponents of slavery led both sets of negotiators to pull back. On December 30, 1853, they signed an agreement on a $15 million purchase of New Mexico's Mesilla Valley and all of Arizona's land south of the Gila River from a point seventy miles below the Yuma Crossing of the Colorado River and then angling eastward to and then along the 31st degree of latitude. This was some six miles above the river's outlet into the Gulf of California but still close enough to eventually secure the Americans a port there. Article XI of the Treaty of Guadalupe Hidalgo on Indian depredations was also abrogated.

The United States Senate debated and tinkered with the proposed treaty, moving the new boundary line northward (a reduction of nine thousand square miles), ending hope for an Arizona port on the Gulf of California (a reduction of 9,000 square miles) and cutting the payment to Mexico by $5 million. Although this shortsighted compromise enraged Gadsden and disappointed Pierce and Davis, the treaty was ratified by the Senate and signed by the president on June 29, 1854. Fresh lines on the map would have to be drawn, and Major William H. Emory was soon headed westward to mark a new international boundary.[18]

Sectional strife blocked the railroad for another thirty years, until the same capitalists who had completed the first transcontinental railroad in 1869 purchased the rights to the Southern Pacific Railroad Company in 1868. Collis P. Huntington, the driving force behind the so-called Big Four of Huntington, Stanford, Hopkins, and Crocker, had rails laid from San Francisco to San Diego and then finally to Yuma by 1877. The line pushed east to Casa Grande, Tucson, and Benson in Arizona and on to Lordsburg and Deming in New Mexico before uniting with Jay Gould's Texas Pacific east of El Paso in 1882, completing the nation's second transcontinental line. The railroad would bring rapid change to the West and to the Apaches, but that was still far in the future when the Gadsden Purchase added nearly 30,000 square miles of territory to the United States. This included the towns of Mesilla and Tucson as well as all the mountains in between. Those mountains made up the heart of Apacheria.[19]

Americans slowly began to trickle into this new land that they called simply the "Purchase" or "the Gadsden strip." Among the first was the self-styled "Father of Arizona," Charles Debrille Poston. Born into a prosperous Kentucky family in 1825, Poston developed an early interest in the law and literature. While still in his teens he secured an appointment as clerk of the Tennessee Supreme Court. A favorable marriage into one of Kentucky's leading families and solid connections within the Whig political party all held promise of a great future for this witty and intelligent young man. His political connections secured him a position in San Francisco's customs-house just after statehood, but a devastating disease left his bride an invalid for life and his dreams of a family shattered. He turned away from law and politics in search of adventure.[20]

The Gadsden Purchase offered Poston just the sort of opportunity he sought. He fell in with Herman Ehrenberg, a German immigrant and skilled mining engineer. The Leipzig-born Ehrenberg had come to the United States in 1834 when still a teenager. He soon enlisted in a band of volunteers bent on liberating Texas from Mexico. The New Orleans Greys fought alongside Jim Bowie in the 1835 defeat of Mexican forces at San Antonio. Ehrenberg avoided death at the Alamo three months later by following those Greys who marched with Colonel James Fannin to Goliad. He had then miraculously escaped the fate of his companions when Fannin's captured troops were murdered by order of General Santa Anna on March 27, 1836. He returned to Germany, wrote a popular book on his Texas adventures, and studied mining engineering and cartography. He found employment with the Hawaiian government before reaching California just in time to join in the Bear Flag Revolt. With the discovery of gold, his services as a mining engineer and cartographer were in high demand. He soon formed a partnership with Poston to explore the land south of Tucson for lost Spanish silver mines.[21]

The American dreamer and the German engineer made a formidable team that quickly attracted the interest of San Francisco financiers. These capitalists now fronted the money for Poston to hire thirty men and purchase weapons and supplies for them. "They were not so bad as reckless," Poston said of his wild recruits, "not ungovernable, but independent."[22]

Poston's party loaded their goods onto a three-masted British vessel of dubious seaworthiness for the journey to Guaymas on the Sonoran coast. From there they would proceed overland to the Santa Cruz Valley. A storm blew their ship off course and dashed her against the rocky shores of an island in the Gulf of California. After much suffering, the shipwrecked adventurers finally reached Guaymas on January 14, 1854.

Poston and Ehrenberg, with just fifteen remaining companions, purchased mules and pushed eastward across Sonora to the lands south of Tucson acquired in the Gadsden Purchase. Mexican officials warned them that the purchase was illegal, for Santa Anna was but a usurper with no right to sell national territory. Poston was not worried about the legality of the purchase, but he was astonished at just how little territory was acquired and outraged to learn that it did not include an American port on the Gulf of California.

He was delighted with the country he crossed over to the south of Tucson but was disappointed in the crumbling old presidio. Tucson contained fewer than three hundred Hispanic residents and was essentially besieged by the Apaches. Poston felt the industrious Pimas farming along the Gila River to be the only productive population he encountered. American settlers would remedy that quickly enough. He could not explore north of the Gila because of the Apaches—who, he noted, "for three hundred years . . . have killed Spaniards, Mexicans, and Americans, which makes about the longest continuous war on record."[23]

Despite the pathetic condition of Tucson and the Apache peril, Poston was enthusiastic about this enchanting land, which was both ancient and new. "The valleys are as fair as the sun ever shone upon, with soil as productive as the valley of the Nile," he wrote. "The rigors of winter never disturb agricultural pursuits in the open. In fact, in the southern portion of the territory there is no winter."[24]

He and Ehrenberg explored the mountains bordering the Santa Cruz Valley for silver veins. Loaded down with promising ore samples, they headed west along the Gila River for Fort Yuma on the Colorado River. They reached the Yuma Crossing in June 1854. Captain Samuel P. Heintzelman issued the famished company rations and listened with rapt attention to Poston's tales of the promise of mineral wealth in this new American acquisition. Poston and Ehrenberg proceeded on to San Diego and then by steamer north to San Francisco to report the results of their reconnaissance to their investors. Poston's remarkable gift for salesmanship did not fail him, for the investors decided to send him to Washington to plead for government assistance in settling Arizona. Troops were needed to provide protection for any mines that were to be established. The Apaches had to be convinced to leave future American settlers alone or they had to be subdued. There were no courts or lawmen either, and the distance to Santa Fe or Mesilla for court proceedings was daunting if not impossible, so creating a new and separate territory seemed essential.

Poston and Ehrenberg traveled the Panama route back to the East Coast. After visiting his invalid wife in Kentucky, Poston proceeded to

Washington to meet with Secretary of War Jefferson Davis. By a fortunate coincidence Captain Heintzelman was also in Washington, and they visited with both President Pierce and Secretary Davis to sing the praises of the potential of the "Purchase." Davis promised to station troops near Tucson as soon as possible.

Poston also visited with the capitalists engaged in creating the Texas Pacific Railroad Company, the southern transcontinental railway so favored by the Pierce administration. He brought them into his Sonora Exploring and Mining Company, organized in Cincinnati on March 24, 1856, with Captain Heintzelman as president, Poston as manager, and Ehrenberg as engineer. Poston was soon on his way to San Antonio with a $100,000 line of credit to hire men, wagons, stock, and arms for his expedition into the Purchase.[25]

Poston found several well-educated German miners about New Braunfels, working on farms and selling lager beer, and they quickly enlisted. He also wisely secured the services of frontiersmen—or "buckskin boys," as he called them—"who were not afraid of the devil."[26]

The party reached El Paso on July 4, 1856, refitted, and pushed on to Fort Thorn on the Rio Grande. From here they would make the dangerous dash across the mountains to Tucson. Fortunately for Poston, Dr. Michael Steck was at the fort.

Steck had come to New Mexico in 1849 as a military contract surgeon. He fell in love with the Southwest. Steck counted among his friends the noted ethnologist Henry Rowe Schoolcraft, who helped secure him appointment as Indian agent for New Mexico's Apaches in 1852. An intelligent man of integrity, compassion, and bedrock honesty, he was reappointed agent by Presidents Pierce, Buchanan, and Lincoln. As agent for the Mescalero and Mimbres Apaches, he gained their confidence and then used them to make the first Indian Bureau contacts with the Chiricahuas, as well the Western Apache bands, the Pinals and Coyoteros. Steck had successfully negotiated with the Mescaleros of southeastern New Mexico in 1855 and had even lured Cuchillo Negro and his Chihenne people to attempt farming near Fort Thorn.[27]

Steck invited Poston to accompany him to the old presidio at Santa Rita del Cobre, where he could introduce the miner to the Apache leaders. Poston readily accepted and selected five men to go with him. Steck had two wagons loaded with corn for Mangas Coloradas's Chihenne band. This corn, Poston observed, was later made into that favorite Apache brew, *tiswin*.

On July 25, Poston and Steck camped at the old presidio, still in somewhat decent shape. Mangas soon brought in 350 of his people and a grand party followed. Poston had his boys put on quite a show for the Apaches with their new revolvers and carbines. The Apaches joined in, and Poston was charmed that they carefully cut the bullets from the trees they used for targets "as they were economists in ammunition if nothing else." Poston and his men "exhibited our new firearms, which were then Sharp's [*sic*] rifles and Colt's revolvers, shot at marks, and drank *tiswin*, roasted venison, and made the Indians some presents." Poston was amused that the most valued gift he could give was matches, which the Apaches carefully wrapped in buckskin.[28]

Steck introduced Poston to Mangas, who impressed the miner as "a fine looking chief," and asked him to protect the Americans as they journeyed to the Santa Cruz River. Mangas promised peace with his new American friend but again warned Steck "that the Spanish and Mexicans had treated them badly and that they would kill them and rob them as long as they lived." Steck talked with Mangas about his desire to establish a reservation for the Chihennes and Bedonkohes on the Mimbres River at Santa Lucia Springs. Even in his brief time in New Mexico, he had noticed a rather dramatic decline in the Apache population as a result of the long war with Mexico. Now was the time to increase rations and farming assistance to induce Mangas and his people to come in and settle down. Unfortunately his pleas would have more success with the Apaches than with his civilian superiors in Santa Fe and Washington.[29]

The visit was a grand success, at least from Poston's perspective. To cement his friendship with Mangas, Delgadito, and the other chiefs, he distributed several little tintypes of himself that he had acquired back in New York. He wanted them to remember him as a friend. Years later he would learn from an Apache woman that a band of warriors lying in ambush had spared him because their leader carried his tintype. "I have generally found the Indians willing to keep faith with the whites," Poston wrote, "if the whites will keep faith with them."[30]

Of course, the Americans would never "keep faith" with the Indians.

Apaches soon discovered that the Americans seemingly worshipped these lines that they drew on paper. The new international line made no sense to the Chiricahuas. It placed many of their relatives in Mexico while leaving others in the United States. It divided in half what they viewed as their country. Soon the Americans would draw even more lines, this time dividing off the western half of New Mexico into a new territory called Arizona. This would further divide the Apaches and in fact make it more complicated for civilian and military authorities to deal with them. The paper lines meant more to the Americans than trade, or efficiency, or family, or justice. So important were these paper lines to the Americans that they were willing to write them in blood.

19

FLIGHT OF THE RAVENS

With the end of the Mexican War, the Santa Fe Trail, that 909-mile road of commerce that had become a pathway for military invasion, was once again bustling with trade caravans. The necessity of supplying the new American military outposts in the vast New Mexico Territory (which included modern New Mexico and Arizona, as well as parts of Nevada and Colorado) added to this traffic. The 1848 discovery of gold in California had led to a brief flurry of emigrants attaching themselves to the caravans, even though the Gila and Old Spanish Trails never became popular with the gold seekers. During the 1848–1849 season alone an army officer at Fort Mann on the Arkansas River counted 3,000 wagons, 12,000 pioneers, and 50,000 head of stock passing his little outpost. This new western territory offered opportunity for all bold enough to challenge its dangers.[1]

Postwar New Mexico held the promise of prosperity and a return to family life for Kit Carson as well. By 1849 he was one of the most celebrated Americans in the world—the inheritor of the buckskin mantle of Boone and Crockett as the nation's preeminent frontiersman. Taciturn and unassuming, Carson did not meet the blood-and-thunder image of the frontier Hercules who emerged from the wild tales that exaggerated his very real adventures.[2]

BY 1849, CARSON DID NOT MUCH CARE ABOUT WHATEVER kind of hero folks expected him to be. In February 1843 he had married María Josefa Jaramillo in Taos. "Her style of beauty was of the haughty, heart-breaking kind," noted a visitor to their home, "such as would lead a man with the glance of the eye, to risk his life for one smile." Her family, while not wealthy, was well-connected in New Mexican social circles. Her sister was married to New Mexico's first territorial governor, Carson's old friend Charles Bent. Carson, devoted to his young wife, whom he called Chepita, and growing family—they eventually had eight children and also adopted a Navajo boy—often lamented to his friends how his service to the government kept him away from home. He was particularly disturbed when this service had him absent from Taos in April 1847 when his brother-in-law, Governor Bent, was brutally murdered while protecting Josefa and her sister from a rebellious mob. That tragedy made Carson all the more anxious to stay nearer home.[3]

"In April, Mr. Maxwell and I concluded to make a settlement on the Rayado. We had been leading a roving life long enough and now was the time, if ever, to make a home for ourselves and children," Carson later recalled. "We were getting old and could not expect to remain any length of time able to gain a livelihood as we had been such a number of years."[4]

Determined to settle down, Carson invested much of the $2,000 he had earned over the years as a government scout, soldier, and transcontinental courier in a ranching and farming enterprise with his old friend Lucien Maxwell. Through marriage, Maxwell had inherited an enormous Mexican land grant along the Cimarron River and was anxious to develop it. They purchased seeds, supplies, and stock and hired workers to erect buildings on Rayado Creek, some fifty miles across the mountains to the southeast of Taos. Although south of the Sangre de Cristos and thus exposed to Plains Indian raiders, this new settlement was favorably located along the Mountain Branch of the Santa Fe Trail. Rayado quickly attracted settlers, who built along the tributaries of the Canadian River. Maxwell moved his family there in the spring of 1849 and was soon joined by another old frontiersman, Robert Fisher. Carson hesitated to resettle his family east of the mountains. He was particularly worried about Indian raids, for by the spring of 1849 no part of the Santa Fe Trail was safe.

Indian affairs in northern New Mexico had deteriorated rapidly following the 1846 American conquest, although the situation had never been even remotely peaceful. The Llaneros (Plains Band) of the Jicarilla Apaches had reached a shaky balance of power with the New Mexicans over the previous generation, but it had quickly broken down once the Americans arrived. Comanche hostility had forced the Llaneros from the plains back onto the traditional homeland that they shared with their more settled cousins the Olleros (Mountain Band) between Taos Valley and the Raton Mountains. The Spanish had named them "La Xicarilla," which translated as "Little Basket Maker," in reference to the beautiful baskets handcrafted by the Jicarilla women. Isolated in their northern mountain homeland or roaming eastward onto the plains, the Jicarillas had been far less influenced by the Spanish settlers than other tribes. Their traditional economy of hunting and gathering continued to flourish, augmented by both trade with and plunder from the Hispanics to the south. By 1849 they numbered about a hundred lodges, which was a population of around five hundred. The Americans, immediately suspicious of all Apaches, sided with their new Hispanic neighbors in all disputes with the Jicarillas. The new territorial government was also determined to limit the ability of the Apaches to follow their traditional roaming patterns. Mistrust, tension, and violence followed.[5]

The Llanero Jicarillas, roving east of the upper Rio Grande and southeast to the Canadian River, now made life miserable for settler and traveler alike. "They are not considered a numerous band," declared New Mexico Indian superintendent James Calhoun from his office in Santa Fe, "but they are bold, daring and adventurous spirits." This increasing hostility was fueled by their northern friends the Utes, who provided a ready market for their plunder, and by rivalry between two chiefs, old Chacon of the Olleros and young Lobo Blanco of the Llaneros, for tribal leadership.[6]

Regular troops and New Mexico Volunteers repeatedly clashed with Lobo's band, driving him southeast of Rayado toward favorite haunts along the Canadian River. Captain Henry Judd, commanding a detachment posted at Las Vegas, reported in late summer 1849 that the Jicarillas had been well supplied by whiskey traders from Mora and "that after leaving their families in a secure place, the Apaches will return to this frontier for plunder." John Greiner, Indian agent in Santa Fe, noted that "there is hardly an American here that stirs abroad without being armed to the teeth, and under his pillow pistols and bowie-knife may always be found."[7]

To the east it was no better along the Santa Fe Trail. The Comanches, noted one army officer, "openly declared that they would cut off all commerce between the United States and Mexico and kill or enslave every

American who might venture to pass the plains." The Santa Fe Trail was fast becoming little better than a killing ground.

Throughout the summer of 1849, it was rare for a wagon train to reach Santa Fe without being attacked or having stock driven off. Calhoun requested more troops on August 15, noting that the Indians were in a particularly bad temper. By October, matters had deteriorated even more. Calhoun wrote that "Mr. St. Vrain, long a citizen here, every way reliable, and intelligent, says a worse state of things has not existed in this country since he has been an inhabitant of it."[8]

Poor Calhoun, who in January 1851 would be appointed governor for the newly organized territory of New Mexico, was fighting a three-front diplomatic war. He had to keep the Hispanic New Mexicans from attacking the Apaches, he had to offer the Apaches some incentive to keep the peace, and he had to persuade reluctant military officers to cooperate with him. On more than one occasion spiteful officers refused to provide military escorts for treaty councils, making it impossible for Calhoun to do his job. The superintendent knew better than to venture into Indian Country without military protection. With the military reluctant to act, Calhoun requested permission to raise a force of local volunteers but was refused. His military counterpart, Lieutenant Colonel Edwin Vose Sumner of the 1st Dragoons, opposed arming any civilian militias. Displaying an equal contempt for Calhoun, the Hispanics of New Mexico, and the Indians, the gruff dragoon officer declared in a letter to the army adjutant general: "This predatory war has been carried on for two hundred years, between the Mexicans & Indians, quite time enough to prove, that unless some change is made the war will be interminable. They steal women and children, and Cattle, from each other, and in fact carry on the war, in all respects, like two Indian nations." Sumner, who had but 885 men scattered about at a handful of posts, wanted additional regular troops—not local militia—to patrol his vast southwestern command.[9]

The army, even if more troops could be sent, offered little hope to the New Mexico settlers or protection to travelers on the trail. The *St. Louis Daily Union*, under a bold headline of "Indian Murders—Apathy of our Government," called for action to punish the Indian raiders. "It is almost useless to send regular forces against Indians. The Indians will elude them, and disperse to their secret haunts," editorialized the *Daily Union*. "Not so, however, with the Texan rangers, or the hunters of our own frontier. Acquainted with Indian life, they will follow the savage to the fastnesses of his own ravines or mountains, hunt him out, and, arm to arm, exact from him the penalty of his depredations."[10]

Despite the dangers, the great trade caravans still gathered. The most experienced of all the wagon train captains, the intrepid François Xavier Aubry, organized a large caravan at Kansas City in mid-September. No wagon train captain was more respected than this young French Canadian who had repeatedly set travel records both with his caravans and as a mail carrier. A friend of both Carson and Frémont, Aubry had battled hostile Indians and severe weather to take three trains to Santa Fe in 1848 alone. In February 1849 he had accompanied Charles White to Chihuahua, then fast becoming the real center of a trade network stretching from St. Louis to Santa Fe and then along the old Camino Real to Mexico City. Aubry's return to Missouri was marked by attacks by both Apaches and Pawnees, but his little band reached Independence on August 23 with no losses. Undaunted, he immediately proceeded to purchase goods for a return to Santa Fe.[11]

Attached to Aubry's caravan were ten wagons owned by Ceran St. Vrain and thirteen wagons owned by James M. White. The White brothers, of Warsaw, Missouri, were among those who sought their fortune in postwar New Mexico. James and Charles White had arrived in Santa Fe in mid-July 1848 to open a mercantile business similar to the general store they operated in Missouri. Their business plan was simple but effective: "Cheap Merchants—Cheaper than the Cheapest" ran their advertisement in the July 24, 1848, issue of the *Santa Fe Republican*. After a successful summer of trade, Charles headed south to explore business prospects between Santa Fe and Chihuahua, while James returned to St. Louis to bank $58,000 in gold and silver coins. He promptly made plans to return to Santa Fe with his family. New Mexico would be their new home. White planned to headquarter his mercantile business in Santa Fe, with yet another branch in El Paso established by his brother and Aubry the previous winter. All of his personal goods were with the wagon train. His wife, Ann Dunn White, and baby daughter, Virginia; a Black employee, Ben Bushman; and a Black female servant made up the White household. They departed Kansas City on September 15.[12]

Despite all the dire warnings of Indian unrest, the journey proved uneventful, although the weather turned cold and blustery. Aubry, when just to the east of Council Grove, decided to send his wagon master, William Calloway, ahead to Santa Fe for fresh mules. White wanted to accompany Calloway in order to get his family to Santa Fe more quickly. Aubry argued against such an action but could not dissuade the merchant. Leaving his wagons with Aubry, White pushed ahead with his family in two carriages on October 18. They were accompanied by Calloway, the baby's Black nursemaid, Ben Bushman, a German traveler named Lawberger, and two of Aubry's New Mexican employees.

By October 24, the little party had hurried down the Santa Fe Trail's Cimarron Cutoff and across Palo Blanco Creek some ten miles east of the Point of Rocks landmark. They were less than one hundred miles from the relative safety of Las Vegas when Lobo Blanco's Jicarillas sprang their ambush. The Indians later claimed that they had attempted to parley with White and were fired on, but the elaborate stone breastworks they had constructed beside the trail told a different story. It must have been over quickly. Calloway was shot through the chest and Lawberger through the neck. The two New Mexicans fell nearby. White fought desperately in defense of his family, falling with several bullet and lance wounds. His loyal servant, Bushman, died not far from him.

The gun smoke had hardly cleared when a party of New Mexican buffalo hunters happened on the scene. The Apaches quickly hid themselves. Rather than burying the dead the hunters proceeded to ransack the carriages for plunder. Then Lobo Blanco struck again. One hunter was killed and his young son terribly wounded as the others beat a hasty retreat.

The injured boy played possum and then managed to reach Point of Rocks, where he encountered the party of Hugh Smith, the New Mexico territorial delegate to Congress, on his way to Washington. The boy's tale horrified the men, who promptly returned to Las Vegas to alert the troops at Santa Fe and Taos.

Englishman Alexander Barclay, whose adobe fort was an important way station along Mora Creek, reached the murder scene on the evening of October 25. He and his companions did not linger, especially after finding White's body with its lower half completely devoured by wolves. They pushed on quickly to camp at Point of Rocks before reaching Barclay's Fort on the morning of the twenty-seventh. Smith was there with the wounded boy. The boy claimed that the Jicarillas had headed to the northwest after killing his father. Barclay, long the factor at Bent's Fort, knew the Apaches well and surmised that they must have headed southeast toward the broken country along the Canadian River. Barclay's party had also encountered several Pueblo Indians who had seen Ann White and her daughter, Virginia, in the Apache camp. It was assumed that the nurse was with them as well, but the Pueblos had not seen her.[13]

Word reached Calhoun in Santa Fe on October 29. He hired Indian trader Encarnacion Garcia to ransom Mrs. White and her daughter from the Apaches. Calhoun offered Garcia $1,000 for the ransom, at the same time confessing to his superiors that "I am left to lament the impotency of my arm, and if the two captives are not to be liberated, it is to be hoped they are dead."[14]

Aubry, reaching Santa Fe the next morning, was stunned by the news and promptly hired both Pueblo Indians and New Mexican friends to rescue the captives. He also offered a reward or ransom of $1,000, a huge sum at that time.

At Las Vegas the wary Captain Judd ordered an escort of twenty men eastward under Sergeant Philip Swartwout to guard the mail wagon bound for "the states." Judd also sent an Indian hostage taken prisoner by Lieutenant Ambrose Burnside the previous August along with the sergeant just in case they should encounter the Apaches. The hostage, Lobo Blanco's daughter, was to be traded for Mrs. White. The first night out, the party camped a few miles east of Point of Rocks, not far from the White murder site. The Jicarilla woman was allowed to climb a nearby knoll, where she awakened the entire camp with her mournful wail. She cried all night. By dawn she appeared calm, sitting quietly next to the campfire, when ordered into a wagon by one of the teamsters. In response she stabbed the man several times with a butcher knife before being knocked down by one of his companions. She then chased her assailant around the camp before, in her wild frustration, stabbing several of the mules, killing one. Swartwout ordered her shot, thus ending all hope of a hostage exchange. What had led to the woman's despondency was never determined, but it seems obvious that she must have discovered some sign of her people that night in the hills above the massacre site.[15]

Troops were also in motion from Taos, where Captain William Grier organized a joint force consisting of his own company of the 1st Dragoons, forty-two men, as well as forty mounted New Mexican Volunteers under Captain José María Valdez and a battery of six-pounders. Grier, an 1835 West Point graduate who had been brevetted major for gallantry during the Mexican War, had not been in New Mexico long. One of his dragoons described him as "a fatherly old man who was designed for a Methodist minister but whose patriotic spirit exceeded his religious zeal." Grier wisely hired Antoine Leroux as his chief of scouts for the expedition. Leroux rivaled even Kit Carson as a mountain man and scout. Born of French-Canadian parents in St. Louis in 1803, Leroux had gone west with William H. Ashley's band of trappers in 1822. An experienced trapper and mountain man, he had settled in New Mexico in 1833 and married into the prominent Vigil clan. During the Mexican War he had won fame as a scout for Colonel Philip St. George Cooke's Mormon Battalion, helping to blaze a wagon road across the Southwest to California.[16]

Also attached to the command was a twenty-two-year-old German emigrant named William Kronig, freshly minted orderly sergeant of Valdez's company. Kronig had immigrated to the United States from Westphalia in 1847. Lured westward by gold fever, he had made it only as far as Santa Fe before running out of cash. In hopes of making enough money to continue on to the California goldfields, he enlisted for two months' service in the New Mexico Volunteers; since he was the only man in his company who could read or write English, he was promptly promoted to sergeant. When the detachment was ordered out, he requested that Captain Grier provide him with a gun but was dismissed with the statement that a saber was enough of a weapon for him.[17]

On the third night out, Grier's detachment reached Rayado. The captain wanted Kit Carson to join his party, even though Leroux was to be chief scout and the noted frontiersmen Robert Fisher, Dick Wootton, and Tom Tobin were also in his company. The story he told Carson was a sad tale as old as the frontier itself and always compelling. The rescue of his daughter from the Shawnees was one of the most famous stories from the life of Daniel Boone, and it in turn had provided the inspiration for James Fenimore Cooper's 1826 novel *The Last of the Mohicans*. While the written manifestations of this tale in the published biographies of Boone and in

Cooper's novel were lost on Carson, who could neither read nor write, the plight of young Ann White certainly stirred him to action.

Carson was the first to reach the slaughter site on November 9. He quickly found the abandoned Apache camp as well. "The letters, papers etc. found strewed about this camp," wrote Grier, "were conclusive evidence that here had been the hiding place of those Indians who, two weeks previously had murdered Mr. J.M. White and his party." Even the rough mountain men of the party were moved by the discovery of Virginia White's little rocking chair.[18]

"It was the most difficult trail that I ever followed," Carson declared later. The Apaches broke into small parties every morning, rejoining at a designated campsite in the late afternoon. The trail, already cold, led Carson and the other scouts to many a dead end.

Ann White was their great ally. "In nearly every camp we would find some of Mrs. White's clothing," Carson noted, "which was the cause of renewed energy on our part to continue the pursuit."[19]

From Point of Rocks, Carson trailed the Jicarillas to the southeast, toward their favored haunts along the Canadian River and its tributaries. After two hundred miles they forded the river only to realize that their quarry had circled back some fifteen miles below the point of their crossing.

"It was the flight of the ravens, which led me to believe that we were nearing the hostiles of whom we were in pursuit," recalled frontiersman Dick Wootton. "The direction of their flight indicated the location of a camp, where they could find the carcasses of dead animals to feed on, and the time of their flight in the afternoon, indicated the distance of the camp from us."[20]

As the trail became fresh, Captain Grier ordered the men to supply themselves with bread for eight days for the final pursuit. They would make only cold camps at night after pushing hard every day. About two hours before sundown on November 16, the scouts found the abandoned Apache camp with cottonwood still smoldering in the ashes of the fires. Scouts were sent out but it was too late in the day to find the Jicarillas. Having traveled a punishing forty miles that day, Grier decided to camp in a grove of nearby cottonwoods to rest his horses and men for the final push forward.

At dawn on November 17, Grier moved his command out at the gallop, the scouts in advance. He gambled that even though they had to travel across the exposed prairie to make speed, the Indians would not spy them until too late. Grier ordered a trot and the soldiers soon came in sight of the Apache pony herd grazing on the hills above the Indian camp. The Jicarillas were encamped on the Canadian River some fifteen miles south of the landmark called Tucumcari Butte.[21]

Carson, far in advance, could see that the Apaches had been alerted to the troops and were breaking camp. As he galloped forward he called back to the men to follow him. Wootton and others in the advance hurried forward to join Carson in charging the camp. Grier suddenly appeared and ordered the men to halt. Wootton, stunned, felt Grier's action "one of the strangest ideas that ever entered the head of a commanding officer, who was about to engage an Indian or any other enemy."[22]

Carson galloped back, cursing Grier and demanding an immediate charge, but Leroux had suggested a parley and the captain was adamant. An enraged volunteer sergeant rode up to Grier and threw down his gun and saber in disgust. By this time Apache warriors were rushing toward the troops, screening the escape of their families. Grier suddenly reeled in his saddle, shot in the chest by one of the Apaches. His gauntlets, stuffed into his coat pocket, saved him by stopping the spent ball. Gasping for breath, he ordered the charge. It was too late.

As the soldiers rushed the village, the last of the Apaches melted away before them with their families safely across the river. Fisher shot one man as he attempted to cross the river. He was the only Apache warrior killed. The Indians, with their fresh horses, easily outdistanced the pursuing soldiers and quickly scattered.[23]

Young James Bennett, who had been with the dragoons only a few months, was among the first into the camp. He saw Ann White struggling to escape from an old Indian woman who was trying to force her to mount a mule. She broke away and ran toward the soldiers but was stopped short by an arrow from the bow of the Indian woman. As Bennett watched in horror, "Mrs. White with a shriek fell, pierced to the heart when we were within 15 paces of her, for which act the squaw paid dearly with her own life."[24]

Carson was quickly beside Ann White's body. She was "perfectly warm, had not been killed more than five minutes," he recalled with some bitterness. "I am certain that if the Indians had been charged immediately on our arrival, she would have been saved." Sergeant Kronig also came on the tragic scene: "It was a pitiful sight to see an American woman so ruthlessly killed by these heartless savages. They still had her baby and the Negro nurse."[25]

With pursuit fruitless, the soldiers gathered up camp equipment, buffalo robes, saddles, and food and tore down some thirty lodges. These were all gathered over Mrs. White's grave and burned so that the Apaches would not find the burial site. "She was a fraile, delicate, and very beautiful woman but having undergone such usage and treatment as she had suffered, nothing but a wreck remained. Her body bore evident signs of brutal treatment," lamented trooper Bennett. "Over her corpse we swore vengeance upon her persecutors."[26]

Nearly two hundred ponies and mules were taken, which Grier gave to the volunteers. Two Apache children were found and Grier turned them over to Jesús Silva to take back to Rayado. (The taking of Indian children as slaves was still commonplace among New Mexicans.)

Mrs. White's baggage was found while gathering the Apache property for destruction. A remarkable discovery was made. Carson never forgot the moment: "In camp was found a book, the first of the kind I had ever seen, in which I was made a great hero, slaying Indians by the hundred, and I have often thought that as Mrs. White would read the same, and knowing that I lived near, she would pray for my appearance and that she might be saved. I did come, but had not the power to convince those that were in command over me to pursue my plan for her rescue."[27]

The book was most likely Charles E. Averill's *Kit Carson, The Prince of the Gold Hunters*, published earlier that year and the first of many novels to wildly exaggerate Carson's heroics. Disgusted, Carson ordered his companions to toss the book into the fire over Ann White's grave.

Later that evening, several of the soldiers heard a muffled cry coming from the willows along the river. Bennett and half a dozen troopers investigated. By the river Bennett discovered an Apache baby, perhaps eight months old, still strapped into its cradle board. When Bennett picked up the child, another soldier pushed forward, declaring, "Let me see that brat!" As the others stood slack-jawed, the soldier lashed a stone to the cradle board and tossed the baby into the river. Within a moment the child vanished into the swirling waters of the Canadian. "You're a little feller now but will make a big Injun bye and bye," the soldier mumbled as he walked away. "I only wish I had more to treat the same way."[28]

On the return home, the column was struck by a sudden blizzard. In the ensuing whiteout most of the captured ponies were lost as the command drifted before the storm. The men suffered terribly. It was even worse for Lobo Blanco's people, caught on the open prairie without any lodges or buffalo robes. A great many of them perished. Carson, Leroux, and Grier, with several of the dragoons, staggered into Captain Judd's camp at Las Vegas on November 24. From there Carson left the command for Rayado.

In 1850, Congress authorized $1,500 to be paid by Calhoun for the return of the White girl. It was too late, for the trail had grown cold. "I have not been able to make any further discovery in relation to the child and servant," Calhoun reported back to Washington in March 1851, "notwithstanding I have had out a number of traders in every direction, who have ventured into the camps of the Utahs, and the Jicarillas and Mescaleros Apaches." Calhoun did everything he could to rescue them, but the White child and her nurse were never found. The Apaches repeatedly reported them to be dead, which was likely the case. The White murders received wide press coverage in the East, so that in response Calhoun got his request for more troops. In 1851, Fort Union, which was to be a pivotal frontier post and supply depot for the next forty years, was built near where the Cimarron and Mountain Branches of the Santa Fe Trail came together just to the southwest of Point of Rocks.[29]

Back in Taos, Sergeant Kronig was ordered to copy the official military report of Grier's expedition. "I copied it and to my surprise I read of the wonders that we had performed," he grumbled. As he was working, Major Benjamin Beall of the 1st Dragoons stepped into the office to inquire how he was doing. When the young German remarked on his surprise on reading of the brilliant campaign that he had participated in but had not witnessed, the old soldier smiled, remarking that it was "paper talk."

Kit Carson now also knew the strange power of paper talk. On the far reaches of the Canadian he had come face-to-face with his own legend in one of the most remarkable moments in all of frontier history: the discovery of Averill's book made it seem as if life were imitating art, but with tragic consequences. His failure to save Ann White and her baby would haunt him all the rest of his days.

20

LAND OF THE JICARILLA

Early in the spring of 1853, Kit Carson embarked on one of the strangest adventures of his storied career. Along with his partner Lucien Maxwell and Daniel Boone's great-grandson Tom Boggs, he led a great trail drive to California, predating the cattle drives up the Chisholm Trail by nearly twenty years. However, it was not cattle that Carson and his companions herded to the California goldfields. It was sheep, 6,500 woolly head that they drove all the way from Santa Fe via Fort Laramie, Wyoming, to the Sweetwater and Green Rivers and across the Great Basin along the California Trail to Sacramento.[1]

After visiting with old friends in California, Carson returned via the Gila Trail to Santa Fe, arriving on Christmas Day. There he learned that he had been appointed federal Indian agent for northern New Mexico (which then included southern Colorado) at a salary of $1,000 a year. This appointment, along with the earlier selection of famed mountain man Thomas Fitzpatrick as agent for the plains tribes, was a rare flash of intelligence on the part of the Washington political class. These positions were usually doled out as patronage favors to politicos of varying degrees of competence and honesty. Even when honest men received such appointments, by the time they finally learned the customs, rituals, and politics of Indian Country, they were usually replaced as another administration took office. Carson's predecessor as agent, John Greiner, who was an honest man, admitted as much upon his return to Washington, where he spoke before Congress. "The great difficulty in our Indian policy is in the selection of Indian agents, who are generally appointed for political services," he testified to the Joint Special Committee on Indian Affairs. "I was changed just as I was about to be of service and became acquainted with the Indians." All could agree, however, that Carson was a superb selection as agent, even if he was illiterate and would have to hire a clerk to write his reports. The forty-four-year-old Carson would serve as Indian agent for the next seven years.[2]

Carson now found himself in charge of his old enemies the Jicarilla Apaches. He felt little but contempt for the small tribe, whom he considered "truly the most degraded and troublesome Indians we have in our department."[3] Headquartered in Taos, his jurisdiction included not only the Jicarillas but also the Mohuache Utes and the Pueblos of Taos. Carson had a particularly warm relationship with the Utes, but the Jicarillas were another matter altogether. New Mexico territorial governor David Meriwether, who had also taken over as Indian superintendent from Calhoun, remarked in 1854 that "no other single band of Indians has committed an equal amount of depredations upon, and caused so much trouble and annoyance to the people of this Territory, as the Jicarillas." Carson and Meriwether feuded constantly, but when it came to the Jicarillas they were in complete agreement.[4]

Former governor and Indian superintendent Calhoun had met with both Chacon and Lobo Blanco at a Santa Fe treaty council in April 1851. The searing memory of the White tragedy made this peace council hard for Carson and others to stomach. The talks went well and the Apache chiefs agreed to stay away from the settlements in exchange for annuities from the federal government. Unfortunately Calhoun, who was already in such ill health that he had a coffin constructed and carried in the wagon with him, since he feared being buried in a shallow grave on the prairie, died on his way to Washington in June 1852. The coffin indeed proved of use—a sad end for a good man. He had traveled east to lobby for his agreement with the Apaches but the treaty died with him.[5]

Dr. Michael Steck, who took over as Indian agent for the southern Apaches late in 1852, was a remarkably able and honest man, if a bit too trusting and idealistic. He now attempted to settle the Jicarilla problem by moving all of them west of the Rio Grande. This seemed an absurdity to Lobo Blanco and his Llaneros, for the plains east of the river were their traditional homeland. But old Chacon and his Olleros, the mountain people, readily agreed to Steck's terms, settling along the Rio Puerco some twenty miles west of Abiquiu. Chacon's people cleared fields and planted crops of corn, wheat, pumpkins, and melons. A delighted Steck urged Congress to secure this land for the Jicarillas and keep the Hispanic and white settlers out.[6]

Steck's dream of peace was but a mirage. The Llaneros raided with impunity, even striking the cattle herd at Fort Union. On February 20, 1854, Lieutenant David Bell led a detachment of the 2nd Dragoons south from Fort Union and down the Canadian River in search of the Jicarillas who had made off with the cattle. Bell, considered by his commanding officer "an officer of great promise, a superb shot and remarkably fine horseman," overtook the Apaches along the Red River after a heart-pounding pursuit. The Apaches signaled for a parley. Bell advanced with twenty-two mounted dragoons, to be met by an equal number of dismounted Jicarillas. They were led by Lobo Blanco himself. No man was more wanted by the dragoons, for the chief had bragged of repeatedly raping Ann White.

This parley was the same gambit that Lobo Blanco had successfully used on Grier. But the lieutenant was not only far less trusting; he was also determined to get his man. With weapon drawn, he ordered the bold chief to surrender. In response, Lobo Blanco dropped to his knee and unleashed an arrow at the lieutenant. Bell reined up his horse and fired back, emptying his revolver into his foe. Even as he reeled from the bullets, Lobo Blanco sent an arrow into the chest of the dragoon next to Bell.

Several of the warriors hurried to rescue their chief, firing arrow after arrow into the charging dragoons. Two soldiers tumbled dead from their horses and four others were wounded within a few moments. Lobo Blanco rose in rage and staggered toward the young officer. Another dragoon shot the chief yet again, and as he fell the soldier picked up a huge rock and crushed in his skull.[7]

The death of Lobo Blanco inflamed the passions of all the Jicarillas—not just his own plains Llaneros but the mountain Olleros as well. Carson attempted to cool their ardor, meeting with Chacon and several of his Ollero warriors on March 25. Chacon condemned the cattle raid on Fort Union and the fight with Bell's dragoons, swearing his peaceful intentions and asking for government rations and protection. Carson could neither feed the Apaches nor protect them, but he urged them to remain near the pueblo of Picuris while he traveled south to Santa Fe to plead their case.[8]

While Carson was gone, a detachment of dragoons, traveling from

Fort Union to Taos, blundered upon Chacon's people, stampeding them into panicked flight. Sixty dragoons were sent from Cantonment Burgwin, near Taos, under orders to find Chacon's Apaches. Lieutenant John W. Davidson, 1st Dragoons, who had been with Carson on Kearny's march, led his men some twenty miles south of Taos into the steep canyon of Embudo Mountain following the Apache trail.

On March 30, Davidson came upon the Jicarillas. Concealed amidst the trees along the steep canyon walls were nearly two hundred Jicarilla and Ute warriors. The dragoons were taken completely by surprise as the Indians unleashed a volley of arrows and musket fire. Davidson, although wounded, rallied his men and sent them charging up the canyon walls against the concealed Indians. Within a few minutes twenty-two of the soldiers were dead and nearly every member of the command wounded. The Apaches quickly flanked the soldiers, rushing upon the horse holders in the rear. In danger of having all his horses stampeded, Davidson ordered a retreat out of the deadly ambush. Leaving their dead and wounded comrades behind in the canyon, the remaining dragoons used their sabers to cut their way out. Young James Bennett had fallen late in the fight, shot through both legs. The desperate dragoon grasped onto the stirrup of a passing horse and was dragged half a mile before mounting and galloping to safety. The Indians, content to capture the remaining horses and loot the dead, let the white soldiers go.

Carson, on his way home to Taos from Santa Fe the next day, passed near the canyon but was unaware of the battle. He soon returned to Cieneguilla, as the army named the battle site, to help bury the dead. "The trap had long been prepared by the Indians," he noted, "it was unknown to the military, and no one could have avoided it."[9]

The acting territorial governor promptly declared that "war existed between the United States and the Jicarilla band of the Apache tribe of Indians, and all their aiders and abettors," remarking that "the highest dictates of humanity demanded their extinction."[10]

As soon as word of the battle reached Fort Union, Lieutenant Colonel Philip St. George Cooke took the field, stripping the fort of every available man. On April 4, Cooke marched westward toward the Rio Grande with Bell's company of the 2nd Dragoons, a detachment of the 1st Dragoons under Lieutenant Sam Sturgis, and a company of the 2nd Artillery serving as infantrymen. Cooke, an aristocratic Virginian by both birth and inclination (his son-in-law was Jeb Stuart), was held in either fear or awe by most who came into contact with him. He had graduated from West Point in 1827 and was one of the first officers selected for the 1st Dragoons. That regiment of mounted infantry had been organized in 1833 in recognition of the needs of frontier expansion. (The U.S. Army had no peacetime mounted forces before that time because of the lingering Revolutionary-era prejudice against the aristocratic pretensions of cavalrymen.) Cooke's 1843 assignment to guard the Santa Fe Trail from attacks from both Indian and Texan raiders had led him into contact with Kit Carson, Ceran St. Vrain, and the Bent brothers. He had failed to endear himself to these New Mexicans. The imperious Cooke impressed Carson as undoubtedly "brave and gallant" but nevertheless "a very peppery man with language, [who] talked through his nose so that you could hardly understand him, but you *had* to understand him!"[11]

When Cooke reached Taos he asked Carson to serve as chief scout for the expedition. Carson recruited thirty New Mexicans from Taos as well as several Pueblo Indians to join the war party. The Pueblos, so long the enemies of the Jicarillas that even the old men had forgotten the original offense, led the way for Cooke's two-hundred-man force. They marched into the teeth of a fierce spring snowstorm. Cooke later reported: "Crossing the Rio Grande, we pursued the enemy through deep snows along the margin of frightful precipices and ravines, over the roughest mountains by sheep-paths, following the devious and scarcely perceptible trail only through the wonderful sagacity of our Pueblo allies, who seemed never at fault."

Cooke's column finally found the Jicarillas in the steep canyon of the Rio Ojo Caliente, a tributary of the Rio Chama, near hot springs that Carson knew to be a favorite Apache campsite. The canyon walls were too steep to descend without alerting the Indians, so the soldiers unleashed a volley on the sleeping village from above. The surprised warriors returned fire as they desperately tried to get their families across the swollen river to safety. Seventeen women and children perished in the icy waters or from exposure afterward.

So prominent was Carson in this fight that the Jicarilla long remembered him as the leader of the white soldiers. Carson was anxious to capture the Apache women and children and hold them as hostages. This might well force the warriors to surrender. The last thing he wanted was for any of them to be killed, for that would leave the men with nothing to live for save vengeance. Another scout, James Quinn, remembered Carson leading the assault into the village ahead of the soldiers: "Carson had always been ahead with the Spy Company and it being no time to swap knives he charged hard on the left with the Mexicans and myself with my Pueblos."[12]

The soldiers quickly secured the camp, although all save five warriors escaped. A dragoon found an infant by the riverbank where his mother had drowned and turned the baby over to one of Carson's Hispanic volunteers. The man carried the child off into slavery in Taos. Cooke, in his report, claimed a grand victory over 150 of Chacon's warriors, with but one soldier killed and another seriously wounded.

Carson was disgusted. Even with his prejudice against the Jicarillas, he had little stomach for Cooke's so-called victory. He soon informed the governor in Santa Fe: "Having become acquainted with the commencement of War on the Apaches about Taos, & accompanied Col. Cooke in his present expedition, I have to report to you, first, that in my opinion, they were driven into the war, by the action of the officers & troops in that quarter."[13]

Cooke's attempt to pursue the fleeing Apaches was frustrated by terrain, weather, and the elusive nature of his foe. "The Jicarilla Apache Indians are the worst that are to be pursued," Carson noted. "They always, after having been attacked, retreat in small parties and have no baggage, and are capable of traveling several days without food so that it is impossible for any command of regular troops to overtake them."[14]

Cooke returned to Fort Union in frustration. Jicarilla war parties, now joined by their Ute allies, struck all along the line of New Mexican settlements on the Rio Grande to the north of Santa Fe. Fearing an alliance of the mountain Jicarillas and Utes with the plains Comanches and Kiowas to the east and the Mescaleros to the south, Cooke ordered Captain James Henry Carleton to take two companies of the 1st Dragoons, along with Captain Quinn's Spy Company, north from Taos into Colorado's San Luis Valley to intercept Jicarilla raiders. Kit Carson was once again to be chief of scouts.

Carson had first met Carleton in the summer of 1851 near the Arkansas River crossing of the Santa Fe Trail. While escorting a dozen of

Maxwell's wagons loaded down with Kansas City goods, he had encountered a large party of sullen Cheyennes. Learning that a Cheyenne chief had recently been flogged by some imperious army officer, Carson realized that his small party was in great danger: "As an Indian very seldom lets pass an injury done him unavenged, and it matters not who may be the victim so that it is of the same nation, I unfortunately, happened to be the first [American] that passed them since the insult was given them. On me they intended to have retaliation."[15]

Carson was worried. He had with him his sixteen-year-old daughter, Adaline, as well as his niece Susan and her new husband. He could ill afford a pitched battle with the Cheyennes. The Indians were in an ugly mood, threatening Carson and his dozen companions. The Cheyennes had withdrawn after a campfire confrontation, with each side pulling out their guns. Carson was a brave man but he was no fool. He sent a messenger galloping westward in search of help. He had the wagons quickly packed up and moved out under cover of darkness. The Cheyennes followed, shadowing the wagons along the trail, waiting for just the right moment to strike. It was Carleton, with thirty men, who arrived just in the nick of time to save the wagon train and escort it to Rayado. Carson never forgot Carleton's rescue and felt a lifelong debt to the dragoon officer for saving not only his life but also those of his daughter and niece.[16]

The rigidly austere army officer from Maine did not immediately warm to the famed frontiersman, feeling Carson's reputation absurdly exaggerated. His opinion quickly changed during their campaign against the Jicarillas. Carson discovered a faint trail made by three warriors in Sangre de Cristo Pass and led Carleton's dragoons out of the mountains and southeast onto the broad prairie that led to Raton Pass. The scout knew this country well. He could tell from the trail sign that the Jicarillas were near. The morning of the sixth day on the trail, Carson told Carleton that they should find the Indians by two o'clock that afternoon. This proved a bit much for that officer's New England skepticism. Carson recalled with delight that Carleton "told me that if such would be the case that he would present to me one of the finest hats that could be procured in New York."[17]

The Jicarilla village was discovered on the benchland on the east flank of Fishers Peak, just to the north of Raton Pass. As Carleton ordered

Quinn's scouts and the dragoons forward, he looked at his timepiece: it was exactly 2:07.

The Jicarillas managed to escape with but few casualties. The soldiers destroyed their camp, recovered forty head of stolen horses, and found considerable evidence of their raids upon the settlements.

"Kit Carson," Carleton confessed in his after-action report, "is justly celebrated as being the best tracker among white men in the world." Sometime afterward a box from New York arrived at Carson's Taos home. Carleton had paid his wager as promised with a beaver hat—"and a fine one it was," stated Carson. Gilt-lettered on the inside band was:

> At 2 o'clock.
> Kit Carson,
> From Major Carleton

With the end of Carleton's expedition, Carson returned to Taos and his agency duties. There he labored to keep the Utes from joining their Jicarilla friends and also worked to keep the Hispanic settlers and military authorities from attacking the Indians. For most New Mexicans—Hispanic farmers, Pueblo tribesmen, and white soldiers alike—all of the northern tribes were viewed simply as hostiles.[18]

Carleton was also finished with field operations for the time being, receiving a choice staff assignment to Philadelphia, where he was to assist Captain George B. McClellan with a report on the Crimean War. He departed Santa Fe on September 26, 1856. No sooner had he settled his family in Philadelphia than all three of his children came down with scarlet fever. His little boy, Guy, died. Carleton's plush Eastern assignment thus began with tragedy. But he learned much from his close study of the Cossack cavalry in the Crimea, and his report led Secretary of War Jefferson Davis to conclude that the Indian tribes in the West could be organized into an irregular cavalry, much like the Cossacks, to augment U.S. regulars on the frontier.[19]

While Carson tended to the Utes and Carleton studied the Cossacks, New Mexico military commanders renewed attacks on the Jicarillas. General John Garland, department commander, augmented his regulars with six companies of New Mexico Volunteers under the command of Carson's old friend Ceran St. Vrain. Among his officers were Captain Manuel Antonio Chaves, a direct descendant of Spanish conquistadores, and Lieutenant Albert Pfeiffer, a young Dutch immigrant who had become Kit Carson's protégé. These troops continually harassed the Jicarillas throughout the spring of 1855.

Carson once again acted as chief scout in the most important of these campaigns in March 1855. St. Vrain's Hispanic volunteers joined with two companies of the 1st Dragoons, an artillery company serving as infantry, and a contingent of Pueblo scouts—a formidable force of five hundred men. It was that perfectly miserable time of year in the Rockies, when the weather danced back and forth between winter and spring. First the men slogged through ankle-deep mud and then knee-deep snow as they labored across Colorado's San Luis Valley in search of the Jicarillas and Utes. They were determined to flush out their foe, for the Indians—now led by a bold young Ute chief—had kept life uncertain for the settlers north of Santa Fe throughout the long "Indian summer" months of the fall of 1854.

At Saguache Pass, at the northern end of the valley, they ran their prey to ground. Painted warriors brandishing long lances and shrieking taunts in Spanish rode to meet the soldiers. Captain Chaves of the volunteers, his shoulder-length black hair streaming behind him, boldly sallied forth to return a young warrior's challenge. The Jicarilla lowered his lance and galloped at the captain, who, reining in his charging horse, steadily took aim with his single-shot rifle, knocking the warrior off his pony. One of the captain's men, Antonio Tapia, promptly scalped the warrior with his Bowie knife as the soldiers surged forward, breaking the Indian line and putting the warriors to flight. It was said that this very same Bowie knife was the one used by Major Richard Weightman to kill famed wagon master François X. Aubry in the Mercure brothers' cantina on the Santa Fe plaza. If so, it was indeed a bloody weapon worthy of its namesake. Two chiefs and six warriors were killed in the battle, and the Indians were forced to scatter into their mountain sanctuaries. While there was never another decisive battle after Saguache Pass, the weary Apaches and Utes finally requested a peace parley that August.[20]

The Jicarillas and Mohuache Utes met with Governor David Meriwether and Carson at Abiquiu in September. Chacon was ill and anxious for peace, but the Llaneros, who had fled south to live with the Mescaleros after Lobo Blanco's death, had now returned to the mountains in as belligerent a mood as ever. The treaty negotiations soured immediately when Meriwether failed to bring enough sheep and rations with him to feed the assembled Indians. This breach of basic Indian Country etiquette was exacerbated when Carson and Meriwether argued in front of the assembled chiefs. The friction between the two men went deeper than sheep, for Carson opposed the treaty offered by Meriwether as unrealistic and unenforceable. The Jicarillas were to receive 160,000 acres of land in the mountains northeast of Abiquiu, part of which Carson knew was involved in a Mexican land grant claim, while the Utes were promised a thousand square miles, including much of Colorado's already partially settled San Luis Valley. Despite Carson's sullen disapproval, the treaties were signed on September 10.

Governor Meriwether, an old frontier hand who nevertheless was a remarkable combination of arrogance compounded by ignorance, had achieved a momentary paper victory that kept the Indians quiet for a few months and gave him a gold star with his federal superiors. He also embarked on a crusade to discredit Carson, which failed miserably. He was left to grumble: "Poor Kit was a good tracker, hunter, and guide, and in the latter capacity, while employed by Colonel Frémont had acquired a reputation which spoiled him, and which in after life and in a higher position he failed to sustain."[21]

Carson well knew that the government would never live up to the treaty terms. Indeed, the treaty was never ratified by the U.S. Senate, no reservations were created, and the governor was soon on his way back to his home in Kentucky. Carson and the Indians were left to pick up the pieces.

Carson later reminded his superiors that "the Indians are the masters of the country." He wisely condemned the practice of having "a grand talk" with the distribution of presents and sacred promises that would soon be broken. He knew the people of the West well—Indian, Hispanic, and Anglo—and spoke from a wealth of experience that no other Indian agent ever possessed. He urged that the Jicarillas and Utes be segregated away from the settlements so they could be protected from Hispanic and Anglo settlers. "They steal from the Indians," he complained in 1857, "and the Indians know no law but that of retaliation, and from such acts commence hostilities . . . and as long as they remain near the Mexican settlements they will be furnished liquor, and the Jicarilla Apaches being notorios [*sic*] for drinking, will be always in difficulty with the citizens of the Territory." His pleas fell on deaf ears.[22]

On March 4, 1861, far to the east, in Washington, Abraham Lincoln was inaugurated as the first Republican president of the United States. Lincoln, like Carson, had been born in Kentucky in 1809 and had spent his formative years on the frontier. His support for a transcontinental railroad and the Homestead Act would dramatically alter the destiny of the West that he loved and saw as the future hope of a dangerously divided nation. Carson had of course supported his old friend John Frémont as the first Republican candidate for president in 1856. Little did he know when first told of Lincoln's election how profoundly that event would forever change his life. For the Apaches and other western tribes that impact would be even more profound.[23]

21

VALVERDE

Taos was no stranger to rebellion. The ancient Tiwa Pueblo, settled two centuries before Columbus, had been buffeted by insurrection before: first in the great Pueblo Revolt of 1680 that drove the Spanish out of New Mexico for a dozen years, and then again in the 1847 rebellion against the Americans that had left Kit Carson's brother-in-law, Governor Charles Bent, beheaded near the plaza. Now up from the south came word that a new rebellion was brewing.

When news of Abraham Lincoln's election reached Taos, Carson and a band of seven loyal Union men confronted a secessionist crowd on the plaza. They raised the Stars and Stripes on a tall cottonwood pole in the center of the plaza and then dared the mob to try to take it down. A guard was posted to make certain it was not disturbed.[1]

The news of Lincoln's election brought a scowl to the deeply lined face of forty-five-year-old Major Henry Hopkins Sibley of the 1st Dragoons. He commanded two dragoon companies at Taos and welcomed secessionist sentiment in the town. On May 13, 1861, he resigned his army commission and headed to the more congenial climes of Texas. "Boys, if you only knew it," he bluntly informed his Unionist fellow officers upon departing, "I am the worst enemy you have!" No one could accuse the man of not being honest.

Within a few weeks of the rebel bombardment of Fort Sumter in April 1861, and President Lincoln's call for volunteers to suppress the Southern rebellion, nearly half of all the military officers stationed in New Mexico and Arizona had resigned and joined the army of the Confederate States of America.[2]

Carson resigned his position as Indian agent on May 24, 1861, to accept a commission as lieutenant colonel of the 1st Regiment of New Mexico Volunteers. The mannered Frenchman Ceran St. Vrain, commanding the regiment, organized his men in Albuquerque. The new Union commander, Colonel Edward Canby, had neither uniforms nor arms with which to equip the volunteers, nor money to pay them. Advanced to regimental colonel on October 4, 1861, when ill health forced St. Vrain to resign, Carson now led his recruits down the Rio Grande to Fort Craig. These men were mostly Hispanic, and while not regular soldiers they were experienced Indian fighters who were particularly anxious to meet their old foes from Texas in combat. Canby, hardly impressed by the volunteers, declared them "worse than worthless."[3]

On Valentine's Day 1862, Canby assigned Carson command of the field operations of the third column of his forces. Carson's 512 men were to be divided into two battalions, one under Lieutenant Colonel José Francisco Chaves and the other under the German immigrant Major Arthur Morrison. Among the regimental officers were experienced men from the Apache campaigns such as Captains Albert Pfeiffer and Rafael Chacon and Lieutenants Andres Tapia and Lawrence G. Murphy, the latter to become famous many years later as the villain of the Lincoln County War. A total of five volunteer regiments were raised, along with several militia companies, and most of these troops were ordered to Fort Craig, where they were soon encamped inside and around its earthen walls.[4]

One month after his resignation from the dragoons, Henry Hopkins Sibley received his commission as a brigadier general in the Confederate army. A West Point graduate of the class of 1838, he was best known in military circles for his invention of a cone-shaped tent popular with both armies during the Civil War as well as for a legendary thirst. Perhaps it was whiskey that fueled his grandiose scheme of a Confederate empire stretching from the goldfields of Colorado across the Southwest to California. He nevertheless sold a notoriously sober Jefferson Davis and the rest of the rebel military hierarchy on his plan. The expansion of slavery into these territories had so long been a central tenet of Southern dogma that perhaps they were all ripe for this sort of delusion. Not only would the western territories soon belong to the Confederacy, but they also coveted the states of northern Mexico. This was not to be a western empire for liberty, as Thomas Jefferson had foreseen, but rather a western empire of slavery.[5]

Sibley's Army of New Mexico consisted of the 4th, 5th, and 7th Texas Mounted Volunteers and the 2nd Texas Mounted Rifles—2,590 men. Lieutenant Colonel John Robert Baylor's troops had easily brushed aside Union resistance in southern New Mexico in July, occupying Mesilla and forcing the surrender of nearby Fort Fillmore. Secessionist sentiment was strong in Mesilla among both the Anglo and Hispanic populations. From Mesilla on August 1, 1861, Baylor proclaimed all the land south of the 34th parallel in New Mexico and Arizona west to the Colorado River as the Confederate Territory of New Mexico.[6]

By January, Sibley's army had united with Baylor in Mesilla. Rebel troops quickly seized the abandoned Fort Thorn some forty miles to the north, at the southern edge of the dreaded desert known as Jornada del Muerto (Journey of Death). As Sibley prepared to move up the Rio Grande, he ordered a small detachment to march west and capture Tucson. The road to California looked open and inviting, but Sibley's besotted gaze was fixed northward on Santa Fe and the Colorado goldfields beyond.

Only Fort Craig, some 160 miles south of Santa Fe, stood in Sibley's way. One young officer described the fort as "an imposing object in this country of small houses." Sibley knew the fortification on the west bank of the Rio Grande that guarded the ancient Camino Real only too well from his service in New Mexico. Fort Craig's twenty-two adobe buildings were surrounded by stout earthen walls ten feet high and well mounted with artillery. The fort had been designed to house two companies but was now required to hold many more. Post commander Lieutenant Colonel Benjamin S. Roberts had done the best he could to place his artillery and prepare his twenty-acre compound for either an assault or a siege.

Canby hurried reinforcements to this last bastion of federal power and they feverishly labored to improve the fortifications. Sibley also knew Canby well. They had been cadets together at West Point, Canby had been best man at Sibley's wedding, and Sibley's last campaign under the Old Flag had been with Canby against the Navajos. By February 1862, Canby had nearly 4,000 men under arms at Fort Craig, 1,200 of them regulars. Among the regulars were Arizona troops from Forts Breckinridge and Buchanan.[7]

Captain James "Paddy" Graydon soon arrived at the fort commanding a volunteer spy company. An Irish emigrant from County Fermanagh, Graydon had come to the United States in his teens. Like many of his countrymen he had enlisted in the army in 1853 and was soon assigned to the 1st Dragoons, stationed in Santa Fe. The congenial twenty-one-year-old recruit soon became a favorite of his company commander, Captain Richard S. Ewell, and saw hard service in campaigns against both the Navajo and the Apache. After the Gadsden Purchase, Ewell's company was sent to the Sonoita Valley, in Arizona, where they established Fort Buchanan far to the south of Tucson.

On April 25, 1858, Captain Ewell reluctantly signed Corporal Paddy Graydon's honorable discharge at Fort Buchanan. Graydon had been on his final campaign with the 1st Dragoons. But Graydon was hardly finished with the army, for he had grand plans to make the most of his military connections.

Several months later, Graydon established the United States Boundary Hotel on Sonoita Creek, just four miles south of Fort Buchanan. The one-story adobe was known to all as Casa Blanca because of its whitewashed walls. Graydon advertised "a fine assortment of wines, liquors, cigars, sardines . . . and good accommodations for the night." Sonoran senoritas sang songs, waited tables, sometimes dealt cards, and always smiled at the rough patrons, laughed at their crude jokes, and helped them to forget just how very far from home they were. It was, remarked one patron, "a pretty tough joint, but a good saloon." Guns and knives often settled disputes over cards, for as Lieutenant Isaiah Moore of the dragoons commented, the "American population" on the Sonoita was "mostly outlaws having everything to gain and nothing to lose."[8]

By 1860, Graydon was the wealthiest man in southern Arizona. "Paddy Graydon had a gin mill just off the fort reservation," remarked an admirer, "and he made more money from it than all the ranchmen put together." The 1860 census listed Graydon's real estate at $3,000 and his personal property at $10,000, a small fortune for that time and place.

Graydon's most profitable venture was likely the partnership he formed at Casa Blanca with the most famous woman on the frontier: Sarah Bowman, truly larger-than-life in every way and known to all as the "Great Western." Jeff Ake, who met her at Graydon's place, was awestruck: "They called her old Great Western. She packed two six-shooters, and they all said she shore could use 'em, that she had killed a couple of men in her time. She was a hell of a good woman." Ake's father, Felix Grundy Ake, spoke of Sarah reverently as simply "the greatest whore in the West."[9]

Sarah was born in Missouri in 1812, her maiden name long ago lost to history. She grew to be an impressive woman over six feet tall and close to two hundred pounds. She was blessed with a well-proportioned if ample figure and an attractive face framed by dark red hair. Sarah had a great appetite for life and for men. She married at least three times and the name of her last husband, a German immigrant in the 2nd Dragoons who was fifteen years her junior, stuck with her. A fellow soldier was suitably impressed by Corporal Albert Bowman's bride. "Today we are reinforced by a renowned female character," Private Sylvester Matson wrote in his diary on May 9, 1852. "They call her Doctor Mary. Her other name is the Great Western." He described her as a "giantess . . . over seven feet tall" with a scar across her cheek from a Mexican saber wound. The camp story was that she had killed the Mexican soldier who wounded her. "She appears here modest and womanly not withstanding her great size and attire," declared Matson. "She has on a crimson velvet waist, a pretty riding skirt and her head is surmounted by a gold laced cap of the Second Artillery. She is carrying pistols and a rifle. She reminds me of Joan of Arc and the days of chivalry."[10]

Her fame was derived from her heroics during the Mexican War. Her second husband, Charles Bourgette of the 5th Infantry, was among the troops assigned to occupy the Nueces Strip in Texas just before the outbreak of the war. Sarah was a laundress and cook attached to General Zachary Taylor's army when it reached Corpus Christi in July 1846. Her husband became ill and was evacuated to Point Isabel on the coast while she drove her wagon south to the Rio Grande.

General Taylor left the 7th Infantry under Major Jacob Brown to finish the construction of earthen fortifications across the river from Matamoros while he took his main force to Port Isabel to secure his line of supply. Sarah remained with the 7th. By this time she had already been nicknamed the Great Western, which was at the time the name of the largest steamboat in the world.[11]

On May 3 the Mexicans opened a fierce bombardment of the fort. Major Brown's guns replied. For five days and nights the Mexican shells rained down on the American fort. Major Brown fell on the fourth day, a shell exploding just above his position. It was a living hell for all the defenders. The Great Western refused to take shelter with the other women. She set up her kitchen tent in the middle of the fort and kept the men on the walls fed despite a bullet dislodging her bonnet. She took water to the parched soldiers and tended to the wounded until General Taylor lifted the siege on May 9, crushing General Mariano Arista's force at Resaca de la Palma.

On May 18 the American army crossed the Rio Grande to occupy Matamoros and prepare for the invasion of northern Mexico. A grand dinner party was held in General Arista's elegant headquarters in Matamoros with Sarah Bowman as a special guest. Lieutenant Braxton Bragg offered a toast to "Great Western—one of the bravest and most patriotic soldiers at the siege of Fort Brown."[12] It was met with cheers from all the officers.

When Taylor's army moved southwest against Monterey, the Great Western followed. Taylor was Sarah's kind of general. The soldiers had affectionately nicknamed him "Old Rough and Ready," for he was always quick to share their privations, discomforts, and dangers. As an old frontier soldier, he cared little for military pomp and, unlike his military rival Winfield Scott, always dressed plainly. Old Rough and Ready may have not looked much like a soldier but he was a fighter, and Sarah admired him as such. At the Battle of Buena Vista on February 23, 1847, a panicked soldier rushed back among the reserves crying out that Taylor was whipped and the army destroyed. Sarah seized the man and, according to Texas volunteer George Washington Traherne, "she just drew off and hit him between the eyes and knocked him sprawling; says 'you damned son of a bitch, there ain't Mexicans enough to whip old Taylor.' "[13]

In Saltillo, Sarah opened an establishment that catered to the many needs of the army of occupation. As the army advanced from Saltillo, she was informed by a bluenosed, by-the-book officer that without a husband she could not join the column.

"All right, Major, I'll marry the whole Squadron and you thrown in but what I go along," she declared. She gave the officer a smart salute and turned her horse to trot down the line of soldiers.

"Who wants a wife with fifteen thousand dollars, and the biggest leg in Mexico!" she cried out. "Come my beauties, don't all speak at once—who is the lucky man?" She soon had a new husband and an official place on the rolls of the dragoons as laundress.

When the war ended she moved her thriving business north to El Paso, where famed Texas Ranger John "Rip" Ford met her. "On our side an American woman known as the Great Western kept a hotel. She was very tall, large and well made," Ford related of his 1849 encounter. "She had a reputation of being something of the roughest fighter on the Rio Grande; and was approached in a polite, if not humble manner by all of us."[14]

From El Paso, Sarah followed the army and her new husband, Corporal Bowman, to Fort Yuma at the Colorado River crossing. She soon had an establishment across the river from the fort that fed the varied appetites of the officers and enlisted men of Fort Yuma. In time a little village grew up around her combination dance hall, restaurant, and brothel called at first Colorado City and finally Yuma, Arizona. Charles Poston and Herman Ehrenberg surveyed the town site in July 1854 on their return journey to California from the "Purchase." Lieutenant Sylvester Mowry, soon to be one of the founding fathers of Arizona, was one of her most ardent admirers. "The Great Western you remember don't you, is the woman who distinguished herself so much at the Fort Brown bombardment just before the battles at Palo Alto and Resaca," he wrote a Rhode Island friend in 1855. "She has been with the Army twenty years and was brought up here where she keeps the officers' mess. Among her other good qualities she is an admirable pimp. She used to be a splendid looking woman and has done 'good service' but is too old for that now."[15]

Despite her profession, or perhaps because of it, when Olive Oatman was ransomed from the Mojaves and brought to Fort Yuma on the last day of February 1856, she was turned over to Sarah for safekeeping.

The nine members of the Oatman family had been traveling westward along the Gila River toward California when they were attacked on March 19, 1851, by a small party of Yavapai warriors. The Yavapais, Yuman speakers related in the distant past to the Mohave and Walapai, often ranged north into central Arizona, so they were usually mistaken for Apaches by the whites. The Indians murdered Royce and his wife, Mary Ann, along with four of their children, and left a teenage son, Lorenzo, for dead while carrying off fourteen-year-old Olive and seven-year-old Mary into slavery.

The Yavapais sold the girls to their Mohave cousins, who took them to their village on the Colorado River. Mary starved to death but Olive survived to grow into an attractive young woman who became quite acculturated to her new life, even participating in a tattooing ritual that left her chin permanently marked with Native designs.

After five years she was ransomed by a Fort Yuma carpenter and his Yuma Indian friend and brought into the post. She had forgotten English and the officers feared for her sanity, but under the tender care of the Great Western she was soon communicating well and anxious to be reunited with her long-lost brother, Lorenzo. After the massacre he had been found by two Pima Indians and taken to Fort Yuma, where he had begged the soldiers to go in search of his sisters. Captain Samuel Heintzelman, post commander, refused to send out a search party, since he barely had enough men to garrison and guard the fort. Lorenzo had moved to El Monte, California, and now rushed to Fort Yuma upon receiving word of his sister's rescue. "She did not know him and he did not know her also," remarked an eyewitness to the reunion, "so much change in five years."[16]

There would also be considerable change for Sarah Bowman, for even as she watched Olive Oatman depart for her new life as a celebrated "redeemed captive," she was preparing to depart Yuma for the new military post south of Tucson. In October 1856, she and Albert, who had left the dragoons, joined a small wagon train headed east, happy to leave Yuma behind. "There was just one thin sheet of sandpaper between Yuma and Hell," she declared upon departing the desert metropolis she had founded. Along the Gila Trail she halted the wagon train long enough to give the victims of the Oatman massacre a decent burial. At first she operated a boardinghouse in Tucson but soon decided to relocate to the Sonoita Valley to be closer to Fort Buchanan. By the summer of 1858, she and her girls were well established with Paddy Graydon at Casa Blanca.[17]

Sonoran ladies by the score came north, and not all came to work for Paddy and the Great Western. "Sonora has always been famous for the beauty and gracefulness of its señoritas," remarked Charles Poston. They found work as cooks at the mines and ranches, some landed husbands, while others served drinks and food, sang songs, and ran the gambling tables at Casa Blanca. "They were experts at cards," Poston recalled from sad experience, "and divested many a miner of his week's wages over a game of Monte."[18]

A gang of young toughs ran roughshod over the valley and were especially brutal in their treatment of the Mexican farmers and laborers. This cowboy element proved so troublesome that it fell to Paddy Graydon to establish some sort of law and order in the valley. Two Mexicans were killed in a saloon brawl with the cowboys at Casa Blanca, and Paddy had a gunfight with one of the drunken toughs. He eventually put together a posse of reliable men who captured several of the outlaws and drove the rest of the gang out of the territory. "He was a true Irishman," noted an admiring Dr. John Hall, a British soldier of fortune who joined Graydon's posse, "easily got into a scrape and just as easily got out of it, and withal he was a dangerous customer to deal with; he possessed in a remarkable degree the cunning of a fox."[19]

In time, Graydon set himself up as a sort of informal lawman. Ewell arranged for the army to pay him a monthly salary to act as a scout and interpreter when needed. Much of this work involved trailing deserters and bringing them back to the fort. Paddy made quite a reputation for himself while adding to his fortune with the army bounty payments.[20]

On January 28, 1861, Johnny Ward, one of Graydon's neighbors who had a ranch a dozen miles south on the Sonoita, arrived at Fort Buchanan. Apaches had raided his ranch, kidnapped his eleven-year-old stepson, and made off with his cattle herd. Captain Ewell was in Albuquerque, so the pursuit of the Apaches was entrusted to young Second Lieutenant George Bascom, 7th Infantry, who rode out early the next morning with fifty-four of his infantrymen mounted on mules. Ward accompanied the column. Bascom made straight for the Butterfield stage station at Apache Pass, for he knew that the Chiricahua chief Cochise camped in the nearby mountains.

The Apache Pass station was one of 141 stations stretching across the southwest some 2,795 miles, providing an all-weather mail route from St. Louis to California. John Butterfield, a former stage driver who cofounded the American Express Company, had won bidding on the federal mail contract worth $600,000 a year. The Butterfield stages were required to deliver mail and passengers within a twenty-five-day one-way trip. Passenger fare was $200 one way. Postage was ten cents a letter. Roads had been graded and bridges built along the route in a truly monumental undertaking. The stations were the vital link in the road, and most of them, like the Apache Pass station, were small forts.[21]

Cochise, undoubtedly influenced by his father-in-law, Mangas Coloradas, had long assisted the Apache Pass station by providing hay and wood. He had forbidden his warriors from attacking the stages and on occasion had returned stolen stock taken by other Apache bands. Like Mangas, he was anxious to keep the peace with the Americans while continuing to raid into Mexico.

Once at the stage station, Bascom had sent a message to Cochise requesting a parley and the chief came in the next morning, accompanied by his wife, young son, brother, and four others. Cochise thought he was coming in for the noonday meal and a cordial talk and so was taken aback when Bascom demanded that he return the kidnapped Ward boy. Cochise truthfully replied that he did not have the child but promised to try to find him. Bascom responded that Cochise and his companions would be held as hostages until the boy was returned and promptly ordered their arrest. Cochise pulled a knife and cut his way out of Bascom's tent, but the others were taken prisoner and one Apache was killed.

Cochise soon returned with scores of warriors to besiege the stage station. His warriors also captured a wagon train and Cochise offered to trade his prisoners for the Apache hostages. Bascom refused and hard fighting followed in which several of the besieged were killed or wounded. Bascom's woes were increased by the arrival of two stages at the station, one of which had fought its way in and had wounded men. Several men now volunteered to go out under cover of darkness to get help from Fort Buchanan.[22]

Post commander Pitcairn Morrison had few troops to spare. Assistant Surgeon Bernard J. D. Irwin, knowing that there were wounded men with Bascom, volunteered to go. The messengers from Bascom all volunteered to go back with Irwin, as did eleven men from H Company. Morrison sent a messenger to Lieutenant Isaiah Moore at Fort Breckenridge requesting assistance from the dragoons and sent another to Casa Blanca to enlist Paddy Graydon. The Irishman, always anxious for an adventure, soon arrived, and the detachment, mounted on mules, departed for Apache Pass. Despite a fierce snowstorm, they covered sixty-five miles the first day, camping at Dragoon Springs that night. Irwin was delighted to have Graydon with his little command, later writing in his official report that "his character for daring and courage needs no commendation at my hands."[23]

Irwin's Fort Buchanan relief party pressed on along the Overland Mail road on Sunday morning, February 10. Along the desolate Playa de los Pinos, on the eastern edge of the Sulphur Springs Valley, the soldiers saw a distant dust cloud and halted to discover the source. It turned out to be a raiding party of Coyotero Apaches heading north with stolen cattle and horses.

This was made to order for Paddy Graydon. He led the mule-mounted infantry in a wild seven-mile chase that captured thirteen cattle, three horses, and, most importantly, three of the Apache raiders. Graydon had the Coyotero warriors bound, then proceeded on with the cattle and horses toward Apache Pass. This strange caravan reached the stage station later that evening. Wild cheers erupted as the besieged men welcomed the desperately needed doctor, who had brought not only medical care but also reinforcements and beef for dinner. For leading this daring rescue ride, Dr. Irwin would later be awarded the Medal of Honor.

Four days later, Lieutenant Moore with two dragoon companies reached the stage station. Bascom had remained immobile since Irwin's arrival, fearful to venture away from his fortified position. He did not know that Cochise and his warriors had killed their prisoners and scattered. Moore, who was now the ranking officer at Apache Pass, organized a reconnaissance in force on February 16, and not far from the overland road they discovered four butchered bodies. In response, Moore and Bascom hanged Cochise's brother and five other prisoners. Apache vengeance would be swift.[24]

Within weeks of the so-called Bascom Affair, the Apaches struck everywhere. Cochise's warriors hit five stage stations, repeatedly attacked the mail coaches, and swept through the Santa Cruz Valley, killing 150 of the hated white settlers. In early June, Cochise's warriors rounded up an entire Fort Buchanan herd of ten mules and twenty-three cattle that were grazing just south of the post near Casa Blanca. Mangas drove the settlers from the Mimbres River Valley and captured all the stock from Fort McLane. By June he had all but closed the road between Mesilla and Tucson.

By August, less than sixty Americans were still in Tucson. The farms and ranches along the Sonoita and Santa Cruz were all abandoned, as were all the mines save for one near the border. On July 9, 1861, an express from New Mexico had reached Fort Buchanan with orders to abandon the post and march to Fort Fillmore on the Rio Grande to meet the new Confederate invasion from Texas. Lieutenant Moore soon arrived with his two dragoon companies from the abandoned and burned Fort Breckenridge to join the two companies of the 7th Infantry on their eastward trek. As the troops departed on July 23 they torched the fort and all the supplies they had left behind. Not even Paddy Graydon was allowed any government goods, for orders were orders, and it was the desire of the government to destroy property rather than turn it over to the citizens of Arizona.

"Well, this country is going to the devil with railroad speed," reported a newspaperman from Tucson on July 17. "Secessionists on one side and Apaches on the other will bring us speedily to the issue, and the issue will be absence or death."[25]

The game was up, and the Americans along the Sonoita and Santa Cruz packed up and left their fields. Tubac, besieged by a large Coyotero war party, was soon abandoned. Most of the Mexican mine and ranch workers fled south to Sonora. Even Paddy Graydon decided to abandon Casa Blanca, for there was no longer any clientele to purchase the services he and the Great Western provided. Sarah sent her girls south to Sonora and parted with the eastbound Graydon. She was going west.

When the fleeing Arizona miners Charles Poston and Raphael Pumpelly arrived at Yuma, they found Sarah and Albert Bowman back in business. They boarded with her, and Pumpelly, later to be a famous explorer and Harvard professor, was mesmerized. "Our landlady, known as the 'Great Western,' no longer young, was a character of a varied past," he wrote in his memoir. "Her relations with the soldiers were of two kinds. One of these does not admit of analysis; the other was angelic, for she was adored by the soldiers for bravery in the field and for her unceasing kindness in nursing the sick and wounded." The Eastern dude watched this magnificent woman's every movement "as with quiet native dignity, she served our simple meal. She was a lesson in the complexity of human nature."[26]

California volunteers soon flooded into Fort Yuma to prepare to march east against the Confederates. Sarah once again did a booming business. Lieutenant Edward Tuttle was in awe. "She was a splendid example of the American frontier woman," he gushed. He was also impressed that she had been awarded "rations for life" by the 4th Infantry. Those rations did not continue for long. Sarah died on December 23, 1866, at Fort Yuma in her fifty-third year, the victim, it was reported, of the bite of a tarantula spider. They buried her in the Fort Yuma cemetery, where the soldiers fired a salute over her grave.[27]

Graydon had departed the Sonoita in July not long after the abandonment of Fort Buchanan and headed east for Mesilla. He followed a path of desolation all along the way. At Apache Pass he encountered the rotting Indian bodies still dangling from a tree in mute testimony of Bascom's folly. Then, not far from Steins Peak, he passed the wreckage of one of the last Butterfield coaches, captured by Cochise the previous April. All the passengers had been slaughtered. A fresher scene of death awaited him to the southeast of the pyramid-shaped landmark that was Cookes Peak, where a party of Butterfield men had been ambushed by Cochise and Mangas Coloradas only days before. Cochise had gone to Janos to trade for guns and lick his wounds; otherwise, Graydon might never have made it through. He had already arranged with Lieutenant Moore of the dragoons to pick up as much information as possible in Mesilla before reporting to Union headquarters. The saloons of the town were packed with loud-talking Texas volunteers. Upon reaching Santa Fe, Graydon made a report on the rebel troop movements and offered his services to the territorial governor. By October 1861 he had his spy company in the field.[28]

Few officers became as popular or as notorious as thirty-year-old Paddy Graydon. The hard-drinking, colorful Irishman had made quite a reputation, both good and bad, in the months between joining the Union army and his arrival at Fort Craig. He had recruited his "Independent Spy Company" quickly, aided by his Catholic faith, long experience in the Southwest, and fluency in Spanish. They were the "hardest cases he could find," one of Canby's officers recalled, and all eighty-four took an oath before "Jesús Christo y Santa María" to faithfully serve Captain Graydon and the U.S. government. They then kissed the Holy Cross that an obliging senorita had sewn onto the company's little blue silk banner. This was a wildly undisciplined but highly effective scouting company in the campaign against Sibley's invading Texans. Captain George H. Pettis of the California Column characterized Graydon as "a brave man, and no undertaking was too hazardous for him to attempt." A fellow volunteer officer from Colorado colorfully described the Irish captain as "the vulture over the carrion" and "an enterprising, fearless leader of a desperate band." Another Colorado soldier admired him simply as "a daredevil and as reckless as can be."

As Sibley's army marched up the Camino Real, Graydon harassed them at every opportunity, taking prisoners, burning supply wagons, rescuing

Yankee prisoners from the invader, and generally making himself a legend to the rank and file huddled around Union campfires. "Paddy Graydon, as he is familiarly called, is quite an ordinary appearing man, but he emphatically deceives his looks," noted Captain O. J. Hollister of the Colorado Volunteers. "He is always hovering around the foe, watching with eagle eye for a chance to strike a telling blow." Even the rebels whispered his name around their campfires. "O'Graydon himself was looking at us when we drilled at Ft. Davis coming on up," Sergeant Alfred Brown Peticolas of the 4th Texas Mounted Volunteers recorded in his diary, "and some of their spys took supper with us every night we were in New Mexico."[29]

In the inky blackness of the night of February 13, Graydon torched a bonfire on the barren north face of Fra Cristobal Mountain to warn Canby at distant Fort Craig of the approach of the rebel army. The next morning he spied a rebel courier some five miles south of the fort and captured him within sight of the rebel advance guard. Two days later, from behind the stout walls of Fort Craig, Graydon sighted the fluttering banners of the rebel host in the distance and promptly sallied forth with his company to challenge them. Paddy rode to within musket range of the rebel line and as they fired turned his gray horse and galloped back into the fort to the cheers of the garrison. He had counted their guns.[30]

Sibley had no stomach for an assault on Fort Craig. On February 19 he began to move his men and wagons across the river at the ford at Paraje, some six miles to the south. He planned to bypass the fort, leaving it isolated and without hope of resupply, or at least hoped to draw the defenders out into an open battle. This was a daring plan, for the rebel soldiers would have to pull their wagons and artillery across rough and broken country blocked by high bluffs from easy access to the river. For the already exhausted mules and horses it would mean two days without water. The weather was miserable, with intermittent sleet and hail following on the heels of a massive sandstorm. Sibley could cross back and regain the Camino Real some four miles upriver from the fort at the northern edge of Mesa del Contadero near the adobe ruins of the abandoned village of Valverde. The Apaches had forced the settlers out decades before.

A full day passed before Canby's scouts discovered the rebel movement. The high bluffs to the east of the river screened the enemy from Fort

Craig's heavy guns, so Canby was obliged to send his cavalry across the river to engage the rebels. A couple of well-placed Confederate artillery shells sent the blue-clad horsemen scurrying back to their fort.

Paddy Graydon now came up with a crazy scheme (perhaps inspired by Drake's fire ships against the Spanish Armada) to stampede the rebel horse herd. Surveying Fort Craig's corral, Graydon selected two ancient mules for a daring mission behind enemy lines. Paddy must have known the famed quip about mules—that they had no pride of ancestry nor any hope for posterity—for this was to be a suicide mission. He and a handful of his best men loaded the mules down with twenty-four-pounder artillery shells to which they attached long fuses. Under cover of darkness they led the sturdy beasts across the frigid river, carefully making their way up the rocky escarpment behind which lay the enemy camp. The rebel campfires lit up the sky beyond the bluff. Graydon could hear voices in the camp. His target was the horse and cattle herd, for he hoped his mules would gravitate toward their rebel cousins. He lit the fuses and with a slap on their rumps sent the patriotic Union mules off toward the camp. Graydon and his men scurried away, delighted to have escaped undetected. Suddenly they realized that they were being followed. Unfortunately, the notoriously stubborn—or loyal—mules had reversed course to follow Graydon. The burning fuses, getting shorter by the second, lit up the night sky. Graydon and his wide-eyed companions beat a hasty retreat. They had not gone far when the inevitable explosions came. The ball of flame sent shock waves through the rebel camp. The martyred mules had not died in vain, for the boom of the exploding shells sent the rebel horse and mule herd into a panic. Already crazed with thirst, they stampeded down to the Rio Grande to drink. Union soldiers collected 150 of them and herded them back to the fort. This escapade endeared the colorful captain all the more to the Yankee soldiers. The rebels were not amused, for the next morning they were forced to burn nearly a quarter of their wagons, since they no longer had teams to pull them.[31]

Before dawn the next morning Graydon's irregulars, along with Captain Rafael Chacon's mounted company of Carson's regiment, splashed across the Rio Grande toward the barren cottonwoods marking the eastern bank. A brisk fire suddenly erupted from the trees and the Battle of

Valverde was underway. Graydon and Chacon discovered Sibley's men not only in the cottonwoods, but also arrayed on the steep sandy mesa rising three hundred feet behind the screen of trees.

As the sun rose, Lieutenant Colonel Benjamin S. Roberts ordered his men across the river to support Graydon and Chacon. Four companies of the newly designated 1st and 3rd Cavalry (formerly the 1st Dragoons and the Mounted Rifles) splashed across the river into a blinding sunrise to drive the outnumbered rebels from the tree line. As more federal reinforcements arrived, including Captain George Bascom's Arizona regulars, they were hurried across the Valverde ford. Supported by an artillery battery of six guns under Captain Alexander McRae, Bascom's infantry held the northern flank of a Union line strung out a considerable distance down the Rio Grande. Graydon raced up and down the extended battle line. A Union officer remembered that "his little battle flag was seen everywhere; now harassing upon one flank, now charging impetuously upon the other." The Texans were certain that "Kit Carson and a thousand Mexicans . . . had gone round to cut off the train." They convinced themselves that the troops left to guard the wagons had fought off Carson's host, but it was actually Graydon's single company of irregulars that they had repulsed. Carson's regiment was held in reserve on the west bank for over three hours as the outnumbered rebels were forced back from the river.

Canby tardily reached Valverde from Fort Craig at around three o'clock in the afternoon, which was just about the same time that his friend Sibley retired from the field to an ambulance. "The commanding general," noted a rebel soldier, "was an old Army officer whose love for liquor exceeded that for home, country or God." Colonel Tom Green, an experienced Indian fighter from the Texas frontier, now took command of the Confederate forces, which was quite unfortunate for the federal cause. Green rallied his men, and 750 Texans came charging down from the bluffs toward McRae's battery on the federal left.

The befuddled Canby assisted the rebels by shifting Carson and the reserves over to the right flank just as Green's men, shrieking their rebel yell, crashed down on McRae. The young captain and his weary men, who had been in combat all day, fought valiantly but were quickly overwhelmed. It was hand-to-hand around the cannons, with federal bayonet against rebel Bowie knife. McRae, calmly emptying his pistol into the advancing rebels, died beside his guns. The rebels swept over the battery and sent the supporting soldiers into a wild retreat. Turning the captured guns around, they proceeded to bombard the fleeing troops. Captain Bascom, architect of the council at Apache Pass with Cochise, fell during this retreat as he attempted to cross the river.

Canby, his mouth firmly clenched on an unlit cigar and on foot, since his horse had been shot out from under him, watched helplessly as his left flank collapsed. As darkness approached, he ordered a retreat back to Fort Craig. Carson's men, on the right flank, were in pursuit of retreating rebels when recalled. "I could not understand the signals to retreat," remarked Captain Chacon, "for we considered that our charge upon the enemy's main cavalry had won the battle." Colonel Green halted the pursuit of the fleeing Yankees, even gallantly agreeing to a two-day truce to gather up the dead and wounded. It had been a costly day. "A spectacle that was horrible," remembered the twenty-eight-year-old Captain Chacon, for the field was covered with dead horses, torn and dismembered limbs, and heads separated from their bodies. Canby had lost 111 dead and 160 wounded, and Sibley had 72 dead and 157 wounded.[32]

Sibley sobered up quickly from his battlefield illness. He marched north to occupy Albuquerque with ease and then settled into quarters in Santa Fe on March 10. Only Fort Union stood between him and the Colorado mines, but nearly a thousand Colorado volunteer troops hurried south to reinforce the fort. Under a fire-breathing Methodist minister, Major John Chivington, they delivered a devastating blow to the Confederate forces near Glorieta Pass, just to the east of Santa Fe, on March 28, 1862. Chivington, later infamous for the 1864 massacre of Cheyenne and Arapaho Indians at Sand Creek, was led over the mountains and to the rear of the rebel army by Manuel Chaves, known throughout New Mexico as the "Little Lion" because of his Indian-fighting bravado. They won the day by destroying the rebel supply train and horse herd. Even though the Texans defeated Union forces a few miles to the east at Glorieta, the destruction of the herd and supply train was a death blow. Sibley, with no supplies or any hope of reinforcements, had no choice but to abandon Santa Fe and Albuquerque on April 12. The rebels were continually harassed by both Yankees and Apaches before the remnant of Sibley's army reached Texas. Sibley had lost over a third of his men through death or desertion.[33]

Carson and his regiment were assigned to garrison Fort Craig. In May, Canby reorganized the New Mexico Volunteer regiments into a single unit under Carson's command. This reorganization retained only the best officers and men from the various regiments for service, with the remainder sent home. Paddy Graydon was selected to command one of Carson's companies. Lawrence Murphy was assigned as Carson's adjutant.

Canby returned to Santa Fe on May 3, 1862. While his forces had lost every battle, they had still won the campaign. His reward was a brigadier general's star and a transfer to the East. After the war ended, he returned to the West, where on April 11, 1873, he became the only general officer in American history to be killed by Indians when assassinated at a California peace conference with the Modocs.[34]

Carson's old dragoon comrade-in-arms, the newly minted brigadier general James Henry Carleton, officially assumed command of the Department of New Mexico on September 8, 1862. With the rebels defeated, the new commander was determined to use his troops to finally crush the Apaches and Navajos decisively. He knew just the man he wanted to lead this campaign: Colonel Kit Carson.

22

MANGAS COLORADAS

Mangas Coloradas was satisfied. His people had indeed successfully thrown back the advance of the American frontier. Mangas and Cochise were certain that the retreat of the soldiers, miners, and settlers was because of the war they had unleashed on the Americans after the Bascom Affair. In his lifetime Mangas had seen first the Spanish and then the Mexicans repulsed, and now he had defeated the Americans. "We were successful," Cochise later proclaimed to an American official, "and your soldiers were driven away and your people killed and we again possessed our land."[1]

This victory would be short-lived. In California, General George Wright, Union commander of the Department of the Pacific, hurriedly organized volunteer regiments to be sent to Utah, Washington, and New Mexico. Wright selected Major James H. Carleton, promoted to colonel of volunteers, to lead the California Column to New Mexico. Wright greatly admired the veteran dragoon officer, whom he described as "an officer of great experience, indefatigable and active." Carleton's many talents were just as often eclipsed by a tyrannical bent and streak of brutality that would make his tenure in New Mexico highly controversial. Indian agent Michael Steck labeled him the "Great Mogul."

Carleton took command of ten companies of his own 1st California Infantry, with Lieutenant Colonel Joseph Rodman West as his second-in-command; five companies of the 1st California Cavalry under Colonel Edward Engle Eyre, reinforced by a company of the 2nd California Cavalry under Captain John Cremony of Bartlett survey fame; and ten companies of infantry and two mountain-howitzer batteries under Colonel George

Washington Bowie. In all, Carleton had 2,350 men under his command for the six-hundred-mile march east along the Gila to Tucson. He wisely spread out the departure dates for his various columns to protect the scarce water resources along the trail. Carleton personally reached Tucson on June 6, 1862.[2]

On June 21, Carleton sent Colonel Eyre forward with two companies—some 140 men—of his cavalry to Mesilla in a reconnaissance in force. They reached the old stage station at Apache Pass on June 25. A little after noon, Cochise appeared with a dozen warriors under a white flag, while a large number of warriors could be seen on the nearby ridgeline. Eyre, anxious to avoid hostilities, boldly advanced with an interpreter to parley.

Cochise, tall and erect in his fiftieth year, impressed the waiting soldiers. "He carried a fine rifle and two six shooters," noted one of Eyre's troopers, "and rides as fine a horse as anybody."

Eyre assured Cochise of his peaceful intentions: "We wished to be friends of the Apaches; at present I was only traveling through their country and desired that he [Cochise] would not interfere with my men or animals; that a great Captain was at Tucson with a large number of soldiers; that he wished to have a talk with the Apache Chiefs and to make peace with them and make them presents."[3]

Cochise, having obtained vital intelligence from the naïve Eyre, accepted some gifts of tobacco and pemmican and promised to return that evening for another talk. While this parley was going on, three of Eyre's men were being butchered in the nearby hills. When the bodies were discovered, the colonel prudently moved his camp two miles to the east. Cochise did not return that evening, but his warriors fired into the soldier camp, wounding Eyre's surgeon. Eyre hurriedly advanced his command to the Rio Grande, where he reoccupied Fort Thorn and learned for the first time of the Confederate defeat and retreat.

Cochise promptly sent runners to Mangas and other Apache leaders to come join him at Apache Pass. They would confront this new soldier chief from Tucson. Mangas arrived with a large band of Bedonkohe warriors, including Victorio and Geronimo. They were joined by Juh and his warriors from Mexico as well as a contingent of eastern White Mountain people under their leader, Francisco. By the second week of July, Mangas and Cochise had gathered over two hundred warriors at Apache Pass.

Carleton, not having heard from Eyre and still in ignorance of the situation with the Confederates in New Mexico, decided to send a force out from Tucson to establish secure supply depots along the route. He identified Apache Pass as of particular importance. Captain Thomas L. Roberts departed Tucson early on July 10, 1862, with his company of the 1st California Infantry, two mountain howitzers, and John Cremony's company of the 2nd California Cavalry. These troops escorted a large wagon train and cattle herd. Supplies from the wagon train were to be used to establish the supply depots for the use of Carleton's main column.

After an exhausting march, Roberts, with sixty-eight men, two wagons, and the howitzers, approached the old stage station around noon on July 15. Cochise and Mangas, with their concealed warriors, quietly waited. The wagons and artillery had fallen behind the main column and made a tempting target. One man was killed and two were wounded in this initial ambush, but Roberts and his infantry hurried back to drive off the Apaches. They then fought their way back to the vital springs near the abandoned stage station. In this hard fighting the mountain howitzers proved decisive.[4]

Roberts sent a sergeant and six cavalrymen back to warn Cremony to hold up the wagon train and not attempt the steep climb up to Apache Pass. No sooner had the troopers reached the flats of Sulphur Springs Valley beyond the pass than some fifty mounted Apaches came galloping in pursuit. The soldiers spurred their horses and, with only one man wounded, somehow managed to outdistance the Apaches.

Private John Teal had dismounted to rest his weary horse just as the Apaches approached. Teal fired at a band of fifteen or so warriors with his breechloader and caused them to back off as he mounted and made a run for it. He did not get far, for a shot from a large, older man whom Teal recognized as the chief brought down his horse. Determined to sell his life as dearly as possible, Teal took careful aim at the chief and sent him tumbling down.

To the young trooper's amazement, the Apaches gathered up the fallen chief and hurriedly rode away. Teal made his way under cover of darkness the eight miles back to Cremony's camp to discover that his companions had reported him dead. Little did Teal realize that the "old chief" he had shot was none other than Mangas Coloradas.

Geronimo and a band of warriors carried Mangas south to Janos, in

Chihuahua, where literally at gunpoint they forced a doctor there to treat his wound. It was not the first wound the great chief had suffered but it was particularly dangerous for a man of his age. It took him some time to recover.

At Apache Pass, Roberts had joined up with Cremony to launch a strong counterattack on the Apaches the next morning. The fate of Mangas had disheartened the Apaches, for they did not know if he was alive or dead, and by late that afternoon they melted away. Roberts had lost two killed and two wounded and thought that his men had killed at least nine Apaches, while Captain Cremony estimated warrior deaths as much higher. Although casualties on both sides were minimal, the Battle of Apache Pass took on added significance because of the serious wound suffered by Mangas and as a result of the loss of access to the vital spring. Carleton would soon order a post—Fort Bowie—to be built there; it would guard the spring and hold the strategic pass until 1894.[5]

By early August, most of Carleton's troops had reached the Rio Grande. The general assumed command of the Department of New Mexico on September 18. Colonel West, soon to be promoted to brigadier general, now took command of the California Column and the District of Arizona, which included the Mesilla Valley. Carleton was determined to use his troops, as well as the New Mexico Volunteers, to crush both the Apaches and the Navajos.

On September 27, Colonel Kit Carson received Special Order No. 176 from his old friend Carleton to take five companies of his command to the Sierra Blanca homeland of the Mescalero Apaches and garrison the abandoned Fort Stanton. Upon reaching the fort on October 26, Carson found it in shambles, with everything of value carried off by rebels or Mescaleros. The abandonment of the post in July of 1861 had naturally delighted the Mescaleros and led them to resume their raids against the scattered Hispanic settlements. Forty-six people had been killed and several others carried off into captivity in the summer of 1862 alone.

Once at the fort, Carson received detailed orders from Carleton: "As your scouts . . . come near the mouth of the Peñasco they will, doubtless, find a plenty of Mescaleros. . . . All Indian men of that [the Mescalero] tribe are to be killed whenever and wherever you can find them. The women and children will not be harmed, but you will take them prisoners, and feed them at Fort Stanton until you receive other instructions about them."

The general was also quick to stroke Carson's ego: "The world-wide reputation of Colonel Carson as a partisan gives a good guarantee that anything that may be required of him, which brings into practical operation the peculiar skill and high courage for which he is justly celebrated, will be well done." Carson did not want to fight the Mescaleros, and Carleton knew it. The flattery was meant to make this bitter pill easier to swallow.[6]

The Mescaleros, like their northern cousins the Jicarillas, were not a numerous people. They made the southern New Mexico mountains their home, often moving about to favorite campsites in the Guadalupes, the Capitans, and the Sacramentos. They harvested the abundant mescal plant, which provided them with a staple food. The Spanish named them Mescalero, or "Mescal Maker," because of their dependence on that huge desert plant. Spanish horses had allowed Mescalero hunters to roam eastward onto the Great Plains in search of buffalo. Despite Comanche resistance, the Mescaleros hunted as far east as the headwaters of the Brazos and Colorado Rivers and south to the Big Bend area of the Rio Grande. By the time of the 1846 American conquest, the Mescaleros held sway over a vast territory. Within a decade, however, the Americans had them hemmed in with five forts, the most important of which was Fort Stanton.

Carleton, nervous about his old friend's scruples when fighting the Indians, also sent out four companies of California troops from Mesilla. They were instructed to cooperate with Carson yet to act independently of him. The Californians received orders from Carleton that "there is to be no council held with the Indians, nor any talks. The men are to be slain whenever and wherever they can be found. . . . They have robbed and murdered the people with impunity too long already." The California troops were soon hunting Mescaleros in the Sacramento and Guadalupe Mountains.[7]

Carson's New Mexican troops saw action first, but it proved controversial. Captain Paddy Graydon had led two companies south from Anton Chico in early October as an escort for a supply train to Fort Stanton. Along the trail they discovered the bodies of three army couriers. At Gallinas Springs, high on the western slope of 8,637-foot Gallinas Peak, Graydon and a scouting party encountered the Mescalero chief Manuelito and a small band and opened fire. The chief and eleven others were killed and two children captured.

Graydon claimed self-defense, but at Fort Stanton, Major Arthur Morrison, who had little use for the flamboyant captain, labeled it a massacre of innocents. The "Gallinas Massacre" quickly became a cause célèbre in both military circles and the territorial press. Even though Graydon was following his direct orders to the troops, Carleton ordered Carson to investigate. At the same time the general bragged to his superiors about Graydon's victory.[8]

Two weeks later, California troops surprised a large Mescalero village in Dog Canyon. This was a favored Sacramento Mountain campsite where U.S. dragoons had first battled the Apaches back in 1849. The soldiers routed the Indians, captured their camp, and demoralized the survivors. This fight, along with the death of Manuelito, convinced the Mescaleros that further resistance was futile.

Led by their chief Cadete, several hundred Mescaleros came to Fort Stanton to surrender to Carson. The colonel disobeyed Carleton's orders, accepted their surrender, and distributed army rations to the Mescalero families. Indian agent Lorenzo Labadie had also just arrived at Fort Stanton. Labadie was a longtime resident of New Mexico and, like Carson, had also married into an important Hispanic family. While not as sympathetic to his charges as Dr. Steck had been, he was still a good friend to the Apaches. He and Carson were also old friends, and they now devised a scheme to send a Mescalero delegation to Santa Fe to make peace with Carleton. Carson would remain at Fort Stanton while Labadie accompanied Cadete and four other Mescalero leaders to Santa Fe.

Carleton, who met with the chiefs on November 24, had already decided on the fate of the Mescaleros. They were to be the first to settle on a new Indian reservation he planned on the plains of eastern New Mexico. He had ordered the construction of a new post on the Pecos River at the Bosque Redondo (Round Forest), where his forty-square-mile reserve would be located. Fort Sumner was to protect New Mexico from Comanche raiders to the east while overseeing the general's grand experiment in Indian removal. The Mescaleros and other tribes were to be imprisoned there and segregated from the Rio Grande settlements. Carleton assured his superiors that he would transform these proud Apache warriors into productive Christian farmers and "have them, in short, become what is called in this country—a pueblo."[9]

Labadie returned to Fort Stanton with the Mescalero chiefs to gather their people for the journey to Bosque Redondo. By March, Carson had nearly four hundred Mescaleros loaded onto government wagons and headed north toward the new reservation.

Carson's most serious problem at Fort Stanton proved not to be with the Mescaleros but with his own undisciplined volunteers. The old mountain man, hardly a stickler for military discipline, allowed his regiment to become, as one observer noted, notorious for "murder, alcoholism, embezzlement, sexual deviation, desertion, and incompetence." Eventually, nearly half of Carson's officers were forced to resign in disgrace.[10]

In early November, these disciplinary issues boiled over upon the arrival of J. M. "Doc" Whitlock at Fort Stanton. The doctor had served as regimental surgeon for the 1st New Mexico Volunteers before its reorganization and transfer to Fort Stanton. Whitlock had come to see Carson about getting a letter of recommendation, and he waited for him in the post sutler's store on the evening of November 4, 1862. Paddy Graydon came in and trouble followed. Whitlock, like Major Morrison, was a serious man who had no use for the happy-go-lucky Irishman. The doctor had just published a bitter denunciation of the murder of Manuelito in a Santa Fe newspaper. Graydon immediately approached Whitlock, who was playing cards with several officers, to demand an apology. The doctor refused but promised to talk with Graydon about it in the morning. He returned to his card game while Paddy stormed out.

Graydon found Whitlock early the next morning having coffee with several officers in front of the sutler's store. Still fuming, he ordered Whitlock from the post: "I am an officer and you are a pimp that follows the army!"

"Captain you are in the wrong," Whitlock retorted as both men drew their pistols. Graydon's first shot missed, but his second hit Whitlock in the wrist. The doctor fired back, striking Graydon in the chest.

"The son-of-a-bitch has killed me," Paddy exclaimed as he fell to the ground.

As Graydon's companions carried the wounded captain to his tent, the doctor, sensing the mood of the crowd, bolted for the sutler's store and then out its back door. He did not get far. Several of Graydon's men pursued Whitlock, gunning him down as he fled. More men of Graydon's company soon gathered. They emptied their pistols and shotguns into the doctor's body, leaving him a bloody pulp.

Carson rushed to the scene and flew into a rage. He ordered regimental assembly and had Graydon's company disarmed. "I'll have you scoundrels to swing before sunset!" he roared.

Cooler heads prevailed. The following day Carson ordered Graydon to resign, but death prevented the captain from complying, so that the irate colonel had to satisfy himself with sending three H Company soldiers to Santa Fe in irons to stand trial for Whitlock's murder. A few days before their trial could begin, the three men escaped from jail and vanished, which seemed a good solution to all save Carson.[11]

Captain Albert Pfeiffer now took command of Graydon's H Company. One of Carson's warmest friends, Pfeiffer had come to New Mexico from Holland in 1846. He had fled the home of his Lutheran minister father at age twenty-two for the American frontier. His education at a military school in Stockholm won him an appointment as Indian agent at Abiquiu for the Utes and Jicarillas. He quickly mastered the Ute language and worked alongside Carson until resigning his position to join the volunteers in 1861. Like Carson, Pfeiffer had taken a lovely Hispanic bride and was counted as a respected member of New Mexican society. His fondness for the bottle often got him into trouble, exasperating his friend Carson, but most agreed with a contemporary account of him as a "very paladin of the frontier . . . probably the most desperately courageous and successful Indian fighter in the West." A personal tragedy would soon turn Pfeiffer into that "paladin."[12]

Soon after New Year's Day 1863, Carson reported the end of the Mescalero campaign to Carleton, assuring the general that "the Bonito and Pecos valleys might now be cultivated without danger of Indian depredations." Carson was being overly optimistic, or perhaps he just wanted to return to his family in Taos. At least a hundred Mescaleros were still at large, some hiding out in the Sacramentos, but most fleeing west to seek sanctuary with their cousins, the Gila Apaches of Mangas Coloradas. In March, a band of Hispanic salt gatherers were slaughtered just to the west of Fort Stanton, and soon after a raid was made on the fort's horse herd. The burned body of a courier to Santa Fe was also discovered not far from the fort, tied to a stake.

To deal with these holdouts, Carleton ordered a new post constructed at Ojo del Muerto (Spring of Death), near the midpoint of the infamous Jornada del Muerto, in hopes of denying the Mescaleros access to a favored campsite on their trail to the Gila country. The Jornada del Muerto was a ninety-mile detour from the Rio Grande north across the desert between Valverde and Las Cruces that avoided a great westerly bend in the river. While travelers had preferred this shorter route since the time of the Spanish conquest, its name clearly bespoke its history.

Colonel Carson now sent his old friend Captain Pfeiffer to Fort McRae to literally dry out. Carson had secured Pfeiffer a commission in the 1st New Mexico Volunteers in the reorganization after the rebel retreat. He had then assigned him to take command of Paddy Graydon's troubled company after the Fort Stanton gunfight. But Pfeiffer, although a superb officer of undoubted courage, was a hopeless alcoholic. The drinking exacerbated a terrible skin condition that plagued the stout, blond, fair-skinned Dutch immigrant.

Pfeiffer established Fort McRae, named for the hero of Valverde, on April 3, 1863, at Ojo del Muerto, near a favorite east-to-west Apache crossing point of the Rio Grande. The river at this place was fairly shallow and free of quicksand. General Carleton hoped that the post might disrupt the movement of the Mescaleros to join with their Warm Springs and Mimbres River cousins. The fort was described by one of the California Volunteers as "a miserable and dirty looking place garrisoned by a company of greasers—tents every which way and brush shanties all around." This sunbaked, rocky desert was hardly a place to induce sobriety, but Carson had allowed his friend to take his wife and son with him in hopes of keeping him off the bottle.

Carson fretted over his dear friend, for he desperately needed him for the upcoming Navajo campaign that he was planning with General Carleton in Santa Fe. "I have been making inquiries of every person who has seen you and they all tell me that your face is not yet well, and that you are again drinking. When will you have sense?" Carson wrote Pfeiffer from Santa Fe on May 8, 1863. "Can't you try and quit whisky for a little while, at least until you get your face cured? If your face ain't well when I next see you, you had better look out."[13]

A few miles from Fort McRae there was a mineral hot springs where

Captain Pfeiffer often bathed in hopes of clearing up his skin condition. On June 20, Pfeiffer, with his wife, two servant girls, and a guard detail of six men, traveled to the hot springs for a picnic.

Pfeiffer was bathing in the springs when the Apaches attacked. They numbered twenty and had waited for just the right moment to strike. The first volley killed two of the Hispanic volunteers. Another soldier fell wounded while the others fled for their lives. Pfeiffer arose from the hot spring and lunged for his pistol on the bank. An arrow dug deep into his leg and then another hit him in the side. He crawled to the cover of some nearby boulders and fired back at the Apaches. The rocks burned his naked skin but still he managed to kill two of the charging warriors. The rest of the Apaches were quickly on the move, herding the soldiers' nine horses and the three women toward the west.

Pfeiffer, alone, naked, and horribly wounded, headed for the fort, nearly nine miles distant. The scorching summer sun deeply burned his fair skin so that, when he finally reached the post and the surgeon extracted the arrows from his body, all the flesh simply peeled away. Near death, he slipped in and out of consciousness, but not before ordering out a detachment after the Apaches.

The trail was easy to follow, and the troopers soon closed in on the fleeing raiders. The Apaches, hard-pressed by the pursuit, butchered the three women, knowing the soldiers would stop once they found the bodies. One of the servant girls survived, but Pfeiffer's wife and the other girl were killed. The soldiers wrapped the bodies in blankets and returned to Fort McRae.

Pfeiffer somehow survived, although it would be nearly two months before he could join Carson for the Navajo campaign. He was a changed man, of course, now possessed of a single-minded determination to hunt down and kill Indians—any Indians. No officer would compile a more outstanding record in the war against the Navajos than Pfeiffer.

After the Navajo War, Pfeiffer returned south to the lands of the Apache. He went alone, sometimes for months at a time, in search of Apaches. He later declared that he was never entirely alone, for a pack of wolves shadowed him.

"They liked me," he said of the wolves, "because they're fond of dead Indians and I feed them well." He roamed the southwestern mountains for the remainder of his fifty years, dealing death to the Apaches whenever he could find them. In 1881 he finally drank himself to death in a ramshackle cabin in Colorado's San Luis Valley. When the undertaker laid him out, he counted seventeen arrow and lance scars on the withered body.[14]

While Carson prepared his regiment for the Navajo campaign, Carleton turned his attention toward the Gila Apaches. "I shall organize and send into the country around the headwaters of the Gila an expedition to punish, for their frequent and recent murders and depredations, the band of Apaches which infest that region," he informed Washington in January 1863. "The Pinos Altos gold mines can then be worked with security."

Carleton was determined to crush the Apaches and Navajos once and for all, even though the two tribes were often mortal enemies. The defeat of the Navajos, and their removal from their homeland, would actually free the Apaches to the south from that threat to the north. "By the time the spring opens the Apaches of the Gila will doubtless have been subdued, when I propose to punish the Navajo Indians for their recent murders and wholesale robberies," he assured the secretary of war on February 1, 1863.[15]

Mangas Coloradas had wearied of war, for the wound suffered at Apache Pass had somewhat tempered his warrior spirit. He was now past seventy and wanted only to return in peace to his Mogollon Mountain homeland on the headwaters of the Gila River. Indian Agent Steck had promised him a reservation at Santa Lucia Springs and he now proposed to accept the offer. He traveled north to Acoma, west of Albuquerque, in September to leave a message for Carleton that he wanted to make a permanent peace.

Captain Julius C. Shaw of the 1st New Mexico Volunteer Cavalry received Mangas's peace overture from a prominent Acoma leader and promptly wrote Carleton that the Apache chief was "now anxious for peace and wishes to return to his former home and pursuits, and to live like a Christian."

General Carleton issued General Order No. 1 to West, instructing him to "immediately organize a suitable expedition to chastise what is known as Mangas Coloradas's Band of Gila Apaches. The campaign to be made by this expedition must be a vigorous one and the punishment of that band of murderers and robbers must be thorough and sharp." Carleton did not have to worry about West, for unlike Carson the new brigadier general had no sympathy for the Indians.[16]

West left Mesilla in early January with 250 men to establish a base of operations at the abandoned Fort McLane to the southeast of the mines at Pinos Altos. Once there, he sought out the frontiersman Jack Swilling, who had recently met with Mangas.

Swilling was a long-haired hard case with a reputation for daring. The Georgia native had fought as a teenager in the Mexican War and afterward had found work on the Leach Wagon Road connecting El Paso and Fort Yuma and then with the Butterfield stage line. The 1860 discovery of gold at Pinos Altos, just to the north of the old copper mines at Santa Rita del Cobre, led Swilling to join the rush to the new diggings. Once the army had abandoned nearby Fort McLane, with the outbreak of war, Swilling had helped to organize an outfit called the Arizona Guards for protection from the Apaches. The guards soon joined the Confederate army and Swilling was part of the rebel occupation of Tucson. With Sibley's retreat, he promptly switched sides to scout for Carleton's California Column.[17]

January 1863 found Swilling at Fort McLane, where he encountered a band of twenty adventurers under Carson's old comrade Joseph Walker. Swilling signed on with Walker, who intended to explore the mountains of central Arizona in search of gold. His party had been repeatedly blocked by the Apaches from crossing the mountains into Arizona.

Swilling had recently met with Mangas at Pinos Altos and they had agreed on another parley in ten days. He now proposed that when Mangas came in to talk, they seize him as hostage in order to secure safe passage through Apache country. Walker agreed to this. Just as they were about to depart for Pinos Altos, West's advance guard of twenty men under Captain Edmund Shirland arrived at Fort McLane. The California captain quickly endorsed this wild scheme, and at dawn on January 16, 1863, Swilling led Walker's men and the soldiers north to the ramshackle mining camp where some thirty families precariously resided. Upon reaching Pinos Altos, they hid the soldiers, raised a white flag, and waited for the return of Mangas Coloradas.

After his journey to Acoma and his meeting with Swilling, Mangas had held a series of councils with his leading warriors to discuss his intention to make peace with the whites at Pinos Altos. The dour Bedonkohe warrior Geronimo argued against this, reminding Mangas of the betrayal of Cochise under a white flag at Apache Pass. Mangas had met with Kearny and Sumner without problems and had in fact won them over, and he was anxious to have Swilling arrange a meeting with this new general. Victorio, bold leader of the Warm Springs people, was also skeptical and insisted that he and several of his warriors accompany Mangas as bodyguards.

It was noon the next day when Mangas appeared. Swilling, along with several of Walker's men, slowly approached the imposing Apache chief.

"Mangas was a large athletic man considerably over six feet in height, with a large broad head covered with a tremendously heavy growth of long hair that reached to his waist," noted one of Walker's adventurers, a young Kentuckian named Daniel Conner. "His shoulders were broad and his chest full, and muscular. He stood erect and his step was proud and altogether he presented quite a model of physical manhood."[18]

Swilling placed his hand on Mangas's shoulder. This was a signal to his men to pull their guns. Swilling, in broken Spanish, told Mangas that he was their hostage to ensure safe passage. Mangas waved off Victorio and the bodyguard with a warning that "they were not fooling with Mexicans here." The Apaches withdrew to wait and watch.

As the Americans backed into the village, Shirland's soldiers, with rifles leveled, emerged from the cabins. It was only then that Mangas realized the full extent of the danger he was in. Shirland ordered the horses brought out to carry his prisoner to Fort McLane.

General West arrived at Fort McLane the next day to claim the prize prisoner as his own. He ordered Mangas confined in one of the post's crumbling adobe huts.

West placed a guard over the prisoner and personally gave them their instructions: "Men, that old murderer has got away from every soldier command and has left a trail of blood for 500 miles on the old stage line. I want him dead or alive tomorrow morning; do you understand?" he snarled out his orders.

"I want him dead," he repeated for emphasis.

Young Conner had drawn sentry duty that night and paced about not far from the adobe Mangas was held in. It was cold, and a large fire illuminated the scene. The young sentry could see that the guards were fretting the prisoner by heating the tips of their bayonets in the fire and then poking the chief with them.

Mangas rose up in rage. He shouted at his tormentors in Spanish only to be met by point-blank musket fire. As Conner watched in horror, a sergeant appeared out of the darkness, pushed the two guards aside, and fired his pistol into the chief's head.

The sergeant then reported to General West that the chief was dead. "Very well, Sergeant," West calmly replied, "then let his guard go to sleep."[19]

The next morning the soldiers rolled the body of Mangas Coloradas into an arroyo and threw some brush over it. Before this hasty burial, one of the soldiers scalped the chief. Shortly afterward assistant surgeon David Sturgeon ordered the men to retrieve the corpse so he might sever the head for scientific purposes. He had the head boiled in a great black kettle and then carefully packed for transport east as a gift to Professor Orson Squire Fowler. The famed phrenologist featured the impressive skull in his 1873 book, *Human Science; or, Phrenology*. He declared it to be a marvel. In time the well-traveled skull probably made its way to the Smithsonian in Washington to be warehoused in its vast collection of Native remains.[20]

West sent Shirland out with a detachment in search of Mangas's people and on January 25 they hit Victorio's village in the nearby mountains. They killed nine Apaches and scattered the rest. At almost the same time Mangas's family came into Pinos Altos in search of him. They were ambushed by soldiers and miners. One of the sons of Mangas was killed along with ten others. The soldiers then rode back into Fort McLane with Apache scalps decorating their bridles and saddles.

West returned to Mesilla in triumph on January 25, 1863. He promptly wrote a duplicitous report to Carleton describing how Mangas had been killed while attempting to escape: "I have dwelt at length upon this matter in order to show that even with a murderous Indian, whose life is clearly forfeited by all laws either human or divine, whenever found, the good faith of the U.S. Military Authorities was in no way compromised."

Carleton did not investigate the matter even though it was common knowledge among West's soldiers what had actually happened at Fort McLane. "He got what he deserved and no one in our command pitied him or cried about it," remarked one of the California soldiers. Carleton gleefully repeated West's lies to Washington.

"Mangas Coloradas, doubtless the worst Indian within our boundaries, and one who has been the cause of more murders and torturing and of burning at the stake in this country than all others together, has been killed," he wrote the War Department, greatly exaggerating the warlike habits of Mangas while praising West's campaign.[21]

Cochise was enraged over this cold-blooded act of betrayal and murder. He swore to avenge his father-in-law and, joined by Victorio, Juh, and Geronimo, attacked all around Tucson as well as along the Rio Grande, slaughtering civilian and soldier alike.

"The killing of an unarmed man who has gone to the enemy under truce was an incomprehensible act," declared one of Victorio's people, "but infinitely worse was the mutilation of his body." The Apache believed that people went into the afterlife in the same mutilated condition as when they died.

To Geronimo it was simply "the greatest of wrongs."[22]

The murder of Mangas Coloradas galvanized Apache resistance to the American invader. A ghastly war would rage on for almost a generation, not ending until the final surrender of Geronimo at Skeleton Canyon in 1886.

23

CANYON DE CHELLY

They called themselves Dine—"the people"—and lived between the four sacred mountains in northwestern New Mexico and northeastern Arizona. The Spanish invader had named them Apaches de Nabajó and called their country Navajo. Unlike their Apache cousins to the south and east, the Navajo were excellent farmers, with large fields of corn and wheat as well as fruit orchards. They proved to be a highly adaptable people, quick to embrace the crops, horses, and sheep used by their new Spanish neighbors. They were a wildly democratic people, with loyalty to the family and the matrilineal clan above all else and with tribal political organization nonexistent. Headmen spoke only for the groups of families they represented and could not sign treaties that bound anyone beyond their relations.

The Navajo came late to the Southwest, migrating south from the far Northwest down the front range of the Rocky Mountains. They came not as a single group, for this slow migration involved hundreds of years and included their Athabaskan-speaking cousins the Apaches. In time they reached the Southwest and split into disparate groups. The Navajo and Apache became mortal enemies and settled separately, some (Navajo) remaining among the canyonlands and mesas of the "Four Corners" region, while others (Apache) traveled south to the mountains of New Mexico, Arizona, and Old Mexico. By 1400 they were well established, with a large population spread from the Rio Grande on the east to the Colorado on the west, the San Juan to the north, and the Little Colorado to the south.

The arrival of the Spanish led to a precipitous drop in population from both disease and warfare. But the Navajo found the trade goods and animals the Spanish introduced attractive. Repulsed by the Spanish missionaries and the new religion they brought, they joined with the Pueblos in the great 1680 uprising that drove the Spanish out of New Mexico for a dozen years. With the reconquest, many Pueblo traditionalists fled west to seek refuge with the Navajo, which in turn had a profound effect on Navajo culture. The following years saw periods of both war and accommodation.[1]

It was the Spanish desire for slaves that made war inevitable and also led the Navajos to develop a partial raiding economy. The Spanish, desperate for labor and servants, raided both Navajo and Apache villages for captives while at the same time subjecting the Pueblo people up and down the Rio Grande to forced labor through peonage. A Spanish friar in New Mexico described enslaved Indians as the "gold and silver" of the province. In many New Mexico towns, Navajo and Apache slaves were sold in the village plaza after Sunday mass. There was also a ready market for Indian captives in both Chihuahua and Sonora.

The New Mexicans rationalized their actions by pointing out that the Indians were baptized and thus by this benevolent act their souls were saved. American observers noted a more practical result. "They are held and treated as slaves," noted Indian agent James L. Collins, "but become amalgamated with the Mexicans and lose their identity." The same thing often happened with New Mexican women and children captured by the Navajos.[2]

The successful Mexican revolution of 1821 and the subsequent opening of the Santa Fe Trail led to increased wealth for New Mexico. The inhabitants, long kept disarmed or poorly armed by the Spanish as a matter of policy, could now acquire American weapons. This gave them a decided advantage over their Navajo enemies and they stepped up their forays and kidnapping raids. The Navajo responded in kind, with devastating results.

"The Navajos were in the habit of making forays upon the ranches and settlements, stealing, robbing, and carrying away captives; the finding of herds and driving off sheep and other animals was carried on to a very ruinous extent; the killing of persons did not seem so much the object of their warfare as an incidental means of succeeding in other depredations," noted American judge Kirby Benedict.[3]

"The war with the Navajos," declared Manuel Armijo, the last Mexican governor of New Mexico, to his superiors in Mexico City, "is slowly consuming the Department, reducing to very obvious misery the District of the Southwest." The Navajos inadvertently aided the American conquest of New Mexico by impoverishing the land and preventing any sense of security. General Carleton felt that the Navajo raids contributed mightily to the "backwardness" of New Mexico.[4]

In one of his first reports to Carleton after opening his Navajo campaign, Kit Carson asked permission to distribute captive Navajos to his Ute allies. "It is expected by the Utes, and has, I believe, been customary to allow them to keep the Women & children, and the property captured by them . . . ," Carson noted. "I am satisfied that the future of the captives disposed of in this manner would be much better than if sent even to the Bosque Redondo," he explained. "As a general thing, the Utes dispose of their captives to Mexican families, where they are fed and taken care of and thus cease to require any further attention on the part of the government."

Carleton's response shocked Carson, who had three Navajos living in his household. "All prisoners which are captured by the troops or employees of your command will be sent to Santa Fe," the flinty general replied. Carleton was well aware of this "custom of the country" and he was equally aware that the United States was currently waging a great war to liberate all enslaved people within the republic.[5]

An additional complexity was the deep divisions within Navajo society. At this time the Navajos were divided into two groups by the New Mexicans: the *ricos*, the wealthy and well established; and the *ladrones* (literally, thieves or robbers), the poorer people without great herds of sheep and horses. The *ladrones* formed the war party that often raided the New Mexican and Pueblo villages, while the *ricos*, with much to lose, formed the peace party. The reprisal forays of the New Mexicans fell heavily on the more settled *ricos* and in some cases impoverished them and their relatives and turned them into *ladrones*. This vicious cycle had been perpetuated for longer than people could remember.

Carson understood the nature of this ancient conflict and sympathized with the plight of the Navajo *ricos*. He blamed settler aggression for most of the troubles but recognized that the Navajo were hardly blameless. "I knew that even before the acquisition of New Mexico there had about always existed an hereditary warfare between the Navajoes and Mexicans; forays were made into each other's country, and stock, women, and children stolen," he declared in 1865 in explaining his campaign. "Since the acquisition, the same state has existed; we would hardly get back from fighting and making peace with them before they would be at war again. . . . There is a part of the Navajoes, the wealthy, who wish to live in peace; the poorer classes are in the majority, and they have no chiefs who can control them."[6]

Early in December 1862, the Navajo chiefs Delgadito and Barboncito led a delegation of sixteen prominent men to Santa Fe to meet with General Carleton. They were concerned that the soldiers were building a post, Fort Wingate, on the eastern edge of their country. The officer in charge of this construction—Lieutenant Colonel José Francisco Chaves—was well-known to them for his many raids against their people. Why was he there now and what was the purpose of this fort?

Carleton's face was taut, his chin, framed by great muttonchop whiskers, jutted forward as he lectured them as if they were pupils and he a New England schoolmaster. He told them that he had no faith in their promises and that if they did not bring their people in, there would be war. In April, Carleton would again meet with Delgadito and Barboncito, this time at Cubero, to hear their response. These peace chiefs hoped to separate their people from the raiders who had caused so much trouble with the New Mexicans, but Carleton would hear none of this.

Barboncito sought a reasonable compromise, promising to keep his people at Fort Wingate. Carleton would not budge: they must all go to the Bosque Redondo, peace party and war party alike. Barboncito replied that he preferred to die at Wingate within the sacred four mountains rather than go east to the Pecos River country. Go back, Carleton told him, and bring all your people in by July 20 or his soldiers would hunt them down.

In late June, Carleton wrote Chaves to send for Delgadito and Barboncito and give them one last chance: "Tell them that I shall feel very sorry if they refuse to come in. That we have no desire to make war upon them and other good Navajoes, but that the troops cannot tell the good from the bad; and we neither can nor will tolerate their staying as a peace party among those against whom we intend to make war. Tell them they can have until the twentieth day of July of this year to come in—they and all those who belong to what they call the peace party. That after that day every Navajoe that is seen will be considered as hostile and treated accordingly. That after that day the door now open will be closed. Tell them to say all this to their people—and that as sure as the sun shines all this will come true."[7]

Carleton did not wait for the deadline to pass. General Order No. 15, dated June 15, 1863, directed "that Colonel CHRISTOPHER CARSON, with a proper military force proceed without delay to a point in the Navajoe country known as *Pueblo Colorado*, and there establish a defensible Depot for his supplies and Hospital: and thence to prosecute a vigorous war upon the men of this tribe until it is considered at these Head Quarters that they have been effectually punished for their long continued atrocities."[8]

Carson was to command nine companies, six mounted and three infantry, a total of 736 men, with another 326, under Lieutenant Colonel José Francisco Chaves, to garrison Fort Wingate. Three of Carson's companies would be delayed—two to remain to corral the remaining Mescaleros, and Pfeiffer's Company H at Fort McRae because of the captain's slow recovery from his wounds.

Carson, who had unsuccessfully attempted to resign rather than lead the campaign, departed the little post at Los Pinos—on the eastern bank of the Rio Grande some sixteen miles to the south of Albuquerque—on July 7, with four companies of his 1st New Mexico Volunteers. He reached Fort Wingate three days later.

Carson rode at the head of the column alongside Kaniache, the leader of the Ute auxiliaries he had recruited for the expedition, followed by colorful Ute and Pueblo warriors with mixed dress and weapons. The dusty line of white and Hispanic soldiers followed. The colonel was tired, looking much older than his fifty-three years, and he was in constant pain. A horse fall while hunting in 1860 had led to unrelenting chest pains that fretted him to no end. He was anxious to have the campaign over with so as to return home to Josefa and the children.

Failure was not an option. Carleton's final admonition reminded him that his fame placed an additional burden on him: "Make *every* string draw. Much is expected of you, both here and in Washington."[9]

The column reached Pueblo Colorado (Red House—now called Ganado, Arizona) on July 23, 1863. On the march, Carson's Ute allies had killed a dozen Navajos and either destroyed or confiscated over 40,000 pounds of Indian wheat. Carson encouraged his Ute, Pueblo, and Zuni allies by payment of a $20 bounty for each captured mule or horse, and a $1 bounty for every sheep. The Navajo had made many enemies among their Native neighbors over the years, and now they reaped the whirlwind.

Carson found the timber and water at Pueblo Colorado inadequate to sustain a major supply depot and so he moved his command twenty-six miles to the northeast, to the site of the abandoned Fort Defiance. The old post, first built in 1851, was renamed Fort Canby and now became the headquarters for the Navajo campaign.[10]

While most of his troops were busy with the construction of Fort Canby and the movement of supplies, Carson prepared for a long scout into the country of the Navajo. Captain Pfeiffer, still nursing his arrow wounds, arrived with H Company on August 2.

On August 5, 1863, Carson led six companies—some four hundred men—southwest to Zuni and then toward the Hopi Mesas. On his return he skirted the Navajo stronghold of Canyon de Chelly. This impressive red sandstone canyon sprawled across some 130 miles in a spiderweb of rock formations that reached nearly a thousand feet in height. This was the ancient land of the vanished Anasazi. Their whitewashed cliff-dweller ruins mutely spoke of their passing. Generations of Navajos had sought security beneath the high sheltering walls of this natural fortification. Carson's Ute and Zuni scouts assured him that the Navajos would flock into the canyon for safety from the troops or flee west beyond the Little Colorado.

The scout, which lasted twenty-seven days and covered nearly five hundred miles, was brutal. The heat was unrelenting, taking a toll on both men and animals. Water and forage were scarce. Carson pushed the men hard but endured every privation alongside them.

"I have seen him reeling in his saddle from fatigue and loss of sleep," reported a sergeant in the regiment, "still pushing forward and hoping to come upon them."[11]

Just to the south of Canyon de Chelly, in an adjacent canyon, Major Joseph Cummings was killed in an ambush. Remarkably his was to be the only military death directly connected to the campaign, although several men were wounded. In this scout, a handful of Navajos were killed, several women and children captured, some horses taken, and several acres of corn destroyed before the troops returned to Fort Canby. It was in fact quite stunning just how few Navajos had been seen, considering that up to 12,000 people lived in the region; they seemed like ghosts to the soldiers. It had not been particularly productive in terms of combat, but Carson had now gained a valuable sense of the landscape in which his troops would operate.

Carson returned to Fort Canby to face serious disciplinary problems. He was more than lax with discipline out of both a lack of knowledge and training as well as a personal contempt for army rules and the martinets who enforced them. His soldiers were a thirsty lot and had early on discovered that their commanding officer was illiterate. In a notorious episode, several men forged requisition orders for whiskey and told Carson they were for molasses. When he later visited with the sutler, he was made aware of his error and after that had all requisitions signed by his adjutant, Lieutenant Lawrence Murphy. Drunken behavior was hardly confined to the enlisted men, for several officers, including Major Arthur Morrison, were cashiered for their drunken behavior. Although only one of Carson's officers was killed in the campaign, nearly half of them were forced to resign or were court-martialed for offenses ranging from alcoholism and embezzlement to murder and "sexual deviation." (A lieutenant, while serving as officer of the day, was discovered to have bedded an enlisted man, and Major Morrison was accused of pimping prostitutes for his fellow officers.) Drunkenness finally subsided when the post sutler exhausted his supply of whiskey.[12]

Carson led a second reconnaissance in force from Fort Canby on September 9, this time with 405 men to the south toward the Little Colorado. The monthlong scout proved frustrating: no battles or victories to report. Carson's Zuni scouts managed to capture a small herd of Navajo sheep, while Captain Pfeiffer pursued a small party of Navajos and captured a child. Another patrol was ambushed near Fort Canby and suffered one man seriously wounded. They killed and scalped a Navajo man. This act horrified and disgusted the Navajo, who, like their Apache cousins, did not take scalps.

"This scout I am sorry to say was a failure as regards any positive injury inflicted on the Navajos," a frustrated Carson reported to Carleton on October 5, 1863, "but the fatigues and hardships undergone by my command are fully compensated for by the increased knowledge of the country, and of the haunts of the Navajoes with their Stock."[13]

Carson's scout had pressed the elusive Navajo harder than he realized. Feeling insecure and unable to protect their families and stock, several small groups of Navajos came into Fort Canby to surrender. Delgadito brought 187 of his people into Fort Wingate in mid-October. Carleton ordered that they all be promptly sent to Bosque Redondo.

On November 1, a worn-out Carson requested a two-month leave to visit Taos, where Josefa was expecting their sixth child. He had been away from his family and in the field for most of the time since May of 1861, with the exception of brief reunions after Valverde and the Mescalero campaign. Carleton coldly denied the request, ordering Carson to instead lead a winter campaign into the sprawling Navajo stronghold of Canyon de Chelly. He reminded his field commander that all Navajos must be sent to the Pecos Valley: "Say to them—'Go to the Bosque Redondo, or we will pursue and destroy you. We will not make peace with you on any other terms. . . . This war shall be pursued against you if it takes years, now that we have begun, until you cease to exist or move.' "

Carleton also advised Carson that all Navajos who voluntarily surrendered might keep the stock and other property they possessed. He hoped this might encourage the *ricos* to lead their people in. To assuage Carson's feelings, he promised that as soon as he secured a hundred Navajo captives, he might come to Santa Fe for a consultation. First, however, he must go into Canyon de Chelly.

"As winter approaches," he reassured Carson, "you will have better luck."[14]

A soldier poet of sorts composed a little ditty that the men put to music to sing on the march. It proved popular enough to be reprinted in the New Mexico press:

Johnny Navajo, Oh, Johnny Navajo!
We'll first chastise, then civilize, bold Johnny Navajo!
Come dress your ranks, my gallant souls, a-standing in a row,
Kit Carson is waiting to march against the foe,
At night we march to Moqui o'er the hills of snow.
To meet and crush the savage foe, bold Johnny Navajo!
Johnny Navajo! Oh, Johnny Navajo!

On January 6, 1864, Carson led his men out of Fort Canby across crusted snow toward Canyon de Chelly. It was freezing and the snow deepened as the command—14 officers and 375 men—labored toward Pueblo Colorado. A journey that normally took but a day consumed the better part of three days, while Carson's stock—horses, mules, and oxen already broken down from the scouts and poor forage—began to perish. Carson had to abandon one wagon. Six days later they arrived at the western entrance to the mysterious Canyon de Chelly. Carson had detached the always reliable Pfeiffer with one hundred men to circle around and enter the canyon from its eastern end. The Navajos would be caught between the two columns.

Carson understood better than most the spiritual significance of Canyon de Chelly to the Navajo. This was the home of their gods, where the flocks and orchards of the people were forever protected from all foes. Deep in the folds of the winding canyon stood mammoth Fortress Rock, soaring almost eight hundred feet from the canyon floor, and atop it hid some three hundred men, women, and children. Here surely they would be safe.

Carson sent scouting parties into the west entrance as well as along the canyon rim. One party of fifty men encountered a small band of Navajos in a side canyon and killed eleven men and captured two women with their two children: first blood.

To the east, Pfeiffer followed a little frozen stream into the canyon and pushed deeper into its shadowed depths on December 11. Although he assumed that he was in the main canyon, he was actually just to the north in the equally formidable Canyon del Muerto. Pfeiffer formed three sapper parties to explore and clear passages into what the captain labeled the "Gibraltar of Navajodom." His pack mules used the stream bed as a trail, although often breaking through the ice and cutting themselves. When the canyon widened out, they came upon fields and orchards. The European captain was particularly impressed with the cliff dwellings built into the canyon walls above him: "solidly built, and remarkable for its substantial and beautiful masonry, and denoting taste on the part of the rude Barbarians."

As the soldiers pressed deeper into the canyon, they were finally confronted by large numbers of Navajos hundreds of feet above them on the canyon rim. "They were enabled to jump about on the ledges of the rocks like Mountain Cats," noted Pfeiffer, "hallooing at me, swearing and cursing, and threatening vengeance on my command in every variety of Spanish they were capable of mustering."[15]

Carson grew increasingly concerned over the fate of his friend. He was overjoyed when the captain's command appeared at the western entrance of Canyon de Chelly with nineteen prisoners on January 13. Pfeiffer had traveled some thirty miles from east to west through the canyon. This called for a considerable celebration, since it was thought that Pfeiffer's little command had been annihilated.

The next day a small Navajo party came in to parley. They were rather pathetic, starving and suffering from the frigid temperatures. Many of the old and the young had already perished from the cold, they told Carson. He promised them food and shelter if they would bring their people in, and he urged them to tell others that he meant the Navajo no harm. If they would come into Fort Canby, they would be fed, clothed, and protected. Then they must go to the Bosque Redondo.

Carson, with a small party and the prisoners, returned to Fort Canby on January 21 after sixteen days in the field. He left the main body of his force behind at the canyon under Captains Pfeiffer and A. B. Carey with orders to traverse the canyon from west to east and destroy all hogans, fields, and orchards. The weather proved too severe to destroy the magnificent Navajo peach orchards where several thousand trees had stood since early contact with the Spanish, but troops would return in the summer to lay waste to them. This was a particularly cruel blow to the Navajo, for they had developed a deep spiritual connection with the trees.

The brief campaign—which had resulted in only one death among the soldiers and but twenty-three among the Navajos—nevertheless had a devastating psychological impact on the Navajo people. Their sense of security was forever shattered and the scorched-earth policy of the soldiers would leave them impoverished. Carson had brought two hundred prisoners with him back to Canby, but that number soon doubled, then tripled, and within only a few weeks numbered in the thousands. The problem now was how to feed and shelter so many people until they could be moved to the east. As news of the conquest spread, bands of armed New Mexicans appeared to steal Navajo women and children. Carson had to use his troops to protect the Indians from these slavers.

"We have shown the Indians that in no place, however formidable or inaccessible in their opinion, are they safe from the pursuit of the troops of this command; and have convinced a large portion of them that the struggle on their part is a hopeless one," Carson reported to Carleton on January 24. "We have also demonstrated that the intentions of the Government toward them are eminently humane; and dictated by an earnest desire to promote their welfare; that the principle is not to destroy but to save them, if they are disposed to be saved."[16]

Carson now journeyed east with 253 prisoners. At the Rio Grande he turned over these first of thousands of Navajos to the troops who would transport them to the Bosque Redondo. He then turned north to Santa Fe to meet with Carleton and receive his reward of a leave to return to Taos and his family. He was greeted as a conquering hero by his military chieftain and the people of Santa Fe. He had done what no warrior—Spanish, Mexican, or American—could accomplish: defeat the Navajo.

"It was reserved for Colonel Carson to be the first to succeed," Carleton wrote to his superiors in Washington, "and I respectfully request the Government will favorably notice that officer and give him a substantial reward for this crowning act in a long life spent in various capacities in the service of his country in fighting the savages among the fastnesses of the Rocky Mountains."[17]

Carson returned home to Taos for a brief respite, but by March he was back at Fort Canby. Captain Carey, the able regular army officer who had been left in command, now had 3,000 Navajos encamped around his little post. The situation was dire as a result of the weather and the inability to properly supply the post with enough rations for the Indians. Over one hundred Navajos perished, many from dysentery as a result of the foreign diet forced on them. It was imperative to get these people to the relative safety of Bosque Redondo. This crisis was compounded by the fact that the enlistments of many of the New Mexico Volunteers were set to expire. A detachment of 52 men under Captain John Thompson was ordered to escort 2,645 Navajos from Canby to Fort Sumner. Thirty-four wagons were all that Carey could spare for the journey. This meant that most people walked. Thompson would lose 197 on the journey before reaching Fort Sumner on April 13. Another group of Navajos, 1,445 in number, departed Fort Wingate for the Bosque at about the same time. This group suffered only ten deaths, although five children were kidnapped along the route by New Mexicans, assisted no doubt by accomplices among the New Mexico Volunteers.

"The meeting between the party which I escorted and those already at the Bosque, was very affectionate, and very touching," reported the escort commander. "Numbers of them shed tears of joy at meeting their parents and brothers and sisters, others wept over the loss of a deceased father or brother."[18]

The Navajos called it the "Long Walk." This journey of some four hundred miles proved to be a nightmare. Those with stock herded their sheep and ponies ahead of the column. This made a tempting target for New Mexican brigands who shadowed the long, strung-out columns. Some, especially the old or ill, fell behind. Navajos would later assert that the soldiers shot those stragglers. When they reached the Hispanic villages along the Rio Grande, the officers had to keep their soldiers on high alert to prevent the citizens from stealing the Navajo children and young women to use as servants or to sell to Comancheros or to Mexican slave traders. To the Navajo people this all left a searing memory.

The Four Sacred Mountains that marked the boundaries of their homeland (the La Plata Mountains of southwestern Colorado to the north, the San Francisco Peaks of north-central Arizona to the west, Blanca Peak near Alamosa, Colorado, to the northeast, and Mount Taylor, some sixty miles west of Albuquerque, to the south), protected them, but now, as they left Mount Taylor (they called it Turquoise Mountain) they knew that their spiritual power would desert them. The crossing of the Rio Grande into the strange land east of the river led to even greater despondency. Even the boldest of the warriors and the wisest of the medicine men now lost hope. The Navajo mothers, clutching their children to their breasts, knew that they must be strong to hold the people together.

Within a matter of months, there were over 8,000 Navajos at the Bosque Redondo. Carleton was astonished. He did not believe that there were that many Navajos. Actually, over a thousand never surrendered, including the bold three hundred atop Fortress Rock. Many had fled beyond the Little Colorado westward to the San Francisco Peaks under Manuelito and other chiefs. Carleton did not care how many were still at large, for he promptly declared victory and turned his attention to the problems of his new reservation.[19]

The success of Carson's scorched-earth campaign—as well as his benevolent treatment that led even more Navajos to surrender than his soldiers did—doomed Carleton's grand reservation experiment on the Pecos. Carleton had to scramble to provide even marginal rations for his wards, placing his own troops on half rations in order to feed the Indians. He was certain that the industrious Navajos would be able to raise enough corn to feed themselves, but their population was beyond the carrying capacity of the land. While this was rich grazing country, it was barely suitable for agriculture—and was of course totally alien to the Navajos.

The Pecos River was so alkaline that it caused severe dysentery among both the Fort Sumner garrison and the Indians. The river often flooded. There was not enough timber in the "Round Forest," which was but sixteen miles long and a half mile wide, to provide firewood, much less building materials for housing. The Navajos wanted to build traditional hogans, but there was simply not enough wood. Much of the forest had already been cut down to construct the buildings for Fort Sumner.

The Mescaleros were naturally nervous about this huge influx of their traditional enemies and before long bolted the reservation. Comanche and Kiowa raiding parties swept across the plains from the east to prey on the Navajo flocks and pony herds. When the first corn crop showed promise, it was discovered to be infested with cutworms. What the moth larvae did not destroy, locusts did.

Despite Carleton's best efforts to provide for them, the Navajos suffered through a long starving time. The army issued them ration tickets and the Navajos quickly became master forgers, but this was discovered before too long. Desperate for rations to feed their families, many women and girls prostituted themselves to the soldiers. Syphilis reached epidemic proportions, with half of the Fort Sumner garrison treated for the dreaded scourge each year by army surgeons.

Carleton begged the government for assistance: "Unless you make . . . all the arrangements here contemplated, you will find this interesting and intelligent race of Indians will fast diminish in numbers, until, within a few years only, not one of those who boasted in the proud name of Navajoe will be left to upbraid us for having taken their birthright and then left them to perish. . . . For pity's sake, if not moved by any other consideration, let us as a great nation, for once treat the Indian as he deserves to be treated."[20]

In response, Congress appropriated $100,000 for food, clothing, and farming implements for the Bosque Redondo Indians, but the supplies that eventually reached the reservation were pathetic and transportation costs exorbitant. The Indians received war-surplus blankets that cost $4.50 to manufacture but were billed to the government at $22. Broken tools and moth-eaten clothing crossed over the Santa Fe Trail at inflated transportation costs only to line the pockets of war profiteers and contractors, leaving the Indians and the army defrauded.

In desperation, Carleton sent Carson to take charge at Bosque Redondo. The Navajos welcomed the arrival of the man they now called "Rope Thrower" because he had corralled them all. They trusted him, believing he must have almost mystical powers, but the mess was too great even for him to solve. Ill-suited to administration and bedeviled by lack of authority over the soldiers at Fort Sumner, the new "military superintendent of Indians" lasted but three months. He threatened again to resign unless reassigned.

Carleton now had a new mission for his favorite officer.

24

ADOBE WALLS

The Santa Fe Trail had become a killing ground. All through the summer and fall of 1864, Cheyenne, Kiowa, and Comanche raiders struck stagecoaches, wagon trains, and military convoys along the Santa Fe Trail as well as on the Saline and Solomon Rivers in Kansas. Many settlers in eastern Colorado abandoned their farms and ranches to seek safety in Denver. The Kiowas were so bold as to successfully raid the horse herd at Fort Larned. Dozens of soldiers, travelers, and settlers were killed, and for every real incident there were rumors of a hundred more. The supplies General Carleton so desperately needed at Bosque Redondo were being slowed to a crawl, while bands of Comanches and Kiowas raided the disarmed Navajos with impunity, driving off stock and kidnapping women and children.

"Unless prompt and efficient steps are at once taken our annual supplies for this department will be cut off and much suffering to the troops in this department ensue, not to mention the complete stoppage of our mails to and from the east," noted Carleton's chief of staff.[1]

Carleton issued orders to Carson on October 22, 1864, to proceed against the Kiowa and Comanche Indians, whom Comanchero traders had reported encamped in their winter haunts along the Canadian River in the Texas Panhandle. The Comancheros ran a lucrative trade with the Kiowas and Comanches in guns, whiskey, and captives in exchange for buffalo robes and stolen horses, cattle, and other booty. Carson was to have two and a half companies of the 1st California Cavalry, two companies of the 1st New Mexico Cavalry, a company of California infantry, as well as two smoothbore twelve-pounder mountain howitzers. Major William McCleave was to command the cavalry, while Lieutenant Colonel Francisco Abreau commanded the infantry. Lieutenant George Pettis had charge of the howitzers. Carson had requested the artillery since he anticipated far more trouble from the Kiowas and Comanches than he had faced from the Navajos. His command consisted of but 14 officers and 321 enlisted men as well as 70 Utes under Kaniache and Buckskin Charley and a handful of Jicarilla Apaches. Carson well knew that he would be greatly outnumbered.

"Your knowledge of the haunts of the Indians of the plains, and the great confidence the Ute Indians have in you as a friend and as a leader, point to yourself as the most fitting person to organize, direct, and bring this enterprise to a successful issue," Carleton told Carson.[2]

Carson was at Maxwell's sprawling ranch on the Cimarron when he received his orders. His old friend was making a fortune providing beef, mutton, corn, wheat, and flour to the Indians at Bosque Redondo. The Utes were camped near his ranch and Carson went there to recruit. He found 250 Utes there, and Kaniache assured him that many would go to fight their old enemies on the plains if their families were properly provided for. Carson added to Maxwell's fortunes by convincing Carleton to pay his friend to provision the Ute families while the men were away. He hoped to have them all back within forty-five days.

Carson led his Indian allies south to the newly constructed Fort Bascom on the Canadian River, where they rendezvoused with the rest of the command. The expedition marched out of the fort on November 12 with Carson and the Utes in the lead. Their destination, some two hundred miles to the northeast, was an abandoned trading post that the Bent brothers had built on the Canadian years before at a place called Adobe Walls.

The soldiers followed the Canadian eastward onto the Staked Plains in steady marches, slowed by their supply wagons and the howitzers. They reached Red River Springs on November 14, and Carson decided to lay over an extra day. This place had special meaning to him, and around the campfire that night he regaled the officers with the sad tale of Mrs. White, who had met her fate at that very spot. Carson was not over his failure to save her. The men listened attentively as Carson described the events of long ago, noted Lieutenant Pettis, "in his usual graphic manner." The evening was made all the more eerie by the strange wails and songs of the Utes engaging in their nightly war dance.

As Carson led the column eastward, the men could not help but notice how ill he looked. Wrapped in an army greatcoat, "his face seemed haggard and drawn with pain," noted one observer. On November 24, Carson's scouts reported hundreds of Comanche and Kiowa lodges on the south bank of the Canadian near the ruins of the old trading post.

"We will have no difficulty finding all the Indians that we desire," Carson assured his officers.[3]

At dusk Carson led all his mounted men and the howitzers forward. Even in the darkness they could make out a large and deeply worn Indian trail. After some fifteen miles Carson halted the men. They were ordered to stand by their horses: no talking or smoking. At dawn they moved out.

"I had a dream the night before, of being engaged with a large number of Indians; your cannons were firing," he whispered to Pettis. The young officer sensed that the colonel put great stock in dreams.[4]

Suddenly the Ute scouts cried out that the enemy was near. Three Kiowas were flushed. Carson ordered McCleve and his cavalry forward, while he remained with Pettis's artillery and the wagons and infantry. Within three miles they came across a village of nearly two hundred lodges, the white hides of the teepees glimmering in the crisp morning sunlight so that the soldiers at first mistook them for Sibley army tents.

The Kiowa warriors, screening the flight of their families, fired as they retreated, but the soldiers quickly captured the village. They found it full of booty taken from the Santa Fe Trail, even including two captured wagons. As the soldiers pulled down the teepees, they discovered a handful of elderly Kiowas. The Utes killed them before Carson arrived. Hundreds of buffalo robes, ready to be traded with the Comancheros, were gathered up and piled with all the Kiowa goods, food, and booty, to be burned along with the teepees. The Utes and Jicarillas busied themselves rounding up the Kiowa pony herd, for Carson had promised them all the horses they could capture.

In the teepees the soldiers discovered evidence of white captives as well as the uniform of a soldier. It was later learned that the Kiowas had a half dozen white women and children in the camp. They had been taken away by the retreating Indian women, who hid them amidst the bushes on the sand hills to the north of the camp.

This was the village of the aged Kiowa chief Little Mountain, so well-known on the southern plains that famed artist George Catlin had painted his portrait long ago when visiting with Colonel Henry Dodge's dragoon expedition. The old chief led his warriors down the Canadian River toward the ruins of the Adobe Walls trading post. Just beyond it, screened by bluffs, was a Comanche village of over three hundred lodges. The gunfire stirred the Comanche camp, and hundreds of warriors now raced to reinforce Little Mountain's people.

McCleave's cavalry, riding in hot pursuit, suddenly pulled up as they reached Adobe Walls. Hundreds of warriors seemingly appeared out of nowhere, galloping to the front of McCleave's troopers. McCleave ordered his men to dismount and set up a skirmish line. William Bent had built this sturdy outpost in 1845. The adobe walls were nine feet high and the compound sprawled over an area of eighty feet by eighty feet. McCleave placed his horses inside the walls while his surgeon set up a medical station in one of the buildings to treat the half dozen wounded men.

Carson passed through the abandoned village, riding to the sound of the guns. Topping a small bluff, he could now see the battle in progress. Carson put spurs to his horse and galloped forward with the rest of the cavalry behind. He had been there before, back in '48, when Bent sent him to open the trading post. Jicarillas had driven him off and Bent decided to abandon the place. Now he was back to fight the greatest battle of his storied career.

Pettis and his lumbering howitzers finally caught up. Before him he saw hundreds of warriors racing back and forth on their ponies, concealing themselves as they fired under the necks of the animals, and behind them on the nearby bluffs were over a thousand more. Carson's men were outnumbered by at least four to one.

"A finer sight I never saw before," noted Pettis, "and probably shall never see again."

The young officer dismounted before Carson and McCleave and saluted.

"Pettis, throw a few shell into that crowd over thar," Carson casually remarked as he pointed to a group of chiefs in their feathered headdresses haranguing the warriors in preparation of a grand charge.

"Battery, halt!" ordered Pettis. "Action right! Load with shell, load! Number one, FIRE! Number two, FIRE!"

The massed warriors pulled up and watched in astonishment as the little howitzers belched forth smoke. By the time a fourth shot exploded among them, they had scattered to race back toward the Comanche village.

Carson called in his skirmish lines and told the men to make breakfast. It was ten o'clock in the morning. After their hardtack and bacon, he planned to burn the captured Kiowa village before advancing against the Comanches. While the men ate, Carson strolled over to a grassy high point to survey the scene with his spyglass. To his amazement, there was not just one Comanche village along the river but several more stretching as far as he could see. Warriors were pouring forth from them all. And it was not hundreds this time but literally thousands—far more than he could count. This great mass of painted and feathered humanity was advancing toward Adobe Walls as fast as their ponies could carry them.

Carson hurried back to his little fortress and again threw out his skirmish lines. Again the bold warriors raced back and forth in front of the soldiers, leaning forward to fire under the necks of their swift mounts. They kept some distance between themselves and the skirmishers. Others crept through the tall grass to snipe at the kneeling troopers. The weather might be cold, but this was hot work for all.

Pettis kept his guns firing, and they proved critical in keeping the warriors at bay. One remarkable shot passed through a Comanche horse, sending its rider flying high into the air. As the soldiers stared with awe and admiration, two Comanches galloped forward, seized the fallen man amidst a volley of gunfire, lifted him up, and carried him away to safety.

One young Hispanic soldier took the only scalp of the day. While in position on the skirmish line that morning, he had been bitten by a rattlesnake. He was treated by the surgeon and sent back to the line, where he promptly brought down a warrior who had ventured too close to the improvised fort. He rushed forward to take his fallen foe's scalp. He later bartered it away to the Utes.

This fighting kept up all afternoon. Carson could see that some of the warriors were circling around him to get to the Kiowa village that had been captured that morning to retrieve their horses and goods. He was also worried about his wagon train, which had but a seventy-five-man guard. It contained all his supplies and extra ammunition.

A little after three that afternoon he ordered a withdrawal back to the

Kiowa camp. The officers all wanted to advance against the Comanche villages, while the Indian scouts felt it was time to retreat. Carson agreed with the Utes. They had captured one village and its large pony herd, faced a formidable and determined foe that vastly outnumbered them, and had wounded to care for. Carson was too old and wise an Indian fighter for reckless, forlorn charges.

The horses were gathered and horse holders led three horses while riding one as the dismounted men provided protective skirmishers. The howitzers brought up the rear to keep the milling warriors at bay. Carson and McCleave led the formation—which was a hollow square with the dozen wounded men in the center—back toward the Kiowa village.

The warriors now set fire to the grass so that the thick smoke might screen their advance. An easterly wind frustrated their plan, allowing Pettis to fire several rounds at them. This fighting was torturously slow, so that the sun was setting by the time Carson reached the village. The Kiowas had beat him to it and now the soldiers had a fight to their front as well as their rear.

The Indians were quickly driven from the village. While half of the men began the work of destruction, the rest kept the Indians away. Hundreds of buffalo robes, ready to be traded to Comancheros, were gathered up, and after Carson set one aside for each soldier, the rest were burned. The Indian lodges and a wide array of plunder taken from wagon trains, along with Kiowa goods as well as a great quantity of food, were all burned. The fires lit the sky as the sun vanished below the horizon.

As darkness set in, the Indians retired back to their villages. Carson led his men in the opposite direction, back toward the supply train. His command, nearly out of ammunition, had three dead and twenty-five wounded and needed to get away from the large Comanche encampments as rapidly as possible. They limped through the darkness back to the wagon train. The exhausted men found comfort that night in their new buffalo robes and the security of the camp. The command rested for a day and then the next morning, Sunday, November 27, started the long march back to Fort Bascom. The Comanches hovered around them for a while but kept their distance. Many of Carson's officers wanted to renew the battle, but the old scout did not wish to tempt fate further. He had destroyed the Kiowa camp, fought an all-day battle, and extricated his command with few casualties while killing over a hundred Indians and wounding many more; that was enough. This was to be his last fight.

Carson's command reached Fort Bascom fifteen days later, on December 10. They had been serenaded every night by the Utes, who conducted a scalp dance over the single scalp they had purchased from the young snakebitten soldier.

From Fort Bascom, Carson wrote his official report to Carleton, in which he claimed victory. "I flatter myself that I have taught these Indians a severe lesson," he dictated to an aide, "and hereafter they will be more cautious about how they engage a force of civilized troops." Carson knew better, of course, and not long afterward William Bent's half-Cheyenne son George said that Carson confessed that "the Indians whipped him in this fight." Buckskin Charley, one of the Ute scouts, told Bent the same thing. Several years later Lieutenant Pettis met two Comancheros at Algodones, just south of Santa Fe, who told him that the Indians had suffered nearly 100 killed and another 150 wounded in the Adobe Walls fight.

"They also said," noted Pettis, "that the Indians claimed that if the whites had not had with them the two guns that shot twice, referring to the shells of the mountain howitzers, they would never have allowed a single white man to escape out of the valley of the Canadian, and I may say, with becoming modesty, that this was also the often expressed opinion of Colonel Carson." Carson's dream had proven prescient.[5]

Carleton gushed to his superiors over Carson's fight, presenting it as a great victory. He also extolled Carson with a commendation: "This brilliant affair adds another green leaf to the laurel wreath which you have so nobly won in the service of your country." Soon after, in March 1865, Carson was rewarded with the brevet (an honorary rank for meritorious service) of brigadier general of volunteers. This was surely gratifying to Carson, who had not forgotten how the Senate had refused to confirm his appointment as a second lieutenant of the Mounted Riflemen back in 1847. For Carson, however, such military glory and rank were but moonglow, giving a little light but no warmth. At fifty-five, he was sick and worn-out and wanted now only to return to Taos and his family, which he finally did in January 1865.[6]

Carson was not to be in Taos for long. He soon testified before the Doolittle congressional committee that had been sent west to investigate the Sand Creek Massacre of November 29, 1864, in which Colonel John Chivington, the hero of Glorieta Pass, had slaughtered a camp of peaceful Cheyenne and Arapaho Indians. Carson knew many of the over two hundred people killed in the village just to the north of Fort Lyon. Four of William Bent's children had been there. He condemned the attack in the strongest terms. General James Rusling recalled Carson's opinion of the massacre and left an account in his version of Carson's unique vernacular:

> *"To think of that dog Chivington, and his hounds, up thar at Sand Creek! Whoever heerd of sich doings among Christians!... So they just pitched into these friendlies, and massa-creed them... in cold blood, in spite of our flag thar—women and little children even!... [T]hat thar d—d miscreant and his men shot down squaws, and blew the brains out of little innocent children—even pistoled little babies in the arms of their dead mothers, and worse than this! And ye call these civilized men—Christians; and the Injuns savages, du ye?*
>
> *"I tell ye what; I don't like a hostile Red Skin any better, than you du. And when they are hostile, I've fit 'em—fout 'em—as hard as any man. But I never yit drew a bead on a squaw or papoose, and I loathe and hate the man who would.... Pore things! I've seen as much of 'em as any white man livin' and I can't help but pity 'em! They'll all soon be gone anyhow."*[7]

With the Civil War over and the great, final push westward about to begin, Carson's advice was sought by policymakers both civilian and military. General William Tecumseh Sherman, soon to be commander of the newly created Division of the Missouri, called him back to St. Louis in the fall of 1865. Sherman and Carson reminisced about their first meeting long years before in California and discussed the Indian situation on the plains. Sand Creek had enraged all the tribes of the Great Plains, but the government wanted to establish a new peace if possible. It was especially important to make safe the roadway for the great transcontinental line pushing across the central plains.

Carson's future was also under discussion, for he had no interest in remaining for much longer in the army. Sherman needed him for now, and orders were soon issued for him to take command of Fort Garland, Colorado, on the western edge of the Sangre de Cristo Mountains. The Utes who lived nearby were uneasy, as the game was being killed off by settlers in the San Luis Valley and the mountain foothills. Carson, the friend of the Utes, was to keep the peace.

Sherman and General Rusling came out to Fort Garland early in September 1866 to meet with the Utes and lay the groundwork for the establishment of a Colorado reservation for them farther to the west. Carson translated for them.

"In talking, I observed, that he frequently hesitated for the right English word; but when speaking bastard Spanish (Mexican) or Indian, he was as fluent as a native," noted Rusling. "Both Mexican and Indian, however, are largely pantomime, which may have helped him along somewhat." Spanish was the language of the Carson home.

Sherman was suitably impressed. "These Red Skins think Kit twice as big a man as me. Why his integrity is simply perfect," Sherman told Rusling. "They know it, and they would believe him and trust him any day before me."

Rusling was somewhat surprised by Carson's defense of the Indians. "Kit seemed thoroughly familiar with Indian life and character . . . he was their stout friend—no Boston philanthropist more so," Rusling later wrote. "He did not hesitate to say, that all our Indian troubles were caused originally by bad white men, if the truth were known, and was terribly severe on the brutalities and barbarities of the border."[8]

Sherman, noting Carson's haggard and deeply lined face as well as the shimmer of silver in his sandy hair, worried about his friend's large family.

"Carson then had his family with him—wife and half a dozen children, boys and girls as wild and untrained as a brood of Mexican mustangs," Sherman remarked about his visit to Fort Garland. "One day these children ran through the room in which we were seated, half clad and boisterous, and I inquired, 'Kit, what are you doing about your children?'"

"He replied: 'That is a source of great anxiety; I myself had no education' (he could not even write, his wife always signing his name to official reports). 'I value education as much as any man, but I have never had the advantage of schools, and now that I am getting old and infirm, I fear I have not done right by my children.'"

Sherman replied that he had received a scholarship to the Catholic

College at South Bend, Indiana (now Notre Dame), and that when Carson's oldest boy was of age he would see that he was educated there. Carson was grateful, and when the time came Sherman proved true to his word.[9]

Sometime after his visit with Carson at Fort Garland, Sherman was appointed to a commission to settle the Navajo on a new reservation. Bosque Redondo had proven too expensive for the government to sustain; this was a time for postwar retrenchment. Carleton was gone from New Mexico by then, removed from his command in September 1866 and transferred to the 4th Cavalry in Texas. There was no one left to protect his grandiose reservation experiment. Sherman, who had spoken with Carson about the Navajo, was inclined to return them to their homeland.

"I think we could better send them to the Fifth Avenue Hotel to board," the flinty general grumbled over the cost of Bosque Redondo.[10]

Sherman, who reached Fort Sumner in late May, moved swiftly and with the same determination as his famous "March to the Sea." Within three days of their arrival he and fellow commissioner Samuel Tappan had drafted a treaty setting out new boundaries for the Navajos in their Four Corners homeland. Signed amidst much ceremony on June 1, 1868, the treaty allowed the Navajo to depart the Bosque Redondo just as soon as military transportation could be arranged. Sherman also promised the Navajo that he would halt the enslavement of their people by the New Mexicans and work to return children to their families. He made good on his pledge.

On June 15, 1868, over 7,000 people, along with thousands of head of livestock and a large train of supply wagons forming a column ten miles long, began the long but joyful exodus back to the land of their fathers. They would never again make war against the Americans.

By the second week of July the long procession had crossed the Rio Grande at Albuquerque and in the distance before them rose Mount Taylor—the "Blue Bead"—their sacred mountain marking the southeastern boundary of their homeland.

"When we saw the top of the mountain from Albuquerque we wondered if it was our mountain," declared Chief Manuelito, "and loved it so, and some of the old men and women cried with joy when they reached their homes."[11]

Kit Carson would not live to see the return of the Navajo to their homeland. He had resigned from the army on account of ill health in July 1867, although he would not officially be mustered out of the service until November and had hopes of securing the appointment as Colorado superintendent of Indian Affairs. With the help of Pfeiffer he removed his family to the Purgatoire River in southeastern Colorado, where his old friend Tom Boggs, who was married to Josefa's niece, had established the little hamlet of Boggsville not far from Fort Lyon. Carson was so ill that he could no longer ride. He now spent his days in the spacious adobe home owned by the Boggs family, surrounded by his children.[12]

In February 1868, Carson was asked by the commissioner of Indian Affairs to lead a delegation of Ute chiefs to Washington to help negotiate a new treaty to move the tribe to the Western Slope of Colorado. He hesitated to go on account of his health, as well as the fact that Josefa was expecting another child, but his sense of duty overcame his trepidation and he decided to go.

It was something of a triumphal journey, for crowds gathered all along the route to see America's greatest frontiersman. Captain Henry Inman met Carson during this time and was amazed to find his childhood hero to be "a delicate, reticent, under-sized, wiry man, as perfectly the opposite of the type my childish brain had created as it is possible to conceive." He presented his hero with a colorful dime novel featuring a buckskin-clad Carson on the cover in heroic stance, clutching a beautiful damsel by the waist while slaying an Indian with his knife. Carson put on his spectacles to carefully study the garish image.

He then pronounced to the great amusement of Inman and his companions: "Gentlemen, that thar may be true, but I hain't got no recollection of it."

Another army officer upon meeting him remarked, "So this is the great Kit Carson, who has made so many Indians run!"

"Yes, sometimes I ran after them," Carson replied, "but most times they war runnin' after me."[13]

He took the stage from Fort Lyon to Fort Hays, Kansas. Nearby Hays City, then the terminus of the Kansas Pacific Railway, had become something of a boomtown, frequented by buffalo hunters, cowboys, soldiers, and a wide assortment of hard cases. While there he met a young buffalo hunter who was already making quite a name for himself as a scout for the army. Bill Cody had escorted General Sherman on part of his 1866 inspection of western posts, although he had not accompanied him to Fort Garland, and had recently performed a similar service for the newly arrived lieutenant colonel of the 7th Cavalry, George Armstrong Custer.

Cody, like so many others, was disappointed upon meeting Carson. He had hoped to extract from the famed scout some tales of hair-raising adventure but could barely get him to speak at all.

"Modesty is a becoming trait, except when it serves to obscure important incidents in the life of a justly historic personage," Cody later complained, "and in Carson this obstacle to a proper knowledge of his career is particularly conspicuous . . . for he seldom spoke of his own deeds, though I hardly think he was so different from other men as to be wholly indifferent to praise." Cody, of course, would never be burdened by undue modesty.[14]

From Fort Hays, Carson traveled by rail to Kansas City and then on to St. Louis, where he was joined by Albert Gallatin Boone, the grandson of Daniel Boone, who as a special commissioner was to assist with the Ute treaty. They traveled together to Washington on the train. Carson found himself to be quite the celebrity in the nation's capital. He was feted at dinners by politicians and generals and photographed by Mathew Brady. On February 5, the twenty-one members of the Ute delegation visited the White House, where Carson met yet another Tennessee president, Andrew Johnson. By March 18, the treaty was completed and presented to the Senate.

Carson also met with General Sherman, who was about to start for New Mexico to treat with the Navajo, and General Phil Sheridan, who was to take command on the southern plains. He had soured on the Bosque Redondo experiment and advised Sherman to let the Navajos return to their homeland.

"General, I'm not so sure the Great Spirit means for us to take over Indian lands," he said. "Let me lead them back while they still have the will to live."[15]

Carson was also reunited with John Frémont, who, despite the fact that his fortunes had declined precipitously, still retained a fairly lavish lifestyle. Frémont was deeply disturbed by Carson's appearance. He arranged for Carson to travel north to New York City to consult with the specialist Dr. Lewis Albert Sayre. Frémont wrote Jessie of how Carson looked "so ill and suffering" and urged her to meet him in the city. After he had seen Sayre, she would take him to their estate on the Hudson to rest.

Carson received permission to take several of the Ute chiefs with him to New York City. They stayed at the Metropolitan Hotel. Jessie Benton Frémont came to visit him and found him somewhat despondent. He had met with Dr. Sayre, who had diagnosed an aneurysm of the aorta, which he told Carson could be fatal at any moment. There was nothing that could be done for him.

Carson told Jessie that he had had a dream of death. "Suddenly the bed seemed to rise with me—I felt my head swell and my breath leaving me. Then I woke up at the window. It was open and my face and head all wet. I was on the floor and the chief was holding my head on his arm and putting water on me. He was crying. He said, 'I thought you were dead. You called your Lord Jesus, then you shut your eyes and couldn't speak.'"

Carson was never outwardly spiritual, but he now confessed that "it's only Him that can help me where I stand now."

Jessie begged him to come up the Hudson with her to their country house, Pocaho, but he refused.

"I must take the chiefs to Boston. They depend on me," he told her. "Then we go home, straight. My wife must see me. If I was to write about this, or died out here, it would kill her. I must get home, and I think I can do it."

His appearance so shocked her that it was difficult for her to keep her emotions in check. In the face of her distress, Carson set aside his melancholy. "Carson," she noted, "was only troubled by my emotion." She felt that he carried himself with "the dignity of coming death." He was, in a way, her creation, for it had been her rewrite of her husband's reports that had made the name of Kit Carson famous throughout the households of America. In later years she would prove to be a zealous keeper of the flame. Knowing that this was their final meeting, she sent an arrangement of violets to his room at the Metropolitan.[16]

The old scout faced his final battle with his usual stoicism. From Boston, he and his Indian friends traveled by rail to Chicago and then on to Cheyenne. By the end of March they reached Denver via stagecoach. He had to rest in Denver, staying for a few days at the Planter's House. Old friends visited him there and, when he was feeling a bit better, took him by wagon to La Junta, some twenty miles from Boggsville. They stopped at Pueblo, where he visited with another doctor, who confirmed the diagnosis of an aneurysm of the carotid artery. It was so prominent that the doctor could see it bulging against the skin. It could burst at any moment. The doctor gave Carson some cherry syrup laced with opium for his cough. Carson could barely breathe, and the constant cough might burst the aneurysm. He had to lie in the back of the wagon on the way to La Junta.[17]

Josefa met him there on April 11 with a little horse-drawn carriage. Although heavy with child, she helped to guide the wagon across the rough road to Boggsville. There on April 13 she gave birth to her baby, a girl, whom Carson named Josefita after her. Then came the fever.

She was but forty, and Dr. Henry Tilton, the post surgeon at Fort Lyon, thought she would surely recover. He was more worried about Carson, who now could barely sit up.

Late in the evening of April 27, Josefa called out, "*¡Cristóbal! ¡Ven acá!*"

Carson hurried to her side, cradling her in his arms as her life ebbed away. It was more than he could bear.

"He just seemed to pine away after mother died," lamented young Charles Carson.

Boggs helped him write to his close friend Aloys Scheurich, a German immigrant and successful merchant, who was married to Teresina Bent, to ask that he bring his wife and her mother (Ignacia, Josefa's sister) to Boggsville to look after the children until he might recover. Of course, he well knew there was no hope for recovery.

"Please tell the old lady," he wrote Scheurich, referring to Ignacia, "that there is nobody in the world who can take care of my children but her, and she must know that it would be the greatest of favors to me, if she would come and stay until I am healthier." He added that he wished that he and Josefa be transported to Taos for burial "as soon as the weather is cool enough to do so." This was to be Carson's last letter.

Scheurich, with Teresina and Ignacia, left on the two-hundred-mile journey to Boggsville three days after receiving the letter. By the time they arrived on May 15, Carson had already been moved to Dr. Tilton's quarters at Fort Lyon. The doctor made his patient as comfortable as possible, propped up on a pile of buffalo robes. Carson did not wish to die in a bed. Tilton administered chloroform to help relieve the coughing spasms. In their time together, Tilton read to Carson from De Witt C. Peters's 1858 book *The Life and Adventures of Kit Carson, the Nestor of the Rocky Mountains*. Scheurich had come to the fort and stayed with his old friend.

On the afternoon of May 23, Carson seemed to brighten. He asked for a "man's meal," and when Tilton nodded in approval, Scheurich went off to cook a large steak and prepare some strong coffee. Carson enjoyed the meal and called for his old clay mountaineer's pipe. As he smoked he talked with Scheurich of old times.

Suddenly, a bloody coughing fit overcame him, and he called out, "Doctor, compadre, adios!"[18]

And he was gone. He was fifty-eight years old. They buried him next to Josefa in the little garden behind the Boggs house. Captain (Brevet Brigadier General) William H. Penrose had the Fort Lyon flag lowered to half-mast and along with most of the garrison attended the funeral ceremony. A 7th Cavalry bugler sounded taps.

The *Rocky Mountain News* (Denver) noted Carson's passing in its May 27, 1868, edition, with a commentary soon echoed by newspapers throughout the country:

"Over what an immense expanse of plains, of snow-clad sierras, of rivers, lakes, and seas, has he cut out the first paths, into which now the locomotives, the steamships, the organized two halves of human society, are massing the activity, the power, the condensed energy of ancient and of modern times.

". . . [H]is guiding instinct has been an innate chivalry, from the practice of which nothing has ever deflected him. He had in him a personal courage which came forth when wanted, like lightning from a cloud."

"Kit Carson," wrote the ever-cynical William Tecumseh Sherman, "was a good type of a class of men most useful in their day, but now as antiquated as Jason of the Golden Fleece, Ulysses of Troy, the Chevalier La Salle of the Lakes, Daniel Boone of Kentucky, Irvin Bridger and Jim Beckwith of the Rockies, all belonging to the dead past."[19]

Part IV

THE PRAIRIE

25

THE BUFFALO RANGE

William Frederick Cody was a true child of the frontier. Born in a log cabin in Scott County, Iowa, on February 26, 1846, Will, as the family called him, was the third child of Isaac and Mary Laycock Cody. Isaac, who was Canadian by birth, moved his family from Iowa to the newly organized Kansas Territory in 1854, settling in the Salt Creek Valley near Fort Leavenworth. Isaac became a prominent advocate of the Free-Soil cause, and while speaking against the extension of slavery into Kansas on September 18, 1854, was pulled from his platform and stabbed by a proslavery man. Although he recovered well enough to win election to the Free-Soil Topeka legislature in 1856, he was continually plagued by the wound, finally dying on March 10, 1857. To young Will, his father was a martyr, having "shed the first blood in the cause of the freedom of Kansas."[1]

With the family in financial straits after his father's death, Will Cody went to work for the freighting company of Alexander Majors and William H. Russell. At first the youth worked as an express boy between the firm's office and the telegraph office, three miles distant at Fort Leavenworth. In 1857 the company contracted with the government to haul supplies for Colonel Albert Sidney Johnston's army during the so-called Mormon War of 1857. President James Buchanan, as one of his first acts, ordered 2,500 troops to Utah to enforce federal law after several territorial appointees had resigned in the face of Brigham Young's theological rule. Despite his mother's objections, the teenage boy was soon on his way to Utah with wagon master Lewis Simpson's twenty-five ox-drawn wagons. The large wagons each carried over 6,000 pounds of supplies for Johnston's army. It was on this trip that Cody struck up a friendship with James Butler Hickok, soon to be known throughout the West as "Wild Bill."

"He was ten years my senior—a tall, handsome, magnificently built and powerful young fellow, who could out-run, out-jump, and out-fight any man in the train. . . and of his bravery there was not a doubt," Cody later wrote. "Wild Bill was my protector and intimate friend, and the friendship thus began continued until his death."[2]

When the firm of Russell, Majors and Waddell initiated the short-lived Pony Express in April 1860, Cody briefly served as a rider. With sectional tension at a flashpoint over the 1860 presidential election, rapid communication between the East and California became vital. Since the transcontinental telegraph was not yet completed, the Pony Express was born. The company promised to complete the nearly 2,000-mile trip in ten days—come hell or high water—and the riders did it. The pony riders might ride sixty miles at a stretch, with relay stations every ten to twenty miles, from St. Joseph, Missouri, to Sacramento, California. Russell's ad for riders ran: "Young skinny wiry fellows not over eighteen. Must be expert riders willing to risk death daily. Orphans preferred."[3]

With the outbreak of the Civil War, Cody joined a band of Kansas Jayhawkers preying upon neighboring Missourians. Anxious to avenge his father's murder and the depredations of Missouri "Border Ruffians," he felt no pangs of conscience about his horse-stealing forays into Missouri.

Cody readily admitted that these were not his best days. "I entered upon a dissolute and reckless life—to my shame be it said—and associated with gamblers, drunkards, and bad characters generally." After one particularly rowdy night in February 1864, Cody enlisted as a private in the 7th Kansas Volunteer Cavalry. He claimed to have passed out under "the influence of bad whiskey" and then awoke to find himself a soldier. Private Cody served in the regiment until the end of the war, participating in several battles as well as acting as scout and dispatch rider.[4]

With the war over, Cody took himself a bride, Louisa Frederici of St. Louis, and attempted to settle down to the life of a hotelkeeper at his Salt Creek Valley home. It was not to be, for he was devoid of business skills, and within a year he headed west to seek employment with the army. Hickok was scouting out of Fort Ellsworth, Kansas, at the time, and he got his friend a job as guide at the post.

During this time Cody became acquainted with Lieutenant Colonel George A. Custer, 7th Cavalry, then just commencing his frontier career. Custer wanted a guide to take him from Fort Hays to Fort Larned, through sixty-five miles of dangerous country. He had but a ten-man escort. Cody agreed to guide Custer, but as they prepared to leave Fort Hays, Custer objected to Cody's mouse-colored mule.

"Cody, I want to travel fast and go through as quickly as possible, and I don't think that mule of yours is fast enough to suit me," the colonel declared. Custer, who rightly prided himself on being a splendid judge of horseflesh, rode a spirited Thoroughbred.

"General, never mind the mule," Cody replied, "he'll get there as soon as your horses. That mule is a good one."

"Very well; go ahead, then," a scowling Custer responded.

As they traveled the first fifteen miles, Cody had a difficult time keeping up. Custer would repeatedly call back to him that his mule was no good.

Once they crossed the Smoky Hill River and hit the sand hills beyond, the old mule hit his stride and Cody had to pull up and wait for Custer and his escort on their fatigued horses. By the time they reached Fort Larned late that afternoon, half of the escort lagged behind.

"General, how about this mule, anyhow?" Cody asked.

"Cody, you have a better vehicle than I thought you had," he replied. He was in a good humor over his defeat and thanked Cody profusely for bringing him straight across a country where there was no trail.[5]

Custer asked Cody to scout for the 7th Cavalry in a proposed summer campaign against the Cheyennes, but an offer to hunt buffalo to feed workers on the Kansas Pacific Railway proved more attractive. The firm of Goddard Brothers had the contract to feed the railway workers, and they employed Cody at the princely sum of $500 a month for this dangerous work. They even supplied him with a butcher to do the really dirty work.

In eight months' time, from October 1867 until May 1868, Cody killed 4,280 buffalo for Goddard Brothers. "My great forte in killing buffaloes from horseback," Cody explained, "was to get them circling by riding my horse at the head of the herd, shooting the leaders, thus crowding their followers to the left, till they would finally circle round and round."

Mounted on his fleet horse Brigham (named after the Mormon patriarch) and armed with a breech-loading .50-caliber Springfield rifle dubbed

Lucretia Borgia, Cody became a familiar and welcome sight in the tough, end-of-track railway camps. The workers conferred on him the sobriquet of "Buffalo Bill," and it stuck. They even composed a ditty that they sang while working on the construction gangs.

Buffalo Bill, Buffalo Bill
Never missed and never will;
Always aims and shoots to kill
And the company pays his buffalo bill.[6]

The American bison that Cody hunted was the largest mammal in North America. It is historically and colloquially referred to as the American buffalo, a name conferred on the animal by early French explorers and fur trappers. The correct scientific term of "bison" was not in use for another century and a half, so that the word "buffalo" entered the colonial American language as the name for the majestic beast that at the time was found throughout what would become the Eastern United States. The buffalo name has remained in common usage and is deeply embedded in American culture and language, thanks in part to its relationship to Buffalo Bill.

Although buffalo roamed across the entire continent in the colonial period, in time they became most clearly identified with the trans-Mississippi West. They had been hunted out or driven from the area east of the Mississippi River by around 1800. In the West they ranged from Alaska across the Canadian prairie and down throughout the U.S. Great Plains to Mexico in astonishing numbers (estimated at between 20 and 50 million in the early nineteenth century). They became closely identified with Native peoples across the West: the Natives often viewed them as sacred symbols, and buffalo were an important part of the creation stories of several Native tribes. Buffalo were not only critical to Plains Indian society and culture; they were instrumental in basic survival and economic prosperity. Their meat fed the people, while their skins provided clothing, tepees, and robes, and their bones were used for weapons and utensils. With the coming of the Europeans, the robe-and-hide trade became essential to the economic well-being of various tribes as they became increasingly dependent on trade goods. The near extermination of the buffalo in the late nineteenth century eventually led to the collapse of Plains Indian tribal autonomy and independence.

The bison was a relative latecomer to North America. Fossil evidence indicates an arrival via the Bering Land Bridge (Beringea) connecting Asia and the Americas about 300,000 years ago and perhaps even later. Within a few thousand years, expanding human populations spread across the continent and, along with a warming climate, wiped out the giant beasts.

Some 10,000 years ago, the smaller buffalo emerged and, with no competition for grazing and a much shorter gestation period than its ancestor, it quickly overspread the continent. The Indians preyed on these animals, but their primitive weapons and small populations did not threaten to inflict too much damage on the ever-expanding herds. Since the horse did not arrive until the European invasion, the range of Indian hunters was limited. Even on foot they still managed to slaughter buffalo by the thousands, sometimes by running them off cliffs in "buffalo jumps" or by drowning them in rivers. Still, massive herds spread across the West from Alaska and Alberta (the wood bison) and south to blanket the Great Plains from Canada to Mexico (the plains bison). They drifted south in the winter and north in the summer in herds numbering in the millions. By 1400 there were some 4 million people in all of North America, with almost 2 million living east of the Mississippi River. This population hardly made a dent in the great buffalo herds. With only humans and wolves as predators, the herds expanded exponentially. Then, in 1492, the Europeans arrived, and everything began to change.

There were perhaps 5 million buffalo east of the Mississippi River in the early eighteenth century. The Indians often set fires in the eastern forests to clear trees and open up grazing for both deer and bison. When Daniel Boone first explored Kentucky, he reported "buffalo as thick as cattle in the settlements." But the days of the buffalo in Kentucky were numbered. Settlers could not resist killing the animals for both food and bragging rights, so that by 1800 the eastern herds were no more.[7]

Of course, the herds in the West were far larger than those in the East, but two events coincided that would eventually lead to disaster for the buffalo. In 1680 the Pueblo Indians of New Mexico expelled their Spanish overlords. As the Spanish retreated back to Mexico (they would not return for a dozen years), their horse herds were either released to roam free or captured by the Indians. The Pueblos began a lively trade in horses with tribes to the north and east. In a remarkably short time many of these tribes—most notably the Comanche, Cheyenne, Kiowa, Crow, Pawnee, and Sioux—became master horsemen. The great era of the mounted Plains Indian buffalo-hunting cultures began. It was to last for another century. At the same time, thousands of horses ran free across the Great Plains, rapidly increasing in population and competing with the buffalo for grass. These feral horses numbered over 2 million by 1800. Since the horse and the buffalo had a dietary overlap of 80 percent, this put considerable stress on the herds.

As the plains tribes developed their new horse and buffalo-hunting culture, they also opened up trade with French, British, Spanish, and later American traders along the Missouri River in the north and the Red and Arkansas Rivers in the south. A lucrative buffalo robe trade developed. By the 1820s 100,000 buffalo robes were being shipped out of New Orleans annually. Within two decades the same number of robes was reaching St. Louis annually, while to the north the British Hudson's Bay Company was trading for 75,000 robes per year. The tribes now became market hunters. Little wonder that the early explorers, and the artists who accompanied them into the West, found buffalo skulls to be a common sight. Both George Catlin and John James Audubon warned that the buffalo were doomed.

By mid-century a remarkable convergence of historical forces descended on the buffalo herds. The animals had to compete with wild horses for grass and water at the same time that a prolonged drought began in the West. The U.S. government had relocated some 80,000 eastern Indians (the infamous Trail of Tears) to the southern plains (Indian Territory, later Oklahoma) by the 1840s, which added further hunting stress to the herds. The highly mobile plains tribes continued to roam across the landscape in search of buffalo for the robe market. At the same time (1840–1850) herds of domestic cattle crossed the plains on both the Oregon Trail and the Santa Fe Trail. These cattle brought brucellosis and anthrax to the plains, resulting in massive die-offs among the exposed buffalo.

The buffalo herds received a brief reprieve with the outbreak of the Civil War, but when the war ended, thousands of young men—many of them veterans in search of work—headed west. Thousands found jobs as buffalo hide hunters—and they delivered the coup de grâce to the already seriously depleted herds. With new long-range Sharps rifles and skinning knives, they swarmed across the southern plains. Just as a previous generation of fur trappers had all but eradicated the beaver population, now the buffalo hunters wiped out the great herds in a twinkling.

Cody's hunting career predated the great slaughter that was to follow. Cody, of course, hunted not from stands but on horseback as the Indians did. The hunters, who usually worked in small groups, would position themselves behind an outcropping of sage, lie flat with their rifles in gun rests made from tree branches, and at about two hundred yards would commence killing. As long as the animals did not see or smell the hunter, they would not stampede even as death was dealt all around them. A skilled buffalo hunter aimed for the lungs; the stricken beast would throw blood from his nose, take a step or two, and drop dead. A shot through the heart would allow the buffalo to run several hundred yards, perhaps taking the herd with him. It also made the work of the skinners harder, as the carcasses would be spread out. The hunter usually carried at least two rifles so one could cool while the other fired. The buffalo would mill about, sometimes bawling out in bewilderment, but would stay put until most were killed. The only thing that might save them was that the hunter would tire out his arm. They were indeed the "monarchs of the plains," but they were not particularly bright. And so they died—by the hundreds, by the thousands, by the millions.[8]

Railroads pushing across the West provided easy access to markets for buffalo hides, for hides now replaced robes as the profitable commodity. A new chemical process back East converted the hides into tough leather for industrial belts. The bodies were left to rot after the hides were harvested, so that the Great Plains were soon littered with bones and skulls. Wolves and coyote packs grew in ever greater numbers as they feasted on the carcasses. The settlers and soldiers put out poison to kill the wolves and in turn ravens and crows feasted on these carcasses and were poisoned. The ground around Dodge City was littered with the bodies of thousands of birds. It was a perfect killing ground.

The military establishment encouraged this destruction in hopes of eradicating the commissary of their Indian foes. When, in 1881, there was talk in Congress of protecting what was left of the herds, General Phil

Sheridan vigorously opposed such action. "If I could learn that every buffalo in the northern herd were killed I would be glad," the western army commander wrote to the War Department. "The destruction of this herd would do more to keep Indians quiet than anything else that could happen. Since the destruction of the southern herd, which formerly roamed from Texas to the Platte, the Indians in that section have given us no trouble." Sheridan got his wish: no government protection was forthcoming. By 1878 the southern herd was gone and within a decade the northern herd joined them. In 1876, 80,000 hides were shipped down the Missouri River from Fort Benton, Montana, but by 1884 not a single hide was shipped out. This slaughter, Cody lamented in 1883, had "been criminally large and useless."[9]

Only the bleaching bones of the buffalo remained, and they were soon collected by the wagonload to be converted into fertilizer, combs, and buttons. The Atchison, Topeka and Santa Fe Railway carried well over a million pounds of bones in a three-year period. The 1870s also saw over $2 million earned by the bone pickers in Kansas alone. Cattle replaced buffalo on the plains, and the buffalo skull became a common decoration over western fireplaces and on fence posts. The passing of the buffalo quickly became a metaphor for the end of the wild and open West.[10]

A combination of bad weather and hostile Indians temporarily halted construction of the Kansas Pacific when end of track reached Sheridan, Kansas. Cody's contract ended in May 1868, but he was not unemployed for long. With a new war brewing with the Cheyennes and their allies, the army promptly hired him. He went to work at Fort Larned for Colonel William B. Hazen, the Indian superintendent for the southern plains, whose job it was to protect friendly or neutral Indians while identifying those who were potentially hostile.

It was while working for Hazen that Cody first came to the attention of Major General Phil Sheridan, the new commander of the Department of the Missouri. Cody was sent from Fort Larned to Fort Hays, a distance of sixty-five miles, to report to General Sheridan that some Kiowas and Comanches had joined the warring bands. This disturbing news forced Sheridan to change his troop dispositions. It was now vital that he get new orders through to Fort Dodge, but he could not find a scout willing to undertake the ride.

"This too being a particularly dangerous route—several couriers having been killed on it—it was impossible to get one of the various 'Petes,' 'Jacks,' or 'Jims' hanging around Hays City to take my communication," Sheridan later recalled. "Cody learning of the strait I was in, manfully came to the rescue, and proposed to make the trip to Dodge, though he had just finished his long and perilous ride from Larned."

Cody carried the dispatches to Fort Dodge, slept for a few hours, and then headed back to Fort Larned with more mail. At Larned, Colonel Hazen immediately recruited him to again make the dangerous ride to Fort Hays with the news that the hostile Kiowas had fled south of the Arkansas River. Cody covered almost three hundred miles in some fifty-eight hours of riding time, often moving parallel to the Indians he was carrying news about.

Sheridan, profoundly impressed by Cody's "exhibition of endurance and courage," personally appointed him chief of scouts for the 5th Cavalry. Although other scouts were hired only for individual expeditions, Cody continuously served as chief of scouts for the 5th from September 1868 until November 1872. He was soon to become the army's most famous scout.

"The mantle of Kit Carson fits more perfectly the shoulders of Cody than those of any other of the great frontiersman's successors," noted Sheridan's quartermaster Henry Inman.[11]

Sheridan, who along with Grant and Sherman had emerged as one of the three great Union generals of the Civil War, had taken command of the Department of the Missouri (consisting of the Indian Territory, the territories of Colorado and New Mexico, and the states of Missouri and Kansas) on September 5, 1867. The stubby little general did not cut a particularly impressive figure. With the hard days of campaigning behind him, the thirty-seven-year-old general had begun to put on weight, which exaggerated his barrel-shaped torso. Below heavy, arched eyebrows, Sheridan's dark Irish eyes sparked with the fire that had made him the victor at Missionary Ridge, the inspirational general whose presence had turned around a routed army at Cedar Creek, and the stern commander who had broken Lee's army at Five Forks. John Schuyler Crosby, his onetime military aide who became the territorial governor of Montana, remarked that "one could tell from his eyes in a moment whether he was serious, sad, or humorous, without noticing another feature of his face."[12]

Sheridan found his department in chaos following General Winfield Scott Hancock's bungled 1867 campaign against the Cheyenne and Sioux. Sheridan's protégé, Lieutenant Colonel Custer, had been made the scapegoat for the failed campaign, court-martialed, and suspended from rank and pay for one year. An enraged Sheridan turned over his Fort Leavenworth quarters to Custer and his wife, convinced that the court-martial was "an attempt by Hancock to cover up the failure of the Indian expedition." The general would recall Custer to duty before the full sentence was served.

Sheridan moved his headquarters to Fort Hays, then the terminus of the Kansas Pacific Railway. The protection of the railroad was one of the army's primary missions. Sheridan met with several leaders of the Cheyennes, Kiowas, and Arapahos camped near Fort Larned. He found them saucy. "Let your soldiers grow long hair, so that we can have some honor in killing them," declared Cheyenne chief Stone Calf. Sheridan replied that he could not, since his soldiers might get lice. He found the warriors utterly contemptuous of his soldiers and sullen over the failure of the government to deliver annuities promised in the 1867 Medicine Lodge Treaty. Oglala Sioux were also down from the north, bragging of how Red Cloud's warriors had wiped out a hundred soldiers at Fort Phil Kearny and closed the Bozeman Trail.

Sheridan's initiation to plains warfare was not going well. Since Indian raids picked up in early August 1868 within the limits of Sheridan's new command, 110 civilians had been killed; 13 women had been raped; several women and children had been captured; over a thousand head of stock had been stolen; farms, stage depots, and rolling stock had been destroyed; and unescorted travel had been halted on all the major roads. Bill Comstock, one of his best scouts, had been killed; George "Sandy" Forsyth, his longtime aide, had been critically wounded; and eighteen troopers had been killed and another forty-five wounded.[13]

With Custer suspended, Sheridan needed an aggressive cavalry commander for his projected campaign. He had requested that the 5th Cavalry be transferred from Reconstruction duty in the South so that most of the regiment was gathered at Fort Harker by late September. The field commander of the 5th, Major Eugene Asa Carr, an 1850 West Point graduate, had served with the Mounted Rifles in campaigns against plains tribes, and Sheridan considered him "always active, competent and brave." In the Civil War, Carr had risen to the rank of brevet major general and won the Congressional Medal of Honor for his actions at the Battle of Pea Ridge. Carr and his new chief of scouts, Cody, took an immediate liking to each other. They soon had several hot skirmishes with Tall Bull's Cheyenne Dog Soldiers. In November the 5th was ordered to Fort Lyon, Colorado, to prepare for a winter campaign against the Indians.[14]

Sheridan's plan called for converging columns of troops to move against those tribes that the government had deemed "hostile," which included all bands who had not reported to the agencies assigned to them by the Medicine Lodge Treaty. This included a large number of Cheyennes, Kiowas, Comanches, and Arapahos. Winter on the Great Plains, with its numbing cold and heavy snow, limited the Indians' mobility and forced them to seek sheltered camps along riverbanks. Their ponies would be weakened by cold and scarce fodder while their owners found warmth in their tepees, lulled into a false sense of security by the bitter weather, which would discourage attacks by the army. However, the railroad had made distance less of a consideration, for Sheridan could now more easily supply his troops in the field. He felt that his well-supplied troopers could withstand the weather just long enough to strike a decisive blow. A winter campaign was generally considered novel and daring, although Kit Carson had only recently engaged in similar campaigns at Canyon de Chelly and Adobe Walls.

Major Andrew Evans led one column east from Fort Bascom, New Mexico, consisting of six companies of the 3rd Cavalry and two companies of the 37th Infantry, some 563 men, on November 18, 1868. Major Carr, with Cody and seven companies of the 5th, marched southeast from Fort Lyon to the North Canadian, where he joined with Captain William H. Penrose, who commanded four companies of the 10th Cavalry (Buffalo Soldiers) and one company of the 7th Cavalry already in the field. This combined force, numbering 650 men, was to proceed toward the Antelope Hills. Sheridan hoped that these troops would drive the Indians eastward, where his main strike force under Custer, with eleven companies of the 7th, along with supporting infantry and several companies of Kansas volunteers, would run the Indians to ground.

Custer struck first, wiping out Black Kettle's Cheyenne village of fifty lodges on the Washita River on November 27, 1868, in a costly (two officers and nineteen enlisted men killed and three officers and eleven enlisted men wounded) and controversial victory. Black Kettle, a well-known "peace chief" of the Southern Cheyennes, had escaped Sand Creek only to die alongside his wife on the Washita. Custer had followed the hot trail of a war party to Black Kettle's village and in the camp was hard evidence of the hostile nature of some of the inhabitants: household goods and photographs taken in raids on Kansas settlers, mail captured from army couriers, and army mules. A nearby village held a white woman and her baby prisoner. They were soon killed by the Indians in revenge for Custer's attack. Custer's men had burned the village and slaughtered over eight hundred Indian horses and mules, dealing a devastating blow to Cheyenne mobility. Over a hundred Cheyennes, including some women and children, had been killed and another fifty-three women and children taken as prisoners. Custer was roundly criticized in the East by friends of the Indians for the Washita "massacre," which they compared to Sand Creek. Sherman and Sheridan defended Custer, who had, after all, taken fifty-three prisoners at Washita. Custer had personally intervened to stop his Osage scouts from killing women and children.

"I do not know exactly how far these humanitarians should be excused on account of their ignorance," Sheridan wrote in defense of his soldiers, "but surely it is the only excuse that gives a shadow of justification for aiding and abetting such horrid crimes."[15]

Major Evans had scouted along the Red River without finding any Indians while suffering greatly from freezing weather and supply problems. On Christmas Day, however, he discovered and attacked a sixty-lodge Nokoni Comanche village near Soldier Spring Creek. Not many Comanches were killed but their village was captured and burned. This impoverished the Indians so that most of them soon surrendered at Fort Bascom.

Carr was not as fortunate as Custer and Evans in terms of combat, but his column saved poor Penrose's men from starvation. Cody again proved his worth as a scout by discovering Penrose's trail in late December despite a brutal snowstorm. Cody found his old friend Hickok with Penrose. The Buffalo Soldiers had all been on quarter rations and had lost two hundred of their animals to weather and starvation.

Carr established a supply depot in what is now the Oklahoma Panhandle and prepared to strike south in search of Indians. His wagons were sent back to pick up more supplies. With five hundred men and a packtrain, Carr pressed south toward the south fork of the Canadian, not far from the site of Carson's battle at Adobe Walls. Cody and Hickok scouted for Carr, along with several New Mexico Hispanics who had been with Penrose. They found no Indians, but Cody and Hickok spied a supply train from Fort Bascom on its way to Evans. On inspection of the train, they discovered a good supply of beer, which they hijacked and took back to Carr's command. The New Mexicans were delighted to sell their brew to Carr's men and save themselves the trouble of finding Evans.

"It was sold to our boys in pint cups, and as the weather was very cold we warmed the beer by putting the ends of our picket-pins heated red-hot into the cups," Cody recalled. "The result was one of the biggest beer jollifications I ever had the misfortune to attend."[16]

Another "jollification" got Cody and Hickok in considerable trouble. Cody, appointed chief scout for the combined command of Carr and Penrose, discovered that considerable bad blood existed between Hickok and Penrose's New Mexican scouts. Cody's appointment over them did not sit well with the Hispanics, and threats were issued. This was not to be tolerated, and a brawl soon followed in which the New Mexicans were severely beaten. Carr was furious.

"It is not to be denied that Wild Bill and myself had been partaking too freely of 'tanglefoot' that evening," Cody confessed.[17]

Carr's anger soon mellowed to bemusement, but to reduce the tension he ordered Hickok east with dispatches for Sheridan and sent Cody out to hunt antelope to feed the command.

Carr's scout along the Canadian proved fruitless and in February 1869 the column returned to Fort Lyon. Once there, they received orders from Sheridan to proceed north to Fort McPherson, Nebraska, near the confluence of the North and South Platte in the Department of the Platte. Sheridan's successful campaign had forced most of the Natives onto their assigned reservations, but Tall Bull's Dog Soldiers, the most warlike of the Cheyennes, had moved north to join with the Sioux. They lingered in their favored haunts along the Republican River, a continuing threat to both the railroads and the settlers. On their way north, Cody discovered a large Cheyenne village on May 13 near the Republican at the mouth of Beaver Creek. Carr attacked and scattered the village in a running fight in which

Cody was wounded. As a result, the Indians began a series of raids in the spring of 1869 against the exposed settlers and even struck the railroad line. In these raids the Cheyennes carried off two white women as prisoners.

Sheridan's winter campaign had won him a promotion to lieutenant general and command of the Division of the Missouri, which included almost all of the West east of the Pacific coastal states. Sherman took Grant's place as a four-star general in command of the entire army. Grant had, of course, been elected president. Sheridan, determined to break the Dog Soldiers, now ordered Carr to prepare an expedition.

At Fort McPherson, Cody made the acquaintance of Major Frank North, commander of the celebrated Pawnee scouts, and his younger brother, Luther, who commanded one of the scout companies. North's scouts, four companies strong, had been raised in the winter of 1866 to guard construction crews of the Union Pacific Railroad. Now three companies of Pawnees, dressed in an amalgam of Native and soldier clothing, were to accompany eight companies of the 5th on the 1869 Republican River Expedition. Cody was to serve as chief of scouts.

Cody admired the Pawnees and he and North became fast friends. As the expedition was being organized, he came to admire a buckskin horse ridden by one of the scouts. North helped negotiate a trade for the horse, which was actually owned by the army. Cody had sold Brigham when he went to work for the army because he feared his cherished horse might be killed. Now "Buckskin Joe" became his favorite and he would ride him until the end of his scouting service in 1872. He then purchased the horse from the government and retired him to his Nebraska ranch.

Cody's fine new horse proved his mettle in the monthlong hunt for the Cheyennes to follow. At Summit Springs, on the South Platte in northeastern Colorado, Cody and several of the Pawnees discovered the Dog Soldier village on July 11, 1869. The village of eighty-four lodges had been heading north toward the Powder River country to join the Sioux. Carr in anticipation of battle had cut back his column to include only the men with fresh horses, some 244 troopers and 50 of the Pawnee scouts.

Cody urged Carr to circle around the Indians to the north to prevent them getting across the South Platte and escaping. By this stratagem Carr indeed managed to surprise the village by avoiding the Cheyenne rearguard scouts. He divided his command, sending Major William Royall with three companies to strike the pony herd while he led the rest of the men to a hill above the village to attack from the northwest. As Carr and Cody reined in atop the hill above the unsuspecting village, the major turned to his bugler and ordered, "Sound the charge!"

"I—I disremember it, sir," the nervous man replied.

Lieutenant Edward Hayes grabbed the bugle from the man's hands and sounded the charge himself. As the men all charged down the hill, Hayes tossed aside the bugle, pulled his pistol, and galloped into the village, blazing away. Carr's three companies took the village completely by surprise. As they swept through it, Royall and his men reappeared and joined in. The Pawnee scouts had scattered and now came into the village from every direction.

It was all over quickly, as the surprised warriors barely had time to seize their weapons before the 5th Cavalry troopers and Pawnee scouts rode them down. As the panicked Cheyennes fled in every direction, a bleeding white woman came running out of a tepee and directly toward the charging troopers. They yelled for her to lie down and the line of horsemen jumped over her. Frank North dismounted and comforted the hysterical captive. The other white captive was tomahawked to death by a Cheyenne woman whom Cody later identified as Tall Bull's wife.

Several warriors, led by a well-mounted chief with a magnificent war bonnet, returned to the village to harass the soldiers and screen the escape of their families. Cody was impressed by this brave chief who courted death as he encouraged his warriors. The scout was even more impressed with the man's horse.

"His horse was an extraordinary one, fleet as the wind, dashing here and there," he recalled, "and I determined to capture him if possible, but I was afraid to fire at the Indian for fear of killing the horse."

Cody circled around the skirmish line to a ravine not far from the chief's position. At about thirty yards Cody fired, dropping the chief. The horse galloped into the soldier line, where a sergeant recovered him soon after and turned him over to Cody, who rode him down into the village where the Cheyenne prisoners were gathered together.

"One of the squaws among the prisoners suddenly began crying in a pitiful and hysterical manner at the sight of this horse, and upon inquiry I found that she was Tall Bull's wife, the same squaw that had killed one of the white women and wounded the other," Cody wrote a few years later. "She stated that this was her husband's favorite war-horse, and that only a short time ago she had seen Tall Bull riding him. I gave her to understand that her liege lord had passed in his mortal chips and that it would be sometime before he would ride his favorite horse again, and I informed her that henceforth I should call the gallant steed 'Tall Bull,' in honor of her husband."[18]

The village was secured by late afternoon and the troopers busied themselves with counting the dead and burning the lodges, buffalo robes, and other property of the Cheyennes. Also captured were 274 horses and 144 mules, 56 rifles, 22 pistols, 40 sets of bows and arrows, and 50 pounds of gunpowder. They counted fifty-two dead on the field and seventeen women and children as prisoners. Over a hundred Cheyennes had fled and, although pursued by the Pawnees, made good their escape. There was considerable booty taken in the raids on the Saline and Solomon Rivers, including over $1,000. Most of this money was given to the liberated captive, Mrs. Maria Weichell, whose husband had been killed when she was captured. She later married the hospital steward at Fort Sedgwick who nursed her wounds. That evening they buried the other captive, Susanna Alderdice, in a solemn ceremony.

The death of Tall Bull, the most celebrated of the hostile chiefs, deflated the war fever among the Cheyennes, and almost all of the holdouts now reported into their agencies. This concluded Sheridan's campaign with its three major goals met: the Indians had been removed from the land between the Platte and the Arkansas and the security of the settlers and railroad lines had been secured; those bands involved in the Kansas raids had been punished; and the southern plains tribes had been settled on reservations as stipulated in the Medicine Lodge Treaty. The Kiowas, Comanches, and Cheyennes, increasingly frustrated by reservation life and horrified by the slaughter of the buffalo herds by the white hide hunters, would rise again in the Red River War of 1874–75. This resulted in their final subjugation.[19]

Although Indian raids, especially by the Sioux, continued sporadically after Summit Springs, it was relatively quiet around Fort McPherson. Cody now found time to supplement his army pay of $100 a month with money earned guiding hunting parties onto the plains. With the completion of the transcontinental line in 1869, it had become easy as well as fashionable for sportsmen to come out to hunt buffalo. Sheridan and other military officers recommended Cody's services as a guide. He guided Sir John Watts Garland in the winter of 1870 and Lord Adare, later the fourth Earl of Dunraven, the following year. Dunraven was quite taken with his two guides, Cody and John "Texas Jack" Omohundro, a former rebel soldier and Texas cowboy. He felt Texas Jack to be the very model of "a typical modern Anglo-Saxon" and described Cody as "dark, with quick searching eyes, aquiline nose, and delicately cut features, and he wore his hair falling in long ringlets over his shoulders, in true Western style."[20]

The most impressive of these celebrity hunts, hosted by General Sheridan, came to be known as the "Millionaire's Hunt." The general's staff had organized this junket as a way to curry favor with influential businessmen and journalists, including James Gordon Bennett of the *New York Herald*; Charles L. Wilson of the *Chicago Evening Journal*; Anson Stager of the Western Union Telegraph Company; financiers Lawrence Jerome and his brother Leonard Walter Jerome, future grandfather of Winston Churchill; and General Henry Davies, who had commanded a division of cavalry under Sheridan in the Shenandoah.[21]

Upon reaching Fort McPherson, they were greeted by Colonel William H. Emory, commander of the 5th, who had fought at San Pasqual with Kit Carson and who treated them to a review of the veterans of Summit Springs led by Major Carr.

Cody, eager to put on a good show for his benefactor Sheridan, rode down to the camp of the hunting party at five in the morning with considerable élan. "I rose fresh and eager for the trip," Cody noted, "and as it was a nobby and high-toned outfit which I was to accompany, I determined to put on a little style myself." Indeed he did. Charles Wilson wrote back to his newspaper that Cody was "the observed of all observers—splendid in form, the beau ideal of the rough rider." General Davies could not have agreed more:

> *The most striking feature of the whole was the figure of our friend Buffalo Bill, riding down from the Fort to our camp, mounted upon a snowy white horse. Dressed in a suit of light buckskin, trimmed along the seams with fringes of the same leather, his costume*

> *lighted by the crimson shirt worn under his open coat, a broad sombrero on his head, and carrying his rifle lightly in his hand, as his horse came toward us on an easy gallop, he realized to perfection the bold hunter and gallant sportsman of the plains.*[22]

Emory provided an escort of a hundred men for the hunters, accompanied by sixteen wagons—including one loaded with ice—and three army ambulances for passengers and baggage. Wall tents were provided as shelter for the guests, their servants, and the cooks. The energetic and able Lieutenant Hayes, quartermaster for the 5th, arranged it all. Each evening Cody entertained the hunting party with hunting and Indian-fighting tales, some of which were actually true.

In ten days the party covered some two hundred miles from Fort McPherson to Fort Hays, leaving a trail of champagne bottles and animal carcasses behind them. They killed over six hundred buffalo, along with a large number of elk, antelope, wild turkeys, and even a handful of prairie dogs. The only mishap on the journey was a serious injury to General Sheridan's greyhound, which he had just brought back from Europe, where he had been an observer of the Franco-Prussian War. The dog eventually recovered. More worrisome was the loss of Cody's prized Buckskin Joe, whom he had loaned to Lawrence Jerome. The hunter went out alone after a particularly large buffalo and incautiously dismounted to get a good shot and let go of the horse's bridle. Buckskin Joe, trained by Cody to run with the buffalo herd, promptly took off after the buffalo, leaving Jerome afoot. The embarrassed hunter tramped back to camp, while Buckskin Joe vanished. Fortunately he turned up back at Fort McPherson several days later.

On October 2, 1871, the hunting party bade Cody a warm farewell and boarded the train at Hays City for the East. Bennett extended an invitation for the young scout to visit New York City as his guest. Cody then returned with the 5th Cavalry escort to Fort McPherson and a reunion with Louisa and their two children.[23]

In November 1872 the 5th Cavalry was transferred to Arizona. Cody had planned to accompany the 5th, even though he knew nothing of Arizona or the Apaches, but he was ordered by Sheridan to remain at Fort McPherson. Delighted with the success of the Millionaire's Hunt, the general wanted Cody retained for the much larger buffalo hunt planned for the Russian grand duke Alexis. The third son of Czar Alexander II was then en route to America, sent on a goodwill tour to allow a romantic scandal to cool off. President Grant, anxious to get Alexis out of Washington, where a bitter feud existed between the secretary of state and the Russian ambassador, thought a western hunt the perfect diversion.

Dr. Morris Asch and Lieutenant Colonel George Forsyth of Sheridan's staff arrived at Fort McPherson in early January to meet with Cody and plan out the hunt. They selected a campsite on Red Willow Creek, some sixty miles from Fort McPherson between the Platte and Republican Rivers. To make certain that the twenty-one-year-old Romanoff got a real glimpse of frontier life, Sheridan asked Cody to secure a hundred Brule Sioux from Chief Spotted Tail's band to join in the hunt and put on some dances to entertain the party. This was a dangerous mission, for while Spotted Tail had long been friendly with the whites, many of his young warriors had fought Pahaska—or "Long Hair," as they called Cody—and might seek revenge.

It was bitterly cold as Cody snuck into the Brule village covered with a blanket as a disguise until he found Spotted Tail's lodge. He was greeted warmly by the chief. Cody explained that a "great chief from across the water" was coming to visit and that it was hoped by General Sheridan that the Brule would join in the big buffalo hunt. This pleased Spotted Tail and he agreed to call his people together in the morning to see who might agree to go. That night Cody remained under the protection of the chief's lodge.

The next morning all gathered to hear the proposition. As Cody was introduced he noticed that several of the warriors looked "daggers at me . . . as if they wished to raise my hair then and there." Spotted Tail recruited quite a large contingent for the hunt and then bade Cody farewell, assuring him that none of the disgruntled warriors would be allowed to follow him.[24]

Cody hurried back to the fort, where preparations were well underway to provide "Camp Alexis" on Red Willow Creek with all the luxuries necessary for royalty. Quartermaster Hayes had also been retained to organize this supply train. On January 12, 1872, a special train with the grand duke's entourage arrived at the North Platte depot. Cody was there, along with a company of the 2nd Cavalry as escort, a half dozen ambulances, and extra saddle horses for the royal party.

"General Sheridan at once introduced me to the Grand Duke as Buffalo Bill," Cody noted, "and said that I was to take charge of him and show him how to kill buffalo."[25]

To make certain that Alexis might hobnob with a famous cavalryman and Indian fighter, Sheridan had recalled Lieutenant Colonel Custer from Reconstruction duty in Kentucky. Custer, who was himself a noted sportsman, was delighted with the opportunity. Sheridan had put together quite the star-studded cast for his frontier show in the still very wild West. No doubt several of Spotted Tail's Brule warriors would be on hand to greet Custer at the Little Big Horn four years later.

"General Custer appeared in his well-known frontier buckskin hunting costume," noted a reporter for the *New York Herald*, "and if instead of the comical sealskin hat he wore he had only had feathers fastened in his flowing hair, he would have passed at a distance for a great Indian Chief. Buffalo Bill's dress was somewhat similar to Custer's." The *Herald* headline for January 14, 1872, read: "The Grand Duke's Hunt—General Sheridan and Buffalo Bill Lead the Way."[26]

The hunting party hurried south to Red Willow Creek, where they were greeted by Spotted Tail and his people. That evening the Brule put on a grand war dance, much to the delight of the grand duke. Cody, well satisfied with the camp and Indian performers, noticed that Custer "carried on a mild flirtation with one of Spotted Tail's daughters, who had accompanied her father thither, and it was noticed also that the Duke Alexis paid considerable attention to another handsome red-skin maiden."[27]

The next morning they were off at nine in search of buffalo. They had not gone far when a sizable herd was spotted and Cody guided the hunters to a good spot from which they could charge down upon them. He had given Alexis Buckskin Joe to ride—and he was soon in among the herd but, firing wildly with his pistol, missed his mark. Anxious to make certain that the Duke got his kill, Cody galloped up and handed him his rifle Lucretia Borgia. He told him to move in close to a nearby bull and, giving Buckskin Joe a swat on his rump, sent them off into the milling animals.

"Now is your time!" Cody shouted as Alexis fired into the big buffalo and brought him down. Mission accomplished. The duke's entourage hurried up to join him and they all began jabbering in Russian, much to Cody's amazement. Sheridan came to join them with a basket of champagne, and corks began to fly.

"We gave him three cheers," Cody reported. "I was in hopes that he would kill five or six more buffaloes before we reached camp, especially if a basket of champagne was to be opened every time he dropped one."[28]

After two more days of hunting, in which Cody regaled the hunting party with tall tales around the evening campfire, the party decamped for North Platte and the railroad. The grand duke and Sheridan rode in a double-seated open carriage—Cody called it an "Irish dogcart"—drawn by four spirited horses, and the general asked Cody to drive.

"Shake 'em up a little, Bill, and give us some old-time stage-driving," the general shouted.

Cody cracked the whip and the horses sped on across the prairie, bouncing along at a rapid gait until they reached a relay station. The general and his royal companion had to hold on for dear life, and once they finally halted, the grand duke announced that he had had enough excitement for one day.

Cody left the party at North Platte. Alexis, quite taken with the picturesque plainsman, gifted him several pieces of valuable jewelry before the royal party departed for more hunting in Colorado.

Sheridan provided his young friend with some sage advice that proved to be far more valuable. Recalling James Gordon Bennett's invitation to visit New York City, the general told Cody that he would "never have a better opportunity to accept that invitation than now." He promised to secure Cody a thirty-day leave of absence with pay and a railroad pass to New York.

Not only had Buffalo Bill, Sheridan, and Spotted Tail invented the Wild West show on the Nebraska prairie that January, "Little Phil" had now set Cody on the greasepaint trail to fame and fortune.

26

WARBONNET CREEK

Custer was dead. The news reached Colonel Wesley Merritt's 5th Cavalry camp at Sage Creek, Wyoming Territory, on July 7, 1876. It had taken a full twelve days for the dispatch to reach a column located perilously close to the scene of the disaster. Chief of Scouts Buffalo Bill Cody brought the Fort Laramie courier to the colonel's tent at midmorning. Everyone was stunned. Custer and every man of five companies of the 7th Cavalry dead on the Little Big Horn—it seemed impossible to believe. But it was true.

Lieutenant Charles King, acting adjutant of the 5th, never forgot that morning: "A party of junior officers were returning from a refreshing bath in a deep pool in the stream, when Buffalo Bill came hurriedly towards them from the general's tent. His handsome face wore a look of deep trouble, and he brought us to a halt in stunned, awe-stricken silence with the announcement, 'Custer and five companies of the Seventh wiped out of existence.'" King sensed that Cody had taken the news hard. "Perhaps no man felt it more than Cody, who had ridden with Custer on many a run for buffalo," he recalled.

Cody had only recently departed his theatrical troupe to rejoin the 5th Cavalry on the northern plains. Reunited with his old friends on June 10, 1876, he was immediately reappointed chief of scouts by Lieutenant Colonel Eugene A. Carr. Enlisted men as well as officers were delighted to have their old scout back, for when Cody galloped into the camp of the 5th Cavalry, a cry of "Here's Buffalo Bill" went out, followed by three rousing cheers.[1]

"There is very little change in his appearance since I saw him last in '69, except that he looks a little worn, probably caused by his vocation in the

East not agreeing with him," noted one enlisted man in a newspaper interview. "All the old boys in the regiment upon seeing General Carr and Cody together, exchanged confidences, and expressed themselves to the effect that with such a leader and scout they could get away with all the Sitting Bulls and Crazy Horses in the Sioux tribe."[2]

The regiment, transferred back north from service against the Arizona Apaches, was serving as part of General George Crook's column moving north from Forts Laramie and Fetterman against the Sioux bands following Sitting Bull, Crazy Horse, Gall, and other non-reservation leaders in defiance of the government's order to report to their reservation. The Grant administration, determined to force the reluctant Sioux to sell the gold-laden Black Hills, blamed the failure to strike a deal on Sitting Bull.

The great Hunkpapa Lakota chief who caused the United States government so much grief was born somewhere on the Missouri River in the year 1831. His father, the elder Sitting Bull (Tatanka-Iyotanka, or Buffalo Bull Sitting on Its Haunches), was a wealthy leader of his people who owned many horses. He gave his son the early name of Jumping Badger, which would be changed when he came of age, although the people nicknamed him Slow because he was so stubborn. The Hunkpapa were a small tribe of the western Sioux (as the whites and their Indian enemies called them), or Lakota, as they called themselves. The other six western Lakota tribes were the Oglala, Brule, Miniconjou, Two Kettle, Sans Arc, and Sihasapa. They were loosely confederated, united mostly by culture and language.

The Lakota were relative newcomers to the Great Plains, having been driven westward by better-armed midwestern tribes. Obtaining horses and then eventually guns, the fugitives quickly overspread the buffalo range—first from the Upper Missouri to the Bighorn Mountains to the west, and north into Canada and south to the Platte and Republican Rivers. They pushed aside rival tribes and by the 1800s claimed a vast empire rich in game of every sort, most notably the buffalo, which was central to both their economic and cultural well-being. They prospered, growing ever more powerful, soon numbering well over twenty thousand people.

Jumping Badger displayed his warrior prowess as a teenager battling the Crow, Assiniboine, and Flathead enemies of his people. These war honors led his father to confer his own name on him so that Jumping Badger now became Sitting Bull. This was a great honor. More honors were to come as the young warrior earned membership in the Strong Heart Society, was elevated to war chief, and in 1857 became head chief of the Hunkpapa. Sitting Bull was only twenty-six.

It was at this time that the whites began to pass through the country of the Lakota in ever-increasing numbers. The Hunkpapa had welcomed early white fur traders and carried on a lucrative trade in buffalo robes with them. Because they lived to the north, they were at first not disturbed too much by the wagon trains and new soldier forts. They took no part in the Fort Laramie Treaty of 1851, although many other tribal leaders took the white man's presents and signed their mark. By this the Sioux, along with Cheyennes, Arapahos, Shoshones, Crows, and other tribes, agreed to cease warfare with each other and to allow the United States to build roads and forts in their country. In return they were to receive an annuity of $50,000 for fifteen years—a rather paltry sum to be divided among so many tribes. The Hunkpapas were surprised to learn that they were bound by this treaty they had not signed, and the issue caused increasing factionalism among the various Sioux tribes.[3]

The Fort Laramie Treaty brought no peace to the prairie. In 1854 a young lieutenant from Fort Laramie blundered into a confrontation with Brule chief Conquering Bear over a stolen cow. He killed Conquering Bear and paid for his folly with his life and the lives of all thirty of his soldiers. In response, the government sent a large force of soldiers up the Missouri to battle the Sioux. Colonel William S. Harney, whom the Indians named "Mad Bear," was in command. He wiped out the Brule village of Little Thunder on Blue Water Creek and marched across the land of the Lakota. Then in March 1856 he summoned the Sioux chiefs to Fort Pierre, where he demanded the surrender of all Indians who had murdered whites and the return of all stolen property. Once this was done, annuities might begin again. He then arrogantly appointed a head chief to each band; for the Hunkpapa that was Bear's Rib. He would later be killed for his appeasement of the whites. All this was unenforceable, but to Sitting Bull, who attended, it was also infuriating. He concluded that his people must avoid these crazy white people.[4]

That proved impossible. In 1862 the Santee Sioux in Minnesota rose in rebellion, killing hundreds of white settlers before they were defeated by the soldiers. Many of the survivors fled westward to the land of the Hunkpapa. To the west, in Montana, gold had been discovered and mining towns sprang up seemingly everywhere. Steamboats brought miners west, but most came up the Bozeman Trail from Fort Laramie to the Montana mines through the heart of Sioux country. The Oglala leader Red Cloud made war on these trespassers, besieged the soldiers in their forts, and closed the trail. In 1868 the government called yet another great treaty council at Fort Laramie and made peace with Red Cloud. The Bozeman Trail forts were to be abandoned and in exchange the Sioux would agree to a reservation that included all of Dakota west of the Missouri River. Those who did not wish to live near the reservation agencies to receive their annuities might continue to hunt in an unceded "Indian Territory" west to the Bighorn Mountains so long as the buffalo remained.

Sitting Bull refused to sign the treaty. "You are fools to make yourselves slaves to a piece of fat bacon, some hard tack, and a little sugar and coffee," he warned those who signed.[5]

The celebrated treaty was soon broken. By 1873, as the Northern Pacific Railway pushed westward across present North Dakota, the army had the Sioux reservation ringed in by forts. Sheridan, who wanted an additional post in the Black Hills, ordered Custer and the 7th out from Fort Abraham Lincoln (across the river from Bismarck, North Dakota, then the end of track for the railroad) on a grand reconnaissance of the mysterious Black Hills. The trail that Custer's thousand men pressed into the hard Dakota sod that summer came to be known by the Sioux as the Thieves' Road. There had long been rumors of gold in the Black Hills, and the financial panic of 1873 only heightened interest. While construction of a fort was allowed under the terms of the 1868 treaty, most observers, both Indian and white, viewed Custer's reconnaissance as a grand prospecting expedition. Custer took some miners along with him as well as a gaggle of newspaper reporters. They soon discovered gold "from the grass roots down." Parties of prospectors were soon organizing to invade the Black Hills.[6]

The Paha Sapa (Hills That Are Black) were both sacred and utilitarian to the Sioux. Here resided rich hunting grounds, beautiful valleys for winter camps, and great forests of lodgepole pines for tepee poles. Sitting Bull was not receptive when a Sioux delegation from the Red Cloud Agency came north to request his attendance at a meeting at the agency in September 1875 to talk of selling the Black Hills. Frank Grouard, a half-white

Polynesian whose Mormon father had sent him to Utah, had been captured by the Sioux and eventually adopted by Sitting Bull. He now acted as an intermediary for the whites and reported back to them Sitting Bull's response:

> *He said he would not sell his land. He said he had never been to an agency and was not going in. He was no agency Indian. He told me to go out and tell the white men at Red Cloud that he declared open war and would fight them wherever he met them from that time on.*[7]

The Allison Commission, sent west under Iowa senator William B. Allison to purchase the Black Hills, met with the agency chiefs at Red Cloud that September and received a chilly reception. Several hundred of Sitting Bull's people came south to observe as well as intimidate. On September 23, 1875, Little Big Man, a close friend to the young Oglala war leader Crazy Horse, led several painted warriors in a mock charge on the white delegation. Little Big Man abruptly reined in his pony before the terrified white officials to announce that he had been sent by Sitting Bull to stop this talk of selling the sacred Black Hills. He would shoot anyone who dared to sign such an agreement.[8]

The commissioners scampered back to Washington to report their mission a failure. They urged the government to fix a price on the Black Hills and force the Sioux to accept it. Thousands of miners had already overrun the Black Hills even though the Grant administration had at first assigned troops to protect the hills. The administration now used depredations by the Sioux on the white invaders, as well as raids on the Crow Indians in Montana, to justify an order to have all the northern Sioux bands depart the unceded hunting grounds and report to their respective agencies. In November the secretary of the interior sent instructions to the various Indian agents "to notify Sitting Bull's band, and other wild and lawless bands of Sioux Indians," to report to their agencies before January 31, 1876, or be forced there by the army. Sheridan, who rightly felt that this order would "be regarded as a good joke by the Indians," had already started to organize his campaign.[9]

Not only had Sitting Bull emerged as a great political leader, but he was also a visionary *wichasha wakan*, a holy man. He had dreams that might well foretell the future. One such dream foreshadowed his death at the hands of his own people. He often underwent the Sun Dance, in which skewers pierced both his chest and back as he danced around a pole, pulling on ropes attached to the skewers in order to break free, all the while praying to Wakan Tanka—the Great Mystery—for a vision.

"He was strong in religion—Indian religion," recalled the Cheyenne Wooden Leg. "He made medicine many times. He prayed and fasted and whipped his flesh into submission to the will of the Great Medicine."[10]

In early June 1876 he again performed the Sun Dance. As he sat before the pole, fifty pieces of flesh were gouged from his arms and legs. As blood streamed down his body, he danced around the pole, gazing at the sun until he fainted. Then, when he awoke, he told the people of his vision: of soldiers falling upside down into their camp. All the soldiers were to die.

Sheridan hoped a winter campaign might drive the Sioux in, but the brutal weather frustrated his plan. One column, moving north from Fort Fetterman, struck a Cheyenne and Oglala village on the Powder River on March 17, 1876, but was repulsed, which ended the winter campaign. Sheridan now reluctantly planned a summer campaign. From the west came Colonel John Gibbon's command out of Fort Ellis with six companies of infantry, four companies of the 2nd Cavalry, and a contingent of Crow scouts. From the east, General Alfred Terry marched from Fort Abraham Lincoln with Custer's 7th Cavalry as his strike force. General George Crook moved north from Fort Fetterman with fifteen companies of cavalry and five of infantry along with over two hundred Crow and Shoshone auxiliaries. Sheridan also ordered the eight available companies of the 5th Cavalry to Fort Laramie to scout between the columns of Crook and Terry. It was assumed that the troops sent into the field might, at most, confront five hundred warriors. That estimate proved wildly inaccurate, for the Indian Bureau agents had lied to the army about the census numbers at their agencies. The soldiers would face not hundreds but thousands of warriors.

Sheridan decided to make a hurried inspection of the agencies himself. On June 14 he reached Fort Laramie, where he was delighted to find Cody. He enlisted his favorite scout to accompany him to the Sioux agencies. With an escort of 5th Cavalry troopers, Sheridan's party reached Camp Robinson the next morning. Sheridan and Cody found it quiet at the White River agencies, which confirmed the general's suspicion that the reports of Indians leaving for the Powder River country were exaggerated.

Convinced that he had nothing to worry about on the White River, Sheridan ordered the 5th north to the Powder River Trail. This trail led from the Red Cloud Agency to the Powder and Yellowstone Rivers, where Sitting Bull's people were assumed to be. The 5th was charged with blocking any reinforcement from reaching the hostiles from the Nebraska agencies of Red Cloud and Spotted Tail. Sheridan also secured the promotion of Wesley Merritt, another of his Civil War protégés, to command the 5th in the upcoming campaign. This last-minute change was a hard blow to Carr, who now was reduced to second-in-command. Sheridan bade Cody—who was disappointed with the change of commanders, although he came to admire the able Merritt—a warm farewell and headed back to his Chicago headquarters. Sheridan hoped that this scout by the 5th might "stir things up and prove advantageous in the settlement of the Indian question."[11]

No sooner had Sheridan settled back behind his Chicago desk than he learned that affairs had indeed been stirred up, but hardly as he had hoped. Crazy Horse checked Crook on Rosebud Creek on June 17, 1876. Crook claimed victory, holding the field, but still fell back to Goose Creek to tend his wounded, reorganize, and await reinforcements. Crook was still hunkered down, licking his wounds, when Custer's 7th, ignorant of his fate, met the same Sioux several miles to the north on Montana's Little Big Horn River on June 25. Sheridan's plan to envelop the Indians had spectacularly failed.

Crook, usually the coolest, most levelheaded of officers, was totally unnerved by the Battle of the Rosebud. Inactive at Goose Creek, at the eastern edge of Wyoming's Big Horn Mountains, Crook now demanded Merritt's 5th Cavalry before he dared advance north against the Sioux. Merritt, however, had received intelligence that hundreds of Cheyennes had left the Nebraska agencies to join Sitting Bull in Montana. Disregarding his orders to reinforce Crook, he instead moved north to block the Powder River Trail. The troops marched a punishing eighty-five miles in thirty-one hours to reach Warbonnet Creek (also called Hat Creek) on the great Indian trail from the agencies to the Powder River country. Cody, astride a strawberry roan some sixteen hands high, was ever in the lead. The exhausted command bedded down late on July 16, 1876. There, among the troopers of the 5th Cavalry, Buffalo Bill was truly in his element. Little did he realize how the next morning's events would forever change his life, for Buffalo Bill

Cody the celebrated actor was about to again become Buffalo Bill Cody the famed scout in a remarkable moment in time when myth and reality were to meld into one at a place called Warbonnet Creek.

SINCE SUMMIT SPRINGS, CODY HAD ADDED TO HIS NAtional fame not only by acting as a guide to celebrity hunting parties but also by continued heroics in action with the Indians. On April 26, 1872, near the south fork of Nebraska's Loup River, Cody led a company of the 3rd Cavalry in a running battle with Indian raiders, which won him the Medal of Honor on May 22, 1872. Captain Charles Meinhold, who had once served with Carson in the New Mexico Volunteers, in the letter of commendation describing the engagement with the Indians, noted that "Mr. William Cody's reputation for bravery and skill as a guide is so well established that I need not say anything else but that he acted in his usual manner." Meinhold's words were typical of the high regard in which frontier soldiers held Cody. William Tecumseh Sherman, Phil Sheridan, William Emory, Eugene Carr, Wesley Merritt, Charles King, Anson Mills, and other army officers lavishly praised Cody both before and after he became nationally famous. Cody's frontier exploits, although later wildly exaggerated by press agents and show business hype, were authentic.[12]

In one twelve-month period, for example, from October 1868 to October 1869, Cody, as chief of scouts for the 5th Cavalry, participated in seven expeditions against the Indians, engaging in nine fights. Few soldiers experienced that much action in a decade of service. All of Cody's frontier exploits, including sixteen Indian battles, occurred before his thirty-second birthday, for after 1876 he devoted his time exclusively to show business.

The grand maestro of Cody's rise to international fame and show business glory was Ned Buntline, an obscure writer of limited talent but unflagging imagination. His real name was Edward Zane Carroll Judson, and he was born in New York in 1823. This stumpy, plump little man was a master of the dime novel, claiming to have written half a dozen of them in one week. He went through several fortunes and six wives, some of whom he was married to simultaneously. Writing and women were Ned's great passions, and he pursued both with a vengeance. He was widely published, even writing for journals as reputable as the *Knickerbocker.*

In his youth he had gone to sea, eventually serving as a midshipman in the "Mosquito Squadron" during the Seminole War in Florida. From this service he acquired his pen name, for a buntline is the naval word for a rope at the bottom of a square sail. This nautical pseudonym was the only thing he shared with another writer of the era: Mark Twain.

Buntline's early career as a writer, which showed some promise, secured him a position as editor of the struggling *Western Literary Journal* in Nashville. His job came to a premature end in 1846 after a romantic dalliance with a lady who was burdened with a jealous husband. A duel followed the unfortunate exposure of the affair. Ned was an excellent shot, a useful talent for an editor, and promptly killed the aggrieved husband. Taken into custody, Ned was hauled from the jail by a mob, dragged to the town square, and strung up. Fortunately, the mob was an impatient bunch, as they left their victim dangling while they retired to a nearby saloon to celebrate. Ned's friends cut him down and whisked him away to safer climes.

Two years later he established a newspaper, *Ned Buntline's Own*, which published his fiction as well as editorials against liquor, gambling, and prostitution. The editor, of course, was acquainted with all these vices. His strongest diatribes were leveled against the Irish and German immigrants then reaching America's shores, and he became quite an advocate of the nativist Know-Nothing Party.

During the Civil War, Ned served in a New York volunteer regiment for two years, briefly attaining the rank of sergeant. He later claimed to have been a colonel. After the war Buntline continued writing, often supplementing his income with temperance lectures. On July 24, 1869, he was scheduled to rail against the evils of strong drink at Fort McPherson. Before the lecture, however, he learned that Major William H. Brown was to lead a detachment of the 5th Cavalry out after an Indian raiding party. Always in search of a good story, Buntline volunteered to accompany the troops. Major Brown introduced the celebrated writer to the 5th Cavalry's chief of scouts. They found no Indians along the Platte, but Buntline discovered Cody to be a treasure trove of frontier lore. When the scouting party ended at Fort Sedgwick, Buntline headed east, promising to keep in touch.

On December 23, 1869, the *New York Weekly* carried the first installment of Buntline's "Buffalo Bill, the King of Border Men." The tabloid story was a fictional reworking of the already well-published Civil War exploits of Cody's friend Wild Bill Hickok. Nevertheless, Buntline's story initiated the legend of Buffalo Bill—a frontier Hercules to match Boone, Crockett, and Carson.[13]

Back at Fort McPherson, the real Buffalo Bill was highly flattered by the tale, even if none of it was true. When his son was born on November 26, 1870, he proposed to name him after Buntline. Cooler heads prevailed, and the lad was instead named Kit Carson Cody.

By February of 1872, not long after the grand duke's hunt, Cody had worked up his courage to head east. Anson Stager provided railroad passes for the trip, while Bennett sent $500 to cover expenses. He first stopped in Chicago, still recovering from the great fire, and stayed with General Sheridan and his brother Michael in their two-story bachelor home at 708 Michigan Avenue. Before venturing forth into society, Cody was taken by Mike Sheridan to Marshall Field's and decked out in appropriate evening wear. Cody did not fancy the top hat that went with his new white tie and tails and so took to sporting his Stetson. In this manner he sallied forth in company with the Sheridan brothers and other alumni from the September hunt.

Sheridan took his bashful scout to a swank ball in nearby Riverside, where Cody got his first taste of high society. "On this occasion I became so embarrassed that it was more difficult for me to face the throng of beautiful ladies, than it would have been to confront a hundred hostile Indians," he declared. "This was my first trip to the East, and I had not yet become accustomed to being stared at."[14]

After a brief sojourn in Chicago, Cody boarded a train for New York City, stopping en route to play the tourist at Niagara Falls. John G. Heckscher, an alumnus of the "Millionaire's Hunt," met him at the railroad station and took him to the Union Club for a welcoming dinner hosted by James Gordon Bennett and Leonard Jerome. This new "Lion of the West" was an immediate success with the swells of New York's upper crust.

Cody was anxious to reunite with his literary benefactor and, with Heckscher as guide, started out through the dark canyons of the city. They found Buntline at the Brevoort Place Hotel, where he was living with his fourth wife (although inconveniently not yet divorced from his third spouse).

Ned, needless to say, did not associate with the Union Club crowd, but he was delighted to see Cody and Heckscher. He insisted that Cody remain at the Brevoort as his guest. This caused Cody quite a quandary, which he solved by agreeing to divide his time between the Brevoort and the Union Club, much to the displeasure of his host Bennett.

"The next few days . . . everything being new and startling, convinc[ed] me that as yet I had seen but a small portion of the world," Cody mused. There were more dinners, including a particularly grand affair at August Belmont's mansion, and a sortie with Bennett to the famous Liederkranz masked ball, where Cody dressed in his buckskins, to the delight of the other Academy of Music guests.

"To me it was a novel and entertaining sight," he declared, "and in many respects reminded me greatly of an Indian war-dance."

Bennett's *New York Herald* reported that Buffalo Bill had "come from the land of the buffalo and red skin to see for himself the difference between an Indian powwow and a genuine masquerade."[15]

The high point of Cody's visit came on February 20, 1872, when he accompanied Buntline to the Bowery Theater—a working-class establishment that was a considerable step down from the Academy of Music—for the opening night of a revival of Fred G. Maeder's 1872 melodrama *Buffalo Bill, the King of Border Men*, based on Buntline's *New York Weekly* stories. Frontier plays were then quite popular thanks to the success of Frank Murdoch and Frank Mayo's play *Davy Crockett; or, Be Sure You're Right, Then Go Ahead*, which premiered in 1872 and ran continuously for twenty-four years in the United States and England. The 1896 death of Mayo, who played Davy, stopped its incredible run. J. B. Studley had the title role of Buffalo Bill in Maeder's play, and—in a moment reminiscent of Crockett's 1833 encounter with Hackett in *The Lion of the West*—the actor introduced the real Buffalo Bill to the audience. The crowd thunderously demanded his appearance on the stage. Timid and embarrassed, Cody went before the footlights for the first time and mumbled a few inaudible words of thanks.

"Bowing to the audience, I beat a hasty retreat into one of the cañons of the stage," recalled Cody. "I never felt more relieved in my life than when I got out of the view of that immense crowd."

He was amazed when the theater manager offered him $500 a week to replace Studley as Buffalo Bill. At first he thought the man was joking but soon realized that he was in earnest. Cody thanked him but quickly declined since he, as he put it, "didn't have the requisite cheek to undertake a thing of that sort."[16]

Sheridan visited New York a few days later and inquired how his young friend was faring. Cody, warming to his celebrity status, informed the general that he had "struck the best camp" he had ever seen. He requested an extension of his leave, which Sheridan gladly granted, but with a warning that Cody would soon be needed for a campaign once the 3rd Cavalry reached Fort McPherson from Arizona.

When Cody returned west and met his new commanding officer, Colonel Joseph J. Reynolds of the 3rd Cavalry, he was wearing a formal evening suit and a top hat. The East had taken ahold of Buffalo Bill and he was a changed man. Reynolds need not have worried too much, for Cody was soon back in his element. His skills as a scout had not been dulled by the trip east, as he soon proved in a sharp engagement with a Sioux raiding party on the south fork of Nebraska's Loup River in May. It was for this engagement that he received the Medal of Honor.

Now, Ned Buntline was not a man to allow opportunity to slip away. He commenced scribbling a new novel, *Buffalo Bill's Best Shot; or, the Heart of Spotted Tail*, which began its serial run in the *New York Weekly* on March 25, 1872, quickly followed in July by *Buffalo Bill's Last Victory; or, Dove Eye, the Lodge Queen*. At the same time Ned barraged Cody with letters promising fame and fortune if he would come east and portray himself on the stage.

Cody finally relented and recruited Texas Jack Omohundro to accompany him to Chicago and join in this novel enterprise. Louisa Cody was hardly optimistic about her husband's future on the boards. She rightly quipped that neither of the two scouts "ever had seen more than a dozen plays in their lives. They had no idea of how to make an entrance or an exit, they did not know a cue from a footlight, and they believed that plays just happened."[17]

The scouts turned actors were met by Buntline in Chicago on December 12. To their amazement they found that Buntline had no script, even though the play was to open at Nixon's Amphitheatre on December 18. Retreating to his hotel room, Buntline penned *The Scouts of the Prairie* in four hours. An unimpressed *Chicago Tribune* theater critic later asked why it had taken Ned so long.

Buntline hired ten aspiring thespians off the Chicago streets to portray Indians in his little drama and acquired the services of a lovely Italian actress, Giuseppina Morlacchi, to play the Indian heroine. Unlike the other members of the cast, Morlacchi actually had stage experience; she was well-known for introducing the cancan to the United States in 1867.

A crowd estimated at 2,500 crowded into Nixon's Amphitheatre for opening night. The play had no discernible plot, which was fine, since Cody forgot all his lines anyway. It did not matter, for the scouts were handsome, Miss Morlacchi fetching as an Italian-accented Indian maiden, and the action nonstop.

The Scouts of the Prairie was a grand success. Even the theater critics had to admit that it might not be art, but it was certainly entertainment of a unique sort. One discerning critic pointed out that the real attraction of the play was in seeing the two real-life Western scouts on the stage "not only as the heroes of the play, but as celebrities whose fame long ante-dates their appearance before the footlights."

"On the whole it is not probable that Chicago will ever look upon the like again," declared the *Chicago Times*. "Such a combination of incongruous drama, execrable acting, renowned performers, mixed audience, intolerable stench, scalping, blood and thunder, is not likely to be vouchsafed to a city a second time—even Chicago."[18]

The Western had been born, with Ned Buntline and Buffalo Bill acting as able midwives, and popular, mass-market entertainment was never to be the same again. The play toured Eastern cities, greeted by enthusiastic audiences, stunned theater critics, and overflowing box office tills. By the time the tour ended in June 1873, Cody was fully committed to a stage career. He no longer had need of Buntline, and they parted company forever that month.

For the 1873–1874 theatrical season, Cody enlisted the pen of Fred G. Maeder to create a new drama for the Buffalo Bill Combination, as his gypsy troupe was now called. *The Scouts of the Plains* opened at Williamsport, Pennsylvania, on September 8. Buffalo Bill and Texas Jack played themselves, of course, with Morlacchi portraying another Indian maiden. Co-starring was another authentic Western hero, Cody's old friend Wild Bill Hickok. By this time Wild Bill had added to his laurels as scout and Indian fighter by serving as marshal in Hays City and Abilene. But the life of a thespian did not suit Hickok. All of Cody's efforts to imbue his friend with a proper respect for show business failed, and after one particularly heated exchange Hickok departed in a huff. They met again only once, in Sage Creek, Wyoming, in July 1876, when Cody was scouting for the 5th Cavalry and Hickok was heading for the Black Hills boomtown of Deadwood. There he had a rendezvous with the "Dead Man's Hand" and an assassin's bullet while playing poker in Saloon No. 10.[19]

For a decade, from 1873 until he left the boards to organize his Wild West show in 1883, Cody toured in various frontier dramas. In every play he starred as Buffalo Bill, with each drama supposedly based on authentic adventures from his own past. It was this connection between history and drama that provided a unique electricity to Cody's stage presence and made his blood-and-thunder plays so popular with the public.

Cody's 1876 tour was a huge success, but it was interrupted in April 1876 in Springfield, Massachusetts, by a telegram informing him that five-year-old Kit was desperately ill with scarlet fever. Returning to his home in Rochester, New York, he was able to hold his son one final time: "I found my little boy unable to speak but he seemed to recognize me and putting his little arms around my neck he tried to kiss me." Kit soon after died in his father's arms.

"My only darling boy is dead. He was too good for this world," Cody wrote Texas Jack. "We loved him too dearly—he could not stay. And now his place is vacant and can never be filled." The loss further strained Cody's increasingly tumultuous marriage to Louisa.[20]

All but broken by his loss, Cody determined to answer the call of Sheridan, Carr, and other army officers to return to the West for what all assumed would be the last great Indian war. After a final show in Wilmington, Delaware, on June 3, Cody and Texas Jack split up the troupe and Buffalo Bill headed west to Cheyenne, Wyoming. Texas Jack, who had married Morlacchi, continued on the stage with some success until his untimely death from pneumonia in Leadville, Colorado, on June 28, 1880, at age thirty-four.

BEFORE DAWN ON JULY 17, 1876, MERRITT ORDERED CODY out to scout Dull Knife's advancing Cheyennes. Oddly, Cody dressed that morning in one of the stage costumes he had brought with him from the East. It was a Mexican vaquero outfit with pants of black velvet, trimmed in scarlet and flared at the bottom, a wide leather belt with a huge solid-silver buckle, a red silk shirt, topped with a broad-brimmed beaver sombrero. Buffalo Bill had certainly dressed for his role that day. He quickly located the Cheyenne village but returned to find the cavalry camp on full alert, as Cheyenne scouts had been spotted nearby. Cody reported to Merritt atop a slight conical hill overlooking the valley formed by Warbonnet Creek.

In the distance a party of Cheyenne scouts formed directly across the little valley from the 5th Cavalry. Merritt ordered Carr to silently saddle up the regiment and prepare to engage the Cheyennes. Cody instantly noticed that the Indians were actually watching a distant supply train laboring to join Merritt's command. Two dispatch riders from the wagon train were galloping toward the cavalry camp and they had caught the attention of the Cheyennes. A party of warriors rushed forth to intercept them.

Cody promptly asked Merritt for permission to engage the Cheyennes with his scouts. The colonel, as he hurried away to rejoin the regiment, gave the go-ahead. Lieutenant Charles King was to watch from the hill and send in the scouts just before the Cheyennes could intercept the two messengers.

"Now, lads, in with you!" cried King just in the nick of time.

Cody's men charged the surprised warriors, turning the tables on their ambush and scattering them with a rifle volley. As Cody's horse splashed across Warbonnet Creek, a Cheyenne warrior turned to meet him. His name was Yellow Hair, and, like Cody, he had dressed splendidly for combat. He wore a magnificent feathered bonnet, a special charm, tin bracelets, and a beautifully beaded belt in which he tucked the blond scalp from which he derived his name. His unique breechcloth had been fashioned from a cotton American flag. As his handful of companions fled, he boldly stood his ground and fired at the long-haired scout.

Yellow Hair's shot missed, but Cody placed a round through the Cheyenne warrior's leg, dropping his calico pony. At the same moment Cody's horse stumbled, sending him tumbling onto the ground. Jumping clear of his horse, Cody fired simultaneously with the wounded Yellow Hair. The Cheyenne missed but Buffalo Bill did not and the warrior fell.

Rushing forward, Cody scalped the fallen warrior, raised the topknot and warbonnet aloft, and cried out, "The first scalp for Custer!"

Merritt ordered the regiment forward and they cheered for their scout as they galloped past in pursuit of the retreating warriors. The 5th Cavalry pursued the Cheyennes back to the Red Cloud Agency, some thirty miles away, where they quickly blended back into the agency population. Darkness had fallen by the time that most of the troops arrived.

Lieutenant King remembered that the Indians were as impressed with Cody as the soldiers were:

> *One and all they wanted to see Buffalo Bill, and whenever he moved they followed him with awe-filled eyes. He wore the same dress in which he had burst upon them in yesterday's fight, a Mexican costume of black velvet, slashed with scarlet and trimmed with silver buttons and lace—one of his theatrical garbs, in which he had done much execution before the footlights in the States, and which now became of intensified value.*[21]

Just as Priam had gone forth to beseech Achilles before the walls of Troy, now Yellow Hair's aged father sought out Cody at the Red Cloud Agency. Cut Nose did not come, as had Priam, for his son's body, but rather for his bracelets, charm, belt, and warbonnet. Cut Nose was poor, but he offered a ransom of four mules for his son's regalia. Cody later claimed some remorse for his failure to accommodate the old man, but he already had grand plans for these war trophies.[22]

An exhausted Cody took a moment that evening to write his wife: "We have had a fight. I killed Yellow Hand [*sic*] a Cheyenne Chief in a single-handed fight. You will no doubt hear of it through the papers. I am going as soon as I reach Fort Laramie the place we are heading for now send the war bonnet, shield, bridal, whip, arms and his scalp to Kerngood [a friend in Rochester] to put up in his window. I will write Kerngood to bring it up to the house so you can show it to the neighbors." When Kerngood brought the scalp to Louisa, she promptly fainted.[23]

The 5th Cavalry now moved north to reinforce General Crook's column and pursue Sitting Bull's people. Crook had over 2,000 men, and this huge command was designated the Big Horn and Yellowstone Expedition.

Buffalo Bill was appointed chief of scouts for Crook's command, with some twenty scouts working under him. But as summer faded into August, the opportunities for additional action faded as well. The triumphant Indians scattered, and the lumbering army columns had no chance of catching them. On August 22, Cody asked for his discharge.

Cody quickly put a new theatrical combination together, featuring a companion from the Great Sioux War, Captain Jack Crawford, the Poet Scout. The new play was entitled *The Red Right Hand; or, Buffalo Bill's First Scalp for Custer.* This five-act monstrosity was, according to Cody, "without head or tail, and it made no difference at which act we commenced the performance." It was his most successful play. Not the least of the show's attractions were the scalp and feathered warbonnet of Yellow Hair. The northeastern press and clergy quickly sent up a howl of protest over this barbaric display, so Cody withdrew his trophies from theater windows and confined himself to brandishing them onstage. This only increased box office receipts as folks hurried to see the controversial scalp.[24]

Was *The Red Right Hand* a case of art imitating life? Or, rather, had the slaying of the unfortunate Yellow Hair been a case of life imitating art? Cody had, in fact, dressed the morning of July 17, 1876, in one of his stage costumes and, attired properly for the part, had gone forth and killed an Indian in a grisly ritual that reaffirmed his status as a true frontiersman. Then he hurried eastward, scalp in hand, to exploit the deed. It was as if the frontier West had become a vast living stage where Cody performed ritualistic acts of heroism for the entertainment of the population of the industrial East. It was a unique moment in time. By 1876 the frontier had already become an anachronism to these Eastern folk. After his premiere performance on Warbonnet Creek, Buffalo Bill simply took the show on the road. *The Red Right Hand* was a rerun, and the residuals proved quite profitable.

27

THE DANCING HORSE

Near the end of the 1882 theatrical season, Bill Cody had a fateful lunch in New York City at the restaurant adjacent to Haverly's 14th Street Theatre with Nate Salsbury. The conversation drifted to an idea Nate had for an arena show featuring a variety of American horsemen—cowboys, Indians, and Mexican vaqueros—in daredevil feats of riding. Such a show needed a headliner and Salsbury felt Cody the perfect man for the part. Cody's stage career had prospered, although he was growing weary of tramping the boards and anxious for a new challenge. The 1879 publication of his autobiography—dedicated to General Sheridan—had enhanced his fame, as had scores of dime novels attributed to him. Cody liked the idea and he liked Salsbury, but the problem was in how to finance such an extravaganza.

Cody returned home to North Platte, where he had built Louisa and the girls a fine house not far from town. In 1877, in partnership with Frank North, he had bought a ranch on the Dismal River and stocked it with cattle. He let North run the outfit while he concentrated on his stage career. He could not get Salsbury's idea for an outdoor cowboy show out of his mind. No sooner had he reached North Platte than he was asked by the city fathers to organize a July Fourth celebration at the local racetrack. Cody, calling it the "Old Glory Blow Out," sent out flyers offering prizes for cowboy entrants to engage in bronco busting, trick riding, cattle roping, and shooting contests. He got over a thousand entries and the people for miles around flocked to the rodeo. It was such a huge success that it inspired Cody to put together a touring cowboy show.

He returned to New York for the remainder of the 1883 theatrical season and approached W. F. "Doc" Carver, the self-styled "Evil Spirit of the Plains," who was a noted marksman, with his idea for an arena show. The sharpshooting dentist agreed, and so they pooled their resources on *Buffalo Bill and Doc Carver's Wild West, Rocky Mountain and Prairie Exhibition*, which opened at the Omaha Fairgrounds on May 19, 1883. They hired John Burke to handle publicity, and he proved to be a master of that craft. Cody wired Salsbury and offered him a partnership but he declined. Nate considered the ill-tempered Carver "a fakir in the show business."[1]

Frank North recruited thirty-six Pawnees for the show as well as young Gordon "Pawnee Bill" Lillie as interpreter. In the first rehearsal the Pawnees proved so enthusiastic in their attack on the Deadwood stagecoach that it almost overturned.

"Bill, if you want to make this damned show go, you do not need me or my Indians," North argued to Cody. "You want about twenty old bucks. Fix them up with all the paint and feathers in the market. Use some old hack horses and a hack driver. To make a go, you want a show of illusion, not realism."[2]

Cody did not take his friend's advice, for he was obsessed with realism. He confessed that he could put a Stetson and red shirt on anyone and invent a cowboy, but he could not invent Indians. He was determined to have only real Indians in his show. The Deadwood stage was the real thing, used by the Cheyenne and Black Hills Stage Line. Cody had ridden in it in 1876. He did, however, in time come to appreciate the power of illusion as well.

The new show proved a success, although it was always difficult to meet expenses, especially since Cody and Carver drank up much of the profit. The *Hartford Courant* declared that Cody had "out-Barnumed Barnum," pointing out that "the real sight of the whole thing is, after all, Buffalo Bill, a perfect model of manly beauty. Mounted on his blooded horse, he rode around the grounds, the observed of all observers. Cody was an extraordinary figure and sits a horse as if he were born in the saddle."[3]

The show lasted but one season, as the partners quarreled constantly, drank incessantly, and, as a result, poorly managed operations. In October, while playing in Chicago, Cody was called home by the illness of eleven-year-old Orra. She died on October 24, and Cody sought even more solace in the bottle. He and Louisa were nearly at the breaking point but held the marriage together for their two remaining daughters, Arta, born in 1866, and Irma, born in 1883.

He soon parted company with Carver and once again turned to Nate Salsbury. They signed a contract to establish *Buffalo Bill's Wild West: America's National Entertainment* that autumn, and Nate began to organize the 1884 season.

Born in Illinois in 1846, Salsbury ran away from home at age fifteen to join the Union army. He saw hard service in the army of William Tecumseh Sherman. "Uncle Billy" was visiting with his soldiers late one evening during the Georgia campaign when he heard "a boyish voice spouting imperfectly, Hamlet's soliloquy, a short distance ahead . . ."

The undiscovere'd country, from whose bourn
No traveller returns, puzzles the will,
And makes us rather bear those ills we have
Than fly to others that we know not of?

". . . Then changing into a rollicking negro melody, accompanied by shouts of laughter . . .

"Standing on the top of a decayed stump of a cedar tree, was a young fellow, who could not have been more than sixteen or seventeen years old, in full uniform, except an old plug hat, that had once been white, that was cocked on the side of his head, after the exaggerated style of the funny men of the minstrel stage, that lent color to the vociferous accents of his vocal efforts," Sherman recalled. "Between the verses of his song he danced a jig to the delight of the lookers on."

This had been a great relief to men who had been under fire continuously for over a month. Sherman told this story at a testimonial dinner in New York City in 1888 and was surprised when Salsbury, also a guest, rose to inform him that he had been that boy and again sang the song—"Oh! Susanna"—for the general. It was a grand reunion.[4]

Not long after the initial Sherman performance, Nate was captured by the rebels and sent to Andersonville prison. In that grim hellhole he entertained his comrades as best he could. After the war he went on the stage, first as a stock actor, and then with his own company—Salsbury's Troubadours. He toured with this company for twelve years before meeting Cody.

It was in many ways a perfect partnership, although there were some bumps along the trail, especially regarding Cody's drinking. In Nate's mind Cody would be the star attraction of the Wild West, which he saw as his invention. But Cody took an active role in management and, even more importantly, in the conception of the show (although he refused to call it a show). He conceived of it as a combination rodeo, outdoor spectacle, and historical pageant. Combined with steer roping, bronc riding, and western animals, including a small herd of buffalo, were historical motifs, some borrowed from his stage plays, such as the Deadwood stage, the attack on the settlers' cabin, the Pony Express, Summit Springs, the first scalp for Custer, and even Custer's Last Stand. In time the historical pageants in the Wild West were updated to include Roosevelt's Rough Riders at San Juan Hill, the Boxer Rebellion, the Philippine Insurrection, and the Boer War, although elements such as the Deadwood stage, the Pony Express, and the first scalp for Custer remained standard fare.

Frontier celebrities, both real and invented, were featured over the years—Frank North, A. H. Bogardus, Dr. Frank "White Beaver" Powell, Pawnee Bill, Lillian Smith, Antonio Esquivel, and, most importantly, sharpshooting Annie Oakley (Phoebe Ann Moses), who signed on in 1885. Cody called her "Little Missie."

"I traveled with him for seventeen years—there were thousands of men in the outfit during that time, Comanches, cowboys, Cossacks, Arabs, and every kind of person," she said of Cody. "And the whole time we were one great family loyal to a man. His words were more than most contracts. Personally, I never had a contract with the show after I started. It would have been superfluous."[5]

The Wild West took the name "cowboy," once a pejorative, and turned it into a heroic term. In time, with an able assist from Owen Wister, Theodore Roosevelt, Charlie Russell, and Frederic Remington, the cowboy became a defining figure of the American character. William "Buck" Taylor, a strapping Texas cowpuncher who had worked on Cody's ranch before joining the show, was billed as "King of the Cowboys," while Johnny Baker, a North Platte waif whom Cody essentially adopted, became the "Cowboy Kid."

One unique celebrity whom Cody was determined to sign was Sitting Bull. "I am going to try hard to get old Sitting Bull," Cody wrote Carver in 1883. "If we can manage to get him our ever lasting fortune is made."[6]

After the Little Big Horn, Sitting Bull, hounded by troops under Colonel Nelson "Bear Coat" Miles, had led his people across the "Medicine Line" into Canada. At that time, war correspondent John F. Finerty had written of him: "He has, at least, the magic sway of a Mohammed over the rude war tribes that engirdle him. Everybody talks of Sitting Bull, and, whether he be a figure-head, or an idea, or an incomprehensible mystery, his present influence is undoubted. His very name is potent."[7]

Potent indeed. When he led his starving people south to surrender at Fort Buford in July 1881, everyone wanted a piece of Sitting Bull. The army had first claim on him. Although he was promised that if he would surrender he and his people were to be settled at the Standing Rock Agency on the Missouri River with those of his people who had surrendered earlier, the army reneged. Instead, he and his 167 followers were loaded onto the steamer *General Sherman* and taken downriver to Fort Randall as prisoners of war, where they were guarded by the Buffalo Soldiers of the 25th Infantry. In May 1883, after twenty months, they were finally allowed to go to Standing Rock, where they pitched their tepees near Fort Yates. A year later Sitting Bull was allowed to move south to the Grand River, where he, his relatives, and close adherents built log cabins.

The Indian agent at Standing Rock was forty-one-year-old James McLaughlin, a twelve-year veteran of the Bureau of Indian Affairs. A somewhat unique figure in the Indian service, he was neither corrupt nor a political hack and, unlike most agents, was genuinely committed, in his paternalistic way, to the well-being of his Native charges. His Dakota wife gave him insights into tribal politics that helped to make him a superior agent. He was reasonably secure in his position thanks to the support of the Catholic Church and the humanitarian reformers of the Indian Rights Association. He was also arrogant and condescending, with an authoritarian streak. Almost at once, he began to clash with Sitting Bull, who could be equally arrogant and stubborn. Most of the Standing Rock Sioux looked to Sitting Bull as their chief and remained loyal to him. This worried McLaughlin, who worked to raise others to power, most notably Gall, the Hunkpapa war chief, who had played a leading role at the Little Big Horn.

"Sitting Bull is an Indian of very mediocre ability, rather dull, and much the inferior of Gall and others of his lieutenants in intelligence,"

McLaughlin declared. "He is pompous, vain, and boastful, and considers himself a very important personage."[8]

Despite the agent's opinion, other people also considered the chief "a very important personage." When Bismarck was selected as the capital of Dakota Territory in September 1883, McLaughlin agreed to bring Sitting Bull to ride in a procession that included former president Grant, Henry Villard of the Northern Pacific Railway, territorial governor Nehemiah Ordway, Secretary of the Interior Henry Teller, and former secretary of the interior Carl Schurz. While in Bismarck, Sitting Bull also discovered that people would pay $2 for his autograph.

John Burke was soon at Standing Rock with an attractive financial package for Sitting Bull to tour with Cody's Wild West. McLaughlin refused, since "the late hostiles are so well disposed and are just beginning to take hold of an agricultural life."[9]

McLaughlin lied to Burke, for he had already agreed to allow the chief, one of his wives, and several other Sioux men and their wives to join Alvaren Allen's troupe the Sitting Bull Combination. To sweeten the deal, Allen agreed to employ the agent's wife and son as interpreters. They traveled to St. Paul, Philadelphia, and New York with a simple program in which the Lakotas sat around a tepee smoking and cooking while a lecturer entertained the audience with stories of Indian life. Sitting Bull, who sometimes briefly spoke, was constantly badgered with questions about Custer and the Little Big Horn. He warmed to his theatrical role with some of his responses even before he took to the stage, as in this response to a *New York Herald* reporter's question on how Custer died:

> **SB:** "It was said that up there where the last fight took place, where the last stand was made, the Long Hair stood like a sheaf of corn with all the ears fallen around him."
> **Reporter:** "Not wounded?"
> **SB:** "No."
> **Reporter:** "How many stood by him?"
> **SB:** "A few."
> **Reporter:** "When did he fall?"
> **SB:** "He killed a man when he fell. He laughed."

Reporter: "You mean he cried out?"
SB: "No, he laughed; he had fired his last shot."

Of course, we may assume that the *Herald* reporter improved upon the translation a bit. Sitting Bull had not actually witnessed the last stand.[10]

The commissioner of Indian Affairs was not amused by reports of the Sitting Bull Combination that he read in the newspapers and demanded an explanation from McLaughlin. The agent shifted blame to others and was happy to have the enterprise ended that October and Sitting Bull safely back at Standing Rock.

Cody remained doggedly on the trail of Sitting Bull, determined to have him for the 1885 summer season. He was firmly rebuffed by Secretary of the Interior Lucius Q. C. Lamar, a former Confederate general, until he enlisted the support of General William T. Sherman.

"Sitting Bull is a humbug but has a popular fame on which he has a natural right to bank," Sherman wrote in support of Cody. The former rebel retreated before the four-star Yankee general.[11]

Burke was promptly off to Standing Rock to strike a deal. The sly old chief played coy, but "Arizona John" was no amateur at this business. Spying a photo of Annie Oakley in Sitting Bull's cabin, he gleefully informed the chief that she had just signed to tour with the Wild West: they would be headliners together on tour. This sealed the deal. Sitting Bull had seen Oakley perform the previous year in St. Paul and had been utterly enchanted. The starstruck chief had sent a request for a photo accompanied by $65 to her.

"This amused me, so I sent him back his money and a photograph, with my love, and a message to say I would call the following morning," Annie recalled. "I did so, and the old man was so pleased with me, he insisted upon adopting me, and I was then and there christened 'Watanya Cicilla,' or 'Little Sure Shot.'"[12]

Sitting Bull gave his new friend a photo of himself as well as a pair of moccasins that he claimed to have worn at the Battle of the Little Big Horn. This was the beginning of a beautiful friendship, perhaps only possible in show business.

Sitting Bull still drove a hard bargain. He was to be paid $50 a week, with a two-week advance, along with the exclusive right to sell his autograph and photographs, as well as a $125 signing bonus. Five Lakota warriors were to go with him at $25 a month, as well as three women for $15 a month, and reservation interpreter William Halsey at $60. Burke also agreed to pay all round-trip travel expenses to and from Standing Rock. The Sioux entourage joined the Wild West in Buffalo, New York, on June 12, 1885. The combination of Sitting Bull, Annie Oakley, and Buffalo Bill proved catnip to audiences. The season played to over a million visitors (at 25 cents for children and 50 cents for adults) and secured the financial stability and future of Cody's show.

The hiring of Sitting Bull posed a problem with the Pawnees in *Buffalo Bill's Wild West*, for they were mortal enemies of the Sioux. Cody solved this by only hiring Sioux and Cheyennes as "show Indians" in the future. Since Frank North had been injured in an arena accident in 1884 and left the show (he died the next year), the termination of the Pawnee connection appeared quite natural. Tryouts for the show would be held at Rushville, Nebraska, near Pine Ridge, and Cody would often attend to personally select the Lakota performers—men, women, and children. He took ninety-seven Lakota performers with him to England in 1887. The Indian village set up on the show-grounds allowed visitors to observe and interact with the Native performers.

The show Indians were somewhat overwhelmed by the abundance of food available to them. They were particularly fond of well-done steak, although Sitting Bull developed a taste for oyster stew and hard candy. Once a year the Lakota performers held a dog feast (even though this was outlawed on their reservation), followed by a "dog dance," in honor of the old days. This treat was something of a holiday for them.

The Indian performers ate in the same dining tent with everyone else, which led one visiting reporter to note that the communal dining experience proved "that in time knowledge and acquaintance will dispel racial prejudices and national hatred and emphasize the fact of all mankind's kindredship."[13]

Sitting Bull was presented with great dignity in the *Wild West*, riding a light gray show horse in parades and in the arena, dressed in all his Lakota finery. Sometimes he was booed in the arena, but that was rare. "Foes in '76, Friends in '85" was used on advertising posters along with a photograph taken in Montreal of Cody and Sitting Bull side by side.

Cody defended Sitting Bull in the press over the Custer battle: "The defeat of Custer was not a massacre. The Indians were being pursued by skilled fighters with orders to kill. For centuries they had been hounded from the Atlantic to the Pacific and back again. They had their wives and little ones to protect and they were fighting for their existence. With the end of Custer they considered that their greatest enemy had passed away. Sitting Bull was not the leader of the Sioux in that battle. He was a medicine man who played on their superstitions—their politician, their diplomat."[14]

The two old foes formed a bond of true friendship. It was bold of Cody to speak up so forcefully in defense of his new friend just nine years after Custer's Last Stand. Even as he celebrated the "winning of the West" in his show, Cody came to understand all that had been lost in that great conquest.

When the *Wild West* played Washington, Cody took Sitting Bull to the White House for a brief audience with the corpulent President Grover Cleveland. The meeting was unsatisfactory for the chief. They also visited with General Sheridan at army headquarters, although Sitting Bull seemed more impressed with the war paintings on the walls than with his military nemesis.

The season ended in St. Louis that October and Sitting Bull and his Lakota companions returned to Standing Rock. He had not kept much of his show money, sending most of it home to his family and giving the rest to bootblacks, beggars, and street urchins. He could not understand how a land so wealthy could also have such poverty. Annie Oakley, who had grown ever closer to the old chief during their four months together, noted that his money "went into the pockets of small, ragged boys. Nor could he understand how so much wealth could go brushing by, unmindful of the poor."[15]

In parting, Cody gave Sitting Bull a size 8 white Stetson and the gray prancing horse that he had ridden in the arena. Sitting Bull treasured both. Once, when a relative dared to put on the hat, he upbraided him: "My friend Long Hair gave me this hat. I value it very highly, for the hand that placed it upon my head had a friendly feeling for me."[16]

When John Burke returned to Standing Rock to recruit Sitting Bull for another season with the *Wild West*, he found McLaughlin intractable. The agent felt that the previous season with Cody had only added to the chief's arrogant self-importance.

"He is inflated with the public attention he received," the agent declared, "and has not profited by what he has seen, but tells the most astounding falsehoods to the Indians."

McLaughlin was also irritated that Sitting Bull had "squandered" all of his show money on feasts and gifts for the Hunkpapas. This was expected of a wealthy chief by the people, but to McLaughlin "he makes no good use of the money he thus earns." Of course, his gifts enhanced his influence over the people and undercut McLaughlin's authority. So spiteful was this man that, rather than get rid of this troublesome chief by allowing him to go out with Cody, he preferred to keep him close and under his thumb to further humiliate and punish him. Sitting Bull's show business career was over.[17]

With Sitting Bull and Annie Oakley as headliners, *Buffalo Bill's Wild West* grossed over a million dollars in 1885 (with $100,000 profit). The cast increased to 240 people, with more Indians as well as the addition of several cowgirls. The crew was organized with military precision, with crew bosses to tackle the setting up and breaking down of the various scenes.

Cody fed his crew well and also regularly put on special dinners and barbecues for guests and visitors. "With Colonel Cody, Mr. Salsbury, his partner, Major Burke and other 'pale-face' chiefs, you find you are in a jolly company at a lavish feast," noted a reporter. The concession sales also contributed greatly to the profit margin, with Cracker Jack being a huge seller. Visitors could purchase a meal for 50 cents.[18]

CODY AND SALSBURY TOOK *BUFFALO BILL'S WILD WEST* to London in 1887 for Queen Victoria's Golden Jubilee; it proved to be a sensation. Over 2 million people would see the show in London. Not since 1066 had the English been so easily conquered. Buffalo Bill gave them, and later other Europeans, a taste of the vanishing frontier that had so enthralled his own countrymen. He exploited the romantic possibilities of the story of the American West, making it intelligible to millions who had no other knowledge of the frontier than what he presented. In turn, he became a buckskin-clad goodwill ambassador, winning the hearts of Europe as no American since Benjamin Franklin had done.

Queen Victoria came to the Earl's Court arena on May 11 for a command performance of the *Wild West*. When the American flag was presented at the top of the show, the queen rose and bowed toward it, as did her entourage. Cody and the other cast members let out a lusty American war whoop, for this was the first time a British monarch had ever saluted the flag of the

United States. Thus did a century of rivalry and resentment melt away, for *Buffalo Bill's Wild West* had conquered the heart of the queen and her people as no army ever could, forging bonds of friendship that would never again be severed. After the show, the queen requested that the leading stars of the show be presented to her. Buffalo Bill, Nate Salsbury, Annie Oakley, Lillian Smith, two Indian women and their babies, and the Lakota headliner Red Shirt were presented. The handsome Red Shirt seemed to particularly catch the attention of the queen and the ladies of her retinue.

Another command performance was called for June 20 so that the royals attending the jubilee might see *Buffalo Bill's Wild West*. In the audience were the kings of Denmark, Greece, Saxony, and the Belgians as well as several crown princes, among them the Prince of Wales (the future Edward VII); his son George of Wales (the future George V), and the crown prince of Germany (the future Wilhelm II).

Cody drove the Deadwood stage during the mock Indian attack with the kings of Denmark, Greece, the Belgians, and Saxony and the Prince of Wales aboard. After the thrilling ride ended, the Prince of Wales remarked to Cody, "Colonel, you never held four kings like these before."

Not missing a beat on the poker metaphor, Cody responded, "I've held four kings, but four kings and the Prince of Wales make a royal flush, such as no man ever held before."[19]

The Prince of Wales, who fancied himself quite the judge of horseflesh, visited the stables with Cody and was particularly taken with Old Charlie, who was then twenty-one and the star horse of the Wild West. Cody had ridden him for fourteen years. "Charlie is an animal of almost human intelligence," Cody informed the royals. He was notoriously sentimental about his horses.[20]

The jubilee tour was one triumph after another, as the whole country seemed to be caught up in the fascination of all things Wild West. Colonel Cody was feted everywhere (he had now adopted "Colonel" as his title, just like Davy Crockett, thanks to an 1887 appointment as colonel in the Nebraska National Guard) and dined with the leaders of British society, including Lord and Lady Randolph Churchill and their young son Winston. Lady Churchill, formerly Jennie Jerome, was the daughter of Leonard Jerome, Cody's companion on the 1871 "Millionaire's Hunt."

"He was probably the guest of more people in diverse circumstances than any man alive," observed Annie Oakley. "Tepee and palace were all the same to him. And so were their inhabitants."[21]

The *Wild West* company returned to the United States in the spring of 1888. The homecoming was saddened by the death of Old Charlie. On May 17, wrapped in canvas and the American flag, Charlie was lowered over the side of the *Persian Monarch* to be buried at sea. Cody was overcome with emotion as he said farewell:

"Old fellow, your journeys are over. . . . Obedient to my call, gladly you bore your burden on, little knowing, little reckoning what the day might bring, shared sorrows and pleasures alike. Willing speed, tireless courage . . . you have never failed me. Ah, Charlie, old fellow, I have had many friends, but few of whom I could say that. . . . I loved you as you loved me. Men tell me you have no soul; but if there is a heaven and scouts can enter there, I'll wait at the gate for you, old friend."[22]

The next year *Buffalo Bill's Wild West* invaded the continent of Europe with equally spectacular results—financially, diplomatically, and culturally. Salsbury planned the tour in order to exploit the 1889 Paris Exposition. The president of France attended the opening, as did Thomas Edison, who happened to be visiting Paris at the time. French artists descended on the *Wild West* grounds. Rosa Bonheur painted a portrait of Cody, mounted on his new white show horse, that became quite famous. The show moved on to Barcelona, where five cast members died of the flu, then sunny Naples, and finally Rome, where the cast had an audience with Pope Leo XIII. Triumphs followed in Florence, Milan, and Venice, where Cody and several Indian companions rode in a gondola. They went north into Germany, where the populace became infatuated with the American West. They played in Berlin for a month to overflow crowds. The summer tour concluded with shows in Vienna, Dresden, Leipzig, Bonn, Coblenz, and Frankfurt before ending in Stuttgart.[23]

Several of the show Indians became ill and were sent home, which led to unfounded rumors that they had been mistreated. In response, and with the show season over, all the Indians were sent home with Burke. Cody soon followed, anxious to visit Washington and defend his treatment of his Native performers. When he landed in New York, he was greeted by reporters who wanted to know what he thought of the Ghost Dance troubles among the western tribes.[24]

These were hard times on the Sioux reservation. New land agreements resulting from the 1887 Dawes Act had reduced the reservation by 60 million acrès. The land was opened to white ranchers and homesteaders, while the Sioux were encouraged to take land allotments of 160 acres, which would eventually lead to citizenship. The government needed Sioux consent to this under the 1868 treaty, but when that was not forthcoming, a commission was sent out led by General George Crook. In concert with McLaughlin, the general exploited Sioux factionalism and secured the required signatures to sell the surplus land for $1.25 an acre (less after three years for unsold land). Sitting Bull opposed this without success.

"Sitting Bull tried to speak after the signing commenced, but I stopped him," Crook wrote in his diary. "Then he tried twice to stampede the Indians away from signing, but his efforts failed, and he flattened out, his wind bag punctured, and several of his followers have deserted him."[25]

Events now moved swiftly. In February 1889 a statehood bill passed bringing North and South Dakota, as well as Montana and Washington, into the Union. Now the two new Dakota states would have even more political clout with the administration of President Benjamin Harrison to demand that surplus Sioux land be thrown open to settlers. At the same time, as an economy measure, the government cut the rations provided to the Indians. In the six new reservations—Standing Rock, Cheyenne River, Lower Brule, Crow Creek, Rosebud, and Pine Ridge—hunger stalked the people. Influenza struck that winter with devastating results. The Lakota, divided by the Indian agents into "progressives" and "nonprogressives," fell into deep despair.

Now came word that, to the west, in Nevada, a Paiute holy man named Wovoka was preaching a new religion called the Ghost Dance. If the people would perform this dance, the buffalo would return along with their deceased ancestors—and the white men would vanish. A Miniconjou named Kicking Bear became the Ghost Dance apostle among the Sioux and won many converts at Rosebud and Pine Ridge. Sitting Bull invited him to preach at Standing Rock, where his sermons won more converts. James McLaughlin responded by ordering him off the reservation. It was too late, for now Sitting Bull's log cabin encampment became the scene of daily dances. Sitting Bull did not dance, but he encouraged others to do so. The tepees of the dancers soon ringed Sitting Bull's cabins. The dancers often fell into trances and saw their dead relatives. More people began to dance. Sitting Bull once again assumed a leadership role, which further troubled McLaughlin.

McLaughlin remained calm, but the other reservation agents became increasingly hysterical over the Ghost Dance, as did nearby settlers. They called for the army to send in troops to disperse the dancers. On November 20, 1890, troops moved to occupy the Pine Ridge and Rosebud agencies with orders to arrest the leaders of the Ghost Dance.

General Nelson A. Miles, son-in-law of General Sherman and the most experienced Indian fighter in the army, now commanding the Division of the Missouri, deluded himself into believing that the Ghost Dance was the greatest crisis since the Little Big Horn.

"It was a threatened uprising of colossal proportions," he wrote, "extending over a far greater territory than did the confederation inaugurated by the Prophet and led by Tecumseh, or the conspiracy of Pontiac, and only the prompt action of the military prevented its execution."[26]

Cody had just returned from Europe when he received a telegram from Miles asking him to hurry to his Chicago headquarters. He had hoped to join Burke in Washington to answer the complaints from the hacks in the Bureau of Indian Affairs over false claims of mistreatment of the show Indians, but instead headed to Chicago from New York. He found Miles fretting over a possible war with the Ghost Dancers.

"He asked me if I could go immediately to Standing Rock and Fort Yates, and thence to Sitting Bull's camp," Cody recalled. "He knew that I was an old friend of the chief, and he believed that if any one could induce the old fox to abandon his plans for a general war I could."

Miles wrote out an order on November 24, 1890, marked "confidential" for Cody to "secure the person of Sitting Bull" and deliver him to the nearest military post. Miles hoped to remove the chief from the scene of turmoil and perhaps bring him to Chicago for a meeting. He also handed Cody his card with orders for army officers to assist him scrawled in pencil on the back.[27]

Cody promptly departed for Fort Yates accompanied by show associates Robert "Pony Bob" Haslam and Frank "White Beaver" Powell, who had been particular friends with Sitting Bull during his season with *Buffalo Bill's Wild West*. This colorful entourage arrived at the Dakota fort on November 28. Cody presented his orders as well as General Miles's calling card to Lieutenant Colonel William F. Drum, the post commander. Drum, who was working closely with the devious McLaughlin, was mortified by these orders. He hurriedly got word off to McLaughlin while he had his officers entertain Cody at the post officers' club. The plan was to get him roaring drunk and delay his journey to Standing Rock until McLaughlin could wire the commissioner of Indian affairs and have the mission canceled. They misjudged their man.

"Colonel Cody's capacity was such that it took practically all the officers in details two or three at a time to keep him interested and busy through the day," noted the post surgeon.[28]

The officers fell by the wayside as Cody closed down the club and retired in good spirits. The next morning he slept in but was still on the road well before noon. He loaded a buckboard with gifts for Sitting Bull and his family—with an emphasis on candy, as he knew the chief had a notorious sweet tooth—and was off on his mission to the Grand River camp.

The increasingly frantic McLaughlin now sent his agency interpreter out to intercept Cody with a false story that Sitting Bull was on his way into the agency by another road. He anxiously awaited a response to his telegram to Washington.

"William F. Cody (Buffalo Bill) has arrived here with commission from Gen. Miles to arrest Sitting Bull," he had written. "Such a step at present is unnecessary and unwise, as it will precipitate a fight which can be averted. . . . Request Gen. Miles's order to Cody be rescinded and request immediate answer."[29]

This was a tissue of lies, for Cody and his unarmed party were in no danger. Cody was not about to force an arrest. It was not in his power to do so even if he had wished to—and he did not. A Chicago newspaperman had been in Sitting Bull's camp the day before, taking photographs of Ghost Dancers without any problem. There was no danger.

"If they had left Cody alone, he'd have captured Sitting Bull with an all-day sucker," noted Buffalo Bill's cowboy star Johnny Baker.[30]

The secretary of the interior hurried to President Harrison with McLaughlin's telegram and the president promptly recalled Cody. The recall order reached Cody's party just before they reached Grand River. Cody said that Harrison later admitted to him that his recall was in error and apologized. Well, he should have, for that order set a great tragedy in motion.[31]

McLaughlin now determined to arrest Sitting Bull with his Indian police. Colonel Drum agreed to cooperate. He would have two companies of cavalry nearby to assist the Indian police if necessary. On December 15, Captain Bull Head, who had fought with Sitting Bull at the Little Big Horn and Rosebud, was to lead forty-four Sioux policemen to arrest the great chief. As he made his plan, he instructed Red Bear and White Bird to go to Sitting Bull's corral and saddle the gray show horse in readiness for the arrest. A little before six that morning, under cloudy skies and an icy drizzle, they reached the Grand River village.

Sitting Bull was asleep in one of his two cabins with his wife and fourteen-year-old son Crow Foot, a small child, and three guests. The rest of his family were in his smaller cabin to the north. They were awakened by barking dogs and a sudden pounding on the cabin door.

The door flew open and dark forms rushed in. A candle was lit.

"Brother, we came after you," announced Sergeant Shave Head.

"How, all right," the surprised chief answered as he was seized and dragged from under his blankets.

He was naked and demanded to be allowed to dress. The police complied but hurried him along, pushing him toward the door. Sitting Bull's wife began to upbraid the police and then to wail.

Bull Head and Shave Head forced Sitting Bull through the door and out into the darkness beyond. Sergeant Red Tomahawk walked behind, his pistol in the chief's back. The gray horse waited, saddled and ready.

The barking dogs had alerted the village and a great crowd now gathered. Angry people shook their fists; some waved rifles. A cry went up: "You shall not take our chief!"

From the doorway, Crow Foot called after his father: "You always called yourself a brave chief. Now you are allowing yourself to be taken by the *ceska maza* [metal breasts, i.e., badges]."

"Then I shall not go," Sitting Bull declared.

Sitting Bull's friend Catch-the-Bear took aim with his rifle and shot Bull Head. As he fell, the policeman shot Sitting Bull in the chest. At the same moment Red Tomahawk fired into the back of the chief's head. Shave Head went down at the same time, shot in the stomach, while policeman Lone Man killed Catch-the-Bear.

Suddenly the gray horse, trained to perform during gunfire, began to prance; it was as if Sitting Bull's spirit had entered his body. In the dim dawn light—amidst the haze of black powder smoke—the horse appeared as if an apparition. He danced around the bloodied body of the great chieftain who had been his master. He danced above the old warriors who had fought beside Sitting Bull on the Yellowstone, at Rosebud, and against Long Hair Custer at the Little Big Horn—all killed, now dead by the hands of their own people. Then the horse sat down on his haunches and raised his hoofs in the air: Was it perhaps a prayer of solace for all that was now lost? For the death of the great chief marked the end of the old ways forever. This was indeed a ghost dance. There was a momentary halt in the shooting as all stared in awe at the mystical horse.

Some of the police retreated into the cabin, while others took cover behind it and in the corral. Now they all began to fire again. The Ghost Dancers took cover in nearby timber, leaving six of their number dead. The spirit horse stood his ground, untouched by the hail of bullets. As the police pulled their wounded comrades into the cabin, they discovered Crow Foot. They asked the mortally wounded Bull Head what to do with the boy.

"Kill him, they have killed me," he snarled.

Red Tomahawk smashed the boy across the head with his rifle butt as two other policemen shot him. Red Tomahawk called Hawk Man to his side and ordered him to mount the gray horse and ride to get help from the soldiers. In a hail of bullets he galloped away—but the magic of the gray horse kept him untouched.

At dawn the cavalry arrived and quickly drove Sitting Bull's people away. Captain Edmond G. Fechet reported that he "saw evidence of a most desperate encounter" with the bodies of eight dead Indians, including Sitting Bull, in front of the cabin, along with two dead horses. Inside the cabin he found four dead policemen and three wounded men, two mortally. He was anxious to depart, a bit unnerved by the constant wails of the women.

Fechet commandeered a nearby wagon and ordered Sitting Bull's body to be put in it. Someone had smashed in the chief's face and he looked particularly gruesome as they tossed him into the wagon. The dead Indian policemen were placed on top of him, and the wagon, soldiers, and Indian police rode north up the trail to Standing Rock.[32]

They took Sitting Bull's mangled corpse to Fort Yates, where on December 17 he was buried in the post cemetery. McLaughlin and three army officers supervised the burial. Wrapped in canvas, the body was placed in a crude wooden coffin that was too small. The soldiers had to sit on the lid to close it. They lowered Sitting Bull into a pauper's grave and poured lime on top before shoveling in dirt.

"We laid the noble Old Chief away without a hymn or a prayer or a sprinkle of earth. Quicklime was used instead," recalled John F. Waggoner, the soldier who had made the coffin. "It made me angry. I had always admired the Chief for his courage and his generalship. He was a man!"[33]

Sitting Bull's death panicked the Ghost Dancers. Hundreds of Hunkpapas fled south to the Cheyenne River Reservation, while some pushed even farther south to the Ghost Dance stronghold at Pine Ridge. Big Foot, the diplomatic leader of the Miniconjous at Cheyenne River, under pressure from his more militant headmen, bolted for Pine Ridge with over three hundred people, including forty-eight of the Hunkpapa refugees. Troops, including Custer's old regiment the 7th Cavalry, were soon in hot pursuit.

Orders from General Miles, now in the Black Hills, were clear: Big Foot's band must be stopped. "Find his trail and follow, or find his hiding place and capture him," Miles directed. "If he fights, destroy him."[34]

Major Samuel Whiteside, with four companies of the 7th and a battery of two Hotchkiss guns, intercepted Big Foot's band on Porcupine Creek, where the chief, near death from pneumonia, surrendered his 120 men and 230 women and children. Whiteside sent a message to Colonel James W. Forsyth, Sheridan's longtime aide, who now commanded the 7th, to bring up the rest of the regiment to the trading post on Wounded Knee Creek to facilitate the disarming of the Indians. Whiteside had noticed marked hostility among Big Foot's young men and hoped this show of force might overawe them "so they would submit quietly to be disarmed." Forsyth, who would take command at Wounded Knee, had over five hundred men and two batteries of Hotchkiss breech-loading mountain artillery.[35]

On the morning of December 29, 1890, Forsyth dispersed his troops, with the Hotchkiss guns on a hill above Big Foot's village, and moved in to disarm the Indians. The Sioux surrendered only a few old guns, so it was decided to search the village. The soldiers soon collected a small arsenal, but again mostly old weapons. Forsyth ordered the assembled warriors to remove their blankets, where he thought their Winchesters were concealed. A Ghost Dance leader named Yellow Bird, who had been dancing and singing the whole time, suddenly tossed two handfuls of dirt into the air. Several young men threw off their blankets and leveled their rifles at the soldiers. Both sides opened fire at point-blank range. Among the first to fall were Captain George D. Wallace, who had survived the Little Big Horn, and Big Foot, both shot through the head. Within five minutes, twenty warriors and thirty soldiers were dead or wounded on the ground. As the Indians broke through the soldier line, Forsyth raced up the hill to the artillery and gave the order to fire. The officers at the guns had hesitated for fear of hitting their own men but now opened up, firing fifty explosive shells a minute. When it was over at least 153 Sioux—many of them women and children—were dead and 44 wounded, along with 25 soldiers killed and another 39 wounded. It had been a perfect slaughter, with large numbers of women and children, as well as several soldiers, indiscriminately cut down by the Hotchkiss guns. General Miles termed it a "massacre."

The campaign, the last of nearly four hundred years of conflict since Columbus first landed, came to its sad end. Buffalo Bill Cody was there, promoted from colonel to general in the Nebraska National Guard and sent by the state governor to confer with Miles. He reported all quiet on Pine Ridge and urged respect for Indian rights: "I think it looks like peace, and if so, the greater the victory." Many of his show Indians were employed as police at Pine Ridge and he fretted over their safety. He also worried about the Ghost Dancers, and when Miles sent nineteen as prisoners to Fort Sheridan at Chicago, Cody interceded and had them released to his custody to accompany the *Wild West* to Europe in the spring.

It all came to a colorful but melancholy end on January 21 in a grand review of over 3,000 soldiers at Pine Ridge. Cody sat his horse next to General Miles as the troops passed in review in a blinding sandstorm. Guidons whipped in the wind while one by one the regiments passed in review. As Whiteside led the 7th in review, the band struck up "Garryowen," Custer's regimental air, and Miles, overcome with emotion, removed his hat in a quiet salute. Thus did centuries of warfare come to an end.[36]

Cody had one last mission to undertake. He sought out the family of Sitting Bull to ask if he might purchase the chief's gray horse from them. They agreed. And so the dancing horse returned to the *Wild West*.

28

WILD WEST

Sitting Bull's gray horse led the grand procession of the newly retitled *Buffalo Bill's Wild West and Congress of Rough Riders of the World* as it made its way to the showgrounds outside the entrance to the 1893 World's Columbian Exposition in Chicago. The midwestern snobs who ran the "White City" had decided not to allow the *Wild West* inside the fairgrounds, but Salsbury had wisely leased a fourteen-acre lot between Sixty-Second and Sixty-Third Streets, outside the entrance.

"Ladies and gentlemen, permit me to introduce to you a Congress of Rough Riders of the World!" boomed the deep voice of the forty-seven-year-old showman as he swept off his white Stetson on opening day, April 3, 1893.

It was his first show in America in four years, and it was bigger than ever. The arena stands could hold 18,000 spectators. There were now six hundred in the entire company, with up to four hundred in the arena at one time. Not only cowboys and Indians followed the gray horse into the arena but also Cossacks, German uhlans, French chasseurs, Mexican vaqueros, Arabs, British lancers, and American cavalrymen—and of course the thirty-seven-member cowboy band. It would prove to be the most successful season yet, with over 3 million tickets sold and a profit of a million dollars. Even more tickets were given away to the orphans and waifs of the "Windy City."

Of course, Buffalo Bill was still the main draw. One admiring female visitor wrote: "Cody is one of the most imposing men in appearance that America ever grew in her kindly atmosphere. In his earlier days a hint of the border desperado lurked in his blazing eyes and the poetic fierceness of his mien and coloring. Now it is all subdued into pleasantness and he is the kindliest, most benign gentleman, as simple as a village priest and learned as a savant of Chartreuse."[1]

Salsbury had new stationery printed featuring a portrait of Columbus on one side and Cody on the other—with "Pilot of the Ocean, the first Pioneer" under the admiral and "Pilot of the Prairie, the last Pioneer" under the colonel.

Indians remained a major component of the show, with seventy-four men and women from Pine Ridge in the company. Cody also brought an additional one hundred from Rosebud, Standing Rock, and Pine Ridge to follow Sitting Bull's gray horse in the opening parade. Cody treated the Lakotas to a day at the Columbian Exhibition at his expense. Amy Leslie, who wrote a column on the fair for the *Chicago Daily News*, noted the visitors' appearance as "a blazing line of character moving along with high, flaunting crests of feathers and flaming blankets which stood out against the gleaming white of the staff dome like a rainbow cleft into remembrances of a lost, primitive glory."[2]

Several of Cody's Lakota guests were former Ghost Dancers, and they must have been amazed to see Sitting Bull's death cabin on the fairgrounds. It had been carefully taken down piece by piece from Grand River and reconstructed on the Midway (a new name coined for the carnival sideshow area that included Little Egypt belly dancing to the "hootchy-kootchy" and the amazing Ferris wheel). Cody arranged a meeting between several of the Indians and Grover Cleveland on the day the president turned on the electric lights for the exposition.

One warm summer evening, fifteen show Indians took over the Midway merry-go-round and proceeded to let loose with full-throated war cries as they rode the brightly painted ponies. A reporter for the *Chicago News Record* noted that the Indians "seem to like being jerked around on a carousel. They prefer it to art galleries, and some people who are not Indians feel the same way."[3]

Amy Leslie, in comparing Cody's show to the highbrow neoclassicism of the White City or the gaudy Midway, noted that it was the "American Exposition" where the visitor could "find Americans, real Americans."[4]

The components of the 1893 program proved so successful that they remained relatively unchanged for the next fifteen years: an overture—"The Star-Spangled Banner"; the Grand Review; Annie Oakley; horse races between the various rough riders of the world; the Pony Express; an attack on a wagon train and rescue by Buffalo Bill and cowboys; Arabian horsemen; Cossacks; Johnny Baker Cowboy Kid, marksman; Mexican vaqueros; a horse race between Prairie, Spanish, and Indian girls; cowboys; military evolutions by world cavalrymen; an attack on the Deadwood stage; an Indian bareback race; customs of the Indians; Colonel Cody sharpshooting; a buffalo hunt with Buffalo Bill and Indians; the Battle of the Little Big Horn, Custer's Last Charge; and the final salute.

An exceedingly awkward moment for Cody occurred near the end of the season in Chicago when Louisa decided to pay a surprise visit. Upon her arrival she inquired at his hotel for Colonel Cody and identified herself, only to be informed that Mrs. Cody was already at the hotel. Charles Whalen, the longtime *Wild West* employee who often told this story, had only sympathy for the colonel. "It was only natural; any man would have done the same, the way women ran after him," he declared. The incident would later come up in the colonel's divorce suit.[5]

A special invitation was extended in July to the historians participating in the lofty "World's Congress of Historians and Historical Students" at the new Art Institute. One historian who could not attend the afternoon Wild West show on July 12 was a rather obscure thirty-two-year-old professor from the University of Wisconsin: Frederick Jackson Turner. He was still tinkering with the paper he was to deliver that evening.

"I am," the notorious procrastinator told his good friend Woodrow Wilson, "in the final agonies of getting out a belated paper."[6]

The gathering had been organized by Henry Baxter Adams, secretary of the American Historical Association, and William F. Poole of Chicago's Newberry Library. There was some difficulty in persuading distinguished Eastern historians to dare the wilds of Chicago.

"I fancy people at the World's Fair will not care much about hearing historical papers," grumbled Adams. Fortunately, the program committee worked to provide enough speakers to listen to the other speakers, as usually happens at such gatherings. The AHA had been organized by Adams in 1884 in an effort to professionalize the historical profession and move away from the "literary history" as practiced by such luminaries as George Bancroft, Francis Parkman, and William H. Prescott. Within a few years there were six hundred members, most of them academics devoted to the new "scientific history" practiced in Germany. (Adams had received his doctorate from Heidelberg University.)

Adams personally invited his former student from Johns Hopkins University, young Fred Turner, who had completed his graduate work in 1888. Turner agreed to give a paper entitled "The Significance of the Frontier in American History."[7]

Turner was himself a child of the frontier, born in Portage, Wisconsin, on November 14, 1861. The town was on a famous fur trade route from Green Bay to the Mississippi River, although by Turner's boyhood it was a lumber town. The boy enjoyed the outdoors, becoming an avid fisherman, but did not neglect his studies. He was educated at the then quite small University of Wisconsin in Madison, where he excelled in history and oratory. After graduating, the gifted student was offered a position substituting for his mentor, Francis Allen, who was on leave. This teaching experience inspired him to pursue a master's degree, which he completed in 1888 on the Wisconsin fur trade. In hopes of securing a permanent position at Wisconsin, Turner entered Johns Hopkins University in 1888 in order to secure his doctorate. It was in Baltimore that he formed warm friendships with Woodrow Wilson and Herbert Baxter Adams. Upon completion of his doctorate, Turner returned to Madison, where he secured a permanent faculty position in 1891.

Turner's turn to speak came the evening of Wednesday, July 12. It had been a stifling hot day, but a lake breeze helped cool the evening a bit. Turner was preceded by four other speakers on such diverse topics as "English Popular Uprisings in the Middle Ages" and "Early Lead Mining in Illinois and Wisconsin." Turner certainly must have given an abbreviated version of his paper to what was left of the small crowd in the hall, and even that remnant seemed bored. There were no questions when he finished.[8]

Little did Turner or anyone else in that room realize that he had just issued a clarion call for a new historical approach to the American story. "The true point of view in the history of this nation is not the Atlantic coast, it is the Great West," he announced in a declaration of independence from the shackles of an Eastern-dominated historiography.

"American democracy was born of no theorist's dream," Turner declared. "It came out of the American forest, and it gained new strength each time it touched a new frontier." Turner shifted the emphasis of our national story from the East to the West with his bold assertion that the distinctiveness of American cultural and political society, as well as our exceptional national character, emerged from the frontier experience. "The existence of an area of free land, its continuous recession, and the advance of American settlement westward, explain American development," he boldly declared. He refuted the then prevailing theory that American institutions had evolved from so-called European germ cells without regard to environmental factors. It was the frontier—which he characterized as "the meeting point between savagery and civilization"—that explained the unique American character: a rejection of class and aristocracy, of established religion, standing armies, and the other trappings of Europe in favor of adaptation, innovation, invention, individualism, and a rough-hewn democracy. The frontier was not only a process; it was also a state of mind. Turner worried about the future of the country now that the frontier had closed.[9]

Turner sent copies of his essay to leading historians and gradually it gained traction. Theodore Roosevelt wrote to congratulate Turner: "I think you have struck some first class ideas, and have put into definite shape a good deal of thought that has been floating around rather loosely." Roosevelt felt he could use the thesis in the completion of the third volume of his monumental *The Winning of the West.* Turner's friend Wilson, even more complimentary, spread the word in academic circles about this remarkable new essay. Others took up Turner's crusade to change the focus of teaching American history to the West, so that by the time of Turner's death in 1932 some 60 percent of the history departments in the nation's major colleges and universities taught classes on frontier or western history. His ideas of American frontier exceptionalism escaped the halls of the academy to influence popular thought as much as Cody's show business inventions had done. Novelists, filmmakers, journalists, and politicians all came to embrace the "Turner Thesis." Turner and Cody had won the West that hot summer in Chicago and placed it firmly as the centerpiece of American thought.[10]

In the years to come, the *Wild West* would play even more venues, giving up long stands in one place for shorter performances. This was the brainchild of James Anthony Bailey (of Barnum & Bailey fame), who leased fifty-two railway cars and moved the show rapidly from venue to venue. In

1895 the show did 131 stands in 190 days over a 9,000-mile route. The next year they did 10,000 miles and 132 stops. Burke went in advance, plastering towns with posters. The printing bill was astronomical, with Cody paying close attention to the detail and quality of the colorful broadsides. It was an amazing organizational feat.[11]

There were setbacks along the way. Annie Oakley was seriously injured in a train wreck in 1901 and retired just before the show's final European tour; Nate Salsbury died on Christmas Eve 1902; a mining venture in Arizona proved financially disastrous; Cody's dream of founding his namesake town in Wyoming's Bighorn Basin near Yellowstone, although successful, was a drain on his fortune; and then in 1905 came a scandalous divorce trial between Cody and Louisa that embarrassed everyone involved. Cody, humiliated before the world, was not granted a divorce. In time, with advancing age, their relationship grew less toxic.

After Salsbury's death, the show went into a slow decline, finally going bankrupt in 1913. Cody, worn-out and in declining health, toured for two more seasons with the Sells-Floto Circus and made his final appearance with the *Miller Brothers 101 Ranch Wild West* show in 1916. The new medium of motion pictures was proving fatal to the big-arena shows. Cody tried his hand at the movies but that failed as well.

Buffalo Bill Cody died on January 10, 1917, at his sister's home in Denver. It was as if a final connection between the modern America of urban blight, industry, automobiles, airplanes, and world wars and the old frontier America of the pristine wilderness, the Pony Express, the stagecoach, and the Indian Wars had been severed. The city of Denver, not about to lose a potential tourist attraction, buried Cody amidst much ceremony atop Lookout Mountain in a steel vault lined with concrete. They feared that the citizens of Cody, Wyoming, the town Buffalo Bill had promoted and made his home after 1902, might attempt to steal the body. Buffalo Bill was a valuable commodity, dead or alive. No doubt Cody would have understood. It was, after all, show business.

William F. Cody was a man seemingly trapped in the distant past, yet one who cared desperately about the onrushing future—for himself, his family, his business, and his country. He was progressive in politics (he favored votes for women long before President Woodrow Wilson came around) and was, for his time and place, enlightened on questions of race and equality. He had risen from poverty to incredible wealth, was fawned over by kings and queens, presidents and captains of industry, and in his time was the living symbol of "The American." President Theodore Roosevelt described him as "an American of Americans. He embodied those traits of courage, strength, and self-reliant hardihood which are vital to the well-being of the nation."[12]

Gene Fowler, who knew Cody in his twilight years, left a more cynical characterization: "The celebrated Colonel's biographers have made him a Sir Galahad of the plains, an Indian fighter and scout superior to the rugged, taciturn Kit Carson. His critics have gone to the other extreme, portraying him as a bellowing faker, a butcher of buffaloes, a glutton for rum and romance. The man himself is lost between legend and calumny. All agreed, obviously, that demigod or satyr, Buffalo Bill was an institution."[13]

He was, like the nation he came to symbolize, a bundle of contradictions: a hunter who became a conservationist; a friend to Indians who was famed as an Indian fighter; a rugged frontier scout best remembered as a sequined showman; a living artifact of a pioneer past playing out his role in a rapidly changing world of telephones, radios, motion pictures, and skyscrapers.

Cody lived the Wild West from 1846 to 1876, then he took it on the road—first in stage shows and then in the greatest arena extravaganza of all time. It was a romantic adventure, a gilded historical pageant, a combination rodeo and circus, and, most importantly, a tale of progress. Cody gave to Americans and then to people all around the world a compelling story of the birth of the United States. He became the physical embodiment of that story and the American spirit, presenting to the world an image of rugged Americanism as important to the nineteenth century as Benjamin Franklin had been to the previous century.

While Cody inherited the frontier crown of Boone, Crockett, and Carson, it was he, along with his contemporaries Frederick Jackson Turner and Theodore Roosevelt, who made the story of the American frontier into the nation's creation myth. Buffalo Bill astride his snow-white stallion presented an image that all the people of a rapidly changing nation could embrace no matter where they had come from.

When Cody died, his country—marching into a future of steam, steel, and international power—paused and reflected on just how far they had come in so short a time. It had all been encompassed in the life of this one man, and with the passing of Buffalo Bill it seemed as if a great page in American history had been turned.

By the time of Cody's death, Frederick Jackson Turner had departed the bracing air of Madison and the University of Wisconsin for the far more rarified atmosphere of Cambridge, Massachusetts, and Harvard. He had reached the pinnacle of his academic life, although he never wrote the "Great Book" that everyone longed for. By then his legions of students had carried his ideas throughout the nation, so that his celebration of the first great period of American history and his anxiety over the close of the frontier became an accepted part of national consciousness. His words have since echoed down through the generations:

"Stand at Cumberland Gap and watch the procession of civilization, marching single file—the buffalo, following the trail to the salt springs, the Indian, the fur trader and hunter, the cattle raiser, the pioneer farmer—and the frontier has passed by."[14]

ACKNOWLEDGMENTS

A book of this nature is built upon a lifetime of research, study, and contemplation. Innumerable debts to librarians and archivists across the country were incurred. Many historians, both academic and literary, grandmasters as well as grassroots, influenced my thinking and writing. Most especially I must acknowledge my professional mentors—Martin Ridge, Robert M. Utley, and David J. Weber. They inspired and guided me throughout much of my career. They are gone now, but all left an indelible mark on the historical profession—and on this author.

As always thanks are due my agent, James Donovan, himself a fine historian and talented writer, who is a master of structure and story technique as well as the nuts and bolts of the publishing world.

David Howe, my talented editor at Dutton, has been a pleasure to work with. His light editorial touch was always insightful and productive. Thanks also to Alice Dalrymple, Ella Kurki, and Nicole Jarvis at Dutton. Once again, Jeff Ward provided superb maps. Brent Howard, my initial editor at Dutton who left to pursue a career as an agent at Gramercy Literary, was an unflagging champion of this book.

Particular thanks are due my University of New Mexico students Jackson Andress, Jason Strykowski, Candolin Cook, David Pafford, and Alexander Marx for research assistance. Professor Durwood Ball, my student who in time became my colleague in the UNM History Department, was always ready to discuss the travails of the historian's craft.

Also in the UNM History Department, Yolanda Martinez, the office manager, continued her enduring support and warm friendship that I have relied upon for forty years. I will miss her wise counsel as I depart from the university this year. Dana Ellison once again went above and beyond in her help with this book, as did Marie Walper. Thanks also to History Department chair Melissa Bokovoy.

Much like Daniel Boone, I am departing academe late in life, after forty-eight years of teaching, to move in search of "elbow room" and adventure on a new professional frontier. Thanks are especially due to Naoma Tate, whose dedication to the cultural values of the American West is inspiring and whom I have worked with for many years on the board of the Buffalo Bill Museum at the Buffalo Bill Center of the West in Cody, Wyoming, an institution we both treasure. Upon the untimely passing of my friend Jeremy Johnston, the curator of the Buffalo Bill Museum, it was Naoma who suggested that I consider taking on the position of interim curator. Thanks also to Mary Anne Dingus, Rebecca West, Karen McWhorter, Terry Harley, Anne Marie Shriver, and Sam Hanna for helping to make this unexpected opportunity a reality.

Many thanks as well to Paul Fees, Marvin Kaiser, Stuart Rosebrook, Elaine Nelson, Kent Blansett, Barton Barbour, Alden Big Man, Jeffrey Pearson, Meg Frisbee, Liping Zhu, Ollie Reed, Greg Lalire, Hampton Sides, William C. Davis, Thom Ross, Rusty York, Jon Belyeu, Faye Oshima Belyeu, Charles Rankin, Eli Paul, Jerome Greene, Brian W. Dippie, Rich Markey, Joel Strom, Andy Marx, Don Fork, Tim Gravenstreter, Bruce Dinges, Vince Heier, Frank Thompson, John Carson, Mark Lee Gardner, Tara Walch, Patty Limerick, Louis Warren, and Stephen Harrigan.

Special thanks are also due to Gary Foreman of Native Sun Productions, Sam Dolan of Warm Springs Productions, and Bill Kurtis, with whom I collaborated on a series of western television documentaries.

Significant contributions were made to this book by Bob Boze Bell of *True West* magazine, who has done more than anyone else on the planet to celebrate our frontier heritage and keep western history alive. David Zucker, who shares my passion for history and especially for our mutual hero Davy Crockett, provided critical advice as well as research materials. Paul Hedren, my friend of half a century, carefully critiqued several chapters.

I would be remiss if I did not mention my steadfast companion throughout the writing of this book—my yellow Labrador, Captain Bucky O'Neill. He was sprawled at my feet every hour that I wrote, and when I fell terribly ill for several months, he never left my side. He passed away just a few weeks before the completion of this manuscript—he has been missed every day since. In a lifetime of wonderful dogs, he was the very best.

My wife, Tracy, suffered through the intense angst I created in the long struggle to complete this book. She proved once again to be my best advisor, critic, patient helpmate, and then tender nurse during my long illness. This book is a testament to her unwavering loyalty, courage, and devotion. As smart as she is lovely, she inspires me every day.

Several readers of *Apache Wars* have written me to comment on my unknown German mother mentioned at the end of the acknowledgments of that book. Through the heroic efforts and dogged determination of my daughter, Lorena, through five years of searching, the mystery has been solved. Lorena wrote countless letters to German officials in search of information. In response we learned the details of my birth, my mother's name—Maria Lina Ingeburg Adler—but not her fate. Then, just weeks before this book went to press, we received a letter from the German Red Cross with the astonishing news that my mother had only recently passed away in August 2021 at the age of ninety-four. It was indeed sad to discover that she was still alive when we began our search and that I might have been able to meet her, but we were gratified to learn the name of my first cousin—Edeltraud Muller—who cared for her in her last years. My mother had kept my birth a secret from her family until the end of her life. We have since contacted my cousin, as well as her son, Philip Muller, and have made an emotional and gratifying connection. From being a lost orphan, I have suddenly discovered a large extended family in Germany. How strange is fate?

This book is dedicated to my children—who are indeed the greatest gift of life.

NOTES

CHAPTER 1: DEATH ON THE MONONGAHELA

1. Neal O. Hammon, ed., *My Father, Daniel Boone: The Draper Interviews with Nathan Boone* (Lexington: University Press of Kentucky, 1999), 41–42.

2. Michael A. Lofaro, *Daniel Boone: An American Life* (Lexington: University Press of Kentucky, 2003), 4–5.

3. Robert Morgan, *Boone: A Biography* (Chapel Hill, NC: Algonquin Books, 2007), 30–32; and Ted Franklin Belue, *The Hunters of Kentucky: A Narrative History of America's First Far West, 1750–1792* (Mechanicsburg, PA: Stackpole, 2003), 87–93. Boone's family history is laid out in four excellent modern biographies: John Mack Faragher, *Daniel Boone: The Life and Legend of an American Pioneer* (New York: Henry Holt, 1992), 9–13; Morgan, *Boone*, 1–21; Lofaro, *Daniel Boone*, 1–9; and Meredith Mason Brown, *Frontiersman: Daniel Boone and the Making of America* (Baton Rouge: Louisiana State University Press, 2008), 3–11. There are also several classic biographies of Boone. The first was John Filson, *The Discovery, Settlement and Present State of Kentucke* (Wilmington, DE: James Adams, 1784), which has the important appendix "The Adventures of Col. Daniel Boon," which is Boone's autobiography. Filson's little book has been reprinted in numerous editions. The first major Boone biography—and a source of considerable information and misinformation—was Timothy Flint, *Biographical Memoir of Daniel Boone, The First Settler of Kentucky* (Cincinnati: N. and G. Guilford, 1833). For a valuable annotated edition of Flint, see Michael A. Lofaro, ed., *Boone, Black Hawk, and Crockett in 1833: Unsettling the Mythic West* (Knoxville: University of Tennessee Press, 2019). Older classic biographies include Reuben Gold Thwaites, *Daniel Boone* (New York: Appleton, 1902); John Bakeless, *Daniel Boone: Master of the Wilderness* (New York: Morrow, 1939); and Stewart Edward White, *Daniel Boone: Wilderness Scout* (New York: Doubleday, 1992). Also see Lyman C. Draper, *The Life of Daniel Boone*, ed. Ted Franklin Belue (Mechanicsburg, PA: Stackpole, 1998), 101–23. It is to Lyman Draper, the secretary of the Wisconsin Historical Society, that we owe a huge debt for his tireless efforts to collect stories from hundreds of early pioneers. His papers at the Wisconsin State Historical Society are a treasure trove of enormous value. Several libraries have microfilm copies.

4. The literature on George Washington is vast and exhaustive, but the best account of his early western activities is to be found in Colin G. Calloway, *The Indian World of*

George Washington (New York: Oxford University Press, 2018), 45–101. Also see Thomas Perkins Abernathy, *Western Lands and the American Revolution* (New York: D. Appleton, Century, 1937); and Kenneth P. Bailey, *The Ohio Company of Virginia and the Westward Movement, 1748–1792* (Glendale, CA: Arthur H. Clark, 1939). For Washington's early career, see Douglas Southall Freeman, *George Washington: Young Washington*, 2 vols. (New York: Charles Scribner's Sons, 1948); James Thomas Flexner, *George Washington: The Forge of Experience 1732–1775* (Boston: Little, Brown, 1965); Peter Stark, *Young Washington* (New York: Ecco, 2018); and Donald Jackson, ed., *The Diaries of George Washington*, vol. 1, *1748–65* (Charlottesville: University of Virginia, 1976). Washington's expedition is covered in Jackson, *Diaries*, vol. 1, 118–61, with the quote about Gist on p. 130; and Freeman, *Young Washington*, vol. 1, 274–326. Washington's report was reprinted in several period newspapers as well as appearing as *The Journal of Major George Washington, Sent by the Hon. Robert Dinwiddie, Esq.; His Majesty's Lieutenant-Governor, and Commander-in-Chief of Virginia, to the Commandant of the French Forces in Ohio. To Which Are Added, the Governor's Letter, and a Translation of the French Officer's Answer* (Williamsburg, VA: William Hunter, 1754).

5. Nicholas B. Wainwright, *George Croghan: Wilderness Diplomat* (Chapel Hill: University of North Carolina Press, 1959), 62–63. Also see Albert T. Volwiler, *George Croghan and the Westward Movement, 1741–1782* (Cleveland: Arthur H. Clark, 1926), 85–88; and James H. Merrell, *Into the American Woods: Negotiators on the Pennsylvania Frontier* (New York: W. W. Norton, 1999), 75–77, 81–83.

6. Calloway, *Indian World*, 84–101, and 97–98 for the Half King quote; Jackson, *Diaries*, vol. 1, 162–210; Freeman, *Young Washington*, vol. 1, 340–411; Fred Anderson, *Crucible of War: The Seven Years' War and the Fate of Empire in British North America* (New York: Alfred A. Knopf, 2000), 50–65; and David A. Clary, *George Washington's First War* (New York: Simon & Schuster, 2011), 68–114.

7. Anderson, *Crucible of War*, 66–70. An equally excellent but much briefer account of these events is to be found in Fred Anderson, *The War That Made America: A Short History of the French and Indian War* (New York: Viking, 2005). Also see Michael N. McConnell, *Army and Empire: British Soldiers on the American Frontier, 1758–1775* (Lincoln: University of Nebraska Press, 2005).

8. Jackson, *Diaries*, vol. 1, 172; and Anderson, *Crucible of War*, 71–73.

9. Benjamin Franklin, *The Autobiography and Other Writings*, ed. Kenneth Silverman (New York: Penguin Books, 1986), 132–36; and Anderson, *Crucible of War*, 77–93. Also see Timothy J. Shannon, *Indians and Colonists at the Crossroads of Empire: The Albany Congress of 1754* (Ithaca, NY: Cornell University Press, 1999).

10. Franklin, *Autobiography*, 136–41; and David Preston, *Braddock's Defeat: The Battle of the Monongahela and the Road to Revolution* (New York: Oxford University Press, 2015), 92–97.

11. Freeman, *Young Washington*, vol. 1, 415–16; Calloway, *Indian World*, 97–99.

12. Freeman, *Young Washington*, vol. 1, 440–41, vol. 2, 10–21.

13. Franklin, *Autobiography*, 141–42; Dale Van Every, *Forth to the Wilderness: The First American Frontier, 1754–1774* (New York: Morrow, 1961), 73–74; and Anderson, *Crucible of War*, 94–96; and Calloway, *Indian World*, 113, for Scarouady's statement. The Mingo leader's son was killed by "friendly fire" during the campaign.

14. Preston, *Braddock's Defeat*, 67–68, 121.
15. Faragher, *Daniel Boone*, 36–37; and Lofaro, *Boone*, 12–15.
16. Don Higginbotham, *Daniel Morgan: Revolutionary Rifleman* (Chapel Hill: University of North Carolina Press, 1961), 4–6; Kenneth Roberts, *The Battle of Cowpens* (Garden City, NY: Doubleday, 1958), 36–37; Lawrence E. Babits, *A Devil of a Whipping: The Battle of Cowpens* (Chapel Hill: University of North Carolina Press, 1998), 23–24; and Preston, *Braddock's Defeat*, 96–97.
17. Hammon, *My Father*, 14; Faragher, *Daniel Boone*, 69–71; Morgan, *Boone*, 47; and Brown, *Frontiersman*, 19–20.
18. Freeman, *Young Washington*, vol. 2, 60–68; Preston, *Braddock's Defeat*, 207–21; and Clary, *Washington's First War*, 131–43.
19. John Marshall, *The Life of George Washington*, 2 vols. (Philadelphia: James Crissy, 1832), vol. 1, 9. Dr. Craik was Washington's close friend and personal physician. During the Revolution he became the physician general of the army. He was also the attending physician at Washington's death.
20. Franklin, *Autobiography*, 142; and Freeman, *Young Washington*, vol. 2, 78–79.
21. The best and most detailed account of the battle is in Preston, *Braddock's Defeat*, 217–67. But also see Anderson, *Crucible of War*, 94–107; Calloway, *Indian World*, 109–13; Clary, *Washington's First War*, 144–66; Van Every, *Forth to the Wilderness*, 74–79; and Walter O'Meara, *Guns at the Forks* (Englewood Cliffs, NJ: Prentice Hall, 1965), 130–51. Orme is quoted in Preston, *Braddock's Defeat*, 248, and Washington in Freeman, *Young Washington*, vol. 2, 76. Also see Winthrop Sargent, ed., *The History of the Expedition Against Fort Duquesne in 1755; Under Major-General Edward Braddock* (Philadelphia: Lippincott/Historical Society of Pennsylvania, 1855), which contains considerable original material, including the journals of Captain Orme and others. For an interesting study of the nature of colonial Indian warfare, see Wayne E. Lee, *The Cutting-Off Way: Indigenous Warfare in Eastern North America, 1500–1800* (Chapel Hill: University of North Carolina Press, 2023).
22. The Orme quote is from Franklin, *Autobiography*, 143–44. Also see Preston, *Braddock's Defeat*, 273.
23. O'Meara, *Guns at the Forks*, 150; Preston, *Braddock's Defeat*, 276–77; and Anderson, *Crucible of War*, 105.
24. Franklin, *Autobiography*, 143; and Freeman, *Young Washington*, vol. 2, 86–87, 103–6.

CHAPTER 2: THE FORKS OF THE OHIO

1. Fred Anderson, *The War That Made America: A Short History of the French and Indian War* (New York: Viking, 2005), 151–56; Douglas Southall Freeman, *George Washington: Young Washington* (New York: Charles Scribner's Sons, 1948), vol. 2, 107–18; and R. A. Brock, ed., *The Official Records of Robert Dinwiddie, Lieutenant-Governor of the Colony of Virginia, 1751–1758*, 2 vols. (Richmond: Virginia Historical Society, 1884), vol. 2, 114, 474.
2. Don Higginbotham, *Daniel Morgan* (Chapel Hill: University of North Carolina Press, 1961), 6–8; Freeman, *Young Washington*, vol. 2, 176–77, 199–203; and Walter O'Meara, *Guns at the Forks* (Englewood Cliffs, NJ: Prentice Hall, 1965), 170–71.

3. Colin G. Calloway, *The Indian World of George Washington* (New York: Oxford University Press, 2018), 27–28. The literature on the history and customs of Native Americans in this period and the crisis they faced is immense. Among the best and most accessible books are Richard White, *The Middle Ground: Indians, Empires and Republics in the Great Lakes Region, 1650–1815* (New York: Cambridge University Press, 1991); Ian K. Steele, *Warpaths: Invasions of North America* (New York: Oxford University Press, 1994); Timothy J. Shannon, *Iroquois Diplomacy on the Early Frontier* (New York: Viking, 2008); Colin G. Calloway, *The Shawnees and the War for America* (New York: Viking, 2007); Colin G. Calloway, *The American Revolution in Indian Country* (New York: Cambridge University Press, 1995); Michael N. McConnell, *A Country Between: The Upper Ohio Valley and Its Peoples, 1724–1774* (Lincoln: University of Nebraska Press, 1992); Sami Lakomaki, *Gathering Together: The Shawnee People Through Diaspora and Nationhood, 1600–1870* (New Haven, CT: Yale University Press, 2014); Gregory Evans Dowd, *A Spirited Resistance: The North American Indian Struggle for Unity, 1745–1815* (Baltimore: Johns Hopkins University Press, 1992); Eric Hinderaker, *Elusive Empires: Constructing Colonialism in the Ohio Valley, 1673–1800* (Cambridge: Cambridge University Press, 1997); Randolph C. Downes, *Council Fires on the Upper Ohio* (Pittsburgh: University of Pittsburgh Press, 1940); Francis Jennings, *The Invasion of America: Indians, Colonialism, and the Cant of Conquest* (Chapel Hill: University of North Carolina Press, 1976); Charles Hudson, *The Southeastern Indians* (Knoxville: University of Tennessee Press, 1976); John R. Swanton, *The Indians of the Southeastern United States* (Washington, DC: Smithsonian Institution Press, 1946); William Sturtevant and Bruce G. Trigger, eds., *Handbook of North American Indians: Northeast*, vol. 15 (Washington, DC: Smithsonian Institution, 1978); and William Sturtevant and Ray Fogelson, eds., *Handbook of North American Indians: Southeast*, vol. 14 (Washington, DC: Smithsonian Institution, 2004). For a dramatic global view of these changes, see Jared Diamond, *Guns, Germs, and Steel* (New York: W. W. Norton, 1997).

4. Calloway, *Indian World*, 33–34, 41–44.

5. Kathryn E. Holland Braund, *Deerskins and Duffels: The Creek Indian Trade with Anglo-America, 1685–1815* (Lincoln: University of Nebraska Press, 1993), 87–89, 96–98; and Calloway, *Indian World*, 42, for the Cherokee quote. Also see Dowd, *Spirited Resistance*, 1–22.

6. Nicholas B. Wainwright, *George Croghan: Wilderness Diplomat* (Chapel Hill: University of North Carolina Press, 1959), 49–50; Calloway, *Indian World*, 55; Albert T. Volwiler, *George Croghan* (Cleveland: Arthur H. Clark, 1926), 76–78; and Lois Mulkearn, "Why the Treaty of Logstown, 1752," *Virginia Magazine of History and Biography* 59 (January 1951): 3–20.

7. Wainwright, *George Croghan*, 96–98; and Benjamin Franklin, *The Autobiography and Other Writings*, ed. Kenneth Silverman (New York: Penguin Books, 1986), 143–45.

8. Wainwright, *George Croghan*, 104.

9. Volwiler, *Croghan*, 17–113; Wainwright, *George Croghan*, 3–134; and Thomas D. Clark, *Frontier America: The Story of the Westward Movement* (New York: Scribners, 1969), 33–35.

10. Wainwright, *George Croghan*, 105; and Volwiler, *Croghan*, 115–42.

11. O'Meara, *Guns at the Forks*, 185–86; and Freeman, *Young Washington*, vol. 2, 303–15, 322–28.
12. Freeman, *Young Washington*, vol. 2, 328–32.
13. Calloway, *Indian World*, 154–55; Anderson, *War That Made America*, 170; and Wainwright, *George Croghan*, 126–34.
14. O'Meara, *Guns at the Forks*, 199–207; Freeman, *Young Washington*, vol. 2, 340–60; and David A. Clary, *Washington's First War* (New York: Simon & Schuster, 2011), 254–57.
15. Calloway, *Indian World*, 158–59; Fred Anderson, *Crucible of War* (New York: Alfred A. Knopf, 2000), 282–85; and Freeman, *Young Washington*, vol. 2, 362–67. The most recent account of the Forbes Campaign is Michael N. McConnell, *To Risk It All: General Forbes, the Capture of Fort Duquesne, and the Course of Empire in the Ohio Country* (Pittsburgh: University of Pittsburgh Press, 2020).
16. O'Meara, *Guns at the Forks*, 213–24; and Anderson, *War That Made America*, 163–72.
17. Freeman, *Young Washington*, vol. 2, 368–99; and Calloway, *Indian World*, 171–88.
18. Neal O. Hammon, ed., *My Father, Daniel Boone* (Lexington: University Press of Kentucky, 1999), 13–14; John Mack Faragher, *Daniel Boone* (New York: Henry Holt, 1992), 38–39; and Robert Morgan, *Boone* (Chapel Hill, NC: Algonquin Books, 2007), 46–47.

CHAPTER 3: BUSHY RUN

1. Robert Rogers, *Journals of Major Robert Rogers* (London: J. Millan Bookseller, 1765), 195–231, quote on p. 218; John R. Cuneo, *Robert Rogers of the Rangers* (New York: Richardson and Steinman, 1987), 129–41; and Ray Allen Billington, *Westward Expansion: A History of the American Frontier* (New York: Macmillan, 1949), 132.
2. Nicholas B. Wainwright, *George Croghan: Wilderness Diplomat* (Chapel Hill: University of North Carolina Press, 1959), 174–77; Albert T. Volwiler, *George Croghan* (Cleveland: Arthur H. Clark, 1926), 154–57; Billington, *Westward Expansion*, 133; and Fred Anderson, *Crucible of War* (New York: Alfred A. Knopf, 2000), 505–6.
3. Milo Milton Quaife, ed., *The Siege of Detroit in 1763: The Journal of Pontiac's Conspiracy and John Rutherfurd's Narrative of a Captivity* (Chicago: R. R. Donnelley/Lakeside Press, 1958), which contains Neolin's speech as related by Robert Navarre, pp. 8–17; David Dixon, *Never Come to Peace Again: Pontiac's Uprising and the Fate of the British Empire in North America* (Norman: University of Oklahoma Press, 2005), 93–97; Howard H. Peckham, *Pontiac and the Indian Uprising* (Princeton, NJ: Princeton University Press, 1947), 112–16; Gregory Evans Dowd, *A Spirited Resistance* (Baltimore: Johns Hopkins University Press, 1992), 33–36; and Richard White, *The Middle Ground* (New York: Cambridge University Press, 1991), 279–85. Also see Gregory Evans Dowd, *War Under Heaven: Pontiac, the Indian Nations and the British Empire* (Baltimore: Johns Hopkins University Press, 2002); and Timothy J. Todish and Todd E. Harburn, *A Most Troublesome Situation: The British Military and the Pontiac Indian Uprising of 1763–1764* (Bovina Center, NY: Purple Mountain Press, 2006). The classic account of Pontiac's uprising, now considered dated but well worth reading, is Francis Parkman, *History of the Conspiracy of Pontiac* (Boston: Little, Brown, 1855).

For the non-academic reader, the books by Peckham and Dixon remain the best modern accounts.

4. Thomas D. Clark, *Frontier America* (New York: Scribner's, 1969), 74. Also see Dixon, *Never Come to Peace Again*, 73–84; Wainwright, *George Croghan*, 177, 180–81; and Anderson, *Crucible of War*, 535–46.

5. For Pontiac's appearance, see Quaife, *Siege of Detroit*, 3; Dixon, *Never Come to Peace Again*, 62; and Peckham, *Pontiac*, 28–29. No portrait from life was ever made of the Ottawa chief. Pontiac's quote is in Quaife, *Siege of Detroit*, 18–20.

6. Wainwright, *George Croghan*, 194–95; O'Meara, *Guns at the Forks*, 233.

7. Ecuyer to Bouquet, May 29, 1763, in *The Papers of Henry Bouquet*, vol. 6, 193. Colonel Bouquet's papers were published in seventeen typescript volumes by the Pennsylvania Historical and Museum Commission in 1940–43. The estimate of 2,000 killed or captured was by Croghan. Also see Dixon, *Never Come to Peace Again*, 136–38; and O'Meara, *Guns at the Forks*, 227–29.

8. Amherst to Bouquet, June 12, 1763, and Bouquet to Amherst, June 29, 1763, in *Bouquet Papers*, vol. 6, 205, 270–71; and O'Meara, *Guns at the Forks*, 234–35.

9. Cyrus Cort, *Col. Henry Bouquet and His Campaigns of 1763 and 1764* (Lancaster, PA: Steinman and Hensel, 1883), 17–18, 23–24.

10. Ecuyer quote in *Bouquet Papers*, vol. 6, 336–37. Also see Dixon, *Never Come to Peace Again*, 182–84; and O'Meara, *Guns at the Forks*, 230–32.

11. Bouquet to Amherst, August 5, 6, 1763, *Bouquet Papers*, vol. 6, 339–43. For the battle, see the reprint of the 1765 edition of William Smith, *Historical Account of Bouquet's Expedition Against the Ohio Indians in 1764* (Cincinnati: Robert Clarke, 1907), 1–23; Niles Anderson, "Bushy Run: Decisive Battle in the Wilderness," *Western Pennsylvania Historical Magazine* 46 (July 1963): 211–45; Cort, *Col. Henry Bouquet*, 34–50; Dixon, *Never Come to Peace Again*, 185–95; and O'Meara, *Guns at the Forks*, 236–44.

12. Dixon, *Never Come to Peace Again*, 190.

13. Mary C. Darlington, ed., *History of Col. Henry Bouquet and the Western Frontiers of Pennsylvania, 1747–1764* (New York: Arno Press, 1971), 196, reprint of the 1920 edition; Bouquet to Amherst, August 6, 1763, *Bouquet Papers*, vol. 6, 343; Dixon, *Never Come to Peace Again*, 193–94; and Parkman, *Conspiracy of Pontiac*, 352–68. Also see Brady J. Crytzer, *Guyasuta and the Fall of Indian America* (Yardley, PA: Westholme Publishing, 2013), 104–12.

14. Darlington, *History of Col. Henry Bouquet*, 209–10; Dixon, *Never Come to Peace Again*, 202; and Wainwright, *George Croghan*, 201.

15. Cort, *Col. Henry Bouquet*, 58–61; and Dixon, *Never Come to Peace Again*, 223.

16. Amherst to Bouquet, July 7, 1763, *Bouquet Papers*, vol. 6, 301, 315; Elizabeth Fenn, "Biological Warfare in Eighteenth-Century North America: Beyond Jeffrey Amherst," *Journal of American History* 86 (March 2000): 1552–80; Philip Ranlet, "The British, the Indians, and Smallpox: What Actually Happened at Fort Pitt in 1763?," *Pennsylvania History* 67 (Summer 2000): 427–41; Dixon, *Never Come to Peace Again*, 153–55; Colin Calloway, *The Indian World of George Washington* (New York: Oxford University Press, 2018), 176–77; Anderson, *Crucible of Empire*, 541–42; and Peckham, *Pontiac*, 226–28.

17. Brooke Hindle, "The March of the Paxton Boys," *William and Mary Quarterly* 3 (October 1946): 461–86; Merrell, *Into the American Woods*, 282–88; and Dixon, *Never Come to Peace Again*, 247–50. Also see Kevin Kenny, *Peaceable Kingdom Lost: The Paxton Boys and the Destruction of William Penn's Holy Experiment* (New York: Oxford University Press, 2009).

18. Alden T. Vaughan, "Frontier Banditti and the Indians: The Paxton Boys' Legacy, 1763–1775," *Pennsylvania History* 51 (January 1984): 1–29. Also see Parkman, *Conspiracy of Pontiac*, 409–25, 602–13.

19. Peckham, *Pontiac*, 201–8; Quaife, *Siege of Detroit*, 200–211; Cuneo, *Robert Rogers*, 162–67; Anderson, *Crucible of Empire*, 547–48; and Dixon, *Never Come to Peace Again*, 181, for the Amherst quote. Also see Parkman, *Conspiracy of Pontiac*, 267–79.

20. Ecuyer to Bouquet, November 10, 1764, *Bouquet Papers*, vol. 6, 464–65.

21. Dixon, *Never Come to Peace Again*, 216–17. Also see John Richard Alden, *General Gates in America: Being Principally a History of His Role in the American Revolution* (Baton Rouge: Louisiana State University Press, 1948).

22. Anderson, *Crucible of Empire*, 617–25; Peckham, *Pontiac*, 254–62; and Parkman, *Conspiracy of Pontiac*, 446–77.

23. Smith, *Historical Account of Bouquet's Expedition*, 24–75; "Conference Minutes," *Bouquet Papers*, vol. 6, 694–707; Dixon, *Never Come to Peace Again*, 234–41; Anderson, *Crucible of Empire*, 625–26; Peckham, *Pontiac*, 262–64; and Parkman, *Conspiracy of Pontiac*, 479–512.

24. Quote in Smith, *Historical Account of Bouquet's Expedition*, 74.

25. Dixon, *Never Come to Peace Again*, 252, 265–67. George III, despite a prohibition on the promotion of foreign-born officers to the rank of general, promoted Bouquet to the rank of brigadier general early in 1765. The new brigadier was ordered to take command of the Southern District with headquarters in Pensacola. General Bouquet arrived on August 25, 1765. He promptly contracted yellow fever and died on September 2, 1765, at the age of forty-seven.

26. Wainwright, *George Croghan*, 218–25; quote in Dixon, *Never Come to Peace Again*, 263.

27. Volwiler, *Croghan*, 195–98; Wainwright, *George Croghan*, 221–22 for quote on Pontiac; Dixon, *Never Come to Peace Again*, 264–65; and Parkman, *Conspiracy of Pontiac*, 539–59.

28. Peckham, *Pontiac*, 311–16; Dixon, *Never Come to Peace Again*, 268–69; Parkman, *Conspiracy of Pontiac*, 568–71; and Dowd, *War Under Heaven*, 260–62. Rumors persisted for years that the British had ordered Pontiac's assassination, but most modern historians now believe it was a personal quarrel that led to the chief's death. The lack of any significant reprisals against either the Peoria tribe or the British for Pontiac's murder support this conclusion.

CHAPTER 4: CUMBERLAND GAP

1. William Edward Myer, "Indian Trails of the Southeast," *Forty-Second Annual Report of the Bureau of American Ethnology to the Secretary of the Smithsonian Institution, 1924–1925*, part 4 (Washington, DC: United States Government Printing Office, 1928),

743–84; Robert L. Kincaid, *The Wilderness Road* (Indianapolis: Bobbs-Merrill, 1947), 25–26; Ted Franklin Belue, *The Hunters of Kentucky* (Mechanicsburg, PA: Stackpole, 2003), 12–15; and Robert Morgan, *Boone* (Chapel Hill, NC: Algonquin Books, 2007), 95–96.

2. Kincaid, *Wilderness Road*, 45–48; and Belue, *Hunters of Kentucky*, 19–33.

3. For Walker's expedition, see J. Stoddard Johnston, ed., *First Exploration of Kentucky: Dr. Thomas Walker's Journal of an Exploration of Kentucky in 1750* (Louisville: The Filson Club, 1898). An electronic version of Walker's journal is available via the internet courtesy of the University of Virginia Center for Digital History (2003). Also see Thomas D. Clark, *A History of Kentucky* (Lexington: John Bradford Press, 1960), 19–31; and David M. Burns, *Gateway: Dr. Thomas Walker and the Opening of the West* (Middlesboro, KY: Bell County Historical Society, 2000).

4. Ray Allen Billington, *Westward Expansion* (New York: Macmillan, 1949), 139–43.

5. Thomas D. Clark, *Frontier America* (New York: Scribner's, 1969), 84.

6. Colin G. Calloway, *The Indian World of George Washington* (New York: Oxford University Press, 2018), 182; and Clark, *Frontier America*, 88.

7. Douglas Southall Freeman, *George Washington: A Biography*, vol. 3, *Planter and Patriot* (New York: Scribner's, 1951), 246–47; Calloway, *Indian World*, 178–81. Also see Roy Bird Cook, *Washington's Western Lands* (Strasburg, VA: Shenandoah Publishing House, 1930); Bernhard Knollenberg, *George Washington: The Virginia Period, 1732–1775* (Durham, NC: Duke University Press, 1964); and Charles H. Ambler, *George Washington and the West* (Chapel Hill: University of North Carolina Press, 1936).

8. George Washington to William Crawford, September 21, 1767, in C. W. Butterfield, ed., *The Washington-Crawford Letters* (Cincinnati: Robert Clarke and Company, 1877), 1–5; and Freeman, *Planter and Patriot*, 101.

9. Washington to Crawford, September 21, 1767, in Butterfield, *Letters*, 4; Freeman, *Planter and Patriot*, 189–91; Calloway, *Indian World*, 185–88; and Ambler, *Washington and the West*, 136–38.

10. Robert N. Thompson, *Disaster on the Sandusky: The Life of Colonel William Crawford* (Staunton, VA: American History Press, 2017), 1–75; and Butterfield, *Letters*, vii–xi.

11. Freeman, *Planter and Patriot*, 257–58; Donald Jackson, ed., *The Diaries of George Washington* (Charlottesville: University of Virginia, 1976), vol. 2, 276–80; and Thompson, *Crawford*, 84.

12. Nicholas B. Wainwright, *George Croghan: Wilderness Diplomat* (Chapel Hill: University of North Carolina Press, 1959), 276–77; Freeman, *Planter and Patriot*, 259–61; Calloway, *Indian World*, 196–99; and Brady J. Crytzer, *Guyasuta and the Fall of Indian America* (Yardley, PA: Westholme Publishing, 2013), 116–18. For the Vandalia speculation, see Billington, *Westward Expansion*, 150–51; and Albert T. Volwiler, *George Croghan and the Westward Movement, 1741–1782* (Cleveland: Arthur H. Clark, 1926), 271–79, 285–86, 295–301.

13. Jackson, *Diaries*, vol. 2, 316–17.

14. Calloway, *Indian World*, 199. Washington details the entire journey in Jackson, *Diaries*, vol. 2, 276–328.

15. Thomas Perkins Abernethy, *Western Lands and the American Revolution* (New York: D. Appleton-Century, 1937), 47; and Calloway, *Indian World*, 178–79.

16. Lyman C. Draper, *The Life of Daniel Boone* (Mechanicsburg, PA: Stackpole, 1998), 139–41; John Mack Faragher, *Daniel Boone* (New York: Henry Holt, 1992), 43–48; Morgan, *Boone*, 48–54; and Michael A. Lofaro, *Daniel Boone* (Lexington: University Press of Kentucky, 2003), 15–17. The fire-hunt story first appeared in Timothy Flint's 1833 Boone biography. The patriarch Morgan Bryan had seven children, and his eldest son, Joseph, was the father of Rebecca.

17. Reuben Gold Thwaites, *Daniel Boone* (New York: Appleton, 1902), 212–13.

18. Belue, *Hunters of Kentucky*, 87–93, 205–14; and Carl P. Russell, *Guns on the Early Frontiers* (Berkeley: University of California Press, 1957), 175–77. Also see John G. W. Dillin, *The Kentucky Rifle* (Washington, DC: National Rifle Association, 1924).

19. "Mrs. Boone was present at the time he told me," Stephen Hempstead told Lyman Draper, "she made her knitting needles fly very fast I can assure you." Hempstead to Draper, February 15, March 6, 1863, Draper Mss., 16C 75–77; Lofaro, *Daniel Boone*, 19–20; Faragher, *Daniel Boone*, 58–59; and Morgan, *Boone*, 73–77.

20. Draper, *Life of Daniel Boone*, 204–8; and Neal O. Hammon, ed., *My Father, Daniel Boone* (Lexington: University Press of Kentucky, 1999), 23.

21. Jackson, *Diaries*, vol. 1, 18; and Billington, *Westward Expansion*, 87–91. Also see John W. Wayland, *The German Element of the Shenandoah Valley of Virginia* (Charlottesville, VA: Michie Company, 1907); and Walter Allen Knittle, *Early Eighteenth Century Palatine Emigration* (Philadelphia: Dorrance, 1937).

22. Billington, *Westward Expansion*, 93. There is a large literature on the Scotch-Irish in America. See Kenneth W. Keller, "What Is Distinctive About the Scotch-Irish?," in Robert D. Mitchell, ed., *Appalachian Frontiers: Settlement, Society, and Development in the Preindustrial Era* (Lexington: University Press of Kentucky, 1991), 69–86; James G. Leyburn, *The Scotch-Irish: A Social History* (Chapel Hill: University of North Carolina Press, 1989); H. Tyler Belhen and Curtis W. Wood Jr., *From Ulster to Carolina: The Migration of the Scotch-Irish to Southwestern North Carolina* (Chapel Hill: University of North Carolina Press, 1998); and Judith A. Ridner, *The Scots Irish of Early Pennsylvania: A Varied People* (Philadelphia: Temple University Press, 2018). A recent popular history is James Webb, *Born Fighting: How the Scots-Irish Shaped America* (New York: Crown, 2005).

23. For the Regulator movement, see Archibald Henderson, *The Conquest of the Old Southwest* (New York: Century Company, 1920), 160–95; Jack M. Sosin, *The Revolutionary Frontier, 1763–1783* (New York: Holt, Rinehart and Winston, 1967), 68–72; John Richard Alden, *The South in the Revolution, 1763–1789* (Baton Rouge: Louisiana State University Press, 1957), 153–63; and Archibald Henderson, "The Origin of the Regulation in North Carolina," *American Historical Review* 21 (January 1916): 320–32. Also see Marjoleine Kars, *Breaking Loose Together: The Regulator Rebellion in Pre-Revolutionary North Carolina* (Chapel Hill: University of North Carolina Press, 2002); and Richard Maxwell Brown, *The South Carolina Regulators: The Story of the First American Vigilante Movement* (Cambridge, MA: Harvard University Press, 1963).

24. John Filson, *The Discovery, Settlement and Present State of Kentucke* (Wilmington, DE: James Adams, 1784), 50–51; Faragher, *Daniel Boone*, 76–79; and Draper, *Life of Daniel Boone*, 204–11.

25. Draper, *Life of Daniel Boone*, 215–16; and Filson, *Discovery*, 51–52.

26. Squire Boone quote in Faragher, *Daniel Boone*, 82. Also see Morgan, *Boone*, 102–7.

27. Quote in Filson, *Discovery*, 52. It seems rather astonishing to think of Daniel Boone reading *Gulliver's Travels* by the light of a campfire deep in the wilds of Kentucky, but such was indeed the case. Boone even named a creek Lulbegrud after a town in the book. Jonathan Swift's 1726 satirical novel was quite popular in both Europe and America. Ironically, the book contributed the word "Yahoo" (a boorish, anti-intellectual lout) to the English language, which is how the Tidewater gentry referred to frontier folk like Boone.

28. Filson, *Discovery*, 55–56. For Stewart's disappearance, see Hammon, *My Father*, 28–30; and Draper, *Life of Daniel Boone*, 235–38.

29. Hammon, *My Father*, 31–32. Nathan Boone told Draper: "It was understood from the way in which he spoke of it that he had shot and killed the Indian; yet he seemed not to care about alluding more particularly to it." Nathan Boone and Abner Boone to Draper, Draper Mss., 1890, 6565, 30C44. This incident is discussed in Lofaro, *Daniel Boone*, 35–36; Meredith Mason Brown, *Frontiersman: Daniel Boone and the Making of America* (Baton Rouge: Louisiana State University Press, 2008), 52; Morgan, *Boone*, 113–14; and Faragher, *Daniel Boone*, 86.

30. Faragher, *Daniel Boone*, 86–87. John Roark told the reunion story to Draper. Draper Mss., 1885, 16, C81.

31. Filson, *Discovery*, 56–57.

CHAPTER 5: THE WILDERNESS ROAD

1. Lyman C. Draper, *The Life of Daniel Boone* (Mechanicsburg, PA: Stackpole, 1998), 284–85; John Mack Faragher, *Daniel Boone* (New York: Henry Holt, 1992), 90–91; John Filson, *The Discovery, Settlement and Present State of Kentucke* (Wilmington, DE: James Adams, 1784), 57; and Robert Morgan, *Boone* (Chapel Hill, NC: Algonquin Books, 2007), 132–34. In 1773, the Boone family consisted of James, sixteen, Israel, fourteen, Susannah, twelve, Jemima, ten, Levina, seven, Rebecca, five, Daniel, three, and baby Jesse. A son, William, was born in 1775 but did not survive infancy, while a final child, Nathan, was born in 1781 (and lived until 1856).

2. Washington to Crawford, September 25, 1773, and Crawford to Washington, November 12, 1773, in C. W. Butterfield, ed., *The Washington-Crawford Letters* (Cincinnati: Robert Clarke & Company, 1877), 29–37; Douglas Southall Freeman, *George Washington: Planter and Patriot* (New York: Scribner's, 1951), 333–35; Charles H. Ambler, *George Washington and the West* (Chapel Hill: University of North Carolina Press, 1936), 152; Michael A. Lofaro, *Daniel Boone* (Lexington: University Press of Kentucky, 2003), 43; and Colin G. Calloway, *The Indian World of George Washington* (New York: Oxford University Press, 2018), 202–6.

3. Lord Dunmore to the Earl of Dartmouth, December 24, 1774, in Reuben Gold Thwaites and Louise Phelps Kellogg, eds., *Documentary History of Dunmore's War, 1774* (Madison: Wisconsin Historical Society, 1905), 371. For Lord Dunmore, see James Corbett David, *Dunmore's New World* (Charlottesville: University of Virginia Press, 2013).

4. Neal O. Hammon, ed., *My Father, Daniel Boone* (Lexington: University of Kentucky Press, 1999), 39–42; Draper, *Life of Daniel Boone*, 283–90; Filson, *Discovery*, 57–58; Faragher, *Daniel Boone*, 91–95; and Morgan, *Boone*, 134–38.

5. Major Arthur Campbell to Colonel William Preston, June 20, 1774, in Thwaites and Kellogg, *Dunmore's War*, 38–39.

6. Crawford to Washington, May 8, 1774, in Butterfield, *Letters*, 46–50; Calloway, *Indian World*, 207–8; and Theodore Roosevelt, *The Winning of the West*, 6 vols. (New York: Current Literature Publishing, 1905), vol. 1, 254–62. Roosevelt's multivolume work, first published in 1889 by Putnam and then in many later editions, often makes use of language regarding Native Americans that is now deemed inappropriate. In this he is no different from almost all writers of his era but he is more roundly criticized because of his international notoriety. Nevertheless his impressive history contains much valuable detail as well as many interesting insights into the author's mindset on the eve of his rise to fame as a war hero and "cowboy president."

7. Filson, *Discovery*, 58–59; Captain William Russell to Colonel Preston, June 26, 1774, and Captain Daniel Smith to Colonel Preston, October 13, 1774, in Thwaites and Kellogg, *Dunmore's War*, 49–51, 248–49.

8. Logan's war message is in Thwaites and Kellogg, *Dunmore's War*, 246–47. Also see Faragher, *Daniel Boone*, 102–5.

9. The Battle of Point Pleasant is detailed in a series of reports and letters reprinted from the Draper Collection in Thwaites and Kellogg, *Dunmore's War*, 253–97. Stuart's quote is in John Stuart, "Narrative by Captain John Stuart of General Andrew Lewis' Expedition Against the Indians in the Year 1774 and the Battle of Point Pleasant, Virginia," part 1, *Magazine of American History* 1 (November 1877): 677–78. Also see Colin G. Calloway, *The Shawnees and the War for America* (New York: Viking, 2007), 55; Roosevelt, *Winning of the West*, vol. 2, 5–27; Dale Van Every, *Forth to the Wilderness* (New York: Morrow, 1961), 334–44; and Alexander S. Withers, *Chronicles of Border Warfare* (Cincinnati: Robert Clarke, 1895), 134–86.

10. Dunmore's account of both the war and the negotiations is in Dunmore to Dartmouth, December 24, 1774, in Thwaites and Kellogg, *Dunmore's War*, 368–95. The description of Cornstalk is in Withers, *Chronicles*, 186.

11. Logan's speech is reprinted in Roosevelt, *Winning of the West*, vol. 2, 30–31. There was considerable controversy over the authenticity of the speech, which Roosevelt discusses at length in an appendix, pp. 312–21. He proves it was authentic. Also see Thwaites and Kellogg, *Dunmore's War*, 305–6; Withers, *Chronicles*, 184; Anthony F. C. Wallace, *Jefferson and the Indians: The Tragic Fate of the First Americans* (Cambridge, MA: Harvard University Press, 1999), 1–20; Barbara Rasmussen, "Anarchy and Enterprise on the Imperial Frontier: Washington, Dunmore, Logan, and Land in the Eighteenth-Century Ohio Valley," *Ohio Valley History* 6, no. 4 (Winter 2006): 1–26; and Robert G. Parkinson, "From Indian Killer to Worthy Citizen: The Revolutionary Transformation of Michael Cresap," *William and Mary Quarterly* 63, no. 1 (January 2006): 97–122. Cresap later raised a company of Maryland riflemen for the Continental Army but fell ill in New York and died on October 18, 1775. He is buried in Trinity Church Cemetery not far from Alexander Hamilton, Horatio Gates, Albert Gallatin, and other notables.

12. Crawford to Washington, November 14, 1774, in Butterfield, *Letters*, 54–57; Withers, *Chronicles*, 184–85; Robert N. Thompson, *Disaster on the Sandusky* (Staunton, VA: American History Press, 2017), 106–8; Don Higginbotham, *Daniel Morgan* (Chapel Hill: University of North Carolina Press, 1961), 17–18; and Thwaites and Kellogg, *Dunmore's War*, 302–4.

13. Higginbotham, *Daniel Morgan*, 19; Thwaites and Kellogg, *Dunmore's War*, xxv, 311; and Roosevelt, *Winning of the West*, vol. 1, 31–33. For the reaction to the Quebec Act, see Freeman, *Washington*, vol. 3, 359; John Richard Alden, *The South in the Revolution* (Baton Rouge: Louisiana State University Press, 1957), 137–39; and Ray Allen Billington, *Westward Expansion* (New York: Macmillan, 1949), 152–53.

14. Alden, *South in the Revolution*, 184–85, 194–95; Thwaites and Kellogg, *Dunmore's War*, 425–28. Colonel Andrew Lewis was so highly regarded in Virginia that Washington recommended him to command the Continental Army in 1775. The Irish-born officer had served with Washington at Fort Necessity and again in the Forbes campaign. He was appointed brigadier general but resigned his commission in 1777 and died just before his sixty-first birthday in 1781.

15. Archibald Henderson, *The Conquest of the Old Southwest* (New York: Century Company, 1920), 104–15, 175–86, 216–25; Thomas D. Clark, *Frontier America* (New York: Scribner's, 1969), 105–7; and Billington, *Westward Expansion*, 168–70. Archibald Henderson was the great champion of Judge Henderson. In his writings he portrayed Boone as essentially the hired man of Henderson from an early date. In this he overstates the length of their relationship and somewhat twists the rather delicate nature of the conflicting interests of the land speculator and the long hunter. Each man represented a powerful strain of the American expansionist impulse and together they contributed mightily to the creation of a new nation that stretched all the way to the Mississippi River. Also see Stephen Aron, *How the West Was Lost: The Transformation of Kentucky from Daniel Boone to Henry Clay* (Baltimore: Johns Hopkins University Press, 1996), 59–70.

16. Felix Walker, "The First Settlement of Kentucky. Narrative of an Adventure in Kentucky in the Year 1775," *DeBow's Review* 16, no. 2 (February 1854): 151.

17. Filson, *Discovery*, 80; Draper, *Life of Daniel Boone*, 333; and Morgan, *Boone*, 159–62.

18. Aron, *How the West Was Lost*, 62–63; Van Every, *Forth to the Wilderness*, 347; Alden, *South in the Revolution*, 136–39.

19. Draper, *Life of Daniel Boone*, 332–33; Van Every, *Forth to the Wilderness*, 347; and Grace Steele Woodward, *The Cherokees* (Norman: University of Oklahoma Press, 1963), 22, 89–90.

20. Filson, *Discovery*, 59; and Faragher, *Daniel Boone*, 112–14.

21. Walker, "First Settlement," 151–53; Draper, *Life of Daniel Boone*, 335–37; and Robert L. Kincaid, *The Wilderness Road* (Indianapolis: Bobbs-Merrill, 1947), 100–103.

22. Walker, "First Settlement," 154; Hammon, *My Father*, 44–45; and Draper, *Life of Daniel Boone*, 337–39. Boone's letter is reprinted in Draper, 339, and in Faragher, *Daniel Boone*, 115.

23. Walker, "First Settlement," 153; and Ted Franklin Belue, *The Long Hunt: Death of the*

Buffalo East of the Mississippi (Mechanicsburg, PA: Stackpole, 1996), 107–10, 132–34, 163–64.

24. Walker, "First Settlement," 153–54. Felix Walker returned to North Carolina in 1775 and soon joined the Patriot forces in the Revolutionary War. In 1816 he was elected to the first of three terms in Congress as a Democratic-Republican (Jeffersonian). In 1820 he won considerable notoriety when, in the midst of a prolonged and heated debate over Missouri statehood, he rose to give a long-winded speech on behalf of his constituents in Buncombe County, the North Carolina county that made up his district. Walker was eventually shouted down by his congressional colleagues and "buncombe" (later changed to "bunkum" or simply "bunk") entered the American lexicon as a term for nonsense. He died in 1828.

25. Draper, *Life of Daniel Boone*, 341; and Kincaid, *Wilderness Road*, 107–9.

26. Kincaid, *Wilderness Road*, 113–16. Benjamin Logan eventually became colonel of the Kentucky militia (the second-in-command) and served with George Rogers Clark in his campaigns north of the Ohio River. He became a leading advocate for Kentucky statehood and was elected to the Kentucky House of Representatives in 1792. He twice ran unsuccessfully for governor and died in 1802 at the age of sixty.

27. Lofaro, *Daniel Boone*, 58–60; and Faragher, *Daniel Boone*, 118–23. Considerable portions of Judge Henderson's manuscript journal for this period are reprinted in Draper, *Life of Daniel Boone*, 344–53.

28. John Shane, Josiah Collins, and Nathaniel Hart interviews, Draper Mss., 12CC97 and 17CC195. Also see Faragher, *Daniel Boone*, 110; and Morgan, *Boone*, 163. Susannah and Will Hays remained married for twenty-five more years before her untimely death in 1800. She bore him ten children before her fortieth year. Not everyone believed the gossip. Josiah Collins later declared: "Susan when I saw her at Bnsbgh was a clever, pretty, well behaved woman. These were stories that were in circulation and not anything I saw." Josiah Collins to John Shane, Draper Mss., 12CC97.

29. Aron, *How the West Was Lost*, 66–67; Draper, *Life of Daniel Boone*, 365–75; Henderson, *Conquest of the Old Southwest*, 243–59; and Billington, *Westward Expansion*, 171–73.

30. Clark, *Frontier America*, 105–10; Aron, *How the West Was Lost*, 63–70; and Faragher, *Daniel Boone*, 123–26. Richard Henderson returned to North Carolina and became increasingly involved (along with his Transylvania Company) in the new settlements along the Cumberland River in what was to become Tennessee. He was a founder of the settlement that became Nashville as well as the author of the "Cumberland Compact" of government for the frontier community. An interesting aspect of that compact, considering Judge Henderson's unhappy involvement in the Regulator Movement, was a provision for the recall of judges. Henderson died in North Carolina on January 30, 1785, and was buried at his farm near Williamsboro. He was only forty-nine years old.

31. Filson, *Discovery*, 60; Lofaro, *Daniel Boone*, 61–63; Draper, *Life of Daniel Boone*, 375, 383–85, 389–90; and Morgan, *Boone*, 186–90.

CHAPTER 6: THE DARK AND BLOODY GROUND

1. Few events in frontier history are as celebrated as the rescue of Jemima Boone and the Callaway sisters. It caused a sensation on the frontier, with events naturally "improved upon" in the many retellings of the tale, and was also eventually featured in several eastern newspapers. Many literary critics consider it to be the inspiration for the main plotline of James Fenimore Cooper's 1826 novel *The Last of the Mohicans*. Boone is generally considered as Cooper's model for his hero Natty Bumppo/Hawkeye character in the "Leatherstocking" novels. For Boone as literary figure, see Michael A. Lofaro, ed., *Boone, Black Hawk, and Crockett in 1833* (Knoxville: University of Tennessee Press, 2019), 160–62; and Richard Slotkin, *Regeneration Through Violence: The Mythology of the American Frontier, 1600–1860* (Middletown, CT: Wesleyan University Press, 1973), 394–516. Boone's brief account of the rescue is in Filson, *Discovery*, 60. Lyman Draper collected a treasure trove of material on the incident from forty Boone family members and acquaintances. See Lyman C. Draper, *The Life of Daniel Boone* (Mechanicsburg, PA: Stackpole, 1998), 411–21; and Neal O. Hammon, ed., *My Father, Daniel Boone* (Lexington: University Press of Kentucky, 1999), 38, 47–51. The Draper Mss. include interviews with Nathan Reid, one of the rescue party, as well as letters from John Floyd. See Draper Mss., Nathan Reid, 31C2, 25-31; John Floyd to William Preston, July 21, 1776, Draper Mss., 335, 300–05; and Evira Coshow Letters, 1885, Draper Mss., 21C 28-29, C37. Also see John Mack Faragher, *Daniel Boone* (New York: Henry Holt, 1992), 131–40; Michael A. Lofaro, *Daniel Boone* (Lexington: University Press of Kentucky, 2003), 68–75; Robert Morgan, *Boone* (Chapel Hill, NC: Algonquin Books, 2007), 201–12; Meredith Mason Brown, *Frontiersman* (Baton Rouge: Louisiana State University Press, 2008), 104–14; and Reuben Gold Thwaites, *Daniel Boone* (New York: Appleton, 1902), 134–36. A recent book entirely devoted to the incident is by the novelist Matthew Pearl, *The Taking of Jemima Boone: Colonial Settlers, Tribal Nations, and the Kidnap That Shaped America* (New York: Harper, 2021).

2. William R. Nester, *The Frontier War for American Independence* (Mechanicsburg, PA: Stackpole Books, 2004), 13; Faragher, *Daniel Boone*, 141–45; Dale Van Every, *A Company of Heroes: The American Frontier, 1775–1783* (New York: Morrow, 1962), 61–62; and Sami Lakomaki, *Gathering Together: The Shawnee People Through Diaspora and Nationhood, 1600–1870* (New Haven, CT: Yale University Press, 2014), 102–13.

3. Van Every, *Company of Heroes*, 61–65; and Reuben Gold Thwaites and Louise Phelps Kellogg, eds., *The Revolution on the Upper Ohio, 1775–1777* (Madison: Wisconsin Historical Society, 1908), 21–28. John Montour, the mixed-blood son of Andrew Montour and a Delaware woman, was born in 1744 and educated in Philadelphia. He had served with Dunmore in 1774 but joined the Patriot ranks in the war and was commissioned as a captain in 1782.

4. Sir William Johnson was replaced as Indian commissioner by his rather ineffectual nephew Guy Johnson. Johnson's failure to match his uncle's influence with the tribes put actual control of British Indian affairs in the hands of the celebrated Mohawk leader Joseph Brant (Thayendanegea). Brant was long rumored to be Sir William's son by the Mohawk woman Owandah. No matter the disputed details of his birth, the intelligent and charismatic Brant was greatly favored by Sir William. Brant's sister Molly was Sir William's consort of twenty-one years and bore him eight children. Brant eventually married the mixed-blood daughter of George Croghan. Despite Brant's diplomatic skill, the Iroquois Confederacy split over which side they should take in the Revolution, with the Oneidas and Tuscaroras siding with the Americans. Brant led the Iroquois in the defeat of American forces at Oriskany on August 6, 1777, and then led his warriors in devastating raids in both New York and Pennsylvania.

Brant felt deeply betrayed by the British with the signing of the Treaty of Paris in 1783, which provided no protection for the Natives. He remained influential after the war and often took a leading role in negotiations with the American government. He died at his Ontario home on November 4, 1807. For Brant, see James O'Donnell, "Joseph Brant," in R. David Edmunds, ed., *American Indian Leaders: Studies in Diversity* (Lincoln: University of Nebraska Press, 1980), 21–40; Timothy J. Shannon, *Iroquois Diplomacy on the Early American Frontier* (New York: Viking, 2008), 170–213; Harvey Chalmers and E. B. Monture, *Joseph Brant: Mohawk* (East Lansing: Michigan State University Press, 1955); and William T. Hagan, *Longhouse Diplomacy and Frontier Warfare* (Albany: New York State American Revolution Bicentennial Commission, 1976). Dale Van Every uses Brant, along with George Rogers Clark, as the two central characters in *A Company of Heroes*, the second volume of his grand narrative history of the early frontier movement. For Croghan's sad fate, see Nicholas B. Wainwright, *George Croghan: Wilderness Diplomat* (Chapel Hill: University of North Carolina Press, 1959), 300–310; and Albert. T. Volwiler, *George Croghan and the Westward Movement, 1741–1782* (Cleveland: Arthur H. Clark, 1926), 323–36.

5. Details of the Fort Pitt council are in Thwaites and Kellogg, *Revolution on the Upper Ohio*, 25–135. Also see Brady J. Crytzer, *Guyasuta and the Fall of Indian America* (Yardley, PA: Westholme, 2013), 163–67; and Randolph C. Downes, *Council Fires on the Upper Ohio* (Pittsburgh: University of Pittsburgh Press, 1940), 183–87. Guyasuta is quoted in Crytzer, *Guyasuta*, 165–66. The American Congress rewarded the old chief for his loyalty with an engraved silver gorget and an honorary commission as colonel in the Continental Army. Such flattery had but slight impact, for in August 1777 he would take a leading role in defeating American militia forces and their Oneida allies at the Battle of Oriskany in New York's Mohawk Valley.

6. Downes, *Council Fires*, 191–94. Henry Hamilton had joined the British army in 1754. In 1758 he served under Amherst at Louisbourg, where he was wounded. He later saw service at Quebec and in the West Indies. He left the army in 1775 to accept an appointment as lieutenant governor, headquartered at Detroit. After his 1779 capture by Clark at Vincennes, he was held as a prisoner in Virginia until exchanged in 1780. He soon after returned to England until appointed lieutenant governor of Canada in 1782. He held that post until 1785 and later served as governor of both Bermuda and Dominica. Hamilton died in September 1796 in Antigua. See Thwaites and Kellogg, *Revolution on the Upper Ohio*, 135–36; Bernard Sheehan, "The Famous Hair Buyer General: Henry Hamilton, George Rogers Clark and the American Indian," *Indiana Magazine of History* 79, no. 1 (March 1983): 1–28; and John D. Barnhart, *Henry Hamilton and George Rogers Clark in the American Revolution with the Unpublished Journal of Lieut. Governor Henry Hamilton* (Crawfordsville, IN: R. E. Banta, 1951).

7. Thwaites and Kellogg, *Revolution on the Upper Ohio*, 14–16; Reuben Gold Thwaites and Louise Phelps Kellogg, eds., *Frontier Defense on the Upper Ohio, 1777–1778* (Madison: Wisconsin Historical Society, 1912), 161; Colin G. Calloway, *The Shawnees and the War for America* (New York: Viking, 2007), 63–64; and Lakomaki, *Gathering Together*, 109–10.

8. John Stuart, "Narrative by Captain John Stuart of General Andrew Lewis' Expedition Against the Indians in the Year 1774 and the Battle of Point Pleasant, Virginia [part 2]," *Magazine of American History* 1 (December 1877): 740–50; Alexander S. Withers, *Chronicles of Border Warfare* (Cincinnati: Robert Clarke, 1895), 208–14; and Thwaites and Kellogg, *Frontier Defense*, 157–63. John Stuart, a Virginian born in 1749,

established the first settlement in what is now Greenbrier County, West Virginia. He served as a captain under Colonel Andrew Lewis at the Battle of Point Pleasant. Before his death in 1823, he wrote a memoir that is a major source for the military campaign, the death of Cornstalk, and the early white settlement of the Greenbrier Valley. His valuable memoir, edited by his son Charles, who also corresponded with Lyman Draper, was first published in 1833 in the *Virginia Historical Collection* and later in two parts in the *Magazine of American History* 1 (November–December 1877): 668–79 and 740–50.

9. Edward Hand to Patrick Henry, December 9, 1777, in Thwaites and Kellogg, *Frontier Defense*, 175–77.

10. Quoted in Nester, *Frontier War*, 1. Also see Faragher, *Daniel Boone*, 144.

11. Van Every, *Company of Heroes*, 80–81; Faragher, *Daniel Boone*, 146. Boonesborough had about fifty women, thirty children, and ten enslaved people within its walls. Also see James Alton James, *The Life of George Rogers Clark* (Chicago: Chicago University Press, 1928), 51–68; and Reuben Gold Thwaites, *How George Rogers Clark Won the Northwest and Other Essays in Western History* (Chicago: A. C. McClurg, 1903), 3–72. George Rogers Clark, born in Virginia in 1752, was a strapping six-footer with red hair and an athletic frame. Although from a well-placed family, he was, like Boone, a natural rover and, like Washington, followed the surveyor's profession from an early age. He was only twenty-one when he served as a militia officer in Dunmore's War. He then settled near the mouth of Fish Creek in Kentucky. He thereafter quickly rose to prominence as a military leader of remarkable talent. Governor Thomas Jefferson secured him a commission as brigadier general of the Virginia militia. His fame for the "winning of the Old Northwest" for the new nation remains a point of considerable historical debate. His younger brother William was a leader of the Lewis and Clark Expedition in 1803–5. After the war, Clark's career spiraled downward as a result of failed land speculations, political misadventures, and alcoholism. He died at Locust Grove, Kentucky, not far from Louisville, on February 13, 1818. The most recent biography is William R. Nester, *George Rogers Clark: "I Glory in War"* (Norman: University of Oklahoma Press, 2012).

12. Lakomaki, *Gathering Together*, 110–11.

13. Chester Raymond Young, ed., *Westward into Kentucky: The Narrative of Daniel Trabue* (Lexington: University of Kentucky Press, 1981), 47; Sarah Graham interview, Draper Mss., 12CC45; and Faragher, *Daniel Boone*, 145–47. The Trabue narrative is in the Draper Mss. as part of the George Rogers Clark Papers, 57J, 1-148.

14. For the story of the salt boilers, see Filson, *Discovery*, 63–66; Draper, *Life of Daniel Boone*, 459–84; Hammon, *My Father*, 53–63; Lofaro, *Daniel Boone*, 82–89; Faragher, *Daniel Boone*, 154–64; Thwaites, *Boone*, 146–58; and Brown, *Frontiersman*, 127–44.

15. Henry Hamilton to Guy Carleton, April 25, 1778, in Thwaites and Kellogg, *Frontier Defense*, 280–88.

16. Filson, *Discovery*, 64–65; Hammon, *My Father*, 59; Faragher, *Daniel Boone*, 165–66; and Morgan, *Boone*, 237–43. It was rumored that Boone took a Shawnee wife during his captivity. See Evira Coshow, 1885, Draper Mss., 31C24, 12-13.

17. Boone's letter is in Louise Phelps Kellogg, ed., *Frontier Advance on the Upper Ohio, 1778–1779* (Madison: Wisconsin Historical Society, 1916), 115. For Boone's escape, see Hammon, *My Father*, 61–62; and Draper, *Life of Daniel Boone*, 475–81.

18. Boone's brief account of the siege is in Filson, *Discovery*, 66–70. Also see Draper, *Life of Daniel Boone*, 495–520; Hammon, *My Father*, 65–69; Faragher, *Daniel Boone*, 177–99; Morgan, *Boone*, 251–75; Lofaro, *Daniel Boone*, 94–105; Thwaites, *Boone*, 160–65; and Brown, *Frontiersman*, 145–60.

19. Boone never spoke of this humiliating incident, nor did his family. Filson does not include it in the Boone autobiographical appendix to his *Discovery* (which is entitled "The Adventures of Col. Daniel Boon; containing a Narrative of the Wars of Kentucke"). The sole source for the court-martial is Daniel Trabue's fascinating and quite reliable narrative in the Draper Mss., Clark Papers, 57J, 1-148, which is reprinted in Chester Raymond Young, ed., *Westward into Kentucky* (Lexington: University Press of Kentucky, 1981), 63–64.

20. Lofaro, *Daniel Boone*, 107–11; Faragher, *Daniel Boone*, 202–7; and Morgan, *Boone*, 282–88.

21. For the remarkable career of William Wells, see Paul A. Hutton, "William Wells: Frontier Scout and Indian Agent," *Indiana Magazine of History* 74, no. 3 (September 1978): 183–222; and William Heath, *William Wells and the Struggle for the Old Northwest* (Norman: University of Oklahoma Press, 2015).

22. Lofaro, *Daniel Boone*, 138; and Hammon, *My Father*, 81.

23. Faragher, *Daniel Boone*, 211–13.

24. Lofaro, *Daniel Boone*, 116–18.

CHAPTER 7: KINGS MOUNTAIN

1. Dragging Canoe's Chickamauga Creek town was near present Chattanooga. For the Cherokee struggle with the Revolutionary pioneers, see Samuel Cole Williams, *Tennessee During the Revolutionary War* (Nashville: Tennessee Historical Commission, 1944), 32–74; James H. O'Donnell, *Southern Indians in the American Revolution* (Knoxville: University of Tennessee Press, 1973), 34–53; Colin G. Calloway, *The American Revolution in Indian Country* (New York: Cambridge University Press, 1995), 182–212; John R. Finger, *Tennessee Frontiers: Three Regions in Transition* (Bloomington: Indiana University Press, 2001), 49–98; Grace Steele Woodward, *The Cherokees* (Norman: University of Oklahoma Press, 1963), 88–116; J. G. M. Ramsey, *The Annals of Tennessee to the End of the Eighteenth Century* (Philadelphia: Lippincott, Grambo, 1853), 143–74; Philip M. Hamer, "The Wataugans and the Cherokee Indians in 1776," *East Tennessee Historical Society's Publications* 3 (January 1931): 108–26; and James H. O'Donnell, "The Virginia Expedition Against the Overhill Cherokee, 1776," *East Tennessee Historical Society's Publications* 39 (1967): 13–25.

2. It was with the birth of Robert Crockett in 1755 that the paper trail on the family began. S. H. Stout, "David Crockett," *American Historical Magazine* 7 (January 1902): 3–21; and Stanley J. Folmsbee and Anna Grace Catron, "The Early Career of David Crockett," in Herbert L. Harper, ed., *Houston and Crockett: Heroes of Tennessee and Texas: An Anthology* (Nashville: Tennessee Historical Commission, 1986), 132–34. Stout, who knew the Crockett family, maintained that they were an old Scottish family and had spent little time in Ireland before migrating to America. After careful study, Stanley J. Folmsbee and James A. Shackford agreed with this. See James A. Shackford and Stanley J. Folmsbee, ed., *A Narrative of the Life of David Crockett of the*

State of Tennessee by David Crockett (Knoxville: University of Tennessee Press, 1973), 14 n. 3. Shackford, however, in his 1955 biography of Crockett, followed the genealogical research of Janie P. C. French and Zella Armstrong, *The Crockett Family and Connecting Lines*, vol. 5 of Notable Southern Families (Bristol, TN: King Printing Company, 1928), which contends that the Crocketts were descended from Antoine de Crocketagne, a wealthy French merchant who was forced to flee to England during Louis XIV's persecution of the Huguenots. The family eventually settled in Bantry Bay, Ireland, and it was from there that Crocketagne's third son, Joseph Louis, departed for America in 1709. Soon after, the family moved to Pennsylvania and then to Virginia around 1718. See James Atkins Shackford, *David Crockett: The Man and the Legend* (Chapel Hill: University of North Carolina Press, 1956), 293 n. 1. Also see William C. Davis, *Three Roads to the Alamo: The Lives and Fortunes of David Crockett, James Bowie, and William Barret Travis* (New York: HarperCollins, 1998), 9–11; and Anna Grace Catron, "The Public Career of David Crockett" (master's thesis, University of Tennessee, 1955), 1–2. David Crockett, in his autobiography, plainly states that his father, John, was of Irish descent and was born either in Ireland or during the voyage to America. It is hard to believe that Crockett confused his father with his great-grandfather and he must remain the best source on his own lineage. *A Narrative of the Life of David Crockett of the State of Tennessee, Written by Himself* (Philadelphia: E. L. Carey and A. Hart, 1834), 14.

3. Ramsey, *Annals of Tennessee*, 133–40; Thomas Perkins Abernathy, *From Frontier to Plantation in Tennessee: A Study in Frontier Democracy* (Tuscaloosa: University of Alabama Press, 1967), 1–43; Stanley J. Folmsbee, Robert E. Corlew, and Enoch L. Mitchell, *Tennessee: A Short History* (Knoxville: University of Tennessee Press, 1969), 48–63; Williams, *Tennessee During the Revolutionary War*, 17–23; and Finger, *Tennessee Frontiers*, 46–48. Also see Ray Allen Billington, *Westward Expansion* (New York: Macmillan, 1949), 157–60; and Thomas D. Clark, *Frontier America* (New York: Scribner's, 1969), 140–41. The Robertson quote is in John Buchanan, *The Road to Guilford Courthouse* (New York: John Wiley and Sons, 1997), 206.

4. There is a rich literature on early pioneer life and culture. See Everett Dick, *The Dixie Frontier* (New York: Alfred A. Knopf, 1948); Grady McWhiney, *Cracker Culture: Celtic Ways in the Old South* (Tuscaloosa: University of Alabama Press, 1988); Harriette Simpson Arnow, *Seedtime on the Cumberland* (Lexington: University Press of Kentucky, 1983); Harriette Simpson Arnow, *Flowering on the Cumberland* (Lexington: University Press of Kentucky, 1984); Thomas D. Clark, *The Rampaging Frontier: Manners and Humors of Pioneer Days in the South and the Middle West* (Indianapolis: Bobbs-Merrill, 1939); Louis B. Wright, *Culture on the Moving Frontier* (New York: Harper, 1961); David Freeman Hawke, *Everyday Life in Early America* (New York: Harper, 1988); and J. E. Wright and Doris S. Corbett, *Pioneer Life in Western Pennsylvania* (Pittsburgh: University of Pittsburgh Press, 1940).

5. Tradition and common sense have placed the date of the attack in April of 1777. This was the time of Dragging Canoe's most concentrated raids on Carter's Valley. It should be noted, however, that the Chickamauga warriors continued their attacks throughout the summer and fall as well. David Crockett and his sons William and John signed a petition dated November 6, 1777, and submitted it to the Virginia House of Delegates requesting the establishment of the county seat for Washington County, Virginia, at a more central location to accommodate the needs of frontier settlers. Since four different copies of this petition were circulated throughout different areas

over a considerable period of time, it is quite possible that David Crockett signed it before his death in April, but it nevertheless certainly calls that death date into question. See Prentiss Price, ed., "Two Petitions to Virginia of the North of Holston Men, 1776, 1777," *East Tennessee Historical Society's Publications* 21 (1949): 95–110; Williams, *Tennessee During the Revolutionary War,* 62; Woodward, *The Cherokees,* 98; and Folmsbee and Catron, "Early Career," 133–34. The Crockett cabin was located near the site of present Rogersville, Tennessee. John Crockett's cabin was on Big Creek some three miles below this site.

6. Folmsbee and Catron, "Early Career," 134; Shackford and Folmsbee, *Narrative,* 15–16; Williams, *Tennessee During the Revolutionary War,* 64–74, 91–99; O'Donnell, *Southern Indians,* 54–59, 83–85; Woodward, *The Cherokees,* 100–101; and Ronald N. Satz, *Tennessee's Indian Peoples: From White Contact to Removal, 1540–1840* (Knoxville: University of Tennessee Press, 1979), 64–71.

7. Folmsbee and Catron, "Early Career," 134; Shackford, *David Crockett,* 293 n. 1; Catron, "Public Career," 3; Louise W. Reynolds, "The Pioneer Crockett Family of Tennessee," *Daughters of the American Revolution Magazine* 55, no. 4 (April 1921): 188. David Crockett proudly described his mother simply as an "American woman." *A Narrative of the Life of David Crockett of the State of Tennessee, Written by Himself* (Philadelphia: E. L. Carey and A. Hart, 1834), 14. Folmsbee and Catron disagree with Shackford's assertion that Rebecca and Sarah Hawkins were sisters. Sarah died in 1780. Also see Hank Messick, *King's Mountain: The Epic of the Blue Ridge "Mountain Men" in the American Revolution* (Boston: Little, Brown, 1976), 104–5.

8. For the war in the South, see John Richard Alden, *The South in the Revolution, 1763–1789* (Baton Rouge: Louisiana State University Press, 1957); John S. Pancake, *This Destructive War: The British Campaign in the Carolinas, 1780–1782* (Tuscaloosa: University of Alabama Press, 1985); Walter Edgar, *Partisans and Redcoats: The Southern Conflict that Turned the Tide of the American Revolution* (New York: William Morrow, 2001); Don Higginbotham, *The War of American Independence: Military Attitudes, Policies, and Practice, 1763–1789* (New York: Macmillan, 1971), 352–419; Robert Middlekauff, *The Glorious Cause: The American Revolution, 1763–1789* (New York: Oxford University Press, 1982), 434–601; and George F. Scheer and Hugh F. Rankin, *Rebels and Redcoats: The American Revolution Through the Eyes of Those Who Fought and Lived It* (New York: Da Capo, 1957), 389–507.

9. For Tarleton, see Robert D. Bass, *The Green Dragoon: The Lives of Banastre Tarleton and Mary Robinson* (New York: Henry Holt, 1957); Oscar E. Gilbert and Catherine R. Gilbert, *Bloody Ban: Banastre Tarleton and the American Revolution, 1776–1783* (El Dorado Hills, CA: Savas Beatie, 2022); and Banastre Tarleton, *A History of the Campaigns of 1780 and 1781 in the Southern Provinces of North America* (London: T. Cadell, 1787).

10. Bass, *Green Dragoon,* 4, 9.

11. Clinton quoted in Lyman C. Draper, *King's Mountain and Its Heroes* (Johnson City, TN: Overmountain Press, 1996; reprint of the 1881 edition), 46. For the Waxhaws, see Buchanan, *Road to Guilford Courthouse,* 80–85; Edgar, *Partisans and Redcoats,* 55–57; and Bass, *Green Dragoon,* 78–83.

12. Henry Clinton, *The American Rebellion: Sir Henry Clinton's Narrative of His Campaigns, 1775–1782,* ed. William B. Willcox (New Haven, CT: Yale University Press, 1954), 44; and Pancake, *This Destructive War,* 69.

13. Buchanan, *Road to Guilford Courthouse*, 194–206; Draper, *King's Mountain*, 48–67; and Messick, *King's Mountain*, 50–58. At the Battle of Brandywine in September 1777, Ferguson had a remarkable encounter with a distinguished-looking American officer. The officer passed within a hundred yards of Ferguson's position. The captain advanced from the screen of woods and ordered the man to halt. The officer stared at the British captain for a moment but then calmly proceeded on. Ferguson declined to shoot him in the back. He later learned that the officer he had encountered was George Washington.

14. For Camden, see Pancake, *This Destructive War*, 91–107; Alden, *South in the Revolution*, 242–46; Edgar, *Partisans and Redcoats*, 107–11; Scheer and Rankin, *Rebels and Redcoats*, 401–11; and Higginbotham, *War of Independence*, 357–60.

15. Greene quoted in John Oller, *The Swamp Fox: How Francis Marion Saved the American Revolution* (Boston: Da Capo, 2016), 15.

16. Clinton, *American Rebellion*, 226–27; and Pancake, *This Destructive War*, 109.

17. Williams, *Tennessee During the Revolutionary War*, 141; Draper, *King's Mountain*, 562; and Ramsey, *Annals of Tennessee*, 223.

18. Wilma Dykeman, *With Fire and Sword: The Battle of Kings Mountain, 1780* (Washington, DC: National Park Service, 1978), 39; and Draper, *King's Mountain*, 562. Shelby's narrative of the battle is reprinted as an appendix in Draper. Modern usage drops the possessive from Kings Mountain.

19. Donald Davidson, *The Tennessee: The Old River* (New York: Rinehart, 1946), 181.

20. Messick, *King's Mountain*, 99–100.

21. Williams, *Tennessee During the Revolutionary War*, 151. Along with smaller groups of unattached men, the breakdown of command was William Campbell, 400; Isaac Shelby, 240; John Sevier, 240; and Joseph McDowell, 120. At Quaker Meadows Benjamin Cleveland, Joseph Winston, and James Williams joined them with 350 more men. There was no shortage of colonels in the militia. J. David Dameron, *King's Mountain: The Defeat of the Loyalists, October 7, 1780* (Cambridge, MA: Da Capo, 2003), 35–36. Rosters for both Patriot and Tory forces have been compiled by Bobby Gilmer Moss, *The Patriots at King's Mountain* (Blacksburg, SC: Scotia-Hibernia Press, 1990), and *The Loyalists at King's Mountain* (Blacksburg, SC: Scotia-Hibernia Press, 1998).

22. Messick, *King's Mountain*, 140–41.

23. For the battle, see Draper, *King's Mountain*, 165–377; Messick, *King's Mountain*, 93–157; Williams, *Tennessee During the Revolutionary War*, 138–62; Pancake, *This Destructive War*, 108–21; Archibald Henderson, *The Conquest of the Old Southwest* (New York: Century Company, 1920), 288–305; Buchanan, *Road to Guilford Courthouse*, 208–42; Ramsey, *Annals of Tennessee*, 221–49; Skinner, *Pioneers of the Old Southwest*, 185–225; and Roosevelt, *Winning of the West*, vol. 3, 121–87. Also see Dykeman, *With Fire and Sword*; Dameron, *King's Mountain*; and Pat Alderman, *One Heroic Hour at King's Mountain* (Johnson City, TN: Overmountain Press, 1968). For participant accounts, see Scheer and Rankin, *Rebels and Redcoats*, 412–21; the appendix in Draper, *King's Mountain*, 484–593; and Robert M. Dunkerly, *The Battle of Kings Mountain, Eyewitness Accounts* (Charleston, SC: History Press, 2007).

24. Arthur Campbell to Thomas Jefferson, January 15, 1781, as quoted in Calloway, *American Revolution in Indian Country*, 204. Also see Messick, *King's Mountain*, 175;

Ramsey, *Annals of Tennessee*, 262–68; Williams, *Tennessee During the Revolutionary War*, 180–92; and Finger, *Tennessee Frontiers*, 89–90.

25. Don Higginbotham, *Daniel Morgan* (Chapel Hill: University of North Carolina Press, 1961), 100–128.

26. Clinton, *American Rebellion*, 228; and Pancake, *This Destructive War*, 132–33.

27. Greene quoted in Higginbotham, *Daniel Morgan*, 129. Also see Buchanan, *Road to Guilford Courthouse*, 305–10.

28. Bass, *Green Dragoon*, 139.

29. Quote in Lawrence E. Babits, *A Devil of a Whipping: The Battle of Cowpens* (Chapel Hill: University of North Carolina Press, 1998), 54–55.

30. Quote in Andrew Waters, ed., *Battle of Cowpens: Primary and Contemporary Accounts* (n.p.: Regiment Press, 2019), 56–57. For Morgan's plan, see Higginbotham, *Daniel Morgan*, 131–34; Babits, *Devil of a Whipping*, 54–56; Buchanan, *Road to Guilford* Courthouse, 315–18; and Roberts, *Battle of Cowpens*, 71–78. Because of the fluid nature of the American militia forces, there is some confusion over the number of men Morgan actually had. Morgan claimed that he had but 800. Babits, who has made the most careful study of the battle, believes that Morgan did not include the militia in his count. Babits puts the total much closer to 2,000 men. Buchanan, Pancake, Roberts, and Higginbotham all estimate Morgan's force at around 1,000 men. Ed and Catherine Gilbert, in their concise but excellent little book, agree with Babits and place Morgan's force at 1,897 men. Ed Gilbert and Catherine Gilbert, *Cowpens 1781: Turning Point of the American Revolution* (New York: Osprey, 2016), 20–27.

31. Thomas Young narrative in Waters, *Battle of Cowpens*, 57–58.

32. Bass, *Green Dragoon*, 157–60.

33. Morgan quote in Higginbotham, *Daniel Morgan*, 142. For the battle, see Babits, *Devil of a Whipping*; Waters, *Battle of Cowpens*; Gilbert and Gilbert, *Cowpens 1781*; and the more-colorful-than-reliable Roberts, *Cowpens*. Also see Clinton, *American Rebellion*, 244–48; Scheer and Rankin, *Rebels and Redcoats*, 422–33; Robert Middlekauff, *The Glorious Cause* (New York: Oxford University Press, 1982), 468–76; Buchanan, *Road to Guilford Courthouse*, 319–33; Higginbotham, *Daniel Morgan*, 119–55; Pancake, *This Destructive War*, 131–40; Bass, *Green Dragoon*, 139–62; and Alden, *South in the Revolution*, 251–55. Babits estimated Morgan's losses at 24 killed and 104 wounded. Babits, *Devil of a Whipping*, 151–53.

34. Charles Stedman narrative, in Waters, *Battle of Cowpens*, 118; Bass, *Green Dragoon*, 160–61; and Buchanan, *Road to Guilford Courthouse*, 327.

35. Cornwallis to Clinton, January 18, 1781, in Clinton, *American Rebellion*, 485; and Waters, *Battle of Cowpens*, 101.

36. Higginbotham, *Daniel Morgan*, 155. Morgan returned to his home in Frederick County, Virginia, but soon returned to the field at the behest of the Marquis de Lafayette. He and Anthony Wayne almost bagged Tarleton on the James River but the sly dragoon escaped. Morgan's health did not hold and he was forced to again retire from the field and missed the climactic Yorktown campaign. After the war he briefly resumed military service in 1794 to deal with the western Pennsylvania "Whiskey Rebellion." In 1797 he was elected as a staunch Federalist to Congress, where he famously denounced the rival Jeffersonians as a "parcel of Egg sucking dogs." He declined to run for reelection in 1799 because of his declining health and died on July 6, 1802, at age sixty-seven. Higginbotham, *Daniel Morgan*, 156–215.

37. Gilbert and Gilbert, *Cowpens 1781*, 86. For the final campaign, see Middlekauff, *Glorious Cause*, 479–95, 559–71; Clinton, *American Rebellion*, 332–50; Alden, *South in the Revolution*, 290–305; Higginbotham, *War of American Independence*, 368–83; Buchanan, *Road to Guilford Courthouse*, 334–83; and Jerome A. Greene, *The Guns of Independence: The Siege of Yorktown, 1781* (El Dorado Hills, CA: Savas Beatie, 2005). Tarleton, wounded at Guilford Courthouse and then captured by the French near Yorktown, returned to England early in 1782 as a celebrated war hero. Once back in London, he became a member of the rakish inner circle of the Prince of Wales and even engaged in a notorious affair with the prince's cast-off and paid-off mistress, the famed actress Mary Robinson. From 1790 until 1812, Tarleton entered politics as a Whig and served in the House of Commons, where he staunchly defended the slave trade, upon which his family fortune was based. Although eventually promoted to general, he never again saw active service and died forgotten in 1833. Lord Cornwallis, on the other hand, had a distinguished military and civil career after Yorktown. He also rather surprisingly returned home a hero—Clinton was made the scapegoat for the loss of America—and enjoyed the patronage of King George III. In 1786 he was knighted and appointed governor-general and commander in chief of Bengal, where he proved an able administrator and distinguished himself in a series of military campaigns against the rebellious sultan of Mysore. After an unhappy stint as lord lieutenant of Ireland, he returned to India, where he died at age sixty-seven in 1805. He is buried in an impressive tomb overlooking the Ganges River. For Cornwallis, see Richard Middleton, *Cornwallis: Soldier and Statesman in a Revolutionary World* (New Haven, CT: Yale University Press, 2022); for Tarleton, see Bass, *Green Dragoon*, and Gilbert and Gilbert, *Bloody Ban.*

38. Clinton, *American Rebellion*, 226. Jefferson quote in Williams, *Tennessee During the Revolutionary War*, 161.

39. Robert N. Thompson, *Disaster on the Sandusky* (Staunton, VA: American History Press, 2017), 190–232.

40. Boone quote in John Filson, *The Discovery, Settlement and Present State of Kentucke* (Wilmington, DE: James Adams, 1784), 80. For the Blue Licks fight, see Peter Houston, *A Sketch of the Life and Character of Daniel Boone* (Mechanicsburg, PA: Stackpole, 1997), 22–27; Neal O. Hammon, ed., *My Father, Daniel Boone* (Lexington: University Press of Kentucky, 1999), 75–80; Michael A. Lofaro, *Daniel Boone* (Lexington: University Press of Kentucky, 2003), 121–32; John Mack Faragher, *Daniel Boone* (New York: Henry Holt, 1992), 217–24; Robert Morgan, *Boone* (Chapel Hill, NC: Algonquin Books, 2007), 316–331; and Neal O. Hammon and Richard Taylor, *Virginia's Western War* (Mechanicsburg, PA: Stackpole, 2002), 155–67.

41. Paul Andrew Hutton, "The Two Worlds of William Wells," *American History Illustrated* 18 (April 1983): 33–41; and Alan D. Gaff, *Bayonets in the Wilderness: Anthony Wayne's Legion in the Old Northwest* (Norman: University of Oklahoma Press, 2004).

42. Boone quote in Lofaro, *Daniel Boone*, 152, 175. Also see Faragher, *Daniel Boone*, 318; Morgan, *Boone*, 423–24; and Paul Andrew Hutton, "The Forgotten Founding Father:

Daniel Boone and the Birth of the Frontier Movement," *True West* 67 (December 2020): 20–27.

43. Boone quoted in Faragher, *Daniel Boone*, 302.

CHAPTER 8: THE COUNCIL FIRE

1. Benjamin W. Griffith Jr., *McIntosh and Weatherford, Creek Indian Leaders* (Tuscaloosa: University of Alabama Press, 1988), 3–6; George Cary Eggleston, *Red Eagle and the Wars with the Creek Indians of Alabama* (New York: Dodd, Mead, 1878), 15–17, 37–46; Lynn Thompson, *William Weatherford: His Country and His People* (Bay Minette, AL: Lavender Press, 1991), 1–29; Andrew K. Frank, *Creeks and Southerners: Biculturalism on the Early American Frontier* (Lincoln: University of Nebraska Press, 2005), 34–35, 68, 120–23; J. Leitch Wright Jr., *Creeks and Seminoles: The Destruction and Regeneration of the Muscogulge People* (Lincoln: University of Nebraska Press, 1986), 167–68; and Claudio Saunt, *A New Order of Things: Property, Power, and the Transformation of the Creek Indians, 1733–1816* (Cambridge: Cambridge University Press, 1999), 167–70, 227.

2. Hawkins quoted in Griffith, *McIntosh and Weatherford*, 2; also see J. F. H. Claiborne, *Life and Times of Gen. Sam Dale* (New York: Harper & Brothers, 1860), 212. For the important role of women in mixed marriages, see Robbie Ethridge, *Creek Country: The Creek Indians and Their World* (Chapel Hill: University of North Carolina Press, 2003), 111–19; and Frank, *Creeks and Southerners*, 26–39.

3. Bartram quoted in John Walton Caughey, *McGillivray of the Creeks* (Norman: University of Oklahoma Press, 1959), 8.

4. Ethridge, *Creek Country*, 99–100, 142–43; and Caughey, *McGillivray*, 7–8.

5. Griffith, *McIntosh and Weatherford*, 1–2; Frank, *Creeks and Southerners*, 1–10; Ethridge, *Creek Country*, 113–19; Caughey, *McGillivray*, 5–6; and Saunt, *New Order*, 167–68. Saunt notes how fences were a new addition to Creek Country, as there were no fences before the 1750s. As more Creeks (and whites like Weatherford who married into Creek society) began to raise hogs and cattle, they fenced their previously open fields. This contributed to a breakdown of community as well as a new sense of private ownership rather than communal property. In time, this sense of private property rights came to also include enslaved African Americans. Saunt, *New Order*, 171–75.

6. Ethridge, *Creek Country*, 47–53, 60–62, 152–54; and Griffith, *McIntosh and Weatherford*, 10–16. Also see Charles Hudson, *The Southeastern Indians* (Knoxville: University of Tennessee Press, 1976), 272–309.

7. Ethridge, *Creek Country*, 31, 94–105; and Hudson, *Southeastern Indians*, 367–70. The Native people who would become known as Creek Indians were descendants of the impressive Mississippian Culture that flourished from around 700 until just before the arrival of the Spanish in the early 1500s. These were the famous Mound Builders, and their cities numbered well over a thousand people living around their temple mounds. This theocratic civilization had all but vanished by the time Hernando de Soto landed on Florida's west coast in 1539 with some six hundred soldiers and potential colonists. His bloody three-year march through the Southeast

proved disastrous to the Native peoples he encountered before he found a watery grave in the Mississippi River in May 1542. Not only did the Spanish slaughter the Natives in battle and loot their food stores, they also unintentionally introduced a wide variety of deadly European diseases across the region from Florida to the Mississippi River. Smallpox proved the most deadly, wiping out whole communities. Within a hundred years, Native populations declined by nearly 90 percent and the survivors coalesced into new, much smaller communities with authority vested in local chiefs. These people now began a lucrative trade in enslaved Natives with both British and Spanish colonists. Most Indian slaves were sent to the Caribbean Islands. In time, the colonial powers decided that it was prudent to end the Native slave trade in order to prevent warfare among their trading partners. At the same time it proved more economical to import Africans to work their fields. Trade now shifted from slaves to furs and deerskins. In this business the Native villages prospered and populations began to rebound. This trade resulted in an increased dependence on European goods even while it allowed the Indians to play the colonial powers off against each other. Eventually, imperial wars and the American Revolution would strictly limit Native options.

There is some controversy over the origin of the Creek name. It became a common appellation by the early eighteenth century as English traders from Charles Town made Indian villages on Ochesee Creek, a branch of the upper Ocmulgee River, a center of trade. These colonial traders soon began to refer to all their Native trading partners in the area as Creeks. Ultimately the term "Creek" was applied by the colonists to all Native bands who were not Cherokees, Choctaws, or Chickasaws. The Seminoles were Creeks who migrated south into Florida and took the name "Cimarrones" from the Spanish. The English translated that name to "Seminole." The Creeks continued to refer to themselves by their village names—Tallassee, Yuchi, Coweta, Coosa, Alabama, Tuskegee, and others—and spoke distinct Muskogee dialects, but gradually began to come together as one people. See Wright, *Creeks and Seminoles*, 1–6; and Ethridge, *Creek Country*, 22–31.

8. Caughey, *McGillivray*, 14.

9. Griffith, *McIntosh and Weatherford*, 23–29; Ethridge, *Creek Country*, 103–4; Hudson, *Southeastern Indians*, 325–27; and John Francis McDermott, ed., *Milford's Memoir* (Chicago: Lakeside Press, 1956), 25, 174–76. Louis LeClerc de Milfort was a French adventurer who, through his friendship with Alexander McGillivray, came to live with the Creeks for nearly twenty years, rising to prominence among them. He married McGillivray's sister and thus became an uncle to William Weatherford. Soon after McGillivray's death he returned to France, where he published a highly romanticized memoir in Paris in 1802. McDermott, the editor of this volume, believed his name to actually be Milford, but most historians accept the name as it appears on the title page of the memoir: Milfort.

10. Ethridge, *Creek Country*, 100–102; and Hudson, *Southeastern Indians*, 408–21. Other southeastern tribes also engaged in ball play.

11. Quote in McDermott, *Milford's Memoir*, 95. For Alexander McGillivray's remarkable career, see Caughey, *McGillivray*, 3–57; James L. Hill, *Creek Internationalism in an Age of Revolution, 1763–1818* (Lincoln: University of Nebraska Press, 2022), 57–74; Albert James Pickett, *History of Alabama and Incidentally of Georgia and Mississippi, from the Earliest Period* (Birmingham, AL: Birmingham Book and Magazine Co., 1962;

reprint of the 1851 edition), 342–432; Dale Van Every, *Ark of Empire: The American Frontier, 1784–1803* (New York: William Morrow, 1963), 62–74; Saunt, *New Order*, 67–89; Arthur P. Whitaker, "Alexander McGillivray, 1783–1789," *North Carolina Historical Review* 5, no. 2 (April 1928): 181–203; Arthur P. Whitaker, "Alexander McGillivray, 1789–1793," *North Carolina Historical Review* 5, no. 3 (July 1928): 289–309; James H. O'Donnell, "Alexander McGillivray: Training for Leadership, 1777–1783," *Georgia Historical Quarterly* 49 (June 1965): 172–86; Colin G. Calloway, *The Indian World of George Washington* (New York: Oxford University Press, 2018), 346–77; and Michael D. Green, "Alexander McGillivray," in R. David Edmunds, ed., *American Indian Leaders* (Lincoln: University of Nebraska Press, 1980), 41–63. McGillivray is also the central character in Milfort's memoir.

12. Adams quoted in Saunt, *New Order*, 75; David Humpheys, Washington's aide-de-camp during the Revolutionary War, quoted in Calloway, *Indian World*, 362.

13. Caughey, *McGillivray*, 73.

14. McGillivray to O'Neill, February 5, 1784, and July 6, 1785, in Caughey, *McGillivray*, 69–70, 90. For the Treaty of Pensacola and the establishment of the trade concession with Panton, Leslie, & Company, see Caughey, *McGillivray*, 75–81, 141–42; Calloway, *Indian World*, 351–53; and Van Every, *Ark of Empire*, 68–71. Arturo O'Neill was an Irish soldier in the service of Spain.

15. Pickett, *Alabama*, 369–71; McDermott, *Milford's Memoir*, 132–37; and McGillivray to O'Neill, April 18, 1787, in Caughey, *McGillivray*, 149–51.

16. McGillivray to O'Neill, June 20, July 10, 1787, in Caughey, *McGillivray*, 153–56.

17. Pickett, *Alabama*, 378–84; Van Every, *Ark of Empire*, 174–84; Kathryn E. Holland Braund, *Deerskins & Duffels: The Creek Indian Trade with Anglo-America, 1685–1815* (Lincoln: University of Nebraska Press, 1993), 175; and McGillivray to O'Neill, August 12, October 30, 1786, in Caughey, *McGillivray*, 127–35.

18. For Bowles, see J. Leitch Wright Jr., *William Augustus Bowles: Director General of the Creek Nation* (Athens: University of Georgia Press, 1967), 1–35; Van Every, *Ark of Empire*, 121–25; and Saunt, *New Order*, 86–88. Bowles's Creek son Billy became a Seminole chief who later battled against the American invasion of Florida. According to Wright, his son by his Chickamauga wife became the famous Chief Bowles, an important Cherokee leader who befriended Sam Houston. He removed his people to Texas to avoid further conflict with American frontiersmen only to be killed in battle with Texas troops on July 16, 1839, at the Battle of Neches. Other sources state that Chief Bowles's father was a Scottish trader. Wright, *Bowles*, 172, 177.

19. For Weatherford's duplicity, see McGillivray to O'Neill, December 3, 1786, Miro to McGillivray, December 13, 1788, and O'Neill to Miro, December 22, 1788, in Caughey, *McGillivray*, 140–41, 209–12; and for McGillivray's quotes, see McGillivray to Panton, January 12, February 1, 1789, in Caughey, *McGillivray*, 214–20.

20. Wright, *Bowles*, 30–54. Also see Pickett, *Alabama*, 410–13; and Hill, *Creek Internationalism*, 81–108.

21. For the Treaty of New York, see Caughey, *McGillivray*, 256–79; Pickett, *Alabama*, 397–407; and Angie Debo, *The Road to Disappearance: The Creek Indians* (Norman: University of Oklahoma Press, 1941), 45–52. The Spanish agent quote is in Van Every, *Ark of Empire*, 213.

22. Howard to Quesada, September 24, 1790, in Caughey, *McGillivray*, 281–84; Pickett, *Alabama*, 403–4; and Griffith, *McIntosh and Weatherford*, 11.

23. Jackson quoted in Caughey, *McGillivray*, 45; Seagrove quoted in Van Every, *Ark of Empire*, 25, 259. For the Treaty of New York, see Calloway, *Indian World*, 357–77; and J. Leitch Wright, "Creek-American Treaty of 1790: Alexander McGillivray and the Diplomacy of the Old Southwest," *Georgia Historical Quarterly* 51, no. 4 (December 1967): 379–400. It was a result of his attempt to receive advice from the Senate on this treaty, and their treatment of him in the Senate Chamber, that led Washington to decide to never again subject himself to such discourtesy. This established the vital precedent by which the president did not again confer with the Senate in person but only sent negotiated treaties to them for consent.

24. Pickett, *Alabama*, 429; Saunt, *New Order*, 194–97; and Hallowing King quoted in Braund, *Deerskins & Duffels*, 175.

25. Howard to Quesada, September 24, 1790, McGillivray to Miró, June 8, 1791, McGillivray to Panton, October 28, 1791, in Caughey, *McGillivray*, 281–84, 290–93, 298–301; Lawrence Kinnard, ed., *Spain in the Mississippi Valley: Problems of Frontier Defense, 1792–1794* (Washington, DC: U.S. Government Printing Office, 1946), xi–xiii. Caleb Swan, a veteran of the Revolutionary War, had served as chief clerk in the War Department before being assigned as agent to the Creeks. He would later serve as paymaster general of the U.S. Army from 1792 to 1808. He died in 1809. Swan wrote an insightful report concerning his time with the Creeks that was published as "Position and State of Manners and Arts in the Creek, or Muscogee Nation in 1791," in Henry Rowe Schoolcraft, *Historical and Statistical Information, Respecting the History, Condition and Prospects of the Indian Tribes of the United States*, 6 vols. (Philadelphia: J. B. Lippincott, 1851–57), vol. 5, 251–83.

26. Knox to Arthur St. Clair, December 2, 1791, *American State Papers*, vol. 1, 184; McGillivray to Panton, October 28, 1791, in Caughey, *McGillivray*, 298–300; and Wright, *Bowles*, 55–59.

27. Wright, *Bowles*, 65–86; and Kinnard, *Spain in the Mississippi Valley*, 12–18.

28. Caughey, *McGillivray*, 46–53, 353–63; Pickett, *Alabama*, 429–32. McGillivray appears to have long suffered from syphilis, which contributed to his chronic maladies and early death. Since he was not a Catholic, McGillivray was denied burial in the Pensacola cemetery and was instead buried in Panton's garden. He left behind a son and two daughters. The boy, Aleck, was sent to Banff, Scotland, to be educated but fell ill with consumption and died in 1802.

CHAPTER 9: THE HEARTH

1. Ray Allington Billington, *Land of Savagery, Land of Promise: The European Image of the American Frontier in the Nineteenth Century* (New York: W. W. Norton, 1981), 202. A marvelous case study of the war against the forest is in William Cronon, *Changes in the Land: Indians, Colonists, and the Ecology of New England* (New York: Hill and Wang, 1983), 108–26.

2. Anna Grace Catron, "The Public Career of David Crockett" (master's thesis, University of Tennessee, 1955), 3; James Atkins Shackford, *David Crockett* (Chapel Hill: University of North Carolina Press, 1956), 5–7; and James A. Shackford and Stanley J. Folmsbee, eds., *A Narrative of the Life of David Crockett of the State of Tennessee*

(Knoxville: University of Tennessee Press, 1973), 20. John Crockett was among those listed on the first tax list for Greene County in 1783. Pat Alderman, *The Overmountain Men* (Johnson City, TN: Overmountain Press, 1986), 239.

3. Stanley J. Folmsbee and Anna Grace Catron, "The Early Career of David Crockett," in Herbert L. Harper, *Houston and Crockett* (Nashville: Tennessee Historical Commission, 1986), 135; and Thomas Perkins Abernathy, *From Frontier to Plantation in Tennessee* (Tuscaloosa: University of Alabama Press, 1967), 64–90. Technically, then, it might be said that David Crockett was born in the unrecognized state of Franklin. Accurately it should be said that he was born in North Carolina, in western territory eventually ceded to the federal government in 1790. Tennessee did not become a state until June 1, 1796. Also see Shackford, *David Crockett*, 6. The land on Mossy Creek may well have been John Crockett's Revolutionary War service bounty.

4. Samuel D. Smith, *Historical Background and Testing of the Davy Crockett Birthplace State Historic Area, Greene County, Tennessee* (Nashville: Division of Archeology, Tennessee Department of Conservation, 1980), 7–14. In response to the renewed interest in Crockett inspired by the 1955 Walt Disney television show and film, a birthplace cabin was reconstructed on the site where local tradition placed John Crockett's cabin. A nearby historic log cabin of the Stonecypher family was dismantled and used to build the Crockett cabin. A doorstep stone reputed to be from the original Crockett cabin was also used. Archaeological excavations at this site in 1977 revealed no evidence of an original cabin at the reconstruction site, now part of a state park. The original cabin may have been nearer to the confluence of the creek and river, but the overall location of the site is certainly accurate. Smith, *Historical Background*, 17, 30–36; and Crockett, *Narrative*, 16–17. David was the fifth son of six sons and three daughters born to John and Rebecca Crockett.

5. For the place of corn in Tennessee pioneer life, see J. G. M. Ramsey, *The Annals of Tennessee* (Philadelphia: Lippincott, Grambo, 1853), 718–20; Harriette Simpson Arnow, *Seedtime on the Cumberland* (Lexington: University Press of Kentucky, 1983), 322–24, 390–97; and Harriette Simpson Arnow, *Flowering of the Cumberland* (Lexington: University Press of Kentucky, 1984), 237–42. Also see Daniel Drake, *Pioneer Life in Kentucky, 1785–1800*, ed. Emmet Field Horine (New York: Henry Schuman, 1948), 41–70; and Everett Dick, *The Dixie Frontier* (New York: Alfred A. Knopf, 1948), 98–106, 289–90.

6. "Journal of André Michaux, 1793–1796," in Reuben Gold Thwaites, ed., *Early Western Travels, 1748–1846*, 32 vols. (Cleveland: Arthur H. Clark Company, 1904–7), vol. 3, 99.

7. For childhood on the frontier, see Arnow, *Flowering of the Cumberland*, 58–81; J. E. Wright and Doris S. Corbett, *Pioneer Life in Western Pennsylvania* (Pittsburgh: University of Pittsburgh Press, 1940), 84–100; and, for a later period, Elliott West, *Growing Up with the Country: Childhood on the Far Western Frontier* (Albuquerque: University of New Mexico Press, 1989).

8. Arnow, *Seedtime on the Cumberland*, 395–97, 401–8, 413–14. Drake, *Pioneer Life*, 45–46. Also see John Rice Irwin, *Alex Stewart: Portrait of a Pioneer* (Atglen, PA: Schiffer, 1985), 25.

9. François André Michaux, "Travels to the West of the Alleghany Mountains," in Thwaites, *Early Western Travels*, vol. 3, 269; and Paul O'Neil, *The Frontiersmen* (Alexandria, VA: Time-Life Books, 1977), 29.

10. Frances Trollope, *Domestic Manners of the Americans*, ed. Donald Smalley (New York: Alfred A. Knopf, 1949), 20–21.

11. R. Carlyle Buley, *The Old Northwest: Pioneer Period, 1815–1840*, 2 vols. (Indianapolis: Indiana Historical Society, 1950), vol. 1, 244, 258. Also see Wright and Corbett, *Pioneer Life*, 129–39.

12. Irwin, *Alex Stewart*, 28.

13. Buley, *Old Northwest*, vol. 1, 247–48; Dick, *Dixie Frontier*, 215–24.

14. Irwin, *Alex Stewart*, 26–27. Also See Buley, *Old Northwest*, vol. 1, 255–56.

15. Buley, *Old Northwest*, vol. 1, 256–70. Also see Madge E. Pickard and R. Carlyle Buley, *The Midwest Pioneer: His Ills, Cures, and Doctors* (New York: Henry Schuman, 1946).

16. W. J. Rorabaugh, *The Alcoholic Republic: An American Tradition* (New York: Oxford University Press, 1979), 5–21.

17. Crockett, *Narrative*, 18–20.

18. Crockett, *Narrative*, 97–99.

19. Joe Swann, *The Early Life and Times of David Crockett in East Tennessee* (Traverse City, MI: Mission Point Press, 2023), 79–80.

20. Swann, *Early Life*, 97–99.

21. Crockett, *Narrative*, 22–23. For Crockett's childhood, see Shackford, *David Crockett*, 3–11; Folmsbee and Catron, "Early Career of David Crockett," 58–85; and Swann, *Early Life*, 1–134.

22. Crockett, *Narrative*, 30–31.

23. Crockett, *Narrative*, 33, 42–43.

24. Crockett, *Narrative*, 49.

25. Swann, *Early Life*, 135–60; Crockett, *Narrative*, 54–59.

26. Crockett, *Narrative*, 67–68.

27. Shackford, *David Crockett*, 14–17; Swann, *Early Life*, 158–60.

28. Crockett, *Narrative*, 85.

29. Crockett, *Narrative*, 162–64. For bear hunting, see Paul Schullery, *The Bear Hunter's Century* (Harrisburg, PA: Stackpole, 1989).

30. Michael A. Lofaro, ed., *Boone, Black Hawk and Crockett in 1833* (Knoxville: University of Tennessee Press, 2019), 345–46. Lofaro presents an annotated version of James Strange French, *The Life and Adventures of Colonel David Crockett, of West Tennessee* (Cincinnati: Published for the Proprietor, 1833), which was soon reprinted in a more popular edition as *Sketches and Eccentricities of Col. David Crockett, of West Tennessee* (New York: J. & J. Harper, 1833). The author was a lawyer and novelist best known for his defense of Nat Turner and other enslaved people involved in the rebellion of 1831. He also wrote *Elkswatawa; or, The Prophet of the West: A Tale of the Frontier* (New York: Harper & Brothers, 1836), a sympathetic novel on the Indians. Authorship of the book is disputed. Lofaro and Hutton agree that French (1807–1886) is the author for the simple fact that he registered the copyright for the book as well as his interest in frontier life. Shackford makes the case that the author was the Pennsylvanian Matthew St. Clair Clarke (1790–1852), who knew Crockett and served seven terms as clerk of the House of Representatives. Noted authors Richard Boyd Hauck and William C. Davis agree with Shackford. See Shackford, *David Crockett*, 258–64; Richard Boyd Hauck, *Crockett: A Bio-Bibliography* (Westport, CT: Greenwood Press, 1982), 3–4; and William C. Davis, *Three Roads to the Alamo* (New York: HarperCollins, 1998), 313–15.

31. Lofaro, *Boone, Black Hawk and Crockett*, 329–53.

32. There are innumerable biographies of Crockett besides Shackford's and Davis's. Among the most useful are Constance Rourke, *Davy Crockett* (New York: Harcourt, 1934); Richard M. Dorson, ed., *Davy Crockett: American Comic Legend* (New York: Rockland, 1939); Walter Blair, *Davy Crockett, Frontier Hero* (New York: Coward-McCann, 1955); Gary L. Foreman, *Crockett: The Gentleman from the Cane* (Dallas: Taylor, 1986); William R. Chemerka, *The Davy Crockett Almanac and Book of Lists* (Fort Worth: Eakin Press, 2000); William Groneman III, *David Crockett: Hero of the Common Man* (New York: Forge, 2005); Michael Wallis, *David Crockett: The Lion of the West* (New York: W. W. Norton, 2011); James C. Kelly and Frederick S. Voss, *Davy Crockett: Gentleman from the Cane* (Washington, DC: National Portrait Gallery, 1986); and Bob Thompson, *Born on a Mountaintop* (New York: Crown, 2013). Also, useful anthologies include Michael Lofaro, ed., *Davy Crockett: The Man, the Legend, the Legacy, 1786–1986* (Knoxville: University of Tennessee Press, 1985); Michael A. Lofaro and Joe Cummings, eds., *Crockett at Two Hundred: New Perspectives on the Man and the Myth* (Knoxville: University of Tennessee Press, 1989); and Herbert L. Harper, ed., *Houston and Crockett: Heroes of Tennessee and Texas* (Nashville: Tennessee Historical Commission, 1986). The most useful edition of the autobiography is the annotated edition by Shackford and Folmsbee, *Narrative*. Also see Joseph J. Arpad, ed., *A Narrative of the Life of David Crockett of the State of Tennessee* (New Haven, CT: College and University Press, 1972); and Paul Andrew Hutton, ed., *A Narrative of the Life of David Crockett of the State of Tennessee* (Lincoln: University of Nebraska Press, 1987).

CHAPTER 10: FORT MIMS

1. For Fort Mims, see Gregory A. Waselkov, *A Conquering Spirit: Fort Mims and the Red Stick War of 1813–1814* (Tuscaloosa: University of Alabama Press, 2006); Karl Davis, "Remember Fort Mims: Reinterpreting the Origins of the Creek War," *Journal of the Early Republic* 22, no. 4 (Winter 2002): 612–36; and Frank L. Owsley Jr., "The Fort Mims Massacre," *Alabama Review* 24 (July 1971): 192–204. For the Creek War (also with much on Fort Mims, of course), see H. S. Halbert and T. H. Ball, *The Creek War of 1813 and 1815* (Chicago: Donohue & Henneberry, 1895), which is the classic older account. Modern studies include Peter Cozzens, *A Brutal Reckoning: Andrew Jackson, the Creek Indians, and the Epic War for the American South* (New York: Alfred A. Knopf, 2023); Howard T. Weir, III, *A Paradise of Blood: The Creek War of 1813–14* (Yardley, PA: Westholme, 2016); David S. Heidler and Jeanne T. Heidler, *Old Hickory's War: Andrew Jackson and the Quest for Empire* (Mechanicsburg, PA: Stackpole Books, 1996); John Buchanan, *Jackson's Way: Andrew Jackson and the People of the Western Waters* (New York: John Wiley, 2001); Frank L. Owsley Jr., *Struggle for the Gulf Borderlands: The Creek*

War and the Battle of New Orleans, 1812–1815 (Gainesville: University of Florida, 1981); Mrs. Dunbar Rowland (Eron Rowland), *Andrew Jackson's Campaign Against the British, or the Mississippi Territory in the War of 1812* (New York: Macmillan, 1926); Joel W. Martin, *Sacred Revolt: The Muskogees' Struggle for a New World* (Boston: Beacon Press, 1991); and Sean Michael O'Brien, *In Bitterness and in Tears: Andrew Jackson's Destruction of the Creeks and Seminoles* (Guilford, CT: Lyons Press, 2003).

2. Hawkins quote in Florette Henri, *The Southern Indians and Benjamin Hawkins, 1796–1816* (Norman: University of Oklahoma Press, 1986), 285–86.

3. Washington quote in Merritt B. Pound, *Benjamin Hawkins, Indian Agent* (Athens: University of Georgia Press, 1951), 99–100. For biographical information on Hawkins, consult both Pound, *Hawkins*, and Henri, *Hawkins*. For William McIntosh, see Benjamin W. Griffith, *McIntosh and Weatherford* (Tuscaloosa: University of Alabama Press, 1988); George Chapman, *Chief William McIntosh: A Man of Two Worlds* (Atlanta: Cherokee Publishing, 1988); and James C. Bonner, "William McIntosh," in Horace Montgomery, ed., *Georgians in Profile* (Athens: University of Georgia Press, 1958), 114–43.

4. For Bowles's adventures and return, see J. Leitch Wright, *William Augustus Bowles* (Athens: University of Georgia Press, 1967), 71–124.

5. Bowles quote in Pound, *Hawkins*, 191–92; and Hawkins quote in Wright, *Bowles*, 132–33. Also see Henri, *Hawkins*, 214–20.

6. Wright, *Bowles*, 142–74; Griffith, *McIntosh and Weatherford*, 50–54; Henri, *Hawkins*, 234–38.

7. Thomas S. Woodward, *Woodward's Reminiscences of the Creek, or Muscogee Indians, Contained in Letters to Friends in Georgia and Alabama*, ed. J. J. Hooper (Montgomery, AL: Barrett & Wimbish, 1859), 89.

8. George Cary Eggleston, *Red Eagle* (New York: Dodd Mead, 1878), 44. For Weatherford's personal life, also see Rowland, *Andrew Jackson's Campaign*, 106–17; Waselkov, *Conquering Spirit*, 93–95; Griffith, *McIntosh and Weatherford*, 253–54; Albert James Pickett, *History of Alabama and Incidentally of Georgia and Mississippi, from the Earliest Period* (Birmingham, AL: Birmingham Book and Magazine Co., 1962; reprint of 1851 edition), 530–31; Halbert and Ball, *Creek War of 1813*, 172–76 (for a letter on Weatherford's life by his grandson Charles Weatherford); Woodward, *Reminiscences*, 88–103; and George Stiggins, *Creek Indian History*, ed. Virginia Pounds Brown (Birmingham: Birmingham Public Library/University of Alabama Press, 1989), 103–5. Also of interest is Lynn Hastie Thompson, *William Weatherford: His Country and His People* (Bay Minette, AL: Lavender Publishing, 1991); and J. Anthony Paredes and Judith Knight, eds., *Red Eagle's Children: Weatherford vs. Weatherford et al.* (Tuscaloosa: University of Alabama Press, 2012).

9. Henri, *Hawkins*, 149–50.

10. For Tecumseh and the Prophet, see Peter Cozzens, *Tecumseh and the Prophet: The Shawnee Brothers Who Defied a Nation* (New York: Alfred A. Knopf, 2020); Peter Stark, *Gallop Toward the Sun: Tecumseh and William Henry Harrison's Struggle for the Destiny of a Nation* (New York: Random House, 2023); John Sugden, *Tecumseh: A Life* (New York: Henry Holt, 1997); John Sugden, *Tecumseh's Last Stand* (Norman: University of Oklahoma Press, 1985); R. David Edmunds, *The Shawnee Prophet* (Lincoln: University of Nebraska Press, 1983); R. David Edmunds, *Tecumseh and the Quest for Indian*

Leadership (Boston: Little, Brown, 1984); Glenn Tucker, *Tecumseh: Vision of Glory* (New York: Bobbs-Merrill, 1956); and Benjamin Drake, *Life of Tecumseh, and His Brother the Prophet* (Cincinnati: E. Morgan, 1841).

11. Dale quote in J. F. H. Claiborne, *Life and Times of Gen. Sam Dale, the Mississippi Partisan* (New York: Harper & Brothers, 1860), 51. For Tecumseh's visit with the Creeks, see Cozzens, *Tecumseh and the Prophet*, 262–74; Edmunds, *Tecumseh*, 146–53; Drake, *Life of Tecumseh*, 143–45; Gregory Evans Dowd, *A Spirited Resistance* (Baltimore: Johns Hopkins University Press, 1992), 144–48, 154–57; Halbert and Ball, *Creek War*, 58–84; and Martin, *Sacred Revolt*, 119–25.

12. For Tecumseh's speech, see Claiborne, *Sam Dale*, 55–62; Stiggins, *Creek Indian History*, 84–87; and Woodward, *Reminiscences*, 87–88. Woodward stated that Dale was not at Tecumseh's speech and he may well be correct. It seems strange that a white man, even one as well-connected with the Creeks as Dale, would be allowed in the council. Dale may well have reconstructed his version of the speech from his friend Weatherford and others who were present. Also see Cozzens, *Tecumseh and the Prophet*, 270–72; Pickett, *Alabama*, 510–17, 567–72 (which also has a fine contemporary biography of Dale); Edmunds, *Tecumseh*, 149–53; Cozzens, *Brutal Reckoning*, 60–70; and Halbert and Ball, *Creek War*, 65–70.

13. Dale quote in Claiborne, *Sam Dale*, 63–64. Also see Griffith, *McIntosh and Weatherford*, 74–87; Woodward, *Reminiscences*, 94–95; Henri, *Hawkins*, 269–71; Cozzens, *Brutal Reckoning*, 68–70; and Drake, *Life of Tecumseh*, 143–45. Eggleston, *Red Eagle*, 59–63, says that Tecumseh and Weatherford formed an immediate alliance, which contradicts all contemporary accounts.

14. Brock quote in Harry L. Coles, *The War of 1812* (Chicago: University of Chicago Press, 1965), 52.

15. Cozzens, *Brutal Reckoning*, 87–90; Coles, *War of 1812*, 45–58, 115–17, 192–95; and Cozzens, *Tecumseh and the Prophet*, 338–45, 356–57. Tecumseh would die in battle with the troops of General William Henry Harrison at the Battle of the Thames on October 5, 1813. Tecumseh's dream of an Indian confederacy died with him.

16. Hawkins quote in Cozzens, *Brutal Reckoning*, 94. Also see Henri, *Hawkins*, 276–79; and Griffith, *McIntosh and Weatherford*, 82–86.

17. Quote in Stiggins, *Creek Indian History*, 101. For the battle, see Claiborne, *Sam Dale*, 69–82; Cozzens, *Brutal Reckoning*, 126–30; Waselkov, *Conquering Spirit*, 98–102; and Weir, *Paradise of Blood*, 117–42.

18. Woodward, *Reminiscences*, 88–96; Stiggins, *Creek Indian History*, 103–14; Thompson, *Weatherford*, 183–203; Weir, *Paradise of Blood*, 158–61; and Waselkov, *Conquering Spirit*, 91–95. Woodward and Stiggins, who both knew Weatherford well, give slightly different versions of why he joined the Red Stick faction, but both agree that it was in response to his children being taken hostage.

CHAPTER 11: THE WAR OF THE RED STICKS

1. *A Narrative of the Life of David Crockett of the State of Tennessee, Written by Himself* (Philadelphia: E. L. Carey and A. Hart, 1834), 72.

2. Andrew Jackson to Willie Blount, June 4, 1812, in Harold D. Moser, Sharon Macpherson, and Charles Bryan Jr., eds., *The Papers of Andrew Jackson*, vol. 2,

1804–1813 (Knoxville: University of Tennessee Press, 1984), 300–301. Also see Robert V. Remini, *Andrew Jackson and the Course of American Empire, 1767–1821* (New York: Harper & Row, 1977), 165–77.

3. Quote in Marquis James, *Andrew Jackson: The Border Captain* (Indianapolis: Bobbs-Merrill, 1933), 31. Also see Remini, *Jackson*, 1–36.

4. Allan Nevins, *Frémont: The West's Greatest Adventurer*, 2 vols. (New York: Harper & Brothers, 1928), vol. 1, 7–8. For the duel, see James, *Border Captain*, 159–63; and Remini, *Jackson*, 181–86.

5. Crockett, *Narrative*, 81–82.

6. Crockett, *Narrative*, 87–90. Also see Peter Cozzens, *A Brutal Reckoning* (New York: Alfred A. Knopf, 2023), 186–90; and Tom Kanon, *Tennesseans at War, 1812–1815* (Tuscaloosa: University of Alabama Press, 2014), 75–77.

7. Howard T. Weir, *A Paradise of Blood* (Yardley, PA: Westholme, 2016), 220.

8. Jackson to Rachel Jackson, December 19, 29, 1813, in Moser et al., *Papers of Andrew Jackson*, vol. 2, 494–95, 515–16. Also see James, *Border Captain*, 169; and Cozzens, *Brutal Reckoning*, 189–90.

9. Quoted in Remini, *Jackson*, 194. Also see Christina Snyder, "Andrew Jackson's Indian Son: Native Captives and American Empire," in Tim Alan Garrison and Greg O'Brien, eds., *The Native South: New Histories and Enduring Legacies* (Lincoln: University of Nebraska Press, 2017), 84–106.

10. William C. Davis, *Three Roads to the Alamo* (New York: HarperCollins, 1998), 29–31; and Crockett, *Narrative*, 95–100.

11. Quote in Cozzens, *Brutal Reckoning*, 223. For Weatherford in the Holy Ground battle, see Benjamin W. Griffith, *McIntosh and Weatherford* (Tuscaloosa: University of Alabama Press, 1988), 126–32; Lynn Thompson, *William Weatherford* (Bay Minette, AL: Lavender Press, 1991), 475–94; J. F. H. Claiborne, *Life and Times of Gen. Sam Dale the Mississippi Partisan* (New York: Harper & Brothers, 1860), 130–42; George Cary Eggleston, *Red Eagle* (New York: Dodd Mead, 1878), 214–29; Gregory A. Waselkov, *A Conquering Spirit: Fort Mims and the Red Stick War of 1813–1814* (Tuscaloosa: University of Alabama Press, 2006), 164–67; Weir, *Paradise of Blood*, 284–300; and Pam Jones, "William Weatherford and the Road to the Holy Ground," *Alabama Heritage* 74 (Fall 2004): 24–32.

12. For the battles at Emuckfau and Enotachopco, see Remini, *Jackson*, 206–13; Cozzens, *Brutal Reckoning*, 265–71; Kanon, *Tennesseans at War*, 89–95; and George Stiggins, *Creek Indian History*, ed. Virginia Pounds Brown (Birmingham: Birmingham Public Library/University of Alabama Press, 1989), 118–20.

13. Houston quote in Marquis James, *The Raven: A Biography of Sam Houston* (Indianapolis: Bobbs-Merrill, 1929), 34. For the Battle of Horseshoe Bend, see Griffith, *McIntosh and Weatherford*, 133–49; Cozzens, *Brutal Reckoning*, 287–99; Remini, *Jackson*, 213–19; Weir, *Paradise of Blood*, 391–428; Kanon, *Tennesseans at War*, 95–107; and Frank L. Owsley Jr., *Struggle for the Gulf Borderlands: The Creek War and the Battle of New Orleans, 1812–1815* (Gainesville: University of Florida, 1981), 72–85.

14. Jackson quote in Albert James Pickett, *History of Alabama and Incidentally of Georgia and Mississippi, from the Earliest Period* (Birmingham, AL: Birmingham Book and Magazine Co., 1962; reprint of 1851 edition), 594–95.

15. Thomas S. Woodward, *Woodward's Reminiscences* (Montgomery, AL: Barrett & Wimbish, 1859), 91–93. For the story of Weatherford's surrender, see Pickett, *Alabama*, 593–96; Griffith, *McIntosh and Weatherford*, 151–55; Angie Debo, *The Road to Disappearance: The Creek Indians* (Norman: University of Oklahoma Press, 1941), 82; Thompson, *Weatherford*, 553–71; James, *Border Captain*, 164–84; Cozzens, *Brutal Reckoning*, 302–7; and Remini, *Jackson*, 218–20.

16. Crockett, *Narrative*, 101, 123–24. For the campaign, see Davis, *Three Roads*, 31–34; and James Atkins Shackford, *David Crockett* (Chapel Hill: University of North Carolina Press, 1956), 28–32.

17. Jackson quote in Cozzens, *Brutal Reckoning*, 324. For the Treaty of Fort Jackson, see Owsley, *Struggle for the Gulf Borderlands*, 86–94; Waselkov, *Conquering Spirit*, 203–10; Florette Henri, *The Southern Indians and Benjamin Hawkins, 1796–1816* (Norman: University of Oklahoma Press, 1986), 295–318; and Remini, *Jackson*, 225–32.

18. Dale quotes in Claiborne, *Sam Dale*, 127–29. Also see Griffith, *McIntosh and Weatherford*, 252–54; Thompson, *Weatherford*, 593–624; Pickett, *Alabama*, 596–97; and Eggleston, *Red Eagle*, 340–46.

CHAPTER 12: THE LION OF THE WEST

1. Crockett quote in David Crockett, *An Account of Col. Crockett's Tour to the North and Down East* (Philadelphia: E. L. Carey and A. Hart, 1835), 33–34.

2. Paulding quote in Paulding to John Wesley Jarvis, "Friday morning," 1830, in Ralph M. Aderman, ed., *The Letters of James Kirke Paulding* (Madison: University of Wisconsin Press, 1962), 112–13; Richard Boyd Hauck, "Making It All Up: Davy Crockett in the Theater," in Michael Lofaro, ed., *Davy Crockett: The Man, the Legend, the Legacy, 1786–1986* (Knoxville: University of Tennessee Press, 1985), 102–23; Joseph J. Arpad, "John Wesley Jarvis, James Kirke Paulding, and Colonel Nimrod Wildfire," *New York Folklore Quarterly* 21, no. 2 (June 1965): 92–106; James Kirke Paulding, *The Lion of the West, Retitled The Kentuckian, or A Trip to New York: A Farce in Two Acts*, ed. James N. Tidwell (Stanford, CA: Stanford University Press, 1954). Crockett's theater career continued with another hit play during the Gilded Age entitled *Davy Crockett; or, Be Sure You're Right Then Go Ahead*, by Frank Murdock and featuring Frank Mayo as Crockett. Mayo became so identified with the role that he could not escape it and acted it repeatedly until his death in 1896. Dustin Farnum re-created the part in the 1916 silent film *Davy Crockett*. Several more films featured Crockett, most notably Walt Disney's *Davy Crockett, King of the Wild Frontier* in 1955. Fess Parker's portrayal of Crockett first aired as a three-part series on the *Disneyland* television show on ABC in December 1954 and January and February 1955. They were a spectacular success and set off the first great merchandizing bonanza of the baby boomer generation. Over 10 million copies of the song "The Ballad of Davy Crockett," written by Tom Blackburn and George Bruns as narrative filler for the television show, were sold as the Bill Hayes recording topped the record charts for thirteen weeks. John Wayne returned as Crockett in his 1960 film *The Alamo*. Wayne not only starred as Crockett but also produced and directed the epic. The casting was inspired: an American icon portraying an American icon. In 2004, Billy Bob Thornton played Crockett in John Lee Hancock's *The Alamo*, which, despite fine performances and a lavish budget, failed to find an audience and proved a box office failure. For the Murdock play, see Isaac Goldberg and Hubert Heffner, eds., *Davy Crockett & Other Plays* (Princeton, NJ: Princeton University Press, 1940). The original stage prompt book for the play has

survived and is in the David Zucker Collection, Los Angeles. For Crockett films, see Paul Andrew Hutton, "The Celluloid Alamo," *Arizona and the West* 28, no. 1 (Spring 1986): 5–22; William Eric Jamborsky, "Davy Crockett and the Tradition of the Westerner in American Cinema," in Michael A. Lofaro and Joe Cummings, eds., *Crockett at Two Hundred* (Knoxville: University of Tennessee Press, 1989), 97–113; Frank Thompson, *Alamo Movies* (East Berlin, PA: Old Mill Books, 1991); Susan Prendergast Schoelwer, with Tom W. Glaser and Paul Andrew Hutton, *Alamo Images: Changing Perceptions of a Texas Experience* (Dallas: DeGolyer Library/Southern Methodist University Press, 1985); and Frank Thompson, *The Alamo: A Cultural History* (Dallas: Taylor Trade Publishing, 2001).

3. James R. Boylston and Allen J. Wiener, *David Crockett in Congress: The Rise and Fall of the Poor Man's Friend* (Houston: Bright Sky Press, 2009), 80, 109–110, 194–95; William C. Davis, *Three Roads to the Alamo* (New York, HarperCollins, 1998), 183–84, 318–19; James Atkins Shackford, *David Crockett* (Chapel Hill: University of North Carolina Press, 1956), 253–56; and Paul Andrew Hutton, "Davy Crockett: Still King of the Wild Frontier," *Texas Monthly* 14 (November 1986): 122–30, 244–48. Interestingly it was the actor James Henry Hackett as Nimrod Wildfire who helped to establish the coonskin cap as Crockett's symbolic headgear (a nod to Benjamin Franklin's fur hat, which so enchanted the French). No portrait or newspaper account mentions such headgear before 1836. The first drawing of Crockett in a fur cap (it is a wildcat skin) graced the cover of *Davy Crockett's 1837 Almanack of Wild Sports in the West* (Nashville, 1836), and it is a copy of a drawing of Hackett as Wildfire that was used to publicize the play. That Crockett did indeed wear a fur cap on occasion there is no doubt, although he also wore other headgear, depending on the setting. James Strange French mentions him wearing "a black fur cap" in *Sketches and Eccentricities* (French, *Sketches and Eccentricities of Col. David Crockett of West Tennessee* [New York: J. & J. Harper, 1833], 115), and his youngest daughter, Matilda, recalled that the morning he left for Texas "he was dressed in his hunting shirt, wearing a coon skin cap" (Gary L. Foreman, *Crockett: The Gentleman from the Cane* [Dallas: Taylor, 1986], 41). James Davis remembered Crockett as wearing "that same veritable coon-skin cap and hunting shirt" when he departed Memphis for Texas (Shackford, *David Crockett*, 212). Alamo survivor Susanna Dickinson reported seeing Crockett's mutilated body between the church and the long barracks and remembered "his peculiar cap by his side" (Shackford, *David Crockett*, 234). For the symbolism of the fur cap, see John Seelye, "Cats, Coons, Crocketts, and Other Furry Critters: Or, Why Davy Wears an Animal for a Hat," in Lofaro and Cummings, *Crockett at Two Hundred*, 153–78. For the song "The Hunters of Kentucky," see John William Ward, *Andrew Jackson: Symbol for an Age* (New York: Oxford University Press, 1955), 217.

4. Quoted in M. J. Heale, "The Role of the Frontier in Jacksonian Politics: David Crockett and the Myth of the Self-Made Man," *Western Historical Quarterly* 4, no. 4 (October 1973): 406. Also see Franklin J. Meine, ed., *The Crockett Almanacks: Nashville Series, 1835–1838* (Chicago: Caxton Club, 1955), ix.

5. *A Narrative of the Life of David Crockett of the State of Tennessee, Written by Himself* (Philadelphia: E. L. Carey and A. Hart, 1834), 126–27; Davis, *Three Roads*, 64–65. David and Elizabeth would have three children (Robert, Rebecca, and Matilda) of their own to add to his three (John, William, and Margaret) and her two (George and Margaret, called Peggy) by their previous marriages. In time they grew distant, especially after he went to Washington to serve in the House of Representatives. In 1854 she moved to Texas with their son and daughter, Robert and Rebecca, and her son George; there

she claimed Crockett's bounty land. She died in Hood County, Texas, in 1860 at age seventy-one and was buried in Acton. In 1913, the state erected a monument over her grave. Shackford, *David Crockett*, 236; Michael Wallis, *David Crockett* (New York: W. W. Norton, 2011), 229–30, 300; and Allen J. Wiener, *David Crockett in Texas: His Search for New Land* (College Station: Texas A&M University Press, 2024), 176–85.

6. Crockett, *Narrative*, 127–38; Shackford, *David Crockett*, 34–45; Richard Boyd Hauck, *Crockett: A Bio-Bibliography* (Westport, CT: Greenwood Press, 1982), 28–33.

7. Crockett, *Narrative*, 168–69, 201–2.

8. The standard biography of Polk remains Charles Sellers, *James K. Polk, Jacksonian, 1795–1843* (Princeton, NJ: Princeton University Press, 1957). A classic earlier work is Eugene Irving McCormac, *James K. Polk, a Political Biography* (Berkeley: University of California Press, 1922).

9. Crockett, *Narrative*, 143–44.

10. French, *Sketches*, 57–59; Shackford, *David Crockett*, 47–53; and Davis, *Three Roads*, 71–78.

11. Crockett, *Narrative*, 144–45.

12. H. S. Turner, "Andrew Jackson and David Crockett: Reminiscences of Colonel Chester," *Magazine of American History* 27 (May 1892): 385–87; Shackford, *David Crockett*, 63–64.

13. French, *Sketches*, 125–27.

14. *Jackson (TN) Gazette*, December 23, 1826; and Boylston and Wiener, *David Crockett*, 147–48.

15. *Nashville Republican Banner*, September 26, 1829.

16. James Erwin to Henry Clay, August 12, September 30, 1877, in James F. Hopkins and Mary W. M. Hargreaves eds., *The Papers of Henry Clay*, vol. 6, *Secretary of State, 1827* (Lexington: University Press of Kentucky, 1981), 892, 1098; and Davis, *Three Roads*, 124–25.

17. Crockett to James Blackburn, February 5, 1828, in Boylston and Wiener, *David Crockett*, 151–52. Born in 1798, Chilton was elected to Congress in the same year as Crockett and, like his close friend, would break with the Jackson forces and become a Whig in the infancy of that party. He played a significant role in writing Crockett's autobiography. He left Congress in 1835 and resumed his law practice. Chilton had studied as a youth for the Baptist ministry and in 1839 took up the pulpit in Alabama. In 1851 he removed to Texas to become pastor of the First Baptist Church of Houston. He died of a heart attack on August 15, 1854, while preaching a sermon in Montgomery, Texas. His grandson Horace Chilton served as a U.S. senator from Texas in 1891–1892 and again from 1895 to 1901.

18. Quoted in George Wilson Pierson, *Tocqueville in America* (Garden City, NY: Doubleday, 1959), 386.

19. French, *Sketches*, 164–65. The speech is partially taken by French (not Crockett) from the play *Lion of the West*.

20. Walter Blair, *Davy Crockett, Frontier Hero* (New York: Coward-McCann, 1955), 135. Also see Walter Blair and Hamlin Hill, *America's Humor: From Poor Richard to Doonesbury* (New York: Oxford University Press, 1978).

21. *Niles Weekly Register*, May 3, 1834.

22. James K. Polk to Davison McMillen, January 16, 1829, in Herbert Weaver and Paul H. Bergeron, eds., *Correspondence of James K. Polk*, vol. 1, *1817–1832* (Nashville: Vanderbilt University Press, 1969), 229–31. For a full discussion of Crockett's land bill, see Shackford, *David Crockett*, 87–107; and Boylston and Wiener, *David Crockett*, 27–42, 57–64. A version of Crockett's land bill (which gave first purchase option at a minimal price to squatters who had pioneered the land ahead of surveyors and organized settlement) was eventually passed in February 1841. It was Crockett's son John Wesley Crockett, elected to Congress in 1839, who successfully pushed through the legislation that had so eluded his less patient father. Vacant lands were awarded to Tennessee under the ruling that pioneers would have preemption purchase rights to them at 12½ cents an acre. For a discussion of Jacksonian land policies, see Daniel Feller, *The Public Lands in Jacksonian Politics* (Madison: University of Wisconsin Press, 1984).

23. *Speeches on the Passage of the Bill for the Removal of the Indians, Delivered in the Congress of the United States, April and May, 1830* (Boston: Perkins and Marvin, 1830), 251–54. Also see Shackford, *David Crockett*, 116–18, who has a cynical view of Crockett's vote; Davis, *Three Roads*, 175–77; Wallis, *Crockett*, 217–23; and Boylston and Wiener, *David Crockett*, 65–75. For Indian removal, see Francis Paul Prucha, *The Great Father: The United States Government and the American Indians*, 2 vols. (Lincoln: University of Nebraska Press, 1984), vol. 1, 179–314; Grant Foreman, *Indian Removal: The Emigration of the Five Civilized Tribes* (Norman: University of Oklahoma Press, 1966); Jeffrey Ostler, *Surviving Genocide: Native Nations and the United States from the American Revolution to Bleeding Kansas* (New Haven, CT: Yale University Press, 2019); J. Leitch Wright Jr., *The Only Land They Knew: The Tragic Story of the American Indians in the Old South* (New York: Free Press, 1981); Michael D. Green, *The Politics of Indian Removal: Creek Government and Society in Crisis* (Lincoln: University of Nebraska Press, 1982); Christopher D. Haveman, *Rivers of Sand: Creek Indian Emigration, Relocation, and Ethnic Cleansing in the American South* (Lincoln: University of Nebraska Press, 2016); John T. Ellisor, *The Second Creek War: Interethnic Conflict and Collusion on a Collapsing Frontier* (Lincoln: University of Nebraska Press, 2010); Anthony F. C. Wallace, *The Long Bitter Trail: Andrew Jackson and the Indians* (New York: Hill and Wang, 1993); Michael Paul Rogin, *Fathers and Children: Andrew Jackson and the Subjugation of the American Indian* (New York: Alfred A. Knopf, 1975); Arthur DeRosier Jr., *The Removal of the Choctaw Indians* (Knoxville: University of Tennessee Press, 1970); Theda Perdue and Michael D. Green, eds., *The Cherokee Removal: A Brief History with Documents* (Boston: Bedford Books, 1995); John Ehle, *Trail of Tears: The Rise and Fall of the Cherokee Nation* (New York: Doubleday, 1988); Thurman Wilkins, *Cherokee Tragedy: The Ridge Family and the Decimation of a People* (Norman: University of Oklahoma Press, 1986); and Ned Blackhawk, *The Rediscovery of America: Native Peoples and the Unmaking of U.S. History* (New Haven, CT: Yale University Press, 2023), 211–88.

24. Crockett to A. M. Hughes, February 13, 1831, in Boylston and Wiener, *David Crockett*, 201–202; Crockett, *Narrative*, 210–11; and Shackford, *David Crockett*, 133.

25. Paul Andrew Hutton, "'Sunrise in His Pocket': The Crockett Almanacs and the Birth of an American Legend," in Robert C. Ritchie and Paul Andrew Hutton, eds., *Frontier and Region: Essays in Honor of Martin Ridge* (Albuquerque: University of New Mexico Press, 1997), 141–67; Paul Andrew Hutton, "'Going to Congress and Making

Allmynacks Is My Trade': Davy Crockett, His Almanacs, and the Evolution of a Frontier Legend," *Journal of the West* 37, no. 2 (April 1998): 10–22; John Seelye, "A Well-Wrought Crockett: Or, How the Fakelorists Passed Through the Credibility Gap and Discovered Kentucky," in Lofaro, *Davy Crockett*, 21–45; and Hauck, *Crockett*, 79–133. The 1839–1841 Nashville almanacs are reprinted in facsimile in Michael Lofaro, ed., *The Tall Tales of Davy Crockett: The Second Nashville Series of Crockett Almanacs, 1839–1841* (Knoxville: University of Tennessee Press, 1987). The Nashville imprint almanacs for 1835–1838 are reprinted in Meine, *Crockett Almanacks*. A compilation of many of the best almanac stories, although without dated attribution, are in Richard M. Dorson, ed., *Davy Crockett: American Comic Legend* (New York: Rockland Editions, 1939), while a delightful if fanciful biography using the almanacs is Irwin Shapiro, *Yankee Thunder: The Legendary Life of Davy Crockett* (New York: Julian Messner, 1944). Also see Michael A. Lofaro, *Davy Crockett's Riproarious Shemales and Sentimental Sisters: Women's Tall Tales from the Crockett Almanacs, 1835–1856* (Mechanicsburg, PA: Stackpole, 2001).

26. French, *Sketches*, 177–78; Chapman quoted in *Galveston Daily News*, January 27, 1895; Curtis Carroll Davis, "A Legend at Full-Length: Mr. Chapman Paints Colonel Crockett and Tells About It," *Proceedings of the American Antiquarian Society* 69 (October 1959): 155–74.

27. Davis, *Three Roads*, 332–35; Hauck, *Crockett*, 60–67.

28. Crockett quote in Stuart A. Stiffler, "Davy Crockett: The Genesis of Heroic Myth," *Tennessee Historical Quarterly* 16, no. 2 (June 1957): 139; Polk to Pryor Lea, February 17, 1829, in Weaver and Bergeron, *Correspondence of Polk*, vol. 1, 240–42; Jackson to Polk, May 12, 1835, in Herbert Weaver and Kermit Hall, eds., *Correspondence of James K. Polk*, vol. 3, *1835–1836* (Nashville: Vanderbilt University Press, 1975), 190–92.

29. Shackford, *David Crockett*, 131.

30. Carlton Jackson, "Another Time, Another Place: The Attempted Assassination of President Andrew Jackson," *Tennessee Historical Quarterly* 26, no. 2 (Summer 1967): 184–90.

31. Adam Huntsman to Polk, January 1, 1835, in Weaver and Hall, *Correspondence of Polk*, vol. 3, 3–4.

32. Shackford, *David Crockett*, 203–4.

33. James D. Davis, *The History of the City of Memphis* (Memphis: Hite, Crumpton, & Kelly, 1873), 143.

CHAPTER 13: THE TEXAS

1. Crockett to George Patton, October 31, 1835, David Zucker Collection, Los Angeles.
2. Atlas Jones (admirer) quote, William C. Davis, *Three Roads to the Alamo* (New York: HarperCollins, 1998), 409; Crockett and Davis quotes in James D. Davis, *The History of the City of Memphis* (Memphis: Hite, Crumpton, & Kelly, 1873), 140–41 (which also describes the bar crawl). Also see Paul Andrew Hutton, "Frontier Hero Davy Crockett," *Wild West* 11 (February 1999): 38–44.
3. Little Rock *Arkansas Advocate*, November 13, 1835; Davis, *Three Roads*, 410–12.
4. *Niles Weekly Register*, August 27, 1836. Isaac Jones returned the watch to Elizabeth

Crockett. James Atkins Shackford, *David Crockett* (Chapel Hill: University of North Carolina Press, 1956), 213–14; and Allen J. Wiener, *David Crockett in Texas* (College Station: Texas A&M University Press, 2024), 62–97.

5. Crockett to Wiley and Margaret Flowers, January 9, 1836, in James R. Boylston and Allen J. Wiener, *David Crockett in Congress* (Houston: Bright Sky Press, 2009), 286–87; Michael Wallis, *David Crockett* (New York: W. W. Norton, 2011), 285–87; Pat B. Clark, *The History of Clarksville and Old Red River County* (Dallas: Mathis, Van Nort, 1937), 12–15; Constance Rourke, *Davy Crockett* (New York: Harcourt, 1934), 171–72.

6. Davis, *Three Roads*, 415–16. For the Texas revolt, see William C. Binkley, *The Texas Revolution* (Baton Rouge: Louisiana State University Press, 1952); Paul D. Lack, *The Texas Revolutionary Experience: A Political and Social History, 1835–1836* (College Station: Texas A&M University Press, 1992); David J. Weber, *The Mexican Frontier, 1821–1846: The American Southwest Under Mexico* (Albuquerque: University of New Mexico Press, 1982), 158–78, 242–55; and Stephen Harrigan, *Big Wonderful Thing: A History of Texas* (Austin: University of Texas Press, 2019), 80–199. Of particular value are John H. Jenkins, ed., *The Papers of the Texas Revolution*, 10 vols. (Austin: Presidial Press, 1973); and Carlos E. Castaneda, ed., *The Mexican Side of the Texan Revolution, by the Chief Mexican Participants* (Dallas: P.L. Turner, 1928). An excellent military history is Stephen L. Hardin, *Texian Iliad: A Military History of the Texas Revolution* (Austin: University of Texas Press, 1994).

7. Santa Anna quoted in Robert L. Scheina, *Santa Anna: A Curse upon Mexico* (Washington, DC: Brassey's Inc., 2002), 12. Along with Scheina, other biographies of Santa Anna include Clarence R. Wharton, *El Presidente: A Sketch of the Life of General Santa Anna* (Austin: Gammel's Book Store, 1926); Frank C. Hanighen, *Santa Anna: The Napoleon of the West* (New York: Coward-McCann, 1934); Wilfrid Hardy Walcott, *Santa Anna: The Story of an Enigma Who Once Was Mexico* (Norman: University of Oklahoma Press, 1936); Ann Fears Crawford, ed., *The Eagle: The Autobiography of Santa Anna* (Austin: State House Press, 1988); Ruth R. Olivera and Liliane Crete, *Life in Mexico Under Santa Anna, 1822–1855* (Norman: University of Oklahoma Press, 1991); and Will Fowler, *Santa Anna of Mexico* (Lincoln: University of Nebraska Press, 2007).

8. Santa Anna quoted in Scheina, *Santa Anna*, 26. Also see Hardin, *Texian Iliad*, 5–102. An invaluable addition to the story of the Texas Revolution, as well as the character of Santa Anna, is Jack Jackson and John Wheat, eds., *Almonte's Texas: Juan N. Almonte's 1834 Inspection, Secret Report and Role in the 1836 Campaign* (Austin: Texas State Historical Association, 2003). Almonte served as Santa Anna's aide-de-camp during the Texas campaign as well as a diplomatic officer to the United States both before and after the Texas war. In an interesting aside while translating a New Orleans newspaper editorial on Texas from March 19, 1834 (*Merchant Daily News*), Almonte described Crockett: "Colonel Crockett is a lunatic politician from the United States of America." Jackson and Wheat, *Almonte's Texas*, 87.

9. Crockett to Wiley and Margaret Flowers, January 9, 1836, in Boylston and Wiener, *David Crockett*, 286–87.

10. Micajah Autry to Martha Autry, January 13, 1836, in Jenkins, *Papers of the Texas Revolution*, vol. 3, 504; and Daniel Cloud quote in Davis, *Three Roads*, 417.

11. Crockett to Gales and Seaton, April 18, 1829, in Boylston and Wiener, *David Crockett*, 178. For Houston, see James L. Haley, *Sam Houston* (Norman: University of Oklahoma

Press, 2002), 63; and Marquis James, *The Raven: A Biography of Sam Houston* (Indianapolis: Bobbs-Merrill, 1929), 73–85. Houston has had many biographers, and Haley and James rank as the two best, but also of note are Amelia W. Williams and Eugene C. Barker, eds., *The Writings of Sam Houston, 1813–1863*, 8 vols. (Austin: University of Texas Press, 1938–1943); Donald Day and Harry Herbert Ullom, eds., *The Autobiography of Sam Houston* (Norman: University of Oklahoma Press, 1954); Llerena B. Friend, *Sam Houston, the Great Designer* (Austin: University of Texas Press, 1954); M. K. Wisehart, *Sam Houston: American Giant* (Washington, DC: Robert B. Luce, 1962); John Hoyt Williams, *Sam Houston: A Biography of the Father of Texas* (New York: Simon & Schuster, 1993); and Marshall DeBruhl, *Sword of San Jacinto: A Life of Sam Houston* (New York: Random House, 1993). Also see Herbert L. Harper, ed., *Houston and Crockett: Heroes of Tennessee and Texas—An Anthology* (Nashville: Tennessee Historical Commission, 1986); Paul Williams, *Jackson, Crockett and Houston on the American Frontier: From Fort Mims to the Alamo, 1813–1836* (Jefferson, NC: McFarland, 2016); and Robert Morgan, *Lions of the West: Heroes and Villains of the Westward Expansion* (Chapel Hill, NC: Algonquin Books, 2011).

12. Houston quote in Houston to Henry Smith, January 20, 1836, in Williams and Barker, *Writings of Houston*, vol. 1, 347. The best biography of Bowie is the Bowie chapters in Davis, *Three Roads*. Also see Raymond W. Thorp, *Bowie Knife* (Albuquerque: University of New Mexico Press, 1948); J. R. Edmondson, *Mr. Bowie with a Knife: A History of the Sandbar Fight* (Haltom City, TX: Watkins Printing, 1998); John Bowie, "Early Life in the Southwest—the Bowies," *DeBow's Review* 13 (October 1852): 378–83; C. L. Douglas, *James Bowie: The Life of a Bravo* (Dallas: Banks Upshaw and Company, 1944); J. Frank Dobie, "Jim Bowie—Big Dealer," *Southwestern Historical Quarterly* 60 (January 1957): 3–23; J. Frank Dobie, *Tales of Old-Time Texas* (Boston: Little, Brown, 1955), 51–77; and J. Frank Dobie, "Bowie and the Bowie Knife," *Southwest Review* 16 (April 1931): 351–68.

13. Bowie to Henry Smith, February 2, 1836, in Todd Hansen, ed., *The Alamo Reader: A Study in History* (Mechanicsburg, PA: Stackpole, 2003), 19–20; and James P. Newcomb, ed., *Antonio Menchaca Memoirs* (San Antonio, TX: Yanaguana Society, 1937), 22. Also see Davis, *Three Roads*, 494–501.

14. Crockett quote in John Sutherland, "The Alamo," in Hansen, *Alamo Reader*, 140. Sutherland was a doctor attached to the garrison. Hansen reprints the manuscript account of his memoir from the John Ford Papers in the Barker Center of the University of Texas. A slightly different version was published as John Sutherland, *The Fall of the Alamo* (San Antonio, TX: Naylor Company, 1936). The Crockett speech is on pp. 11–12. Sutherland was sent as a messenger to Gonzales and thus escaped death in the Alamo.

15. Newcomb, *Menchaca Memoirs*, 22–23. For Menchaca, also see Timothy Matovina, Jesús F. de la Teja, and Justin Poché, eds., *Recollections of a Tejano Life: Antonio Menchaca in Texas History* (Austin: University of Texas Press, 2013). For Travis, see the chapters on him in Davis, *Three Roads*. Also see Archie P. McDonald, *Travis* (Austin: Jenkins, 1976); Martha Anne Turner, *William Barret Travis: His Sword and His Pen* (Waco: Texian Press, 1972); and Robert E. Davis, ed., *The Diary of William Barret Travis* (Waco: Texian Press, 1966).

16. Davis, *Three Roads*, 535. The literature on the Alamo is extensive. Along with Davis, *Three Roads*, and Hansen, *Alamo Reader*, see James Donovan, *The Blood of Heroes: The 13-Day Struggle for the Alamo—and the Sacrifice That Forged a Nation* (New York: Little, Brown, 2012); Alan C. Huffines, *Blood of Noble Men: The Alamo Siege and Battle*

(Austin: Eakin Press, 1999); Jeff Long, *Duel of Eagles: The Mexican and U.S. Fight for the Alamo* (New York: William Morrow, 1990); J. R. Edmondson, *The Alamo Story: From Early History to Current Conflicts* (Plano: Republic of Texas Press, 2000); William Bruce Winders, *Sacrificed at the Alamo: Tragedy and Triumph in the Texas Revolution* (Abilene, TX: State House Press, 2004); H. W. Brands, *Lone Star Nation: The Epic Story of the Battle for Texas Independence* (New York: Doubleday, 2004); William C. Davis, *Lone Star Rising: The Revolutionary Birth of the Texas Republic* (New York: Free Press, 2003); Stephen L. Hardin, *The Alamo, 1836: Santa Anna's Texas Campaign* (New York: Osprey, 2001); Bill Groneman, ed., *Eyewitness to the Alamo* (Plano: Republic of Texas Press, 1996); and James E. Crisp, *Sleuthing the Alamo: Davy Crockett's Last Stand and Other Mysteries of the Texas Revolution* (New York: Oxford University Press, 2005). Four older classic accounts of the battle are Walter Lord, *A Time to Stand* (New York: Harper & Row, 1961); Lon Tinkle, *13 Days to Glory* (New York: McGraw-Hill, 1958); John Myers Myers, *The Alamo* (New York: E. P. Dutton, 1948); and Amelia W. Williams, "A Critical Study of the Siege of the Alamo and of the Personnel of Its Defenders" (Ph.D. diss., University of Texas, 1931), which was partially published in the *Southwestern Historical Quarterly* 36–37 (1932–1934). For alternative interpretations of the heroic Alamo story, see Richard R. Flores, *Remembering the Alamo: Memory, Modernity, and the Master Symbol* (Austin: University of Texas Press, 2002); and Bryan Burrough, Chris Tomlinson, and Jason Stanford, *Forget the Alamo: The Rise and Fall of an American Myth* (New York: Penguin, 2021).

17. Sutherland, *Fall of the Alamo*, 19–20.

18. Paul Andrew Hutton, "'It Was but a Small Affair': The Battle of the Alamo," in Paul Andrew Hutton, ed., *Western Heritage: A Selection of Wrangler Award–Winning Articles* (Norman: University of Oklahoma Press, 2011), 219–38 (Esparza quote on 230); Hansen, *Alamo Reader*, 202; and Groneman, *Eyewitness to the Alamo*, 148–49. Also see Paul Andrew Hutton, "Santa Anna: Out on a Limb," *Wild West* 30 (February 2018): 38–45.

19. Travis to Houston, February 25, 1836, reprinted in *Arkansas Gazette* (Little Rock), April 12, 1836. For the famous Travis letter of February 24, see Donovan, *Blood of Heroes*, 212–13. For the 32 from Gonzales, see Lord, *A Time to Stand*, 125–31.

20. Esparza quote in Groneman, *Eyewitness to the Alamo*, 150–51.

21. Soldana quote in Hansen, *Alamo Reader*, 470.

22. Susanna Dickinson quote in Groneman, *Eyewitness to the Alamo*, 68.

23. For the final assault, see Donovan, *Blood of Heroes*, 259–97; Davis, *Three Roads*, 553–63; Long, *Duel of Eagles*, 235–67; and Lord, *A Time to Stand*, 154–79. The story of the line drawn by Travis and the escape of Moses Rose has been controversial since William Zuber first related it in the 1857 *Texas Almanac* (pp. 80–85). Also see W. P. Zuber, "The Escape of Rose from the Alamo," *Texas Historical Association Quarterly* 5 (July 1901): 1–11. Although initially dismissed as fiction, subsequent research has proven it to be true. Susanna Dickinson confirmed it in interviews with the *National Police Gazette*, May 4, 1878, and the *San Antonio Daily Express*, April 28, 1881, as did Enrique Esparza in the *San Antonio Daily Express* in 1901. In 1939 a dogged amateur historian named R. B. Blake discovered court and land records in Nacogdoches County that provided proof that Rose, who operated a meat market in Nacogdoches, had escaped from the Alamo. So the shining legend of the line in the dust—where each defender, in a moment of sublime democratic choice, made a personal decision to remain and die for liberty—is true. "But nobody forgets the line," wrote J. Frank Dobie in 1939. "It is drawn too deep and straight . . . a grand canyon cut into the bedrock of human emotions and heroical impulses." J. Frank Dobie, "Rose and His Story of the Alamo," in J. Frank Dobie, Mody C. Boatright, and Harry H. Ransom, eds., *In the Shadow of History* (Austin: Texas Folk-Lore Society, 1939), 9–41. Also see Paul Andrew Hutton, "The Alamo: Well Remembered," *Wild West* 23 (February 2011): 26–35; Donovan, *Blood of Heroes*, 351–74; and Lord, *A Time to Stand*, 201–4.

24. Dickinson (also known by later married names of Belles and Hannig) quote in Groneman, *Eyewitness to the Alamo*, 68–70. Also see Hansen, *Alamo Reader*, 41–69, which includes all the extant Susanna Dickinson interviews, including the quote on Crockett's body from 1874. Mrs. Dickinson was escorted from the Alamo church by an English-speaking officer who she presumed was Almonte. That officer would also play a role in the most debated moment of the Alamo story: the death of Crockett. De la Peña quote in Carmen Perry, trans. and ed., *With Santa Anna in Texas: A Personal Narrative of the Revolution, by José Enrique de la Peña* (College Station: Texas A&M University Press, 1975), 52–54. This remarkable military memoir was first published in Mexico in 1955 as J. Sánchez Garza, ed., *La rebelión de Texas: manuscrito inédito de 1836 por un oficial de Santa Anna* (Mexico D.F.: A. F. de Sánchez, 1955). It is without question the best account of the battle of the Alamo by a participant. For years the book was believed to be a diary first published in Matamoros, Mexico, in 1836, but the careful research of Professor James Crisp revealed that the diary had been reworked by de la Peña while he languished in a Mexico City prison (where the young officer died in 1840) in hopes of publishing it as a book. His death ended that hope, so it was not until 1955 that Jesús Sánchez Garza rescued the manuscript from oblivion and published it. Walter Lord, as a result of a faulty translation, identified the diary as an 1836 publication in 1961 in *A Time to Stand*, pp. 206–7, and many historians (including this author) followed his lead. For a generation of Alamo scholars Lord's wonderful book was gospel. (See introduction by James E. Crisp to the 1997 expanded edition of Perry, *With Santa Anna in Texas* [College Station: Texas A&M University Press, 1997], xi–xxv.) The collection of de la Peña manuscripts was purchased from Sánchez Garza by wealthy Texas collector John Peace, who hired Carmen Perry to translate it, and it now resides in the Center for American History at the University of Texas, Austin. The papers were subjected to extensive forensic tests and declared to be authentic. Also see Phil Guarnieri and Richard L. Range, *David Crockett Went Down Fighting* (Dallas: Red River Press, 2024).

Despite the value of young de la Peña's narrative of the Texas campaign as a historical document of immense significance, it is a single page describing the death of Crockett that created a storm of controversy. A tsunami of magazine articles and at least three books have dealt with this issue: Dan Kilgore, *How Did Davy Die?* (College Station: Texas A&M University Press, 1978), which defended the de la Peña account and presented six additional Mexican accounts of Crockett's execution; Bill Groneman, *Death of a Legend: The Myth and Mystery Surrounding the Death of Davy Crockett* (Plano: Republic of Texas Press, 1999), which labeled the de la Peña account a forgery and fraud, concluding that it is impossible to know how Crockett actually died; and Crisp, *Sleuthing the Alamo*, which disproved the allegations of forgery and fraud leveled by Groneman and others.

The controversial de la Peña passage reads:

> *Some seven men had survived the general carnage and, under the protec-*

> *tion of General Castrillon, they were brought before Santa Anna. Among them was one of great stature, well proportioned, with regular features, in whose face there was the imprint of adversity, but in whom one also noticed a degree of resignation and nobility that did him honor. He was the naturalist David Crockett, well known in North America for his unusual adventures, who had undertaken to explore the country and who, finding himself in Béjar at the very moment of surprise, had taken refuge in the Alamo, fearing that his status as a foreigner might not be respected. Santa Anna answered Castrillon's intervention in Crockett's behalf with a gesture of indignation and, addressing himself to the sappers, the troops closest to him, ordered his execution. The commanders and officers were outraged at this action and did not support the order, hoping that once the fury of the moment had blown over, these men would be spared; but several other officers who were around the president and who, perhaps, had not been present during the moment of danger, became noteworthy by an infamous deed, surpassing the soldiers in cruelty. They thrust themselves forward, in order to flatter their commander, and with swords in hand, fell upon these unfortunate, defenseless men just as a tiger leaps upon his prey. Though tortured before they were killed, these unfortunates died without complaining and without humiliating themselves before their torturers.*

The execution story was widespread in Texas after the battle, although Crockett was not always identified. Sam Houston wrote James Fannin at Goliad on March 11, 1836, that "after the fort was carried, seven men surrendered and called for Santa Anna and quarter. They were murdered by his order" (Williams and Barker, *Writings of Houston,* vol. 1, 362–63), and several Eastern newspapers carried the execution story. The most prominent of the early newspaper accounts was the July 9, 1836, *Morning Courier and New-York Enquirer,* which was the first to report Crockett as among the handful executed. The Mexican eyewitness who reported this was not identified but may have been Almonte. That officer was identified as the source of a similar account identifying Crockett contained in a July 19, 1836, letter from Texas soldier George M. Dolson to his brother in Michigan that was reprinted in the *Detroit Democratic Free Press* on September 7, 1836. The newspaper article was discovered by a researcher in 1960 and published as Thomas Lawrence Connelly, "Did David Crockett Surrender at the Alamo? A Contemporary Letter," *Journal of Southern History* 26, no. 3 (August 1960): 368–76. Almonte's version of Crockett's death was quite close to that related by de la Peña. (Almonte was captured at San Jacinto, while de la Peña was not at that battle, having been detached with General Vicente Filisola's column in the division of the Mexican forces after the Alamo.) It is in fact rather surprising that we have so much detail on Crockett's death. It is of course possible that he was misidentified, although both de la Peña and Almonte, our main eyewitnesses, were intelligent officers of sterling character. There is no eyewitness account of Crockett's death in battle, and the historian must be guided by available sources and not legendary tales. For more on this topic, see Donovan, *Blood of Heroes,* 446–53; Hansen, *Alamo Reader,* 431–52, 783–98; Groneman, *Eyewitness to the Alamo,* 36–41; Crisp, *Sleuthing the Alamo,* 61–138; and Davis, *Three Roads,* 737–38.

25. Esparza quote in Groneman, *Eyewitness to the Alamo,* 157–58.

26. Groneman, *Eyewitness to the Alamo,* 57; Hardin, *Texian Iliad,* 155.

CHAPTER 14: THE MOUNTAIN MEN

1. There is a rich literature on the American fur trade. Excellent overviews include Hiram Martin Chittenden, *The American Fur Trade of the Far West*, 2 vols. (New York: Press of the Pioneers, 1935); Bernard DeVoto, *Across the Wide Missouri* (Boston: Houghton Mifflin, 1947); David Lavender, *The Fist in the Wilderness* (Garden City, NY: Doubleday, 1964); LeRoy R. Hafen and Francis M. Young, *Fort Laramie and the Pageant of the West, 1834–1890* (Glendale, CA: Arthur H. Clark, 1938); Robert M. Utley, *A Life Wild and Perilous: Mountain Men and the Paths to the Pacific* (New York: Henry Holt, 1997); Eric Jay Dolin, *Fur, Fortune, and Empire* (New York: W. W. Norton, 2010); Theodore J. Karamanske, *Fur Trade and Exploration: Opening the Far Northwest, 1821–1852* (Norman: University of Oklahoma Press, 1983); Robert Glass Cleland, *This Reckless Breed of Men* (New York: Alfred A. Knopf, 1950); Dale Morgan, *Jedediah Smith and the Opening of the West* (Indianapolis: Bobbs-Merrill, 1953); Peter Stark, *Astoria: John Jacob Astor and Thomas Jefferson's Lost Pacific Empire* (New York: Ecco, 2014); James P. Ronda, *Astoria & Empire* (Lincoln: University of Nebraska Press, 1990); David J. Weber, *The Taos Trappers: The Fur Trade in the Far Southwest, 1540–1846* (Norman: University of Oklahoma Press, 1971); and the invaluable LeRoy R. Hafen, ed., *The Mountain Men and the Fur Trade of the Far West*, 10 vols. (Glendale, CA: Arthur H. Clark, 1965–72). It is impossible to form any exact idea of the magnitude of the trade, but an interesting calculation was made by Indian agent John Dougherty in 1832 of the extent of the trade between 1815 and 1830 in St. Louis. He estimated 26,000 buffalo robes per year, 25,000 beaver skins per year, 4,000 otter skins per year, 12,000 coonskins per year, 37,500 muskrat skins per year, and 150,000 pounds of deer skins. At $4 each, beaver skins were the most profitable. He estimated an annual profit of $110,000 per year. Losses were high, both monetary and human, as a result of conflict with the Indians. At least two hundred to three hundred trappers were killed during this period. Chittenden, *American Fur Trade*, vol. 1, 7–10.

2. Lindsey Carson was born in 1754 in North Carolina of Scotch-Irish stock. His ancestors had come to Pennsylvania early in the eighteenth century and like so many others migrated south into the Carolinas. Lindsey and his brother Andrew were both veterans of the Revolutionary army. Lindsey moved up the Wilderness Road to Madison County, Kentucky, in 1792 after the death of his first wife. The eldest boy of this first marriage, William (there were four children) married Millie Boone of the Kentucky Boones and thus secured a distant Carson connection to Daniel Boone. Lindsey and his son Moses (Kit's stepbrother) both served in the Missouri home guards during the War of 1812, and Lindsey was wounded in an Indian fight. Lindsey married Rebecca Robinson, of Greenbriar County, Virginia, in 1797. She would bear him ten children, four girls and six boys. Christopher Houston Carson was the fifth child. Amazingly for the period, all of Lindsey Carson's children survived into adulthood. All his sons would become involved in either the Santa Fe Trail trade or the fur trade. Edwin Legrand Sabin, *Kit Carson Days, 1809–1868: Adventures in the Path of Empire*, 2 vols. (New York: Press of the Pioneers, 1935), vol. 1, 5–8; and Quantrille D. McClung, *Carson-Bent-Boggs Genealogy* (Denver: Denver Public Library, 1962). The place to start when considering Carson is the autobiography he dictated in 1856 but which was not published until 1926 as Blanche Grant, ed., *Kit Carson's Own Story of His Life* (Taos, NM: privately printed, 1926) and did not become widely available until Milo M. Quaife located the original manuscript in Chicago's Newberry Library, edited it, and released it as one of his famous Christmas "Lakeside Classics"—although he unfortunately cleaned up the syntax and grammar to make it more

readable for a modern audience. Milo M. Quaife, ed., *Kit Carson's Autobiography* (Chicago: Lakeside Press, 1935). It has often been reprinted. The best edition of the autobiography, as well as an invaluable addition to the Carson literature, is the heavily annotated book by Harvey L. Carter, *Dear Old Kit: The Historical Christopher Carson, with a New Edition of the Carson Memoirs* (Norman: University of Oklahoma Press, 1968). Carson's friend Dr. DeWitt Clinton Peters used the memoir as the basis for his 1858 biography of Carson entitled *The Life and Adventures of Kit Carson, the Nestor of the Rocky Mountains, from Facts Narrated by Himself* (New York: W. R. C. Clark, 1858). The book proved quite successful. Another valuable contemporary piece is George D. Brewerton, "A Ride with Kit Carson," *Harper's New Monthly Magazine* 7 (August 1853): 306–45. This was expanded and reprinted as Stallo Vinton, ed., *Overland with Kit Carson: A Narrative of the Old Spanish Trail in '48* (New York: Coward-McCann, 1930). Nineteenth-century biographies by John Abbott, Edward S. Ellis, William F. Cody, and Charles Burdett mostly parrot Dr. Peters. Edwin L. Sabin, a popular writer of Western fiction, produced one of the best biographies of Carson in 1914, which he greatly expanded into the 1935 two-volume set already cited. Sabin had unfortunately fallen under the spell of Oliver Perry Wiggins, a Denver old-timer who told imaginary tales of his time with Carson. With the exception of the Wiggins material, the book is quite valuable. Less notable is Stanley Vestal's *Kit Carson, the Happy Warrior of the Old West* (Boston: Houghton Mifflin, 1928), which has more literary than historical value. Two later biographies—Bernice Blackwelder, *Great Westerner* (Caldwell, ID: Caxton, 1962), and M. Morgan Estergreen, *Kit Carson: A Portrait in Courage* (Norman: University of Oklahoma Press, 1962)—are hagiographic pieces with little new in them. Interestingly, Blackwelder and the earlier cited McClung in turn inspired a work deconstructing their motives as well as modern western historiography in Susan Lee Johnson, *Writing Kit Carson: Fallen Heroes in a Changing West* (Chapel Hill: University of North Carolina Press, 2020). The best modern biography is Hampton Sides, *Blood and Thunder: An Epic of the American West* (New York: Doubleday, 2006). Other valuable works include Thelma S. Guild and Harvey L. Carter, *Kit Carson: A Pattern for Heroes* (Lincoln: University of Nebraska Press, 1984); David Roberts, *A Newer World: Kit Carson, John C. Frémont, and the Claiming of the American West* (New York: Simon & Schuster, 2000); Tom Dunlay, *Kit Carson and the Indians* (Lincoln: University of Nebraska Press, 2000); R. C. Gordon-McCutchan, ed., *Kit Carson: Indian Fighter or Indian Killer?* (Niwot: University Press of Colorado, 1996); Marc Simmons, *Kit Carson and His Three Wives* (Albuquerque: University of New Mexico Press, 2003); and David Remley, *Kit Carson: The Life of an American Border Man* (Norman: University of Oklahoma Press, 2011).

3. Carson quote in Carter, *Dear Old Kit*, 38. *Missouri Intelligencer* (Franklin, MO), October 6, 1826.

4. Ray Allen Billington, *The Far Western Frontier, 1830–1860* (New York: Harper and Brothers, 1956), 35–36. For the Santa Fe Trail, see Josiah Gregg, *Commerce of the Prairies*, 2 vols. (New York: Henry G. Langley, 1844), which has often been reprinted; Henry Inman, *The Old Santa Fe Trail: The Story of a Great Highway* (New York: Macmillan, 1898); R. L. Duffus, *The Santa Fe Trail* (New York: Longmans, 1930); David Dary, *The Santa Fe Trail* (New York: Alfred A. Knopf, 2000); Marc Simmons, ed., *On the Santa Fe Trail* (Lawrence: University Press of Kansas, 1986); and Seymour V. Connor and Jimmy M. Skaggs, *Broadcloth and Britches: The Santa Fe Trade* (College Station: Texas A&M University Press, 1977). For Becknell, see William Becknell, "Journal of Two Expeditions from Boon's Lick to Santa Fe," *Missouri Intelligencer* (Franklin, MO), April 22, 1823; and Larry M. Beachum, *William Becknell: Father of the Santa Fe Trade* (El Paso: Texas Western Press, 1982).

5. Carter, *Dear Old Kit*, 42–50; Sabin, *Kit Carson Days,* vol. 1, 33–64; Guild and Carter, *Kit Carson,* 16–45; Cleland, *Reckless Breed*, 215–45; and Weber, *Taos Trappers*, 124–54.
6. For Fitzpatrick, see LeRoy R. Hafen, *Broken Hand: The Life of Thomas Fitzpatrick: Mountain Man, Guide and Indian Agent* (Denver: Old West Publishing, 1973).
7. Utley, *Life Wild and Perilous*, 57–71, 83–102; Hafen, *Broken Hand,* 89–171; Sabin, *Kit Carson Days*, vol. 1, 137–43.
8. Frances Fuller Victor, *The River of the West* (Hartford, CT: Columbian Book Company, 1870), 64–65. Also see Enos A. Mills, *In Beaver World* (Boston: Houghton Mifflin, 1913); and Stanley Vestal, *Joe Meek* (Caldwell, ID: Caxton, 1952).
9. Carter, *Dear Old Kit*, 60–61.
10. Samuel Parker, *Journal of an Exploring Tour Beyond the Rocky Mountains* (Ithaca, NY: Andrus, Woodruff and Gauntlett, 1838), 78–80.
11. Parker, *Journal*; Carter, *Dear Old Kit,* 63–65; Simmons, *Three Wives*, 7–22; Sabin, *Kit Carson*, vol. 1, 257–60; Utley, *Life Wild and Perilous,* 161–63.
12. Chouinard's fate is a point of some debate. Neither Parker nor Carson clarify the man's condition after the duel. Later, Carson told a Taos friend that Chouinard was "the only man he ever killed that he was pleased with [him]self for doing it." Simmons, *Three Wives,* 14; Vestal, *Kit Carson*, 115–25.
13. John Charles Frémont, *Memoirs of My Life* (Chicago: Belford, Clarke & Co., 1887), 74; and Gerald Thompson, *Edward F. Beale and the American West* (Albuquerque: University of New Mexico Press, 1983), 24.
14. Carter, *Dear Old Kit*, 79.
15. For Bent's Fort, see David Lavender, *Bent's Fort* (Garden City, NY: Doubleday, 1854).
16. Victor, *River of the West*, 264.

CHAPTER 15: THE OREGON TRAIL

1. John Charles Frémont, *Memoirs of My Life* (Chicago: Belford, Clarke & Co., 1887), 74.
2. Harvey L. Carter, *Dear Old Kit* (Norman: University of Oklahoma Press, 1968), 81.
3. Frémont remains one of the more controversial figures in American history. The standard biography is still Allan Nevins, *Frémont,* 2 vols. (New York: Harper and Brothers, 1928), which is quite positive in its treatment of its subject. A far more negative view was presented by Cardinal Goodwin, *John Charles Frémont: An Explanation of His Career* (Stanford, CA: Stanford University Press, 1930). A psychological study can be found in Andrew Rolle, *John Charles Frémont: Character as Destiny* (Norman: University of Oklahoma Press, 1991). Two excellent modern biographies are Ferol Egan, *Frémont: Explorer for a Restless Nation* (New York: Doubleday, 1977), and Tom Chaffin, *Pathfinder: John Charles Frémont and the Course of the American Empire* (Norman: University of Oklahoma Press, 2002). Two campaign biographies of some value are John Bigelow, *Memoir of the Life and Public Services of John Charles Frémont* (New York: Derby & Jackson, 1856), and Charles W. Upham, *Life, Explorations and Public Services of John Charles Frémont* (Boston: Ticknor and Fields, 1856). Frederick S. Dellenbaugh, *Frémont and '49* (New York: G. P. Putnam's Sons, 1914) also contains valuable material. Invaluable to any study of

Frémont is Donald Jackson and Mary Lee Spence, eds., *The Expeditions of John Charles Frémont*, 3 vols. (Urbana: University of Illinois Press, 1970–84). This masterful work of documentary editing also contains a supplementary volume on the court-martial and a map portfolio. Frémont's 1886 memoir is also an invaluable source. He intended to write two volumes but never completed the second, so the book ends with the conquest of California. For the important scientific role Frémont played in the exploration of the West, see William H. Goetzmann, *Exploration and Empire: The Explorer and the Scientist in the Winning of the American West* (New York: Alfred A. Knopf, 1966). For Jessie Benton Frémont, see Pamela Herr, *Jessie Benton Frémont: A Biography* (New York: Franklin Watts, 1987); Sally Denton, *Passion and Principle* (New York: Bloomsbury, 2007); and Pamela Herr and Mary Lee Spence, eds., *The Letters of Jessie Benton Frémont* (Urbana: University of Illinois Press, 1993).

4. Herr, *Jessie*, 58. For Thomas Hart Benton, see Ken S. Mueller, *Senator Benton and the People* (DeKalb: Northern Illinois University Press, 2014); William Nisbet Chambers, *Old Bullion Benton: Senator from the New West* (Boston: Little, Brown and Company, 1956); and Theodore Roosevelt, *Thomas H. Benton* (Boston: Houghton, Mifflin, 1899).

5. Quoted in Chaffin, *Pathfinder*, 14–15. For the expedition, see Frémont, *Memoirs*, 73–123.

6. Frémont, "Report," in Jackson and Spence, *Expeditions*, vol. 1, 253.

7. Jessie quote in Egan, *Frémont*, 117–18. Frémont quote in Frémont "Report," in Jackson and Spence, *Expeditions*, vol. 1, 270. For the writing of the report, see Frémont, *Memoirs*, 162–63; Herr, *Jessie*, 77–82; Denton, *Passion and Principle*, 84–86; and Nevins, *Frémont*, 125–37. The report was published in 1843 as Senate Doc. 243, 27th Congress, 3rd Session, "A Report of an Exploration of the Country Lying Between the Missouri River and the Rocky Mountains on the Line of the Kansas and Great Platte Rivers," and is conveniently reprinted in Jackson and Spence, *Expeditions*, vol. 1, 168–338. For the Oregon Trail, see John D. Unruh Jr., *The Plains Across: The Overland Emigrants and the Trans-Mississippi West, 1840–60* (Urbana: University of Illinois Press, 1979); John Mack Faragher, *Women and Men on the Overland Trail* (New Haven, CT: Yale University Press, 1979); John Phillip Reid, *Law for the Elephant: Property and Social Behavior on the Overland Trail* (San Marino, CA: Huntington Library, 1980); David Dary, *The Oregon Trail* (New York: Alfred A. Knopf, 2004); W. J. Ghent, *The Road to Oregon* (New York: Longmans, Green, 1929); Will Bagley, *South Pass: Gateway to a Continent* (Norman: University of Oklahoma Press, 2014); Merrill J. Mattes, *The Great Platte River Road* (Lincoln: University of Nebraska Press, 1969); Will Bagley, *So Rugged and Mountainous: Blazing Trails to Oregon and California, 1812–1848* (Norman: University of Oklahoma Press, 2010); Martin Ridge, ed., *Westward Journeys: Memoirs of Jesse A. Applegate and Lavinia Honeyman Porter, Who Traveled the Overland Trail* (Chicago: Lakeside Press, 1989).

8. *Niles' National Register*, May 6, 1843.

9. J. Abert to Frémont, March 10, 1843, in Jackson and Spence, *Expeditions*, vol. 1, 160–61; Talbot quote in Egan, *Frémont*, 126–27. Also see Frémont, *Memoirs*, 164–76; and Chaffin, *Pathfinder*, 147–49.

10. Charles Preuss, *Exploring with Frémont: The Private Diaries of Charles Preuss, Cartographer for John C. Frémont*, ed. Erwin G. Gudde and Elisabeth K. Gudde (Norman: University of Oklahoma Press, 1958), 86. Also see Frémont, *Memoirs*, 169–236.

11. Frémont, "Report," in Jackson and Spence, *Expeditions,* vol. 1, 516; and Billington, *Far Western Frontier,* 199, 208–10.

12. Preuss, *Exploring,* 91.

13. Preuss, *Exploring,* 95; Frémont, *Memoirs,* 275–76.

14. Frémont, *Memoirs,* 279–80.

15. Frémont, "Report," in Jackson and Spence, *Expeditions,* vol. 1, 574–75; and Carson quote in Carter, *Dear Old Kit,* 89. Also see Egan, *Frémont,* 181–98.

16. Carson quote in Carter, *Dear Old Kit,* 90–91. For the mountain crossing, see Frémont, *Memoirs,* 324–50: Preuss, *Exploring,* 104–19; Nevins, *Frémont,* vol. 1, 163–80; Chaffin, *Pathfinder,* 209–21; and Egan, *Frémont,* 199–222.

17. For John Sutter, see Erwin G. Gudde, *Sutter's Own Story* (New York: G. P. Putnam's Sons, 1936); James P. Zollinger, *Sutter: The Man and His Empire* (New York: Oxford University Press, 1939); Kenneth N. Owens, ed., *John Sutter and a Wider West* (Lincoln: University of Nebraska Press, 1994); and Albert Hurtado, *John Sutter: A Life on the North American Frontier* (Norman: University of Oklahoma Press, 2006).

18. Carter, *Dear Old Kit,* 93. For the Old Spanish Trail, see LeRoy R. Hafen and Ann W. Hafen, *The Old Spanish Trail: Santa Fe to Los Angeles* (Glendale, CA: Arthur H. Clark, 1968).

19. Preuss, *Exploring,* 127–28; Frémont, *Memoirs,* 374; Carter, *Dear Old Kit,* 91–93.

20. Preuss, *Exploring,* 130–31; Frémont, *Memoirs,* 375–410.

21. Carter, *Dear Old Kit,* 95.

CHAPTER 16: MANIFEST DESTINY

1. *New York Morning News,* December 27, 1845. For the concept of Manifest Destiny and its consequences, see Frederick Merk, *Manifest Destiny and Mission in American History: A Reinterpretation* (New York: Alfred A. Knopf, 1963); Albert K. Weinberg, *Manifest Destiny: A Study of Nationalist Expansion in American History* (Baltimore: Johns Hopkins University Press, 1935); Bernard DeVoto, *The Year of Decision: 1846* (Boston: Little, Brown, 1943); William H. Goetzmann, *When the Eagle Screamed: The Romantic Horizon in American Expansionism, 1800–1860* (New York: John Wiley, 1966); Sam W. Haynes and Christopher Morris, eds., *Manifest Destiny and Empire: American Antebellum Expansionism* (College Station: Texas A&M Press, 1997); and Walter Nugent, *Habits of Empire: A History of American Expansion* (New York: Alfred A. Knopf, 2008).

2. Robert W. Merry, *A Country of Vast Designs: James K. Polk, the Mexican War, and the Conquest of the American Continent* (New York: Simon & Schuster, 2009), 49–111; Paul H. Bergeron, *The Presidency of James K. Polk* (Lawrence: University Press of Kansas, 1987), 12–22; John Seigenthaler, *James K. Polk* (New York: Henry Holt, 2004), 87–99; and Charles Sellers, *James K. Polk: Continentalist, 1843–1846* (Princeton, NJ: Princeton University Press, 1966), 32–161.

3. Stephen Harrigan, *Big Wonderful Thing: A History of Texas* (Austin: University of Texas Press), 23–35; Marquis James, *The Raven* (Indianapolis: Bobbs-Merrill, 1929), 338–58; and Sam W. Haynes, *Unsettled Land: From Revolution to Republic, the Struggle for Texas* (New York: Basic Books, 2022), 329–44. The best account of the Texas and

Oregon crisis remains David M. Pletcher, *The Diplomacy of Annexation: Texas, Oregon, and the Mexican War* (Columbia: University of Missouri Press, 1973).

4. Almonte quote in Harrigan, *Big Wonderful Thing*, 238.

5. Merry, *Country of Vast Designs*, 190–221; Pletcher, *Diplomacy*, 352–77; K. Jack Bauer, *The Mexican War, 1846–1848* (New York: Macmillan, 1974), 4–29; and Amy S. Greenberg, *A Wicked War: Polk, Clay, Lincoln, and the 1846 U.S. Invasion of Mexico* (New York: Alfred A. Knopf, 2012), 76–79. From 1853 until 1861, Congressman John Slidell (1793–1871) would serve as a senator from Louisiana and was one of the loudest and most intemperate of the secessionists. He was appointed as a Confederate diplomat to France and became famous when captured by the Union Navy in the 1861 *Trent* affair. After the war, he went into exile in Paris.

6. Frémont, *Memoirs of My Life* (Chicago: Belford, Clarke & Co., 1887), 410–19; Buchanan quoted in Allan Nevins, *Frémont* (New York: Harper and Brothers, 1928), vol. 1, 229. Frémont's report is conveniently reprinted as "A Report of the Exploring Expedition to Oregon and North California in the Years 1843–44" in Donald Jackson and Mary Lee Spence, eds., *The Expeditions of John Charles Frémont*, 3 vols. (Urbana: University of Illinois Press, 1970–84), vol. 1, 426–806.

7. Frémont quote in Frémont, *Memoirs*, 422; J. J. Abert's orders in Jackson and Spence, *Expeditions*, vol. 1, 395–97. Also see Tom Chaffin, *Pathfinder* (Norman: University of Oklahoma Press, 2002), 252–53, and Nevins, *Frémont*, vol. 1, 231–37.

8. Thomas S. Martin, *With Frémont to California and the Southwest, 1845–1849* (Ashland, OR: Lewis Osborne, 1975), 2.

9. Frémont, *Memoirs*, 427; Harvey L. Carter, ed., *Dear Old Kit* (Norman: University of Oklahoma Press, 1968), 95–96. Also see Robert V. Hine, *Edward Kern and American Expansion* (New Haven, CT: Yale University Press, 1962), 1–24; Ferol Egan, *Frémont: Explorer for a Restless Nation* (New York: Doubleday, 1977), 290–96; and Chaffin, *Pathfinder*, 258–60.

10. Pletcher, *Diplomacy*, 312–51, 402–17. Also see Frederick Merk, *The Oregon Question: Essays in Anglo-American Diplomacy and Politics* (Cambridge, MA: Harvard University Press, 1967).

11. Bauer, *Mexican War*, 16–78, 392–99; Greenberg, *Wicked War*, 96–110, 256–71; and Merry, *Country of Vast Designs*, 190–204, 238–52, 448–51. The regular army swelled to 42,587 men during the war, while the bulk of the American forces consisted of 73,532 men in various volunteer regiments. A total of 1,721 died as a result of battle wounds, while another 11,155 died from disease or accidents, and 4,102 were wounded, thus making the conflict quite costly in terms of percentage of casualties. The war cost about $60 million, with another $15 million paid to Mexico along with the assumption of Mexican debts to the United States as a result of the Treaty of Guadalupe Hidalgo. The United States acquired 529,017 square miles of territory to fulfill its "continental destiny." The war poisoned national politics over the question of the extension of slavery into the new western territories and contributed to the outbreak of the Civil War. Already politically unstable, Mexico now descended into an even more chaotic political crisis, which resulted in civil war and the brief establishment of the monarchy of the French puppet Maximilian. Mexico never quite recovered from the conflict, while the war secured for the United States a place of economic and political world power. Besides Bauer, standard military histories of the

Mexican War include Justin H. Smith, *The War with Mexico,* 2 vols. (New York: Macmillan, 1919); Otis Singletary, *The Mexican War* (Chicago: University of Chicago Press, 1960); John S. D. Eisenhower, *So Far from God: The U.S. War with Mexico, 1846–1848* (New York: Random House, 1989); David A. Clary, *Eagles and Empire: The United States, Mexico, and the Struggle for a Continent* (New York: Bantam, 2009); George Winston Smith and Charles Judah, eds., *Chronicles of the Gringos: The U.S. Army in the Mexican War, 1846–1848; Accounts of Eyewitnesses and Combatants* (Albuquerque: University of New Mexico Press, 1968); James M. McCaffrey, *Army of Manifest Destiny: The American Soldier in the Mexican War, 1846–1848* (New York: New York University Press, 1992); William A. DePalo Jr., *The Mexican National Army, 1822–1852* (College Station: Texas A&M University Press, 2004); and Richard Bruce Winders, *Mr. Polk's Army: The American Military Experience in the Mexican War* (College Station: Texas A&M University Press, 1997).

12. Allan Nevins, ed., *Polk: The Diary of a President, 1845–1849* (London: Longman, Green, 1952), 50–53, 148–50; Wilfrid Hardy Callcott, *Santa Anna: The Story of an Enigma Who Once Was Mexico* (Norman: University of Oklahoma Press, 1936), 229–38. See Robert L. Scheina, *Santa Anna: A Curse upon Mexico* (Washington, DC: Brassey's, 2002), 47–49, for a Mexican liberal quote. Alexander Slidell Mackenzie was the younger brother of John Slidell, the brother-in-law of Commodore Matthew C. Perry, and the father of the famed cavalry officer and Indian fighter Ranald Slidell Mackenzie. He was controversial as a result of a mutiny on his ship the *Somers* in December 1842. Mackenzie hanged the suspected ringleaders, one of whom was the son of the secretary of war. This naturally caused a national scandal, and although Mackenzie was cleared by a court of inquiry, his reputation suffered. He was also an accomplished writer of travel accounts and naval history. He died unexpectedly of a heart attack on September 13, 1848, in New York.

13. Callcott, *Santa Anna,* 243.

14. Frémont to Jessie Benton Frémont, January 24, 1846, in Jackson and Spence, *Expeditions,* vol. 2, 46–48. Also see Robert V. Hine and Savoie Lottinville, eds., *Soldier in the West: Letters of Theodore Talbot During His Services in California, Mexico, and Oregon, 1845–53* (Norman: University of Oklahoma Press, 1972), 11–14, 20; Frémont, *Memoirs,* 424–54; Egan, *Frémont,* 280–315; Chaffin, *Pathfinder,* 257–83; and Nevins, *Frémont,* vol. 1, 231–61.

15. "Castro Proclamation," in Jackson and Spence, *Expeditions,* vol. 2, 81; Talbot to Mother, July 24, 1846, in Hine and Lottinville, *Soldier in the West,* 35–44. Also see Dale L. Walker, *Bear Flag Rising: The Conquest of California, 1846* (New York: Forge, 1999), 91–97.

16. Frémont to Larkin, March 9, 1846, in Jackson and Spence, *Expeditions,* vol. 2, 81–82.

17. Frémont quote in John C. Frémont, "The Conquest of California," *Century Magazine* 19 (April 1891), 924. Also see Frémont, *Memoirs,* 459–90; Egan, *Frémont,* 323–29; and Nevins, *Frémont,* vol. 1, 269–84.

18. Carter, *Dear Old Kit,* 103–5; Martin, *With Frémont,* 8–10; and Frémont, *Memoirs,* 480–93.

19. Martin, *With Frémont,* 10–11.

20. Carter, *Dear Old Kit,* 105–6, 228; Frémont, *Memoirs,* 492–95; Thelma S. Guild and Harvey L. Carter, *Kit Carson* (Lincoln: University of Nebraska Press, 1984), 148–50;

Hampton Sides, *Blood and Thunder* (New York: Doubleday, 2006), 106–10; David Roberts, *A Newer World* (New York: Simon & Schuster, 2000), 159–62; and Edwin Legrand Sabin, *Kit Carson Days* (New York: Press of the Pioneers, 1935), vol. 1, 443–46.

21. There is considerable confusion over the actual date of Frémont's attack on the Sacramento River Indians, with white participants in disagreement over both the timing and the nature of the incident. Both Carson and Martin place the attack at the time of Frémont's first visit to Peter Lassen's Ranch (March 30 to April 5), while Frémont and Thomas Breckenridge place it during the return visit at Lassen's after Oregon (April 11 to April 24). Frémont's detailed explanation of his logic in agreeing to the attack certainly makes more sense after his return from Oregon. He was by then in a much more militant frame of mind as a result of Gillespie's messages and the fight with the Klamaths. No matter the date, the attack seems to have been unprovoked and the result was a terrible slaughter of innocents. This was the initiation of the cruel war waged by the Americans, either authorized by state or federal forces or carried out by civilians, that led to the near extermination of the California tribes over the next forty years. It has been estimated that 150,000 Natives resided in California before the American conquest (down from perhaps 300,000 at the time of the first Spanish settlements). This was the largest Native population north of Mexico. Disease took a devastating toll on the Natives, who for the most part were bucolic, disorganized, and rarely warlike. The American period saw the systematic slaughter of the Indians, especially during the gold rush period, so that by 1880 the census recorded only 16,277 Natives. This was a human tragedy of epic proportions and gives California the dubious distinction of having the worst record of Indian-white relations in all of American history. See Benjamin Madley, *An American Genocide: The United States and the California Indian Catastrophe* (New Haven, CT: Yale University Press, 2016), 1–15, 42–66. For California Indian population figures, consult Sherburne F. Cook, *The Population of the California Indians, 1769–1970* (Berkeley: University of California Press, 1976), and William C. Sturtevant and Robert F. Heizer, eds., *Handbook of North American Indians: California* (Washington, DC: Smithsonian Institution, 1978), 91–127. The Carson quote is in Carter, *Dear Old Kit*, 101. Also see Martin, *With Frémont*, 7–8; Frémont, *Memoirs*, 516–17; Chaffin, *Pathfinder*, 290–91, 312–13, 518; Nevins, *Frémont*, vol. 1, 294–96; Egan, *Frémont*, 338–40; Roberts, *Newer World*, 148–57; and Spence and Jackson, *Expeditions*, vol. 2, 124–25.

22. Todd and Marshall quotes in Egan, *Frémont*, 344; Frémont quote in Frémont, *Memoirs*, 509. Also see Walker, *Bear Flag*, 88–89, 116–30; DeVoto, *Year of Decision*, 200–21; Nevins, *Frémont*, vol. 1, 296–310; and Chaffin, *Pathfinder*, 313–27.

23. This unfortunate incident does not reflect well on either Carson or Frémont. The three Californios—José de los Reyes Berreyesa and his twin nephews, Ramón and Francisco de Haro—were civilians. Carson later related the story of what happened to William Boggs in 1853. See LeRoy R. Hafen, ed., "The W. M. N. Boggs Manuscript About Bent's Fort, Kit Carson, the Far West and Life Among the Indians," *Colorado Magazine* 7, no. 2 (March 1930), 62–63. Alexis Godey gave his version of the executions in the *New York Evening Post*, October 30, 1956. He claimed that the men resisted arrest. Godey's account was a response to a negative article in the *Los Angeles Star*, September 27, 1856, that featured accounts by José S. Berreyesa, the son of Don José, who at the time of the killings was a prisoner of the Americans, and Jasper O'Farrell, a Bear Flagger who claimed to be an eyewitness, that were both quite

critical of Frémont. Since the article appeared during Frémont's presidential campaign, the motive for its appearance is somewhat suspect. O'Farrell claimed to have been standing near Frémont when Carson approached him about the three prisoners. O'Farrell said that he had later spoken to Carson about the incident in 1853 and that "he assured me that then and since he regretted to be compelled to shoot those men, and says he intended to make them prisoners; but Fremont was blood-thirsty enough to order otherwise; and he further remarked that it was not the only brutal act he was compelled to commit while under his command." This seems at odds with Carson's slavish devotion to Frémont. If anyone could be a stone-cold killer on occasion it was Carson. The accounts by Berreyesa, O'Farrell, and Godey are reprinted in Sabin, *Kit Carson Days*, vol. 1, 479–81. Frémont disingenuously claimed in his memoirs that the Delawares had killed the three men to avenge Cowie and Talbot. *Frémont, Memoirs,* 525. But in a letter to Benton he stated, "Three of Castro's party having landed on the Sonoma side in advance, were killed on the beach; and beyond this there was no loss on either side." Frémont to Benton, July 25, 1846, in Jackson and Spence, *Expeditions*, vol. 2, 181–86. Talbot, in a letter home, said simply, "We killed three spies." Hine and Lottinville, *Soldier in the West*, 43, 45. Also see Alonzo Jackson, *The Conquest of California: Alonzo C. Jackson's Letters in Detail of the Seizure of Monterey in 1842 and His Letter on the Final Conquest of 1846* (Los Angeles: Edward Eberstadt & Sons, 1953), 24–25; Sides, *Blood and Thunder,* 119–20; Carter, *Dear Old Kit*, 107–10; Egan, *Frémont*, 355–56; Nevins, *Frémont,* vol. 1, 310–11; Chaffin, *Pathfinder,* 332; and Roberts, *A Newer World,* 169–71.

24. Jackson, *Conquest of California*, 25–26; Walker, *Bear Flag,* 142–45; Egan, *Frémont,* 359–63.

25. Walpole quote in Frémont, *Memoirs,* 533–34. American midshipman Alonzo C. Jackson of the U.S. frigate *Savannah* was equally impressed by Frémont's frontiersmen. In a July 26, 1846, letter to his uncle in Schenectady, New York, he gave a brief but informative account of the California campaign up to that date. Like Lieutenant Forbes Walpole of the Royal Navy (who gave his view of Frémont's men in his 1849 book *Four Years in the Pacific in Her Majesty's Ship "Collingswood" from 1844 to 1848*), Jackson was fascinated by Frémont and his men: "As they came up we gave three cheers which were answered most heartily by Frémont's party. Each man of this party is dressed in buckskin, seldom wearing cloth of any kind. The Indian mocassins is in every case made to supply the place of boots and shoes, and with the exception of saddles and arms there is scarcely an evidence of civilized life among them . . . Many times have I been reminded of old Leatherstocking by the honest simplicity of the backwoodsmen . . . Frémont certainly deserves a great deal of credit for his perseverance and undying energy. Not one man in a hundred could suffer the privations and hardships which have fallen to his share, and like him be energetic and persevering to the last." Jackson, *Conquest of California,* 27–28.

26. Frémont, "Conquest of California," 925–27; Frémont, *Memoirs,* 534–67; Carter, *Dear Old Kit*, 110–11; Martin, *With Frémont*, 16–18; Walker, *Bear Flag*, 155–62. Frémont's acts in this campaign—especially his bold actions in turning from exploration to open warfare before learning of a formal declaration of war and his encouragement of the Bear Flag Revolt—were later bitterly criticized by historians Josiah Royce, H. H. Bancroft, and, to a lesser extent, Bernard DeVoto. Frémont's biographers—most notably Nevins but also Egan; Jackson and Spence; and Chaffin—have vigorously defended this young officer's relatively bloodless conquest of California, his benevolent attitude toward the Hispanic settlers (if not the Indians), and his expansive vision of his nation's future.

CHAPTER 17: CALIFORNIA

1. Dale L. Walker, *Bear Flag Rising: The Conquest of California* (New York: Forge, 1999), 160–62; Allan Nevins, *Frémont,* vol. 1 (New York: Harper and Brothers, 1928), 328–30.

2. John C. Fremont, *Memoirs of My Life* (Chicago: Belford, Clarke & Co., 1887), 567.

3. Harvey Lewis Carter, ed., *Dear Old Kit: The Historical Christopher Carson* (Norman: University of Oklahoma Press, 1968), 111–12.

4. There was no more experienced frontier soldier in the American army than Brigadier General Kearny. Born in New Jersey in 1794 to a wealthy family, he had left King's College (later Columbia University) to enlist in the army at the outbreak of the War of 1812. As a lieutenant in the 13th Infantry Regiment, he was captured, along with his commander, Lieutenant Colonel Winfield Scott, at the Battle of Queenston Heights in October 1812. He was soon exchanged but spent the rest of the war on recruiting duty. After the war he was transferred to Council Bluffs on the Missouri River and from that time on his military career would be spent in the West. He was with General Henry Atkinson's march into Nebraska in 1819 and on the Yellowstone expedition of 1826. In 1826, Captain Kearny took command of the new Jefferson Barracks just to the south of St. Louis. He soon entered the social whirl of the booming frontier metropolis, where he counted among his friends Senator Thomas Hart Benton and Indian Superintendent William Clark (of Lewis and Clark Expedition fame). In 1830 he married Clark's stepdaughter Mary Radford, one of the most sought-after belles of the frontier river city. With the organization of the 1st Dragoons (which eventually would be designated as the 1st Cavalry at the outbreak of the Civil War), Kearny received the appointment of lieutenant colonel under Colonel Henry Dodge. In 1836, Kearny was promoted to colonel and command of the new regiment. In the spring of 1845 he led the dragoons on an expedition from Fort Leavenworth to South Pass on the Oregon Trail and then back to Leavenworth via Bent's Fort and the Santa Fe Trail, some 2,000 miles. With the outbreak of the Mexican War, Kearny was assigned command of the Army of the West and as of June 30, 1846, promoted to brigadier general. See Dwight L. Clarke, *Stephen Watts Kearny, Soldier of the West* (Norman: University of Oklahoma Press, 1961); Durwood Ball, "Stephen W. Kearny," in Paul Andrew Hutton and Durwood Ball, eds., *Soldiers West: Biographies from the Military Frontier* (Norman: University of Oklahoma Press, 2009), 43–71; and Ralph P. Bieber, ed., *Marching with the Army of the West, 1846–1848* (Glendale, CA: Arthur H. Clark Co., 1936). Also see Ralph Emerson Twitchell, *The History of the Military Occupation of the Territory of New Mexico from 1846 to 1851* (Denver: Smith-Brooks, 1909), 38–94, 203–6; W. H. Emory, *Lieutenant Emory Reports: A Reprint of Lieutenant W. H. Emory's Notes of a Military Reconnoissance*, ed. Ross Calvin (Albuquerque: University of New Mexico Press, 1951); Winston Groom, *Kearny's March: The Epic Creation of the American West, 1846–1847* (New York: Alfred A. Knopf, 2011), 6–7, 59–91; and Bernard DeVoto, *The Year of Decision: 1846* (Boston: Little, Brown, 1943), 229–42.

5. Johnston quote in Groom, *Kearny's March*, 147.

6. Carson and Apache chief quote in Calvin, *Lieutenant Emory Reports,* 100–101; Griffin

quoted in John S. Griffin, *A Doctor Comes to California: The Diary of John S. Griffin, Assistant Surgeon with Kearny's Dragoons, 1846–1847*, ed. George Walcott Ames Jr. (San Francisco: California Historical Society, 1953), 24–25.

7. Edwin R. Sweeney, *Mangas Coloradas: Chief of the Chiricahua Apaches* (Norman: University of Oklahoma Press, 1998), 68–158; Paul Andrew Hutton, *The Apache Wars: The Hunt for Geronimo, the Apache Kid, and the Captive Boy Who Started the Longest War in American History* (New York: Crown, 2016), 3–33. Also see Brian DeLay, *War of a Thousand Deserts: Indian Raids and the U.S.-Mexican War* (New Haven, CT: Yale University Press, 2008).

8. Dwight L. Clarke, ed., *The Original Journals of Henry Smith Turner* (Norman: University of Oklahoma Press, 1966), 102–3.

9. Kearny quote in Clarke, *Kearny*, 185; Griffin quote in Griffin, *Assistant Surgeon*, 31; Turner quote in Clarke, *Turner Journals*, 89–90.

10. Kearny and Griffin quotes in Griffin, *Assistant Surgeon*, 36–37.

11. Calvin, *Emory Reports*, 147–66; Griffin, *Assistant Surgeon*, 38–42; Clarke, *Turner Journals*, 115–24; Clarke, *Kearny*, 186–92.

12. Frémont, *Memoirs*, 569–81; Walker, *Bear Flag*, 196–201; Nevins, *Frémont*, vol. 1, 328–32; Talbot to Mother, January 15, 1847, in Robert V. Hine and Savoie Lottinville, eds., *Soldier in the West* (Norman: University of Oklahoma Press, 1972), 50–56. For Beale, see Gerald Thompson, *Edward F. Beale and the American West* (Albuquerque: University of New Mexico Press, 1983); Lewis Burt Lesley, ed., *Uncle Sam's Camels: The Journal of May Humphreys Stacey Supplemented by the Report of Edward Fitzgerald Beale (1857–1858)* (Cambridge, MA: Harvard University Press, 1929); Forrest Bryant Johnson, *The Last Camel Charge: The Untold Story of America's Desert Military Experiment* (New York: Berkley Caliber, 2012); and Paul Andrew Hutton, "Camels Go West," *Wild West* 20, no. 4 (December 2007), 40–47. Beale (1822–1891) came from a wealthy and prominent American family. His maternal grandfather was Commodore Thomas Truxtun, hero of the Revolution and the 1798 undeclared naval war with France. His father, also a naval officer, was a hero of the War of 1812 and had won the hand of Truxton's youngest daughter, Emily, in 1819. Young Beale received a personal appointment as a navy midshipman from President Jackson in 1836. After the Mexican War, Beale proved to be a great booster for California and served as the first superintendent of Indian affairs for the new state. His tenure, highly controversial, ended in May 1854, but he soon received another government appointment to survey a wagon road from New Mexico to California. Part of his survey duties was to experiment with the use of imported camels for desert travel. At the same time, he acquired a huge California ranch called Rancho El Tejon. An early adherent to the Republican Party, he numbered among his friends Lincoln and Grant. In 1872 he purchased the Decatur House, which faced Lafayette Park, across from the White House. He and his wife, Mary, soon made it the center of Washington society life. In 1876, Grant appointed Beale minister to the Court of Vienna. He was an early advocate of a canal across Central America, but his canal company failed. He died in the Decatur House on April 22, 1892, and among his pallbearers were Vice President Levi Morton, Senator Henry Cabot Lodge, and Supreme Court Justice Stephen J. Field.

13. For the Battle of San Pasqual (sometimes spelled "Pascual"), see Clarke, *Turner Journals*, 144–48; Calvin, *Emory Reports*, 168–70; Carter, *Dear Old Kit*, 112–14; Griffin,

Assistant Surgeon, 45–46; Smith and Judah, *Chronicles of the Gringos*, 157–59; Clary, *Eagles and Empire*, 240–45; Groom, *Kearny's March*, 198–208; Clarke, *Kearny*, 195–232; Edwin L. Sabin, *Kit Carson Days*, vol. 2 (New York: Press of the Pioneers, 1935), 525–40; Walker, *Bear Flag*, 210–19; Arthur Woodward, "Lances at San Pascual," *California Historical Society Quarterly* 25, no. 4 (December 1946), 289–308, and part 2, *California Historical Society Quarterly* 26, no. 1 (March 1947), 21–62; and Cecelia Holland, "The Old Woman's Gun," *MHQ: The Quarterly Journal of Military History* 3, no. 4 (Summer 1991): 58–67.

14. Hampton Sides, *Blood and Thunder* (New York: Doubleday, 2006), 192–98; Griffin, *Assistant Surgeon*, 47–49.

15. Emory quote in Calvin, *Emory Reports*, 171–73.

16. Pico quote in Sides, *Blood and Thunder*, 200–203; Carter, *Dear Old Kit*, 115–16; Carson quote in Sabin, *Kit Carson Days*, vol. 2, 535–39.

17. José de Jesús Pico story in Frémont, *Memoirs*, 598–99. Also see Ferol Egan, *Frémont: Explorer for a Restless Nation* (New York: Doubleday, 1977), 385–86, 397–99; Walker, *Bear Flag*, 202–4, 233–34; Nevins, *Frémont*, vol. 1, 331–34; and Tom Chaffin, *Pathfinder: John Charles Frémont and the Course of the American Empire* (Norman: University of Oklahoma Press, 2002), 353–61.

18. Stockton quote in Frémont, *Memoirs*, 601.

19. Emory quote in Calvin, *Emory Reports*, 178–87. Also see Griffin, *Assistant Surgeon*, 61–64; Clarke, *Kearny*, 233–55; Groom, *Kearny's March*, 223–26; and Walker, *Bear Flag*, 229–41.

20. Griffin quote in Griffin, *Assistant Surgeon*, 66. Also see Frémont, *Memoirs*, 601–2; Walker, *Bear Flag*, 244–50; and Egan, *Frémont*, 402–5.

21. Stockton quote in Walker, *Bear Flag*, 258; Nevins, *Frémont*, vol. 2, 345–66; and Clarke, *Kearny*, 256–87. Stockton (1795–1866) seems to have patched up his quarrel with Kearny by the time of the Frémont court-martial. His testimony proved surprisingly neutral. He left the navy in 1850 and the next year was elected as a Democrat to the U.S. Senate from New Jersey. He was a member of the 1861 peace delegation that failed to solve the secession crisis. His later years were spent in business pursuits. He died at Princeton, New Jersey, on October 7, 1866.

22. For the Taos Rebellion, see Lewis H. Garrard, *Wah-to-yah and the Taos Trail* (Norman: University of Oklahoma Press, 1955), 114–22, 170–73; Sides, *Blood and Thunder*, 214–29; Sabin, *Kit Carson Days*, vol. 2, 558–63; and Twitchell, *Military Occupation of New Mexico*, 122–45. Also see James A. Crutchfield, *Tragedy at Taos: The Revolt of 1847* (Plano: Republic of Texas Press, 1995).

23. Carson quote in Frémont, *Memoirs*, 74. Also see Guild and Carter, *Kit Carson*, 167–70; Carter, *Dear Old Kit*, 116–17; Sabin, *Kit Carson Days*, vol. 2, 564–69; Sally Denton, *Passion and Principle: John and Jessie Frémont* (New York: Bloomsbury, 2007), 132–35; and Jessie Benton Frémont, *The Will and the Way Stories* (Boston: D. Lothrop, 1891), 23–50.

24. Allan Nevins, ed., *Polk: The Diary of a President, 1845–1849* (London: Longman, Green, 1952), 240–41.

25. Carson quote in Frémont, *Will and Way Stories*, 40.

26. Godey quote in Egan, *Frémont,* 435. Also see Nevins, *Frémont,* vol. 2, 353–66; Walker, *Bear Flag,* 259–73; and Clarke, *Kearny,* 288–342.

27. Jessie Frémont quote in Denton, *Passion and Principle,* 136. Also see Nevins, *Polk: Diary,* 242–44.

28. William Tecumseh Sherman, *Memoirs of Gen. W. T. Sherman* (New York: Charles L. Webster, 1892), vol. 1, 74–75.

29. Nevins, *Polk: Diary,* 274.

30. The full proceedings of the court-martial, including Polk's order remanding the sentence, are reprinted in Donald Jackson and Mary Lee Spence, eds., *The Expeditions of John Charles Frémont,* vol. 2, *Supplement Proceedings of the Court Martial* (Urbana: University of Illinois Press, 1973). Also see Nevins, *Polk: Diary,* 271–75, 300–303; Nevins, *Frémont,* vol. 2, 367–87; Egan, *Frémont,* 443–63; and Clarke, *Kearny,* 347–73.

31. Frémont, *Memoirs,* 602.

32. Denton, *Passion and Principle,* 154. Also see Janet Lecompte, "A Letter from Jessie to Kit," *Bulletin of the Missouri Historical Society* 29 (July 1973): 260–63.

33. Denton, *Passion and Principle,* 156. Also see Clarke, *Kearny,* 382–85.

34. Sherman, *Memoirs,* vol. 1, 68–69.

35. Sherman, *Memoirs,* vol. 1, 75–79, 82, 85–86. Also see J. S. Holliday, *Rush for Riches: Gold Fever and the Making of California* (Berkeley: University of California Press, 1999), 51–88; and Kevin Starr, *California: A History* (New York: Modern Library, 2005), 73–83.

36. George Douglas Brewerton, *Overland with Kit Carson: A Narrative of the Old Spanish Trail in '48* (New York: Coward-McCann, 1930), 37–38.

37. Carter, *Dear Old Kit,* 121.

CHAPTER 18: LINES ON PAPER

1. John C. Cremony, *Life Among the Apaches* (San Francisco: A. Roman, 1868), 23–29.

2. William H. Goetzmann, *Exploration and Empire: The Explorer and the Scientist in the Winning of the American West* (New York: Alfred A. Knopf, 1966), 261–64; William H. Goetzmann, *Army Exploration in the American West* (New Haven, CT: Yale University Press, 1960), 167–208; and Dan L. Thrapp, *Encyclopedia of Frontier Biography,* 3 vols (Glendale, CA: Arthur H. Clark, 1988), vol. 1, 68–69. Also see John Russell Bartlett, *Personal Narrative of Explorations and Incidents in Texas, New Mexico, California, Sonora, and Chihuahua,* 2 vols. (New York and London: D. Appleton, 1854).

3. Edwin R. Sweeney, *Mangas Coloradas* (Norman: University of Oklahoma Press, 1998), 229–30; and Thrapp, *Encyclopedia of Frontier Biography,* vol. 1, 342–43.

4. Bartlett, *Personal Narrative,* vol. 1, 300–327; Sweeney, *Mangas Coloradas,* 232–33; and Ruth McDonald Boyer and Narcissus Duffy Gayton, *Apache Mothers and Daughters: Four Generations of a Family* (Norman: University of Oklahoma Press, 1992), 43–44.

5. Cremony, *Life Among the Apaches,* 21, 47–48. Although they called themselves Dine or Indeh, which means "the people," they were universally known as Apache, a name

given to them by their Zuni rivals. It meant simply "the enemy." Although culturally united as Apaches, they were divided into several distinct bands and no chief, not even Mangas, held sway over them all. To the east in New Mexico's Sierra Blanca lived the Mescaleros, who sometimes roamed eastward onto the Texas prairie. The Chiricahuas lived in the mountains of western New Mexico and southeastern Arizona as well as the Sierra Madre of Sonora and Chihuahua in Mexico. The Jicarilla lived in the New Mexico mountains far to the north, as well as roaming eastward onto the Great Plains. And to the south along the Pecos River in Texas lived the Lipans. The Western Apaches lived throughout the mountains of eastern and central Arizona. The five Western Apache bands, unlike their eastern cousins, separated along clan lines and also practiced some agriculture, as did the Navajos to the north. They were far less influenced by the Pueblos and Spanish to the east than the New Mexico Apaches. There was little sense of tribal unity among any of the Apache tribal groups. At the time of American contact they numbered between eight and ten thousand people.

6. Bartlett, *Personal Narrative*, vol. 1, 303–9, 398–405; Goetzmann, *Army Exploration*, 179–80; Cremony, *Life Among the Apaches*, 52–58. A rich literature has developed around the issue of captivity, much of which began with the seminal work by James F. Brooks, *Captives and Cousins: Slavery, Kinship, and Community in the Southwest Borderlands* (Chapel Hill: University of North Carolina Press, 2002).

7. Cremony, *Life Among the Apaches*, 59–61; and Bartlett, *Personal Narrative*, vol. 1, 310–12.

8. Sweeney, *Mangas Coloradas*, 235–37; Cremony, *Life Among the Apaches*, 61–66; and Bartlett, *Personal Narrative*, vol. 1, 312–17.

9. Cremony, *Life Among the Apaches*, 66–72. For the full exchange between Bartlett and the Apaches, consult Cremony, *Life Among the Apaches*, and Bartlett, *Personal Narrative*, vol. 1. They differ only slightly as it seems Cremony used Bartlett as his source.

10. Sweeney, *Mangas Coloradas*, 237–40; and Bartlett, *Personal Narrative*, vol. 1, 331–39, 351–54.

11. Jerry D. Thompson, "With the Third Infantry in New Mexico, 1851–1853: The Lost Diary of Private Sylvester W. Matson," *Journal of Arizona History* 31, no. 4 (Winter 1990): 361–65; and Sweeney, *Mangas Coloradas*, 240, 244–47.

12. Thompson, "With the Third Infantry," 372.

13. Sweeney, *Mangas Coloradas*, 251–59.

14. Durwood Ball, *Army Regulars on the Western Frontier, 1848–1861* (Norman: University of Oklahoma Press, 2001), 20–23, 66–67; and Robert M. Utley, *Frontiersmen in Blue: The United States Army and the Indian, 1848–1865* (New York: Macmillan, 1967), 89–90.

15. James A. Bennett, *Forts and Forays: James A. Bennett, A Dragoon in New Mexico, 1850–1856,* ed. Clinton E. Brooks and Frank D. Reeve (Albuquerque: University of New Mexico Press, 1948), 38–39; Sweeney, *Mangas Coloradas*, 259–60; and Ball, *Army Regulars*, 21–22. A copy of the treaty is in the Michael Steck Papers, University of New Mexico Library.

16. Goetzmann, *Army Exploration*, 186–95.

17. Louis Bernard Schmidt, "Manifest Opportunity and the Gadsden Purchase," *Arizona and the West* 3, no. 3 (Autumn 1961): 253. For the impact of Apache and Comanche raids on northern Mexico, see Brian DeLay, *War of a Thousand Deserts* (New Haven, CT: Yale University Press, 2008), 297–340; and Joseph F. Park, "The Apaches in Mexican-American Relations, 1848–1861: A Footnote to the Gadsden Treaty," *Arizona and the West* 3, no. 2 (Summer 1961): 129–46. The standard work on the treaty remains the 1923 study by Paul N. Garber, *The Gadsden Treaty* (Gloucester, MA: Peter Smith, 1959). Also see Rachel St. John, *Line in the Sand: A History of the U.S.-Mexico Border* (Princeton, NJ: Princeton University Press, 2011), for a modern interpretation.

18. Goetzmann, *Army Exploration*, 194–97; and Schmidt, "Manifest Opportunity," 245–64. Useful pictorial representations of the various border proposals are in Henry P. Walker and Don Bufkin, *Historical Atlas of Arizona* (Norman: University of Oklahoma Press, 1978), 18–22; and Warren A. Beck and Ynez D. Haase, *Historical Atlas of New Mexico* (Norman: University of Oklahoma Press, 1969), 26–29.

After San Jacinto, Santa Anna had been held for seven months as a prisoner before Sam Houston finally secured his release. He traveled to Washington, where he met with President Jackson before returning to Veracruz on an American warship. He was greeted as a hero in Mexico and briefly retired to his estates before returning to military service in 1838 to meet a French invasion force in the so-called Pastry War. In this brief conflict, Santa Anna lost his left leg below the knee, was carried back to Mexico City on a litter, and was named president for the fifth time. In the years to come the scheming general moved in and out of power. At the end of the Mexican War, he fled into exile in Jamaica as others made peace at Guadalupe Hidalgo. He returned to power for the eleventh and final time in April 1853 and, desperate for money, negotiated the Gadsden Purchase. Forced yet again into exile by his liberal opponents, he did not return to Mexico until 1874. During his exile in New York City, Santa Anna employed young Thomas Adams (1818–1905) as a secretary. Adams noticed Santa Anna chewing on a foreign substance he discovered to be chicle from Mexico. Santa Anna suggested that this had potential as a profitable product, and Adams took this to heart. He experimented with chicle, adding sweetener to it, and founded the American Chicle Company in 1899. The result was the American chewing gum industry—certainly Santa Anna's most positive contribution to American culture. The old general died impoverished, nearly blind, and all but forgotten on June 21, 1876. History has not been kind to his memory.

19. Thomas E. Sheridan, *Arizona: A History* (Tucson: University of Arizona Press, 2012), 65–66, 119–26; Marshall Trimble, *Arizona: A Panoramic History of a Frontier State* (Garden City, NY: Doubleday, 1977), 121–23, 130–38; and Thomas Edwin Farish, *History of Arizona*, 8 vols. (San Francisco: Filmer Brothers, 1915), vol. 1, 183–98.

20. For Poston's career, see Charles D. Poston, *Building a State in Apache Land* (Tempe, AZ: Aztec Press, 1963), 11–38; J. Ross Browne, *A Tour Through Arizona, 1864: or Adventures in the Apache Country* (Tucson: Arizona Silhouettes, 1951), 235–54; Frank C. Lockwood, *Arizona Characters* (Los Angeles: Times-Mirror Press, 1928), 28–47; and A. W. Gressinger, *Charles D. Poston: Sunland Seer* (Globe, AZ: Dale Stuart King, 1961). Also see C. Gilbert Storms, "Adventures in the Apache Country: J. Ross Browne and Charles Poston Try to Revive Arizona's Fortunes—and Their Own," *Journal of Arizona History* 53, no. 1 (Spring 2012): 35–60.

21. Natalie Ornish, *Ehrenberg: Goliad Survivor, Old West Explorer* (Dallas: Texas Heritage Press, 1997); James E. Crisp, ed., and Louis E. Brister and James C. Kearney, trans., *Inside the Texas Revolution: The Enigmatic Memoir of Herman Ehrenberg* (Austin: Texas State Historical Association, 2021); Herman Ehrenberg, *With Milam and Fannin: Adventures of a German Boy in Texas' Revolution* (Austin: Pemberton Press, 1968); James E. Crisp, "In Pursuit of Herman Ehrenberg: A Research Adventure," *Southwestern Historical Quarterly* 102, no. 4 (April 1999): 422–39; and Thrapp, *Encyclopedia of Frontier Biography*, vol. 1, 455. Ehrenberg was murdered in California in 1866.

22. Poston, *Apache Land*, 48.

23. Gressinger, *Poston*, 13–18; Poston, *Apache Land*, 54; C. L. Sonnichsen, *Tucson: The Life and Times of an American City* (Norman: University of Oklahoma Press, 1982), 41–43.

24. Poston, *Apache Land*, 49.

25. Jerry Thompson, *Civil War to the Bloody End: The Life and Times of Major General Samuel P. Heintzelman* (College Station: Texas A&M University Press, 2006), 62–70; Poston, *Apache Land*, 55–60; and Gressinger, *Poston*, 19–23.

26. Poston, *Apache Land*, 64.

27. Thrapp, *Encyclopedia of Frontier Biography*, vol. 3, 1361–62; and Sweeney, *Mangas Coloradas*, 331–32, 512. The Pinals and Coyoteros were names given to bands of the Western Apache, of eastern Arizona. Other Western Apache bands included the White Mountain people, the Tontos, the Cibecue people, and the Aravaipa. For the Western Apache, see Richard J. Perry, *Western Apache Heritage* (Austin: University of Texas Press, 1991); Morris E. Opler, ed., *Grenville Goodwin Among the Western Apache: Letters from the Field* (Tucson: University of Arizona Press, 1973); and Grenville Goodwin, *The Social Organization of the Western Apache* (Tucson: University of Arizona Press, 1969). For an overview of Apache history and culture, see William C. Sturtevant and Alfonso Ortiz, eds., *Handbook of North American Indians: Southwest*, vol. 10 (Washington, DC: Smithsonian Institution, 1983); James L. Haley, *Apaches: A History and Culture Portrait* (New York: Doubleday, 1981); Morris E. Opler, *An Apache Life-Way* (Chicago: University of Chicago Press, 1965); Frank C. Lockwood, *The Apache Indians* (New York: Macmillan, 1938); Donald Worcester, *The Apaches: Eagles of the Southwest* (Norman: University of Oklahoma Press, 1979); Dan L. Thrapp, *The Conquest of Apacheria* (Norman: University of Oklahoma Press, 1967); and Paul Andrew Hutton, *The Apache Wars* (New York: Crown, 2016).

28. Poston, *Apache Land*, 66–67; and Lockwood, *Apache Indians*, 92–94.

29. Sweeney, *Mangas Coloradas*, 333–34.

30. Poston, *Apache Land*, 67.

CHAPTER 19: FLIGHT OF THE RAVENS

1. David Dary, *The Santa Fe Trail: Its History, Legends and Lore* (New York: Alfred A. Knopf, 2000), 208–10; and Paul Andrew Hutton, "Kit Carson's Ride," *Wild West* 19, no. 6 (April 2007): 28–37.

2. DeWitt Clinton Peters, *The Life and Adventures of Kit Carson* (New York: W.R.C. Clark, 1858), 356–57.

3. Lewis H. Garrard, *Wah-to-yah and the Taos Trail* (Norman: University of Oklahoma Press, 1955), 181.

4. Harvey Lewis Carter, ed., *Dear Old Kit* (Norman: University of Oklahoma Press, 1968), 123–24.

5. Veronica E. Velarde Tiller, *The Jicarilla Apache Tribe: A History* (Lincoln, NE: University of Nebraska Press, 1983), 4–6, 12–30; and Veronica E. Tiller, "Jicarilla Apache," in William C. Sturtevant and Alfonso Ortiz, eds., *Handbook of North American Indians: Southwest*, vol. 10 (Washington, DC: Smithsonian Institution, 1983), 440–61. Also see Delores A. Gunnerson, *The Jicarilla Apaches: A Study in Survival* (DeKalb: Northern Illinois University Press, 1974); Doug Hocking, *Terror on the Santa Fe Trail: Kit Carson and the Jicarilla Apache* (Helena, MT: TwoDot, 2019); and Gregory F. Michno, *Depredation and Deceit: The Making of the Jicarilla and Ute Wars in New Mexico* (Norman: University of Oklahoma Press, 2017).

6. Annie Heloise Abel, ed., *The Official Correspondence of James S. Calhoun* (Washington, DC: U.S. Government Printing Office, 1915), 69.

7. Hutton, "Kit Carson's Ride," 31–32.

8. Abel, *Correspondence of Calhoun*, 20, 42.

9. Durwood Ball, *Army Regulars on the Western Frontier, 1848–1861* (Norman: University of Oklahoma Press, 2001), 20–22.

10. Hutton, "Kit Carson's Ride," 32; Hampton Sides, *Blood and Thunder* (New York: Doubleday, 2006), 241–43; and Tom Dunlay, *Kit Carson and the Indians* (Lincoln: University of Nebraska Press, 2000), 9–10, 138–40.

11. *Santa Fe Republican*, July 24, 1848; and Donald Chaput, *François X. Aubry: Trader, Trailmaker and Voyageur in the Southwest, 1846–1854* (Glendale, CA: Arthur H. Clark, 1975), 77–86.

12. Calhoun's report of the tragedy is the most detailed and is in Abel, *Correspondence of Calhoun*, 63–66, 68–69, 72, 88. Also see Peters, *Life and Adventures*, 349–50; Edwin L. Sabin, *Kit Carson Days* (New York: Press of the Pioneers, 1935), vol. 2, 618–22; Sides, *Blood and Thunder*, 247–48; Hocking, *Terror on the Santa Fe Trail*, 80–87; and Harry C. Myers, "Massacre on the Santa Fe Trail: Mr. White's Company of Unfortunates," *Wagon Tracks: Santa Fe Trail Association Quarterly* 6, no. 2 (February 1992): 18–25. John Greiner left a detailed account in the *Los Angeles Star*, June 25, 1853.

13. Abel, *Correspondence of Calhoun*, 64.

14. Tiller, *Jicarilla Apache*, 35; James A. Bennett, *Forts and Forays: A Dragoon in New Mexico, 1850–1856*, ed. Clinton E. Brooks and Frank D. Reeve (Albuquerque: University of New Mexico Press, 1995), 17.

15. For Leroux, see Forbes Parkhill, *The Blazed Trail of Antoine Leroux* (Los Angeles: Westernlore, 1965).

16. Charles Irving Jones, "William Kronig, New Mexico Pioneer, from His Memories of 1849–1860," *New Mexico Historical Review* 19, no. 3 (July 1944): 200–203.

17. Myers, "Massacre," 8–12; and Hutton, "Kit Carson's Ride," 34.

18. Carter, *Dear Old Kit*, 124.

19. Howard Louis Conard, *"Uncle Dick" Wootton: The Pioneer Frontiersman of the Rocky Mountain Region* (Chicago: W. E. Dibble, 1890), 210–11.

20. Jones, "Kronig," 204–5.

21. Conard, *Wootton*, 211–12.

22. Carter, *Dear Old Kit*, 124–25; Jones, "Kronig," 205–6; and Conard, *Wootton*, 212–13.

23. Bennett, *Forts and Forays*, 24–25.

24. Carter, *Dear Old Kit*, 125; and Jones, "Kronig," 206.

25. Bennett, *Forts and Forays*, 25.

26. Carter, *Dear Old Kit*, 125–26. Also see Sides, *Blood and Thunder*, 256–59; Hocking, *Terror on the Santa Fe Trail*, 90–96; Sabin, *Kit Carson Days*, vol. 2, 620–22; Michno, *Depredation and Deceit*, 59–67; and Alvin R. Lynn, *Kit Carson and the First Battle of Adobe Walls* (Lubbock: Texas Tech University Press, 2014), 20–22.

27. Bennett, *Forts and Forays*, 25.

28. Abel, *Correspondence of Calhoun*, 308.

29. Jones, "Kronig," 210.

CHAPTER 20: LAND OF THE JICARILLA

1. Edwin L. Sabin, *Kit Carson Days* (New York: Press of the Pioneers, 1935), vol. 2, 634. Tom Boggs, a great-grandson of Daniel Boone through his mother, Panthea Boone Boggs, was the son of Missouri governor Lilburn Boggs (famous for expelling the Mormons from Missouri). He had married Josefa Carson's niece Rumalda Bent, the daughter of Governor Charles Bent, in 1846. Boggs was away from Taos serving as an army dispatch rider at the time of the 1847 Taos Rebellion and was thus spared. Rumalda, however, was with her mother, Ignacia, and aunt Josefa and witnessed the murder of her father. Barbara Schultz, *Josefa: The Lifetime of Maria Josefa Jaramillo Carson, 1828–1868* (Taos, NM: Kit Carson Home and Museum, 2017), 53–64.

2. Sabin, *Kit Carson Days*, vol. 2, 639.

3. Sabin, *Kit Carson Days*, vol. 2, 651.

4. Tom Dunlay, *Kit Carson and the Indians* (Lincoln: University of Nebraska Press, 2000), 157.

5. Durwood Ball, *Army Regulars on the Western Frontier, 1848–1861* (Norman: University of Oklahoma Press, 2001), 21–22; and Annie Heloise Abel, ed., *The Official Correspondence of James S. Calhoun* (Washington, DC: U.S. Government Printing Office, 1915), 517–41.

6. Veronica E. Velarde Tiller, *The Jicarilla Apache Tribe: A History* (Santa Barbara, CA: Greenwood, 2011), 40–42.

7. Theophilus F. Rodenbough, comp., *From Everglade to Canyon with the Second United States Cavalry* (Norman: University of Oklahoma Press, 2000), 176–78, 485–86; Sabin, *Kit Carson Days*, vol. 2, 622; James A. Bennett, *Forts and Forays: A Dragoon in New Mexico, 1850–1856*, ed. Clinton E. Brooks and Frank D. Reeve (Albuquerque: University of New Mexico Press, 1995), 48; Gregory F. Michno, *Depredation and Deceit:*

The Making of the Jicarilla and Ute Wars in New Mexico (Norman: University of Oklahoma Press, 2017), 175–79; and Doug Hocking, *Terror on the Santa Fe Trail: Kit Carson and the Jicarilla Apache* (Helena, MT: TwoDot, 2019), 142–47.

8. Tiller, *Jicarilla Apache*, 37; and Dunlay, *Kit Carson and the Indians*, 162–63.

9. For Davidson's battle, see Homer K. Davidson, *Black Jack Davidson: A Cavalry Commander on the Western Frontier* (Glendale, CA: Arthur H. Clark, 1974), 69–72; Bennett, *Forts and Forays*, 54; and Michno, *Depredation and Deceit*, 183–91.

10. Tiller, *Jicarilla Apache*, 47.

11. Sabin, *Kit Carson Days*, vol. 2, 661. Also see Jeffrey V. Pearson, "Philip St. George Cooke," in Paul Andrew Hutton and Durwood Ball, eds., *Soldiers West: Biographies from the Military Frontier* (Norman: University of Oklahoma Press, 2009), 93–121; Albert G. Brackett, *History of the United States Cavalry* (New York: Harper & Brothers, 1865), 34–52, 134–36; and Randy Steffen, *The Horse Soldier, 1776–1943*, 3 vols. (Norman: University of Oklahoma Press, 1991), vol. 1, 84–177.

12. Sabin, *Kit Carson Days*, vol. 2, 662; Dunlay, *Kit Carson and the Indians*, 164–65; and Tiller, *Jicarilla Apache*, 48.

13. Alfred Barnaby Thomas, *The Jicarilla Apache Indians: A History, 1598–1888* (New York: Garland, 1974), 9.

14. Dunlay, *Kit Carson and the Indians*, 165. For Cooke's campaign, see Otis Young, *The West of Philip St. George Cooke, 1809–1895* (Glendale, CA: Arthur H. Clark, 1955), 255–60; Cooke's narrative in Rodenbough, *From Everglade to Canyon*, 178–80; and Carson's account in Harvey Lewis Carter, ed., *Dear Old Kit* (Norman: University of Oklahoma Press, 1968), 135–38. Also see Michno, *Depredation and Deceit*, 193–99; and Hocking, *Terror on the Santa Fe Trail*, 166–77.

15. Carter, *Dear Old Kit*, 130.

16. Carter, *Dear Old Kit*, 132.

17. Hampton Sides, *Blood and Thunder* (New York: Doubleday, 2006), 319–20; Carter, *Dear Old Kit*, 142. For the campaign, see Aurora Hunt, *Major General James Henry Carleton, 1814–1873* (Glendale, CA: Arthur H. Clark, 1958), 137–41.

18. DeWitt Clinton Peters, *The Life and Adventures of Kit Carson* (New York: W.R.C. Clark, 1858), 459; Sabin, *Kit Carson Days*, vol. 2, 665; and Dunlay, *Kit Carson and the Indians*, 168.

19. Adam Kane, "James H. Carleton," in Hutton and Ball, *Soldiers West*, 128; and Hunt, *Carleton*, 165–70.

20. Tiller, *Jicarilla Apache*, 52–53; and Donald Chaput, *François X Aubry: Trader, Trailmaker and Voyageur in the Southwest, 1846–1854* (Glendale, CA: Arthur H. Clark, 1975), 156–66. For Ceran St. Vrain, see Ronald K. Wetherington, *Ceran St. Vrain* (Santa Fe, NM: Sunstone, 2012), 13–89; and Dan L. Thrapp, *Encyclopedia of Frontier Biography*, 3 vols (Glendale, CA: Arthur H. Clark, 1988), vol. 3, 1260. For the fight at Saguache Pass, see Dunlay, *Kit Carson and the Indians*, 171; and Sabin, *Kit Carson Days*, vol. 2, 668. Also see Marc Simmons, *The Little Lion of the Southwest* (Chicago: Sage Books, 1973).

21. David Meriwether, *My Life in the Mountains and on the Plains: The Newly Discovered*

Autobiography, edited by Robert A. Griffen (Norman: University of Oklahoma Press, 1965), 231–32; Dunlay, *Kit Carson and the Indians*, 174–84. For the treaty, see Tiller, *Jicarilla Apache*, 51–55; and Thomas, *Jicarilla Apache*, part 3, 14–15.

22. Dunlay, *Kit Carson and the Indians*, 172, 184–85.

23. Thelma S. Guild and Harvey L. Carter, *Kit Carson* (Lincoln: University of Nebraska Press, 1984), 212–13.

CHAPTER 21: VALVERDE

1. Edwin L. Sabin, *Kit Carson Days* (New York: Press of the Pioneers, 1935), vol. 2, 674; and Hampton Sides, *Blood and Thunder* (New York: Doubleday, 2006), 285–86.

2. Sibley quote in Sides, *Blood and Thunder*, 277. Also see Durwood Ball, *Army Regulars on the Western Frontier, 1848–1861* (Norman: University of Oklahoma Press, 2001), 189–203; Ray C. Colton, *The Civil War in the Western Territories* (Norman: University of Oklahoma Press, 1959), 7; and Alvin M. Josephy Jr., *The Civil War in the American West* (New York: Alfred A. Knopf, 1991), 34–37.

3. Max L. Heyman Jr., *Prudent Soldier: A Biography of Major General E. R. S. Canby, 1817–1873* (Glendale, CA: Arthur H. Clark, 1959), 141–47.

4. Sabin, *Kit Carson Days*, vol. 2, 679–85; and Jacqueline Dorgan Meketa, ed., *Legacy of Honor: The Life of Rafael Chacon, a Nineteenth-Century New Mexican* (Albuquerque: University of New Mexico Press, 1986), 121–45.

5. Flint Whitlock, *Distant Bugles, Distant Drums: The Union Response to the Confederate Invasion of New Mexico* (Boulder: University Press of Colorado, 2008), 22–23. Also see Megan Kate Nelson, *The Three-Cornered War* (New York: Scribner, 2020).

6. John P. Wilson, *When the Texans Come: Missing Records from the Civil War in the Southwest, 1861–1862* (Albuquerque: University of New Mexico Press, 2001), 1–4, 17–51; and Josephy, *Civil War in the American West*, 31–60.

7. Sabin, *Kit Carson Days*, vol. 2, 674–85; and Sides, *Blood and Thunder*, 275–82. For Fort Craig. see Jerry D. Thompson, ed., *New Mexico Territory During the Civil War; Wallen and Evans Inspection Reports, 1862–1863* (Albuquerque: University of New Mexico Press, 2008), 97–110; Edward Eckert and Nicholas J. Amato, eds., *Ten Years in the Saddle: The Memoir of William Woods Averell, 1851–1862* (San Rafael, CA: Presidio Press, 1978), 123; and Paul Andrew Hutton, "The Fearless Leader of a Desperate Band: Paddy Graydon in the Apache and Civil Wars," *New Mexico Historical Review* 91 (Fall 2016): 373–408.

8. For Paddy Graydon, see Jerry D. Thompson, *Desert Tiger: Captain Paddy Graydon and the Civil War in the Far Southwest* (El Paso: Texas Western Press, 1992), 24–34.

9. Ake quotes in James B. O'Neil, *They Die But Once: The Story of a Tejano* (New York: Knight, 1935), 29; James H. Tevis, *Arizona in the '50s* (Albuquerque: University of New Mexico Press, 1954), 161; and *Tubac Weekly Arizonian*, March 3, 1859.

10. Matson quote in Jerry D. Thompson, ed., "With the Third Infantry in New Mexico, 1851–1853: The Lost Diary of Private Sylvester W. Matson," *Journal of Arizona History* 31, no. 4 (Winter 1990): 371–72; Brian Sandwich, *The Great Western: Legendary Lady of the Southwest* (El Paso: Texas Western Press, 1991), 5–6; J. F. Elliott, "The Great

Western: Sarah Bowman, Mother and Mistress to the U.S. Army," *Journal of Arizona History* 30, no. 1 (Spring 1989): 1–4; Paul Andrew Hutton, "The Great Western," *True West* 64 (September 2017): 34–43; and Jana Bommersbach and Bob Boze Bell, *Hellraisers and Trailblazers* (Cave Creek, AZ: Two Roads West, 2022), 60–63.

11. *Spirit of the Times* (New York), July 25, 1846; *Niles' National Register*, August 15, 1846; and Sandwich, *Great Western*, 9–13.

12. Bragg quote in Sandwich, *Great Western*, 9–13. Also see Hutton, "Great Western," 37.

13. Elliott, "Great Western," 6–9.

14. Sandwich, *Great Western*, 20–24. Also see Samuel E. Chamberlain, *My Confession* (New York: Harper & Brothers, 1956), 241–42.

15. Elliott, "Great Western," 18; and Jerry Thompson, *Civil War to the Bloody End* (College Station: Texas A&M University Press, 2006), 62–63.

16. Margot Mifflin, *The Blue Tattoo: The Life of Olive Oatman* (Lincoln: University of Nebraska Press, 2006), 118; Bommersbach and Bell, *Hellraisers*, 88–96; and Victoria Smith, *Captive Arizona, 1851–1900* (Lincoln: University of Nebraska Press, 2009), 1–35. Also see Brian McGinty, *The Oatman Massacre: A Tale of Desert Captivity and Survival* (Norman: University of Oklahoma Press, 2005); and R. B. Stratton, *Captivity of the Oatman Girls* (San Francisco: Whitton, Towne, 1857).

17. O'Neil, *They Die But Once*, 30; Sandwich, *Great Western*, 49–52; and Elliott, "Great Western," 19–20.

18. O'Neil, *They Die But Once*, 30; Sandwich, *Great Western*, 49–52; and Elliott, "Great Western," 19–20.

19. J. Hall, *Sonora: Travels and Adventures in Sonora* (Chicago: J. M. W. Jones, 1881), 175–96, 201–5; O'Neil, *They Die But Once*, 28–31; and Virginia Culin Roberts, "Jack Pennington in Early Arizona," *Arizona and the West* 23, no. 4 (Winter 1981): 317–34.

20. *Tucson Weekly Arizonian*, July 7, 1859; and Thompson, *Desert Tiger*, 15–18.

21. Oscar Osburn Winther, "The Southern Overland Mail and Stagecoach Line, 1857–1861," *New Mexico Historical Review* 32, no. 2 (April 1957): 81–106; Robert N. Mullin, *Stagecoach Pioneers of the Southwest* (El Paso: Texas Western Press, 1983), 32–34; Waterman L. Ormsby, *The Butterfield Overland Mail* (San Marino, CA: Huntington Library, 1991), 80–87; and Oscar Osburn Winther, *The Transportation Frontier* (New York: Holt, Rinehart & Winston, 1964), 48–51.

22. For the "Bascom Affair," as it came to be known, see Paul Andrew Hutton, *Apache Wars* (New York: Crown, 2016), 34–55; Edwin Sweeney, *Cochise: Chiricahua Apache Chief* (Norman: University of Oklahoma Press, 1991), 142–65; Dan L. Thrapp, *The Conquest of Apacheria* (Norman: University of Oklahoma Press, 1967), 15–18; Robert M. Utley, "The Bascom Affair: A Reconstruction," *Arizona and the West* 3, no. 1 (Spring 1961): 59–68; Benjamin Sacks, "New Evidence on the Bascom Affair," *Arizona and the West* 4, no. 3 (Autumn 1962): 261–78; David L. Roberts, *Once They Moved Like the Wind: Cochise, Geronimo, and the Apache Wars* (New York: Simon & Schuster, 1993), 21–29; and James L. Haley, *Apaches: A History and Culture Portrait* (Garden City, NY: Doubleday, 1981), 224–30. Also see Doug Hocking, *The Black Legend: George Bascom, Cochise and the Start of the Apache Wars* (Helena, MT: TwoDot, 2019); and Terry Mort, *The Wrath of Cochise* (New York: Pegasus Books, 2013).

23. Benjamin Irwin Papers, MS 376, Arizona Historical Society, Tucson; Sacks, "New Evidence," 264–65; and Thompson, *Desert Tiger*, 20–21.

24. Hutton, *Apache Wars*, 50–55; and Thompson, *Desert Tiger*, 22–24.

25. Constance Wynn Altshuler, *Latest from Arizona! The Hesperian Letters, 1859–1861* (Tucson: Arizona Pioneers Historical Society, 1969), 202.

26. Raphael Pumpelly, *My Reminiscences*, 2 vols. (New York: H. Holt, 1918), vol. 1, 258–59.

27. Sandwich, *Great Western*, 56–66; and Elliott, "Great Western," 20–22. Fort Yuma was abandoned in 1883 and six years later the remains from the post graveyard, including those of Sarah Bowman, were reinterred in the national cemetery at the Presidio in San Francisco.

28. Thompson, *Desert Tiger*, 24–34; and Meketa, *Chacon*, 165–66.

29. Ovando J. Hollister, *History of the First Regiment of Colorado Volunteers* (Denver: Thomas Gibson, 1863), 155–56; Alonso Ferdinand Ickis, *Bloody Trails Along the Rio Grande* (Denver: Old West Publishing, 1958), 74; George H. Pettis, "The Confederate Invasion of New Mexico and Arizona," in *Battles and Leaders of the Civil War*, vol. 2 (New York: Century Company, 1887), 105; and Don E. Alberts, ed., *Rebels on the Rio Grande: The Civil War Journal of A. B. Peticolas* (Albuquerque: University of New Mexico Press, 1984), 119.

30. Paul Andrew Hutton, "The Fearless Leader of a Desperate Band: Paddy Graydon in the Apache and Civil Wars," *New Mexico Historical Review* 91 (Fall 2016): 373–408; and Thompson, *Desert Tiger*, 34.

31. Josephy, *Civil War in the American West*, 66–67; Thompson, *Desert Tiger*, 35–37; Sides, *Blood and Thunder*, 287–88; and Pettis, "Confederate Invasion," 105.

32. For the Battle of Valverde, see Josephy, *Civil War in the American West*, 68–74; Heyman, *Prudent Soldier*, 165–70; Theophilus F. Rodenbough, *From Everglade to Canyon with the Second United States Cavalry* (Norman: University of Oklahoma Press, 2000), 239–41; Wilson, *When the Texans Came*, 242–56; Sabin, *Kit Carson Days*, vol. 2, 674–93, 843–46; and John Taylor, *Bloody Valverde: A Civil War Battle on the Rio Grande, February 21, 1862* (Albuquerque: University of New Mexico Press, 1995). Also see Meketa, *Chacon*, 163–86; and Sides, *Blood and Thunder*, 286–93.

33. Josephy, *Civil War in the American West*, 67–92; Walter E. Pittman, *New Mexico and the Civil War* (Charleston, SC: History Press, 2011), 52–109; Wilson, *When the Texans Came*, 258–74; and Hollister, *History of the First Regiment*, 71–184.

34. Heyman, *Prudent Soldier*, 181–87, 349–84.

CHAPTER 22: MANGAS COLORADAS

1. Edwin R. Sweeney, *Cochise* (Norman: University of Oklahoma Press, 1991), 190–91; Paul Andrew Hutton, *Apache Wars* (New York: Crown, 2016), 61; Constance Wynn Altshuler, ed., *Latest from Arizona* (Tucson: Arizona Pioneers Historical Society, 1969), 202; and Charles D. Poston, *Building a State in Apache Land* (Tempe, AZ: Aztec Press, 1963), 101–5.

2. Wright quote in Aurora Hunt, *Major General James Henry Carleton* (Glendale, CA: Arthur H. Clark,1958), 198. Steck quote in W. P. Baker to Steck, November 15, 1863,

Steck Papers, University of New Mexico. Also see Robert M. Utley, *Frontiersmen in Blue* (New York: Macmillan, 1967), 219, 231–34; Hunt, *Carleton*, 193–233; Hutton, *Apache Wars*, 64–65; and Aurora Hunt, *The Army of the Pacific, 1860–1866* (Glendale, CA: Arthur Clark, 1961), 19–51. Also see Darlis A. Miller, *The California Column in New Mexico* (Albuquerque: University of New Mexico Press, 1982).

3. Eyre and trooper quotes in Sweeney, *Cochise*, 197.

4. For the Battle of Apache Pass, see John C. Cremony, *Life Among the Apaches* (San Francisco: A. Roman, 1868), 155–67; Allan Radbourne, ed., "Battle for Apache Pass: Reports of the California Volunteers," *English Westerners Brand Book* 34 (Spring 2001), 1–32; Albert J. Fountain, "Battle of Apache Pass," in Joseph Miller, ed., *Arizona Cavalcade* (New York: Hastings House, 1962), 30–35; Hutton, *Apache Wars*, 56–70; Douglas McChristian, *Fort Bowie, Arizona: Combat Post of the Southwest* (Norman: University of Oklahoma Press, 2005), 48–63; Sweeney, *Cochise*, 198–201; and Robert M. Utley, *A Clash of Cultures: Fort Bowie and the Chiricahua Apaches* (Washington, DC: National Park Service, 1977), 25–27.

5. Henry P. Walker, ed., "Soldier in the California Column: The Diary of John W. Teal," *Arizona and the West* 13, no. 1 (Spring 1971): 33–82; Edwin R. Sweeney, *Mangas Coloradas* (Norman: University of Oklahoma Press, 1998), 430–39; Cremony, *Life Among the Apaches*, 160; and Eve Ball, *Indeh: An Apache Odyssey* (Provo, UT: Brigham Young University Press, 1980), 19–20.

6. Carleton quotes in Edwin L. Sabin, *Kit Carson Days* (New York: Press of the Pioneers, 1935), vol. 2, 701–3.

7. William A. Keleher, *Turmoil in New Mexico, 1846–1868* (Santa Fe: Rydal Press, 1952), 286–87; C. L. Sonnichsen, *The Mescalero Apaches* (Norman: University of Oklahoma Press, 1973), 13–64; and Morris E. Opler, "Mescalero Apache," in William C. Sturtevant and Alfonso Ortiz, eds., *Handbook of North American Indians: Southwest* (Washington, DC: Smithsonian Institution, 1983), vol. 10, 419–39.

8. The "Gallinas Massacre" is highly controversial. Graydon's account is in his letter of October 23, 1862, Letters Received, Dept. of New Mexico, RG 393, National Archives. Morrison's report is October 24, 1862, Letters Received, Dept. of New Mexico, RG 393, National Archives. Also see Sonnichsen, *Mescalero Apaches*, 111–12; Lawrence C. Kelly, *Navajo Roundup: Selected Correspondence of Kit Carson's Expedition Against the Navajo, 1863–1865* (Boulder, CO: Pruett, 1970), 12–14; Sabin, *Kit Carson Days*, vol. 2, 704; and Dale F. Giese, ed., *My Life with the Army in the West: Memories of James E. Farmer* (Silver City, NM: Dale Giese, 1993), 49–50.

9. Sonnichsen, *Mescalero Apaches*, 113; Tom Dunlay, *Kit Carson and the Indians* (Lincoln: University of Nebraska Press, 2000), 244–47; Kelly, *Navajo Roundup*, 16–17; and Sabin, *Kit Carson Days*, vol. 2, 705.

10. Kelly, *Navajo Roundup*, 15.

11. *Santa Fe Gazette*, November 15, 1862; *New York Times*, December 9, 1862; *Daily Alta California* (San Francisco), February 14, 1863; B. C. Hernandez, "The Tragical Death of Doctor J. M. Whitlock in 1868 at Fort Stanton, New Mexico," *New Mexico Historical Review* 16, no. 1 (January 1941), 104–6; Jacqueline Dorgan Meketa, ed., *Legacy of Honor: The Life of Rafael Chacon, a Nineteenth-Century New Mexican* (Albuquerque: University of New Mexico Press, 1986), 269–73; Giese, *My Life with the Army*, 49–51;

Keleher, *Turmoil in New Mexico*, 289–91, 485; and Jerry D. Thompson, *Desert Tiger* (El Paso: Texas Western Press, 1992), 56–63, which is the most reliable account of the gunfight.

12. Sabin, *Kit Carson Days*, vol. 2, 901; and Kelly, *Navajo Roundup*, 26.

13. Hampton Sides, *Blood and Thunder* (New York: Doubleday, 2006), 351; and Dunlay, *Carson and the Indians*, 294.

14. Sabin, *Kit Carson Days*, vol. 2, 901–5; Laura C. Manson White, "Albert H. Pfeiffer," *Colorado Magazine* 10, no. 6 (November 1933): 217–22; and Thelma S. Guild and Harvey L. Carter, *Kit Carson* (Lincoln: University of Nebraska Press, 1986), 230.

15. Keleher, *Turmoil in New Mexico*, 291–92.

16. Sweeney, *Mangas Coloradas*, 444.

17. For Swilling, see Albert R. Bates, *Jack Swilling: Arizona's Most Lied About Pioneer* (Tucson: Wheatmark, 2008).

18. Conner quote in Daniel Ellis Conner, *Joseph Reddeford Walker and the Arizona Adventure*, ed. Donald J. Berthrong and Odessa Davenport (Norman: University of Oklahoma Press, 1956), 34–42. Also see Sweeney, *Mangas Coloradas*, 450; Ball, *Indeh*, 19; and Eve Ball, *In the Days of Victorio* (Tucson: University of Arizona Press, 1970), 47–48.

19. Sweeney, *Mangas Coloradas*, 454–58; Conner, *Walker*, 37–39; Hutton, *Apache Wars*, 95–102; and Lee Myers, "The Enigma of Mangas Coloradas' Death," *New Mexico Historical Review* 41, no. 4 (October 1966): 287–304. Clark Stocking of the California Column also left an eyewitness account that differs somewhat from Conner's account: see Clark B. Stocking File and William Fours File, Hayden Collection, Arizona Historical Society. A version of Stocking's account is in James H. McClintock, *Arizona*, 3 vols. (Chicago: S. J. Clarke, 1916), vol. 1, 177–78.

20. Orson S. Fowler, *Human Science: or, Phrenology* (Philadelphia: National Publishing, 1873), 1195–97. A drawing of the skull appears on p. 1196.

21. Sweeney, *Mangas Coloradas*, 459; and Conner, *Walker*, 40–41.

22. S. M. Barrett, ed., *Geronimo's Story of His Life* (New York: Duffield, 1906), 119; Ball, *Days of Victorio*, 48; and Ball, *Indeh*, 20.

CHAPTER 23: CANYON DE CHELLY

1. William C. Sturtevant and Alfonso Ortiz, eds., *Handbook of North American Indians: Southwest* (Washington, DC: Smithsonian Institution, 1983), vol. 10, 489–557. Also see Ruth M. Underhill, *The Navajos* (Norman: University of Oklahoma Press, 1956); Frank McNitt, *Navajo Wars: Military Campaigns, Slave Raids and Reprisals* (Albuquerque: University of New Mexico Press, 1972); Jack D. Forbes, *Apache, Navaho, and Spaniard* (Norman: University of Oklahoma Press, 1960); Clyde Kluckhohn and Dorothea Leighton, *The Navaho* (Cambridge, MA: Harvard University Press, 1946); and Peter Iverson, *Dine: A History of the Navajos* (Albuquerque: University of New Mexico Press, 2002).

2. Paul Andrew Hutton, *Apache Wars* (New York: Crown, 2016), 107; and Tom Dunlay, *Kit Carson and the Indians* (Lincoln: University of Nebraska Press, 2000), 253–54.

3. Benedict quote in Dunlay, *Carson and the Indians,* 253. For the Indian slave trade, see Andrés Reséndez, *The Other Slavery: The Uncovered Story of Indian Enslavement in America* (New York: Houghton Mifflin Harcourt, 2016); James F. Brooks, *Captives and Cousins: Slavery, Kinship, and Community in the Southwest Borderlands* (Chapel Hill: University of North Carolina Press, 2002); and L. R. Bailey, *Indian Slave Trade in the Southwest* (Los Angeles: Westernlore Press, 1966).

4. Armijo quote in McNitt, *Navajo Wars,* 90.

5. Carson to Carleton, July 24, 1863, and Carleton to Carson, August 18, 1863, in Lawrence C. Kelly, ed., *Navajo Roundup: Selected Correspondence of Kit Carson's Expedition Against the Navajo, 1863–1865* (Boulder: Pruett Publishing, 1970), 30–32.

6. Carson testimony in *Condition of the Indian Tribes: Report of the Joint Committee, Appointed Under Joint Resolution of March 3, 1865* (Washington, DC: Government Printing Office, 1867), 96–98.

7. Carleton quoted in Kelly, *Navajo Roundup,* 18–20; and Dunlay, *Carson and the Indians,* 274–75. Also see Aurora Hunt, *Major General James Henry Carleton* (Glendale, CA: Arthur H. Clark, 1958), 271–80.

8. Kelly, *Navajo Roundup,* 22–24.

9. Carleton quote in Kelly, *Navajo Roundup,* 35. Also see Kelly, *Navajo Roundup,* 21–26, for troop dispositions.

10. Kelly, *Navajo Roundup,* 28–32.

11. Raymond E. Lindgren, ed., "A Diary of Kit Carson's Navajo Campaign, 1863–1864," *New Mexico Historical Review* 21, no. 3 (July 1946): 226–46; and Kelly, *Navajo Roundup,* 53.

12. Kelly, *Navajo Roundup,* 15, 34, 44–51.

13. Carson to Carleton, October 5, 1863, in Kelly, *Navajo Roundup,* 55.

14. Carleton to Carson, September 19, 1863; Carson to Carleton, November 1, 22, 1863; Carleton to Carson, December 5, 1863, in Kelly, *Navajo Roundup,* 52, 68-71.

15. For the Song "Johnny Navajo," see *Rio Abajo Weekly Press* (Albuquerque), December 8, 1863. Also see William A. Keleher, *Turmoil in New Mexico, 1846–1868* (Santa Fe: Rydal Press, 1952), 314; and Hunt, *Carleton,* 284. Pfeiffer quote in Kelly, *Navajo Roundup,* 102–5.

16. Carson's report, January 24, 1864, in Kelly, *Navajo Roundup,* 98–101. For the Canyon de Chelly campaign, see Hampton Sides, *Blood and Thunder* (New York: Doubleday, 2006), 346–59; Megan Kate Nelson, *The Three-Cornered War* (New York: Scribner, 2020), 185–99; Edwin L. Sabin, *Kit Carson Days* (New York: Press of the Pioneers, 1935), vol. 2, 707–24; Dunlay, *Carson and the Indians,* 292–300; and Thelma S. Guild and Harvey L. Carter, *Kit Carson* (Lincoln: University of Nebraska Press, 1984), 231–49. The standard work on the Navajo War remains Clifford E. Trafzer, *The Kit Carson Campaign: The Last Great Navajo War* (Norman: University of Oklahoma Press, 1982).

17. Carleton to Adjutant General Lorenzo Thomas, February 7, 1864, in Kelly, *Navajo Roundup,* 107–9.

18. Joseph Berney quoted in Kelly, *Navajo Roundup,* 116.

19. For the Long Walk, see Broderick H. Johnson, ed., *Navajo Stories of the Long Walk* Period (Tsaile, AZ: Navajo Community College Press, 1973); and Lynn R. Bailey, *The*

Long Walk (Los Angeles: Westernlore Press, 1964). Also see Sides, *Blood and Thunder,* 359–69; Keleher, *Turmoil in New Mexico,* 368–85; Trafzer, *Kit Carson Campaign,* 169–223; and Dunlay, *Carson and the Indians*, 300–324.

20. Carleton to Thomas, March 12, 1864, in Kelly, *Navajo Roundup*, 126–28. For Bosque Redondo, see Gerald Thompson, *The Army and the Navajo* (Tucson: University of Arizona Press, 1976). Also see Underhill, *Navajos*, 127–43; Hutton, *Apache Wars,* 105–15; Hunt, *Carleton*, 273–96; and Keleher, *Turmoil in New Mexico,* 409–58.

CHAPTER 24: ADOBE WALLS

1. Robert M. Utley, *Frontiersmen in Blue* (New York: Macmillan, 1967), 281–87, 297–99; Tom Dunlay, *Kit Carson and the Indians* (Lincoln: University of Nebraska Press, 2000), 325; and George E. Hyde, *Life of George Bent: Written from His Letters* (Norman: University of Oklahoma Press, 1968), 110–36.

2. Dunlay, *Carson and the Indians*, 326; and Edwin L. Sabin, *Kit Carson Days* (New York: Press of the Pioneers, 1935), vol. 2, 730.

3. George H. Pettis, *Kit Carson's Fight with the Comanche and Kiowa Indians at the Adobe Walls on the Canadian River, November 25, 1864* (Santa Fe: New Mexico Historical Society, publication no. 12, 1908), 7–13. Pettis's account was reprinted from the *Santa Fe Weekly New Mexican*, March 22, 29, and April 5, 1879. Also see Alvin R. Lynn, *Kit Carson and the First Battle of Adobe Walls* (Lubbock: Texas Tech University Press, 2014), 16–60; Sabin, *Kit Carson Days*, vol. 2, 732–36; and Carson quote in Hampton Sides, *Blood and Thunder* (New York: Doubleday, 2006), 371–73. Another version of Pettis's valuable memoir was published in 1878 by S. S. Rider of Providence, Rhode Island, as part of a Civil War series.

4. Pettis, *Kit Carson's Fight,* 14; and Sabin, *Kit Carson Days,* vol. 2, 738–39.

5. Quoted in Pettis, *Kit Carson's Fight,* 34–35, and for the battle, 14–33. Also see Sabin, *Kit Carson Days*, vol. 2, 746–48; and Hyde, *George Bent,* 244–46. For the Battle of Adobe Walls, see Lynn, *Adobe Walls,* 58–89; Sides, *Blood and Thunder,* 369–79; Thelma S. Guild and Harvey L. Carter, *Kit Carson* (Lincoln: University of Nebraska Press, 1984), 250–60; Sabin, *Kit Carson Days,* vol. 2, 725–48; and Dunlay, *Carson and the Indians*, 326–39. Also see David Pafford, "Kit Carson's Last Fight: The Adobe Walls Campaign of 1864" (PhD diss., University of New Mexico, 2017).

6. Sabin, *Kit Carson Days*, vol. 2, 748–51.

7. James F. Rusling, *Across America* (New York: Sheldon, 1874), 138.

8. Sherman quote in Edward S. Ellis, *The Life of Kit Carson* (New York: Grosset & Dunlap, 1889), 254–257.

9. Ellis, *Life of Kit Carson*, 248–49.

10. Paul Andrew Hutton, *Apache Wars* (New York: Crown, 2016), 115. Carleton died of pneumonia at age fifty-eight at San Antonio, Texas, on January 7, 1873. He was buried at Mount Auburn Cemetery, Cambridge, Massachusetts. Aurora Hunt, *Major General James Henry Carleton* (Glendale, CA: Arthur H. Clark, 1958), 344–48.

11. Manuelito quote in Gerald Thompson, *The Army and the Navajo* (Tucson: University of Arizona Press, 1976), 140. Also see William A. Keleher, *Turmoil in New Mexico* (Santa

Fe: Rydal Press, 1952), 277–459; Megan Kate Nelson, *The Three-Cornered War* (New York: Scribner, 2020), 245–46; and Broderick H. Johnson, ed., *Navajo Stories of the Long Walk Period* (Tsaile, AZ: Navajo Community College Press, 1973), 232–72.

12. John Hough quoted in Sabin, *Kit Carson Days*, vol. 2, 793. Also see Guild and Carter, *Kit Carson*, 276–78; and Sides, *Blood and Thunder*, 389–91. The fate of the Carson children is of interest. William (1852–1889), the eldest, was sent by Tom Boggs to General Sherman, who, true to his pledge, had him educated at the Catholic College at South Bend, Indiana (the future Notre Dame), but the boy proved to be a poor scholar. In 1870, Sherman attempted to get the boy an appointment as a second lieutenant in the 9th Cavalry, but while President Grant promptly made the appointment, William could not pass the required official examining board. "By nature," Sherman noted, "he was not adapted to modern uses." So William went back to work with Boggs on his cattle ranch. In time he moved to Fort Garland, Colorado, where he married the daughter of his father's old mountain man friend Tom Tobin. He was elected sheriff of Costilla County but soon after was killed in a shooting accident at age thirty-seven in 1889. Teresina (1855–1916) married in 1871 and continued to live near Boggsville, in southeastern Colorado. She died on July 6, 1916, and was buried in Trinidad, Colorado. Christopher (1858–1929) married Maria "Lupe" Richards in 1890 and they had seven children. An untamed spirit, he was found guilty of manslaughter in the killing of his father-in-law but served no prison time. He was also involved in the shooting of his brother's father-in-law, Tom Tobin, but charges were not pressed. He died in 1829 at La Junta, Colorado. Charles (1861–1938) became a successful cattleman in Colorado. In 1912 he married Mary Alice Gallagher, an Iowa-born schoolteacher, and they had five children. He died at La Junta at age seventy-seven on July 21, 1938. Rebecca (1863–1885) married in 1883 and died by suicide two years later. She is buried near her parents in Taos. Estefana (1866–1898) married in 1884 and bore four children before dying at age thirty-two. The youngest child, Josefita (1868–1902), suffered through two abusive marriages before being placed in a mental hospital in Las Vegas, New Mexico, where she died at age thirty-four in 1902. She is buried near her parents in Taos. Juan Carson, the Navajo boy adopted by the Carsons, married a Hispanic girl but died young. Charles Bent Carson (1849–1851) died at age two in Taos. Adaline (1837–1862), Kit's daughter by Waa-Nibe, married a former trapper named Louis Simmons in 1851 but the marriage failed. She turned up at the gold diggings near Mono Lake, California, in 1859 with a new husband, George Stilts, a fiddle player from Santa Fe, but died under mysterious circumstances in 1862 at age twenty-five. She was buried near Mono Lake. The name of Carson's second child by Waa-Nibe has not come down to us. The toddler was killed in an accident at Bent's Fort around 1841. Teresina Bent Scheurich, whom the Carsons took into their home after her father's murder, became one of the great ladies of Taos society. She died in 1920, and she and her husband, Aloys Scheurich, are both buried in the Taos cemetery. Kit Carson's great-grandson (yes, just one "great") John Carson presently lives in southeastern Colorado not far from Boggsville. For the Carson family, see Quantrille D. McClung, *Carson-Bent-Boggs Genealogy* (Denver: Denver Public Library, 1962); Marc Simmons, *Kit Carson and His Three Wives* (Albuquerque: University of New Mexico Press, 2003); and Barbara Schultz, *Josefa* (Taos: Kit Carson Home & Museum, 2017). Also see Robert G. Athearn, "The Education of Kit Carson's Son," *New Mexico Historical Review* 31, no. 2 (April 1956): 133–39.

13. Henry Inman, *The Old Santa Fe Trail* (New York: Macmillan, 1897), 380–81; and Guild and Carter, *Kit Carson*, 278.

14. William F. Cody, *Story of the Wild West and Camp Fire Chats* (Chicago: Thompson and Thomas, 1902), iv–v.

15. Carson quoted in Dunlay, *Carson and the Indians*, 415–17. For the Ute delegation, see *Boston Daily Journal*, February 4, 1868, and *Daily National Intelligencer*, February 6, 1868. The other white members of the delegation included Colorado governor and Indian superintendent Alexander Hunt, Ute agent Daniel Oakes, Albert Gallatin Boone, and several clerks and interpreters. The ten-member Ute delegation was led by Chiefs Ouray, Kanaiche, and Ankatosh. Jessie Benton Frémont, *The Will and the Way Stories* (Boston: D. Lothrop, 1891), 43–47.

16. Pamela Herr, *Jessie Benton Frémont* (New York: Franklin Watts, 1987), 386–87; Pamela Herr and Mary Lee Spence, eds., *The Letters of Jessie Benton Frémont* (Urbana: University of Illinois Press, 1993), 402–3, 478–79; Guild and Carter, *Kit Carson*, 280.

17. Sabin, *Kit Carson Days*, vol. 2, 794–98; Simmons, *Three Wives*, 138–41; and Guild and Carter, *Kit Carson*, 279–81.

18. H. R. Tilton to J. Abbott, January 7, 1874, in John S. C. Abbott, *Christopher Carson, Known as Kit Carson* (New York: Dodd, Mead, 1901), 343–48; Simmons, *Three Wives*, 141–45; Schultz, *Josefa*, 110–13; and Sabin, *Kit Carson Days*, vol. 2, 799–811.

19. *Rocky Mountain News*, May 27, 1868. Sherman quoted in Ellis, *Kit Carson*, 252.

CHAPTER 25: THE BUFFALO RANGE

1. The literature on Cody is vast and varied. The place to begin is with his autobiography, which is reasonably reliable: William F. Cody, *The Life of Hon. William F. Cody Known as Buffalo Bill: The Famous Hunter, Scout and Guide* (Hartford, CT: Frank E. Bliss, 1879), which has been reprinted many times, with the best annotated edition being Frank Christianson, ed., *The Life of Hon. William F. Cody, Known as Buffalo Bill* (Lincoln: University of Nebraska Press, 2011). Also by Cody are *Buffalo Bill's Life Story: An Autobiography* (New York: Rinehart, 1920), which is the last of several updates to the autobiography; William F. Cody, *True Tales of the Plains* (New York: Cupples and Leon, 1908); Stella Adelyne Foote, ed., *Letters from Buffalo Bill* (Billings, MT: Foote Publishing, 1954); and Sarah J. Blackstone, ed., *The Business of Being Buffalo Bill: Selected Letters of William F. Cody, 1879–1917* (New York: Praeger, 1988). The two best biographies are Louis S. Warren, *Buffalo Bill's America: William Cody and the Wild West Show* (New York: Alfred A. Knopf, 2005), and Don Russell, *The Lives and Legends of Buffalo Bill* (Norman: University of Oklahoma Press, 1960). Also worthwhile are Richard J. Walsh and Milton S. Salsbury, *The Making of Buffalo Bill: A Study in Heroics* (Indianapolis: Bobbs-Merrill, 1928); Henry Blackman Sell and Victor Weybright, *Buffalo Bill and the Wild West* (New York: Oxford University Press, 1955); Nellie Snyder Yost, *Buffalo Bill: His Family, Friends, Fame, Failures and Fortunes* (Chicago: Swallow Press, 1979); Joseph G. Rosa and Robin May, *Buffalo Bill and His Wild West* (Lawrence: University Press of Kansas, 1989); Robert A. Carter, *Buffalo Bill Cody: The Man Behind the Legend* (New York: Wiley, 2000); and Steve Friesen, *Buffalo Bill: Scout, Showman, Visionary* (Golden, CO: Fulcrum, 2010). Among the many memoirs associated with Cody are Louisa Frederici Cody and Courtney Ryley Cooper, *Memories of Buffalo Bill* (New York: D. Appleton, 1919); Helen Cody Wetmore, *Last of the Great Scouts* (Duluth, MN: Duluth Press Publishing, 1899); Elizabeth Jane Leonard and Julia Cody Goodman, *Buffalo Bill: King of the Old West* (New York: Library

Publishers, 1955); John M. Burke, *Buffalo Bill from Prairie to Palace*, ed. Chris Dizon (Lincoln: University of Nebraska Press, 2012); Charles Eldridge Griffin, *Four Years in Europe with Buffalo Bill* (Albia, IA: Stage Publishing, 1908); Dan Muller, *My Life with Buffalo Bill* (Chicago: Reilly and Lee, 1948); Alexander Majors, *Seventy Years on the Frontier* (Chicago: Rand McNally, 1893); and Gene Fowler, *Timber Line: A Story of Bonfils and Tammen* (New York: Blue Ribbon Books, 1933). Also see, for the Buffalo Bill of legend, *Buffalo Bill and the Wild West: Brooklyn Museum Exhibit Catalog* (Pittsburgh: University of Pittsburgh Press, 1981); Paul Fees and Sarah E. Boehme, *Frontier America: Art and Treasures of the Old West from the Buffalo Bill Historical Center* (New York: Harry N. Abrams, 1988); Henry Nash Smith, *Virgin Land: The American West as Symbol and Myth* (Cambridge, MA: Harvard University Press, 1950); Richard Slotkin, *Gunfighter Nation: The Myth of the Frontier in Twentieth-Century America* (New York: Atheneum, 1992); Daniel Justin Herman, *Hunting and the American Imagination* (Washington, DC: Smithsonian Institution Press, 2001); and William H. Goetzmann, *The West of the Imagination* (New York: W. W. Norton, 1989).

2. Cody, *Life*, 72. Also see Joseph G. Rosa, *They Called Him Wild Bill: The Life and Adventures of James Butler Hickok* (Norman: University of Oklahoma Press, 1974), 22–23, 31.

3. Russell, *Lives and Legends*, 44–54; Walsh and Salsbury, *Making of Buffalo Bill*, 67–76; Sell and Weybright, *Buffalo Bill*, 26–32; Friesen, *Buffalo Bill*, 7–9; Carter, *Buffalo Bill*, 48–61, quote on 50; Cody, *Life*, 103–18; Wetmore, *Last of the Great Scouts*, 69–74; and Warren, *Buffalo Bill's America*, 3–6, 18–21. There is considerable debate over Cody riding for the Pony Express. Don Russell says he did, and most authors follow him, but Louis Warren says he did not. Support for Warren comes from noted researcher John S. Gray in "Fact Versus Fiction in the Kansas Boyhood of Buffalo Bill," *Kansas History* 8, no. 1 (Spring 1985): 2–20. Gray carefully critiqued Cody's autobiography and found numerous inconsistencies in it, especially concerning the Pony Express and the Simpson Wagon Train. Most of his evidence, however, is simply negative, and while it is clear Cody was careless with facts and dates and was not above embellishing his tales of adventure, Gray does not prove his case. If Gray is right, then Cody and many of his contemporaries, including Alexander Majors, who founded the Pony Express, are wrong. Frankly, Cody had no reason to invent his Pony Express connection when he wrote his 1879 memoir. By then Cody was a national figure and the short-lived Pony Express was all but forgotten. It was Cody, through his book and Wild West show, who immortalized the Pony Express.

4. Cody, *Life*, 125–40, quote on 135. Also see Russell, *Lives and Legends*, 55–72; Warren, *Buffalo Bill's America*, 32–39; Leonard and Goodman, *Buffalo Bill*, 114–38; and Wetmore, *Last of the Great Scouts*, 98–122.

5. Cody, *Life*, 145–47; and Warren, *Buffalo Bill's America*, 134–38.

6. Cody, *Life*, 172; and Russell, *Lives and Legends*, 84–99.

7. Boone quote in John Filson, *The Discovery and Settlement of Kentucke* (Wilmington, DE: James Adams, 1784), 50–51. Also see John Mack Faragher, *Daniel Boone* (New York: Henry Holt, 1992), 76–79. For the history of the bison/buffalo, see Martin S. Garretson, *The American Bison* (New York: New York Zoological Society, 1938); Frank Gilbert Roe, *The North American Buffalo: A Critical Study of the Species in Its Wild State* (Toronto: University of Toronto Press, 1951); David A. Dary, *The Buffalo Book* (Chicago: Swallow Press, 1974); Tom McHugh, *The Time of the Buffalo* (New York:

Alfred A. Knopf, 1972); Francis Haines, *The Buffalo* (Norman: University of Oklahoma Press, 1995); Steven Rinella, *American Buffalo: In Search of a Lost Icon* (New York: Random House, 2008); Dan Flores, *Wild New World: The Epic Story of Animals and People in America* (New York: W. W. Norton, 2022); and Dayton Duncan and Ken Burns, *Blood Memory: The Tragic Decline and Improbable Resurrection of the American Buffalo* (New York: Alfred A. Knopf, 2023).

8. For the destruction of the great herds, see William Temple Hornaday, *The Extermination of the American Bison* (Washington, DC: Smithsonian Institution Press, 2002; reprint of the 1889 edition); Mari Sandoz, *The Buffalo Hunters* (New York: Hastings House, 1954); Wayne Gard, *The Great Buffalo Hunt* (New York: Alfred A. Knopf, 1960); Andrew C. Isenberg, *The Destruction of the Bison: An Environmental History, 1750–1920* (Cambridge: Cambridge University Press, 2000); Michael Punke, *Last Stand: George Bird Grinnell, the Battle to Save the Buffalo, and the Birth of the New West* (New York: HarperCollins, 2007); Dan Flores, "When the Buffalo Roamed," in Paul Andrew Hutton, ed., *Western Heritage* (Norman: University of Oklahoma Press, 2011), 3–14; Dan Flores, "Bison Ecology and Bison Diplomacy: The Southern Plains from 1800 to 1850," *Journal of American History* 78, no. 2 (September 1991): 465–85; and Flores, *Wild New World,* 221–56.

9. Sheridan quoted in Paul Andrew Hutton, *Phil Sheridan and His Army* (Lincoln: University of Nebraska Press, 1985), 246. Cody quoted in Steve Friesen, *Galloping Gourmet: Eating and Drinking with Buffalo Bill* (Lincoln: University of Nebraska Press, 2023), 162. Also see Russell, *Lives and Legends,* 342–53; Warren, *Buffalo Bill's America,* 125–49; and Herman, *Hunting and the American Imagination,* 200–217.

10. Dary, *Buffalo Book,* 134–43.

11. Philip H. Sheridan, *Personal Memoirs of P. H. Sheridan, General, United States Army,* 2 vols. (New York: Charles L. Webster, 1888), vol. 2, 300–301; Cody, *Life,* 188–99; and Henry Inman, *The Old Santa Fe Trail* (New York: Macmillan, 1897), 366.

12. Lincoln and Crosby quoted in Hutton, *Phil Sheridan,* 2.

13. Lincoln and Crosby quoted in Hutton, *Phil Sheridan,* 33–35; "Tabular Statement of Murders, Outrages, Robberies and Depredations Committed by Indians in Department of Missouri and Northern Texas, 1868," and "List of Murders, Outrages, and Depredations Committed by Indians from 3rd August to 24th October, 1868," in Box 68, Philip H. Sheridan Papers, Library of Congress.

14. Sheridan to Adjutant General, December 17, 1881, Box 30, Sheridan Papers. For Carr, see James T. King, *War Eagle: A Life of General Eugene A. Carr* (Lincoln: University of Nebraska Press, 1963); and George F. Price, *Across the Continent with the Fifth Cavalry* (New York: Antiquarian Press, 1959), 259–65.

15. "Report of Lieutenant Colonel G. A. Custer, 7th Cavalry, Brevet Major General, U.S.A., of the attack on Black Kettle's Camp," November 28, 1868, Box 83, Sheridan Papers; *Report of the Secretary of War,* 1869, vol. 1 (Washington, DC: Government Printing Office, 1869), 47–48; Sherman to Sheridan, January 19, 1869, Division of the Missouri Letters Sent, RG 393, National Archives; and Hutton, *Phil Sheridan,* 56–100. For the Washita, see T. J. Stiles, *Custer's Trials: A Life on the Frontier of a New America* (New York: Alfred A. Knopf, 2015), 295–328; George Armstrong Custer, *My Life on the Plains* (New York: Sheldon, 1874), 139–83; Sheridan, *Personal Memoirs,* vol. 2, 307–22; Robert M. Utley, *Cavalier in Buckskin: George Armstrong Custer and the Western Military*

Frontier (Norman: University of Oklahoma Press, 1988), 57–78; De Benneville Randolph Keim, *Sheridan's Troopers on the Border: A Winter Campaign on the Plains* (Philadelphia: Claxton, Remsen & Haffelfinger, 1870); Stan Hoig, *The Battle of the Washita* (Garden City, NY: Doubleday, 1976); and Jerome A. Greene, *Washita: The U.S. Army and the Southern Cheyennes, 1867–1869* (Norman: University of Oklahoma Press, 2004).

16. Cody, *Life*, 218–26; Russell, *Lives and Legends*, 108–14; Rosa, *They Called Him Wild Bill*, 122–27; Price, *With the Fifth Cavalry*, 132–33; King, *War Eagle*, 87–90; Morris F. Taylor, "The Carr-Penrose Expedition: General Sheridan's Winter Campaign, 1868–1869," *Chronicles of Oklahoma* 51, no. 2 (Summer 1973): 159–76; and Carl Coke Rister, ed., "Colonel A.W. Evans' Christmas Day Indian Fight (1868)," *Chronicles of Oklahoma* 16, no. 3 (September 1938): 299–300.

17. Cody, *Life*, 227–28.

18. Cody quotes are from Cody, *Life*, 243–62. For Summit Springs, see King, *War Eagle*, 95–116; Cody, *True Tales of the Plains*, 150–57; Walsh, *Buffalo Bill*, 142–54; Price, *With the Fifth Cavalry*, 138–41; Russell, *Lives and Legends*, 129–48; Hutton, *Phil Sheridan*, 110–12; George E. Hyde, *The Life of George Bent* (Norman: University of Oklahoma Press, 1968), 328–35; Warren, *Buffalo Bill's America*, 109–12; George Bird Grinnell, *The Fighting Cheyennes* (Norman: University of Oklahoma Press, 1956), 310–18; Jeff Broome, *Dog Soldier Justice: The Ordeal of Susanna Alderdice in the Kansas Indian War* (Lincoln: University of Nebraska Press, 2009), 163–86; and Clarence Reckmeyer, "The Battle of Summit Springs," *Colorado Magazine* 6, no. 6 (November 1929): 212–16. For Frank North, his brother Luther, and the Pawnee scouts, see George Bird Grinnell, *Two Great Scouts and Their Pawnee Battalion* (Cleveland: Arthur H. Clark, 1928), and Donald F. Danker, ed., *Man of the Plains: Recollections of Luther North, 1856–1882* (Lincoln: University of Nebraska Press, 1961). Cody's role in the battle and the death of Tall Bull is yet another controversial topic. Walsh, Grinnell, and Warren all conclude that Cody did not kill Tall Bull. Luther North is the main source for this, since he claimed that his brother Frank killed Tall Bull and that Cody was not in the battle at all (which is contradicted by the accounts of Carr and other officers). See Danker, *Man of the Plains*, 113–19. Luther North was also Grinnell's informant. Warren dismisses Cody's claim as show business press agency and points out that it is impossible to know for certain who killed the chief. Russell presents a detailed defense of Cody's version. In a careful reconstruction of the incident, Jeff Broome concludes that Sergeant Daniel McGrath killed Tall Bull, although he also does not entirely dismiss Cody's claim. To add to the confusion, General Carr gave three different accounts, crediting at different times McGrath, Cody, and the Pawnee scouts. Jeff Broome, "Cody and Summit Springs," *Denver Westerners Roundup* 76 (May–June 2020): 3–24.

19. Robert M. Utley, *Frontier Regulars* (New York: Macmillan, 1973), 142–62; Peter Cozzens, *The Earth Is Weeping: The Epic Story of the Indian Wars of the American West* (New York: Alfred A. Knopf, 2016), 76–111; and Hutton, *Phil Sheridan*, 95–114. Also see S. C. Gwynne, *Empire of the Summer Moon* (New York: Scribner, 2010), and Pekka Hämäläinen, *Indigenous Continent: The Epic Contest for North America* (New York: Liveright, 2022).

20. Marshall Sprague, *A Gallery of Dudes* (Boston: Little, Brown, 1966), 150–53; Russell, *Lives and Legends*, 164–68; John I. Merritt, *Baronets and Buffalo: The British*

Sportsman in the American West, 1833–1881 (Missoula, MT: Mountain Press Publishing, 1985), 160–74; and William F. Cody, "Famous Hunting Parties on the Plains," *Cosmopolitan* 17 (June 1894): 131–43.

21. Paul Andrew Hutton, ed., *Ten Days on the Plains by Henry E. Davies* (Dallas: Southern Methodist University Press, 1985), 3–49; and Cody, *Life*, 281–90.

22. Cody quote in Cody, *Life*, 282; Wilson quote in *New York Times*, October 7, 1871; Davis quote in Hutton, *Ten Days*, 83; and Cody, "Famous Hunting Parties," 137–40.

23. Cody, *Life*, 286; Hutton, *Ten Days*, 105–6; Russell, *Lives and Legends*, 170–73.

24. Cody, *Life*, 295–98. For Spotted Tail, see George E. Hyde, *Spotted Tail's Folk: A History of the Brulé Sioux* (Norman: University of Oklahoma Press, 1961), and Pekka Hämäläinen, *Lakota America: A New History of Indigenous Power* (New Haven, CT: Yale University Press, 2019), 226–31, 304–10, 373–74. Spotted Tail was murdered by his rival Crow Dog, in 1881. Such an act was not uncommon among the Sioux.

25. Cody, *Life*, 299.

26. *New York Herald*, January 14, 16, 1872; and *Cincinnati Inquirer*, January 18, 1872.

27. Cody, *Life*, 300.

28. Cody and Sheridan quotes in Cody, *Life*, 302–4. For the grand duke's hunt, see Russell, *Lives and Legends*, 174–84; Sprague, *Gallery of Dudes*, 95–117; Stiles, *Custer's Trials*, 359–60; Warren, *Buffalo Bill's America*, 147–49, 158–59; Hutton, *Phil Sheridan*, 212–16; Cody, *True Tales of the Plains*, 166–76; Cody, "Famous Hunting Parties," 131–43; James Albert Hadley, "A Royal Buffalo Hunt," *Transactions of the Kansas State Historical Society* 10 (1907–08): 564–80; John I. White, "Red Carpet for a Romanoff," *American West* 9, no. 1 (January 1972): 5–9; William F. Zornow, "When the Czar and Grant Were Friends," *Mid-America* 43, no. 3 (July 1961): 164–81; and Walsh, *Making of Buffalo Bill*, 168–69. For a contemporary account compiled from newspaper stories, see *The Grand Duke Alexis in the United States of America* (New York: Interland Publishing, 1972; reprint of the 1872 edition); and for Grand Duke Alexis's entire visit, see Lee A. Farrow, *Alexis in America: A Russian Grand Duke's Tour, 1871–1872* (Baton Rouge: Louisiana State University Press, 2014).

CHAPTER 26: WARBONNET CREEK

1. Paul L. Hedren, *First Scalp for Custer: The Skirmish at Warbonnet Creek, Nebraska, July 17, 1876* (Glendale, CA: Arthur H. Clark, 1980), 51; King quoted in Charles King, *Campaigning with Crook* (Norman: University of Oklahoma Press, 1964; reprint of the 1890 edition), 22–23; Don Russell, *Campaigning with King: Charles King, Chronicler of the Old Army*, ed. Paul L. Hedren (Lincoln: University of Nebraska Press, 1991), 62–63; Charles King, "The Story of a March," *Journal of the United States Cavalry Association* 3, no. 9 (June 1890): 121–29; Paul Andrew Hutton, "Buffalo Bill," *Wild West* 21, no. 5 (February 2009), 26–35; and Charles King, "My Friend, Buffalo Bill," *Cavalry Journal* 41 (September–October 1932): 17–20.

2. Don Russell, *The Lives and Legends of Buffalo Bill* (Norman: University of Oklahoma Press, 1960), 220.

3. For Sitting Bull and the Lakota, see Robert M. Utley, *The Lance and the Shield* (New York: Henry Holt, 1993); Mark Lee Gardner, *The Earth Is All That Lasts: Crazy Horse, Sitting Bull, and the Last Stand of the Great Sioux Nation* (Boston: Mariner Books,

2022); Stanley Vestal, *Sitting Bull: Champion of the Sioux* (Norman: University of Oklahoma Press, 1957; reprint of the 1932 edition); Stanley Vestal, *Warpath: The True Story of the Fighting Sioux Told in a Biography of Chief White Bull* (New York: Houghton Mifflin, 1934); Stanley Vestal, *New Sources of Indian History, 1850–1891* (Norman: University of Oklahoma Press, 1934); George E. Hyde, *Red Cloud's Folk: A History of the Oglala Sioux Indians* (Norman: University of Oklahoma Press, 1957); Raymond J. DeMallie, ed., *The Sixth Grandfather: Black Elk's Teachings Given to John G. Neihardt* (Lincoln: University of Nebraska Press, 1982); William C. Sturtevant and Raymond J. DeMallie, eds., *Handbook of North American Indians: Plains,* 2 vols. (Washington, DC: Smithsonian Institution, 2001); Jeffrey Ostler, *The Plains Sioux and U.S. Colonialism from Lewis and Clark to Wounded Knee* (New York: Cambridge University Press, 2004); and Pekka Hämäläinen, *Lakota America: A New History of Indigenous Power* (New Haven, CT: Yale University Press, 2019).

4. Utley, *Lance and Shield*, 44–47. Also see R. Eli Paul, *Blue Water Creek and the First Sioux War, 1854–1856* (Norman: University of Oklahoma Press, 2004).

5. Sitting Bull quote in Charles Larpenteur, *Forty Years a Fur Trader on the Upper Missouri, 1833–1872* (Lincoln: University of Nebraska Press, 1989; reprint of the 1933 edition), 359–60. For the treaty, see Gardner, *Earth Is All That Lasts*, 152–64; Hämäläinen, *Lakota America,* 286–93; and Ostler, *Plains Sioux*, 48–51.

6. *Report of the Secretary of War* [1874], vol. 1 (Washington, DC: Government Printing Office, 1874), 24; Sheridan to Sherman, May 1, 1874, Box 11, Sheridan Papers; and Donald Jackson, *Custer's Gold: The United States Cavalry Expedition of 1874* (New Haven, CT: Yale University Press, 1966).

7. Utley, *Lance and Shield*, 125. Also see Joe De Barthe, *Life and Adventures of Frank Grouard* (Norman: University of Oklahoma Press, 1957).

8. Hyde, *Red Cloud's Folk,* 240–48; John G. Bourke, *On the Border with Crook* (New York: Charles Scribner's Sons, 1891), 243–44; Hämäläinen, *Lakota America,* 350–52; and Utley, *Lance and Shield*, 125–27.

9. Sheridan to Secretary of the Interior, February 4, 1876, Box 91, and Sheridan to Alfred Terry, February 8, 1876, Box 14, Sheridan Papers; *Report of the Secretary of War* [1876], 4 vols. (Washington, DC: Government Printing Office, 1876), vol. 1, 440–41; and Paul Andrew Hutton, *Phil Sheridan and His Army* (Lincoln: University of Nebraska Press, 1985), 298–301.

10. Quote in Thomas B. Marquis, *A Warrior Who Fought Custer* (Minneapolis: Midwest Company, 1931), 178–79.

11. Sheridan to Crook, June 18, 20, 1876, Sheridan to Carr, June 20, 1876, Division of the Missouri, Letters Sent, RG 393, Records of the United States Army, National Archives. For the campaign, see Hutton, *Phil Sheridan and His Army,* 302–30; Robert M. Utley, *Frontier Regulars: The United States Army and the Indian, 1866–1890* (New York: Macmillan, 1973), 236–66; Paul Magid, *The Gray Fox: George Crook and the Indian Wars* (Norman: University of Oklahoma Press, 2015), 215–362; Hämäläinen, *Lakota America*, 337–79; Gardner, *Earth Is All That Lasts*, 221–310; and Peter Cozzens, *The Earth Is Weeping: The Epic Story of the Indian Wars for the American West* (New York: Alfred A. Knopf, 2016), 191–312. Also see James Donovan, *A Terrible Glory: Custer and the Little Bighorn* (New York: Little, Brown, 2008); Charles E. Rankin, ed., *Legacy: New Perspectives on the Battle of the Little Bighorn* (Helena: Montana Historical Society

Press, 1996); Paul L. Hedren, *Rosebud, June 17, 1876: Prelude to the Little Big Horn* (Norman: University of Oklahoma Press, 2019); Neil C. Mangum, *Battle of the Rosebud* (El Segundo, CA: Upton & Sons, 1987); Paul L. Hedren, *Fort Laramie in 1876: Chronicle of a Frontier Post at War* (Lincoln: University of Nebraska Press, 1988); Jerome A. Greene, ed., *Battles and Skirmishes of the Great Sioux War, 1876–1877: The Military View* (Norman: University of Oklahoma Press, 1993); Jerome A. Greene, ed., *Lakota and Cheyenne: Indian Views of the Great Sioux War, 1876–1877* (Norman: University of Oklahoma Press, 1994); Jerome A. Greene, *Slim Buttes, 1876: An Episode of the Great Sioux War* (Norman: University of Oklahoma Press, 1982); Jerome A. Greene, *Yellowstone Command: Colonel Nelson A. Miles and the Great Sioux War, 1876–1877* (Lincoln: University of Nebraska Press, 1991); and Paul L. Hedren, ed., *The Great Sioux War, 1876–77* (Helena: Montana Historical Society Press, 1991).

12. Russell, *Lives and Legends,* 186–88.

13. *New York Weekly,* December 23, 1869. For Ned Buntline see, Russell, *Lives and Legends,* 149–55, 159–61; Louis S. Warren, *Buffalo Bill's America* (New York: Alfred A. Knopf, 2005), 112–16; and Jay Monaghan, *The Great Rascal: The Life and Adventures of Ned Buntline* (Boston: Little, Brown, 1951).

14. William F. Cody, *The Life of Hon. William F. Cody Known as Buffalo Bill* (Hartford, CT: Frank E. Bliss, 1879), 306–8; Russell, *Lives and Legends,* 180–81; and Louisa Frederici Cody and Courtney Ryley Cooper, *Memories of Buffalo Bill* (New York: D. Appleton, 1920), 220–23.

15. *New York Herald,* February 16, 1872; Cody, *Life,* 308–10; and Richard J. Walsh, *The Making of Buffalo Bill* (Indianapolis: Bobbs-Merrill, 1928), 169–70.

16. Cody, *Life,* 310–11; Monaghan, *Great Rascal,* 14–16; and Warren, *Buffalo Bill's America,* 153–60.

17. Louisa Cody quoted in Sandra K. Sagala, *Buffalo Bill on Stage* (Albuquerque: University of New Mexico Press, 2008), 19.

18. Cody, *Life,* 312, 320–28; Russell, *Lives and Legends,* 196; Monaghan, *Great Rascal,* 19–33; Sagala, *Buffalo Bill on Stage,* 17–41. For Texas Jack, see Matthew Kerns, *Texas Jack: America's First Cowboy Star* (Helena, MT: TwoDot, 2021); and Herschel C. Logan, *Buckskin and Satin: The Life of Texas Jack* (Harrisburg, PA: Stackpole, 1954).

19. Joseph G. Rosa, *They Called Him Wild Bill* (Norman: University of Oklahoma Press, 1974), 242–61, 285–88; Kerns, *Texas Jack,* 150–59; Sagala, *Buffalo Bill on Stage,* 43–60. Also see Joseph G. Rosa, *The West of Wild Bill Hickok* (Norman: University of Oklahoma Press, 1982), 140–70, for a marvelous pictorial account of Hickok and Cody on stage.

20. Quote in Kerns, *Texas Jack,* 181. Also see Russell, *Lives and Legends,* 204–13; Warren, *Buffalo Bill's America,* 517–18; Cody, *Life,* 337–39; and Cody and Cooper, *Memories of Buffalo Bill,* 261–66.

21. King, *Campaigning with Crook,* 38.

22. Cody, *Life,* 347; and Cody and Cooper, *Memories of Buffalo Bill,* 275–76.

23. Cody quoted in Russell, *Lives and Legends,* 230; King quoted in King, *Campaigning with Crook,* 31–38. The best account of the affair is Hedren, *First Scalp for Custer,* 61–81. Also see Warren, *Buffalo Bill's America,* 170–73; Walsh, *Making of Buffalo Bill,*

189–205; Cody, *True Tales*, 203–12; and Cody, *Life*, 340–52. The skirmish at Warbonnet is not without controversy, which Don Russell addresses at length in *Lives and Legends*, 214–35. The first account of the fight claiming that "Yellow Hand, a young Cheyenne brave, came foremost, singling Bill as a foeman worthy of his steel," appeared in the *New York Herald*, July 23, 1876.

24. Quote in Cody, *Life*, 360. Also see Sagala, *Buffalo Bill on Stage*, 77–100; Russell, *Lives and Legends*, 252–58; King, *Campaigning with Crook*, 38–40; and Cody and Cooper, *Memories of Buffalo Bill*, 266–76.

CHAPTER 27: THE DANCING HORSE

1. Salsbury quoted in Richard J. Walsh, *The Making of Buffalo Bill* (Indianapolis: Bobbs-Merrill, 1928), 222; Don Russell, *Lives and Legends* (Norman: University of Oklahoma Press, 1960), 285–93; Nate Salsbury, "The Origin of the Wild West Show," *Colorado Magazine* 32, no. 3 (July 1955): 204–14; Henry Blackman Sell and Victor Weybright, *Buffalo Bill and the Wild West* (New York: Oxford University Press, 1955), 125–56. Also see Don Russell, *The Wild West; or, A History of the Wild West Shows* (Fort Worth: Amon Carter Museum, 1970); and Joy S. Kasson, *Buffalo Bill's Wild West: Celebrity, Memory, and Popular History* (New York: Hill & Wang, 2000).

2. Russell, *Lives and Legends*, 294.

3. Walsh, *Making of Buffalo Bill*, 228–29.

4. Walsh, *Making of Buffalo Bill*, 219–22.

5. Oakley quote in Russell, *Lives and Legends*, 313. Oakley's name was Phoebe Ann Moses; her actual name is sometimes given as Mosey. There are several biographies of Annie Oakley. The two best modern works are Glenda Riley, *The Life and Legacy of Annie Oakley* (Norman: University of Oklahoma Press, 1994), and Shirl Kasper, *Annie Oakley* (Norman: University of Oklahoma Press, 1992). Also see Courtney Ryley Cooper, *Annie Oakley: Woman at Arms* (New York: Duffield, 1927); Walter Havighurst, *Annie Oakley of the Wild West* (New York: Macmillan, 1954); Larry McMurtry, *The Colonel and Little Missie: Buffalo Bill, Annie Oakley, and the Beginnings of Superstardom in America* (New York: Simon & Schuster, 2005); and Chris Enss and Howard Kazanjian, *The Trials of Annie Oakley* (Helena, MT: TwoDot, 2022). Annie Oakley, who along with Calamity Jane, Pocahontas, and Sacagawea eventually emerged as the most famous of all frontier heroines, was in many ways a product of John Burke's talent as a publicist. Her shooting skill was of course unparalleled, but it was Burke who shaped a star persona for her. In the twentieth century that image reached new heights thanks to the brother-sister team of Dorothy and Herbert Fields and Irving Berlin with the 1946 Broadway production of *Annie Get Your Gun* starring Ethel Merman (later filmed by MGM in 1950 starring Betty Hutton). The great irony was that the talented Darke County, Ohio, sharpshooter was not a westerner at all. The musical portrayed her as a "tomboyish" female version of Davy Crockett. The real Annie was quite conscious of presenting a prim, proper, and dignified image at all times. She received star billing in the show and, next to the Colonel, was paid the highest salary. She proved to be a sensation in Europe and back home became "America's Sweetheart" long before Hollywood adopted that tagline for its stars. She also paved the way for women athletes to be taken seriously in the United States. And, of course, she lent her name to a complimentary ticket to a show, punched with a hole to resemble the cards she shot at in the arena. She left Cody's

show after a 1901 train accident injured her back, although she continued to perform until 1913. Annie died in November 1926 at age sixty-six, and her husband and manager, Frank E. Butler, died eighteen days later. They are buried in the Brock cemetery near Greenville, Ohio. Will Rogers, in his foreword to Cooper's 1927 biography, noted, "Whenever I think of Annie Oakley I stop and say to myself, 'It's what you are, and not what you are in, that makes you.'"

6. Louis S. Warren, *Buffalo Bill's America* (New York: Alfred A. Knopf, 2005), 219.

7. Finerty quoted in *Chicago Times*, August 1, 1879. Also see Robert M. Utley, *Frontier Regulars* (New York: Macmillan, 1973), 269–91; and Robert M. Utley, *The Last Sovereigns: Sitting Bull and the Resistance of the Free Lakotas* (Lincoln: University of Nebraska Press, 2020), 16–20.

8. McLaughlin quote in Robert M. Utley, *The Lance and the Shield* (New York: Henry Holt, 1993), 250. Also see Mark Lee Gardner, *Earth Is All That Lasts* (Boston: Mariner Books, 2022), 311–24; and Stanley Vestal, *Sitting Bull* (Norman: University of Oklahoma Press, 1957), 214–34.

9. Quoted in Utley, *Lance and Shield,* 263. For Cody and Sitting Bull, see L. G. Moses, *Wild West Shows and the Images of American Indians, 1883–1933* (Albuquerque: University of New Mexico Press, 1996), 23–31; Bobby Bridger, *Buffalo Bill and Sitting Bull: Inventing the Wild West* (Austin: University of Texas Press, 2002); and Deanne Stillman, *Blood Brothers: The Story of the Strange Friendship Between Sitting Bull and Buffalo Bill* (New York: Simon & Schuster, 2017).

10. *New York Herald*, November 16, 1877.

11. Sherman quote in Utley, *Lance and Shield*, 264. Also see Bridger, *Buffalo Bill and Sitting Bull*, 314–17; Walsh, *Making of Buffalo Bill*, 254–57; Russell, *Lives and Legends*, 315–17; and Warren, *Buffalo Bill's America*, 253–55.

12. Oakley quote in Stillman, *Blood Brothers,* 21.

13. Quote in Steve Friesen, *Galloping Gourmet* (Lincoln: University of Nebraska Press, 2023), 88–90; Moses, *Wild West Shows*, 23–31; Russell, *Lives and Legends*, 316.

14. Cody quote in Sell and Weybright, *Buffalo Bill*, 147–48.

15. Oakley quote in Vestal, *Sitting Bull*, 250-51.

16. Vestal, *Sitting Bull*, 251.

17. McLaughlin quote in Utley, *Lance and Shield*, 265–66.

18. Friesen, *Galloping Gourmet,* xi, 70, 146–55; and *New York Times,* August 26, 1894.

19. Cody quote in William F. Cody, *The Wild West in England*, ed. Frank Christianson (Lincoln: University of Nebraska Press, 2012), 85–87. Also see Russell, *Lives and Legends*, 330–331; Kasson, *Buffalo Bill's Wild West*, 76–82; John M. Burke, *Buffalo Bill from Prairie to Palace*, ed. Charles Dizon (Lincoln: University of Nebraska Press, 2012), 210–41; and Walsh, *Making of Buffalo Bill*, 266–72.

20. Cody quote in Sell and Weybright, *Buffalo Bill*, 167.

21. Oakley quote in Friesen, *Galloping Gourmet*, 134.

22. Cody quote in Sell and Weybright, *Buffalo Bill*, 176; and Russell, *Lives and Legends*, 341. For Cody and his horses, see Agnes Wright Spring, *Buffalo Bill and His Horses* (Denver: Bradford-Robinson, 1968); and Lillian Turner, "The Golden Horse on the Silver Screen," *Montana: The Magazine of Western History* 45, no. 4 (Autumn/Winter 1995): 2–19.

23. Kasson, *Buffalo Bill's Wild West*, 83–91; Sell and Weybright, *Buffalo Bill*, 177–90; and Russell, *Lives and Legends*, 350–53.

24. Warren, *Buffalo Bill's America*, 366–74; Kasson, *Buffalo Bill's Wild West*, 162–219; Moses, *Wild West Shows*, 60–105; and Walsh, *Making of Buffalo Bill*, 279–81.

25. Crook quote in Martin F. Schmitt, ed., *General George Crook: His Autobiography* (Norman: University of Oklahoma Press, 1946), 288. Also see Warren, *Buffalo Bill's America*, 374–77; James McLaughlin, *My Friend the Indian* (Lincoln: University of Nebraska Press, 1989), 272–76; Jeffrey Ostler, *The Plains Sioux and U.S. Colonialism from Lewis and Clark to Wounded Knee* (New York: Cambridge University Press, 2004), 217–39; and Utley, *Lance and Shield*, 268–80.

26. Miles quote in Nelson A. Miles, *Serving the Republic* (New York: Harper & Brothers, 1911), 238. For General Miles, see Robert Wooster, *Nelson A. Miles and the Twilight Frontier Army* (Lincoln: University of Nebraska Press, 1993). For the Ghost Dance and Wounded Knee, see Louis Warren, *God's Red Sun: The Ghost Dance Religion and the Making of Modern America* (New York: Basic Books, 2017); Robert M. Utley, *The Last Days of the Sioux Nation* (New Haven, CT: Yale University Press, 1963); Raymond J. Demallie, "The Lakota Ghost Dance: An Ethnohistorical Account," *Pacific Historical Review* 51, no. 4 (November 1982): 385–405; Jeffrey Ostler, "Conquest and the State: Why the United States Employed Massive Military Force to Suppress the Lakota Ghost Dance," *Pacific Historical Review* 65, no. 2 (May 1996): 217–48; James Mooney, *The Ghost Dance Religion and the Sioux Outbreak of 1890* (Washington, DC: Government Printing Office, 1896); Jerome A. Greene, *American Carnage: Wounded Knee, 1890* (Norman: University of Oklahoma Press, 2014); Rex Alan Smith, *Moon of Popping Trees* (New York: Reader's Digest Press, 1975); Heather Cox Richardson, *Wounded Knee: Party Politics and the Road to an American Massacre* (New York: Basic Books, 2010); Jerome A. Greene, ed., *"All Guns Fired at One Time": Native Voices of Wounded Knee, 1890* (Pierre: South Dakota Historical Society Press, 2020); and Richard E. Jensen, R. Eli Paul, and John E. Carter, *Eyewitness at Wounded Knee* (Lincoln: University of Nebraska Press, 1991).

27. Cody quote in Russell, *Lives and Legends*, 358–60; and Buffalo Bill (William F. Cody), *True Tales of the Plains* (New York: Cupples & Leon, 1908), 252–59.

28. Quote in Vestal, *Sitting Bull*, 281; Warren, *Buffalo Bill's America*, 377–80; and Stanley Vestal, *New Sources of Indian History, 1850–1891* (Norman: University of Oklahoma Press, 1934), 2–3.

29. Quote in McLaughlin, *My Friend the Indian*, 207–10. Also see Utley, *Lance and Shield*, 291–95; Stillman, *Blood Brothers*, 212–16; and Bridger, *Buffalo Bill and Sitting Bull*, 387–81.

30. Baker quoted in Vestal, *Sitting Bull*, 280.

31. Cody, *True Tales of the Plains*, 255.

32. For the death of Sitting Bull, see Vestal, *Sitting Bull*, 286–307; Utley, *Lance and Shield*, 291–307; Gardner, *Earth Is All That Lasts*, 356–75; Stillman, *Blood Brothers*, 216–21; Smith, *Moon of Popping Trees*, 157–60; Dee Brown, *Bury My Heart at Wounded Knee* (New York: Holt, Rinehart & Winston, 1970), 436–38; Havighurst, *Annie Oakley*, 149–51; Bridger, *Buffalo Bill and Sitting Bull*, 382–86; Edmund G. Fechet, "The True Story of the Death of Sitting Bull," *Cosmopolitan* 20 (March 1896), 493–501; Warren, *Buffalo Bill's America*, 379–81; Utley, *Last Days of the Sioux Nation*, 146–66; Greene, *American Carnage*, 173–90; and Louis S. Warren, *God's Red Son: The Ghost Dance Religion and the Making of Modern America* (New York: Basic Books, 2017), 281–84. For official reports by both the army and the Indian Bureau as well as contemporary accounts, see John M. Carroll, ed., *The Arrest and Killing of Sitting Bull: A Documentary* (Los Angeles: Arthur H. Clark, 1986). The story of Sitting Bull's dancing horse has aroused some controversy, and several prominent historians, such as Utley (who first accepted the story but later dismissed it), Greene, and Gardner, have rejected it, while others—Vestal, Brown, Havighurst, Russell, Warren, Stillman, Smith, and Bridger—accept it. The story originated with Stanley Vestal's sources at Standing Rock in the 1920s and first appeared in his 1932 biography of Sitting Bull. Vestal, the pen name of Professor Walter S. Campbell of the University of Oklahoma, was a Rhodes scholar and prolific author who has been criticized for his uncritical use of Indian informants and his romantic literary style. Nevertheless, he ranks as one of the most enduring and popular of all Western historians. In an interesting and measured 1995 article by William E. Lemons, a professor in the English department of the University of South Dakota, the author argued that some of Vestal's key informants were not reliable and that the author, well known for his tendency toward the romantic in history, embraced the horse story based on a spurious tall tale told by a mixed-blood interpreter at Standing Rock. Eyewitness accounts from the scene mentioned the gray horse but not the dance, and there were no contemporary reports of Sitting Bull's death that mentioned the amazing spectacle. Lemons's argument is entirely based on negative evidence, of course—no one reported the dancing horse before Vestal—but that does not make the story untrue or negate its power. William E. Lemons, "History by Unreliable Narrators: Sitting Bull's Circus Horse," *Montana: The Magazine of Western History* 45, no. 4 (Autumn/Winter 1995): 64–74.

33. Waggoner quote in Vestal, *Sitting Bull*, 309–10. Cody viewed Sitting Bull's death as an assassination and told a reporter for the *Chicago Tribune* so. He later confronted President Harrison about the incident. Cody claimed that Harrison apologized. *Chicago Tribune*, February 4, 1891. For the suspicion that Sitting Bull's death was a planned assassination, see Greene, *American Carnage*, 188–90; Vestal, *Sitting Bull*, 310–12; and Utley, *Lance and Shield*, 309–12.

34. Miles quote in Utley, *Last Days of the Sioux Nation*, 193. Also see Peter R. DeMontravel, "General Nelson A. Miles and the Wounded Knee Controversy," *Arizona and the West* 28, no. 1 (Spring 1986): 23–44.

35. Whiteside quote in Utley, *Last Days of the Sioux Nation*, 197. For the Wounded Knee Massacre, see Utley, *Last Days*, 200–250; Warren, *God's Red Son*, 271–94; Miles, *Serving the Republic*, 233–47; Greene, *American Carnage*, 191–337; Ostler, *Plains Sioux*, 313–60; Brown, *Bury My Heart*, 439–45; and Cozzens, *Earth Is Weeping*, 419–67.

36. Cody quote in Russell, *Lives and Legends*, 367. Also see Utley, *Last Days of the Sioux Nation*, 268–70; and Warren, *Buffalo Bill's America*, 381–89.

CHAPTER 28: WILD WEST

1. Richard J. Walsh, *The Making of Buffalo Bill* (Indianapolis: Bobbs-Merrill, 1928), 298–302; Don Russell, *Lives and Legends of Buffalo Bill* (Norman: University of Oklahoma Press, 1960), 374–75; Louis S. Warren, *Buffalo Bill's America* (New York: Alfred A. Knopf, 2005), 418–21; Nellie Snyder Yost, *Buffalo Bill* (Chicago: Swallow Press, 1979), 236–40; Richard Slotkin, *Gunfighter Nation* (New York: Atheneum, 1992), 63–87; and Joy S. Kasson, *Buffalo Bill's Wild West* (New York: Hill & Wang, 2000), 93–121.
2. L. G. Moses, *Wild West Shows and the Images of American Indians, 1883–1933* (Albuquerque: University of New Mexico Press, 1996), 134–38; and Bobby Bridger, *Buffalo Bill and Sitting Bull* (Austin: University of Texas Press, 2002), 403–5.
3. Yost, *Buffalo Bill*, 240. For two memoirs by Lakota performers in the Wild West, see Luther Standing Bear, *My People the Sioux* (Boston: Houghton Mifflin, 1928), and John G. Neihardt, *Black Elk Speaks: Being the Life Story of a Holy Man of the Oglala* (New York: William Morrow, 1932). Also see Raymond J. DeMallie, ed., *The Sixth Grandfather* (Lincoln: University of Nebraska Press, 1982), 245–55.
4. Warren, *Buffalo Bill's America*, 420.
5. *Buffalo Bill's Wild West and Congress of Rough Riders of the World: Historical Sketches and Programme* (New York: Cody and Salsbury, 1893); Yost, *Buffalo Bill*, 243; and Warren, *Buffalo Bill's America*, 498–519.
6. Turner quote in Ray Allen Billington, *Frederick Jackson Turner: Historian, Scholar, Teacher* (New York: Oxford University Press, 1973), 126.
7. Billington, *Frederick Jackson Turner*, 124–27. Also see Allan G. Bogue, *Frederick Jackson Turner: Strange Roads Going Down* (Norman: University of Oklahoma Press, 1998), 91–118.
8. Martin Ridge, ed., *History, Frontier, and Section: Three Essays by Frederick Jackson Turner* (Albuquerque: University of New Mexico Press, 1993), 1–26; Billington, *Frederick Jackson Turner*, 3–107; and Bogue, *Frederick Jackson Turner*, 3–89. Also see Martin Ridge, ed., *Frederick Jackson Turner, Wisconsin's Historian of the Frontier* (Madison: State Historical Society of Wisconsin, 1986), 1–25.
9. Frederick Jackson Turner, "The Significance of the Frontier in American History," in Ridge, *History, Frontier, and Section*, 59–91. Also see John Mack Faragher, ed., *Rereading Frederick Jackson Turner* (New York: Holt, 1994).
10. Billington, *Frederick Jackson Turner*, 129–31; Bogue, *Frederick Jackson Turner*, 113–16; and Slotkin, *Gunfighter Nation*, 29–62.
11. Walsh, *Making of Buffalo Bill*, 308–29; Russell, *Lives and Legends*, 378–85, 439–72; and Henry Blackman Sell and Victor Weybright, *Buffalo Bill and the Wild West* (New York: Oxford University Press, 1955), 191–260.
12. Roosevelt quoted in Russell, *Lives and Legends*, 469.
13. Gene Fowler, *Timber Line* (New York: Blue Ribbon Books, 1933), 371.
14. Frederick Jackson Turner, "The Significance of the Frontier in American History," in *Proceedings of the State Historical Society of Wisconsin at Its Forty-First Annual Meeting Held December 14, 1893* (Madison: Democrat Printing Company, State Printer, 1894), 89; and Ridge, *History, Frontier, and Section*, 67.

INDEX

Note: Italicized page numbers indicate material in photographs or illustrations.

ABOUT THE AUTHOR

Paul Andrew Hutton is the author of *The Apache Wars*. He is an American cultural historian, author, documentary writer, and television personality. He is also Distinguished Professor of History Emeritus at the University of New Mexico, a former executive director of the Western History Association, and a past president of the Western Writers of America. He currently serves as interim curator of the Buffalo Bill Museum at the Buffalo Bill Center of the West, in Cody, Wyoming.